Verse in English from Eighteenth-Century Ireland

Verse in English
from Eighteenth-Century Ireland

edited by Andrew Carpenter

CORK UNIVERSITY PRESS

First published in 1998 by
Cork University Press
Cork
Ireland

© Cork University Press 1998

British Library Cataloguing in Publication Data
A CIP catalogue record for this book is available from the British Library.

ISBN 1 85918 103 1 hardback
1 85918 104 X paperback

Typeset by Phototype-Set Ltd., Dublin
Printed by MPG Books Limited, U.K.

for Dorothy

CONTENTS[1]

Introduction   1
A Note on the Texts   34

Part I: 1687-1725

Six poems from the Williamite wars, **1687-91**
    Lilliburlero   37
    A Cruel and Bloody DECLARATION ...   39
    from: The Irish Hudibras or, Fingallian Prince   42
    The Irishmen's Prayers to St. Patrick ...   49
    Epitaph on the Duke of Grafton   51
    An *Irish* Song   53

Nahum Tate (1652-**1698**-1715)
    from: Panacea: A Poem upon Tea   54
    Song of the Angels at the Nativity of Our Blessed Saviour   56

John Toland (1670-**1700**-1722)
    from: Clito: a Poem on the Force of Eloquence   58

William King (1663-**1704**-1712)
    from: Mully of Mountown   61

George Farquhar (1678-**1707**-1707)
    To a Gentleman who had his *Pocket* Pick'd ...   65
    An Epigram on the Riding-House in *Dublin,* made into a Chappel   66

William Congreve (1670-**1710**-1729)
    Doris   67

Thomas Parnell (1679-**1713**-1718)
    To ———   70
    On the Castle of Dublin, *Anno* 1715   71
    Bacchus or the Drunken Metamorphosis   72

Mary Monck (c.1678-**1715**-1715)
    An Elegie on a Favourite Dog   75
    A Tale   76

1. Authors (except Swift and members of his circle, whose work is grouped together in Part II) are normally listed chronologically by the publication date of the earliest of their poems included in this anthology, or by its composition date if this is known to be significantly earlier, or by the date of the poet's death if the poetry was published posthumously. Three dates are given for each author whose works are listed chronologically: birth, date of publication of first work in this anthology, and death.

James Ward (1691-**1718**-1736)
from: *Phoenix* Park   77
The Smock Race at Finglas   79

Morrough O'Connor (fl. **1719**-40)
An Eclogue in Imitation of the first Eclogue of Virgil   83

Matthew Concanen (1701-**1720**-1749)
from: A Match at Football ...   90

Anonymous poems current **1710-25**
from: The Signior in Fashion   99
A Petition to the Ladies of DUBLIN ... *by the Old* WASH-WOMEN   101
from: The Cavalcade: A Poem On the RIDING the FRANCHISES   103
An Irish Wedding between Dick and Moll   107
The Irish Absentee's new Litany   112
The Humble Petition of a Beautiful Young Lady *To the
Reverend Doctor B–rk—y*   115
from: Hesperi-neso-graphia: or, A Description of the Western Isle 116
The Royal Black Bird   126

Nicholas Browne (c.1699-**1722**-1734)
from: The North Country Wedding   128

Mary Davys (1674-**1725**-1732)
from: The Modern Poet   135

Ambrose Philips (1674-**1725**-1749)
To Miss Georgiana   138
Namby Pamby ... [a response by Henry Carey, (d.1743)]   140

Part II: Swift and his Irish contemporaries (1713-45)

Jonathan Smedley (c.1672-**1713**-1729)
Verses fix'd on the Cathedral Door ...   145
An Epistle to his Grace the Duke of Grafton ...   147

Jonathan Swift (1667-1745)
His Grace's Answer to Jonathan   151
To Charles Ford Esqr. on his Birth-day ...   153

Esther Johnson (1681-1728)
To *Dr Swift* on his Birth-day ...   158

Jonathan Swift
    Stella at Wood-Park ...   160

Thomas Sheridan (1687-1738)
    A Description of Doctor Delany's Villa   164

Patrick Delany (c.1685-1768)
    An Epistle to His Excellency John *Lord* Carteret, &c.   166

Jonathan Swift
    An Epistle upon an Epistle from a certain Doctor ...   170
    A LIBEL on D[octor] D[elany] and a Certain Great Lord   174

Jonathan Swift, Patrick Delany, Thomas Sheridan and others
    Riddles, street cries and other short verses   182

Thomas Sheridan
    To the *Dean*, when in England, in 1726   187
    A True and Faithful Inventory ...   189

Jonathan Swift
    Mary the Cook-Maid's Letter to Dr Sheridan   190
    A Pastoral Dialogue ...   192

Mary Barber (c.1685-**1728**-1755)
    An Unanswerable Apology for the Rich   194
    To Mrs Frances-Arabella Kelly   195
    The Recantation: to the same Lady   196

Matthew Pilkington (1701-**1731**-1774)
    The Invitation: To Doctor Delany at Delville, MDCCCIX   197
    Anacreon Paraphras'd, Ode viii   199

Laetitia Pilkington (c.1708-**1732**-1750)
    The Petition of the Birds   201

Constantia Grierson (c.1705-**1732**-1732)
    To Miss *Laetitia Van Lewen*   203
    from: Lines to an unnamed Lady   205

William Dunkin (c.1709-**1734**-1765)
    from: The Parson's Revels   207
    A Receipt for Making a Doctor   214
    On the Omission of the Words *Dei Gratia* in the late Coinage ...   220

Jonathan Swift

    A Character, Panegyric, and Description of the LEGION CLUB ...   222

James Arbuckle (c.1700-**1745**-c.1747)

    On Swift's leaving his Fortune to Build a Mad-House   231

Part III: 1735-60

Henry Brooke (c.1703-**1735**-1783)

    from: Universal Beauty   235

Anonymous poems from the **1730**s and **1740**s

    The Kerry Cavalcade ...   241

    from: The Upper Gallery   244

    An Elegy on the much lamented Death of ... all the *Potatoes* ...   248

James Sterling (1701-**1737**-1763)

    from: A Friend in Need is a Friend in Deed   253

Wetenhall Wilkes (fl. **1737**, d.1751)

    from: The Humours of the Black Dog   260

Robert Nugent, Earl Nugent (1702-**1740**-1788)

    Epistle to Pollio, from the Hills of Howth in Ireland   265

John, Earl of Orrery (1707-**1741**-1762)

    from: The First Ode of the First Book of Horace Imitated ...   268

John Winstanley (1677-**1742**-1750)

    Miss Betty's Singing-Bird   271

    Upon *Daisy*, being brought back from *New Park* to *Stoneybatter*   273

    The Poet's Lamentation for the loss of his Cat ...   275

    To the Revd Mr —— on his Drinking Sea-Water   277

Laurence Whyte (c.1683-**1742**-c.1753)

    A POETICAL Description of Mr. NEAL's new Musick-Hall ...   278

    from: The Parting Cup or The HUMOURS of Deoch an Doruis ...   281

James Eyre Weekes (c.1720-**1743**-c.1754)

    from: The Intrigues of *Jove*: a Ballad   296

    Two Poems   297

Sir Arthur Dawson (1698-**1749**-1775)

    Bumpers, 'Squire Jones   299

Anonymous songs and poems from the **1750**s
    Drinking Song 302
    On Deborah Perkins of the county of Wicklow 303
    The Clerk's Song 304
    TIT for TAT, or the Rater rated 305
    On the *Spaw* at *Castle-connel*, in the County of *Limerick* 307
    A New Ballad on the Hot-Wells at Mallow 309
    The Rakes of Mallow 310
    Scew Ball 312

Thomas Mozeen (fl.**1750**, d.1768)
    A Description of a Fox-Chase 314
    An Invitation to OWEN BRAY's at Laughlin's town 317

Thomas Newburgh (c.1695-**1758**-1779)
    The *BEAU WALK*, in *STEPHEN'S GREEN* 319

Samuel Whyte (1733-**1758**-1811)
    from: A Familiar Epistle to J.H. Esq; near Killarney 320

Art Mac Cumhaidh (c.1715-**1760**-1773)
    Tagra an Dá Theampall ('The Disputation of the Two Churches') 323

Liam Inglis (1709-**1760**-1778)
    Do Tharlaigh Inné Orm ('I met yesterday ...') 327

Part IV: 1760-90

Dorothea Dubois (1728-**1764**-1774)
    The Amazonian Gift 331
    Song 332
    from: A True Tale 333

Anonymous poems from the **1760**s
    Description of Dublin 338
    The Rakes of Stony Batter 339
    The May Bush 340

Olivia Elder (fl. **1769**-80)
    from: To Mrs D.C.H., an account of the Author's manner of
      spending her time 343

Oliver Goldsmith (1728-**1770**-1774)
    from: The Deserted Village   347
    Song (from *She Stoops to Conquer*)   355

Richard Brinsley Sheridan (1751-**1771**-1816)
    Lines by a Lady of Fashion   356
    Song (from *The School for Scandal*)   357

Gerald Fitzgerald (1740-**1773**-1819)
    from: The Academick Sportsman   359

Mary Shackleton (1758-**1774**-1826)
    The Welcome to Liberty   364
    On the Murder of a Cat   366
    To Sarah Shackleton on her beating me with the bed-stick ...   368

William Preston (1753-**1776**-1807)
    from: An heroic Epistle from Donna Teresa Pinna ÿ Ruiz   369

Lady Clare (c.1755-**1776**-1844)
    Motto inscribed on the bottom of chamber-pots beside a portrait
        of Richard Twiss   375

Turlogh Carolan (1670-1738); translated by
Joseph Cooper Walker in **1776**
    Carolan's Receipt   376

Elizabeth Ryves (c.1750-**1777**-1797)
    Ode to Sensibility   377

James Delacourt or De-La-Cour (1709-**1778**-1781)
    In praise of a Negress   378

George Sackville Cotter (1755-**1778**-1831)
    from: Epistles from Swanlinbar   379

Gorges Edmond Howard (1715-**1782**-1786)
    The Modern Lass in High Dress in MDCCLVI   383

Eoghan Rua Ó Súilleabháin (c.1748-**1782**-1784)
    Letter to Father Fitzgerald   385

Chapbook verse of the **1780**s
 Connelly's Ale: a new song 387
 The Connaughtman's Visit to DUBLIN 388
 The Maiden's Resolution, or an Answer to the Farmer's Son 393
 The Sailor Dear 393
 The Coughing Old Man 395
 A Drop of Dram 396
 Corporal Casey 398
 Darby O'Gallagher, or the Answer to Morgan Rattler 399
 The New Dhooraling 400
 Hush Cat from under the Table 402

Anonymous verse from newspapers and books of the **1780**s
 Description of a Country Assizes 405
 The Agent's Downfall: a new ballad 408
 Description of an Unfortunate Woman of the Town 410
 The Lord Mayor's Ball 412
 A New Song 414
 Advertisement Extraordinary 416
 Garry Own Naugh Glora, or The Limerick Rakes 417

Anonymous Irish/English poems from the **1780**s
 The Rake's Frolick or *Stauka an Varaga* 420
 The Answer to *Stauka an Vauraga* 423
 Pléaráca an Bhráthar: A New Song called the Friar's Jigg ... 425

John Taylor (fl. **1787**)
 On a Beef's being stole which was promis'd to the AUTHOR 428

Four Dublin underworld poems from the **1780**s
 De Night afore Larry was stretch'd 430
 Luke Caffrey's Kilmainham Minit 434
 A New Song call'd Luke Caffrey's Gost 437
 Lord Altham's Bull 442

Brian Merriman (c.1749-**1789**-1805)
 from: The Midnight Court (translated in 1789 by Denis Woulfe) 446

Charlotte Brooke (c.1740-**1789**-1793)
 Song for Gracey Nugent (translated from the Irish of Carolan) 453

Thomas Dawson Lawrence (c.1730-**1789**-c.1810)
 Epitaph on an orphan beggar child 455

Part V: 1790-1805

L. O'Reilly (fl. **1790**)
Elegy on the death of ... Miss Bridget Burne   459

Mary O'Brien (fl. **1790**)
The Freedom of John Bull   462

Henrietta Battier (1751-**1791**-1813)
from: The Kirwanade   464
Lines addressed to the late Lord Clifden ...   466

Pat O'Kelly (1754-**1791**-c.1812)
from: The Itinerary ...   468
The Litany for Doneraile   470

Ellen Taylor (fl. **1792**)
Written by the Barrow side ...   473

Henrietta O'Neill (1758-**1792**-1793)
Ode to the Poppy   475

Thomas Dermody (1775-**1792**-1802)
An Ode to Myself   477
Ode to the Collegians   478

Edward Rushton (1756-**1793**-1814)
Mary le More   480

Samuel Thomson (1766-**1793**-1816)
To a Hedge-hog   482
The Hawk and Weazle   484
The Country Dance   485

Edward Walsh (1756-**1793**-1832)
Rapture!   490
The Epigram   491

John Anketell (c.1750-**1793**-1824)
from: Stramore Patron   492
from: Description of Sunday Evening, spent in a
    Coffee-House in ... Dublin   496

Four anonymous 'rambling' songs
    The Peregrinations of Fiachra McBrady   498
    The Irish man's Ramble: a new song   500
    McClure's Ramble   502
    Shales's Rambles, or the Lurgan Weaver   503

Anonymous poems from the **1790**s
    The Colleen Rue   507
    The Irish Phœnix   508
    The Siege of Troy   510
    Paddy MacShane's Seven Ages   511
    Sally Mac Gee   513
    Paddy the Piper   514
    The Ladies Dress, or the Downfall of the Stay-Makers   515
    A New Song call'd The Lord Lieutenant's Farewell to the
        Kingdom of Ireland   517
    A New Song on the Half-Pence being cry'd down ...   518
    Sweet Castle-Hyde   520

Richard Alfred Milliken (1767-**1800**-1815)
    The Groves of Blarney   523

Samuel Burdy (c.1754-**1796**-1820)
    from· The Transformation   526

Jane Elizabeth Moore (1738-**1796**-?)
    A Question to the Society of Freemasons (answered by an
        anonymous Dublin freemason)   530
    Answer   531
    To T.W.M———a, Esq.   531
    A rejoinder to Mrs Jane Eliz Moore's Repledum   532
    Answer to the above Replication   533

William Drennan (1754-**1797**-1820)
    The Wake of William Orr   535

Mary Alcock (c.1742-**1798**-1798)
    The Chimney-Sweeper's Complaint   537

Joseph Atkinson (1743-**1798**-1818)
    from: Killarney: a poem   539

James Orr (1770-**1798**-1816)

    Song composed on the Banks of Newfoundland   542

    The Passengers   544

    The Execution   550

Hugh Porter (1780-**1799**-1812)

    To the Reverend T[homas] T[ighe], Parson's Hill   552

John Philpot Curran (1750-**1799**-1817)

    The Deserter's Meditation   556

Nationalist verse of the **1790**s

    Liberty and Equality or Dermot's Delight   557

    The Star of Liberty   559

    Paddy's Advice to John Bull   560

    from: The United Irishmen: A Tale, founded on Facts   561

    Come all you Warriors   566

    Dunlavin Green   569

    The Croppy Boy   570

    The Patriot Mother   571

    Green upon the Cape   573

    The Exiled Irishman's Lamentation   574

Three Orange Songs

    Lisnagade   576

    Protestant Boys   577

    The Tree of Liberty   578

Robert Emmet (1778-**1799**-1803)

    Lines written on the Burying-Ground of Arbour Hill ...   580

Edward Lysaght (1763-**1800**-1810)

    Song   582

    Love *versus* the Bottle   583

Mary Tighe (1772-**1800**-1810)

    Written at Rossana, November 18, 1799   585

    Written at Killarney, July 29, 1800   586

Daniel Roderick O'Conor (fl. **1800**)

    from: The Author's Farewell to Dublin: a poem   587

Thomas Moore (1779-**1800**-1852)
      Translation of Ode IX by Anacreon   589
      Song   590

W. Kertland (fl. **1805**)
      The DUBLIN Fancy WARE-HOUSE, No. ONE, *Lower* ORMOND-QUAY   592

Glossary   597
Sources of the texts   605
Index   615

ACKNOWLEDGEMENTS

I thank the staff of the following libraries and institutions who have been unfailingly helpful to me while I have been working on this book: Trinity College Dublin, University College Dublin, The National Library of Ireland, The Royal Irish Academy, The Gilbert Collection in the Pearse Street Library Dublin, The Irish Folklore Commission Library at University College Dublin, The Irish Traditional Music Archive, St Patrick's College Maynooth, University College Cork, Queen's University Belfast, The Belfast Public Library, The Linen Hall Library Belfast, The British Library, The National Library of Wales at Aberystwyth, The Library Company of Philadelphia, The Free Library in Philadelphia, The University of Pennsylvania Library in Philadelphia, The Folger Shakespeare Library in Washington D.C., The Henry Huntington Library in Pasadena, The James Andrews Clarke Memorial Library in Los Angeles, and The Harry Ransom Humanities Research Center at the University of Texas at Austin.

Within University College Dublin, my colleague Ray Astbury of the Department of Classics cheerfully translated the Latin I brought him, even material as painful for a true classicist as 'A Cruel and Bloody Declaration' and Father Fagan's bog-Latin in 'The Parson's Revels', and Terry Dolan of the Department of English gave me the benefit of his experience in sorting out the more peculiar aspects of the texts in Hiberno-English; I am very grateful to them both. In addition, I owe a particular debt of gratitude to Alan Harrison of the Department of Modern Irish, who has been an enthusiastic collaborator on this project from the beginning; as anyone using the book will soon see, I have called on his expertise in almost every part of it. Arch Elias of Philadelphia played a major part as well, not only by giving me practical help and guidance in many ways, but also by providing me with invaluable bibliographical data. Without his help, my time in the United States of America would have been far less productive. In addition, special thanks are due to Maurice Craig, Fonsy Mealy, Sara Wilbourne and Jonathan Williams, who all played substantial roles in helping me get this book finished, and to the staff at Cork University Press.

In addition, I thank the following for help of various kinds: Bruce Arnold, Charles Benson, Terence Brown, Nicholas Carolan, Danielle Clarke, Pierce Colbert, Bryan Coleborne, Louis Cullen, Simon Davies,

Eamonn de Burca, Rob and Janice Dey, Terry Dolan, Susan Elias, Neville Figgis, Jack Gamble, Luke Gibbons, the Knight of Glin, David Hayton, Norma Jessop, James Kelly, Mary Kelly, Máire Kennedy, Fiona Keogh, Vincent Kinnane, Marie-Louise Legg, Rolf and Magda Loeber, Linde Lunney, Patricia Lysaght, Joe McMinn, James Maguire, Robert Mahony, Jim Mays, Kenneth Milne, Seamus Ó Catháin, Kate O'Dwyer, Dáithí Ó hÓgáin, Hugh and Margaret Ormsby-Lennon, Mary Pollard, Hermann Real, Peter Rowan, Gregory Schirmer, Brian Summers, Tony Sweeney, Richard Wall, Kevin Whelan, Nicholas Williams, Penny Woods, James Woolley, and Susan Overend Woolley; also Patricia Bourke, Róisín Collins, Cían Gallagher, Sandra McElroy, Elizabeth McWey, Sarah News, Darragh O'Grady and Paul Thomas, members of the Modern English M.A. class at University College Dublin in 1995/96 and 1996/97.

Financial assistance has been provided by the the Faculty of Arts and by the President's Committee for Research, University College Dublin, and I am grateful to both bodies.

I acknowledge, with thanks, permission to quote from materials in the possession of the Board of Trinity College Dublin, the Trustees of National Library of Ireland, and the Board of Trustees of the National Library of Wales.

Dublin, September 1997

INTRODUCTION

(I)

At the beginning of 1759, Oliver Goldsmith confessed to his brother that he found poetry a much easier and 'more agreeable species of composition' than prose. If it were possible to make a living out of poetry, he continued, 'it were no unpleasant employment to be a poet'.[1] Only a handful of those who lived in eighteenth-century Ireland wanted to make money out of the writing of verse, but hundreds — probably thousands — of them, like Goldsmith, considered it a very agreeable pastime. The verse they wrote to and about each other survives today in broadsheets, printed volumes, chapbooks,[2] manuscripts and newspapers, and from this remarkable quantity of material, emerge lively, energetic and distinctive voices. Many of these voices have not been heard for two hundred years, and my aim in this anthology has been to include as many of them as possible. The book also contains well-known voices — that of Swift in 'The Legion Club', that of Goldsmith in 'The Deserted Village' and those of the political song-writers of the 1790s. Without them, no collection of verse in English from eighteenth-century Ireland could pretend to be representative. However, much of the material in this book will be unknown to most readers and the perspectives it brings to life in eighteenth-century Ireland will be new and, perhaps, surprising.

Life in Ireland changed radically between the battle of the Boyne and the Act of Union, and the poems in this volume, stretching from just before the first of these events to just after the second of them, reflect many of these changes. The poems have not been chosen specifically because they reflect social change however, but because they stand out, from the thousands which survive from eighteenth-century Ireland, as

---

1. *The Collected Letters of Oliver Goldsmith* ed. Katharine Balderston (Cambridge, 1928), p. 65.

2. There is some disagreement about how to describe these 'chapbooks'. J.R.R. Adams described them, correctly, as small booklets each 'consisting of a single sheet of paper folded to give sixteen or thirty-two pages' (*The Printed Word and the Common Man* (Belfast, 1987), p.33). He made a distinction between these one-sheet chapbooks, which normally sold for a penny, and dearer works which cost up to sixpence, and which contained extended narratives or arguments. Other modern commentators, for example G-D Zimmerman in his *Songs of Irish Rebellion* (Dublin, 1967), sometimes call single-sheet chapbooks containing songs 'garlands', and John Wardroper describes them as 'songsters' in his *Lovers, Rakes and Rogues* (London, 1995). There is a good discussion of terminologies in Harry B. Weiss, *A Book about Chapbooks* (Hatboro, 1969), p. 1, and I follow him in calling these single-sheet booklets 'chapbooks', even when they contain songs.

authentic, honest, direct statements of the feelings, thoughts and prejudices of the people of eighteenth-century Ireland or because they describe or represent a side of eighteenth-century life which is worth recalling. Thus several informal verse letters are included not because they contain great 'poetry' but because they offer unique insights into life on a farm in County Derry in the 1760s, or the activities of a slightly raffish set at a spa in County Cavan in the 1770s, or the behaviour of small gentry in County Westmeath in the reign of Queen Anne. The *Hesperi-neso-graphia* is included because it contains fascinating details about the lifestyle, eating habits, education and recreations of substantial, Irish-speaking tenant farmers at the beginning of the century, and *The United Irishmen* is included because it gives a harrowing account of the horrors of a skirmish in the 1798 Rising from the point of view of those armed with pitchforks. Equally, we learn a lot about life in eighteenth-century Dublin from the account of the debtors' prison, or the tale of the rowdy young bucks who set out to insult ordinary citizens in the streets, or the admonitory verse to schoolgirls not to misbehave on their way to school. Many poems from the Irish countryside are included — poems about sports, local festivities and weddings — and such works, like those which recount the adventures of countrymen visiting Dublin, are not only enjoyable in themselves, but are also often remarkably revealing about lesser-known sides of life in eighteenth-century Ireland.

Above all, the voices are of those who lived through the events or emotions they describe. This is not a book 'about' life in Ireland in the eighteenth century, but rather a book by those who lived that life and since, of all groups in society, the voices of the marginalised and the poor are the least heard, I have given considerable space to them in this book. Perhaps most unexpected and memorable of all the poems in the anthology are the halting and almost incoherent outpourings of unfortunate women, living in the depths of rural Ireland in the 1770s and 1780s, caught in the webs of inflexible social structures or in the traps of marriage or addiction, such as 'The Coughing Old Man' and 'A Drop of Dram'. Equally unusual are the ballads written in English by the Irish-speaking ballad-makers, such as the moving elegy for Miss Bridget Burne and some of the strange anonymous poems from the 1790s. The Dublin underworld poems too, though they may have been touched up by an educated hand before reaching print, reflect vividly the world of the hopelessly poor, for whom death by hanging seemed an inevitable end. At the other end of the scale, the poems of Swift's circle remind us that the world of lords lieutenant and the clergy of the established church was not so much a gilded one as a brittle one, where the barbed shaft of wit could inflict cruel and vicious wounds and where the fear that one might lose one's security and one's income was very real.

For the rising middle classes of eighteenth-century Ireland, poetry offered an outlet and, sometimes, a source of income. From Nahum Tate and Dorothea Dubois to Jane Elizabeth Moore and Daniel Roderick O'Conor, Irish poets of limited means sought to be paid for their work in the eighteenth century. In the case of women who published their verse by subscription, the money raised could save them from destitution or provide for the education of their children. For more secure figures such as Mary Barber, the writing of verse may not have been a financial necessity but it became a moral one, for women's voices needed to be heard. Even the young Mary Shackleton knew that her criticism of the patriarchal world which surrounded her had to be expressed, and expressed forcibly.

In much of the verse in this anthology, the influence of Gaelic Ireland, its language, its metrical forms and its culture, can be clearly seen and heard. This is most obvious in poems written partly in English and partly in Irish, such as the examples by Art Mac Cumhaidh and Liam Inglis. However, the chapbook and anonymous verse of the period 1770-1800, as well as the work of Irish-speaking balladeers like L. O'Reilly, demonstrates the depth of the interaction between the two cultures, for here we find not only the influence of the language and syntax of Irish in verse written in English but of Gaelic prosody. This important aspect of the cultural life of eighteenth-century Ireland is covered later in this introduction.

It is clear, though, that the widespread idea that there were only two cultures in eighteenth-century Ireland — that of English-speakers and that of Irish-speakers — is quite inadequate to explain the actual cultural situation. In fact, during the period covered by this anthology, Ireland was made up of many distinct but inter-dependent and interwoven social and cultural communities in which two main languages, English and Irish — or versions of them — were living side by side, and influencing each other at a local level. There were many forms of English and many forms of Irish, and many places (hedge-schools for instance) where, in their local forms, these languages rubbed against and influenced each other. As the century progressed, economic conditions changed and travel became easier, which meant that rural communities gradually became less isolated from each other and cultural interaction occurred on an ever-widening stage; but still, as the new language of commerce and progress collided with the older ways of Irish life, strange, culturally hybrid forms of writing came into existence in many parts of Ireland. Some of the most memorable English-language verse of the age is the product of this cross-pollination of form, syntax and vocabulary between the cultures and languages of eighteenth-century Ireland — and one is not referring here simply to cross-pollination between English and Irish, but also to the influence of Scots on the language of Ulster. As the linguistic and cultural heritage of Gaelic Ireland lies behind much poetry written in eighteenth-century Munster, Leinster and Connaught, so the heritage of Scotland lies behind the work of the Ulster weaver poets, enabling them to create a distinct brand of eighteenth-century Irish writing in the wonderfully free and expressive medium of Ulster-Scots.

This cross-cultural writing has not been considered at all in general accounts of eighteenth-century Ireland. In fact, the literary culture of the age, as a whole, has received scant attention, and there has been hardly any interest in eighteenth-century Irish poetry. Apart from that of Swift and Goldsmith, little verse was even in print until recently. Matters have improved in the last decade with editions of the work of Thomas Parnell (1989), Thomas Sheridan (1994), Mary Barber (1992) and Laetitia Pilkington (1997). There is a fine selection of eighteenth-century Anglo-Irish poetry edited by Bryan Coleborne in the *Field Day Anthology of Irish Writing* (1991) and a valuable and wide-ranging collection of Irish verse in English in Patrick Fagan's *Georgian Celebration* (1989). Still, as I worked on this anthology, I was constantly astonished at the quality and interest of the material I found in research libraries. I was impressed not only by the sheer volume of unknown, and distinctly 'Irish' verse I came across, but also by the energy, vigour and originality of it. What makes much of the verse particularly valuable is the fact that the poets were writing about themselves and their lives; thus the verse they produced is full of social as well as cultural interest, and reflects an extraordinarily wide range of Irish life.

The intention of a book such as this is not to reflect all aspects of life, however, and I have had to exclude some categories of verse altogether. There is little 'public' verse, in particular none of the annual odes for the birthdays of sovereigns or addresses of welcome to lords lieutenant which fill many collections of verse of the age. There is no 'polite' verse, such as one finds in the anthologies edited by Joshua Edkins (1790), verse in which gently cultured (and mostly moneyed) Anglo-Irish poets write in pastoral or Augustan style of the Phyllises in their groves. There is also none of the vigorous satirical verse thrown up by the politics of the period 1770-1800. The reason for this omission is that a high level of annotation is needed to make the very specific allusions to persons, reputations and events intelligible and that, as experience taught me, the vigorous invective of this verse loses its bite if the allusions have to be exhaustively explained.

Another category of verse which does not appear in this book is dramatic verse, particularly the prologues and epilogues written for the Irish theatre. Dramatic texts are beyond the scope of this work and the prologues and epilogues, though often entertaining in themselves, can appear stilted and rhetorical when compared with other verse of the age. Still, a fascinating book could be compiled from this rich field. Work needs to be done on the ballad operas of the eighteenth century and also on the songs in the operas of Irish playwrights working in London — for instance, those of John O'Keeffe (1747-1833), who wrote about fifty plays which contain songs, many of which are of Irish interest.

In general, then, this anthology is a set of first-hand accounts of or comments on life in eighteenth-century Ireland by those who lived through it. Swift and his circle are given a section to themselves not simply because Swift is the best-known Irish poet of the age, but because the circle in which he lived and wrote is an interesting cultural phenomenon in itself. Considerations of space have forced me to exclude some poets whom I would have liked to include, such as Samuel Shepherd and Philip Francis — though Philip Francis was included until I discovered that several of his best translations from Ovid were in fact by his friend William Dunkin. I regret also that there is not more space for the work of Dunkin and two other fine mid-century poets, Laurence Whyte and John Winstanley. All three deserve to be brought to new readers in new editions, particularly Dunkin, who is the most seriously neglected Irish poet writing in English of any generation. It is also clear that much more work needs to be done on the women poets of the age — about sixty of whom published books of verse — and scholarly work is needed on Irish chapbooks and broadsheets, particularly the rare survivals of provincial printing from the period 1770-1800.

(II)

Interaction between Languages and Cultures

The verse in this anthology provides interesting evidence of extensive contact between the languages and cultures of eighteenth-century Ireland. The three main languages in use were Irish, Ulster-Scots and English, each of which existed in different forms in the parts of the country where it was spoken. The languages also interacted with each other.

As its title makes clear, this anthology contains only verse which is wholly or substantially in English, but readers who seek to encounter the Irish-language verse of eighteenth-century Ireland will find a memorable selection in *An Duanaire 1600-1900: Poems of the Dispossessed* (Dublin, 1981), where Irish texts from the period, selected and edited by Seán Ó Tuama, are faced by eloquent translations into English verse by Thomas Kinsella.

Ulster-Scots poets in this anthology include Samuel Thomson, James Orr and Hugh Porter. In addition, Olivia Elder, though she is represented here by a poem in English, wrote many poems in Ulster-Scots. Eighteenth-century Ulster-Scots was closely related to Lowland Scots, as used by Robert Fergusson and by Burns. Those interested in this vigorous and colourful language should consult the *Concise Ulster Dictionary* ed. C. I. Macafee (Oxford, 1996), the ten-volume *Scottish National Dictionary*, which treats Ulster-Scots as a variant of Scots, and *The English Dialects of Ulster* (Ulster Folk Museum, 1986), a collection of seminal articles by G. B. Adams.

The anthology provides numerous examples of the two most clearly distinguishable types of English current in eighteenth-century Ireland: English which shows little influence of the Irish language, and 'Hiberno-English', as English influenced by the Irish language is normally called.[3] Among the named poets whose work is represented in this anthology, all but a handful wrote in an English virtually indistinguishable from that used by others of their class and education in England. This is despite the fact that most of them had been born into English-speaking families in Ireland and, like Oliver Goldsmith, presumably spoke with the famous Irish brogue, the characteristics of which Thomas Sheridan recorded in his 'Rules to be observed by the Natives of Ireland in order to attain a just

---

[3.] Only one other language, Latin, appears in the anthology, but it is always in a debased and comic form.

Pronunciation of English' in the introduction to his *A General Dictionary of the English Language* (London, 1780). Though these poets were better educated than many of those to whom Sheridan addressed his remarks, and certainly better educated than the planters whose Hiberno-English Swift recorded so carefully[4] — more than thirty of the poets in this anthology being graduates of Trinity College, Dublin — it is still surprising how little Hiberno-English is found in their work.

However, particularly in the anonymous verse, Hiberno-English in its various forms is common throughout the anthology. Its vocabulary can be seen in words or phrases from the Irish language and its pronunciation detected in the choice of words for rhyme or for assonance. Specifiable varieties of Hiberno-English are found in poems containing direct speech, such as *The Irish Hudibras* and the *Hesperi-neso-graphia*, and in the Dublin underworld poems. These poems in Hiberno-English come from the cultural points at which the languages and cultures of English- and Irish-speakers were meeting and interacting with each other. Hiberno-English is found in just over half the seventy-eight anonymous poems in the anthology, and in the poem by L. O'Reilly.

The Hiberno-English in these texts is of two distinct types, the first of which is a form of the language written by Irish-speaking poets who had an incomplete or faulty knowledge of English, but who were striving to communicate in a language they were in the process of acquiring. The second Hiberno-English is closer to a 'Stage-Irish'; it is a language consciously crafted by authors with a good knowledge of English whose aim was to show Irishmen speaking English in an exaggerated or even parodied 'Hibernian' accent and idiom.[5]

'Natural' Hiberno-English

The more natural and spontaneous Hiberno-English is found in anonymous ballad sheets and chapbooks, printed mostly in Irish provincial towns during a comparatively short period of time — between about 1770 and 1800. It is clear that those who composed these songs wrote also in Irish — indeed some interesting material can be found in bilingual poems in which Irish and Hiberno-English are interwoven.

---

4. *'A Dialogue in Hybernian Stile between A and B' and 'Irish Eloquence' by Jonathan Swift* edited by Alan Bliss (Dublin, 1977).

5. Martin J. Croghan has coined the word 'brogue-write' for this type of Hiberno-English; I prefer to call it 'contrived' Hiberno-English. See Martin J. Croghan, 'Swift, Thomas Sheridan, Maria Edgeworth and the Evolution of Hiberno-English', *Irish University Review* vol. 20, no. 1 (Spring 1990), Special Issue, *The English of the Irish*, ed. T. P. Dolan, pp. 19-34.

Though the knowledge these poets had of English was considerable, it was incomplete, and the use they made of the language was unconventional. They were also using the Irish *amhrán* or song metres, which meant that they would sometimes choose a word more for its sound or metrical value than for its meaning. Some of the songs they wrote are comic or bawdy, but others tell of the horrors of dipsomania, of hopeless love, of forced emigration or of unhappy marriages. The poems reflect real and powerful emotions and the Hiberno-English in which they are written is entirely unselfconscious and natural. Like many writers in post-colonial environments who start working in the language of the cultural coloniser, these poets knew nothing of lexical definitions or of rules about writing 'correct' English. The poet who wrote 'The Maiden's Resolution', for example, was expressing her unrequited love in an unfamiliar medium, borrowing vocabulary and modes of expression from her native Irish as she did so. The effect is poignant, powerful and fresh.

> Draw near each constant female, while I my ruin revealing,
> My grief's beyond concealing, for ever I'm undone;
> As on my bed I leaned, of my darling's pain I dreamed,
> My mind was then enflamed to love my Farmer's Son.

The chapbooks and ballad sheets in which these songs occur were printed in provincial towns such as Monaghan, Limerick, Newry, Tralee and Wexford, as well as in Dublin. The chapbooks would be sold to chapmen, who then hawked them around the towns and through the countryside, selling them on to ballad-singers. The songs would then be sung on street corners, at fairs and patterns,[6] in cottages, kitchens and shebeens,[7] or wherever an audience could be found. Whereas the Irish-language tradition had been one of manuscript and oral transmission, these songs in English (or Irish and English) were transmitted in printed form.[8] The verse is often of immediate interest — commemorating local or national events — and seems to have been written close to the places where it was printed. The texts are sometimes incomplete or garbled, and often contain compositors' mistakes which were not corrected before printing.

Though English was not the normal language for communication in the Irish countryside in the last thirty years of the eighteenth century, it was taught, after a fashion, by hedge-schoolmasters who had often

---

6. 'Pattern' or 'patron' days were the festivals of the patron saints of particular churches, noted for revelry after the religious observances.

7. Ir. *síbín*, a country bar.

8. cf. L. M. Cullen, 'Patrons, Teachers and Literacy in Irish: 1700-1850' in *The Origins of Popular Literacy in Ireland: Language Change and Educational Development 1700-1920*, ed. by Mary Daly and David Dickson (Dublin, 1990), pp. 15-44 (p. 38).

learned the language from books and not from native speakers.[9] The value of English as the language of commerce was widely acknowledged, and many people strove to acquire some competence in it.[10] The evidence of the chapbooks and ballad sheets is that the singing of songs in English was a popular occupation throughout Ireland, and the survival of so many macaronic songs, for the appreciation of which a knowledge of both English and Irish was normally required, suggests practical bilinguilism on a large scale.[11]

If language acquisition in Ireland followed the patterns usual elsewhere — and there is no reason to suppose that it would not have done so — the parents of these songwriters and of their audience would mostly have been monoglot Irish-speakers. Though the poets themselves and the compositors who set the texts in type would, by the 1780s, have been able to speak English fairly fluently, they would have had little formal schooling in it, which would explain why their texts exhibit considerable orthographical uncertainties. Those responsible for printing the 'Stauka an Varaga' poems, for instance, had only a hazy idea of how to represent particular sounds on the page.

The 'natural' Hiberno-English we find in these texts had a short life. As the eighteenth century gave way to the nineteenth, the English language became more widely used and better taught throughout Ireland. The next generation would have been ashamed of the linguistic and emotional rawness of these tentative, 'Irish-sounding' songs and would have wanted to forget the fact that their authors expressed themselves in such an untutored way. Songs such as the 'Colleen Rue' remained popular, but by the mid-nineteenth century, amended by succeeding generations, they had lost the immediacy of the eighteenth-century printings, and had become the comparatively anodyne texts known today.

Despite the short life of this species of Hiberno-English and the fragility of the chapbooks and ballad sheets in which it is found, there is still a surprising amount of it extant. The texts I have included in this anthology are from Monaghan, Limerick and Dublin, but examples exist from all four provinces. A study of these poems could perhaps provide

---

9. See P. J. Dowling, *The Hedge Schools of Ireland* (Cork, 1968) and P. W. Joyce, *English as We Speak it in Ireland*, ed. T. P. Dolan (Dublin, 1979), pp. 149-63.

10. Dáithí Ó hOgáin, 'Folklore and Literature: 1700-1850' in Daly and Dickson, pp. 1-13 (p. 7).

11. See Diarmaid Ó Muirithe, *An tAmhrán Macarónach* (Baile Átha Cliath, 1980). But see also the story told about Donncha Rua Mac Conmara's Gaelic and English distychs in Joep Leerssen, *Mere Irish and Fíor-Ghael: Studies in the Idea of Irish Nationality, Its Development and Literary Expression prior to the Nineteenth Century,* second edition (Cork, 1996), p. 242.

information about the characteristics of the Hiberno-English spoken in different parts of Ireland in the late eighteenth century.

'Contrived' Hiberno-English

The second form of Hiberno-English in these texts is 'contrived'. Although it too is usually found in anonymous poems, these are the work of writers highly skilled in their use of English, who use, in effect, a form of 'Stage-Irish'. The authors of poems such as 'Lilliburlero', 'The Irishmen's Prayers to St. Patrick' or 'The Connaughtman's Visit to Dublin' wrote in exaggerated Hiberno-English to make the audience laugh at the speakers in the poems. Everything about these texts — spelling, vocabulary, idiom — was designed to give an exaggerated impression of the way a typical Irishman was popularly perceived to speak English. Though each separate element in the speech of a character such as Teede in 'The Irishman's Prayers to St. Patrick' reflects accurately some element of Hiberno-English pronunciation or idiom, the compression of so many of these elements into one line or passage is highly unnatural.

> Den now broder *Teague*, vat more can I shay,
> I fear dat King *Yeamus* he will soon run away,
> Ven he hears dat Duke *Scomberg* and his Army is come,
> He'll sheek for *Fader Petre* to help him to *Rome*,
> Vhile ve shall be left to Shaint *Patrick* to pray,
> Dat he vud be pleas'd for to help us I shay; ...

Though the Hiberno-English in passages like this is exaggerated for dramatic, artistic or political effect, the individual elements which make up the speech are authentic and of great interest. The best modern study of this type of Hiberno-English is Alan Bliss's *Spoken English in Ireland 1600-1740* (Dublin, 1979).[12]

Most of the poems written in this contrived Hiberno-English were designed for singing or reciting, and any 'actor' allowing himself to be guided by the spelling would give a convincing, if parodic, impression of extreme Hiberno-English speech. The motive behind this desire to make the Irishman the butt of laughter for his absurd pronunciation of English and his use of 'bulls'[13] changed between 1687 and 1760. The late

---

12. See also the Glossary for a list of words purposely 'misspelled' in these texts to mimic Hiberno-English pronunciation.
13. Expressions involving ludicrous inconsistencies which are often, by English writers of the eighteenth century, put into the mouths of Irishmen; they are sometimes referred to as 'Irish bulls'.

seventeenth-century poems of this type in the anthology, all printed in England and primarily designed for an English anti-catholic and anti-Irish audience, sprang from the common English fear of the time that English protestantism was threatened by Irish catholicism, particularly if the Irish were in league with Jesuits and the Pope. Fear lay behind the ridicule in these early poems. Later poems in this mode, such as 'The Connaughtman's Visit to Dublin', were written when years of penal legislation had removed any such threat; by this time, the Irish countryman was merely a figure of fun, both in Dublin and in England, and his pronunciation and idiom nothing more than comic. By the early nineteenth century, songs about the misfortunes of the wandering Irish countryman were very common.

The anthology also contains poems written in an exaggerated cant or underworld 'Stage-Irish' such as 'De Night afore Larry was stretch'd' and 'Lord Altham's Bull'. These songs are again humorous in intent and have come down to us in a form designed for performance — as the spoken 'patter' at the end of stanzas in some of the texts makes clear. The poems are full of exaggerated 'Hibernicisms' of spelling and vocabulary, but it is interesting to note that some of the more unusual words in them belong to the underworld slang of eighteenth-century England.[14] The dialogues and the attitudes of the protagonists in the poems reflect, convincingly, the world of Dublin criminals in a period of particularly brutal law enforcement and, though tradition states that these poems were written by lawyers or clergymen of the time, I believe they were composed by the criminals themselves and merely 'collected' by someone else. The texts have suffered over the years in the process of transmission, and it is interesting to compare the energetic and brutal 1788 manuscript text of 'De Night afore Larry was stretch'd' in this anthology with the anodyne versions of the song printed in modern collections.

Many other poems in this anthology contain passages in Hiberno-English of various kinds. In *The Irish Hudibras*, for instance, the anonymous poet uses several subtly different versions of the Hiberno-English spoken in late seventeenth-century Fingal, north of Dublin. The main text of the poem is written in one version of this speech, but the incidence of suggestively Hiberno-English spellings, and of idioms borrowed from Irish, increases dramatically in the passages of direct speech. Two of the characters in the poem, the author explains, 'gabble ... down-right Fingallian' while two others 'had both their Education at the *English* Court, which something refin'd their *Gibberish*; yet not so much, but that there is still a *Brogue* discernible on their Tongue; Words ...

---

14. See *Lexicon Balatronicum: A Dictionary of Buckish Slang, University Wit, and Pickpocket Eloquence* (London, 1811).

dropping out so naturally, as very often betray their Country and Extraction'.[15] The author of *The Irish Hudibras* was clearly fascinated by Hiberno-English and those who spoke it, and he appended a glossary of the language and idiom of late-seventeenth century Fingal at the end of the poem.

William Dunkin created a particularly vigorous form of Hiberno-English for Father Fagan in 'The Parson's Revels', and the anonymous author of 'The Connaughtman's Visit to Dublin' entered so fully into the spirit of the exercise of orthographical representation of extreme Hiberno-English pronunciation that his poem is barely intelligible. Other registers are employed by Richard Milliken in 'The Groves of Blarney' (his parody of 'Sweet Castle-Hyde') in some of the political poems on the nationalist side, and in 'comic Irishman' poems such as 'Paddy the Piper'. Equally unexpected is the Hiberno-English of 'The Siege of Troy', which is merely a sample of many such poems. It is worth stressing that a very substantial quantity of eighteenth-century verse containing passages in Hiberno-English — of many different kinds — is extant, each poem carrying its own subtle linguistic, political and cultural messages. Only when these poems are brought to public attention and deciphered will it be possible to make any assessment of the culture of eighteenth-century Ireland.

(III)

The Influence of the Irish Language and of Irish Metrics on
Verse Written in English

Most previous anthologists of eighteenth-century Anglo-Irish verse — trained to consider the English way of writing verse somehow superior to all others — have found it hard to hear or to appreciate the subtle influences of the Irish language and of Irish metrics on that verse. Instead of trying to determine how the influence of Irish might enrich verse in English, they have treated any signs of connection with ridicule. Writing in 1790, Joshua Edkins described the verse written in English by a strolling ballad-writer called L. O'Reilly as so ridiculous that it had to be 'translated' into traditional English verse before it could be understood by the Dublin-based readers of his *Collection of Poems* (1790).[16] Thomas

---

15. *The Irish Hudibras* (London, 1689), 'To the Reader'.
16. *A Collection of Poems, mostly original, by Several Hands*, ed. Joshua Edkins (Dublin, 1790), p. 141.

12

Crofton Croker, writing in the 1830s but referring back to the eighteenth century, wrote disparagingly of '... ignorant Irish village bards with a vast fondness for rhyme, an imperfect knowledge of the English language, and a pedantic ambition to display the full extent of their classical knowledge', and approved of those who made fun of them.[17] In the shadow of such scorn, even writers sympathetic to Irish culture, such as P. W. Joyce, have been inclined to see the verse written by the hedge-schoolmasters and wandering poets of eighteenth-century Ireland as laughable.[18]

The struggle experienced by Irish-speakers to express themselves in the foreign language of English was complicated by the facts of education in eighteenth-century rural Ireland. The bardic schools had died out in the seventeenth century and, under the Penal Laws enacted after the defeat of catholic Ireland at the battle of the Boyne and the siege of Limerick, catholics were prohibited from setting up schools to educate their youth. Only protestants could attend charter or classical schools and so, although in fact there were many catholic schoolmasters and some convents operating clandestinely in Dublin and other cities and towns, a catholic living in the countryside could normally depend for education only on the local hedge-schoolmaster. On the evidence of this anthology, hedge-schoolmasters taught their scholars many useful skills, as well as something of the classics and how to read and write English. In the poem in which he advertises his school (p. 385), Eoghan Rua Ó Súilleabháin — himself a scribe and one of the best poets in the Irish language — lists the subjects he teaches as catechetics, book-keeping, mensuration, navigation, trigonometry, geometry, arithmetic and English grammar. He also taught his students how to deal with legal documents and how to write in rhyme. The emphasis, it will be noted, was on a practical education and on the English language. There is no mention in this poem of the teaching of Irish, though some schoolmasters certainly did teach it while others, particularly in County Kerry, taught Latin and Greek to high standards. But the English taught in the countryside must have varied from school to school. It was taught without the benefit of texts of any kind and often by a master for whom it was a second language and who might have learned it, substantially, from books. The schoolmasters were learned men, but, according to P. W. Joyce, it was hard for them to be certain of the foundations on which their learning was based. He tells of hedge-school masters in rural Ireland engaging in long, public disputations on minute

---

17. *Popular Songs of Ireland*, ed. Thomas Crofton Croker, second edition (London, 1886), p. 138. The first edition of this work appeared in 1839.

18. P. W. Joyce, *English as we Speak it in Ireland*, second edition (Dublin, 1979), pp. 78-80.

points of English grammar, such as the rules governing the use of the verb 'to be'.[19]

Thus when these hedge-schoolmasters or their pupils wrote verse in English, they were using a language with which they were not entirely familiar, and it is not surprising that they often transferred into the new language the metrical patterns they were accustomed to use in Irish verse. In its form, subject matter and tone, the English verse they wrote is far removed from the polished verse produced by middle-class rhymers in Dublin or Cork; but the work of these country poets shows vividly what happened in eighteenth-century Ireland when Irish culture and English culture met each other face to face.

Metrics: the *amhrán* or song metre, and assonance

Throughout the eighteenth-century, English verse was normally written in accentual-syllabic metres, whether it appeared on the page as blank verse, in couplets or in stanzas. Each line was measured by the number of 'feet' it contained, each 'foot' being made up of a fixed number of stressed and unstressed syllables and named after the pattern of those stressed and unstressed syllables (iamb, trochee etc.). Most poets used rhyme, seeking full rather than half-rhymes, and end-rhymes rather than internal ones. Swift, for example, wrote mostly in rhyming iambic tetrameters (lines made up of four iambic feet, with full end-rhymes, arranged in couplets) while Goldsmith wrote in rhyming iambic pentameters (lines made up of five iambic feet, with full end-rhymes, arranged in couplets).

Those writing verse in Irish, on the contrary, commonly used stressed rather than accentual-syllabic metres. The number of syllables in a line of Irish verse was not important, but the number of stresses was. Consonance of sound was sought not in full end-rhymes but in assonance between stressed syllables within, as well as at the end of, lines. Thus the rules of prosody as applied to English and Irish poetry in the eighteenth century differed considerably from each other.

These Irish metres are known as *amhrán* or song metres, and one of them in particular, the *ochtfhoclach*, is found in a number of the anonymous songs in English in this anthology. The basic unit of the *ochtfhoclach* is the couplet. Within couplets, the last stressed syllable of the first line rhymes assonantally with the last stressed syllable of the second line. In addition, there is, within each line, an additional (and different) assonantal rhyming pattern which is repeated three times.

19. Joyce, pp. 152-53. See also Dowling, pp. 35-61.

14

In an Irish poem of this metre, there are usually four couplets in each verse. Sometimes each couplet in a verse will have exactly the same internal assonantal rhyming scheme, but sometimes the pattern changes regularly. Within a verse, the final stressed rhyme is nearly always the same and often is maintained throughout the poem. In the following example of a stanza of the *ochtfhoclach* type written by John Philpot Curran, the different assonantal rhymes are shown in italics and bold type:

> If sadly *thinking*, with spirits *sinking*, ‖ Could, more than *drinking*,
>   my cares com**pose**,
> A cure for *sorrow* from sighs I'd *borrow*, ‖ And hope *tomorrow* would
>   end my **woes**.
> But as in *wailing* there's nought *availing*, ‖ And Death *unfailing* will
>   strike the **blow**,
> Then for that *reason*, and for a *season*, ‖ Let us be *merry* before we **go**.

There are examples of this metre in the work of nearly every major poet writing in Irish between 1650 and 1800 and in folksongs of the period.

When the *ochtfhoclach* is used in English, the result is surprising and powerful. The echoic effect of the triple assonance, repeated so closely, can be used for comic effect (as in 'Connelly's Ale' or Milliken's parody of 'Sweet Castle-Hyde') but it can also — since the chiming is not of full rhymes but sometimes of no more than a vowel — create a haunting undercurrent in a sad poem, as in 'The Maiden's Resolution' or 'The Sailor Dear'. English ears, used to the almost brutal thump of the end-rhyme in English verse, have often found it hard to hear the subtle assonantal interweavings in such verse.[20]

In order to appreciate the effect being sought by eighteenth-century Irish poets who used internal, assonantal rhyme in poems written in English, the verse has to be read aloud and some account taken of the way English was pronounced in Ireland at the time, particularly of the fact that the vowel sounds were more akin to those of Elizabethan English than to those of modern English.[21] As Thomas Sheridan pointed out in his 1780 *Dictionary of the English Language*, eighteenth-century Irishmen pronounced words like *tea*, *sea*, *please* as *tay*, *say*, *plays*. They also

---

20. The best-known serious poem in the *ochtfhoclach* metre in English is 'The Deserter's Meditation' by John Philpot Curran (partly quoted above, and see p. 556). Byron, who knew Curran, is the only major English poet, to my knowledge, to have tried the metre. See 'Stanzas', *The Poetical Works of Lord Byron* (Oxford Standard Authors, 1957), pp. 106-07. The best-known comic poem in *ochtfhoclach* metre in English is Milliken's 'The Groves of Blarney' (see p. 523).

21. For an explanation of the reasons for this linguistic stagnation, see A. J. Bliss, *Spoken English in Ireland 1600-1740* (Dublin, 1979), pp. 186-88.

pronounced *patron, matron* as *pahtron, mahtron* and *calm, psalm* as *cawm, psawm*. Sheridan's other examples include *deceit, receive* pronounced as *desate, resave*, and individual words *onion* as *inion, catch* as *ketch*, and *gather* as *gether*. The most striking differences between Irish pronunciation and that of the standard English of the time is in vowel sounds, and it is vowels on which assonantal rhyme is based.[22]

In addition to Sheridan's examples above, the texts in this anthology will provide scores of other cases where the assonantal rhyme used by the poet suggests a variation in pronunciation between standard English and Hiberno-English. The assonantal rhymes in the first stanza of 'The Sailor Dear' are shown below.

> Ye maidens *pretty* in town and *city* ‖ Pray hear with *pity* my mournful **strain**,
> A maid con*founded* in sorrow *drowned*, ‖ And deeply *wounded* with grief and **pain**.
> 'Tis for the *sake* of a lovely *sailor*, ‖ I'm still *bewailing*, melting in **tears**,
> Whilst other *maidens* are fondly *playing*, ‖ I'm *grieving* for my Sailor **Dear**.

Assonances which suggest Hiberno-English vowel values in the example above are *founded, drowned, wounded* and *maidens, playing, grieving*. More unexpected examples occur in many other poems, for instance in the last two stanzas of 'The Maiden's Resolution' (p. 393). In this case, however, some of the unusual assonances may result from the poet's unfamiliarity with the standard pronunciation of certain English words or from her inability to find appropriate rhyming sounds:

> Blessed was the *hour*, I entered his sweet *bower*, ‖ Bedeckt with fragrant *flowers* where silver streams do **run**;
> And Sol's beams were *shining* with beauty most *surprising*, ‖ All things were still *delighting* my country Farmer's **Son**.
> Tho' my ambitious *parents* doth like for to make *varience*, ‖ Who said he was *inferior* to their great **dignity**;
> Cupid has *inspir'd me* and Hyme has *desir'd me* ‖ To hail the wound *I gave him* with sweet **chestity**.

In addition to unusual assonances such as *parents* and *varience* with *inferior* (which the poet probably pronounced *infarior*) and *inspir'd* and *desir'd* with *gave*, this poem provides the spellings *hail* for *heal* and *chestity* for *chastity*. The second may be a printer's error, but the first is a classic Hiberno-English pronunciation.

22. For further information on this topic, see Bliss, pp. 198-225, and E. J. Dobson, *English Pronunciation 1500-1700*, second edition (Oxford, 1968); for examples, see P. W. Joyce, op. cit., pp. 91-104.

16

Vocabulary

The vocabulary of the Irish-speaking poets and schoolmasters who began writing in English in eighteenth-century Ireland also shows extensive 'interference' from the Irish language. Since they lived in isolated rural communities and seldom heard English spoken by a native speaker, these poets and schoolmasters spoke and wrote in an English which had changed little from that spoken and written by the first English-speaking settlers in their areas who had arrived early in the seventeenth century. Both their vocabulary and pronunciation were distinctly archaic by the end of the eighteenth century. In addition, lacking contact with other English-speakers and teaching themselves the language from books, they sometimes made mistakes in their use of words. Thus in their work we find words and expressions incorrectly used, words and expressions which have crossed over from the Irish language, and archaic English phrases and words. In *English as we Speak it in Ireland* (1910), P. W. Joyce explained what happened

> The Irish schoolmasters knew Irish well, and did their best — generally with success — to master English. This they did partly from their neighbours, but in large measure from books, including dictionaries. As they were naturally inclined to show forth their learning, they made use, as much as possible, of long and unusual words, mostly taken from dictionaries, but many coined by themselves from Latin. Goldsmith's description of the village master with his 'words of learned length and thundering sound' applies exactly to a large proportion of the schoolmasters of the eighteenth and early nineteenth century all over Ireland.... As might be expected, the schoolmasters, as well as others, who used these strange words often made mistakes in applying them, which will be seen in some of the following examples. Here is one whole verse of a song about a young lady, 'The Phoenix of the Hall'.

> > I being quite captivated and so infatuated
> > I then prognosticated by sad forlorn case;
> > But I quickly ruminated — suppose I was *defaited*,
> > I would not be implicated or treated with disgrace;
> > So therefore I awaited with my spirits elevated,
> > And no more I ponderated let what would me befall;
> > I then to her *repated* how Cupid had me *thrated*
> > And thus expostulated with the Phoenix of the Hall.

This poem belongs to the same tradition as several of the chapbook poems of the 1780s included in this anthology, and examples of the misunderstanding of the true meanings of certain English polysyllables, similar to those which Joyce is demonstrating in the example above, can be seen in several of the poems selected for this book, though in no case is it as concentrated as in 'The Phoenix of the Hall'.[23]

Spoken Hiberno-English, particularly if it includes unusual pronunciation and words used incorrectly, can sound comic to speakers of standard English, a fact which has been exploited constantly by those writing 'Stage-Irish' from Shakespeare's time to the present day.[24] However, many of the poems in this anthology in which words are used in unusual ways are not comic, nor were they intended to be. They were written, and were intended to be read, seriously. When English words appear in unusual contexts or are used in an unfamiliar register, as in L. O'Reilly's 'Elegy on Miss Bridget Burne' or in the version of 'The Colleen Rue' in this collection, the reader is startled into reassessing them, and the very lack of 'correctness' in the poems in which such 'misused' words occur gives the poems themselves a memorable freshness and poignancy.

The elegy by L. O'Reilly also shows the influence of the mood and tone of Gaelic poetry. Were it in Irish, this poem would be seen as a fairly standard elegy, written to commission, complete with hyperbole and traditional similes. In English, however, the poem acquires an exotic status; the register is quite unfamiliar to English ears and the work sounds as if it comes (as indeed it does) from a completely different poetic culture. The voice of L. O'Reilly in his 'Elegy on Miss Bridget Burne' is an original voice from eighteenth-century Ireland and one which has not been acknowledged before. 'Sweet Castle-Hyde' too — another survival of the work of a wandering Irish poet written, in English, for money — contains such 'un-English' hyperbole and praise that the landlord to whom it was presented, assuming it to be a mockery instead of hearing it as the praise poem it was intended to be, had the poor poet driven from the gate of Castle Hyde. Crofton Croker, who tells the story and who was clearly as deaf to the poem as was the owner of Castle Hyde, adds the view that, 'in fact, a more nonsensical composition could scarcely escape the pen of a maniac'.[25]

23. 'The Phoenix of the Hall' also provides interesting examples of assonantal rhyme based on Hiberno-English rather than standard vowel values. Joyce italicised the words *defaited*, *repated* and *thrated* to highlight the fact that these spellings represented the pronunciation of *defeated*, *repeated* and *treated*.

24. Swift, Behan and O'Casey are among those who have exploited these aspects of Hiberno-English for comic effect. See also Leerssen, pp. 77-150, and Bliss, pp. 312-16.

25. Croker, p. 137.

Chapbooks

Much of the material written by Irish poets in English survives only in the chapbooks printed in Irish provincial centres between 1770 and 1810, particularly in Monaghan, Limerick, Newry and Tralee. Some of the verse in the chapbooks was well-known, but much of it seems to have been written locally, some of it commemorating local duels or riots and naming local personalities. The chapbooks, printed cheaply on poor-quality paper, often without even a woodcut illustration, were sold to the chapmen who wandered through the countryside at this time. The chapmen, who carried the poems around in their packs, with the needles, patent medicines and trinkets which made up their wares, sold them in rural communities. Here, presumably, they were sung, to popular tunes, in kitchens and shebeens.[26]

The distinguishing characteristic of this verse is its unbourgeois nature. It reflects the interests and obsessions, the passions and miseries of ordinary people living in rural Ireland in the eighteenth century; in its language, its concerns and its often subversive tone, it is far removed from the world of Thomas Moore, Mary Tighe or the piano-playing daughters of the rising middle classes of the 1790s in Waterford or Newry. The voices here are from the margins of society and are often voices which seek to question or subvert that society. Some of the songs are rebel songs, others are bawdy or frankly obscene, some are moving laments and elegies, others bilingual songs which exploit fully the freedom of movement between two languages. All are, in a very particular way, 'Irish', the products of a world in which at least two cultures are struggling to come to terms with each other and to interact. All these poems are worth reading. I would take serious issue with the view expressed in 1976 by James F. Kilroy, that no Irish poet writing in English before the late nineteenth century spoke 'in a voice distinct from the English' or wrote 'for a popular Irish audience'.[27] Many of the Irish poets whose English verse appears in this anthology did just that, and their contribution should be acknowledged and seen in the context of other Irish verse of the age. Where the culture of English-speaking Ireland and that of Irish-speaking Ireland meet from the mid-eighteenth century onward, the poetic voices which emerge are fresh and memorable.

However, it is only now, when the literary canon is a thing of the past and there is an openness towards writing of all kinds, that these poems can

---

26. An important and pioneering article on this neglected area is Hugh Shields, 'Printed Aids to Folk Singing 1700-1900' in Daly and Dickson, pp. 139-152.

27. James F. Kilroy, 'Nineteenth-Century Writers' in *Anglo-Irish Literature: A Review of Research* ed. Richard J. Finneran (New York, 1976), pp. 24-47 (p. 24).

be valued. In the early nineteenth century, the increasingly prosperous middle classes wanted to forget their roots in the Irish language and its culture, and closed their minds to anything that reminded them of their rural past. It would have been hard for the average Irishman or woman of the time to look at the anonymous chapbook verse of the eighteenth century without despising its inelegancies and infelicities. The brutal realism of 'A Drop of Dram' or 'The Coughing Old Man' was best forgotten for social reasons as well as for reasons of literary 'taste', and such a reader would feel much happier with the polished cadences and romantic perceptions of 'Erin' to be found in the Moore's *Irish Melodies*. In addition, the horrors of the last decade of the eighteenth century — agrarian violence, rebellions, risings, economic devastation, forced emigration and eviction — made the early nineteenth century a period of almost obsessive demands for a society and a culture of calm and reason. There was also the rising power of puritanical Maynooth-trained priests, many of whom wanted, with an almost missionary zeal, to drag their parishioners from a dark Irish-speaking past into a bright English-speaking future; for such men, poems such as those circulated by the chapmen reflected the very world from which they themselves were trying to escape, and a world which their parishioners would do well to forget. During most of the present century, perceptions of the Irish literary past have been defined by agendas into which the chapbook verse of the late eighteenth century does not fit at all comfortably.

Translations and macaronic verse

Considering late seventeenth-century English attitudes towards the native culture of Ireland as expressed in, for example, *The Irish Hudibras*, it is surprising how many translations of Irish verse into English verse were made during even the early eighteenth century. Apart from 'A Description of an Irish Feast' — Swift's famous 'translation' of Hugh Mac Gauran's 'Pléaráca na Ruarcach' — at least four other eighteenth-century verse translations of that poem are extant,[28] and Dermod O'Connor's 1723 translation of Geoffrey Keating's *Foras Feasa ar Éirinn* contains fine

28. See Andrew Carpenter and Alan Harrison, 'Swift's "O'Rourke's Feast" and Sheridan's "Letter": Early Transcripts by Anthony Raymond' in *Proceedings of the First Münster Symposium on Jonathan Swift* ed. Hermann J. Real and Heinz J. Vienken (Munich, 1985), pp. 27-46, and Frank Llewelyn Harrison, 'Charles Coffey and Swift's "Description of an Irish Feast"', *Swift Studies*, 1 (1986), pp. 32-38. The other translations are in British Library MS. Egerton 150, in Charles Henry Wilson, *Select Irish Poems Translated into English* (Dublin, 1772) and in two of Charles Coffey's ballad operas.

renditions in English verse of the Irish poetry in that text. Songs were often translated from one language to the other — as is clear happened in the world of Carolan — and even Arthur Dawson's 'Bumpers Squire Jones' (see p. 299) is said to be a translation.[29] Fragments of verse translated into English are not infrequently embedded in Irish manuscripts of the period and there are regular mentions of English-speaking gentlemen and ladies being entertained by Irish harpers and of their being furnished with translations of Irish songs.[30]

Following the publication of James MacPherson's *Fragments of Ancient Poetry Collected in the Highlands of Scotland* in 1760, educated people throughout 'the British Isles' developed a strong interest in things Celtic. This interest embraced the native culture of Ireland as well as that of Scotland and Wales. The *Transactions* of the Royal Irish Academy and, later, of the Gaelic Society of Dublin, contain interesting translations from Irish poetry into English verse, and translations were also published by Joseph Cooper Walker in *Historical Memoirs of the Irish Bards* (London, 1786) and, most notably, by Charles Henry Wilson in his *Poems Translated from the Irish Language into the English* (Dublin, 1782) and by Charlotte Brooke in her *Reliques of Ancient Irish Poetry* (Dublin, 1789) (see pp. 376 and 453). The most influential of these volumes was Brooke's *Reliques*, the preface to which contains the following memorable passage about the Irish language:

> It is really astonishing of what various and comprehensive powers this neglected language is possessed. In the pathetic, it breathes the most beautiful and affecting simplicity; and in the bolder species of composition, it is distinguished by a force of expression, a sublime dignity, and rapid energy which it is scarcely possible for any translation fully to convey; as it sometimes fills the mind with ideas altogether new, and which, perhaps, no modern language is entirely prepared to express.

It is in the context of this growing interest in and enthusiasm for poetry in the Irish language on the part of readers of 'polite literature' that translations began to appear in the 'Poetry' sections of various periodicals in the last two decades of the century. Many of them were translations of heroic verse, but in October 1793 a Philip McKernan of Belturbet, County

---

29. But see Donal O'Sullivan, *Carolan: The Life, Times and Music of an Irish Harper*, two volumes, second edition (Louth, Lincolnshire, 1983), II, 40-43.

30. See, for instance, *The Correspondence of Jonathan Swift*, ed. Harold Williams, 5 vols. (Oxford, 1963), II, 441 where Swift talks of Irish harpers in County Cavan, and Charles Henry Wilson, *Brookiana*, 2 vols. (London, 1804), I, 86, where there is an account of Henry Brooke receiving translations of Irish poems.

Cavan, sent the editor of the *Anthologia Hibernica* the Irish text of a comic poem, 'Seachran Fhiachra mhic Bradaigh', which he described as having been 'composed some years ago by a gentleman of this country of the name of Brady, many of whose productions are still current here, all abounding with real humour'.[31] The editor requested a translation and, when this appeared two months later, it followed, with remarkable fidelity, the metrics of the original Irish text (p. 498). It is a pity that the author of this translation remained anonymous, for his or her wonderfully vigorous recreation in English of the playful Irish text is one of the best extant eighteenth-century translations into English verse from Irish.

Another example of enthusiastic and faithful translation is the English version by Denis Woulfe of Brian Merriman's *Cúirt an Mheán Oíche*. What is surprising about this translation is not that one schoolmaster would put into English the Irish poem written by another, but that Woulfe's translation should be so little known. Portions of the text appeared in a Clare newspaper during the nineteenth century and in *The Irishman* in 1880, but the full text of this translation was printed only in 1982.[32] As an Irish eighteenth-century poem, the translation reflects remarkably well the anarchic force of its original. Like many others, Woulfe was determined to allow those who did not read or speak Irish the chance to hear and enjoy poetry written in that language.

Irish and English culture also meet head to head in macaronic poems written partly in Irish and partly in English. Such poems, scores of which were written during the eighteenth century, presuppose an audience able to understand both languages. Three types of such poems are included in this anthology, of which the most interesting is probably Art Mac Cumhaidh's 'Tagra an Dá Theampall' or 'The Disputation of the Two Churches'. Here the Irish and English languages are used symbolically to represent the two dominant cultures, as a ruined catholic chapel and a newly built protestant church debate the religious and political issues of the 1760s. The catholic chapel speaks in the Irish language and the protestant church speaks in English. The protagonists present their cases in the traditional manner, but the catholic chapel is forced to admit that protestantism is, for the moment, in the more powerful position of the two. Even though Art Mac Cumhaidh was writing for an audience predominantly made up of Irish-speakers, he clearly expected them not

---

31. *Anthologia Hibernica* for October 1793, p. 298. The fact that eight mistakes were made in the Irish text as printed in the October issue (see the errata printed in December on p. 458) suggests that the Dublin proof-correctors of the magazine could not read Irish.

32. Liam P. Ó Murchú, *Cúirt an Mheán-Oíche* (Baile Átha Cliath, 1982) pp. 84-109.

22

only to enjoy hearing a debate between the two churches as if it were between two clerics, but also to be able to follow what the protestant church said in English. The interaction here is not just of language but of the whole range of cultural, religious and political realities of life in eighteenth-century Ireland.

Of the other macaronic verse in the anthology, 'Do Tharlaigh Inné Orm' is typical of many poems in which an English-speaking girl is accosted by an Irish-speaking boy. The poet exploits the difference in meaning between Irish and English words which sound the same — the Irish *mhama* ('breasts') being mistaken for English 'mama' for instance, with comic effect. The Irish portion of the text in the two 'Stauka an Varaga' poems is interesting for a different reason, however. Here, the Irish is not spelled correctly but phonetically; when read aloud, it is (just about) intelligible as Irish to an Irish-speaking audience. This suggests that these texts were being printed for sale to ballad-singers who, though they could read English and speak both English and Irish, could not read Irish. This is not surprising if we remember that it was the ability to write in English rather than in Irish which was taught in the hedge-schools in late eighteenth-century Ireland and that though almost everyone in rural Ireland spoke Irish at this time, few could write or read it.[33]

Both the translations and the macaronic poems included in this anthology give some indication of the linguistic interaction between English and Irish in eighteenth-century Ireland, but more research needs to be done on the cultural context in which some of this work was produced or printed.[34] In particular, it would be interesting to know more about the phonetic spelling of the Irish language in materials for popular consumption. More work needs to be done also on verse translation from Irish to English in polite circles and on the extent to which people who heard Irish songs in, say, the drawing rooms of Dublin or Cork, understood what they meant.

33. See two relevant articles in Daly and Dickson: Louis Cullen, 'Patrons, Teachers and Literacy in Irish 1700-1850' (pp. 15-44) and Nial Ó Cíosáin, 'Printed Popular Literature in Irish 1750-1850: Presence and Absence' (pp. 45-58). See also Nial Ó Cíosáin, *Print and Popular Culture in Ireland, 1750-1850* (London, 1997), particularly pp. 158-69.
34. Though Diarmaid Ó Muirithe's anthology *An tAmhrán Macarónach* (Baile Átha Cliath, 1980) contains several interesting examples taken from primary eighteenth-century sources, many of his texts are later. The fullest discussion of the matter is in Ó Cíosáin, *Print and Popular Culture*, chapter 9.

(IV)

Daily Life in Eighteenth-Century Ireland:
the Evidence of the Poems

Much of the material in this anthology contains contemporary or near-contemporary views of life in eighteenth-century Ireland. Nicholas Browne and John Anketell, for instance, when describing a wedding in County Tyrone and a 'pattern' at a holy well in County Monaghan, are both describing events which they undoubtedly witnessed. Neither seeks to colour the description with political prejudice and each account contains interesting details about the conditions of ordinary life in eighteenth-century Ireland.

Other poetic descriptions in this anthology were intended as records of a dying way of life, particularly Laurence Whyte's 'The Parting Cup or the Humours of Deoch an Doruis'. Whyte wrote this poem in his old age to record life as it had been in County Westmeath in the reign of Queen Anne. There may be exaggeration in the poem but, on the whole, the account of ordinary life which it gives is entirely convincing, and Whyte's political purpose — to deplore the actions of greedy, absentee landlords — is very evident. The political agenda behind the anonymous *Hesperi-neso-graphia* is clear enough also, but although there is religious and political bigotry in some passages in this poem, it is full of authentic details about life in a community more typical of the seventeenth century than of the eighteenth, one seemingly untouched by the Penal Laws or dispossession.

Some poems are valuable because they provide details of eighteenth-century events or situations about which we otherwise know very little — whaling off the coast of County Donegal or the realities of confinement in the Dublin debtors' prison, for instance. In other poems, it is the artless enthusiasm of the poets which makes their descriptions so appealing, whether they are describing a fox-chase or a bull-baiting, a group of young ladies struggling ashore from an upturned pleasure boat, or a smock race. Equally memorable are Morrough O'Connor's description of his farm in Kerry, James Orr's two poems on the horrors of the emigrant ship, and William King's eulogy of the bovine Mully of Mountown, destined for the butcher's knife despite her beauty and her productivity. Other poems provide intimate and sometimes unexpected details about coffee-houses and whiskey-shops, football games and sea-bathing, charity concerts and weddings, activities at patterns, fairs and assizes, life in rich houses and life in poor houses.

So many modern accounts of eighteenth-century Ireland are based on political events that it is surprising to see how few poets of the age were actively concerned with politics until the last twenty years of the century. Jacobite hopes were normally expressed in the Irish language, though they do lie behind 'The Blackbird' and a small number of Jacobite songs in English which are found embedded in Irish manuscripts of the period, as Diarmaid Ó Muirithe has shown.[35] In addition, Murray Pittock has pointed to links between some of the Scottish Jacobite verse and Ireland.[36] A generalised but not very aggressive Jacobitism lies behind the worlds portrayed by Laurence Whyte in 'The Parting Cup or the Humours of Deoch an Doruis' and by the anonymous author of the *Hesperi-neso-graphia*; equally, there is a generalised support for England and things English behind much of the verse in this anthology, from drinking songs to Matthew Concanen's account of a football match, for instance.

It is in the writings of Jonathan Swift that eighteenth-century Ireland finds its most powerful political poet. Since Swift's public verse concerning the Wood's Halfpence controversy of the 1720s can easily be found elsewhere, it is not included in this anthology, though it must not be forgotten that verse from his pen, and that of others, played a major part in the swaying of public opinion of the time. Swift's later, violent attack on the Irish parliament, 'The Legion Club', is included, however, as the most significant Irish political poem of the century. Other members of Swift's circle did not write memorable political verse, and the poets who later supported Lucas or Grattan did not do so in ways which compelled me to include their work in this volume. Once the Volunteer movement began, in the 1770s, the volume of political poetry increased dramatically, though again, most of those who wrote rousing songs supporting the Volunteers or demanding 'Free Trade' did so in less than memorable verse. The verse surrounding Hely-Hutchinson[37] is of a party-political nature and not really of general interest. Only when we reach the late 1780s and the 1790s, do national political events become as central to Irish poetry in English as they had been in the 1720s and 1730s.

---

35. Diarmaid Ó Muirithe, "'Tho' not in full stile compleat": Jacobite songs from Gaelic Manuscript Sources', *Eighteenth-Century Ireland / Iris an dá Chultúr*, VI (1991), pp. 93-103.

36. Murray G. H. Pittock, *Poetry and Jacobite Politics in Eighteenth-Century Britain and Ireland* (Cambridge, 1994).

37. John Hely-Hutchinson (1724-94), lawyer and statesman, secretary of state and provost of Trinity College Dublin.

It was the ideals of the French Revolution which struck a chord with Irish poets on all sides of the political spectrum, and the 'liberty tree' became a powerful symbol for all those who wished to see Ireland 'free', whether the colour of their flag was the white of the Jacobite, the orange of the Orangeman, the blue of the true protestant, or the green that would become the colour of nationalism. Space has been made in this collection for the texts of some of the lesser-known of the thousands of good ballads written in Ireland in the 1790s, though the best-known ballads have been omitted since they are easily available elsewhere.[38] Space has also been made for a Dublin ballad-singer's loyal song in praise of the departing Lord Lieutenant, Earl Fitzwilliam, for a moving poem by Robert Emmet and for part of *The United Irishmen*, a harrowing tale of 1798. In general though, and with the exceptions noted above, it is remarkable how little the political events of eighteenth-century Ireland are reflected in its verse.

Economic matters were of more importance to the poets whose work appears in this anthology, however. A particular problem was posed by the tithes payable to the clergy of the established (protestant) Church of Ireland. These caused considerable economic hardship to the poorer farmers and, since they produced no tangible benefit, they were resented more than rents. The clergy needed tithes, and they felt that the foundations of the establishment were undermined if tithes were questioned — as Swift showed in 'The Legion Club'. But tithes were demanded of all occupiers of land, whatever their religious affiliation, and members of churches other than the Church of Ireland found them particularly irksome. The anonymous Lagan farmer in 'Tit for Tat; or the Rater Rated' is delighted when his wife gives the rector's wife a piece of her mind instead of just paying the tithes quietly.

The problems associated with a life on the land occur in many eighteenth-century Irish poems, and are a central concern of Laurence Whyte in 'The Parting Cup'. As rents rise and the value of produce falls, so older ways of life disappear and improving farmers are turned off their land by greedy landlords determined to rack rents as high as they can.

> Thus Farmers liv'd like Gentlemen
> E're Lands were raised from five to ten,
> Again from ten to three times five,[39]
> Then very few cou'd hope to thrive,

38. See, for instance, Zimmerman and *The Complete Irish Street Ballads* ed. Colm Ó Lochlainn (London, 1965).

39. i.e. rents per acre were raised from five shillings to ten, to fifteen, and finally to twenty shillings (one pound) per annum.

> But tug[g]'d against the rapid Stream,
> Which drove them back from whence they came;
> At length, 'twas canted[40] to a Pound,
> What Tenant then cou'd keep his Ground?
> Not knowing which to stand or fly,
> When Rent-Rolls[41] mounted Zenith high,
> They had their choice to run away,
> Or labour for a Groat a Day,
> Now beggar'd and of all bereft,
> Are doom'd to starve, or live by Theft,
> Take to the Mountains or the Roads,
> When banish'd from their old Abodes;
> Their native Soil were forc'd to quit,
> So Irish Landlords thought it fit,
> Who without Cer'mony or Rout,
> For their Improvements turn'd them out.[42]
> Embracing still the highest Bidder,
> Inviting all Ye Nations hither,
> Encouraging all Strollers, Caitiffs,[43]
> Or any other but the Natives.

In this typically energetic passage, Whyte, more clearly than any other poetic commentator in Ireland, noted the social effect of the greed of landlords in the face of changing economic circumstances. This is also the theme of Goldsmith's 'The Deserted Village' and, as early commentators noticed, Whyte and Goldsmith came from the same part of County Westmeath — though Goldsmith was a generation younger. Farming and the production of food were of central importance to most of the inhabitants of eighteenth-century Ireland and it is not surprising that the price and quality of food and drink are recurring themes in their poetry; in poems where food is available in abundance, there is almost always a description of a gargantuan feast. Other poems, in which food is scarce, give harrowing accounts of the effect of shortage and famine.

Economic reality is also at the centre of James Sterling's plea to Arthur Dobbs to support plans for a whale-fishery in County Donegal in the 1730s, and Sterling's poem 'A Friend in Need is a Friend in Deed' is

---

40. sold at auction.

41. The rents payable on the rent-roll or landlord's list of rented land.

42. Whyte returned to this theme in a poem entitled 'Gaffer and Gammer, with the Humours of a bad Landlord: a Tale' in his 1742 *Original Poems on Various Subjects*, pp. 14-17. In that poem, he tells of an improving farmer who entertains his landlord well and, as a consequence, 'Next Year poor Gaffer was turn'd out / For brewing Ale so very stout, / For being generous and free, / As Farmers whilom us'd to be.'

43. villains.

remarkable for its fifty-six-line poetic summary of Ireland's economic history, a prologue to the argument. A poetic appeal to an eighteenth-century government official, which would be read in coffee-houses and streets as well as in parliament, might be more politically effective than the same thing in prose. Equally, two beneficed clergymen of the established church, Smedley and Delany, thought that a poetic appeal to a Lord Lieutenant for a better living might be more effective than any other approach; in each case, however, their appeal was ridiculed.

Religion and religious affiliation surface less than one might expect in eighteenth-century Irish verse in English. The defeat of Jacobite Ireland in 1691 brought to an end the sort of anti-catholic bigotry which suffuses the early Williamite poems, but it is interesting to see, two generations later, Art Mac Cumhaidh's 'Tagra an Dá Theampall' ('The Disputation of the Two Churches') present the difference between the catholic and protestant churches in theological and historical terms rather than in polemics. It is the church buildings, rather than their occupants, which converse in that poem. Apostasy from catholicism is a theme in many eighteenth-century poems in Irish and recurs here in the 'Pléaráca an Bhráthar'. Mass-going is mentioned fairly regularly, particularly in the anonymous chapbook verse, and patterns and other festivals are described respectfully, even by protestant observers. In Irish verse in English from the eighteenth century as a whole, however, catholic clergy feature more frequently as objects of satire than as serious protagonists.

Life in Ulster

We know a considerable amount, from poetic sources, about late eighteenth-century Ulster, since ordinary life was faithfully recorded by the weaver poets and their work has been more carefully tended than has the popular verse written in English in the other Irish provinces.[44]

Although it is primarily the energy with which they celebrate the local life of late eighteenth-century Ulster which makes the weaver poets so attractive, the Ulster-Scots they use is also of interest. This language has an uninhibited freshness and freedom in both vocabulary and syntax which allows it to represent experience in a particularly vivid way. In this anthology, one has only to read the two poems written by James Orr on the emigrant ship taking him to Delaware to experience this difference at

---

44. See John Hewitt, *Rhyming Weavers* (Belfast, 1974) and the series *The Folk Poets of Ulster* (Bangor, Co. Down, 1992, 1993) in which the poems of Samuel Thomson, James Orr and Hugh Porter have been reprinted under the editorship of J. R. R. Adams, P. S. Robinson and others.

first hand. While the poem in 'standard' English is fluent enough, the poem in Ulster-Scots is far more effective; it has a vivid immediacy in the description and an urgency in the dialogue not found in comparable poems in English.

Another field in which the Ulster poets of the eighteenth century excelled was nature poetry. Even in the 1752 *Ulster Miscellany*, there exists a strong sense of the interaction between man and nature and, towards the end of the period, Samuel Thomson emerges as the most impressive nature poet of the century. Again it is the colourful and concrete vocabulary of Ulster-Scots, together with Thomson's willingness to use vivid dialogue in almost all circumstances, which give this verse a particular strength.

Swift and his Irish contemporaries

Jonathan Swift was clearly the most important poet of eighteenth-century Ireland and his Irish verse, whatever he thought of it, is central to his poetic achievement.[45] He was the leading figure in the intellectual life of Dublin between about 1718 and the end of the 1730s, and around him gathered many active poets, men like Thomas Sheridan, William Dunkin and Patrick Delany, women like Mary Barber, Constantia Grierson and Laetitia Pilkington. To all, Swift acted as a kind of mentor, an avuncular chairman of a *Senatus Consultum*,[46] prepared to give advice on the shaping of verses and on much else.

Behind the verse of Swift, and that of any poets with whom he would have been in contact, was the assumption that the writing of verse was a civilised and a civilising activity. The male poet, in particular, felt himself linked to the world of the classics, ancient and modern: Horace and Martial, Dryden and Pope breathed over his shoulder. Wittily chosen classical epigraphs headed each poem, the muses were invoked, classical gods and goddesses were constantly referred to, and the whole exercise of communicating with one's friends in verse was carried on with an air of

---

45. Swift's attitude toward his verse was ambiguous. On the one hand, he could be disparaging about the poems he wrote in Ireland, describing them as 'trifles' which fell from him, 'amusements in hours of sickness or leisure, or in private families, to divert ourselves and some neighbours, ... never intended for publick view' (Swift to Rev. Henry Jenner, 8 June 1732, Swift's *Correspondence*, ed. Williams, iv, 27). On the other hand, Swift corrected verse he knew was going to the printer — Faulkner for instance — with great care.

46. Delany's name, according to Laetitia Pilkington, for the gatherings convened at Delville, his house at Glasnevin near Dublin, at which Swift would 'correct' the verse of members of his circle. *Memoirs of Laetitia Pilkington* ed. A. C. Elias Jr., two vols. (Athens, Georgia, 1997), I, 283.

relaxed urbanity. So far as the subject-matter of the verse was concerned, poets and readers alike recognised when the fine line between the heroic and the mock-heroic was being crossed, and relished that moment when the writer's savage (or merely venomous) indignation turned an innocent-looking description into a devastating personal attack. Adepts at the poetic art — like Swift himself or William Dunkin — knew how to play the various instruments in this complicated ensemble with consummate skill; others — Patrick Delany or Jonathan Smedley, for instance — could, and did, get the register wrong, so that their heroic epistles ended up the objects of mockery.

The men in Swift's world had all received a classical education and knew — or should have known — how to write and read verse of this type. The classical schoolmasters of the age, Thomas Sheridan and (later) Samuel Whyte, would have expected their better students to write like this and certainly to be able to read verse written in this mode. Sheridan prepared his schoolboys for such a world when he made them perform classical plays in the original languages and it is significant that it was Swift who used to adjudicate the performances in Sheridan's school, and indeed to examine the students in their Latin and Greek. This was the schooling which produced an appreciative audience for the mock-heroic and the mock-pastoral during the first thirty years of the Irish eighteenth century, for poems such as James Ward's 'Smock Race at Finglas', Matthew Concanen's 'A Match at Football', and Nicholas Browne's 'The North Country Wedding'.

It also produced the male poets of Swift's circle, Sheridan, Delany, the Rochfords, the Jacksons and the Grattans. The poems these men wrote to each other were meant to echo, light-heartedly and wittily, the world of Horace and his friends. The atmosphere of these poems, and such poems as 'Stella at Wood Park', is one of lightly worn urbanity. Poets who wrote like this did so for each other, knowing that they were all members of a club, a very particularly trained club, the members of which could pick up nuances not just of subject matter but of tone. A classical schooling was an essential prerequisite to entry into such a world — though a classical schooling did not mean that one could not write with lightness and humour, as Sheridan and Dunkin prove in this collection. The world-view which stems from a classical education extends, in this anthology, well beyond Swift's circle, but it has its centre there.

The women poets who were part of Swift's coterie came with different skills. Most of them had received a haphazard, practical education involving little or no study of the classics, and it is notable that they did not emulate the men in their classicism. Even Constantia Grierson — classical scholar as well as midwife — did not try to write with the Horatian urbanity of the male poets of the group. On the contrary, her poems, like those of Mary Barber and Laetitia Pilkington, were in quite a different register. These women poets wrote with confidence about their own experiences — about motherhood, getting old, being lonely, feeling the need to champion the feminine. Their work springs from a need to express different kinds of emotions from those in, for instance, Sheridan's work, and their verse lacks the cynicism which can be found in Dunkin or Arbuckle.

However, Swift himself stands high above all others of his age, women and men, in his ability to see the hollowness of the institutions of eighteenth-century Ireland and to rage against those who lived off them. 'A Character, Panegyric, and Description of the Legion Club' remains the greatest poem of eighteenth-century Ireland for its unremitting and savage stripping bare of the hypocrisies of the age. It is, in many ways, the central poem of this anthology — far more powerful than any other political poem written in eighteenth-century Ireland. It is not surprising that it appeared anonymously.

Women as poets in eighteenth-century Ireland

About sixty Irish women published verse under their own names in the eighteenth century, and scores of others composed songs which were printed, anonymously, in chapbooks and broadsheets. Nothing is known about those whose work appeared in chapbooks, and little enough is known about the named women authors of volumes of verse, only two of which have been reprinted.[47]

Almost without exception, these women poets wrote trenchantly about their own experiences, and many railed against their position in society. Dorothea Dubois and Jane Elizabeth Moore, for instance, made no secret of their views that women wronged by patriarchal society should not only protest strenuously but strive to beat the men at their own game. Mary Barber and Constantia Grierson, less militant maybe, still left their readers in no doubt about the injustice of the social structures in which

---

47. *The Poetry of Mary Barber, ?1690-1757*, ed. Bernard Tucker (Lampeter, 1992) which contains the texts of Mary Barber's *Poems on Several Occasions* (London, 1734), and *Memoirs of Laetitia Pilkington*, ed. Elias, which contains Mrs Pilkington's poems, and those of some of her contemporaries.

women were always deemed less important than men, particularly in social and intellectual matters. Laetitia Pilkington unequivocally urged women to free themselves from the restraints of male domination. Henrietta Battier and Mary O'Brien were equally determined to assert women's right to be heard and to take an active part in political and literary life. There is astonishing energy and political venom — considering the fact that women could take no part in ordinary politics — in the verse of the last two of these women poets. It is strange that so little is known about them — or indeed about Jane Elizabeth Moore, who issued so ringing a challenge to the Freemasons of Dublin in 1796.

In general, very little has been written about women writers in eighteenth-century Ireland. Scholarly work has been done on the Dublin-based poets Laetitia Pilkington, Mary Barber and Constantia Grierson, but we know nothing about the hundreds of women who were writing verse throughout Ireland, in provincial towns, in country houses, in rectories and in farms. Their work appears — sometimes anonymously, sometimes attributed — in provincial newspapers and journals, in Dodsley's *Miscellanies* and in Edkins's *Collections*, but there must be much interesting material in archives and manuscript collections awaiting discovery and publication — of which the manuscripts of Olivia Elder and the early poems of Mary Shackleton are the most obvious examples of unpublished material.

Women also emerge in this anthology as pacifists, as amazons and as humorists. Some of the most poignant poems are by the women poets of the chapbooks, forced into lives of misery by the social mores of the day, and the verses written by Ellen Taylor, a domestic servant sent to wash linen in the river Barrow, are equally memorable. The contrast between the servile role allocated to Ellen Taylor by the world, and the freedom promised to her soul by the poetic sensitivity she feels, drives her to an eloquent despair.

> Thrice happy she, condemned to move
>   Beneath the servile weight,
> Whose thoughts ne'er soar one inch above
>   The standard of her fate.
>
> But far more happy is the soul,
>   Who feels the pleasing sense;
> And can indulge without control
>   Each thought that flows from thence.

Since naught of these my portion is,
   But the reverse of each,
That I shall taste but little bliss,
   Experience doth me teach.

Could cold insensibility
   Through my whole frame take place,
Sure then from grief I might be free:
   Yes, then I'd hope for peace.

These lines tell with uncompromising honesty what it felt like to be one of those marginalised in late eighteenth-century Ireland. The wonder is that Ellen Taylor, and others like her, were able to see their work in print.

(v)

In fact, the cultural environment of eighteenth-century Ireland was surprisingly kind to those who wrote verse and wanted to see it in print. Dublin was second only to London in the English-speaking world as a centre for publishing and printing, and it also had an appreciative and active book-buying public throughout the century.[48] But this situation was changed dramatically by the Act of Union of 1801. Following the passing of that act, Dublin sank almost overnight from being a capital city to being no more than a provincial backwater within the British empire. All its civil servants and politicians left for London, as did many of its writers and, perhaps more significantly, many of its book-buying citizens. New copyright laws were enacted, the economic structure of the book-trade was entirely changed, and the vibrant literary world which had existed in Dublin throughout the eighteenth century disappeared. According to Sir John Gilbert, the number of books published in the city dropped, after the Union, by eighty percent.[49] The world in which the poems in this anthology were produced, printed and circulated disappeared for ever.

48. See M. Pollard, *Dublin's Trade in Books 1550-1800* (Oxford, 1989), pp. 165-226, and Richard Cargill Cole, *Irish Booksellers and English Writers 1740-1800* (Atlantic Highlands, New Jersey, 1986), pp. 23-39.
49. John T. Gilbert, *A History of the City of Dublin*, 3 vols, second edition (Dublin, 1978), I, 188.

A NOTE ON THE TEXTS

The aim of this anthology is to present the reader with texts that are both true to their original sources, printed or manuscript, and yet readable. Thus the original spelling and capitalisation have been retained, even where there is inconsistency within a text, and proper names also retain their original forms. Obvious misprints have been silently corrected and, where the original punctuation might cause confusion, it has been amended or supplied. Since typographical conventions changed radically between 1700 and 1800, texts in the earlier part of the volume may appear significantly more 'old-fashioned' than later ones; but to reduce all the texts to homogeneity would be to lose the flavour and immediacy of the originals. The sources from which the texts have been taken are listed at the end of the volume.

SHORT TITLES FOR WORKS FREQUENTLY CITED

Bliss	Alan Bliss, ed., *Spoken English in Ireland 1600-1740: Twenty-seven Representative Texts* (Dublin: Cadenus Press and Dolmen Press, 1979)
Brewer	E. Cobham Brewer, *The Dictionary of Phrase and Fable*, new edition (New York: Avenal, 1978)
DNB	*Dictionary of National Biography*
Fagan	Patrick Fagan, *Georgian Celebration: Irish Poets of the Eighteenth Century* (Dublin: Branar, 1989)
Foxon	D. F. Foxon, ed., *English Verse 1701-50: A Catalogue of Separate Printed Poems ...* 2 vols (Cambridge: Cambridge University Press, 1975)
Johnson	Samuel Johnson, *A Dictionary of the English Language* (London, 1755)
Leerssen	Joep Leerssen, *Mere Irish and Fíor-Ghael: Studies in the Idea of Irish Nationality, its Development and Literary Expression prior to the Nineteenth Century*, second edition (Cork: Cork University Press, 1996)
OED	*Oxford English Dictionary*
Partridge	Eric Partridge, *The Routledge Dictionary of Historical Slang* (London: Routledge Kegan Paul, 1973)

PART I
1687-1725

SIX POEMS FROM THE WILLIAMITE WARS
(1687-91)

The events of the reign of James II reverberate throughout eighteenth-century Ireland, as do the songs written at the time. Most Irish Jacobite verse of this period was aimed at an Irish-speaking audience and was written in the Irish language: little of it is therefore represented in this anthology. Williamite verse, on the other hand, was designed for an English-speaking audience. If, as it often was, its aim was to burlesque or ridicule Irish attitudes, it was written in stage-Irish or, more interestingly, in Hiberno-English. The Williamite poems which follow are typical, both in their attitude towards the Irish-speaking inhabitants of Ireland and in their language, of the many which survive.

Lilliburlero, the most famous protestant song of eighteenth-century Ireland, was probably written in 1687 by Thomas Wharton (1648-1715), a notorious rake who was lord lieutenant of Ireland from 1708 to 1710. For the first ten stanzas of the song, two Irish catholics, speaking an exaggerated Hiberno-English, congratulate each other on the impending arrival in Ireland of the new lord deputy appointed by James II, Richard Talbot, Earl Tyrconnell (1630-91), noting that he is expected to bring about the triumph of catholics over protestants in every walk of Irish life; in contrast, the last two verses (which are not in Hiberno-English) give a more cynical assessment of the new lord deputy and his brother, the catholic archbishop of Dublin. The ballad ridicules catholic expectations that James II or his agents would succeed in sweeping their co-religionists to power in Ireland in the late 1680s and, following the defeat of catholic Ireland in 1690-91, the song (which was set to music by the English composer Henry Purcell) became the standard protestant triumphalist anthem.

Lilliburlero

Ho! brother Teague,[1] dost hear de decree,
    Lilli burlero bullen a la;[2]
Dat we shall have a new debittie,[3]
    Lilli burlero bullen a la,
    Lero, lero, lero, lero, Lilli burlero bullen a la,
    Lero, lero, lero, lero, Lilli burlero bullen a la.

Ho! by my shoul[4] it is a Talbot,
    Lilli, &c.
And he will cut all the English throat,[5]
    Lilli, &c. &c.   10

1. Irish proper name *Tadhg*. See Glossary.
2. On the probable significance of this apparently meaningless refrain, see Breandán Ó Buachalla, 'Lilliburlero agus Eile', *Comhar*, Vol. 46, Nos. 3-7 (Máirt-Iúl 1987).
3. Tyrconnell was appointed lord deputy of Ireland in January 1687.
4. soul.
5. cf. the common view of Englishmen in Ireland that Irishmen were always about to massacre them (as they believed had happened in 1641).

Though by my shoul de English do prat,[6]
    Lilli, &c.
De law's on dare[7] side, and Chreist knows what,
    Lilli, &c. &c.

But if dispense[8] do come from de pope,
    Lilli, &c.
We'll hang Magno Carto[9] and demselves in a rope,
    Lilli, &c. &c.

And the good Talbot is made a lord,
    Lilli, &c.
And he with brave lads is coming aboard,
    Lilli, &c. &c.

20

Who all in France[10] have taken a swear,
    Lilli, &c.
Dat dey will have no Protestant heir,[11]
    Lilli, &c. &c.

O! but why does he stay behind?
    Lilli &c.
Ho by my shoul 'tis a Protestant wind,[12]
    Lilli, &c. &c.

30

Now Tyrconnell is come ashore,
    Lilli &c.
And we shall have commissions gillore,[13]
    Lilli, &c. &c.

6. prate; i.e. the English boast that the law is on their side.
7. their.
8. dispensation.
9. Magna Carta, the famous charter of liberties granted by King John to the English people in 1215.
10. The catholic French were traditional supporters of the catholic Irish.
11. i.e. that they will not let their land pass to a protestant.
12. A westerly gale delayed Tyrconnell at Holyhead on his way to Ireland to take up the position of lord deputy early in 1687. The wind is 'protestant' not because of its direction but because it frustrates catholic hopes.
13. Galore (from Ir. *go leor*, plenty) i.e. great numbers of protestant army officers will be replaced by catholics.

And he dat will not go to mass
    Lilli, &c.
Shall turn out[14] and look like an ass,
    Lilli, &c. &c.

Now, now de heretics all go down,[15]
    Lilli, &c.   40
By Chreist and St. Patrick de nation's our own,
    Lilli, &c. &c.

There was an old prophecy found in a bog,
    Lilli, &c.
That Ireland should be rul'd by an ass and a dog:
    Lilli, &c. &c.

And now this prophecy is come to pass,
    Lilli, &c.
For Talbot's the dog, and Tyrconnell's the ass,[16]
    Lilli &c. &c.   50

A Cruel and Bloody DECLARATION
Publish'd by the Cardinals at *Rome*, against *Great-Britain*, and *Ireland*[1]

Heu dolor anxietas! Suspira rumpite pectus:
Fraudibus est, oh prop, cum conjuge Papa detectus.
Nunc Babylona jacet, Meretrix, That's cloathed in scarlet
Cum nudis coxis, A base Pox'd Pick-pocket Harlet:
Nullus nunc Anglus, Will buy her *Commodities,*

14. i.e. be turned out. Attendance at the protestant church service was obligatory for army officers and the point of the line is that, in future, any officer who does not attend the catholic mass will lose his commission.
15. i.e. the heretic English will become the underdogs.
16. Tyrconnell's brother, Peter Talbot (1620-80) was at this time catholic archbishop of Dublin; hence the two brothers are satirised as the 'rulers' of catholic Ireland.

1. Despite the imprint on the only surviving copy of this ribald macaronic (*Rome* Printed, and Re-printed in *Dublin, Nov.* 12. 1725), the verse dates from the last month of Tyrconnell's period as lord deputy of Ireland, specifically after William had been declared king of Britain (12 February 1689) and before the arrival of James II in Ireland (12 March 1689). The broadsheet is addressed to a presumably learned protestant audience in Ireland — perhaps in Trinity College, Dublin. Bawdy fantasies about the Pope and the catholic church are fused with Irish protestant fears about Tyrconnell's determination to wrest land from those currently in possession.

Omnis at Hereticus, Will whip her Pockify'd *Nates.*
Nunc ubi T————l *cum Bogtrottantibus Horsis?*
Qui Bonny-clabber *edens jurat per millia* Crosses:
Potuit ille quondam nihil memorable but plot;
Attamen, heu, Prorex, Is turn'd a beggarly Cut-Troat.   10
O tu dulce decus! More sugar sweet than a *Dear Joy!*
Usquebahum bibitans, With Snush, Tobacco, and *Beer Boy:*
Tuq; quoad possis, drink healthum Jemmy Mack Nero.
Et Chorus, interea, cantabit Lilliburlero.[2]
Roma est Impostor, qui per mental Reservations,
Et Hocum Pocum, *potest decipere* Nations;
Et calcare Anglos qui nunc, Do kick at the Popes Toe,
Donec, Papa Peter will make them all to the Pot go.
Proteret & Reges rabidos, ut once Fredericum,
Atq, Devil's Breado poysonabit ut once Henericum.[3]   20
Fulmine confundet Populos, virtute corona[e]
Triplicis; & capiet, per Criss-Cross, *omnia Bona:*
Templa he will pull down, *vomitans* fire-out like *Vulcano:*
Sic volo sic jubeo was still *de jure Romano.*
Perq; Deum pistum jurat, sine Limite latrans,
Per Nunnam, Friarum, Priests, & unmannerly Matrons,
Quod Vallæ Sham *Princeps, ignoto emptus ab illo*
Patre, partus parvide, (Cut pluttra Nailes, like a Pillow)
Est, Lodovici lege, Hæres sceptro aureo trino,
Britanno, Gallo, Witness Cardinal M————o.   30

---

2. Alas! Grief! Anxiety! Sigh, burst your breast; by deception, oh alas!, the Pope has been
discovered with a wife. Now Babylon, the whore, lies, *that's clothed in scarlet* with
naked hips, *a base pox'd pick-pocket Harlot*: Now no Englishman *will buy her*
Commodities. But every heretic *will whip her Pockify'd* arse. Now where [is]
T[yrconnel]l with [his] bogtrotting horses? Who, eating *Bonny-clabber,* swears by a
thousand *crosses*; once he could [do] nothing memorable *but plot*: yet alas, the regent *is*
turn'd a beggarly cut-throat. O thou sweet glory! *more sugar sweet than a Dear Joy!*
Drinking endlessly, with *snuff, tobacco and Beer Boy*; you, too, as long as you can, drink
the health of *Jemmy Mack Nero,* and the choir meanwhile will sing *Lilliburlero.*
Comments on note 2: the whore of Babylon] anti-catholic propaganda often repre-
sented the Roman Catholic Church in general and the papacy in particular as a powerful,
red-robed woman and linked her to the mystical 'Babylon' of the Apocalypse; bonny-
clabber] see Glossary; the regent] Tyrconnell was lord deputy February 1687-March
1689; Dear Joy] see Glossary; Jemmy Mack Nero] James II; Lilliburlero] see above p. 37.
3. Rome is an impostor who, by means of *mental reservations* and hocus pocus, can deceive
nations and trample on Englishmen who now *do kick at the Pope's toe,* until Pope *Peter*
will make them all to the pot go, and will tread under foot ravening kings as *once*
[he did] Frederick, and with the devil's bread will poison [them], as *once [he did]*
Henry. **Comments on note 3:** Frederick] Frederick I, Barbarossa, Holy Roman Emperor
1155-90, a well-known antagonist of the Pope; Henry] Henry VII, Holy Roman Emperor
1308-13, who is said to have died from poisoned sacramental bread and wine.

Ipse King that's Catholick *rigabit* Spanish Armadoes,
And the Pope will bless him with a thousand great mouth-Granadoes.
Ultima Fata canet Rex Gallus *finitimorum:*
Et vorare vovet Regum Malum *Britannorum.*
Ille Roman Catholick *qui* Christ *crudeliter edet,*
Nil surfeits *Stomachum nil* leather Conscience *lædit:*[4]
Perpetrat hoc Papa, qui vult send *Maurice & Teagum,*
Down *baterare* London, & quite *evitare* Hagum.
Denudent liberos, matres cum patribus, slay all,
Et papa omne Nefas will purge, both pardon, and pay all.   40
Omnibus Hereticis Brutum, cui coccea vestis,
Anglicis & Scotis will be a perpetual *Pestis.*[5]
Flectite vos Papæ, digitum osculamini Pedis,
Atque hoc præveniet præscripta crudelia cædis.
Reliquias mittet Sanctorum munere vobis;
With Bushels of Peter's Teeth, *capitusque duobus.*

---

4. He will confound peoples with a thunderbolt, by virtue of his triple crown, and he will seize, by means of *criss-cross*, all property; temples *he will pull down*, belching *fire out like a volcano;* 'Thus I wish', 'Thus I command' *was still* in accord with Roman law. And he swears by his baked God, barking endlessly, by nun, friar, *priests and unmannerly matrons,* because *the sham* prince *of Wales,* bought by that unknown Father, offspring of ..., (*cut pluttra nails, like a pillow*), is, by Ludwig's law, heir to the threefold golden sceptre, British, French, *Witness Cardinal M[azarin]o. The king* himself, *that's catholic,* will launch Spanish armadoes, *and the Pope will bless him with a thousand mouth-granadoes.* The French king will sing the final fates of his neighbours, and he will vow to devour the wicked king of the British — that *Roman Catholic* who cruelly eats *Christ;* nothing *surfeits* his stomach, nothing damages *[his] leather conscience.* **Comments on note 4:** triple crown] the triple crown of the papacy; baked God] a disparaging reference — like that to 'eating Christ' below — to the catholic doctrine of transubstantiation; prince of Wales] the extended reference to the sham prince of Wales refers to protestant assertions that the son born to James II and Mary of Modena in June 1688 was suppositious and had been smuggled into the queen's bedchamber in a warming pan, or even that the child's father was James's confessor, Father Petrie. The phrase 'cut pluttra nails, like a pillow' is obscure; Ludwig's law] the law of Louis XIV, king of France 1643-1715; Cardinal Mazarino] Jules Mazarin (1602-61), French cardinal and statesman, architect of Louis XIV's successful foreign policy; Spanish armadoes] a reference to the Spanish armada of 1588 and to the fact that Spain, like France, was expected to send assistance to James in his fight to maintain control of Ireland; king of the British] presumably this refers to William of Orange who, with his wife Mary, accepted the throne of Britain and Ireland on 12 February 1689.

5. The pope perpetuates this who wishes *[to] send Maurice and Teague* to batter *down London, and quite* to kill *Hagus.* They will strip children, *slay all,* mothers along with fathers, and the Pope *will purge* all wickedness, *both pardon and pay all.* To all heretics, to English and to Scots, the brute who has a scarlet garment *will be a perpetual* plague. **Comments on note 5:** to batter down London] a commonly expressed fear was that Irish forces ('Teagues'), if they once got to England — presumably aided by Frenchmen (generically called 'Maurice') — would destroy London and massacre its people; Hagus] the Hague, capital of the United Provinces of which William III of England was also ruler (stadholder); brute who has a scarlet garment] the Pope, the 'whore of Babylon'.

Ille vobis send *vult Papissæ* Placket & *partum*:
Et Nunnas castas, & sweet St. *Anthony's fartum.*
Vobis remittet præsentia atque futura
Omina peccata without Pennance *atque censura.*   50
Ille libertatem præbebit to Rogue & *Whorare,*
To Rant, to Swear, to Pick-Pocket, *atque potare,* }
Et Dæmon in illo est qui plus vult desiderare.[6] }

from: The Irish Hudibras or, Fingallian Prince

Taken from the Sixth Book of Virgil's Ænæids, and Adapted to the Present Times[1]

... For here the Old *Scullogues*[2] were all
In a large Field as warm as Wooll;
And had (exempted from our Cares,)
Their own, both Sun, and Moon, and Stars.[3]
A Slut[4] supplies the place of Candle,

6. Bend [the knee] to the pope! Kiss the toe of his foot, and this will forestall his cruel commands of slaughter — and he will send you as a gift relics of saints, *with bushels of Peter's teeth*, and two heads. He wishes to send to you the Popess's *placket and* pudenda, and chaste nuns, *and sweet St. Anthony's fart.* He will forgive you all your present and future sins *without penance* and censure; he will give freedom *to rogue* and to whore, *to rant, to swear, to pick-pocket* and to drink — and there is a demon in that man who wishes to desire more!

1. *The Irish Hudibras* is — to quote Alan Bliss — 'a humorous retelling of the events of Book VI of Virgil's *Æneid*, transferred to an Irish locale and ingeniously adapted to fit the circumstances of Stuart Ireland' (p. 47). The poem follows Nees (cf. Æneas and the Irish personal name Naois) through various adventures in the underworld or purgatory and is written, in part, in a dialect of Hiberno-English described by the author as 'Fingallian'. Fingal is an area north of Dublin and, apart from its use of the local dialect, *The Irish Hudibras* also contains descriptions of the life and customs of the native Irish in that part of the Pale in the late seventeenth century. Though the author is clearly not of Irish stock himself, he knows the people of Fingal intimately. He is not, however, sympathetic to them: in fact, his perspective is that of a bigoted protestant outsider whose aim is to portray the native Irish as superstitious, ignorant and uncivilised. This anti-Irish xenophobia can also be seen in other works of the time, including *Teague-land Jests* (which predates *The Irish Hudibras*) and three violently anti-Irish dramatic pamphlets published in London in 1690, *The Bloody Duke*, *The Abdicated Prince* and *The Late Revolution* (see Leerssen, pp. 98-102). In all these works, the authors portray the native Irish not as they really were but rather as Englishmen expected them to be.

   However, the main significance of *The Irish Hudibras* for the modern reader lies in the fact that the author had an intimate knowledge of the Hiberno-English of late seventeenth-century Ireland, particularly that used in Fingal, and of the lifestyle of those living in the Pale; thus, even though the poem savagely caricatures Irish customs and the people of Fingal, it remains an important source of information on life and language in Ireland at the time.

   The poem draws heavily on two earlier Irish texts, the *Purgatorium Hibernicum* and the *Fingallian Travestie* (see Bliss, p. 47) as well as on similar 'Travesties' by Charles

42

In Socket of split Deal, for Handle:
With Rushes steept in Kitchin-Scurf,[5]
And stuck in Candlestick of Turf:
And Fire enough to Tost their Nose.
Some Exercise, and some Repose;   10
On Rushes some, and some on Pallets;[6]
Some Vermin pick, and some pick Sallets:[7]
Some pace the Whip, some trot the Hay,[8]
Some at their Beads,[9] and some at play.
Have you, in the gay Town of *Lusk*,[10]
Observ'd their Sports about the Dusk
Of *Patrons*-Eve,[11] when all the Rout
Of Raggamuffins flock about;
Men, Maids, and Children, Dogs and all,
To Celebrate the Festival;   20
So were they here assembled from
Each Corner of the Nation; some
Of every Rank, and had the Rogues
A Thousand merry gay Gamshogues.[12]
The Old Men play'd at Blind-man-Buff,

Cotton (1630-87) and others who, in turn, derived the genre from the French writer Paul Scarron (1610-60). Though this poem is more a paraphrase than a translation of the *Æneid*, the reader's attention is constantly drawn to footnotes that give the words of Virgil's Latin which each passage is said to 'translate'. The first extract printed here, which corresponds closely to *Æneid* vi 638-56, describes the visit of Nees to the 'Limbo Patrum' or limbo of the fathers, where he encounters the dead heroes of the Irish past (as Æneas had encountered the dead heroes of the Greek past in an equivalent 'Land of Joy'). After the wild adventures of the earlier part of the poem, Nees is delighted to find himself in such a peaceful spot.

2. Ir. *scológ*: yeoman farmer. [The marginal note reads 'Old Rogues'.]

3. cf. *Æneid* vi, 638-42 where it is explained that the inhabitants of the limbo of the blest fathers have their own sun and moon.

4. Ir. *sloit*: a wick placed in a shallow bowl of oil.

5. kitchen grease (?).

6. straw-filled bags or mattresses.

7. salads: wild leaves such as shamrock and watercress.

8. The names of two dances.

9. rosary beads.

10. A town in Fingal, north of Dublin.

11. On Patron or Pattern Day, large numbers of people would attend masses in honour of the patron saint of a church, after which there would be revelry. In some areas, Pattern Day was celebrated in mid-August. Patterns were prohibited under the Penal Laws. [See Kevin Danagher, *The Year in Ireland* (Cork, 1972), pp. 180-86.]

12. Ir. *geam* or *geám* (from English 'game') + *seoigh*: fun or sport. [The marginal note reads 'Sports'.]

Some Roast Pottados, some grind Snuff:[13]
At five Cards some, some wipe out scores
At One and Thirty, and All-Fours.[14]
The Priests that Lodge upon this Common,
Do play at Irish, and Bac-Gammon;[15]   30
For Prayers, for Kisses, and for Beads,
For Masses, and for Maiden-heads:
The Lay-men Box, and Fight, and Wrestle;
And some make Ropes of Twisted Hasle.[16]

Some Trip a Dance upon the Grass,
And every Culleen[17] has his Lass;
All Exercised, great and small,
All at some Game, and some at all:
For all were Gentlemen that play'd,
Not any one that had a Trade.[18]   40
E're in Mechanicks *Teague* wou'd Toil,
He'd run for sixpence forty Mile.

There was *O Threicy*, with *Old Darcy*,
Playing all Weathers at the Clarsey:[19]
The Irish harp, whose rusty Mettle,
Sounds like the patching of a Kettle.
Mageen,[20] yea, and be[21] he cou'd play,
Lilly-Boleer, Bulleen a la;
Skipping of *Gort*, tripping of *Swords*,

13. i.e. grind tobacco to make snuff.
14. Five Cards, One and Thirty and All-Fours were card games.
15. Backgammon or 'tables' was a common game in the eighteenth century. Presumably 'Irish' gammon was a variant form of backgammon.
16. hazel. [The marginal note reads 'Gads' (Ir. *gad*: a straw rope).]
17. Ir. *coilín*: used to signify the small farmers of Fingal. [The marginal note reads 'Bore' i.e. 'boor' or tenant.] Whereas a *scológ* (l.1 above) was probably a yeoman farmer, a *coilín* was a tenant farmer.
18. A scornful marginal note at this point reads '*Teague* a Trade! *Il-lil lil-loo*'. Comments to the effect that Irishmen thought of themselves as gentlemen and considered all work demeaning are commonly found in eighteenth-century anti-Irish writing. The next two lines could be loosely interpreted: 'An Irishman would run forty miles to get sixpence rather than do a day's work'.
19. i.e. playing the harp (Ir. *cláirseach*) in all weathers.
20. The tunes 'Margery Cree' [marginal note], and (in the next line) 'Lilliburlero'.
21. 'and be!' is frequently used as a mild asseveration in Hiberno-English texts of this period (Bliss, p. 260); it is roughly equivalent to the phrase 'to be sure' and is probably a literal translation of Irish '*agus is ea*'.

Frisk of *Baldoil* best he affords:[22]   50
And for variety *Cronaans*,[23]
Ports and *Portrinkes*, and *Strin-kans*.

They had no Anthems for to Chuse,
Their Hallelujes, were *Hull-lil-loos*:[24]
And so as merry as the day
Is long, they past the Time away:
Here did the Antient Heroes grace
The Warriers of former days.[25]
Heber, and *Hereman*, *Nynvillagh*,[26]
Twarthy de Dane, and *Neil Noyhillagh*,   60
Eoghy O Finn, and *Cahir Moro*,
Con Kedcagh, yea and *Bryan Boro*,
And great *O Mile*, that was the first
Of all our Nation, here was thrust:
Was *Nees*[27] great Wonder make on a'me,[28]
To see the Rebels look so tame.
Stalking about the Bogs and Moors,
Together with their Dogs and Whores;
Without a Rag, Trouses, or Brogues,[29]
Picking of Sorrel and Sham-rogues:[30]   70
Their war-like Horses grazing round about,
And bloody Clubs fixt in the ground about
That fertile ground, where the tall Grass
Did grow too fast upon the Place,
Should you o're Night a Gelding turn in,

---

22. Gort, Swords and Baldoyle are settlements in Fingal and 'skipping', 'tripping' and 'frisk' presumably refer to local dances.
23. Ir. *cronán*: humming; Ir. *port*: tune; Ir. *port rince*: dance tune; Ir. *streancán*: air, tune. [The marginal note glosses 'Ports' as 'Lessons' and 'Portrinkes' as 'Jiggs'.]
24. An attempt to represent the sound of lamentation, probably based on the Ir. *uaill*: howl (cf. n.17 above).
25. cf. *Æneid* vi. 647 where there is a list of 'Teucer's ancient dynasty'.
26. The next six lines contain crude anglicisations of the names of figures from Irish history and mythology, and are intended as a parody of the genealogical lists common in Irish texts.
27. The hero of the tale (cf. Æneas).
28. 'on a'me' = on them (Bliss, p. 286). This couplet means: 'Nees was surprised to see the rebels looking so docile.'
29. For information on the close-fitting Irish trousers (Ir. *triús*) and on Irish footwear (Ir. *bróg*), see Bliss, pp. 268-69. See also the Glossary.
30. Sorrel and shamrock were two of the wild plants eaten at this time in Ireland.

You'd hardly find him the next Morning:
For whatsoe're they fancy'd most,
Thieving or War, the donny[31] Ghost,
Now they were dead, with the same Vigour
Did imitate in Mood and Figure....   80

Towards the end of *The Irish Hudibras*, the poet applies Virgil's text to '*the Late Abdication, and the present Accession of His Majesty, King William the Third*'. This second extract from the poem begins at the point where Nees's father has described the 'Hero's and Warriers' of Ireland, paying particular attention to Tyrconnel whose attempts to promote catholics to positions of power while he was lord deputy were still very much in protestant minds in 1689. Echoing the speech of Anchises in the *Æneid* vi, 755 *et seq.*, Nees's father goes on to forsee military defeat and a disastrous future for the Irish race.

    ... Then clapping hands, as sign of wonder,
'Behold (says he) that Son of Thunder,
Tyrconnel, with his Spoils possest,
The bravest King of all the rest.
His Haughtiness bred in the Bogs,
Shall call his Betters, Rogues and Dogs.
From Butchers Bratt, rais'd to a Peer,
To be a K[ing] in Shamrogshire.[32]

This Devil shall do that which no Man
Cou'd yet effect, restore the Roman;   90
And in his time establish Popery,
Which Curse ye Meroz calls a Foppery.[33]
Chappels shall up, the Churches down,[34]
And all the Land shall be our own.
He shall secure our Titles[35] here,
By a Rebellion each Sheir,[36]
An Army shall Collect the Rent,

---

31. Ir. *donaí*: poor, wretched, small. [Marginal note: 'Little'.]
32. Tyrconnell's father, Sir William Talbot (d.1633) was not a butcher but a distinguished Irish politician. Shamrogshire = 'Shamrock-shire', a disparaging name for Ireland.
33. Perhaps a reference to Sir Thomas Meres (1635-1715), MP for Lincoln, a committed protestant who introduced a bill into the English House of Commons in 1685 seeking to compel all foreigners settled in England to adopt the liturgy of the Church of England.
34. i.e. 'catholic' chapels and 'protestant' churches.
35. documents proving ownership of land.
36. i.e. in each county (shire).

Confirm our Rights by Parliament.
The Act of Settlement shall bate,[37]
And Nees shall get his own Estate,   100
If by the Monsieur not supplanted,
Who for a Sum has Covenanted;
And both their Interests be not lost
By the prevailing British Host.[38]
He shall subdue the Heretick,
To bring in trusty Catholick.
Humble the Peer, Exault the Peasant,
Without Assize of damage-Feisant.[39]
And shall advance the meanest sort
To highest place of Camp and Court: 110
All shall be common as before;
No more shall Justices, no more
Shall Court of Claims, or Council-Table,
Or Formidon,[40] be formidable.
Drink down Excise, know no Committe,[41]
But Routs and Riots in each City;
Cut Throats; in Massacre skill'd well;[42]
And Plunder, tho' it were in Hell.
Thus shall he rule the Rebel Rout,
Till by the Monsieur[43] josled out;   120
Reduc'd to such a low Condition,
He shan't to Curse have a Commission....

---

37. i.e. the 1662 Act of Settlement (which had deprived many Irish catholic landowners of their estates) shall be overturned.

38. These six lines suggest the complexities of the Irish land question in 1689. In addition to Nees's own claim to his estate, there is a current occupier supported by the restoration Act of Settlement. 'The Monsieur' in lines 101-02 is either Louis XIV, whose support of James II would give him rights to all land in Ireland, or perhaps the lines refer to someone else who has agreed to buy the estate or holds a mortgage on it; finally, lines 103-04 refer to the possibility that a Williamite victory could bring in an entirely new settlement, in which all existing claimants would be replaced by a new owner.

39. Damage-feasant: 'said of a stranger's cattle found trespassing and doing damage' (*OED*).

40. The court of claims administered the restoration land settlements: the 'council-table' referred to was the Irish privy council; formedon: 'a writ of right formerly used for claiming entailed property' (*OED*).

41. i.e. pay no attention to excise officers or others collecting taxes or enforcing regulations.

42. A reference to the belief that, during the 1641 Rebellion, protestants had massacred their catholic neighbours.

43. i.e. Louis XIV.

But now the Night, like thickning Smoak
That dwells in *Crates*,[44] possession took
O'th'Firmament, when he begun,
With weeping, thus t'advise his Son.

Oh *Nees*, poor *Nees*, do not importune,
To know thy Countrey-mens misfortune,
That will befal them by Adventurers,
By *English*, *Dutch*, and *Scotch* Debentures:[45]   130
Our Lands possest, we put to rout,
By two Brigades of Horse and Foot:
Transported some, and some Transplanted,
Whilst the prevailing Party Ranted.
Till he's[46] restor'd, with all his Train;
But here's the Devil on't again;
The Fates will only shew his Reign,
To hope for more, is but in vain....
And truly, *Nees*, there's ne'er a one
For us to crack of,[47] when he's gone;   140
Not one, like Him, will e'er appear
Again, to grow in *Shamrogeshire*....
Lilli-bo-lero, lero sing,
Tyrconnel is no longer K[ing]....

44. Houses, or temporary habitations constructed of hurdles (Bliss, p. 270). Since such buildings had no chimneys, they were constantly filled with smoke from the open fire. cf. Ir. *creat(a)*: frame, ribs of a house roof.
45. The reference is to adventurers and others to whom the English government issued debenture notes allocating them land in Ireland in lieu of payment for services: the fear is that a new generation of adventurers, armed with debentures issued by various governments, will descend on Ireland.
46. i.e. James II.
47. to boast about; 'he' in this line is Tyrconnel.

The Irishmen's Prayers to St. Patrick, to make their peace with K. William and Q. Mary:

being a dialogue between two *Teagues*, concerning the Army sent over to
Ireland, Commanded by *Mareschal d' Scomberg*.[1]

Teede[2] *speaks*: 'O broder *Teague*, and *Teague* my Roon,[3]
Arra vat shall ve do full quickly and soon;
De brave *Ingalish* Army is coming ve hear,
And brave General *Scomberg* in de front vill appear:
O den ve must leave all our Citys Dear-Joys,[4]
And yield them unto those *Ingalish* brave boyes;
   Because dat der Canons will make such a noise,
   Dey'l spoil all de *French*, and our *Ierish* Imploys.[5]

Tho now new Devil[6] in bot *Corke* and *Kingshail*,
Wid *Galloway, Limbrick*, and bony *Youghail*,[7]   10
And all de Citys in de North but von,
And dat's *London-derry,* dats quite lost and gone.
Dat plash[8] our Army most sadly destroys,
Because all dats in it are Protestant boys;
   Der Canons against us do make such a noise,
   Dat dey kill all de *French*, and our *Ierish* Dear-joys.

---

1. Like *The Irish Hudibras*, this poem was the work of someone well acquainted with seventeenth-century Hiberno-English. It was probably written in the summer of 1689 following the relief of Derry and the arrival in Ireland of the Williamite forces under Schomberg. The state of the Jacobite army at this time was such that its defeat was widely anticipated (Bliss, p. 59) and this poem would have confirmed the common hope of its (presumably) English readers that Irish mistrust of James and fear of the English would lead to a speedy English victory. For clarification of the type of Hiberno-English used in this text, see the introduction and the Glossary.

2. The name 'Teede' does not correspond to any known Irish name. For 'Teague' see Glossary.

3. cf. Ir. *(a) rú(i)n*: darling.

4. see Glossary.

5. trades or occupations.

6. i.e. though there is now new fighting spirit or energy in ... (Partridge: s.v. *devil* 7).

7. James and his forces arrived at Kinsale on 12 March 1689 and proceeded to Cork and Dublin. During the summer of 1689, Galway, Limerick, Youghal and most other Irish towns and cities, with the exception of Derry, were controlled by James. Derry was in Williamite control after the lifting of the siege on 31 July.

8. place.

Den now broder *Teague*, vat more can I shay,
I fear dat King *Yeamus*[9] he will soon run away,
Ven he hears dat Duke *Scomberg* and his Army is come,
He'll sheek for *Fader Petre* to help him to *Rome*,[10]   20
Vhile ve shall be left to Shaint *Patrick* to pray,
Dat he vud be pleas'd for to help us I shay;
    But der Canon against us so strongly will play,
    Dat unto de Bogs, we must all take our way.[11]

Now *Tyrconel* lies shick of de old Cursed Plot,[12]
Vhile ve for his knavery shall ne'er be forgot;
Now the Priests are all ready to bite off der nailesh,
To tink of de losh of de young Prince of *Wailesh*,[13]
Vhile ve must be forsht for to stand the deveat,
For der putting on ush dat curshed great Sheat,[14]   30
    For der Canons against us will make such a noise,
    Dey'll spoil all our shaying, Come on my brave Boys.'

Teague replies: 'Alas broder *Teede* dis thing it is hard,
    And ve of our Lands now vill all be debarr'd,
    Dey'll make all our Lords, and our Shentry[15] bow,
    And vat vill become of us, I do not vell know;
    Dey'll make us surrender both City and Town,
    And yield 'em to de honour of *Ingalands* great Crown;
        For der Canons against us so strongly will play,
        Ve shall not have hearts to withstand 'em one fray.[16]   40

And vhen de whole power the *Ingalish* hash got,
O den broder *Teede* vat vill fall to our lot,
I fear dat de sheif and de best of our fellows,
Dat are left, vill be forsht for to die on de Gallows,
Because in Rebellion so long we have stood,
Against all de *Ingalish* and Protestant good;
    Der Canons against us will tunder so loud,
    Ve shall not be able our selves for to shroud.

---

9. i.e. Seamus = James.
10. Father [Edward] Petrie S.J. (1631-99), confessor to James II.
11. When defeated in battle, the Irish traditionally retired to the bogs of Ireland.
12. Tyrconnel was in poor health in 1689; it was rumoured that he was being poisoned (*DNB*).
13. The infant prince of Wales was, at the time of this poem, in France.
14. i.e. cheat.
15. gentry.
16. assault.

De boggs dey vill signify little to us,
For being so Loyal to Second *Yeamus*,   50
Altho dat our Priests and our Shesuits swore,
Dat ve should have Lands and Livings *Gillore*,[17]
Not only in *Ireland*, but *Ingaland* too,
Dat makes us in shorrow look pityful blue;[18]
    Because by der Canons dose Slats[19] from us flew,
    Voud the Tivel had had all dose Jesuite crew.

So to conclude, de best vay dat I know for to take,
Is to pray to Shaint *Patrick* our Peace for to make,
And quite leave off fighting for *Yeamus* late King,[20]
And put Ropes round our Necks, and repent for our sin.[21] 60
So dus[22] by repentance ve may be forgiven,
And find mercy bot from great King *Willam* and Heaven.
    Tho ve have Rebell'd at dish Curshed great rate,
    Yet ve may find mercy of *Ingalands* great State.'

Epitaph on the Duke of Grafton[1]

    Beneath this place
    Is stow'd his Grace
    The Duke of G——;
    As sharp a Blade
    As e'er was made
    Or e'er had Haft on;

17. i.e. galore.
18. fearful, low-spirited.
19. Ir. *slat*: stick, skinny person. The line means 'Because those skinny persons (i.e. priests and Jesuits) deserted us when they saw the canons'.
20. From the realistic point of view of this speaker, James is no longer to be considered king of Ireland.
21. Those wishing to make public penance for their sins sometimes paraded through the streets with a hangman's rope round their necks.
22. thus.

1. Henry Fitzroy, first Duke of Grafton (1663-90), a natural son of Charles II, was a courageous sailor and soldier. He was mortally wounded at the siege of Cork in 1690.

Mark'd with a Star
Forg'd for War
Of Metle true
As ever drew   10
Or made a Pass
At Lad or Lass.

This nat'ral Son of Mars
Ne're hung an Arse
Or turn'd his Tail
Tho' shot like Hail
Flew 'bout his Ears.
Through Pikes and Spears
So thick they hid the Sun
He'd boldly lead them on   20
More like a Devil than a Man.

He valued not the Balls of Gun
He ne're would dread
Shot made of Lead
Or Cannon Ball
Nothing at all.

Yet a Bullet of *Cork*
Soon did his Work
Unhappy Pellet
With Grief I tell it   30
It has undone
Great *Cæsar*'s Son.

A Statesman spoil'd
A Soldier soil'd;
G— rot him
That shot him,
A Son of a Whore;
I say no more.

An *Irish* Song[1]

Hub ub, ub, boo;[2]
Hub ub, ub, boo;
Dish can't be true,
De War dees cease,
But der's no Peash,
I know and find,
'Tis Sheal'd and Sign'd,[3]
But won't believe 'tis true,
Hub ub, ub boo, hub ub, ub, boo.

A hone, a hone,[4]   10
Poor *Teague*'s undone,
I dare not be
A Rapparee,[5]
I ne'er shall see,
Magraw Macree,[6]
Nor my more dear Garone,[7]
A hone, a hone.

Awa, awa,
I must huzza,
'Twill hide my Fears,   20
And save my Ears,
The Mob appears,
Her'sh to *Nassau*,
Dear Joy 'tis *Usquebaugh*,[8]
Huzza, Huzza, Huzza.

---

1. The speaker in this poem has just heard of the signing of the Treaty of Limerick (3 October 1691) and decides to switch his allegiance to the winning side. Though presumably written in England and for an English audience, the poem shows sympathy for the plight of individuals on the losing side in Ireland.
2. The normal anglicization of the Ir. *ababú*, an exclamation of displeasure or disgust. For clarification of the Hiberno-English in this poem, see introduction and Glossary.
3. i.e. the Treaty of Limerick.
4. Alas! Ir. *Ochón*.
5. In the later seventeenth century, many of the dispossessed Irish went on the run and became outlaws: they were known as 'rapparees' from the Ir. *rapairí*; see Bliss, p. 267.
6. Ir. *mo ghrá, mo chroí*: my love, my dear.
7. Ir. *gearrán*: horse.
8. whiskey. See Glossary.

NAHUM TATE
(1687-**1698**-1715)

Nahum Tate — his father was the poet Faithfull Teate and Nahum dropped the first 'e' in his name only in adulthood — was born in Dublin and educated at Trinity College where one of his classmates was William King, future archbishop of Dublin (to whom Tate wrote seeking employment many years later). Tate earned a living as a dramatist and poet in London and is perhaps best known for rewriting Shakespeare's *King Lear* to give the play a happy ending. He also collaborated with Dubliner Nicholas Brady on a metrical version of the psalms which became one of the best-selling books of the eighteenth century and was almost universally used in the established church in both England and Ireland for more than a century. Tate's most famous work is undoubtedly the hymn 'While shepherds watched their flocks by night', but *Panacea: A poem upon Tea* was also very popular when it appeared. Like Pope's *The Rape of the Lock*, the poem celebrates the civilised urban life of those who could afford newly available imported luxuries such as tea, coffee, and spices.

from: Panacea: A Poem upon Tea

... Rich in Improvements of his well-spent Time,
The Bard returns to his dear Native Clime:[1]
The neighb'ring Shepherds[2] who his Absence mourn'd,
Visit with Joy their wand'ring Friend return'd.
Short Salutation past, he feasts their Eyes
With pleasing View of *Eastern* Rarities.
Nature and Art's choice Gift, the *Goa-Stone*,[3]
With Plants and Herbs to *Western* Swains unknown.
Yet, more surpriz'd, they found their Senses chear'd
Soon as the verdant fragrant TEA appear'd;   10
It's Nature, Use, confus'dly they demand,
What Name it bore? The Product of what Land?
''Twill Time require to have at full exprest'
The Bard reply'd, 'what you in hast[e] request.
Come to my Bow'r, and I'll inform you there,
What curious Souls must needs be pleas'd to hear.'

He said, and with his willing Guests withdrew,
Where a new Scene of Wonders charm'd their View;
On burning Lamps a silver Vessel plac'd,

1. The poet, Palæmon, has just returned from a visit to the Orient.
2. Symbolic friends for a pastoral poet — not real tenders of sheep.
3. Probably a lump of black manganese ore mined in Goa, a region of India which was at this time a Portuguese colony.

A Table with surprising Figures grac'd,   20
And *China*-Bowls to feast their Sight and Tast:
The Genial Liquor, decently pour'd out,
To the admiring Guests is dealt about.
Scarce had they drunk a first and second Round,
When the warm *Nectar*'s pleasing Force they found;
About their Heart enliven'd Spirits danc'd,
Then to the Brains sublimer Seat advanc'd.
(Such Transports feel young Prophets when they Dream:
Or Poets slumb'ring by *Pirene*'s Stream.)[4]
With silent Wonder mutually they Trace   30
Bright Joys reflected on each other's Face.
Then thus the Bard: 'Fear no *Circæan* Bowls,[5]
This is the Drink of Health, the Drink of Souls!
The Virtues This, and This the Graces quaff,
Like *Nectar* chearful, like *Nepenthe* safe.[6]
Not such a Plant which *Bacchus* first did nurse,
Heav'ns Blessing chang'd by Mortals to their Curse.
Ah Syren-Pleasure, to Destruction turn'd![7]
Ah woeful Mirth to be for ever Mourn'd!
How much more blest —   40
You Swains who drink, with Birds, the running Spring,
And Innocent, like them, like them can sing.
Another Round — Then, of your Patience hold,
I shall the Charming History unfold
How this rare Plant at first divinely sprung,
Nor shall its Sov'reign *Virtues* rest unsung,
For which our *Phœbus*[8] oft his Harp has strung....'

4. A celebrated fountain in Corinth.
5. In Homer's *Odyssey*, the enchantress Circe gave Odysseus and his men bowls of drugged food and drink which turned them into swine.
6. Nectar: the drink of the Greek gods, which made those who drank it immortal; Nepenthe: a drug which takes away grief (Homer, *Odyssey*, IV, 221); the 'virtues' and 'graces' of the previous line are classical deities representing high moral action, grace and charm.
7. The plant of Bacchus is the vine. In Greek mythology, the sirens were fabulous creatures (usually women) who lured men to destruction with their song.
8. Phœbus Apollo in Greek mythology was (among his other attributes) the god of music.

... Hail Queen of Plants, Pride of *Elysian* Bow'rs![9]
How shall we speak thy complicated Pow'rs?
Thou Wond'rous *Panacea*, to asswage   50
The Calentures[10] of *Youth*'s fermenting Rage,
And Animate the freezing Veins of Age.

To *Bacchus* when our Griefs repair for Ease,
The Remedy proves worse than the Disease:
Where Reason we must lose to keep the Round,
And drinking others Healths, our Own confound:
Whilst *TEA*, our Sorrows safely to beguile,
Sobriety and Mirth does reconcile:
For to this Nectar we the Blessing owe,
To grow more *Wise*, as we more chearful grow.   60
Whilst Fancy does her brightest Beams dispense,
And decent Wit diverts without Offence.
Then in Discourse of Nature's mystick Pow'rs
And Noblest Themes, we pass the well-spent Hours,
Whilst all around the *Virtues* Sacred Band,
And list'ning *Graces* pleas'd Attendants stand.[11]
Thus our *Tea*-Conversation we employ,
Where with Delight, Instruction we enjoy;
Quaffing, without the wast of Time of Wealth,
The Sov'reign Drink of *Pleasure* and of *Health*.   70

Song of the Angels at the Nativity of Our Blessed Saviour

While Shepherds watch'd their Flocks by Night, all seated on the Ground,
The Angel of the Lord came down, and Glory shone around.
'Fear not,' said he (for mighty Dread had seiz'd their troubled Mind)
'Glad Tidings of great Joy I bring to you and all Mankind;

---

9. Tate imagines the tea-plant growing in Elysium, the place where those favoured by the
   gods of Greek mythology enjoyed after death a full and pleasant life.
10. fevers, burning passions.
11. See above n. 6.

To you, in *David*'s Town this Day is born of *David*'s Line,
The Saviour, who is Christ the Lord; and this shall be the Sign:
The heav'nly Babe you there shall find to humane view display'd,
All meanly wrapt in swathing Bands, and in a Manger laid.'

Thus spake the Seraph, and forthwith appear'd a shining Throng
Of Angels praising God, and thus addrest their joyful Song;   10
'All Glory be to God on high, and to the Earth be peace;
Goodwill, henceforth, from Heav'n to Men, begin and never cease.'

JOHN TOLAND
(1670-**1700**-1722)

John Toland, who was born in Inishowen, Co. Donegal and was a native speaker of Irish, rejected catholicism at the age of fifteen. After studying in Glasgow, Leyden and Oxford, he became a freethinker, a deist and a fervent controversialist. Toland wrote many theological and political pamphlets and edited the works of the famous republicans John Milton and James Harrington. He became a well-known radical and his most famous work, *Christianity not Mysterious*, was burned in Dublin by order of the Irish House of Commons in 1697. In the poem which follows, Toland explains confidently how he intends to publicise his political views and to expose the hypocrisy of churchmen and churchwomen of most denominations.

from: Clito: a Poem on the Force of Eloquence

In common Words I vulgar things will tell,[1]
And in Discourse not finely speak, but well.
My Phrase shall clear, short, unaffected be,
And all my speech shall like my Thoughts be free;
Not grave enough to fright the Young away,
Nor yet for elder Company too gay.
But when the Crowd I'm chosen to persuade
By long Orations for the purpose made;
Or by what reaches more with more success,
The labour'd Composition of the Press:[2]   10
Then shall my fertil Brain new Terms produce,
Or old Expressions bring again in use,
Make all Ideas with their Signs agree,[3]
And sooner Things than Words shall wanting be.
Harmonious Sounds th'attentive Ear shall please,
While artful Numbers Passions lay or raise;
Commanding Vigour shall my Thoughts convey,
And Softness seal the truth of all I say:
I'll sooth the raging Mob with mildest Words,
Or sluggish Cowards rouse to use their Swords.   20
As furious Winds sweep down whate'er resists,
So shall my Tongue perform whate'er it lists,

---

1. i.e. I will use simple language when speaking about ordinary things to the uneducated.
2. i.e. the printing press.
3. The link between a word and the object to which it refers was the subject of considerable theoretical speculation at this time, both on the Continent and in England and Ireland.

With large impetuous Floods of Eloquence
Tickle the Fancy and bewitch the Sense;
Make what it will the justest Cause appear,
And what's perplex'd or dark, look bright and clear....

Thus arm'd, thus strong, thus fitted to persuade,
I'll Truth protect, and Error straight invade,
Dispel those Clouds that darken human Sight,
And bless the World with everlasting Light.   30
A Noble Fury does possess my Soul,
Which all may forward, nothing can controul;
The fate of Beings, and the hopes of Men,
Shall be what pleases my creating Pen....

O Glorious Liberty![4] for thee I'll prove
The firmest Patron that e'er Tongue did move;
I'll always execute what you decree,
And be the fatal Scourge of Slavery.
Ambitious Tyrants, proud and useless Drones,
I'll first expose, then tumble from their Thrones: 40
Some their foul Crimes shall expiate by Death,
And some in Exile draw their hated Breath,
Their warlike Troops I shall with ease disband,
And conquer those who all beside command;
I've known a Senate with some magic words
For Forks and Spades transform their bloody Swords:
Those hect'ring Braves, who vaunt their Force so loud,
A Patriot's Tongue can humble with the Crowd....

No longer thus the World shall be misled
By him that's falsly call'd th'Unerring Head.[5]   50
His Triple Crown I scornfully will spurn,
And his proud Seat to heaps of Rubbish turn,
Fright all his Vassals into Dens and Caves,
Then smoak to death his sacrilegious Slaves.
The swarming Herds of crafty Priests and Monks,
The Female Orders of Religious Punks,

4. A typical theme of protestant writers of the time was that liberty and catholicism could not coexist: thus nations ruled by catholic monarchs were in a state of slavery.
5. Toland once described himself as having been 'educated from the cradle in the grossest superstition', and he became well-known for his anti-catholic views. The 'Triple Crown' (l. 51) refers to the crown worn by the pope.

Cardinals, Patriarchs, Metropolitans,[6]
Franciscans, Jesuits, Dominicans,
And such like barbarous Names Ecclesiastic,
Such superstitious, villainous, fantastic,   60
Coz'ning Rogues I'll evermore disturb;
Sense shall their Doctrines, Force their Malice curb.
Nor will I here desist; all Holy Cheats
Of all Religions shall partake my Threats,
Whether with sable Gowns they show their Pride,
Or under Cloaks their Knavery they hide,
Or whatsoe'er disguise they chuse to wear
To gull the People, while their Spoils they share.
As much as we revere those worthy Men,
Who teach what's peaceful, necessary, plain;   70
So much we shou'd such Hypocrites impeach,
As only Jargo[n], Strife, and Empire preach.
Religion safe, with Priestcraft is the War;[7]
All Friends to Priestcraft, Foes to Mankind are.
Their impious Fanes[8] and Altars I'll overthrow,
And the whole Farce of their feign[9] Saintship show;
Their pious Tricks disclose; their Murd'ring Zeal,
And all their awful Mysteries reveal;
Their lying Prophets, and their jugling Thieves
Discredit quite; their foolish Books (as Leaves   80
From Trees in Autumn fall) I'll scatter wide,
And shew those Fables which they fain wou'd hide....

---

6. Senior bishops or archbishops.
7. Like Swift in *A Tale of a Tub*, Toland is attacking the 'gross corruptions' of religion and what he calls 'priestcraft', rather than religion itself.
8. banners.
9. i.e. feigned.

WILLIAM KING
(1663-**1704**-1712)

William King, an English miscellaneous writer once described by Swift as a 'poor, starving wit', was appointed to the post of judge of the admiralty court of Ireland (a sinecure) in 1701. Shortly afterwards, he spent some months at the country house of a Judge Upton at Mountown, seven miles south-east of Dublin. This poem celebrates the cow which provided milk for the house at Mountown, but such was King's reputation as a wit that, when it was first published, readers suspected that it was a 'state poem', that is, a poem full of hidden meanings and secret allusions to English state affairs. In fact, as King wrote in the 1707 edition of his collected works, "twas only made ... for Country Diversion'. The poem is printed here for its insight into country life near Dublin in the first years of the eighteenth century.

from: Mully of Mountown

MOUNTOWN! Thou sweet Retreat from *Dublin* Cares,
Be famous for thy *Apples* and thy *Pears*;
For *Turnips, Carrots, Lettice, Beans* and *Pease*;
For *Peggy*'s Butter, and for *Peggy*'s Cheese.
May Clouds of *Pigeons* round about thee fly;
But condescend sometimes to make a *Pye.*
May fat *Geese* gaggle with melodious Voice,
And ne'er want Gooseberries or Apple-sauce:
Ducks in thy *Ponds*, and *Chickens* in thy *Pens*,
And be thy *Turkeys* numerous as thy *Hens*:   10
May thy black *Pigs* lie warm in little Stye,
And have no Thought to grieve them till they die.
Mountown! The *Muses* most delicious *Theam*;
Oh! may thy *Codlins*[1] ever swim in *Cream*:
Thy *Rasp-* and *Strawberries* in *Bourdeaux*[2] drown,
To add a redder Tincture to their own:
Thy *White-Wine, Sugar, Milk,* together Club,
To make that gentle Viand *Syllabub*.[3]
Thy *Tarts* to *Tarts, Cheese-cakes* to *Cheese-cakes* join,
To spoil the Relish of the flowing *Wine*.   20
But to the fading *Palate* bring relief,

---

1. A codlin or codling was a variety of cooking apple.
2. i.e. red wine from Bordeaux.
3. sillabub, a drink made of sweetened milk curdled by the addition of wine or cider. viand = food.

By thy *Westphalian-Ham,* or *Belgick-Beef* [4]
And to complete thy Blessings in a Word,
May still thy *Soil* be Generous as its *Lord.*

Oh! *Peggy, Peggy,* when thou go'st to *Brew,*
Consider well what you're about to do;
Be very *Wise,* very sedately *think*
That what you're going now to make is *Drink*:
Consider *who* must drink that *Drink,* and then,
What 'tis to have the Praise of *Honest* Men: 30
For surely, *Peggy,* while that Drink does last,
'Tis *Peggy* will be *Toasted* or *Disgrac'd.*
Then if thy *Ale* in *Glass* though wouldst confine,
To make its sparkling Rays in Beauty shine,
Let thy clean Bottle be entirely dry,
Lest a white Substance to the Surface fly,
And floating there, disturb the curious Eye.
But this great *Maxim* must be understood,
Be sure, be very sure, thy Cork *be Good.*
Then future Ages shall of *Peggy* tell,   40
That Nymph that *Brew'd* and *Bottled Ale* so well....

MULLY a Cow sprung from a Beauteous Race,
With spreading Front,[5] did *Mountown*'s Pastures grace.
Gentle she was, and with a gentle *Stream,*
Each Morn and Night gave *Milk* that equal'd *Cream.*
Offending None, of *None* she stood in Dread,
Much less of *Persons* which she daily *Fed*:
But Innocence cannot it self Defend,
'Gainst treacherous Arts, veil'd with the Name of Friend.

ROBIN of *Darby-shire,* whose Temper shocks   50
The Constitution of his Native Rocks;
Born in a Place,[6] which if it once be nam'd
Wou'd make a blushing Modesty asham'd:
He with Indulgence kindly did *appear,*
To make poor *Mully* his peculiar Care,

4. Cured ham from Westphalia (now in Germany), and cured beef from Belgium.
5. i.e. horns.
6. *The Devil's Arse of Peak* [original note]. The reference is to an area in the English Peak District.

But *inwardly* this sullen churlish Thief,
Had all his Mind plac'd upon *Mully*'s Beef;
His Fancy fed on her, and thus he'd cry,
'*Mully*, as sure as I'm *Alive* you *Die*;
'Tis a brave Cow, O Sirs, when *Christmas* comes,   60
These *Shins* shall make the *Porridge* grac'd with *Plumbs*,
Then midst our *Cups*, whilst we profusely *Dine*
This *Blade* shall enter deep in *Mully's Chine*,[7]
What *Ribs*, what *Rumps*, what *Bak'd, Boil'd, Stew'd and Roast*?
There shan't one single *Tripe* of her be lost.'

When *Peggy*, Nymph of *Mountown*, heard these Sounds,
She griev'd to hear of *Mully*'s future Wounds,
What Crime, says she, has gentle *Mully* done?
Witness the Rising and the Setting *Sun*,
That knows what *Milk* she constantly would give,   70
Let *that* Quench *Robin*'s Rage, and *Mully* Live.

Daniel, a sprightly Swain that us'd to flash
The Vigorous Steeds that drew his Lord's Calash,[8]
To *Peggy*'s Side inclin'd, for 'twas well known
How well he lov'd those Cattel[9] of his own.

Then *Terence* spoke, Oraculous[10] and sly,
He'd neither grant the Question, or deny;
Pleading for *Milk*, his Thoughts were on *Mince-Pye*:[11]
But all his Arguments so dubious were
That *Mully* thence had neither Hopes nor Fear.   80
'You've spoke,' says *Robin*, 'but now let me tell ye
'Tis not fair spoken *Words* that fill the *Belly*;
Pudding and Beef I Love and cannot stoop
To recommend your *Bonny Clapper Soop*;[12]
You say she's *Innocent*, but what of *that*,

---

7. The part of the meat next to the backbone, the 'saddle'.
8. i.e. to show off the powerful horses which drew his lordship's calash (a light-weight carriage).
9. In the seventeenth and eighteenth centuries, the term 'cattle' referred to horses as well as cows.
10. i.e. like an oracle.
11. Mince pies usually included minced beef as well as raisins, currants and spices at this time.
12. See Glossary.

'Tis more than *Crime* sufficient that she's *Fat*,
And that which is prevailing in this Case
Is, there's another *Cow* to fill her place.
And granting *Mully* to have Milk in store
Yet still this other *Cow* will give us more. 90
She *Dies'* — stop here my *Muse*, forbear the rest,
And veil that Grief which cannot be exprest.

GEORGE FARQUHAR
(1677-**1707**-1707)

George Farquhar, the son of a clergyman, was born in Derry. It is said that he fought on the Williamite side at the battle of the Boyne. He entered Trinity College, Dublin in 1694 but left without a degree in order to take up acting. In 1697, he moved to London where he wrote several comedies. Later, to mend his fortunes, he joined the army which gave him the subject of *The Recruiting Officer* (1706). His most famous play, *The Beaux' Stratagem*, was completed shortly before he died, probably from tuberculosis, in 1707.

To a Gentleman who had his *Pocket* Pick'd of a *Watch* and *Money* by a *Mistriss*

You know the Ancient Writings say,
That men shou'd *Watch* as well as *Pray*;
Had you but *Watch'd* your *Fob*,[1] dear *Tony*,
You'd not been rob'd of *Watch* and *Money*;
However, *Friend*, to leave off punning,
I much admire the *Doxy*'s[2] cunning,
Who was resolv'd to make all sure,
And of your *Mettal* be secure;
But faith, I think, it was a crime
Basely to rob you of your *Time*,   10
Sly Devil! she knew her *Minute* Hand
Cou'd in a *Moment Hours* command,
So *wound* you up to her own liking,
And stole the *Watch* while you were *striking*.

Well, since 'tis gone, ne'er fret and vex,
Necessitati non est Lex;[3]
You say, for your *lost Time* you grieve,
Why? *Money* can your *Time* retrieve;
But then which is the worst *Mishap*,
You say, you fear some *After-clap*;   20
Suppose the worst, your *Old Friend* CASE,[4]

1. A small pocket in the waistband of the breeches used for carrying money or a watch.
2. A common slang term for a prostitute.
3. A variant of a maxim from Roman law '*Necessitas non habet Legem*': 'Necessity has no law'.
4. Dr Case was a London doctor who specialised in the treatment of 'the clap' — venereal disease.

Still Practices in the same place,
Send him but word, he'll send you down
A *perfect Cure* for half a Crown,
Therefore take Heart, your Courage rouze,
Things aren't so bad as you suppose;
And tak't from me —
The *Mettal*'s stronger that's well souder'd,[5]
And *Beef* keeps sweeter once 'tis powder'd.[6]

An Epigram, on the Riding-House in *Dublin*, made into a Chappel

A *Chappel* of the Riding-House is made;
We thus once more see *Christ* in Manger laid,
Where still we find the Jocky trade supply'd;
The *Laymen* bridled, and the *Clergy* ride.

---

5. to souder = to solder, used not only of joining metals with a fusible metallic alloy, but also in medicine of causing wounds to heal.
6. 'powder'd' refers to the use of powdered mercury in treating venereal diseases.

WILLIAM CONGREVE
(1670-**1710**-1729)

Congreve was a school fellow of Jonathan Swift at both Kilkenny School and Trinity College, Dublin. His adult life was spent in London where he became a successful playwright; he also wrote a novel and some verse, including well-known translations of Ovid and Juvenal. The theme of the poem which follows is a common one of the age.

Doris

DORIS, a Nymph of riper Age,
    Has every Grace and Art
A wise Observer to engage,
    Or wound a heedless Heart.
Of Native Blush, and Rosy Dye
    Time has her Cheek bereft,
Which makes the prudent Nymph supply
    With Paint, th' injurious Theft.
Her sparkling Eyes she still retains,
    And Teeth in good Repair;   10
And her well-furnish'd Front[1] disdains
    To grace with borrow'd Hair.
Of Size, she is not short, nor tall,
    And does to Fat incline
No more than what the *French* wou'd call
    Aimable Embonpoint.[2]
Farther, her Person to disclose
    I leave — let it suffice,
She has few Faults but what she knows,
    And can with Skill disguise.   20
She many Lovers has refus'd,
    With many more comply'd,
Which, like her Clothes, when little us'd
    She always lays aside.
She's one who looks with great contempt
    On each affected Creature,
Whose Nicety would seem exempt
    From Appetites of Nature.

1. forehead.
2. Fr. *aimable*: agreeable, attractive; *en bon point*: in good condition.

She thinks they want or Health or Sense,
    Who want an Inclination,[3]   30
And therefore never takes Offence
    At him who pleads his Passion.
Whom she refuses, she treats still
    With so much sweet Behaviour,
That her refusal, through her Skill,
    Looks almost like a Favour.
Since she this Softness can express
    To those whom she rejects,
She must be very fond, you'll guess,
    Of such whom she affects.   40
But here our *Doris* far outgoes
    All that her Sex have done;
She no Regard for Custom knows
    Which Reason bids her shun.
By *Reason*, her own *Reason*'s meant,
    Or if your please, her *Will*:
For when this last is Discontent,
    The first is serv'd but ill.
Peculiar therefore is her Way;
    Whether by Nature taught,   50
I shall not undertake to say,
    Or by Experience bought.
But who o'er-night obtain'd her Grace,
    She can next Day disown,
And stare upon the Strange man's Face
    As one she ne'er had known.
So well she can the Truth disguise,
    Such artful Wonder frame,
The Lover or distrusts his Eyes,
    Or thinks 'twas all a Dream.   60
Some censure this as Lewd and Low
    Who are to Bounty blind,
For to forget what we bestow
    Bespeaks a noble Mind.
Doris, our Thanks nor asks nor needs
    For all her Favours done:
From her Love flows, as Light proceeds
    Spontaneous from the Sun.

---

3. i.e. she thinks that anyone who does not want to make love to her must be ill or mad.

On one or other still her Fires
    Display their Genial Force;   70
And she, like *Sol*, alone retires,
    To shine elsewhere, of Course.

THOMAS PARNELL
(1679-**1713**-1718)

Thomas Parnell was born in Dublin and educated at Trinity College. He was ordained into the Church of Ireland, in 1706 was appointed archdeacon of Clogher and in 1716 became vicar of Finglas, near Dublin. He visited London frequently and became friendly with Swift, Pope and other members of the Scriblerus Club. Pope, who greatly admired Parnell's verse, edited his poems after his death.

To ——————[1]

Thanks to the Friend whose happy Lines cou'd cheer
In Derry's oaten Soil[2] and frozen Air!
When to the City late I bid farewell,
Beneath my firm Resolves, my Scribling fell:[3]
The Ghost of my departed Muse you raise,
And tune her Tongue to long-forgotten Layes.
Thus a poor Girl by Passion over-run
Tires with the Folly and forsakes the Town,
But if her Shades present a pow'rfull Swain,
She feels the Woman stirr — and loves again.   10

Your Thoughts are just! Your Words fall in with ease:
Who wou'd not be abused in lines like these!
Mindless of all the Ill they say of me,
I read them and admire their Poetry;
So when a charming Beauty strikes the Heart,
We slight the Wound to gaze upon the Dart.
But Oh! my Friend! Of writing *much* beware!
If once you're charm'd, you're fix'd for ever there!
Fame all abroad, and loose Desires within
Intice a giddy Creature to the Pen;   20
A 'Cælia' soon he getts to whom to write,
And the brisk Bottle must compleat the Witt.

---

1. This verse letter to an unknown friend is taken from one of Parnell's early manuscript notebooks, and is hard to date. However, after 1706 when he became archdeacon of Clogher, Parnell could well have been staying in Derry, the next diocese and county.
2. Oats were considered a suitable crop only for the colder parts of Ireland in the eighteenth century.
3. i.e. though I had resolved to give up 'scribbling', I failed to do so.

Then every Minute of succeeding Time ⎫
Invents a frolick, or creates a Whim ⎬
Which his lov'd[4] absent Friend must hear in Rime; ⎭
You'll think (and others have been thus undone) ⎫
Your Reason can the growing Passion shun — ⎬
But did you know its Strength, you'd doubt your own. ⎭

Your best Endeavours on the Law bestow:
Rough as it is, 'tis proffitable too.   30
Cowel and Blunt have words, and Cook[5] the way ⎫
To keep the wrangling Sons of Earth in play; ⎬
Then, if your Books you use, your Clients pay! ⎭

Stay Muse! — in Paths you never trod you rove! ⎫
My lean Advice does my Presumption prove; ⎬
But can it show my Fault and not my Love? ⎭
Kindly accept what I in Kindness send,
And think me, as I think myself, your Friend.

On the Castle of Dublin, *Anno* 1715

This House and Inhabitants both well agree,
And resemble each other as near as can be;
One half is decay'd, and in want of a Prop,
The other new built, but not finish'd a-top.[1]

---

4. Parnell's modern editors, Claude Rawson and F. P. Lock (*Collected Poems*, 1989), interpret this word as 'leud'. However, 'lovd' is a possible reading and seems a more appropriate one in the context.
5. John Cowell (1554-1611), Thomas Blount (1618-79) and Sir Edward Coke (1552-1634), authors of famous legal texts.

---

1. The 'decay'd' part of Dublin Castle at this time was the ruinous Bermingham Tower: the 'new-built' part was the reconstructed privy council chamber. The 'Inhabitants' of the Castle referred to are the new lords justices appointed in September 1715: the 'decay'd' one was the aged Earl of Galway, the 'new built' one, 'not finish'd a-top', was the incompetent second Duke of Grafton.

Bacchus or the Drunken Metamorphosis[1]

As Bacchus ranging at his leisure,
(Io![2] Bacchus! king of pleasure)
Charm'd the wide world with Drink and Dances,
And all his thousand airy Fancies,
Alas! he quite forgot the while
His fav'rite Vines in Lesbos Isle.

The God returning e'er they dy'd,[3]
'Ah! see! my jolly Fawns,' he cry'd,
'The Leaves but hardly born are red
And the bare Arms for pity spread.   10
The Beasts afford[4] a rich Manure;
Fly, my Boys, to bring the Cure,
Up the Mountains, o'er the Vales,
Thro' the Woods, and down the Dales;
For this, if full the Cluster grow,
Your Bowls shall doubly overflow.'

So, chear'd with more officious haste,
They bring the Dungs of ev'ry Beast;
The Loads they wheel, the Roots they bare,
They lay the rich Manure with care,   20
While oft he calls to labour hard,
And names as oft the red Reward.

The Plants refresh'd, new Leaves appear;
The thick'ning Clusters load the Year;
The season swiftly Purple grew,
The grapes hung dangling, deep with Blue.

---

1. The first printing of this poem is in Parnell's *Works in Verse and Prose* (Glasgow: Foulis, 1755) where it is entitled 'Bacchus: or the Vines of Lesbos'. Bacchus was one of the names of Dionysus, the classical god of riot, particularly that induced by intoxication, and is usually pictured (as in this poem) surrounded by rioting companions — satyrs or fawns. Lesbos is a large island off the coast of modern Turkey — the birthplace of the famous Greek poet Sappho.
2. A traditional shout of welcome.
3. Vines look as if they are dead during the winter.
4. i.e. animals are capable of yielding rich manure.

A Vineyard ripe, a Day serene,
Now calls them all to Work again.
The Fawns thro' every Furrow shoot,
To load their Flaskets[5] with the Fruit;   30
And now the Vintage early trod,
The Wines invite the jolly God.

Strow the Roses, raise the Song,
See the Master comes along!
Lusty Revel join'd with Laughter,
Whim and Frolick follow after.
The Fawns aside the Vats remain,
To shew the Work, and reap the Gain.
All around, and all around,
They sit to riot on the ground.   40
A Vessel stands amidst the Ring,
And there they laugh, and there they sing;
Or rise a jolly, jolly Band,
And dance about it hand in hand;
Dance about and shout amain[6]
Then sit to laugh and sing again,
Thus they drink and thus they play
The Sun and all their Wits away.

But, as an antient Author sung,[7]
The Vine manur'd with ev'ry Dung   50
From ev'ry Creature, strangely drew
A Tang of brutal Nature too.
'Twas hence in drinking on the Lawns
New turns of Humour seiz'd the Fawns.

Here one was crying out 'By Jove!'
Another 'Fight me in the Grove!'
This wounds a Friend, and that the Trees;
The Lyon's Temper reign'd in these.

---

5. long, shallow baskets (Johnson).

6. vehemently.

7. According to Rawson and Lock, there is no known classical original for this story, nor is there any particular connection between Bacchus and Lesbos (*Collected Poems,* p. 575).

Another grins and leaps about,
And keeps a merry world of Rout, 60
And talks impertinently free,
And twenty talk the same as he,
Chatt'ring, Idle, Airy, Kind:
These take the Monkey's turn of mind.

Here one who saw the Nymphs that stood
To peep upon them from the Wood,
Skulks off to try if any Maid
Be lagging late beneath the Shade,
While loose Discourse another raises,
In naked Nature's plainest Phraises; 70
And ev'ry Glass he drinks enjoys
With change of Nonsense, Lust and Noise;
Mad and careless, hot and vain,
Such as these the Goat retain.

Another drinks and casts it up,
And drinks and wants another Cup,
Is very silent and sedate,
Ever long and ever late,
Full of Meats and full of Wine:
This takes his Temper from the Swine. 80

There some who hardly seem to breathe
Drink and hang the Jaw beneath;
Gaping, tender, apt to weep:
Their Nature's alter'd by the Sheep.

'Twas thus one Autumn all the Crew,
(If what the Poets say be true)
While Bacchus made a merry Feast
Inclin'd to one or other Beast.
And since, 'tis said for many a Mile,
He spread the Vines of Lesbos Isle. 90

MARY MONCK

(1678?-**1715**-1715)

Mary Monck was the daughter of Robert, first Viscount Molesworth, of Brackenstown near Swords, Co. Dublin. Despite the fact that her father seems to have disapproved of the education of women (see his introduction to *Marinda*), Mary was able to read several languages and had a good knowledge of the classics. Her husband, George Monck, who was MP for Philipstown (a borough controlled by her father) in the Irish parliament from 1703-1713, suffered periodic bouts of insanity, and evidence suggests that she lived apart from him for a while (see Roger Lonsdale, *Eighteenth-Century Women Poets* (Oxford, 1989), pp. 70-71). On her (early) death in 1715, poems were found in her desk and her father hastened to publish them as hers in a volume entitled *Marinda* which he dedicated to the Princess of Wales. It seems likely that Mary Monck was a member of a literary coterie and that not all the poems in the volume were actually by her; but some definitely are, and the two which follow reflect the classical influence noticeable in much of her verse.

An Elegie on a Favourite Dog
To her Father

Who can forbid the Muses Tears to flow?
On such a Subject to Indulge her Woe?
Where-e'er Fidelity and Love are join'd,
They claim the Tribute of a grateful Mind.
Birds have had Funeral Rites, and with swol'n Eyes
Fair *Lesbia* grac'd her Sparrow's Obsequies;[1]
His warlike Steed Young *Ammon*[2] did lament,
And rais'd a City for his Monument.
That bright celestial Dog that decks the Skies,[3]
Did by his Merit to that Honour rise: 10
And all the Virtues by which Men renown'd
To Heavenly Seats have climb'd, in Dogs are found.
None dare in glorious Dangers farther go,
None are more watchful to repel the Foe;
Nor are those tend'rer Qualities of Mind
That most endear us, Strangers to this Kind.
In human Race, alas! we seldom prove
So firm a Friendship, so unfeign'd a Love.

---

1. Lesbia, mistress of the Latin poet Catullus, wept on the death of her pet sparrow.
2. Alexander the Great founded the city of Buchephala on the spot where his favourite horse, Buchephalus, died in 326 B.C. Alexander added the name Ammon to his own after being hailed as the son of the god Zeus Ammon in Egypt in 331 B.C.
3. The 'dog-star', Sirius, is the brightest star in the night sky.

Can any then, your grateful Labours blame,
Or wonder, you shou'd to your Favourite's Name   20
The last just Honours pay? it were not fit
So bright a Merit shou'd in darkness sit,
That he who so distinguish'd liv'd, shou'd dye,
And in the common Herd forgotten lye.
No; let a Monumental Marble tell
How dear he liv'd, and how bewail'd he fell.

Press gently on him Earth, and all around
Ye Flowers spring up, and deck th'enamel'd Ground;
Breathe forth your choicest Odours, and perfume
With all your fragrant Sweets his little Tomb.   30

A Tale

A Band of *Cupids* th'other Day
Together met to Laugh and Play,
When on a sudden, 'Come, who flies?'   ⎫
Says one; 'But whither?' t'other cries.   ⎬
'Why, whither, but to *Cloe*'s Eyes'   ⎭
Reply'd a third. The wanton Crew
(Like swarms of Bees to Roses) flew
Around the beauteous *Cloe*'s Face,
And crowded hard to get a place.
This on her nether Lip does fix,   10
Whilst on her Cheek another sticks.
This swings upon her flowing Hair,
In her fair Eyes a lovely pair
Of Youths stand with their Torches lit;
Two others on her Eye-brows sit,
Each with his Bow; Amongst the Rest
One miss'd her Chin, and on her Breast
Fell head-long, but soon looking up did cry
'None of you've got so good a Place as I!'

JAMES WARD
(1691-**1718**-1736)

James Ward was a contemporary of Swift's friend Thomas Sheridan, both at school in Dublin and at Trinity College, from which both men graduated in 1711. Like Sheridan, Ward was ordained into the Church of Ireland and he eventually (1726) became Dean of Cloyne. He was a friend of Lord Orrery, who tried to get him promoted to a bishopric. He contributed poems to several of the earliest collections of Irish verse in English, including *A New Miscellany of Poems and Translations* (Dublin, 1716) and Matthew Concanen's *Miscellaneous Poems* (London, 1724). 'Phoenix Park' is the first substantial example of a topographical poem set in Ireland, and 'The Smock Race at Finglas' is one of the liveliest descriptions of Irish country life in the early eighteenth century.

from: *Phoenix* Park[1]

... Shall *Cooper's-hill* majestick rise in Rhyme
Strong as its Basis, as its Brow sublime?[2]
Shall *Windsor* Forrest win immortal Praise,
It self outlasting in its Poets Lays?
And thou, O *Phoenix* Park! remain so long
Unknown to Fame, and unadorn'd in Song?

... What Scene more lovely, and more form'd for Bliss,
What more deserves the Muse's Strain than this?
Where more can boundless Nature please, and where
In Shapes more various, and more sweet appear?   10

Now when the Centre of the Wood is found,
With goodly Trees a spacious Circle bound,
I stop my wandring — while on ev'ry Side,
Glades op'ning to the Eye, the Grove divide,
To distant Objects stretch my lengthen'd View,
And make each pleasing Prospect charm anew....

1. Phoenix Park, to the west of Dublin, was laid out as a public park in the reign of Charles II. It is still one of the largest public parks within the city boundaries of any European city, and comparatively 'wild'. See Maurice Craig, *Dublin 1660-1860* (Dublin, 1969), pp. 13-17.
2. One of the most famous topographical poems of the seventeenth century was 'Cooper's Hill' (1642) by Sir John Denham. The poem glorified the countryside of the Thames valley and influenced many poets, including Alexander Pope, whose popular pastoral poem 'Windsor Forest', is mentioned in the next couplet.

... Deep in the Vale old *Liffy* rolls his Tides,
Romantick Prospects crown his rev'rend Sides;[3]
Now thro' wild Grotts, and pendant Woods[4] he strays,
And ravish'd at the Sight, his Course delays,   20
Silent and calm — now with impetuous Shock
Pours his swift Torrent down the steepy Rock;
The tumbling Waters thro' airy Channels flow,
And loudly roaring, smoak, and foam below.

Fast by his Banks stands, high above the Plain,
A Fabrick rais'd in peaceful *Charles*'s reign,[5]
Where vet'ran Bands, discharg'd from War, retire,
Feeble their Limbs, extinct their martial Fire:
I hear methinks, I hear the gallant Train,[6]
Recount the Wonders of each past Campaign: 30
Conquests, and Triumphs in my Bosom roll,
And *Britain*'s Glory fills my wid'ning Soul:
Here blest with Plenty, and maintain'd at Ease,
They boast th'Adventures of their youthful Days;
Repeat exhausted Dangers o'er again,
And sigh to speak of faithful Comrades slain.
Silent the list'ning Audience sit around,
Weep at the Tale, and view the Witness Wound:
What mighty Things each for his Country wrought
Each tells, — and all how bravely *Marlbro*' fought.[7]   40

There, o'er wide Plains, my lab'ring Sight extends,
And fails itself e'er the long Landskape ends:
Where Flocks around the rural Cottage seen,
Brouze the young Buds, or graze the tufted Green;
And Fields bespread with golden Crops appear,
Ensuring Plenty for the following Year....

---

3. Phoenix Park was larger in the seventeenth century than it is today and the Liffey then
   flowed through — rather than as it flows today, alongside — the park.
4. i.e. through wild grottos and past low-hanging trees.
5. The Royal Hospital at Kilmainham, founded to provide a home for retired soldiers, had
   been completed in 1674, during the reign of Charles II.
6. group of people, in this case of old soldiers.
7. John Churchill (1650-1722), duke of Marlborough, commander of the English and
   Dutch forces during the War of the Spanish Succession (1704-13).

... There the broad Ocean spreads his Waves around,
With anchor'd Fleets a faithful Harbour crown'd:
By whose kind Aid we num'rous Blessings share,
In Peace our Riches, and our Strength in War.   50
While thus retir'd, I on the City look,
A Groupe of Buildings in a Cloud of Smoak;
(Where various Domes for various Uses made,
Religion, Revels, Luxury, and Trade;
All undistinguish'd in one Mass appear,
And widely diff'ring are united here)
I learn her Vice and Follies to despise,
And love that Heav'n which in the Country lies.
The Sun in his Meridian mounted high,
Now warns me to the covert Bow'r to fly;   60
Where Trees officious croud about my Head,
And twisted Woodbine forms a fragrant Shade.
No noisy Ax thro' all the Grove resounds,
No cruel Steel the living Branches wounds:
Rev'rend in Age the wide-spread Beech appears,
The lofty Oak lives his long Date of Years.

Here careless on some mossy Bank reclin'd,
Lull'd by the murm'ring Stream, and whistling Wind;
Nor poys'nous Asp I fear, nor savage Beast,
That wretched Swains in other Lands infest: 70
Fir'd with the Love of Song, my Voice I raise,
And woo the Muses to my Country's Praise.

The Smock Race at Finglas[1]

Now did the bag-pipe in hoarse notes begin
The expected signal to the neighbouring Green,
While the sun, in the decline of day,
Shoots from the distant West a cooler ray.
Alarmed,[2] the sweating crowds forsake the Town,

---

1. Everyday activities provided many opportunities for eighteenth-century poets to write mock-heroic or mock-epic poems, the most famous of which is Alexander Pope's 'The Rape of the Lock'. The humour is more at the expense of the literary genre than of the participants. Finglas, the site of this race for a smock or chemise, is a few miles north of Dublin and was, at the time of Ward's poem, a country village.
2. excited (rather than 'frightened') (*OED* s.v. *alarm*, 3).

Unpeopled Finglas is a desert grown;
Joan quits her cows which with full udders stand
And low unheeded for the milker's hand.
The joyous sound the distant reapers hear,
Their Harvest leave and to the Sport repair;   10
The Dublin Prentice at the welcome call
In hurry rises from his cakes and ale;
Handling the flaunting seamstress o'er the plain,
He struts a Beau among the homely swain.

The Butcher's soggy Spouse amidst the throng,
Rubbed clean, and tawdry dressed, puffs slow along;
Her pon'drous Rings the wond'ring Mob behold,
And dwell on ev'ry finger heaped with Gold.
Long to Saint Patrick's filthy Shambles[3] bound,
Surpris'd, she views the rural scene around;   20
The distant ocean there salutes her eyes,
Here, tow'ring hills in goodly order rise;
There, fruitful valleys long extended lay,
Here, sheaves of corn and cocks of fragrant hay;
While whatsoe'er she hears, she smells or sees
Gives her fresh transports, and she dotes on trees,
Yet (hapless wretch) the servile thrift of Gain
Can force her to her stinking stall again.

Nor was the Country Justice wanting there,
To make a penny of the rogues that swear;[4]   30
With supercilious looks he awes the Green
'Sirs, keep the peace — I represent the Queen.'[5]
Poor Paddy swears his whole week's gains away
While my young squires blaspheme and nothing pay.
All on the mossy turf confused were laid
The jolly rustic and the buxom maid,
Impatient for the sport, too long delayed.

---

3. There were butcher's stalls and slaughter-houses in and near the market beside St Patrick's cathedral.
4 At this time, a fine could be levied on anyone who swore in public.
5. i.e. Queen Anne — which helps date this poem to her reign, 1702-14.

When, lo, old Arbiter,[6] amid the crowd,
Prince of the annual games, proclaimed aloud:
'Ye virgins that intend to try the race,   40
The swiftest wins a smock enriched with lace:
A Cambrick[7] kerchief shall the next adorn,
And Kidden Gloves[8] shall by the third be worn.'
This said, he high in air displayed each prize;
All view the waving smock with longing eyes.

Fair Oonah at the Barrier first appears,
Pride of the neighbouring mill, in bloom of years;
Her native brightness borrows not one grace,
Uncultivated charms adorn her face,
Her rosy cheeks with modest blushes glow,   50
At once her innocence and her beauty show:
Oonah the eyes of each spectator draws,
What bosom beats not in fair Oonah's cause?

Tall as a pine, majestic Nora stood,
Her youthful veins were swelled with sprightly blood,
Inured to toils, in wholesome gardens bred,
Exact in every limb and formed for speed.

To thee, O Shevan,[9] next what praise is due?
Thy youth and beauty doubly strike the view,
Fresh as the Plumb that keeps the Virgin Blue![10]   60
Each well deserves the smock — but Fates decree
But one must wear it though deserved by three.

Now side by side the panting rivals stand
And fix their eyes upon th'appointed hand:
The signal given, spring forward to the race,
Not famed Camilla[11] ran with fleeter pace;

---

6. A generalised name for the organiser of the day's events, and judge of the race.
7. Cambric was a kind of fine white linen originally made at Cambray in Flanders (*OED*).
8. gloves made of kid skin.
9. Siobhán.
10. i.e. as fresh as a plum still covered with its (bluish) bloom. The phrase may also carry echoes of the fact that the Virgin Mary is often shown wearing a blue cloak to signify her modesty.
11. A maiden-warrior in the *Æneid*, so swift-footed that she could run across a field of corn without bending the blades.

Nora, as lightning swift, the rest o'erpassed,
While Shevan fleetly ran, yet ran the last;
But Oonah then hadst Venus on her side
At Nora's petticoats the goddess plied   70
And in a trice the fatal string untied.
Quick stopped the maid nor would to win the race
Expose her hidden Charms to vulgar gaze;
But while to tie the treacherous knot she stayed
Both her glad rivals pass the weeping maid.
Now in despair she plies the race again,
Not winged winds dart swifter o'er the plain,
She (while chaste Diana[12] aids her hapless speed)
Shevan outstripped, — nor further could succeed,
For with redoubled haste; bright Oonah flies,   80
Seizes the Goal and wins the noblest Prize.

Loud shouts and acclamations fill the place,
Though chance on Oonah had bestowed the race;
Like Felim none rejoiced, — a lovelier swain
Ne'er fed a flock on the Fingallian plain.[13]
Long he with secret passion loved the maid,
Now his increasing Flame itself betrayed.
Stripped for the race how bright did she appear,
No covering hid her feet, her bosom bare,
And to the wind she gave her flowing hair.   90
A thousand charms he saw, concealed before,
Those, yet concealed, he fancied still were more.

Felim, as night came on, young Oonah wooed,
Soon willing Beauty was by Truth subdued;
No jarring Settlement their bliss annoys,
No licence needed to defer their joys.
Oonah e'er morn the sweets of wedlock tried,
The smock she won a virgin, wore a bride.

12. A classical goddess particularly worshipped by women.
13. i.e. the plains of Fingal, north of Dublin, where Finglas is situated.

MORROUGH O'CONNOR
(fl.**1719**-40)

Morrough (or Murroghoh or Morgan) O'Connor — see below for further variants of the first name — is only known for five poems, despite his description of himself in one of them as 'a profess'd poet'. He was the sub-tenant of a farm in County Kerry which was owned by Trinity College Dublin, and all his poems were written in connection with his eviction from the farm and his subsequent reinstatement on the instructions of the Provost and Fellows. The poem which follows is the first of three dialogues between O'Connor and another college tenant, Owen O'Sullivan. O'Sullivan had also been evicted from his farm, but he had not made representations to the College and the farm had been leased to 'a captain of that country', according to an explanatory note in the first edition.

An Eclogue
in Imitation of the first Eclogue of Virgil

Owen: My old acquaintance and my dearest friend,
                My Morroughoo,[1] what joys on you attend;
                Ten thousand blessings seem at once to shine
                Upon your farm and house of Ballyline.[2]
                Since you're restored to native land and ease,
                The world's your own and use it as you please:
                Now tell the glories of your noble name,
                How prince O Connor from Hispania came;
                Sprung from Milesian race[3] of great renown,
                By right of conquest made this isle his own;   10
                Landing at Shannon's mouth, that noble flood,
                Enrich'd Ierna with his royal blood;
                For from his loins as from our flowing springs,
                Our Irish veins are fill'd with blood of kings;
                But I alas! can no such honours boast,
                Since sweet Rincaharough, dear Evraugh,[4] is lost;
                My blood runs low, I'm poor and in disgrace,
                And dare not own I'm of Milesian race:
                You top the world, as great a monarch are,

1. Ir. proper name *Murchú*.
2. A townland near Listowel, Co. Kerry.
3. A long and complex note in the original edition gives the mythology surrounding the original settlement of Ireland. See Glossary.
4. Ir. *Rinn Cathrach* and *Íbh Ráthach*, the farm and townland from which Owen has been evicted.

As Connor Sligo,[5] Connor Failge[6] were;   20
And at your ease beneath Arbutus[7] laid,
Leaning against the mossy tree your head;
With harp and voice the College praises sing,
Till woods and rocks the College praises ring.

Morrough:[8]   'Tis true, to sing her praises is my choice,
She shall for ever have my harp and voice;
To her I owe the happiness you see,
'Twas she restor'd my farm and liberty;
For which full meathers[9] to her health we'll drink,
And to the bottom stranded hogsheads sink;[10]   30
Good stranded clarret, wreck'd upon our shore,
And when that's out, we'll go and search for more;
Whole nights we'll spend, till break of day sit up,
Then Dough an Dorres[11] for the parting cup.

Owen: My dearest Morrough, I am glad to find
So much content and pleasure in your mind;
But I, poor Owen, grieve, lament and moan;
You see I'm packing up, and must be gone;
My bended shoulders with my burthen bow,
And I can hardly drive this limping cow;   40
Not long ago, which gave me cause to fret,
A sea hog at the Shallogs[12] broke my net,
The sea did not up to Rincaharough flow,
Margarton's[13] top was black and wanted snow;

5. 'O Connor Sligo descended from Conn Ceadchathach of the hundred Battles, who was monarch of Ireland in the year of Christ 125, and of the royal line of Heremon.' [original note].

6. 'O Connor Faly, or Failge, descended from Rosa Failge, eldest son of Cathaoir More, sirnamed the Great, who was monarch of Ireland in the year of our Lord 122, and of the race of Heremon.' [original note].

7. The arbutus is a wild evergreen shrub or tree, common in County Kerry.

8. A long note at this point in the original edition traces the heredity of Morrough O Connor back to the earliest inhabitants of Ireland.

9. maddors. Ir. *meadar*, wooden drinking cup, often square in shape.

10. i.e. we will drink dry the casks of wine [looted] from ships wrecked on the Kerry coast.

11. Ir. *Deoch an dorais*. 'The spur-drink, or a drink at the door.' [original note].

12. Sea-hog = Ir. *muc mara,* porpoise. The original note at this point refers to 'the Shallogs' (Ir. *Seallóg*) as: 'A fishery near Owen's farm.'

13. 'An hill which has snow on it all the year.' [original note]. Mt. Mangartan is near Killarney.

With mournful song lamenting the Bantee[14]
Foretold the ruin of my house and me;
When all those omens met at once, I knew
What sad misfortune must of course ensue;
But tell me, Morrough, what the College is,
There's nothing more I long to know than this.   50

Morrough: Owen, I was so foolish once, I own,
To think it like our little school in Town;
Or like the school that's in Tralee, you know,
Where we to assizes and to sessions go;
And when arrested, stand each other's bail,
And spend a cow or two in law and ale.
I might compare Drumcun to Knock a Nore,[15]
Currock of Ballyline[16] to Lanamore[17]
With much more reason; but, my dearest friend,
The College does our school so far transcend   60
Of all the schools that ever yet I saw,
As Kerney's[18] cabbin is below Lexchnaw.[19]

Owen: But what good fortune led you to that place?

Morrough: To tell my sufferings and explain my case.
To be restor'd, to find a just redress
From those who glory'd to relieve distress:
It's true I lost my landlord's favour by't,
But then, dear Owen, I regain'd my right;
All my renewal fines with him[20] were vain,
Nor prayers nor money could my farm obtain: 70
What could I do but to the College run?
And well I did, or I should be undone.
There did I see a venerable board,
Provost and Fellows, men that keep their word;

14. Ir. *bean sí*, banshee. The original note at this point reads: 'An Irish spirit which bewails the signal calamity of any antient remarkable family.'
15. 'One a small hill, the other a great hill.' [original note]. Knockanore (Ir. *Cnoc an Óir*) is a mountain in the MacGillicuddy Reeks, Co. Kerry
16. 'A scrub on Morrough's wood.' [original note].
17. 'The great College wood.' [original note].
18. 'A cotter on Morrough's farm.' [original note].
19. Lixnaw near Listowel; 'The earl of Kerry's house.' [original note].
20. i.e. the landlord. Renewal fines were fees paid by the tenant when a lease was being renewed.

Sincere and just and honest, fair and true,
Their only rule is to give all their due;
No bribes or interest can corrupt their minds,
Unbyass'd laws the rich and poor man finds;
Alike to all their charity extends,
Ev'n I, a stranger, found them all my friends;   80
Such were the saints that once possest this isle,[21]
And drew down blessings on our happy soil:
They soon (for justice here knows no delay)
Gave this short answer, 'Morrough, go your way;
Return, improve your farm as heretofore,
Be gone, you shall not be molested more.'

Owen: Happy Milesian, happiest of men!
Then Ballyline is now your own again;
'Tis large enough, tho' not a whole plow land,[22]
And has a lovely prospect of the strand;   90
Tho' boggs and rocks deform that spot of earth,
Consider, Morrough, that it gave thee birth;
Those boggs and rocks, your cows and sheep surround,
Keep them from trespass, pledge, and starving pound;[23]
Thrice happy you who, living at your ease,
Have nought to do but see your cattle grase;
Speak Latin[24] to the strangers passing by,
And on a Shamrough Bank[25] reclining lye;
Or in the grassy sod, cut points to play
Backgammon, and delude the live long day;[26]   100
When night comes on, to pleasing rest you go,

---

21. 'Ireland, from the prodigious number of holy men and apostles of nations which it produced, was justly call'd the Island of Saints by the Christian World ...' [the original note goes on to list the missionary achievements of about a dozen early Irish saints and to quote Camden and Bede in praise of Ireland's reputation as 'the great mart of learning'].

22. The unit of assessment of land in the northern and eastern counties of England, after the Norman Conquest, based upon the area capable of being tilled by one plough-team of eight oxen in the year (*OED*). It is interesting to see this English land-measurement being used in Co. Kerry.

23. i.e. do not let them stray on others' lands, or be used as sureties for debts, or be impounded.

24. 'It is natural for the cow-boys in the county of Kerry to speak Latin.' [original note].

25. i.e. a bank covered in (growing) shamrock plants.

26. 'Kerry men are such lovers of backgammon that they cut points in the sod, and have potatoes and turnips for men.' [original note].

Lull'd by the soft Crownawn,[27] or sweet Speakshew;[28]
When kerchief'd Shela strains her warbling throat
In tuneful hum, and sleeps upon the note.

Morrough: Dingle and Derry[29] sooner shall unite,
Shannon and Cashin[30] both be dry'd outright,
And Kerry men forsake their cards and dice,[31]
Dogs be pursu'd by hares and cats by mice,
Water begin to burn, and fire to wet,
Before I do my College friends forget.   110

Owen: But I must quit my dear Evraugh, and roam
The world about to find another home;
To Paris go, with satchel cramm'd with books,[32]
With empty pockets, and with hungry looks;
Or else to Dublin, to Tim Sullivan,
To be a drawer, or a waiting man;[33]
Or else, perhaps, some favourable chance
By box and dice my fortune may advance;
At the groom porter's,[34] cou'd I find a friend,
That wou'd poor Owen kindly recommend;   120
There I cou'd nicely serve, and teach young men
The art to cogg,[35] and win their coin again.
But shall this foreign captain[36] force from me
My house, my land, my wayers,[37] my fishery?

27. Ir. *crónán* song. The original note reads: 'An Irish ground.' ['ground' is here used in the musical sense, i.e. 'a melody on which a descant is raised' *OED*].
28. 'An old woman in the chimney corner humming of a tune.' [original note]. cf. Ir. *port béil*, literally = 'mouth tune', and Ir. *seo/seothín* = lullaby. In Irish, songs are not 'sung' but 'spoken'.
29. i.e. the very north and the very south-west of Ireland.
30. The river Cashin which flows into the mouth of the Shannon.
31. 'Kerry men are so fond of cards and dice that they carry them always about them.' [original note].
32. 'A Kerry shift, when broke, to go to Paris and beg as poor scholars.' [original note].
33. 'Tim kept the London tavern (i.e. a tavern so named in Dublin), and was kind to his countrymen.' [original note]. 'Drawer' = one who draws liquor: a tapster at a tavern.
34. The groom-porter was an officer who regulated gaming within the precincts of the [English] royal court, furnished cards and dice and decided disputes arising at play; the position was abolished in the reign of George III. Again, it is interesting to find an English rather than an Irish allusion.
35. to cog = to cheat when playing at dice.
36. 'Captain Magee who came from the North.' [original note].
37. Perhaps 'weirs' but more probably connected with the word 'ware' which, in Scots law, was the right to gather seaweed or 'ware' on the shore.

Was it for him I those improvements made?
Must his long sword turn out my lab'ring spade?
Adieu my dear abode. ——
I shall no more with Brogue Bounscribu[38] climb
Steep Mollabert,[39] enthon'd on top sublime;
Head of my clan, determine ev'ry case,   130
To make my vassals live at home in peace;
To teach them justice a much cheaper way,
Keep them from lawyers fees, and courts delay;
Nor shall I see you, Curakenawye,[40]
Full often have I made a song for thee;
Least[41] some disaster should attend my life,
My tender children, or my loving wife:
Nor thee Cnuckdrum,[42] where our forefathers set
Upon thy lofty top, the insiduous net
To catch Desmonian wild, a sight more rare   140
To British eyes than Scandanavian [*sic*] bear:
Valentia too, I bid farewel to thee,
Title to best of men, great Anglesey.[43]
Desmond tho' last, not least belov'd, farewel,
By whose great lord[44] whole troops of Britons fell;
Thy glory shall in distant lands be known,
And all the world superior Desmond own.

Morrough: But stay, dear Owen, coucher[45] here this night,
            Behold, the rooks have now begun their flight;

---

38. 'A brogue with a scallop'd heel, which none but gentlemen were allow'd to wear.' [original note]. Ir. *bonn scríobtha* = scraped sole or heel.

39. 'An hill in Evanraugh where the head of the clan decides all controversies.' [original note].

40. 'An hill in that country, where those who pass must make a rhime for it, lest any mischance should happen them in their journey.' [original note].

41. i.e. lest.

42. 'A brake that was set on this hill to catch Desmonians.' [original note]. Presumably this was the site of an ambush designed to capture members of the Fitzgerald of Desmond family or clan (the 'Desmonians' of l.140) when they were fugitives during the Elizabethan wars.

43. One of the titles held by eighteenth-century Viscounts Valentia was that of Earl of Anglesea.

44. 'The earl of Desmond in the reign of queen Elizabeth.' [original note]. The reference is to Gerald Fitzgerald, fifteenth earl of Desmond (d. 1583) who led the rebellion against Queen Elizabeth I in Munster 1579-83.

45. A Hiberno-English borrowing from the Ir. *cóisir*, feast. The original edition has a long note on 'what the antient Irish call couchering' or accepting free hospitality in the house of a kinsman.

And to their nests in winged troops repair;   150
They fly in haste, and shew that night is near.
The sheep and lambkins all around us blate,[46]
The sun's just down, to travel 'tis too late;
Slewcawn[47] and Scollops shall adorn my board,
Fit entertainment for a Kerry lord:
In egg-shells then we'll take a parting cup,
Lye down on rushes, with the sun get up.

46. i.e. bleat.
47. Ir. *sleabhcán,* laver or sloke (an edible seaweed or algae).

MATTHEW CONCANEN
(1701-**1720**-1749)

Matthew Concanen is generally said to have been born in Ireland in 1701 and to have trained for the law before turning to literature; however, it seems hard to believe that a nineteen-year-old law student could produce as accomplished and ambitious a poem as *A Match at Football*, and more research needs to be done on his background. Before leaving Dublin for London to earn his living as a miscellaneous writer, Concanen also wrote *Wexford Wells*, a lively comedy; but his fame rests on the two poetic anthologies which he edited in London in 1724 and 1729. The 1724 *Miscellaneous Poems* is particularly important as the first substantial collection of verse in English from Ireland: it includes work by Delany, Smedley, Swift, Sheridan, Sterling, Parnell, Ward, Philips and Concanen himself. Concanen was appointed attorney general of Jamaica in 1732. He died, apparently of consumption, in London in 1749.

from: A Match at Football: A Poem in Three Cantos[1]

from: Canto I

I Sing the Pleasures of the Rural throng,
And Mimick Wars, as yet unknown to Song.[2]
Whilst on Weak Wings uncommon flights I Soar,
And lead the Muse thro' Tracts untried before.[3]
Ye *Sylvan* Maids,[4] be present to my Lays,
Inspire my Numbers, and my fancy raise.

The Distant Sun now Shoots a feeble Ray,
And Warms, with fainter Beams, the fading Day;
Now Cooler Breezes, fan the Sultry Glade,
And Waving Trees project a longer Shade,   10
When on a wide Extent of Level Ground,
Which spreading Groves, and rising hillocks bound,

---

1. From its invocations, its Latinate vocabulary and its terminology of 'cantos' to the intervention of gods such as Flora and Pan in the action, *A Match at Football* follows the customary pattern of the Augustan mock-heroic or (as Alexander Pope styled it) the 'Heroi-Comical' poem. Though football had been played in Ireland for two thousand years before this poem was written, it had developed by 1720 into a violent game governed by no recognised rules. This explains why handling the ball and using the unorthodox methods of tackling described in this poem merited no censure.

2. The first couplet echoes the beginning of Virgil's *Æneid*; *mimick*: to represent or describe.

3. The second couplet probably echoes Milton's *Paradise Lost* i, 12-16: 'I thence / Invoke thy aid to my adventurous song, / That with no middle flight intends to soar / Above the Aonian mount, while it pursues / Things unattempted yet in prose or rhyme.'

4. maids of the woods, i.e. the muses.

The Num'rous Crowd, with wonder and delight,
At once Confound,[5] and entertain the sight.
Here Troops of Horsemen throng the Varied Scene,
Or view the Goal, or Gallop o're the Plain.
There Jolly Rusticks, in their best Array,
Impatient for the Sport, the Field Survey;
Tir'd with preceding Mirth, the Buxom Lass,[6]
Reclines her wearied Limbs upon the Grass: 20
There lay'd at ease, receives her Lovers treats,
Or makes new Conquests, or old Vows repeats.
Some Laugh and Chat, some Dance, while others run,
But all agree, to wish the Sport begun.

At length Old *Hobbinol*[7] the Crowd addrest,
And Words like these, with Son'rous Voice express'd:
'Attend Ye lusty Swains Assembled here,
Ye men of *Soards*, and Ye of *Lusk*,[8] give ear,
Who e're would try their Fortune at the Ball,
And bravely conquer, or as bravely fall.   30
Six *Holland Caps*[9] (the Victor's lawful Prize,)
With *Ribbands* bound, here wave before your Eyes.
Tho' such as win, Immortal Honour gain,
Yet shall the Vanquish'd not contend in vain;
Of *Gloves* full twice three Pair, a Gift as great,
Shall help to reconcile them to their fate.
Besides our *Squire*, the Conq'rours Hearts to Cheer,
Will treat them with a Cask of Humming Beer.[10]
View here my Lads, the Prizes you may win,
So — save the King — and let the Game begin.'   40

---

5. perplex.
6. 'It is customary for the maids to dance for cakes and have several other sports before the football is begun.' (Concanen's note).
7. A generalised name for a countryman — from Spenser's use of the word as a proper name in *The Shepherd's Calendar* (1579).
8. 'Lusk and Swords are two baronies in the County of Dublin, whose inhabitants are famed for dexterity at this game and are always at variance for a superiority of skill.' (Concanen's note).
9. Caps made of 'Holland' linen, originally so called because woven in the Netherlands.
10. strong (probably frothing) beer.

When Lo! Six Men of *Soards* (a goodly sight)
Their Active Limbs, all loosely Clad in White,
Move towards the Barrier[11] with a Sprightly Pace;
A joyful Pride, sat Smiling on each Face;
A Crimson *Ribband*, trimly ty'd behind,
Hung from each Cap and wanton'd in the Wind.

Young *Terence* led the Van,[12] a Blither Swain
Ne're charm'd with Tuneful Song, the Neighb'ring Plain;
Than him none better skill'd, his Flocks to Feed,
The Sires to Fatten, or Encrease the Breed.   50
To Crop the Woolly *Fleece* with Artful Care,
Or from his *Fold* the Wily *Fox* to Scare.

Mov'd by no Thirst of Gain, he seeks the Prize,
No Sordid Passions in his Bosom rise;
All that he hopes, his Labours to beguile,
Is from bright *Norah* one approving Smile.
Norah with Pleasure view'd the gallant Youth,
Proud of his Love, and grateful for his Truth,
And sure severest Censure might Excuse
The fair Ones Pride, when so much merit Sues.   60
In Country Weeds[13] the Lovely *Nymph* was drest,
A Flow'ry Chaplet deck'd her Snowy Breast.
Of new blown Roses she compos'd the wreath,
Fresh as her Face, and fragrant as her Breath.
Terence on her his Watchful Eyes had set,
And as he gazed their changing glances met;
Amaz'd, confus'd — she strove to look around,
Then fixt her modest Eyes upon the Ground;
A sudden rising blush at once display'd,
The Modesty and Beauty of the Maid....   70

Two Brothers next of equal size came on,
The Elder DARBY,[14] and the Younger *John*;
For Singing this, and that for Dancing fam'd,

11. Presumably a light fence erected around the playing field.
12. i.e. was at the front of the advancing team. The names of the footballers indicate both Old English and native Irish ancestry.
13. clothes.
14. As Edward MacLysaght explains, 'The (Irish) forename *Diarmuid* is anglicised 'Darby' as well as 'Dermot' (*The Surnames of Ireland*, 6th edition (Dublin, 1985), p. 80).

This ne're was rude, and that was ne're asham'd;
Both swift of foot in artful grappling skill'd,
Born on the Confines of the fatal[15] Field.

The next to these in place was sturdy *Hugh*,
His sinews tougher than the twanging Eugh.[16]
Far hence on *Wicklow*'s steepy Mountains bred,
With strength'ning Pig-nuts[17] and Potato's fed.   80
But now, (so Fate Ordain'd) our better Cheer
Has charm'd the wandring Wight,[18] and fix'd him here.

How shall I, *Felim*, thy just Praise set forth?
Words can but faintly represent thy worth;
Though three times Twenty rolling Years have shed
Their Hoary[19] Honours on thy rev'rend Head;
Entellus[20] like, thou could'st not brook to stay
A bare Spectator[21] on this glorious Day.
Practice and Years to thee the knack impart,
To shift[22] with Cunning, and to trip with Art.   90

Last *Daniel* came, to *Oxman-town*[23] long known,
In many a well fought Field his skill was shown.
At good defence his chiefest Talent lay,
His prudent conduct oft retriev'd the Day.

Before them march'd (and as he March'd he play'd)
Ventoso[24] in his newest Weeds Array'd.
From Leathern Baggs he squeez'd th'obstrep'rous[25] tone,

---

15. destined — or perhaps meaning the field where fate will decide the outcome of the game.
16. Yew — 'twanging' because of the use of yew trees for bows.
17. Also known as the earth-nut, the earth-chestnut and the ground-nut, these underground nuts (the tubers of *Bunium flexuosum*) were a source of food in eighteenth-century Ireland.
18. person.
19. ancient.
20. A friend of Æneas and a famous athlete in Virgil's *Æneid*.
21. i.e. you could not tolerate being a mere spectator....
22. to manage matters.
23. Oxmantown, a Dublin suburb, was famous for its large open green, the site of annual May Day celebrations. Concanen notes that: 'Oxmantown Green in Dublin is frequently the scene of these kinds of sports.'
24. Latin: *full of wind*; i.e. the piper.
25. noisy: from Latin *obstrepere*: to make a noise against.

Which humming issued thro' the Concave drone; ...
And now once more it cheers the Champions hearts,
A joyful Vigour to each Youth imparts,   100
And fires with ardour to obtain the prize;
It's Notes, though sweet, were drown'd in shriller Cries,
Loud Acclamations fill the spacious round
Whilst distant Rocks repeat the joyous sound.

On t'other hand the Green begins to clear,
And see! six lusty Lads of *Lusk* appear;
Supple their Sinews are, their bodies light,
Their Aspects cheerful, and their Dresses white.
A Ribband in his Cap of Azure hue,
Distinguish'd each bold Champion to the View.   110

With these young *Paddy* holds the foremost place,
In shape to none Inferior or in Face;
In Gardens bred, Herbs were his choicest fare,
And *FLORA*[26] made him her peculiar Care;
Fond of Inglorious ease, he shun'd the Green,
Nor ever was at Rural Pastimes seen,
Nor with Heroic Sentiments inspir'd,
'Till *Norah*'s lovely Eyes his Bosom fir'd.
Desist vain youth, thy hapless fate to Learn!
The Gods are just, and *Norah* can discern!   120
The Gods to more desert decree the prize,
And form to Merit yields, in *Norah*'s Eyes.[27]

Him follow'd *Kit*, near *Nanny-water* bred;[28]
But now by thirst of reputation led,
A Denizen[29] of *Lusk*; none better skill'd,
To Crop with Dextrous art the waving Field,
To tedd the Grass[30] upon the new shorn plain,
Or from the well crush'd Ear divide the Grain.

26. The Roman goddess of flowers and gardens; she intervenes in the football match to assist Paddy.

27. i.e. the gods decree that the prize goes to the one who deserves it most; and, in Norah's eyes, merit is more important than good looks (or perhaps 'than athletic performance'?).

28. Christopher; Concanen notes that Nanny-water is 'a place in the County Meath, about six or seven miles distant from this' — i.e. from Lusk. The river Nanny flows through Julianstown, Co. Meath.

29. one who has moved to an area, an inhabitant.

30. to spread out new-mown grass (hay) for drying. The next line describes threshing.

Next *Neal* and *Cabe*,[31] whom poverty sent forth,
From the bleak regions of the rugged *North*;   130
Wasted with Toils, and starv'd on scanty Oats,
With tatter'd Shirts, and destitute of Coats,
To *Lusk* they came; but now indulg'd in ease,
With Strength'ning Turneps fed and Fat'ning Pease,
Joyful they trip the Field, and long to shew,
Their active Courage on so brave a Foe.

Le'nard succeeds,[32] for strength and skill renown'd,
No Wight like him in all *Fingal* is found,
So swift to gain, and firm to keep his Ground.
See surly *Dick* the *Miller* last appear,   140
And with a gloomy look bring up the Rear,
Nor fir'd with pleasure, nor with danger aw'd;
Strong were his knitted Limbs, his Shoulder broad.
Few better skill'd than him to play the Game,
Or toss the Foot-Ball with a surer aim.

Hail'd by no Friendly Voice they take their stand.
No Prosp'rous Omens chear the luckless band;
Before them Struts, and with his thrumming Song
Uninterrupted, Charms the list'ning throng,
Old *Tim*, supported by one Leg of Wood;   150
Yet, tho' his Limbs were maim'd, his Heart was good.
Of *Hounds* and *Foxes* he could Fights rehearse,
And sing Saint *Patrick*'s praise in Splay-Foot Verse.
Whole Fights and Sieges, to his Song could joyn,
And tell Old Tales of *Aughrum* and the *Boyn*.[33]

from: Canto II

While the bold youths arrang'd on either hand,
Around the field in decent order stand,
Amid the Throng lame *Hobbinol* appear'd,
And Wav'd his Cap in order to be heard.
The Green stood silent as the Midnight-Shade,

---

31. O'Neill and MacCabe are two Ulster surnames.
32. comes next.
33. The battles of Aughrim (1691) and the Boyne (1690).

All tongues but his were still, when thus he said:
'Ye Champions of fair *Lusk*, and Ye of *Soards*,
View well this Ball, the present of your lords.
To outward View, three Folds of Bullocks-hide,
With Leathern Thongs fast bound on ev'ry side: 10
A Mass of finest Hay conceal'd from sight,
Conspire at once, to make it firm and light.
At this you'll all contend, this bravely strive,
Alternate thro' the adverse Goal to drive,
Two Gates of *Sally* bound the Spacious Green,[1]
Here one, and one on yonder Side is seen.
Guard that Ye Men of *Soards*, Ye others this;
Fame waits the careful, Scandal the remiss.'
He said, and high in Air he flung the Ball;
The Champions Crowd, and anxious wait its fall.   20

First *Felim* caught; he pois'd and felt it soft,
Then whirld it with a sudden stroke aloft.
With Motion smooth and swift he saw it glide,
'Till *Dick*, who stop'd it on the other side,
A Dextrous Kick, with artful fury, drew;
The light Machine, with force unerring, flew
To th'adverse goal where, in the sight of all,
The watchful *Daniel* caught the flying Ball.
He proudly joyful in his Arms embrac'd
The welcome Prize, then ran with eager haste.   30
With lusty Strides he measur'd half the Plain,
When all his Foes surround and stop the Swain;
They tug, they pull; to his assistance run
The Strong-limb'd *Darby* and the Nimble *John*.
Paddy with more than common ardour fir'd,
Out-singl'd *Daniel*, while the rest retir'd.
At grapp'ling now their mutual Skill they Try;
Now Arm in Arm they lock, and Thigh in Thigh.
Now turn, now twine, now with a furious bound,
Each lifts his fierce Opposer from the ground.   40
Till *FLORA* who perceiv'd the dire debate,
Anxious and trembling for her Darling's fate,

---

1. 'The goals are formed by sticking two willow twigs in the ground, at a small distance,
   and twisting the tops, so that they seem a gate.' (Concanen's note). *sally* = sallow, the
   willow tree.

Round *Daniel*'s leg, (unseen by human Eyes)
Nine Blades of Grass, with artful Texture ties:
From what slight causes rise our Joy or Grief,
Pleasure or Pain, Affliction or Relief?[2]
Th'entangled Youth, but faintly seems to stand,
Bound by one Leg, Incumber'd in one hand;
For yet he held, nor till his hapless fall
Dropt from his Arms, the long contended Ball.   50

As when a Mountain Oak its ruin finds,
Which long had brav'd the fury of the Winds,
In vain it stands against the dreadful blast,
And, tho' reluctant, must submit at last,
Such *Daniel* was thy fall, nor can it be,
To thy reproach, since by the Gods decree.

And now both bands in close embraces met,
Now Foot to Foot, and Breast to Breast was set;
Now all Impatient grapple round the Ball,
And heaps on heaps in wild confusion fall.   60

Thus when of Old the *cloud-begotten* Guest
Disturb'd the Revels, and embroil'd the Feast,[3]
With sudden frenzy fir'd, All rise to Arms,
And rend Heaven's Azure Vault with loud alarms;
With Drunken Rage and Resolution Steel'd,
The mingling Warriors bustle thro' the Field.
Centaur's and *Lapithae* (a dreadful sight)
Mix in the throng and, Void of order, Fight;
Thro' the wide waste, Death and Confusion Reign,
And cover all around with heaps of Slain.   70

Thy trip, O *Terence*, felled the lusty *Neal*;
Kit dropt by *Felim, Hugh* by *Paddy* fell;
Toss'd down by *Darby, Dick* forbore to Play,
John tugg'd at *Cabe*; while thus confus'd they lay,

---

2. cf. 'What mighty contests rise from trivial things.' *The Rape of the Lock*, i. 2.
3. Concanen's note at this points draws attention to a story in the twelfth book of Ovid's
    Metamorphoses, where Eurytus the Centaur, 'under the sway of drunken frenzy,
    intensified by lust, lost all control of himself' during a wedding feast and tried to carry
    off the bride: a famous and memorably violent battle ensued between the centaurs and
    the Lapithæ (the children and followers of Lapithes, one of the sons of Apollo).

Sly *Le'nard* struck th'unheeded Ball, and Stole,
With easy Paces, tow'rds th'unguarded Goal.
This *Daniel* saw, who rising from the ground,
Where, like *Antaeus*,[4] he new strength had found,
Flew to his Post, and Hallow'd to his Crew.
They start, and swift the flying Foe pursue;   80
Le'nard observing, stood upon his Guard,
And now to Kick the rolling Ball prepar'd,
When careful *Terence*, fleeter than the Wind,
Ran to the Swain, and caught his Arm behind;
A Dextrous *Crook*[5] about his Leg he wound,
And laid the Champion Grov'ling on the ground,
Then toss'd the Foot-Ball in the Ambient Air,
Which soon was stop'd by nimble *Paddy*'s care.
Now FLORA to the *Zephyrs*[6] Cell repairs,
And bribes the Deities with ardent Prayers,   90
To waft the Ball from him with certain aim,
And by his stroke to end the doubtful game.
The *Zephyrs* smiling, promis'd all their Aid,
Flew by the Swain, and with his vesture Play'd.

Pleas'd with the Sign, he list'ned to the call,
And when the Goddess urg'd him, struck the Ball.
No feather'd Shaft sent from the sounding Eugh
E're went so straitly, or so swiftly flew.
For on their Wings (to mortal eyes unseen,)
The careful *Zephyrs* bore the light Machine;   100
Daniel despairing of his promis'd Prize,
Jumps up, and strives to stop it as it flyes;
They to avoid his Fury upwards soar;
'Till past the Goal, the pond'rous load they bore:
At this advantage all the Forces pause,
And the Field eccho's with the loud applause....

Canto III contains, among other things, a blow-by-blow account of the second half of the
football match. Eventually, with the aid of the god Pan, Terence scores another goal for the
men from Swords, who thereby defeat those from Lusk. The poem ends with Terence also
winning the hand of Norah — the prize he really wants.

4. A giant in Greek mythology who received fresh strength whenever he touched the
   ground in a contest.
5. 'So they term the artful way of tripping which they use.' (Concanen's note).
6. The west wind.

ANONYMOUS POEMS
(current **1710-25**)

from: **The Signior in Fashion: or the Fair maid's Conveniency:**
A poem on Nicolini's Musick-Meeting[1]

All Hail ye soft Mysterious Pow'rs, which charm
The coldest Breast, and all our Passions warm.
Sweet Thieves, which like Great Nature's Master-Key, }
Thro' the pleas'd Ear, direct your secret way, }
Unlock the Heart, and steal our Souls away. }
See, at your Call, Obsequious Tories meet,
Melt for the Church, and by Subscription sweat:[2]
The dripping Fair, distills from ev'ry Pore,
'Gods, 'Tis too much!' she cryes, and 'I can hear no more,
How sweet's his Voice, how tender is his Air?   10
But oh! They cost th' Unhappy Youth too dear.'
The gentle Beau, that Ever-dying Swain, }
Beats the slow time, and Sighs with pleasing Pain; }
And lisps the tender Accents back again. }
Ev'n the rough Soldiers[3] mov'd, the dusty Field,
And the big War to softer Pleasures yield;
Such is the Force of the enchanting Strains,
Where Caesar[4] listens, but Grimaldi Reigns.

When the fam'd Greek[5] to native Shoars design'd,
Had left in Flames unhappy Troy behind,   20

---

1. The famous Italian castrato, Nicolo Grimaldi — known universally as Nicolini —
   brought his opera company to Dublin in the summer of 1711 and, among other
   engagements, mounted a concert — the 'Musick-Meeting' referred to in this poem — in
   the hall of the Blue Coat School in Blackhall Place. Nicolini, whose fine soprano voice
   and convincing acting had been widely praised in London, seems to have been equally
   popular — if for different reasons — in Dublin.
2. The Musick-Meeting was a subscription concert, part of the proceeds of which went to
   benefit 'the church'. Tories patronised the event because they were in the ascendant in
   Dublin in the summer of 1711, following the arrival of an energetic new Tory lord
   chancellor, Sir Constantine Phipps. The hall apparently became uncomfortably hot
   during the concert.
3. Presumably this refers to senior army officers who were present; rough = used to a rough
   life.
4. The lord lieutenant, the Duke of Ormond — the king's (Caesar's) representative.
5. Odysseus. The sirens (l. 21) were beautiful sea nymphs whose song was so bewitching that
   it drew mariners to their death. In Homer's *Odyssey*, Odysseus outwitted them and survived.

T'unbend his Mind the sweetest Syrens fail'd,
His Nobler Arts o'er all their Pow'rs prevail'd;
Had sweeter Nic. been in the Syren's Place,
And, fond of Conquest, shone in ev'ry Grace,
Th'unguarded chief had on his Accents hung,
And fall'n the noblest Triumph of his song;
His Eyes no more, had seen the Graecian Coast,
But tristful Pen had mourn'd her Hero lost.

Mankind destroy'd, to former Vigour sprung,
From Stones which Pirrha and Ducalion[6] slung,   30
Such was the way as witty Ovid taught,
Strange was the Miracle, and odd the Thought;
Tho' Nic. wants PEBLES for a Work so course,
His Voice alone had shewn a nobler Force,
A stranger Species from his Notes had sprung,
A tuneful Race, and ready cut[7] for Song,
Whose airy Forms had Warbled in a Paste,
More soft than Man's, and more than Woman's chaste.

Lament ye Beaus, and Sigh ye powder'd Swains,
Curse your dull Snuff, and hurl away your Canes;   40
Tear, Tear your Wigs which could of Conquest boast;
They could alas! but now their Empire's lost;
Fair Chloe's Heart a mightier Rival charms;
Cold to the kneeling World, to Him she warms.
Her Nicolini is the moving Theme,   ⎫
He, happy He, who softens every Dream;   ⎬
Ah the Plump, Tender Thing, there's Musick in his name! ⎭
Her once lov'd Poll now mourns his abject Fate,
His Noise grows dull, and idle is his Prate,
And Prince,[8] the darling of her Soul before,   ⎫   50
Half Famish'd lies neglected on the Floor;   ⎬
Pensive he shakes his Ears, and cocks his Tail no more. ⎭

6. After the world had been destroyed by a great flood in the first book of Ovid's
   Metamorphoses, Deucalion and Pyrrha were instructed by an oracle to throw stones
   behind them; the stones turned into men and women.
7. i.e. already castrated.
8. Her dog.

Ye blooming Nymphs who warily begin
To dread the Censure, but to love the Sin,
Who with false Fears from your Pursuers run,
And filthy Nudities in Picture shun,
From Scandal free, this pretty PLAY-THING meet,
Cool as May Dew, and as it's Butter sweet.
Such is the YOUTH, Resist him if ye can,
This Foreign Curiosity of Man;   60
Who gently leaning on the Far Ones Breast,
May sooth her Griefs, and lull her into Rest.
And should He, should He like her Squirril creep
To her soft Bosome when she's fall'n asleep;
Ev'n then she's safe, nor need she fear Him more
Than those kind Aids which eas'd her Heart before....

A Petition to the Ladies of *DUBLIN* from *DUNLARY* Written by the Old *WASH-WOMEN*[1]

Tu quamcunque Deus tibi fortunaverit Horam
Grata sume Manu, nec dulcia differ in Annum.[2]

YE Females of *Dublin* make Haste and repair
In Coach or on Carr to *Dunlary Wash-Fair*,[3]
Pass by the *Black-Rocks*,[4] you'll quickly be there.

Mirth lasts all the Day without Anger, or Strife,
No *Citizen* there but may venture his *Wife*,
Tho' he lov'd Her as dear as his Wealth or his Life.

---

1. Dun Laoghaire lies a few miles from Dublin city on the south shore of Dublin Bay. In the eighteenth century, sea-bathing was undertaken as a cure for various medical conditions rather than for pleasure. Bathers would disrobe in bathing machines — wooden huts mounted on wheels — after which the bathing-machine would be towed into the sea by a horse. The bather would descend a ladder into the sea and would be ducked below the waves by the 'wash-woman' who had rented the bathing-machine.
2. Horace, *Epistles*, I, 11, 22-23. 'And with a grateful Hand the Bliss receive // If Heaven an Hour more fortunate shall give.' (tr. Philip Francis).
3. The 'season' for sea-bathing was from June to September (see l. 25).
4. Blackrock, now a suburb of Dublin but at the time of this poem a village between Dublin and Dun Laoghaire.

Be sure She will here no Immodesty meet
Altho' She should walk on each Side of the Street,[5]
And when she comes Home she'll be healthy, and sweet.

The *Beaux* ne're come here with their powdered Locks   10
Their Skins are too tender to meet the rough Rocks,
Besides, the salt Water's not good for their P–x.[6]

No *Sharpers*[7] are here with Cheats to entrap Ye,
And sometimes You'll find too a Cup of good Nappy;[8]
But bring Meat, and Wine with you, and you'll be happy.

Your Daughters are free from a sham Wedlock there;[9]
For the black *Couple-Beggars* here seldom repair,
And *Dublin* best serves their Clandestine Affair.

A Widdow may here if she watches espy
A Man for her Turn when she comes out to dry;   20
But I beg her not have a covetous Eye.

No Bullies nor Fops e're come with rude Laughter
To make Madam run squeeking out of the Water;
But still have kept due Distance, and will hereafter.

Our Fair is thus long, from June to September,
And pretty Miss Molly, I'd have her remember,
May strip here as safely as in her own Chamber.

---

5. Presumably a reference to a street one side of which was unfashionable — perhaps a place frequented by prostitutes?

6. pox = venereal disease.

7. Sharpers persuaded the unwary to play cards and fleeced them of their money, often with the help of an accomplice (a cheat).

8. Nappy-ale was strong, foaming ale.

9. Couple-beggars were disreputable priests who could be engaged to conduct marriage services between abducted heiresses and their abductors.

from: The Cavalcade:
A Poem On the RIDING the FRANCHISES[1]

Ye Tuneful Nine,[2] your Poet's Mind inspire,
And fill his Soul with your Celestial Fire:
Aid his Invention, and assist his Verse,
While he attempts in Numbers[3] to rehearse
How great *Eblana*'s Denizons[4] appear
In shining Arms, each Third returning Year:
Mounted on Neighing Steeds they tread the Ground,
And ride the City *Franchises* around.

O thou, bright *Phœbus*, Ruler of the Day,
Expel rough Winds, and drive the Clouds away,   10
Reserve ill Weather for the silent Night,
Nor let rude Showers disturb the Glorious Sight:
Then will each Heroe at the Nights approach,
Come home with dry *Cockade*[5] without a *Coach*,
And own great GEORGE and *Jove*[6] alternate sway,
Jove rules the Night, and GEORGE commands the Day.

Assist ye tuneful Nine, while I declare
How all against[7] the glorious Day prepare:
Some for Themselves, some for their Steeds[8] provide:
The Glittering Sword is fitted to the Side: 20

---

1. Throughout the eighteenth century, a well-known highlight of Dublin life was the colourful mounted procession which, on 1 August every third year, 'rode the franchises' or marked the boundaries of the civic jurisdictions defined by the city charters. The Lord Mayor of Dublin led the procession, in which each of the twenty-five trade guilds had an immense carriage with a wide platform on which were demonstrated the various trades. The printers, for example, had a printing-press on which broadsheets were printed, and the weavers wove ribbons which they threw to the crowd. The mock-heroic poem which follows exists in several variant texts and seems to have been reissued throughout the eighteenth century whenever the 'cavalcade' took place. Perhaps it was actually printed on the moving printing-press during the parade. This text probably dates from 1716.
2. The muses.
3. verse.
4. *Eblana*: a Latin form of the name Dublin.
5. A ribbon, knot of ribbons or rosette worn in the hat as part of a livery dress.
6. George I and the classical god Jove.
7. in preparation for.
8. The guild-masters were all mounted, their apprentices and journeymen on foot.

Some pour on rusty Pistols, cleansing Oyl,
Others at Bridle and the Saddle toil.
Chloris[9] secures the Cockade in its Place,
And binds the *Beaver*[10] round with splendid *Lace*.
The chief contention and the only care
Is, who shall best equipt and arm'd appear.

Soon as the rolling Years brings on the Day,
That snatch'd great ANNA best of Queens away,[11]
And in her place, upon the *British Throne*,
Plac'd Mighty GEORGE to wear *Britania*'s Crown: 30
Soon as *Aurora*[12] with her Rosy Light,
With her bright Rays puts twinkling Stars to flight,
The Silver Trumpet with its loud Alarms
Proclaims the Day, and rouses up to Arms.
The drowsy God, affrighted at the Noise,
Too soon disturb'd, to peaceful Regions flies.
Wak'd with the Sound, all fly inglorious rest;
The neighing Steeds in various Colours drest
In richest Trappings at each Door are ty'd,
The trusty Weapon sits on ev'ry Side.   40
And now the glorious *Cavalcade*'s begun,
Ye Muses, open all your Helicon,[13]
Inspire my Verse, aid and assist my Song,
While I relate how each Troop moves along.

The City Prætor[14] mounted on his Steed
With Ribbons drest, leads on the *Cavalcade*:
Before his Lordship, with a Solemn Grace,
They bear the Sword of Justice and the Mace,
His Gown of richest Scarlet, in his Hand
Majestical he holds the powerful Wand: 50

---

9. A generalised classical name for the wife of a guild-master.
10. Hats made of beaver fur were important possessions in the eighteenth century. (Swift, for instance, listed his three beaver hats separately in his will, leaving each to a different person.)
11. Queen Anne died on 1 August 1714; the riding of the franchises also took place on 1 August.
12. The classical goddess of dawn.
13. The mountain sacred to the muses.
14. i.e. the Lord Mayor of Dublin; prætors were the chief magistrates in ancient Rome.

In awful Pomp and State on either Side
The City Sheriffs in like Triumph ride,
Attended by a Band whose griping Paw,
Poor Debtors dread,[15] and keep them still in awe.

Next march the Guild who plough the froathy Main,
In Depth of Winter for the Hopes of Gain;
To distant Climes our Beef and Wooll Convey,
And barter wholsome Food for Silk and Tea.
Through dang'rous Seas to distant countries run
And visit Kingdoms parch'd by scorching Sun: 60
Fearless of Rocks, they seek the unknown Shoar,
And bring from thence the glitt'ring, [tempting][16] Ore.

The Cross-leg'd Taylors next in order go.
Taylors to creeping Louse Eternal Foe:
Nor Bosome-Friends, nor Backbiters they spare,
Their Thumb Nails stain'd with blood of slain appear.[17]
Men fit for Battle, knowing how to charge,
And as their Bills their Consciences are large:
Twelve Shillings only for the Suit they count,
Thread, Silk and Stay-Tape makes the Bill amount: 70
By such Extortions, by such Arts they thrive,
By such long Bills to Grandeur they arrive.

Next march the Smiths, Men bravely us'd to fire,
Without whose aid all Arts must soon expire:
Before them clad in Armour in his Pride
A brawny *Vulcan*[18] doth in Triumph ride;
Not like the limping God whom Poets feign
In Bands of Wedlock join'd to Beauty's Queen:
But like the God of War, prepar'd to charge,
So broad his Shoulders and his Limbs so large.   80

---

15. One of the main duties of eighteenth-century sheriffs in Dublin was to bring debtors to the debtors' prison; their 'men' were often rough.

16. Added in later editions.

17. *double-entendres* relating the the tailors' killing the lice they find in the clothes they make or mend.

18. The Roman god of fire or divine blacksmith; also (and this is the point of the reference in the next couplet) identified with the lame greek god Hephæstus, who was said to have been married to Aphrodite.

Next come the Barbers, who can soon repaire
Nature's Defects, and load the Bald with Hair:
Suit all Complexions, and with little Pains
Supply the Scull with Wigs that lacketh Brains.

Next come the well bred Men, who know the way
To please the Ladies in their Bread for Tea.
And with their White, their Wheaten, and their Brown,
Can please the Palate of the Lord or Clown.

Next march the Butchers, Men inur'd to Toil,
Their brawny Limbs like Champions shine with Oyl: 90
Murder and Slaughter, knocking on the Head
Are their Delight, the Trade to which they're bred:
Not great *Pelides*[19] on the *Trojan* Plain
E're slaughter'd more; each has his Thousand Slain;
Their pointed Steels have many Widows made,
And sent vast Colonies to *Pluto*'s[20] Shade....

Next march the Saddlers, glorious to behold,
On Sprightly Beasts, their Saddles shine with Gold:
A Warlike Steed most proudly walks before,
Richly attir'd, led by a Black-a moor.   100
Proud of his Furniture[21] he paws the Ground,
And champs the Bit and throws the Foam around;
Just such a Colour, Limbs, and such a Size
Old *Saturn* took, when fearing Jealous Eyes
Of angry Spouse, who caught him in a Rape,
The Letcher gallop'd off and made his 'scape.[22]

Next march the Cooks, who study Day and Night
With costly Fare to please the Appetite:
With these the Vintners ride: Did they refine
As much as they adulterate the Wine,   110
Their Praises ev'ry Month would gladly sound,
And with what Pleasure wou'd the Glass go round....

---

19. Pelides is a patronymic name for Achilles, the hero of *The Iliad.*
20. i.e. the afterlife: Pluto or Hades was god of the underworld in classical mythology.
21. harness.
22. The classical god Saturn turned himself into a horse in order to escape the watchful eye of his wife as he seduced Philyra; the result of the seduction was Chiron, a centaur.

Next march the Goldsmiths who can form and mould
In sundry Shapes and Forms the ductile Gold;
Men call them Traytors, Rebels, and what not,
Nor King nor Queen they spare, all goes to pot:
The splendid Shilling either bent or broken,
And giv'n by parting Lover for a Token,
No Pity meets; in the devouring Fire
Monarchs and Chamber-Pots and Rings expire....   120

In order thus, they ride the City round,
View well the Limits, and observe each Bound,
Then homewards steer their Course without Delay,
And fall to drink, the business of the Day;
Next Morning send their Horse and borrow'd things away.

An Irish Wedding between Dick and Moll[1]

Let that Heroick Muse that sings
The Marriages of Gods and Kings
Lay by her Harp, and stack her strings:
Let him that Writes how first his Head
Bright Phœbus dropt in Thetis's Bed;
Or first how Thames did Isis wed
Be Idle[2]

And lett some Merry Muse now smile,
And Guide me in a pleasant stile,
Tune you Erato[3] for a while   10
My Fidle.

---

1. There are many lively verse descriptions of weddings from eighteenth-century Ireland. This clever and energetic text occurs both in the Whimsical Medley (TCD MS 879), a manuscript collection of verses (mostly from Ireland) compiled before 1722, and in the *Anthologia Hibernica*, a Dublin monthly magazine, for December 1794. The unusual stanza form is found in English poems of the seventeenth century (e.g. 'The Ramble' by Alexander Radcliffe [*Penguin Book of Restoration Verse*, pp. 47-52]) and is also used by William Dunkin in *The Parson's Revels* (see below pp. 207-14). Some details in the text of this poem suggest that it may be an adaptation to an Irish milieu of an English poem.

2. Phœbus Apollo (the sun) fathered children by many women — but not by Thetis: the name may be a mistake for Æthusa. The English river Thames is often called the Isis in and around the city of Oxford, through which it flows, and also in verse (e.g. Spenser, *Faerie Queene* iv, ix, 24). The word 'Isis' may be a corruption of the word 'Isca', the British (and Irish) word for 'water'.

3. The muse of amorous poetry.

107

Come Bacchus[4] too, your sprightly drink,
  Infuses Mirth into my Inck
  And makes Erato look, I think,
    More Jolly;

Tell then, my Muse, where I have been
  The pleasant Wedding I have seen
  'Twixt Country Dick on Yonder Green
    And Molly

Dick thought himself, that's without doubt,   20
  A lad as pritty and as stout
  As any youngster all about
    The village;

Of bullocks he had half a score
  He had as many Goats or more;
  Of rented land he had good store,
    For Tillage.

He was a Lusty Lad and Tall,
  And wou'd not care to try a fall
  With anny Sturdy Lout in all   30
    The Mannor.[5]

'Twas that made Moll so plaguy Mad;
  To have this well sett, proper Lad,
  Whose Mungrell[6] Father was by trade
    A Tanner.

Moll wore a wastecoat not a mant,[7]
  Which she had got from Kate her aunt,
  She was a very comely Plant,
    God bless her.

---

4. The classical god of wine.
5. The manor (i.e. the land belonging to a lord of the manor) is an English, rather than an Irish, unit of territorial organisation; this (like the reference to the Thames in the first stanza) may suggest an English origin for this poem.
6. of mixed parentage.
7. mantle or cloak — typical female attire in Ireland at the time.

Her Petty Coat was red, her Gown   40
    No further than her waste hung down;
    She had the Maids of all the Town
        To dress her.

Two Mutton Fists she had, a Bum
    As Round and sound as anny drum;
    She had a plaguy fatt and thum-
        ping Belly.

A Face as broad as anny Platter
    I'm sure no Pork was ever fatter;
    She was the daughter of an Hatter   50
        Call'd Kelly.

Her Ears wore never anny drops,
    Her Head no Lofty Musslin Tops
    But a plain Coife[8] about her Chops
        Did dangle.

Nor was her Nose so very small,
    But it might serve to fish withall
    For Rod, for Hook, for Bait and all
        To Anglc.[9]

Meanwhile came Reverend Father Dan: 60
    He'd kiss a lass or Toss a can
    With any priest or anny Man
        In Dry-bridge.

Who there by Jolly Dick's commands
    Stood ready now to joyn their hands
    In those Long-wish'd-for pleasant Bands
        of Marriage.

But faith! I stay too long a time:
    My muse will starve before I dine
    And she no longer will to Rhyme   70
        Be able;

8. A coif was a close-fitting cap which covered the top, back and sides of the head; the comparison is made with grander, more expensive head-dresses made of muslin.
9. to catch fish.

Since, then, I've shewn the Pair compleat,
    Aid me, my Muse, and I'll relate,
    The Noble Guests and what they eat
        Att table.

Good store of Milk they brought, so thick
    That in the Midle you might stick
    A knife upright;[10] Yet they did lick
        The Platter.

And with their Milk they also gott   80
    Some few Potatoes piping hot
    Whether from Ashes or the pott,
        No Matter.

Their Butter sadly stunck, their Ale
    Was neither fresh, nor was it stale;
    They had great heaps of Butter'd Kale
        and garlick;

A Pye of Pork: of Rye the walls,
    In which Potatoes served for Balls,
    Was Eat thro' by These Haniballs,   90
        Most Warlick.[11]

Meanwhile the Priest did please and cram
    His Holy Gutts with Pork and Lamb,
    And call'd for Ale and for a Dram
        Of Brandy,

Which Nelly poured from the Great Black Jugg
    And gave him Brandy in a Mugg
    Which he much better lov'd than Sug-
        ar Candy.

Then tasteing it, quoth he: 'O Nell   100
    By Patrick's Cross, I do you tell
    There's no such drink in Dennis's Well,
        My Daughter!

10. A description of Bonnyclabber. See the Glossary.
11. i.e. warlike.

110

'Tis wholesome, by the Pope's Great Toe,
    And Nelly, Lett me never go,
    But it is better than our Ho-
                ly Water.

Now he that does of Nectar[12] sing,
    His heav'nly Lyre away may fling;
    For Brandy is the Noblest Thing   110
                In Nature;

Prometheus needed not desire
    To filch from Heav'n enlivening Fire[13]
    Had He but Brandy to inspire
                His Creature.'

But now the sacred Dan said Grace,
    And Twice or Thrice he Cross'd his Face;
    To Dancing then they fell apace
                In Braces.

In good March Beer their care they drown,   120
    Now ev'ry Lass and ev'ry Clown
    Did dance untill the sweat ran down
                Their Faces.

But Dick no longer now wou'd stay,
    But call'd for Lights; then carried they
    Rush Candles, 'stead of Hymene-
                us taper.[14]

Now Dick blew out the lights and then
    Amongst the Crowd I lost my pen
    And cou'd not find my Inck again   130
                Nor paper.

---

12. The drink of the classical gods.
13. According to Greek mythology, Jupiter (king of the gods) punished mankind by removing fire from the earth. However, Prometheus climbed into heaven, stole it from the sun and gave it back to man.
14. Hymen or Hymenæus was the Greek god of marriage; he was often shown carrying a burning torch.

The Irish Absentee's new Litany[1]

From a Country full of *Rebellion* and *Treason*;
From a People not *Honest*, but void of all *Reason*;
From *running* of *Goods*,[2] which is ne'er out of *Season*,
     Good Lord deliver us.

From dry'd up Potatoes, without any Butter;
From unwholsom Waters, which gives the wild Squitter;[3]
From Priests that in Latin to Blockheads do mutter,
     Good Lord deliver us.

From an *Absentee Irishman*, with large Estate,
Who leaves his dear Country, in *England* to wait;   10
And spends his whole *Substance* to make himself Great,
     Good Lord deliver us.

From whoring *Bogtrotters*, of Footman's Degree;
Who come here and swear that their Pedigree,
First sprung from late *Ormond*'s[4] brave Family,
     Good Lord deliver us.

From *Women* whose Features would frighten the Devil;
From *Children*, whose Skins are like Orange of *Seville*,
And are bred from the Womb to all Manner of Evil,
     Good Lord deliver us.   20

From thick *Bonny-Clauber*,[5] Medicine for Witches,
From *Usquebaugh*, lov'd by all drunken Bitches;
From *Vermin*, which makes 'em scratch where it itches,
     Good Lord deliver us.

---

1. Though satirical parodies of the litany were not uncommon in eighteenth-century Ireland, they are usually too closely linked to specific events to be of lasting interest. The litany which follows, however, reflects, with particular vigour, the bitterness of a protestant Englishman forced to spend time in Ireland, and contains some unusual details about Irish life in the early eighteenth century. Despite the reference to absentee Irishmen in the third stanza of this poem, the title presumably refers to a 'bold Briton' (l. 35) who feels an 'absentee' in Ireland.
2. smuggling.
3. diarrhoea.
4. James Butler, first duke of Ormond (1610-88), lord lieutenant of Ireland for much of the reign of Charles II.
5. For *Bonny-Clauber* and *Usquebaugh* (l. 22), see the Glossary.

From getting[6] of *Children*, and nothing to keep 'em;
From getting of *Corn-Fields*, where idle *Lubbers* wont reap 'em;
From *Fleas* where People by Bushels may sweep 'em,
    Good Lord deliver us.

From wretchedly living in a damn'd low Condition;
From *Beggars*, whose Pride for great Places Petition   30
Or else from the Dung-hill wou'd bear a *Commission*,
    Good Lord deliver us.

From *Irish* Officers where-ever they be,
Who fight against *England* by Land or by Sea,
And treat bold *Britons* with damn'd Cruelty;
    Good Lord deliver us.

From *Mayors* full as foolish as guzzling *Church-Wardens*;
From *Dublin* as full of Whores as the *Spring Gardens*;[7]
From a *Papist* whose Heart against *Protestant* hardens,
    Good Lord deliver us.   40

From running o'er *Bogs*, in all sorts of Weather;
From wearing flat *Brogues* of nasty hard Leather;
From wearing slight *Trowsers*, which scarce hang together,
    Good Lord deliver us.

From going bare-foot, both *Summer* and *Winter*;
From wearing a *Smock*[8] 'till its blacker than Tinder;
From *Poets* whose Parts will never reach *Pindar*,[9]
    Good Lord deliver us.

From *Knights* of the *Post*,[10] against *Innocents* swearing;
From *Doxies*,[11] whose Mouths for *raw Flesh* are staring,   50
And their Presumption of *Men's Breeches* wearing,
    Good Lord deliver us.

---

6. i.e. begetting.
7. A popular haunt for prostitutes in early eighteenth-century London.
8. a shift or chemise (undergarment for women): 'tinder' was black, partially charred linen which was highly inflammable and was used to catch the spark in tinder-boxes and so to make fire.
9. i.e. whose abilities will never equal those of the Greek lyric poet, Pindar.
10. professional perjurers.
11. prostitutes.

From *Lice*, *Itch* and *Scabs*, the *Plague* of the Nation;
From *Pimps*, who claim rich Men to be their Relation,
And of their blind Way of gaining Salvation,
>*Good Lord deliver us.*

From *Cook-Maids* as nasty as any *Gold-finder*;[12]
From *Pastors* as blind as a *Beetle*, or blinder;
From *Strumpets* whom *Money* make never the kinder
>*Good Lord deliver us.*   60

From trading with *France* to get ourselves Riches,[13]
From often cooling our *Courage* in Ditches;
T'asswage the rebellious *Flesh* in the *Breeches*,
>*Good Lord deliver us.*

From *Blind* leading *blind Folks*, and *Cripples* the *Cripple*;
From going to *Church* without any *Steeple*;
From *Ropes* without *Bells*, to ring in the *People*,
>*Good Lord deliver us.*

From *Rapparees* meddling with *Travelers Purses*;
From *Servants* as base, as damn'd *Parish Nurses*;   70
From *Teaguelanders*[14] full of *Damnation* and *Curses*,
>*Good Lord deliver us.*

---

12. An emptier of privies (Partridge).
13. Although trading between Ireland and France was illegal while England was at war with Louis XIV, it continued unabated, and fortunes were made out of it. It is interesting to see the poet align himself with the native Irish — as one who makes money out of illegal trade.
14. Irishmen. See the Glossary.

The Humble Petition of a Beautiful Young Lady
To the Reverend Doctor B–rk——y[1]

Dear Doctor, here comes a young Virgin untainted
To your *Shrine* at *Bermudas* to be Married and Sainted;
I am Young, I am Soft, I am Blooming and Tender,
Of all that I have I make you a Surrender;
My Innocence led by the Voice of your Fame
To your Person and Virtue must put in it's Claime:
And now I behold you, I truly believe
That you'r as like *Adam*, as I am like *Eve*,
Before the dire Serpent their Virtue betray'd,
And Taught them to Fly from the *Sun* to the *Shade*;　　　　10
But you, as in you a new Race has begun,
Are teaching to fly from the *Shade* to the *Sun*;
For you, in Great Goodness, your Friends are Persuading
To go, and to live, and be wise in your *Eden*.
Oh! let me go with you, oh! Pity my Youth,
Oh! take me from hence, let me not loose[2] my Truth;
Sure, you that have Virtue so much on your mind
Can't think to leave me, who am Virtue, behind;
If you make me your Wife, Sir, in Time you may fill a
Whole Town with your Children, and likewise your Villa;　　　20
I Famous for Breeding, you Famous for Knowledge,
I'll found a whole Nation, you'll found a whole Colledge.
When many long Ages in Joys we have Spent,
Our Souls we'll resign with utmost content;
And gently we'll Sink beneath *Cypress* and *Yew*,[3]
You lying by me, and I lying by you.

---

1. This clever lampoon on George Berkeley, philosopher, idealist and Bishop of Cloyne, who published his plan for the establishment of a university in Bermuda in 1725, was probably written by a member of the circle surrounding Swift. There is a poem to Mrs Percival (a close friend of Constantia Grierson and sister-in-law of Berkeley's friend, Lord Percival) on her 'desisting from the *Bermudan* Project' in Mary Barber's *Poems on Several Occasions* (1734), pp. 138-39. See also A.C. Elias Jr., 'On a Manuscript Book of Constantia Grierson's', *Swift Studies* 2 (1987), pp. 33-56 (p. 51, n. 28). Respectably married and father of several children, Berkeley must have been surprised to hear that his worthy project was being ridiculed in a broadsheet sold on the streets of Dublin.

2. lose.

3. trees associated with graveyards.

from: Hesperi-Neso-Graphia: or,
A Description of the Western Isle[1]

from: Canto I

In Western Isle renown'd for Bogs,
For Tories,[2] and for great Wolf-Dogs,
For drawing Hobbies by the Tail,[3]
And threshing Corn with fiery Flail;[4]
Where Beer, and Curds, for Truth I tell it,
Are made without a Pot or Skillet,
And without Pan, and without Kettle,
Or any thing that's made of Mettle;[5]
Where, in some Places, Cows shite Fire,[6]
And Dogs such Soap as some desire;   10

---

1. This is one of four long poems dating from the late seventeenth and early eighteenth centuries which burlesque the native Irish and their lifestyle, the other three being the 'Purgatorium Hibernicum' (National Library of Ireland MS 470), the 'Fingallian Travesty' (British Library, MS Sloan 900) and *The Irish Hudibras* (see above pp. 42-48). There are many similarities between these texts, and all are of linguistic and cultural interest as the poets had considerable knowledge not only of the native Irish of the period but also of the variety of Hiberno-English they used. *Hesperi-neso-graphia* — the title comes from the Greek 'graphein' (to write), 'hesperos' (western) and 'nesos' (an island) — is clearly for an English audience and is the best-known of the three poems; it was written during the reign of William III and was reprinted frequently after its first appearance in 1716. Though it is anonymous, most eighteenth-century editions ascribed it (on no discernible evidence) to a school-master from Killala, Co. Mayo named William Moffat. The poem recounts, at great length and in an exaggerated and burlesque manner, the life and lifestyle of Gillo, his wife Shuan (Siobhán?) and their large household. Despite the patronising attitude of the poet towards him, Gillo was obviously a substantial farmer, a member of an important economic and cultural group which has been fully described by Kevin Whelan in 'An Underground Gentry? Catholic Middlemen in Eighteenth-Century Ireland' in *The Tree of Liberty* (Cork University Press, 1996). The passage printed here contains an interesting description of a large native Irish house and household of the time (cf. Whelan p. 17), as well as a classic account of an Irish feast. I should like to thank Professor Seamus Ó Catháin and members of the Department of Irish Folklore at University College, Dublin for help in annotating this poem.

2. Ir. *tóraí*: originally this word meant a pursuer, but it came to mean 'a hunted man' and ultimately was used to describe any Irish 'rebel' or, as the editor of the 1795 edition of this poem puts it: 'a kind of troublesome gentry' put off their lands by 'John Bull'. See Bliss, p. 267.

3. In Ireland, working horses (also known as 'hobbies') were sometimes secured to ploughs and carts not by harness but by their tails.

4. i.e. separating the ears of corn from the husks by burning the sheaves rather than by threshing them.

5. These lines refer to the custom of warming milk or beer by putting stones which had been heated in a fire into bowls filled with the liquid, rather than by using 'skillets' or cooking pots over the fire.

6. Cow-dung was widely used as fuel in parts of Ireland where turf was scarce or absent.

And where, in Bowels of the Ground
There are great Heaps of Butter found,[7]
Of which, with Blood of living Beast,
The Natives make a dainty Feast;[8]
And where, in leathern hairy Boat,[9]
O'er threatening Waves bold Mortals float,
Like *Gulls*, who[10] never yet were found,
By Strength of Water to be drown'd;
And free from Fear, and Danger ride
On Back of Waves 'gainst Wind and Tide;   20
And where the Mountains, once a Year,
In Flames, like *Ætna*,[11] do appear;
And burn (believe me) Day and Night,
To Strangers a most dreadful Sight;
One *Gillo* liv'd, the Son of *Shane*,
Who was the Son of *Patrick Bane*,[12]
Who was the Son of *Teige* the Tory,
Who, to his great and endless Glory,
Out of a Bush a Shot let fly,   ⎫
And kill'd a Man that passed by,   ⎬   30
For which he was advanced high.   ⎭
This *Teige* was Son of *Gill Christ*,[13]
And he the Son of *Hugh* the Priest;
For Priests in *Shamrogshire*,[14] they say,
Can Women kiss, as well as pray.
This *Hugo*, rampant Priest, was Son,
And only Heir to *Dermot Dun*,
Who was the Son of *Teige Mc Shane*
Who was the Son of *Terlaugh Grane*,

---

7. Butter used to be stored in the bogs (where it can last for many years). See Bliss, pp. 273-74.
8. The custom of bleeding cattle and consuming the blood.
9. i.e. a curragh — a light boat made of animal hides stretched over a wooden frame.
10. i.e. which.
11. Mount Etna, a volcano in Sicily. The reference is to the annual practice of burning gorse and heather on mountainsides to encourage young growth which could be grazed by sheep.
12. Gillo: Ir. *giolla*, a servant or attendant. Shane: Ir. *Seán*, John. Bane: Ir. *bán*, white. Teige: Ir. *Tadhg*, a proper name which was generally applied to any native Irishman. See the Glossary.
13. Ir. *giolla Chríost*, servant of Christ.
14. A burlesque name for Ireland.

Who was the Son of *Phelim Fad*,[15]   40
Who, on each Hand, Six Fingers had;
Could twist Horse-Shoes, and at one Meal,
With Ease, could eat the greatest Veal;
With's Head instead of Hammer cou'd
Knock Nail into a Piece of Wood,
And with his Teeth, without least Pain,
Could pull the Nail from thence again:...

from: Canto II

... In spacious Plain, within a Wood
And Bog, the House of *Gillo* stood;
A House well built, and of much Strength,
Almost Two Hundred Foot in Length:
A House with Mountains fortify'd,
Which in the Clouds their Heads did hide.
At one of th'Ends he kept his Cows,
At th'other End he and his Spouse
On Bed of Straw, without least Grumble,
Nay, with Delight, did often tumble;   10
Without Partition, or a Skreen,
Of spreading Curtains drawn between;
Without Concern expos'd they lay,
Because it was their Country Way;
And when Occasion did require,
In midst of House a mighty Fire,
Of black dry'd Earth and swingeing Blocks,[1]
Was made, enough to roast an Ox;
From whence arose such Clouds of Smoak,
As either you or me wou'd choak: 20
But *Gillo* and his Train inur'd
To Smoak, the same with Ease endur'd;
And sitting low, on Rushes spread,
The Smoak still hover'd over head;[2]

---

15. This passage is a parody of an Irish genealogy: Dermot Dun: Ir. *Diarmaid donn*, brown-haired Dermot. Teige Mc Shane: Ir. *Tadhg Mac Seáin*, Teigue, son of John. Terlaugh Grane: Ir. *Toirealach gránna*, ugly Turlagh. Phelim Fad: Ir. *Féilim fada*, tall Phelim.

1. i.e. of turf and huge blocks of wood.

2. Visitors to Ireland often commented on the lack of chimneys in country dwellings. The smoke escaped under the thatch. Floors were usually covered with rushes.

And did more Good than real Harm,
Because it kept the long House warm,
And never made their Heads to ake;
Therefore no Chimney he wou'd make....
... And if perhaps you do admire,
That this great House did ne'er take Fire,   30
Where Sparks, as thick as Stars in Sky,
About the House did often fly,
And reach'd the sapless wither'd Thatch,
Which like dry Spunge the Fire wou'd catch,
And where no Chimney was erected,
Where Sparks and Flames may be directed;
St. *Bridget*'s Cross[3] hung over Door,
Which did the House from Fire secure.
As *Gillo* thought, O powerful Charm!
To keep a House from taking Harm: 40
And tho' the Dogs and Servants slept,
By *Bridget*'s Care the House was kept.
Directly under *Bridget*'s Cross,
Was firmly nail'd the Shoe of Horse
On Threshold, that the House might be,
From Witches, Thieves, and Devils free,
For *Patrick* o'er the Iron did pray,
And make it holy, as they say;
And banisht from the Hills and Bogs,
All sort of Serpents, Toads and Frogs,   50
By Cross and Iron: You may guess,
What Faith this *Gillo* did profess;[4]
A Faith St. *Paul* did never teach,
Altho' to *Romans* he did preach;
A Faith that makes you to deny
The Testimonium of your Eye;[5]
A Faith obliges you to pray,
Altho' you know not what you say;[6]
A Faith which to the Mother Maid
Commands Ten Ave's[7] should be said;   60

---

3. A small cross woven from rushes or straw on St Briget's Eve (the last day of January), and believed to protect the household from fire and other harm.

4. i.e. the Roman catholic faith, the practices and beliefs of which are satirised in the next few lines. St Patrick's blessing of iron is undocumented.

5. A reference to the doctrine of transubstantiation.

6. i.e. because you pray in Latin.

7. The prayer beginning with the Latin words *Ave Maria*, Hail Mary.

And that we only should direct
One Pater[8] to the Architect
Of Heaven, from whom our Life doth flow,
And ten to one is Odds you know.
But let his Faith be good or bad,
He in his House great Plenty had
Of burnt Oat-Bread, and Butter found,
With Garlick mixt, in boggy Ground;
So strong, a Dog with Help of Wind,
By scenting out, with Ease might find.　　　　　70
And this they count the bravest Meat,[9]
That hungry Mortal e'er did eat.
This grunting Sow would sooner take,
And eat a T—d than Sugar-Cake.

from: Canto III

Now listen well and you shall hear,
With what vast prodigious Chear,
And with what Heaps of various Meat,
His Friends and Neighbours he did treat.
The Day of Feasting come, each Man,
Invited to the Dinner, ran
With winged haste, and with his Skeen,[1]
Or rather Cleaver sharp and clean.
Most of the Guests their Umbra's[2] brought,
And Sauce[3] that never Money bought;　　　　　10
Great Heaps of thick three corner'd Bread,
And hairy Butter Van did lead.[4]
Next came the Flesh of Mountain Goat,
As rank[5] as ever slipt down Throat.
And then Four Quarters of a Foal,
And Three sing'd[6] Sheep entire and whole.

---

8. *Pater Noster* are the first words of the Lord's Prayer in Latin.
9. i.e. food. See canto I, line 12.

---

1. Ir. *scian*, knife or cleaver.
2. Uninvited guests accompanying the invited ones. From Latin *umbra*, shade.
3. sauciness, impertinence.
4. i.e. First to be carried in were great heaps of thick three-cornered bread and quantities of butter; 'hairy' seems to mean either that the butter was mouldy or that animal hairs had fallen into it during milking.
5. having an offensively strong smell; rancid.
6. i.e. cooked three times.

Then Four great Swine, as fat and good
As ever rutted[7] in a Wood
(Or turned the Earth of Garden, where
Belov'd Potatoes growing were)   20
Came in, on brawning[8] Shoulders born,
And laid in Lossels[9] to be torn; ...
... Abortive, well smok'd shrivell'd Calf,
A rary Show[10] whereat to laugh,
Brought up the Reer in stately wise;
But not a Guest it did surprise.
For they, 'bove any Nation,
Love Meat drest by Fumigation;
And hence they took Occasion, to
Admire what Smoke (like Salt) could do.   30
Besides all this, vast Bundles came
Of Sorrel, more than I can name;
And many Sheaves, I hear there was
Of Shamrogs, and of Water-Grass,
Which there for curious Sallads pass.[11]
Yet this great Feast was not compleat,
Unless they had the following Meat;
I'lands of Curds did float in Sea
Of hot, and sweet cerulian Whey.[12]
Of Rushes there was Benches[13] made,   40
On which the Meat was partly laid:
But all the Mutton that was sing'd,
Was laid on Doors that were unhing'd;
So that we all may truly say,
Gillo kept open House that Day.

---

7. copulated.
8. i.e. brawny.
9. wooden food-trays or baskets. cf. Ir. *losaid*, a shallow food-basket.
10. a show or spectacle (from the mispronunciation of the words 'rare show', *OED*).
11. Sorrel, shamrock and water-cress, herbs and plants which grow wild in Ireland, were used as food in the eighteenth century.
12. curds and whey — a traditional dish in areas dependent on dairy products. The word cerulean (blue) suggests Gernon's list of Irish foodstuffs (1620); 'You shall have no drink but Bonnyclabber... nor no meate but mullagham [Ir. *mulchán*], a kind of choke-daw cheese, and blew butter' (quoted by Bliss, p. 273). Fresh buttermilk can be a pale blue colour.
13. Either long wooden forms covered with rushes, or 'súgán' chairs, the seat of which is woven from ropes made of hay, straw or rushes.

The rest was plac't in stately sort
On Planks which Firkins[14] did support;
As for the Guests, when Grace was said,
And all in *Latin* Tongue had pray'd,
Some ran to this, some ran to that,   50
And what they catcht, they thereon sat;[15]
Some sat on Stones, some sat on Blocks,
Some sat on Churns, some on Wheel-Stocks;
Some sat on Cars, some sat on Ladders,
And, for shift, some sat on Madders[16]
Of which Utensils, at the Feast,
There was that Day Threescore at least.
The brisk young Sparks,[17] with their kind Wenches,
Did place themselves on rushy Benches; ...
The Rabble, and the brawny Kearns[18]   60
Well pleas'd, sat down on Heaps of Fearns;
Gillo the noble, as most fit,
At Head of all the Guests did sit:
At Head of table, I'll not say,
For in his House was none that day;
But those at which the Gamesters play.
In mighty State, by *Gillo*'s side,
Her Sex's Envy, th' Island's Pride;
Fair *Shuan*,[19] *Gillo*'s Wife took Place,
Descended from *Milesian* Race.[20]   70
They both on Bench of Rushes sat,
Commixt with Flags,[21] both wonderous fat;
His Hair was black, but hers as red,
As ever grew on Woman's Head.
He swarthy was, she wond'rous fair,
As many in that I'land are.

14. small barrels.
15. Variants of this passage occur in *The Irish Hudibras* (p. 43) and in two poems by James Orr, 'Song composed on the Banks of Newfoundland' (p. 542) and 'The Passengers' (p. 544).
16. wheel-stocks:wheel-hubs; cars:carts; for shift:by necessity; madder: Ir. *meadar*, wooden cup.
17. elegant young men, beaux.
18. Ir. *ceithearn*, foot-soldier, outlaw.
19. Possibly an anglicisation of the Irish proper name Siobhán.
20. i.e. descended from the original inhabitants of Ireland.
21. The seat of this 'súgán' bench is made of rushes interwoven with either wild yellow 'flag' irises (*Iris pseudacorus*) or other coarse grasses. (s.v. flag *sb*1, meanings 1 and 2, *OED*).

Her Legs were short and fat, 'tis true,
And to a mighty Thickness grew;
As did her bulky Waste, which scarce
With clasped Hands you cou'd embrace.   80
Her Head Ten Hundred Linnen[22] bound,
As white and fine as could be found;
But his indented Cappeen[23] wore,
Which he had never us'd before;
'Twas of fine Frize,[24] and without doubt,
Adorn'd with curious Cuts about;
As was the new made Brogues,[25] which they
Both wore for Honour of the Day....
Black hafted[26] Knife and Keys were ty'd,
With leathern pouch, unto her side;   90
In which a black, short dirty Pipe
She kept, which she did never wipe.
For being short it warmed her Nose,
When e'er she smoak'd, altho' it froze;
And from its wheezing Throat she drew,
Most grateful Blasts of darkish blue.
Into this Purse, when there was need,
She put long Twists of *Indian* Weed;[27]
And into it did often thrust
Full Bladders of Tobacco Dust.[28]   100
Her Beads[29] moreover in it lay,
Unless when she was pleas'd to pray;
And Dice for Gamesters, as they say.
And in it she, with Care, did put
Her Money, and her double Nut;[30]
A holy Hazel-Nut, that she
Might be from all Misfortune free....

22. i.e. strips of linen.
23. skull cap; cf. Ir. *caipín.*
24. frize = frieze; a kind of coarse woollen cloth, ... especially of Irish make (*OED*). The meaning of the word 'cuts' is uncertain: it seems to refer to designs on both cap and brogues — perhaps made with a woodblock?
25. shoes, as made and worn by the native Irish. See Glossary.
26. A black-handled knife was a sign of luck — good or ill.
27. tobacco.
28. snuff.
29. Rosary beads.
30. cf. the Halloween custom of putting nuts in the fire to predict love and marriage.

Her lee-washt[31] plaited tresses hung,
That day from shoulders to her bum;
In which she took no little pride,   110
As in her banlon-garb[32] beside....

Now *Gillo* noble, free and brave,
An Hundred Thousand Welcomes gave[33]
To every Friend and Neighbour, that
Came there to eat, to drink and chat;
And for strong Usquebah[34] doth call,
And gives his Service to them all.
The Cup went round and round again,
A noble Cup, that cou'd contain
A Pint, which every Man did drain,   120
With as much Ease as any here
Could drink new Milk or Table-Beer.
Mean while the Harp, conjoin'd with Voice,
Thro' all the House made charming Noise,
Of such Effect, that it did make
Most of the Guests their Heels to shake:
Nay, Trump itself,[35] there seldom fails
To make old Women bob their Tails.
To Dancing they are so inclin'd,
That even the very Lame and Blind,   130
If Trump or Bag-Pipe they do hear,
In dancing Posture do appear,
As strange their Steps, their Shape and Mien,
As e'er in Beggars Bush[36] was seen;
Baldoyle, or yellow Stockings[37] plaid,
Gives nimble Feet to every Maid,

31. washed in lye, a simple cleaning agent.
32. Ir. *banlámh*, a cubit, a traditional measure for cloth; hence this phrase probably means her best clothes.
33. The traditional Irish welcome, *Céad míle fáilte*.
34. whiskey; Ir. *uisce beatha*, water of life.
35. i.e. even the sound of the trumpet or other loud noise.
36. Beggars' Bush in south Dublin is so called because it was a traditional assembly-point for country vagrants; they are shown meeting there in an early print of Dublin Bay. (Peter Somerville-Large, *Dublin* (London, 1979), p. 195).
37. The names of two dance-tunes, the first of which was called after a town in Fingal of the same name.

And Younker,[38] who such Pains do take,
In frisking, that they often leak,
And render Savour from behind,
Let out some Puffs of stiffled Wind;   140
And after all, 'tis there confest,
The longest Dancer dances best.

Gillo to dance was often pray'd,
Courted, and pull'd by every Maid;
But he, by holy Vestment, swore,
And's Beard, he'd never dance before
Ignatius, or his Father *James*,
Came sailing up the rowling *Thames*,
In Pomp and Grandeur to obtain
His ancient Crown, and Right again;[39]   150
With that he thumpt his angry Breast,
And said, 'My Soul shall ne'er take Rest;
Nor shall my Beard divorced be
From Chin, till I that Day do see.'
At this he swore by *Patrick*'s Tooth,
And by black Bell, which finds out Truth,[40]
And by the Bones of one St. *Ruth*,[41]
Whose Sword and Hands was often wet
With reeking Blood of Hugonet;
And who to *James* was firm and good,   160
Whilst Head upon his Shoulders stood!
Whose Bones expos'd to ev'ry Eye
In *Aghrims* Plains now blanching ly[42]....

---

38. a (usually fashionable) young man.

39. Gillo swears by the holy vestments (of Christ?) that he will never dance until James II is restored to the throne of Ireland; secondly he vows that he will not cut his own beard until that day. James had been deemed to have abdicated from two thrones, that of Britain as well as that of Ireland — which explains the reference to the Thames. The mention of St Ignatius Loyola reflects the protestant view that James was heavily influenced by the Jesuits.

40. See C. Plummer, *Vitae Sanctarum Hiberniae,* I, cv, clxxvii.

41. Charles Chalmont, marquis de St Ruhe (d. 1691), normally known in Ireland as 'St Ruth', was a Jacobite hero. As a general in the French army, he had been a relentless hunter of Huguenots and he was sent by Louis XIV to assist the Jacobite cause in Ireland after the battle of the Boyne. He commanded the Jacobite army at the disastrous battle of Aughrim where, at the height of the fighting, his head was blown off by a Williamite cannonball (which explains the reference in line 161).

42. The bodies of the 7,000 Jacobites who lost their lives at Aughrim were not buried but left on the field of battle.

The Royal Black Bird[1]

Upon a fair morning for soft recreation,
    I heard a fair lady making her moan,
With sighing and sobbing and sad lamentation
    Saying, my Black Bird most royal is flown;
        My thoughts they deceive me,
        Reflections do grieve me,
And I am over-burthened with sad misery,
        Yet if death it should blind me,
        As true love inclines me,
My Black Bird I'll seek out wherever he be.   10

Once in fair England my Black Bird did flourish
    He was the chief flower that in it did spring —
Prime ladies of honour his person did nourish,
    Because he was the true son of a king.[2]
        But this false fortune
        Which still is uncertain,
Has caused this parting between him and me,
        His name I'll advance
        In Spain and in France,[3]
And seek out my Black Bird, wherever he be.   20

The birds of the forest they all met together —
    The turtle was chosen to dwell with the dove,
And I am resolved in fair or foul weather
    To seek out until I find my true love;
        He's all my heart's treasure,
        My joy and my pleasure,

---

1. Most Irish Jacobite songs are in Irish, and the anti-Hanoverian sentiments in the few which are in English are disguised. The earliest printed version of this, the best-known of these songs, dates from about 1718, but the song was popular throughout the eighteenth century and may have had its origins as early as 1640 (see Murray Pittock, *Poetry and Jacobite Politics in Eighteenth-Century Britain and Ireland* (Cambridge, 1994), p. 48). The blackbird in this version of the song is the exiled Jacobite claimant to the throne of Ireland, James III, the Old Pretender (1688-1766). Diarmaid Ó Muirithe prints eleven other Jacobite songs in English, taken from Irish manuscripts of the period, in "'Tho' not in full stile compleat": Jacobite songs from Gaelic manuscript sources', *Eighteenth-Century Ireland/Iris an dá Chultúr*, vi (1991), 93-103.

2. The Old Pretender, the only son of James II and Mary of Modena, had been born in London while his father was still king of England and Ireland.

3. Many Jacobite supporters were in France and Spain; the Jacobite court was near Paris.

126

And justly, my love, my heart will follow thee,
   Who is constant and kind,
   And courageous of mind,
All bliss to my Black Bird wherever he be.   30

In England my Black Bird and I were together,
   Where he was still noble and generous of heart,
And woe to the time that he first went thither,
   Alas, he was forced from thence to depart.
    In Scotland he is deemed,
    And highly esteemed,[4]
In England he seemed a stranger to be,
    Yet his name shall remain
    In France and in Spain,
All bliss to my Black Bird, wherever he be.   40

What if the fowler my Black Bird has taken?
   Then sighing and sobbing shall be all my tune;
But if he is safe, I will not be forsaken,
   And hope yet to see him in May or in June.[5]
    For him through the fire,
    Through mud and through mire
I'll go, for I love him to such a degree,
    Who is generous and kind,
    And noble of mind,
Deserving all blessings wherever he be.   50

It is not the ocean can fright me with danger,
   For tho' like a pilgrim I wander forlorn,
I may meet with friendship from one that's a stranger
   More than from one that in England was born.
    Oh! Heaven so spacious,
    To Britain be gracious,
Tho' some there be odious both to him and to me,
    Yet joy and renown
    And laurel shall crown
My Black Bird with honour wherever he be.   60

---

4. The Old Pretender accompanied an abortive French expedition to Scotland in 1706 and led the unsuccessful Jacobite rising there in 1715-16.

5. Rumours of imminent Jacobite landings were not uncommon in eighteenth-century Ireland.

NICHOLAS BROWNE

(c.1699-**1722**-1734)

Nicholas Browne was the son of Rev. Nicholas Browne, the Church of Ireland rector at Rossgarn, Co. Fermanagh, who was an Irish speaker. After a childhood spent in County Fermanagh, Browne was sent to school in England, but he returned to Ireland and entered Trinity College, Dublin in 1716. He was ordained and became rector of Timolin in the diocese of Leighlin. Browne seems to have published only two poems, both when he was in his early twenties, the one which follows and 'The Fire' — a poem describing the discomforts of life in Trinity College and the consequent attractions of the nearby alehouse run by Nurse Musgrove. The two poems appeared in Dublin in 1722 and again in Matthew Concanen's 1724 *Poems by Several Hands*. The 'north country' of the poem's title is the area of counties Tyrone and Fermanagh.

from: The North Country Wedding

Now through the Welkin[1] wide the rosy Morn
Display'd her Charms, and with her Ray dispenc'd
Joy to the World; but greater Joy to none,
Than dawning glow'd in *Willy*'s am'rous Breast;
This Day the Term[2] of all his wonted Woe,
Of doubtful Wooings, and of jealous Fears,
Gave to his Breast the matchless *Moggy*'s Charms;
A blither Lass than whom, with rustick Grace,
Ne'er bore the Bell, at Maypole-Dance or Ring;[3]
She too with am'rous Flame his Flames return'd,   10
And with alternate Hopes and Fears bid hail
Th'auspicious Light, that crown'd their mutual Joy.

Th'attendant Maids, with ornamental Hands,[4]
Now wait, with Gear less natural to deck
That Shape, which Heaven more adorn'd before,
Than all th' unwieldy Weight of artful Tire;[5]

1. the sky. This poetic usage establishes the mock-heroic nature of the poem.
2. end.
3. May Day festivities, including dancing round the maypole, fetching the May Bush and carrying the May Ring (a hoop wreathed with rowan and marsh marigold suspended within which were two balls representing the sun and the moon) were popular in Ireland throughout the eighteenth century. See Constantia Maxwell, *Country and Town in Ireland under the Georges* (London, 1940) p. 274 and Sir James Frazer, *The Golden Bough* (London, 1911), II, 63.
4. i.e. hands ready to adorn the bride with 'gear' (clothes, apparel).
5. attire, dress.

Each, in her proper Sphere, the Work begins,
And now confirms, now alters what begun,
Dislikes, commends, as Envy or as Art
Directs her Words; while she[6] submissive stands   20
The Test of Eyes, on other Thoughts intent.

Nor less concern'd the Bridegroom was t'adorn
His crispéd Locks, and bid his gay Attire
With outward Glare[7] bespeak his inward Joy;
Nor wanted he maternal Care, to add
The nicest homespun Line, or Kenting[8] rare,
The Work of tedious Hour or dreary Night:
His Hands, too proud to bear th'inclement Air,
Lay close invelopt in his Hand-spurs[9] neat;
These once his antient Grandame's Shoulders grac'd,   30
Her Neck incircling in their candid[10] Folds,
When great *Eliza* rul'd the willing World.
Three massy[11] Rings upon his Fingers shone,
Such as the *Roman* Chiefs were wont to wear,
To fence[12] their softer Hands from wintry Blasts.

A doughty[13] Knight his Steps did near attend,
Mc Farrell hight, whose Ancestors well known
For unmatch'd Deeds, and warlike vast Exploits,
Stand foremost in the antient Rolls of Fame;
Proud of his Birth, in Majesty he stalks,   40
Snuffs, and looks big, and glories in his Name,

6. i.e. the bride.

7. bright, sparking appearance.

8. homespun linen ('line') or homemade lace ('kenting'). The latter word is probably derived from the Dutch *kanten* 'lace', since lace pattern-books from Flanders were widely available during the seventeenth century.

9. 'Hand-spurs' seems to describe a muff. The fur-skins now lining the muff had previously been part of the fur collar of a cape worn by Willy's grandmother during the reign of Elizabeth I.

10. white.

11. heavy.

12. protect.

13. valiant. Like the word 'hight' (i.e. 'named') in the next line, this is a consciously archaic and jocular usage; in fact, the whole paragraph gently parodies descriptions of medieval knights errant such as those found in Spenser. In the 1724 edition of this text, Concanen inserts a long note at this point defending Browne's portrait of McFarrell from the charge that it cast aspersions on the Irish nation. On the contrary, suggests Concanen, 'the lines mentioned must be strained to be made satirical, and then are so slight that they rather should provoke laughter than rage from any'.

His Name being all which he is Heir to now;[14]
A trusty Blade fast by his Side was girt,
Which once had arm'd his aged Grandsire's Hand,
With Rebel-Rage, t'oppose his Monarch's Right.
A Silver Circle round his Beaver[15] shone,
Nor wanted he, his manly Hair to deck,
The graceful Ribband; which, with artful Tie,
Low pendant rustled in the sportive Air;
A True-love Knot in Ribband too y'wrought,   50
The Badge of his high Office,[16] grac'd his Brow,
And with fierce Glare confronted ev'ry Eye;
As who shou'd say, beneath Love's Banner thus
Confirm'd, I dare the proudest Foe to Arms.

And now attendant Troops in order wait;
This Party claims the beauteous Bride their care,
And that awaits the Bridegroom's high Behests.
The Bride, the fairest of the Female-Throng,
Up-mounted sat upon a Jennet[17] fair,
Fairer than that, which from the neighb'ring Copse,   60
As Poets sing, *Adonis* Steed[18] entic'd,
Whilst him in vain the *Cyprian Goddess* woo'd.

The Bridegroom, next in gayety and place,
Rode high exalted on a stately Steed,
Whose bounding Feet indignant spurn'd the Ground:
Before him, near his Saddle's sturdy Bow,
Two Pistols shone, within whose Iron-Wombs
Dread Thunder lurk'd, to fright the Rival World.

Before them, Leader of the jovial Crew,
Old son'rous *Sawney*[19] rode, on such a Steed   70
As great *La Mancha*'s Knight[20] bestrode of Old:

---

14. i.e. McFarrell is a dispossessed, 'native' Irish landowner.
15. A hat made of beaver fur.
16. i.e. as groomsman or 'best man' to the bridegroom.
17. A small horse.
18. horse. Venus, the classical goddess of love — 'Cyprian' because she appeared from the sea near the island of Cyprus — loved the young god Adonis. The reference is to Shakespeare's poem *Venus and Adonis*.
19. A contraction of the name Alexander, used as a general name for a Scotsman (cf. Paddy from Ireland). 'Sonorous' (of persons) means 'having a full, rich voice'.
20. Don Quixote, hero of Cervantes's novel, came from a region of Spain called La Mancha.

Down from his Drone[21] a Scarlet Flag there hung
Ensign of War, but War of am'rous Strife,
Of meeting Joys, and combating Desires.
Beneath his Arm a Leathern Bag he plac'd,
Where Mirth and Dole in Magick durance bound,
Lay close immur'd,[22] and as the Time and Place
Requir'd, with artful Squeeze he both dispenc'd;
Not the famed Youth,[23] whose Name long since enroll'd
In *British* Story, yet cou'd equal thee,   80
Tho' list'ning Crowds his tuneful Hand obey'd,
And naked *Step-Dame* and performing *Fryar*,
From all the Joys, that Love and Beauty yield,
He led triumphant thro' sharp bri'ry Brakes,[24]
Thro' devious Mountains and unpittying Rocks;
Whilst they, unheedful of the Pains they bore,
Charm'd by the Notes, thro' all th'encircling Harms
Dance on ensanguin'd.[25] Thus the jovial Crew
Move on, and with gay Chat, and wanton Glee
Shorten the Way, until the sacred Dome   90
They nigh approach, when each deft Country Lad,
With awkward Compliment, and rural Cringe,
Closes the Side of the gay rustick Fair;[26] ...

And now, the sacred Ceremony past,
Each Party moves in slow process along....

And now elated by the sprightly Fair,[27]
And Cup enchanting, ev'ry jolly Swain
Culls from the Crowd, the Mistress of his Breast;
Here with full many a wanton Maze they tread
Alternate Measures, and with airy bound   100
Grace oft the various Motion and the Dance;

---

21. The bass pipe of a set of bagpipes.
22. i.e. where both happy and sad melodies lay forcibly imprisoned....
23. A note at this point in the first edition alludes to 'the Ballad of *Jack* and the Fryar'; though this ballad is, so far, untraced, the story it tells can be guessed from lines 82-83.
24. briary: full of brambles or briars; brake: a clump of bushes, a thicket.
25. stained with blood — presumably caused by scratches from briars and thorns
26. i.e. each handsome country lad comes near (and joins the group around the bride), making a formal expression of courtesy or respect (a bow or obeisance) towards the beautiful bride.
27. i.e. by the sight of the beautiful bride.

Now Face to Face, whilst merry Sounds inspire,
They meet, retire alternate, and pursue,
With many a Wheel, and sounding plause of Hand,
In honour of the Bride and Bridegroom giv'n,
They crown the Dance, and end the sportive Fray....

No sooner dark, but ev'ry Table show'd
Crown'd with a mighty Bowl, replenish'd well
With that fam'd Liquor, Mortals here below
Strong *Bolcan*[28] stile, but by the Gods above,   110
Life's Liquor[29] named; for Gods above full well
This Liquor ken, from whose enliv'ning Warmth,
They circling Youth, and deathless Lustre gain....

Here all around each jolly Toper sat,
Great as a God, with Wine and Beauty crown'd.
Health to the Bride, a joyful Glass is drunk;
Health to the Groom the second Cup proclaims:
The Mistress next the flowing Bumper crowns,
Full as their Love, and flaming as their Breast;
Nor wanted here full many a wanton Wile,   120
And Nod, and secret Beck, and am'rous Leer,
Whereby each Lass right certainly might ken,
Whose Name inscrib'd sat deepest in the Breast
Of Youth enamoured....

... The Bride withdraws, whilst modest Fears attend,
But Fears, by Love and strong Desire, allay'd:
And now undrest, by those whose Hands before
Late drest her, more by unadorning deckt,
Pure, in her native Innocence she shone,
The more outshining, that the less she shone   130
In borrow'd Ornament; Her Snow-white Skin,
The truest Emblem of her spotless Mind,
As soft and fair as Down Cygnean[30] show'd:
But Gods forbid, that ev'ry mortal Eye
Such Charms shou'd view, lest ev'ry mortal Eye
Seduc'd, shou'd hold your sacred Laws in vain.

28. A spirituous liquor (Fagan).
29. whiskey. See Glossary.
30. i.e. her snow-white skin was [also] as soft as the down feathers of a young swan (cygnet).

The joyful Bridegroom, lusty as the Sun,
When from the East his Mattin-Carr he drives,[31]
Attended by a Train of Youth, whose Blood
Fresh in their sprightly Vigour mantled high,
And with a morning Blush their Cheek distain'd,   140
Full boldly enters; whilst their Leader caught
By the fair Object, with a wide fix'd Look,
Firmly his Eye encenters on her Charms;
'Till recollecting, with a vig'rous Spring
He storm'd the Bed, and seiz'd the trembling Prey.
So the keen Eagle when aloof he spies
A milk-white Swan; with Eyes intent, around
He views her well, and meditates the Prey;
Then with a Sowse[32] impetuous downward darts,
And in his Talons holds the Captive bound.   150

The Stocking thrown, the Posset next came on,[33]
In slow Procession by a Matron born,
Who with full many an Olive-branch had dekt
The good Man's Table; whilst he, nigh her side,
With Breeches wide display'd, the Bed approach'd,
And thrice in Magick compass, round their Heads,
The wide containers of his Manhood wav'd:
'Be ye', says he, 'as in our time we've been,
The joyful Parents of a num'rous Brood:
But take my Councel, Son, this Adage true,   160
I've often prov'd, by long Experience taught;
Not he, who swiftest from the Barrier breaks,
Ay gains the wish'd-for Prize;[34] an easy Pace,
And hanck retaining Hand still farthest wends;[35]

31. The sun is imagined, as in classical mythology, driving his chariot ('carr') across the heavens from the east, where it is in the morning ('mattin'), to the west.
32. The act of a hawk in swooping down upon a hunted bird.
33. Three marriage customs are mentioned in these lines; first, a stocking thrown by the bride is caught by one of the bridesmaids — the one who is therefore deemed most likely to be married within a year; next, a cup of posset (hot milk curdled with liquor and sweetened with spices) is brought, in procession, to the bridal chamber for the bride and groom to drink; but before they drink it, the bride's father lowers his trousers and walks round the bridal bed three times giving advice on procreation. After this ceremony, the bride and groom drink the posset and are left alone.
34. i.e. the one who is first to start the race is not always the one who wins the prize.
35. i.e. you will get furthest if you adopt a slow, easy pace, like the weaver who works slowly and retains the hank or coil of thread in his hand longer.

Then spare the Spurs; and, as a Pledge of Love,
This from my Hand receive.' Thus the grave Sage;
And to his Hand presented straight the Cup,
Where various Sweets in grateful Mixture joyn'd,
Breath'd Aromatick,[36] requisite to rowse
The Soul, by Labour too lethargick grown: 170
Thus, provident, when o'er the oozy Marsh,
Or bellying Bog the wild *Hybernian* roams,
With Care in Plyde, or Breeches he reconds,
(If these entire) th'enliv'ning cordial Warmth
Of roast Potatoe, which he still applies
To Mouth, when drooping, and from this regains
His pristine Vigour.[37]
And now, my Muse, be grateful[38] to the Pair,
Withdraw the Crowd; extinguish ev'ry Light;
Leave them no Glimpse, but what their Blushes raise;   180
Give them the Dark, the pleasing Scene of Love;
Leave them encircled in each other's Arms,
To reap the Harvest of a plenteous Bliss;
Thou too withdraw, and with a grateful Hand,
Close up the modest Curtains of the Night.

36. i.e. the cup containing the posset.
37. This unusual passage suggests that Irishmen would revive themselves during a day working in the fields with a meal of warm potatoes which they has been carrying in their breeches or plaids. (A 'plaid' was a long piece of woven cloth which Scotsmen and Irishmen wrapped around themselves as an outer garment.) reconds = stores or hides away (Latin: *recondere*, to stow away).
38. i.e. do something kind or acceptable to the pair.

MARY DAVYS
(1674-**1725**-1732)

Following the death of her husband, Peter Davys, who was the schoolmaster at St Patrick's Cathedral School, Dublin, and a protégé of Swift, Mary Davys found herself in want and went to England where she earned a living running a coffee-house in Cambridge, and writing plays, novels and some poetry. Like several other women writers of the time, Mary Davys was criticised for taking up her pen, but she hit back at her detractors in the preface to her *Works* (1725) where she observes acidly that '... a Woman left to her own Endeavours for Twenty-seven Years together, may well be allow'd to catch at any Opportunity for that Bread, which they that condemn her would very probably deny to give her ...' (p. viii). Her acutely observed, satirical portrait of an impoverished young 'modern' poet, part of which follows, reminds the reader of later works in this genre by, among others, Swift.

from: The Modern Poet

... Behind moth-eaten Curtain, 'stead of Press,[1]
Hung up the tatter'd Relicks of his dress:[2]
A thread-bare Coat, at Elbows quite worn out,
Buttonless Waistcoat with an old Surtout;[3]
Breeches with Pockets gone, for the Abuse
Of Master's Wit had made them of no Use;[4]
A Hat some ten times dress'd,[5] much on the rust,
Was laid in Box, to keep it from the Dust;
On wooden Peg hung piss-burnt Perriwig,[6]
A little out of Curl, but very big;   10
In Days of yore it had a noble Master,
And given to set up the Poetaster;[7]
For Pride has oftentimes appear'd in Tatters,
And strives to make us imitate our Betters:
It gave him Airs to strut about the Town,
Flatt'ring my Lord, and railing at the Gown.[8]

1. cupboard.
2. clothing.
3. overcoat.
4. i.e. the poet had no money to put in them because he had abused his wit (by becoming a poet).
5. repaired: 'much on the rust' means that there was rust-coloured staining or mould on the hat.
6. A large, old-fashioned wig, perhaps yellow with age and so looking as if stained with urine.
7. i.e. undistinguished or inferior poet. A previous owner had given the wig to the poet to 'set him up'.
8. i.e. churchmen.

With brazen-hilted Bilbo[9] to attack
All those, who dare call Names behind his Back;
Tho' certain 'tis, a Poet's only Weapon
Should be his Pen, when People are mistaken.   20
But some, alas! have to their Sorrow found
His Passion, not his Reason, kept its Ground;
He thought it hard he should a Scene run through
Of Beggary,[10] and be insulted too.

His Dress and Person thus describ'd, I come,
To say a Word or two on Lodging Room,
The Height of which already has been said;[11]
Furniture next comes in, and first the Bed,
On which coarse dirty Linnen might be seen,
With Store of those dear Creatures (Bugs) between;   30
A shaggy Rug, as useful as his Meat,
It kept out Winter's Cold, and Summer's Heat:
Beside, that every thing might live at ease,
He laid it on as refuge for the Fleas.
In Closet dark stood what is often useful,
Which Decency forbids to call a ———,[12]
From whence Effluvia rose, which could allay
Vapours in Wits, like Assafœtida.[13]
In Corner of the unswept Room there lay
A Heap of blunted Pens, as who shou'd say,   40
Behold the Fate of all things in this World,
When we have done our best, away we're hurl'd,
And if our Pains but little Profit brought,
Our Guider, not ourselves, was in the Fault!
In Table-drawer whole Quires[14] most neatly writ
Lay useless by, and now for nothing fit,
Unless minc'd Pyes, or some such Use inferiour,

---

9. A sword of high quality – so named because fine swords were made in Bilbao, Spain.
   Also a sword belonging to a bully (Partridge).
10. i.e. he thought it hard he should be as poor as he was, and be insulted too.
11. i.e. earlier in the poem.
12. i.e. close-stool or commode.
13. Asafœtida is a resinous gum famed for its strong and highly unpleasant smell. The
    passage means that the smell arising from the poet's close-stool is sufficient, like the
    smell of asafœtida, to reduce depression ('the vapours') in witty people.
14. A pile of folded sheets of paper (each sheet covered in the poet's handwriting).

As lighting Pipes, or clapping to Posteriour.[15]
Two Dedications[16] he with Sighs laid by,
Because his Patrons did his Suit deny,   50
Nor wou'd with his Necessities comply.
On Chimney-piece, instead of China set,
A Standish,[17] Razor, and old Pen-knife met,
Tobacco-Box, two dirty Pipes with Sticks
Of scented Wax, and Wafers there did mix.
For want of Window-Curtains in his Room,
Two Lordly Cobwebs from the Spider's Loom,
Spread them all o'er with Care, lest too much Light
Shou'd spoil the Student's Eyes, when set to write.
Two chairs there were, one of them had no Back,   60
The other, like his verse, a Foot did lack:
Thus Poetry and Poverty were join'd,
And left the Marks of both their Plagues behind.
If any knocks, away in haste he runs,
Having a strange Antipathy to Duns;[18]
Nor dares he any see, lest they shou'd prove,
The only thing on Earth he cannot love.

The kind Good-natured Mice would often come,
To make him Visits in his empty Room:
Like modern Visitors made short their Stay,   70
And like them too, untreated[19] went away;
Because our Bard's Provision was but scant,
The Mice and he did oft their Dinners want.
And now dear Readers, if this cannot win ye
Strait to turn Poets, sure the Devil's in ye.

---

15. Until the nineteenth century, paper was an expensive commodity, and sheets of paper which had been written on were often used a second time, sometimes to line pie-dishes in a bakery.
16. i.e. essays dedicating his volumes to patrons.
17. inkstand.
18. debt-collectors.
19. i.e. not given any food.

AMBROSE PHILIPS and HENRY CAREY
(1674-**1725**-1749) (d.1743)

Ambrose Philips, an English pastoral poet who was an 'intimate' friend of Swift in London between about 1707 and 1710, came to Ireland as secretary to Hugh Boulter, the whig archbishop of Armagh, in 1724. By this time, he and Swift were estranged (for reasons of both politics and personality) and when Philips, in an attempt to ingratiate himself with the lord lieutenant, Lord Carteret, wrote miniature poems praising Carteret's daughters — poems known as 'flams' — Swift joined in the derisive laughter which greeted their (unauthorised) appearance in broadsheet form on the streets of Dublin in 1725. Philips's detractors coined for him the name 'Namby Pamby', representing a child's efforts to say his name. Many entertaining parodies of Philips's poems appeared, the most memorable of which is by Henry Carey, a prolific miscellaneous writer who was in Dublin at the time.

To Miss Georgiana
Youngest Daughter to Lord Carteret.

August 10, 1725

Little charm of placid mien,
Miniature of beauty's queen,
Numbering years, a scanty nine,
Stealing hearts without design,
Young inveigler, fond in wiles,
Prone to mirth, profuse in smiles,
Yet a novice in disdain,
Pleasure giving without pain,
Still caressing, still caress'd,
Thou, and all thy lovers bless'd,   10
Never teiz'd, and never teizing,
O for ever pleas'd and pleasing!

Hither, *British* muse of mine,
Hither all the *Grecian* nine,
With the lovely graces three,
And your promis'd nurseling see:
Figure[1] on her waxen mind
Images of life refin'd;
Make it, as a garden gay,
Every bud of thought display,   20

---

1. impress.

Till, improving year by year,
The whole culture shall appear,
Voice, and speech, and action, rising,
All to human sense surprising.

Is the silken web so thin
As the texture of her skin?
Can the lily and the rose
Such unsully'd hue disclose?
Are the violets so blue
As her veins expos'd to view?   30
Do the stars, in wintry sky,
Twinkle brighter than her eye?
Has the morning lark a throat
Sounding sweeter than her note?
Whoe'er knew the like before thee?
They who knew the nymph that bore thee.

From thy pastime and thy toys,
From thy harmless cares and joys,
Give me now a moment's time:
When thou shalt attain thy prime,   40
And thy bosom feel desire,
Love the likeness of thy sire,
One ordained, through life, to prove
Still thy glory, still thy love.
Like thy sister, and like thee,
Let thy nurtur'd daughters be:
Semblance of the fair who bore thee,
Trace the pattern set before thee.

Where the *Liffy* meets the main,
Has thy sister heard my strain:[2]   50
From the *Liffy* to the *Thames,*
Minstrel echoes sing their names,
Wafting to the willing ear
Many a cadence sweet to hear,
Smooth as gently breathing gales
O'er the ocean and the vales,

---

2. Philips had already written a poem (dated 31 July 1725) to Georgiana's elder sister when she was suffering from smallpox.

While the vessel calmly glides
O'er the level glassy tides,
While the summer flowers are springing,
And the new fledg'd birds are singing.60

Namby Pamby: or, a PANEGYRIC on the NEW VERSIFICATION address'd to *A—— P——*.[1]

Naughty pauty Jack-a-Dandy,
Stole a Piece of Sugar-Candy
From the Grocer's *Shoppy-Shop,*
And away did hoppy-hop.

All ye Poets of the Age,
All ye Witlings of the Stage,
Learn your Jingles to reform,
Crop your Numbers and conform,
Let your little Verses flow
Gently, sweetly, Row by Row:
Let the Verse the Subject fit,
Little Subject, little Wit:
Namby Pamby is your Guide;
Albion's Joy, *Hibernia*'s Pride,10
Namby-Pamby Phillip-is,
Rhimy pim'd on Missy Miss;
Tartaretta Tartaree
From the Navel to the Knee;
That her Father's Gracey-Grace
Might give him a Placey-Place.
He no longer writes of Mammy
Andromache and her Lammy,
Hanging panging at the Breast
Of a Matron most distrest.[2]20

---

1. This parody is the work of Henry Carey. Iona and Peter Opie (*The Oxford Book of Nursery Rhymes*, 1951) suggest that Carey's quotations from nursery rhymes in this ballad are meant to show that 'Philips's verses were no better than the old common-place jingles sung by children'. They note that many nursery rhymes are echoed in the poem and quote a version of the 'Jack-a-Dandy' verse from 1701 (p. 233).

2. Philips's earlier work had included pastorals and an adaptation of Racine's tragedy *Andromaque,* which includes a famous scene in which Andromache has to part from her son Astyanax.

Now the venal Poet sings
Baby Clouts[3] and Baby Things,
Baby Dolls, and Baby Houses,
Little Misses, little Spouses,
Little Play-things, little Toys,
Little Girls and little Boys.
As an Actor plays his Part,
So the Nurses get by Heart
Namby Pamby's little Rhimes,
Little Jingles, little Chimes,   30
To repeat to little Miss,
Piddling Ponds of Pissy-Piss;
Cacking packing like a Lady,
Or By-bying in the Crady.
Namby Pamby ne'er will die —
While the Nurse sings *Lullabye*.
Namby Pamby's doubly mild
Once a Man, and twice a Child;
To his Hanging Sleeves[4] restor'd;
Now he foots it like a Lord: 40
Now he pumps his little Wits,
Shitting writes, and writing *shits*,
All by little tiny Bits.
Now methinks I hear him say,
Boys and Girls come out to play,[5]
Moon do's shine as bright as Day.
Now my *Namby Pamby*'s found
Sitting on the *Friar's Ground*,
Picking Silver, picking Gold,
Namby Pamby's never old.   50
Bally-Cally they begin,
Namby Pamby still keeps in.
Namby Pamby is no Clown,
London-*Bridge is broken down*:
Now he *courts the gay Ladee*,
Dancing o'er the Lady-Lee:
Now he sings of *Lick-spit Lyar*,
Burning in the Brimstone Fire;

3. clothes.
4. Loose open sleeves hanging down from the arm.
5. This passage contains a series of references to nursery rhymes, some well known, some very difficult to trace.

141

Lyar, Lyar, Lick-spit, Lick,
Turn about the Candle-stick: 60
Now he sings of *Jackey Horner*
Sitting in the Chimney-Corner,
Eating of a Christmas-Pye,
Putting in his Thumb, Oh fie!
Putting in, Oh fie! *his Thumb,*
Pulling out, Oh strange! *a Plumb.*
And again how *Nancy-Cock,*
Nasty Girl! *beshit her Smock.*
Now he acts the *Granadier,*
Calling for *a Pot of Beer*:   70
Where's his Money? He's forgot:
Get him gone, a drunken Sot.
Now on *Cock-Horse* does he ride;
And anon on Timber stride,
See-and-Saw and Sacch'ry-down
London *is a gallant Town.*
Now he gathers Riches in,
Thicker, faster, Pin by Pin;
Pins apiece to see his Show;
Boys and Girls flock Row by Row;   80
From their Cloaths the Pins they take,
Risque a Whipping for his Sake;
From their Frocks the Pins they pull,
To fill *Namby*'s Cushion full.
So much Wit at such an Age,
Does a Genius great presage.
Second Childhood gone and past,
Should he prove a Man at last,[6]
What must second Manhood be
In a Child so bright as he!   90

Guard him, ye Poetick Powers;
Watch his Minutes, watch his Hours;
Let your tuneful *Nine*[7] inspire him:
Let Poetick Fury fire him:
Let the Poets one and all
To his Genius Victims fall.

---

6. According to the *DNB*, Philips was 'rather dandified in appearance'.
7. The Muses.

PART II
Swift and his Irish contemporaries

Swift lived in Ireland for more than fifty of his seventy-eight years, and the country of his birth was a recurrent subject for his writing. For much of the period between 1714, when he returned to Dublin from England, and 1737, when he stopped writing verse, Swift was at the centre of an enthusiastic circle of Dublin poets and poetasters, women and men – a group he called 'my fav'rite clan'. He wrote much verse during this time, sometimes addressing serious themes such as 'fair liberty', at other times playing endlessly with puns and witty rhymes, or exchanging light-hearted poetic squibs with his friends. He helped many lesser poets to improve their verses and recommended their works to his English friends. He was, in fact, the leading light of Dublin's literary world at a time when it was exceptionally vigorous. The poems which follow have been chosen not so much to shed light on Swift himself or on his views on Ireland (which are well known) but to reflect the Irish world in which he and his friends and enemies moved. If Swift was at the centre of the Dublin literary web, the spiders working at its margins could spin fine and witty lines and engage in memorable poetic badinage and repartee.

JONATHAN SMEDLEY
(c.1672-**1713**-1729)

Jonathan Smedley was born in Dublin. He was student at Trinity College in the early 1690s and was ordained into the Church of Ireland, becoming rector and vicar of Rincurran, Co. Cork (a living later held by Swift's friend Thomas Sheridan). He was a strong supporter of the Whig party and of the Hanoverian succession — which may explain, in part at least, why he and Swift engaged in such public squabbles. Smedley was appointed chaplain to the lord lieutenant of Ireland after the accession of George I in 1714, and later held the deanships of Killala and of Clogher. His *Poems on Several Occasions* appeared in London in 1721 and his well-known attack on Swift and Pope, *Gulliveriana*, in 1728. He died at sea in 1729 on the way to take up a chaplaincy in India – a move probably intended to improve his always precarious finances.[1]

Verses fix'd on the Cathedral Door, the Day of Dean *Gulliver*'s Installment[2]

Today, this Temple gets a *Dean*,
Of Parts and Fame, uncommon;
Us'd, both to Pray, and to Prophane,
To serve both *God* and *Mammon*.

When *Wharton* reign'd, a *Whig* he was;
When *Pembroke*, that's Dispute, Sir:
In *Oxford*'s Time, what *Oxford* pleas'd;[3]
Non-Con, or *Jack*, or *Neuter*.[4]

---

1. The best account of Smedley's life and works is in James Woolley's edition of *The Intelligencer* (Oxford: Clarendon Press, 1992), pp. 135-6 and 217-19.
2. It is not clear that these verses were actually fixed to the door of St Patrick's Cathedral, Dublin on the day of Swift's installation as dean, 13 June 1713, as Smedley claimed. Their first published appearance is in *Gulliveriana* (London, 1728), p. 77. Internal evidence suggests, however, that they were written in 1713, though the present title must have been added after the publication of *Gulliver's Travels* in 1726.
3. These lines refer to Swift's change in political allegiance from Whig to Tory in the period 1708-13. Though Swift himself disliked Thomas Wharton, first Earl Wharton (whom he implied was an expert at the art of 'political lying'), Wharton was a leading Whig at the time when Swift supported that party. Swift was more friendly with Thomas Herbert, eighth Earl of Pembroke, who shared his fondness for puns and word-games: Pembroke was neither Whig nor Tory but rather served the crown during his long political career. Wharton and Pembroke both 'reigned' as lords lieutenant of Ireland. Swift's Tory credentials are seen clearest in his close relationship with Robert Harley, first Earl of Oxford, leader of the Tory administration which he served so assiduously after 1710.
4. These lines refer to Swift's attitude towards religious conformity. The implication is that, for political expediency, Swift would at one time support non-conformity (i.e. high-church non-jurors), at another time 'Jack' (a reference to John Calvin and the presbyterians), and at another time neither.

This Place[5] He got by Wit and Rhime,
And many Ways most odd;   10
And might a Bishop be, in Time,
Did he believe in God.[6]

For High-Churchmen and Policy[7]
He swears he prays, most hearty;
But wou'd pray back again, wou'd be
A *Dean* of any Party.

Four *Lessons*! *Dean,* all, in one Day;[8]
Faith! it is hard, that's certain:
'Twere better hear *thy'own Peter* say,
G–d d—n thee, *Jack* and *Martin.*[9]   20

Hard! to be plagu'd with Bible, still,
And Prayer-Book before thee;
Hadst thou not Wit, to think, at Will,
On some diverting Story?

Look down, St. *Patrick*, look, we pray,
On thine own *Church* and *Steeple*;
Convert thy *Dean*, on this *Great Day*;
Or else God help the People!

And now, whene'er his *Deanship* dies,
Upon his Tomb be graven,   30
A Man of *God* here buried lies,
Who never thought of *Heaven*.

---

5. i.e. the deanery of St Patrick's.
6. i.e. if he believed in God. It was widely reported that Queen Anne thought that Swift's *A Tale of a Tub* attacked God, and was therefore unwilling to appoint him to a bishopric. The book is actually an attack on 'gross corruptions' in the Christian churches.
7. Tory values.
8. The installation ceremony (which contained two readings from the scriptures) was followed by evensong, which contained two more.
9. In *A Tale of a Tub*, the three brothers Peter, Jack and Martin stand for, respectively, the Roman catholic church, the presbyterian church and the anglican church.

An Epistle to his Grace the Duke of Grafton, Lord Lieutenant of Ireland[1]

Non Domus & Fundus —— Hor.[2]

It was my Lord, the dextrous Shift,[3]
Of t'other *Jonathan*, viz. *Swift*,
But now, St. *Patrick*'s sawcy Dean,
With Silver Verge,[4] and Surplice clean,
Of *Oxford*, or of *Ormond*'s grace,
In looser Rhyme, to beg a Place:
A Place he got, yclyp'd a *Stall*,[5]
And eke a Thousand Pounds withal;
And, were he a less *witty Writer*,
He might, as well, have got a *Mitre*.[6]   10

Thus I, *The Jonathan of Clogher*,[7]
In humble Lays, my Thanks to offer,
Approach your Grace, with grateful Heart;
My Thanks and Verse both void of Art:
Content with what your Bounty gave;
No larger Income do I crave:
Rejoicing, that, in *better Times*,
GRAFTON requires my *Loyal Rhimes*.[8]

---

1. Charles Fitzroy, second duke of Grafton (1683-1757), grandson of Charles II and the Duchess of Cleveland, lord lieutenant of Ireland 1720-24. Smedley wrote this poem in the spring of 1724, before he had heard that Lord Carteret had replaced Grafton as lord lieutenant.

2. 'A house and land does not ...' Horace, *Epistles* 1.ii. 47. The full sentence runs: *Non domus et fundus, non aeris acervus et auri // Aegroto domini deduxit corpore febris, // Non animo curas.* 'A house and land, a pile of bronze and gold, does not take away fevers from their owner's sick body, nor cares from his mind.'

3. stratagem.

4. The rod or wand of office carried in processions by a verger before the dean of a cathedral.

5. The official seat of a dean (or other dignitary) in a cathedral; yclept = called (a conscious and comic archaism). The lines may be glossed: 'It was, my lord, the clever stratagem of the other Jonathan (i.e. Swift) ... to beg a preferment from Oxford or Ormond [politicians in power when Swift was appointed dean of St Patrick's cathedral] in rhyme: the place he got is called a "stall" and has a stipend of £1000.'

6. See n. 6 to the previous poem.

7. Smedley was appointed dean of Clogher, Co. Tyrone in the spring of 1724, just before he wrote this poem.

8. Smedley was an inveterate Whig, so loyal to the Hanoverian succession.

Proud! while my *Patron* is *Polite*,
I likewise to the Patriot write: 20
Proud! that, at once, I can commend,
King George's and the *Muse*'s friend.
Endear'd to *Britain*: And to *Thee*
(Disjoin'd, *Hibernia*, by the Sea)
Endear'd by twice three anxious Years;
Endear'd by Guardian Toils and Cares!

But where shall SMEDLEY make his Nest,
And lay his wandring Head to Rest?
Where shall he find a decent House,
To treat his Friends, and chear his Spouse?   30
Oh! *Tack*,⁹ my Lord, some pretty Cure,
In wholesome Soil, and Æther¹⁰ pure.
The Garden stor'd with artless Flowers,
In every Angle, shady Bowers.
No gay Parterre,¹¹ with costly Green,
Within the ambient¹² Hedge be seen;
Let Nature, freely, take her Course,
Nor fear from me ungrateful Force:
No Shears shall check her sprouting Vigour:
Nor shape the Yews to antick Figure.   40
A limpid Brook shall *Trouts* supply
In *May*, to take the mimick Fly;¹³
Round a small Orchard may it run,
Whose *Apples* redden to the Sun:
Let all be snug and warm and neat,
For *Fifty-turn'd*,¹⁴ a fit Retreat:
A little *Euston*¹⁵ may it be:
Euston I'll carve on every tree:
But then, to keep it in Repair,
My Lord — *Twice Fifty Pounds a Year*   50

9. i.e. something tacked on or added. The grammar of this phrase may be uncertain, but the
   meaning is clear. Smedley is urging the lord lieutenant to give him an additional 'pretty
   cure' (i.e. a parish where he can live, the income of which will be added to that of his
   deanery). 'Tack' also means 'foodstuff' or 'money'.
10. air.
11. A level space in a garden occupied by ornamental flowerbeds.
12. surrounding.
13. i.e. the fly-fisher's imitation fly.
14. i.e. someone who has just reached the age of fifty.
15. The country seat of the Dukes of Grafton was Euston Hall, Norfolk.

Will barely do: But if your Grace
Could make them *Hundreds* — Charming Place!
Thou then would'st shew another Face.

Clogher! far North, my Lord, it lies,
Beneath *High Hills*, and *Angry Skies*.
One shivers with the *Artick* Wind,
One hears the *Polar Axis* grind.[16]
Good *John*,[17] indeed, with Beef and Claret,
Makes the Place warm, that one may bear it;
He has a Purse to keep a Table,   60
And eke a Soul as hospitable:
My Heart is good, but Assets fail
To fight with Storms of Snow and Hail;
Besides, the Country's thin of People,
Who seldom meet, but at the Steeple:
The *Strapping Dean*, that's gone to *Down*,[18]
Ne'er named the Thing without a Frown.
When much fatigued with Sermon-Study,
He felt his Brain grow dull and muddy,
No fit Companion could be found,   70
To push the lazy Bottle round:
Sure then, for want of better Folks,
To pledge his *Clerk* was Orthodox.[19]

Ah! how unlike to *Gerard-street*,[20]
Where *Beaus* and *Belles*, in Parties meet;
Where gilded Chairs and Coaches throng,
And jostle, as they trowl[21] along;
Where Tea and Coffee, hourly, flow;
And *Gape-seed*[22] does, in Plenty, grow;

---

16. An imaginary line passing through the North and South poles around which the earth might be supposed to revolve, making (Smedley's exaggeration suggests) a grinding noise audible even in Clogher, Co. Tyrone.
17. John Stearne, Swift's predecessor as dean of St Patrick's and, from 1717 to 1745, bishop of Clogher.
18. Rev. William Gore (1680-1732), dean of Clogher 1716-24, dean of Down 1724-32.
19. i.e. it was acceptable to drink the health of his clerk. (A clergyman would not normally drink with his parish clerk.)
20. In London.
21. troll, move around easily.
22. Something stared at by a crowd (*OED*).

And *Griz*[23] (no Clock more certain) cries, 80
Exact at Seven, *Hot Mutton Pyes*:
There Lady *Luna*, in her Sphere,
Once shone, when *Paunceforth* was not near;
But now she *wains*, and as 'tis said,
Keeps sober Hours, and goes to Bed.[24]
There — But 'tis endless to write down,
All the Amusements of the Town:
And Spouse will think herself quite undone,
To trudge to *Clogher*, from sweet *London*;
And Care we must our Wives to please, 90
Or else — we shall be ill at Ease.

You see, my Lord, what 'tis I lack,
'Tis only some convenient TACK,
Some Parsonage House, with Garden sweet,
To be my late, my last Retreat;
A decent Church, close by its Side,
There preaching, praying, to Reside,
And, as my Time securely rolls,
To save my own, and others Souls.

23. A proverbial name for a meek, patient wife.
24. Luna (or Diana) was said, in classical mythology, to oversee childbirth. 'Paunceforth' may be the name of a male-midwife. The lines seem to refer to Mrs Smedley's being past childbearing.

JONATHAN SWIFT
(1667-1745)

His Grace's Answer to Jonathan[1]

Dear *Smed* I read thy Brilliant Lines,
Where Wit in all its Glory shines;
Where Compliments with all their Pride
Are by thy Numbers dignify'd.
I hope to make you yet as clean,
As that same viz. St. *P———k's Dean.*
I'll give thee *Surplice, Verge*, and *Stall*,
And maybe something else withall.
And were you not so good a Writer
I should present you with a *Mitre*.   10
Write worse then if you can — be wise —
Believe me, 'tis *the Way to Rise.*
Talk not of *making of thy Nest,*
Ah! never lay thy Head to Rest!
That Head so well by Wisdom fraught!
That writes without the Toil of Thought.
While others wrack their busy Brains,
You are not in the least at Pains.
Down to your *Deanery* repair
And build *a Castle in the Air.*[2]   20
I'm sure a Man of your fine Sense
Can do it with a Small Expence.
There your *Dear Spouse* and you together
May breathe your Bellies full of *Æther.*
When *Lady Luna* is your Neighbour
She'll help your *Wife* when she's in Labour.
Well skill'd in Mid-wife Artifices;
For she her self oft *falls in Pieces.*[3]
There you shall see a *Rary-Show*[4]
Will make you scorn this *World below.*   30

---

1. This poem echoes the previous one in words and phrases. See notes to the previous poem.
2. A splendid but imaginary building. The phrase is proverbial.
3. i.e. the moon is waning or, fancifully, a piece has fallen off her every night.
4. A peep-show carried around in a box (Brewer); any spectacular display.

When you behold *the Milky Way*
As White as Snow, as bright as Day;
The Glitt'ring Constellations Roll,
About the grinding artick Pole;
The lovely tingling in your Ears,
Wrought by the Musick of the Spheres ——[5]
Your Spouse shall there no longer hector
You need not fear a Curtain-Lecture.[6]
Nor shall she think that she is *un-done*
For quitting her beloved *London*.   40
When she's exalted in the Skies,
She'll never think of *Mutton Pies*.
When you're advanc'd above Dean VIZ.
You'll never think of Goody GRIZ.
But ever ever live at Ease,
And strive, and strive, *your Wife to please*.
In her you'll center all your Joys,
And get Ten thousand Girls and Boys.
Ten thousand *Girls* and *Boys* you'll get
And they like *Stars* shall *Rise* and *Set*.   50
While *you and Spouse* transform'd, shall soon
Be *a New Sun*, and *a New Moon*.
Nor shall you strive your *Horns to hide*,
For then your *Horns* will be your *Pride*.[7]

5. According to Pythagoras, the spheres of the universe made a perfectly harmonious music as they moved in unison with each other.
6. In his *Dictionary* (1755), Dr Johnson defined this as 'a reproof given by a wife to her husband in bed'.
7. The horns of the cuckold or deceived husband.

To Charles Ford Esqr. on his Birth-day
Janry. 31st for the Year 1722-3[1]

Come, be content, since out it must,
For, Stella[2] has betray'd her Trust,
And, whisp'ring, charg'd me not to say
That Mr Ford was born to day:
Or if at last, I needs must blab it,
According to my usuall habit,
So bid me with a Serious Face
Be sure conceal the Time and Place,[3]
And not my Compliment to spoyl
By calling This your native Soyl;   10
Or vex the Ladyes, when they knew
That you are turning fourty two.
But if these Topicks should appear
Strong Arguments to keep You here,
We think, though You judge hardly of it,
Good Manners must give Place to Profit.

The Nymphs with whom You first began
Are each become a Harridan;[4]
And Mountague[5] so far decayd,
That now her Lovers must be payd;   20
And ev'ry Belle that since arose
Has her Cotemporary Beaux.
Your former Comrades, once so bright,
With whom you toasted[6] half the Night,

---

1. i.e. 1723. Charles Ford (1682-1741) was really forty-one when this poem was written rather than forty-two as stated in line 12. The poem is ostensibly an appeal by Swift to Ford, who was one of his closest friends, to return from England to Ireland, but it was also an opportunity for Swift to express his frustration at the state of affairs in England under the Whigs and, in contrast, to paint life in Ireland as relatively attractive. Although Ford owned a pleasant estate at Woodpark, Co. Meath, where Swift was always welcome, he lived much of the time in London, and acted as Swift's agent there from time to time. In his later years, Ford became over-fond of the bottle and he died after falling down the stairs in his London lodgings.

2. Swift's friend, Esther Johnson. Ford was also a valued friend of Stella.

3. Ford was born in Dublin. See also note 1.

4. Swift and Ford were close companions in London in the period 1710-13 and Swift is referring to friends Ford had at that time. Dr Johnson defines a harridan as 'a decayed strumpet'.

5. Lady Mary Montagu, a daughter of the Duke of Marlborough.

6. drank toasts.

Of Rheumatism and Pox complain,
And bid adieu to dear Champain:
Your great Protectors, once in Power,
Are now in Exil, or the Tower,[7]
Your Foes, triumphant o'er the Laws,
Who hate Your Person, and Your Cause,   30
If once they get you on the Spot
You must be guilty of the Plot,
For, true or false, they'll ne'r enquire,
But use You ten times worse than Pri'r.[8]

In London what would You do there?
Can You, my Friend, with Patience bear,
Nay would it not Your Passion raise
Worse than a Pun, or Irish Phrase,
To see a Scoundrel Strut and hector,
A Foot-boy to some Rogue Director?   40
To look on Vice triumphant round,
And Virtue trampled on the Ground:
Observe where bloody Townshend[9] stands
With Informations in his Hands,
Hear him Blaspheme; and Swear, and Rayl,
Threatning the Pillory and Jayl.
If this you think a pleasing Scene
To London strait return again,
Where you have told us from Experience,
Are swarms of Bugs and Hanoverians.   50

I thought my very Spleen would burst
When Fortune hither drove me first;[10]
Was full as hard to please as You,
Nor Persons Names, nor Places knew;
But now I act as other Folk,
Like Pris'ners when their Gall is broke.[11]

---

7. The Earl of Oxford and Lord Bolingbroke, both disgraced after the accession of George I.
8. Lines 29-34 refer to Walpole's attempts to impeach Bishop Atterbury for his contact with the Old Pretender 1722-23 ('the Plot') and to the imprisonment of the poet Matthew Prior on political charges in 1715.
9. Charles Townshend, second Viscount Townshend (1674-1738), a leading member of Walpole's ministry. By 'Informations', Swift probably means false affidavits, as used in the Atterbury case.
10. i.e. when appointed dean of St Patrick's in 1713 and so driven to return to Ireland.
11. i.e. when their spirit is broken into submission.

154

If you have London still at heart
We'll make a small one here by Art:
The Diff'rence is not much between
St. James's Park and Stephen's Green;[12]   60
And, Dawson street will serve as well
To lead you thither, as Pell-mell,[13]
(Without your passing thro the Palace
To choque[14] your Sight, and raise your Malice)
The Deanry-house may well be match't
(Under Correction) with the thatcht,[15]
Nor shall I, when you hither come,
Demand a Croun a Quart for Stumm.[16]
Then, for a middle-aged Charmer,
Stella may vye with your Mountharmar:[17]   70
She's Now as handsom ev'ry bit,
And has a thousand times her Wit.
The Dean and Sheridan,[18] I hope,
Will half supply a Gay and Pope,
Corbet,[19] though yet I know his Worth not,
No doubt, will prove a good Arbuthnot:[20]
I throw into the Bargain, Jim:[21]
In London can you equall Him?

What think you of my fav'rite Clan,
Robin, and Jack, and Jack, and Dan?[22]   80
Fellows of modest Worth and Parts,
With chearfull Looks, and honest Hearts.

12. City parks in, respectively, London and Dublin.
13. City streets in, respectively, Dublin and London (Pall Mall).
14. choke.
15. Swift and Ford had often dined together, in earlier days, at a London tavern called 'The Thatched'.
16. fermented grape-juice.
17. Another of the titles of the Duchess of Montague (see above l. 70).
18. For a note on Thomas Sheridan, see below p. 164.
19. The Rev. Francis Corbet (1688-1775), a prebendary of St Patrick's cathedral and a friend of Stella.
20. Dr John Arbuthnot (1667-1735), doctor to Swift (and to Queen Anne), poet and medical writer.
21. Probably Rev. James Stopford (1697-1759), friend of Swift and of Stella; later bishop of Cloyne.
22. Four of Swift's Irish clergyman friends, all punsters: Robert and John Grattan, John and Daniel Jackson.

Can you on Dublin look with Scorn?
Yet here were You and Ormonde[23] born
Oh, were but You and I so wise
To look with Robin Grattan's Eyes:
Robin adores that Spot of Earth,
That litt'rall Spot which gave him Birth,
And swears, Cushogue[24] is to his Tast,
As fine as Hampton-court at least.   90

When to your Friends you would enhance
The Praise of Italy or France
For Grandeur, Elegance and Wit,
We gladly hear you, and submit:[25]
But then, to come and keep a Clutter[26]
For this, or that Side of a Gutter,[27]
To live in this or t'other Isle,
We cannot think it worth your while
For, take it kindly, or amiss,
The Diff'rence but amounts to this,   100
You bury, on our Side the Channell
In Linnen, and on Yours, in Flannell.[28]
You, for the News are ne'r to seek,
While We perhaps must wait a Week:[29]
You, happy Folks, are sure to meet
A hundred Whores in ev'ry Street,
While We may search all Dublin o'er
And hardly hear of half a Score.

---

23. James Butler, second duke of Ormond (1665-1745), a scion of one of the great families of Ireland and lord lieutenant in the reigns of William II and of Anne. Ormond was later attainted as a Jacobite.
24. The Irish name of Belcamp, the house and estate of the Grattan family, north of Dublin. Ir. *cuiseog*, tall-stemmed grass.
25. In her *Memoirs*, Laetitia Pilkington, after describing Ford as 'one of the oddest little Mortals I ever met with', asserts that he would monopolize a conversation with accounts of his own continental travels. (*Memoirs* [London, 1748] I, 65-6).
26. make a noise or a fuss about.
27. i.e. the Irish Sea. The references in the next line are to the 'islands' of Britain and Ireland.
28. The English law required corpses to be buried in shrouds made of wool, the Irish law that they be buried in linen; in each case the purpose was to stimulate demand for the home-produced material.
29. Contrary winds often delayed the packet boat between England or Wales and Ireland.

You see, my Arguments are Strong;
I wonder you held out so long,   110
But since you are convinc't at last
We'll pardon you for what is past.

So — let us now for Whisk prepare;
Twelvepence a Corner, if you dare.[30]

---

30. In the last couplet, Swift imagines the company — presumably including Ford, now that
he has yielded to the entreaty to return to Ireland (ll. 109-12) — sitting down to a game
of whist and staking twelvepence a point (a 'corner').

ESTHER JOHNSON
(1681-1728)

To *Dr Swift* on his Birth-day
November 30, 1721[1]

St. Patrick's dean, your country's pride,
My early and my only guide,
Let me among the rest attend,
Your pupil and your humble friend,
To celebrate in female strains
The day that paid your mother's pains;
Descend to take that tribute due
In gratitude alone to you.

When men began to call me fair,
You interpos'd your timely care;   10
You early taught me to despise
The ogling of a coxcomb's[2] eyes;
Shew'd where my judgment was misplac'd;
Refin'd my fancy and my taste.

Behold that beauty just decay'd,
Invoking art to nature's aid;
Forsook by her admiring train
She spreads her tatter'd nets in vain;[3]
Short was her part upon the stage;
Went smoothly on for half a page;   20
Her bloom was gone, she wanted art,
As the scene chang'd, to change her part:
She, whom no lover could resist,
Before the second act was hiss'd.

---

1. Swift first met Esther Johnson, who was almost certainly the illegitimate daughter of Sir William Temple, when he was acting as Temple's secretary (and, according to this poem, as Esther's tutor) at Moor Park in Surrey in the 1690s. After Temple's death, 'Stella', as she was generally known, moved to Dublin with her companion Rebecca Dingley (a distant cousin). Here 'the ladies' saw Swift almost every day, and he acted as an affectionate guardian to them. When he was in London 1710-13, Swift wrote to Stella and Dingley every day in the series of letters known as the *Journal to Stella,* and for the rest of her life Stella remained Swift's 'most valuable friend'. From about 1719, Swift and Stella often marked each other's birthday with the gift of a poem.
2. coxcomb = conceited young man, fop.
3. Beauty spreading her nets to 'catch' men.

Such is the fate of female race
With no endowments but a face;
Before the thirti'th year of life
A maid forlorn, or hated wife.

STELLA to you, her tutor, owes
That she has ne'er resembled those;   30
Nor was a burthen to mankind
With half her course of years behind.
You taught how I might youth prolong
By knowing what was right and wrong;
How from my heart to bring supplies
Of lustre to my fading eyes;
How soon a beauteous mind repairs
The loss of chang'd or falling hairs;
How wit and virtue from within
Send out a smoothness o'er the skin: 40
Your lectures cou'd my fancy fix,
And I can please at thirty-six.[4]
The sight of CHLOE at fifteen
Coquetting, gives not me the spleen;
The idol now of every fool
'Till time shall make their passions cool;
Then tumbling down time's steepy hill;
While STELLA holds her station still.
Oh! turn your precepts into laws,
Redeem the women's ruin'd cause,   50
Retrieve lost empire to our sex,
That men may bow their rebel necks.

Long be the day that gave you birth
Sacred to friendship, wit, and mirth;
Late dying may you cast a shred
Of your rich mantle o'er my head;
To bear with dignity my sorrow,
One day *alone, then die to-morrow.*

4. In fact, Stella was forty when she wrote this poem.

JONATHAN SWIFT

Stella at Wood-Park,
A House of *Charles Ford*, Esq; eight Miles from *Dublin*[1]

——*Cuicunqu; nocere volebat*
Vestimenta dabat pretiosa.[2]

Written in the Year 1723

Don *Carlos*[3] in a merry Spight,
Did *Stella* to his House invite:
He entertain'd her half a Year
With gen'rous Wines and costly Chear.[4]
Don *Carlos* made her chief Director,
That she might o'er the Servants hector.
In half a Week the Dame grew nice,[5]
Got all things at the highest Price.

Now at the Table-Head she sits,
Presented with the nicest Bits: 10
She look'd on Partridges with scorn,
Except they tasted of the Corn:
A Haunch of Ven'son made her sweat,
Unless it had the right *Fumette*.[6]
Don *Carlos* earnestly would beg,
Dear Madam, try this Pigeon's Leg;
Was happy when he could prevail
To make her only touch a Quail.
Through Candle-Light she view'd the Wine,
To see that ev'ry Glass was fine.   20
At last grown prouder than the Devil,
With feeding high, and Treatment civil,

1. English and Irish measurements of distance differed from each other in the eighteenth century. Eight 'Irish' miles would have been about eleven 'English' miles.
2. Horace, *Epistles* I, xviii, 31-2. '[Eutrepalus], if he wished to hurt someone, used to give him expensive clothes.'
3. A nickname for Ford, who often told tales about his visits to continental Europe.
4. Stella and Dingley did, in fact, spend several months at Woodpark in 1723.
5. choosy, (too) particular.
6. The smell of game-meat when 'high' and ready to eat.

Don *Carlos* now began to find
His Malice[7] work as he design'd:
The Winter-Sky began to frown,
Poor *Stella* must pack off to Town.
From purling Streams and Fountains bubbling,
To *Liffy*'s stinking Tide in *Dublin*;
From wholesome Exercise and Air
To sossing[8] in an easy Chair;   30
From Stomach sharp and hearty feeding,
To piddle like a Lady breeding:[9]
From ruling there the Houshold singly,
To be directed here by *Dingly*:
From ev'ry Day a lordly Banquet,
To half a Joint, and God be thank it:
From ev'ry Meal *Pontack*[10] in plenty,
To half a Pint one Day in twenty.
From *Ford* attending at her Call,
To visits of Archdeacon Wall;[11]   40
From *Ford*, who thinks of nothing mean,
To the poor Doings of the Dean.
From growing Richer with good Chear,
To running out by starving here.

But now arrives the dismal Day:
She must return to *Ormond Key*:[12]
The Coachman stopt, she lookt, and swore
The Rascal had mistook the Door:
At coming in you saw her stoop;
The Entry[13] brusht against her Hoop: 50
Each Moment rising in her Airs,
She curst the narrow winding Stairs:

7. Used here to mean 'teasing'.
8. lounging about.
9. i.e. toying with her food like a pregnant woman (Stella is known to have had a small appetite).
10. A sweet French wine.
11. Thomas Walls (c. 1672-1750), clergyman and friend of Swift and Stella. In the first printing of this poem (Faulkner, 1735), dashes replace the name. Faulkner also prints 'Devil' (l. 21) as D——l, and 'Dean' (ll. 42 and 72) as D—n.
12. Ormond Quay, beside the Liffey in Dublin, where Stella and Dingley's lodgings were situated.
13. (narrow) entrance hall. At this time, ladies wore hoops inside their dresses.

Began a Thousand Faults to spy;
The Ceiling hardly six Foot high;
The smutty Wainscot full of Cracks,
And half the Chairs with broken Backs:
Her Quarter's out at *Lady-Day*,[14]
She vows she will no longer stay,
In Lodgings, like a poor *Grizette*,[15]
While there are Lodgings to be lett.   60

Howe'er, to keep her Spirits up,
She sent for Company to sup;
When all the while you might remark,
She strove in vain to ape *Wood-Park*.
Two Bottles call'd for, (half her Store;
The Cupboard could contain but four;)
A Supper worthy of her self,
Five *Nothings* in five Plates of *Delph*.[16]

Thus, for a Week the Farce went on;
When all her County-Savings gone,   70
She fell into her former Scene.
Small Beer,[17] a Herring, and the Dean.

Thus far in jest. Though now I fear
You think my jesting too severe:
But Poets when a Hint is new
Regard not whether false or true:
Yet Raillery gives no Offence,
Where Truth has not the least Pretence;
Nor can be more securely plac't
Than on a Nymph of *Stella*'s Taste.   80
I must confess, your Wine and Vittle[18]
I was too hard upon *a little*;
Your Table neat, your Linnen fine;
And, though in Miniature, you shine,

---

14. i.e. her lease expires on Lady Day (25 March).
15. working girl.
16. Glazed earthenware dishes, such as are made in the Dutch city of Delft.
17. weak, every-day ale. Herrings are often mentioned in eighteenth-century Irish verse as a
    staple part of the diet.
18. victuals, food.

Yet, when you sigh to leave *Wood-Park*,
The Scene, the Welcome, and the Spark,[19]
To languish in this odious Town,
And pull your haughty Stomach[20] down;
We think you quite mistake the Case;
The Virtue lies not in the Place: 90
For though my Raillery were true,
A Cottage is *Wood-Park* with you.

---

19. A person of an elegant appearance, in this case Ford himself.
20. temper.

THOMAS SHERIDAN
(1687-1738)

Thomas Sheridan — 'classicist, schoolmaster, translator, priest, poet, essayist and wit'[1] — was born in County Cavan. He was educated at Trinity College, Dublin and ordained into the Church of Ireland. He was the closest of Swift's Irish friends and, like Swift, was addicted to language games, outrageous rhymes and riddles. For many years, he kept one of Dublin's best-known classical schools, noted for its performances of classical plays in the original languages. Despite an unhappy marriage, Sheridan was father of many children, including the playwright, actor-manager, lexicographer and biographer of Swift, Thomas Sheridan the younger; thus the elder Sheridan was father-in-law of Frances Sheridan, the novelist, poet and playwright, and grandfather of the dramatist Richard Brinsley Sheridan. Swift wrote several poems about his visits to Sheridan's delapidated country house at Quilca, Co. Cavan, and collaborated with him on the short-lived *Intelligencer*. In the affectionate poem which follows, Sheridan describes the famous 'country house' at Glasnevin, near Dublin, on which Dr Patrick Delany, mutual friend of Swift and Sheridan, spent so much more than he could afford.

A Description of Doctor Delany's Villa

Would you that *Delville* I describe?
Believe me, Sir, I would not gibe;
For who would be Satirical
Upon a Thing so very small?

You scarce upon the Borders enter,
Before you're at the very Centre.
A single Crow can make it Night,
When o'er your Farm he takes his Flight;
Yet in this narrow Compass, we
Observe a vast Variety;   10
Both Walks, Walls, Meadows and Parterres,[2]
Windows, and Doors, and Rooms, and Stairs,
And Hills, and Dales, and Woods and Fields,
And Hay, and Grass, and Corn it yields;
All to your Haggard[3] brought so cheap in,
Without the Mowing or the Reaping.
A Razour, tho' to say't I'm loath,
Wou'd shave you and your Meadows both.

---

1. James Woolley's succinct and accurate list (*The Intelligencer* ed. Woolley (Oxford, 1992), p. 6).
2. Ornamental parts of the garden, containing flowerbeds.
3. A yard where hay or straw is stacked.

Tho' small's the Farm, yet here's a House
Full large to entertain a Mouse,   20
But where a Rat is dreaded more
Than savage *Caledonian*[4] Boar;
For, if 'tis enter'd by a Rat,
There is no Room to bring a Cat.

A little Riv'let seems to steal
Down thro' a Thing you call a Vale
Like Tears along a wrinkled Cheek,
Like Rain along a Blade of Leek;
And this you call your sweet *Meander*,
Which might be suck'd up by a Gander,   30
Could he but force his nestling Bill
To scoop the Channel of the Rill.
I'm sure you'd make a mighty Clutter,
Were it as big as City Gutter.

Next come I to your Kitchen-Garden,
Where one poor Mouse wou'd fare but hard in;
And round this Garden is a Walk,
No longer than a Taylor's Chalk:[5]
Thus I compute what Space is in it,
A Snail creeps round it in a Minute.   40
One Lettice makes a shift to squeeze
Up thro' a Tuft you call your Trees;
And once a Year a single Rose
Peeps from the Bud, but never blows;[6]
In vain then you expect its Bloom!
It cannot blow for want of Room.

In short, in all your boasted Seat,
There's nothing but yourself that's Great.

---

4. Scottish.
5. i.e. no longer than could be made by a tailor using his chalk (for marking cloth).
6. flowers.

PATRICK DELANY
(c.1685-1768)

Born in County Laois (King's County) of a modest family, Patrick Delany was educated at Trinity College, Dublin and ordained into the Church of Ireland. He held a number of positions in the university and the church and was appointed Dean of Down in 1744. Delany was a well-known preacher, a convivial and generous companion and one of the central figures in Swift's Dublin circle. However, his expenditure on Delville, his house at Glasnevin (see previous poem), ran him into debt. He needed to augment his income and so sent the following rather blunt poetic request for additional preferment to the lord lieutenant of the day. Though the poem did bring him a modest increase in income, it also brought Swift's gentle ridicule. Yet Swift and Delany remained good friends and, after Swift's death, it was Delany who defended Swift's reputation against Lord Orrery's unjust criticisms in his *Observations upon Lord Orrery's Remarks on the Life and Writings of Dr Jonathan Swift* (London, 1754).

An Epistle to His Excellency John *Lord* Carteret, &c.

Credis ob hoc, me, Pastor, opes fortasse rogare,
Propter quod, vulgus, crassaq; turba rogat: Mart. Epig. lib.9[1]

Thou wise, and learned Ruler of our Ile,
Whose Guardian Care can all her Griefs beguile;
When next your generous Soul shall condescend,
T'Instruct, or entertain your humble Friend,[2]
Whether retiring from your weighty Charge,
On some high Theme you learnedly enlarge;
Of all the Ways of Wisdom reason well,
How RICHLEU rose, and how SEJANUS fell:[3]
Or when your Brow less thoughtfully unbends,
Circled with SWIFT, and some delighted Friends;   10
When mixing Mirth and Wisdom with your Wine,
Like that your Wit should flow, your Genius shine,
Nor with less Praise the Conversation guide,
Than in the publick Councils you decide:
Or when the *Dean*,[4] long privileg'd to rail,
Asserts his Friend with more impetuous Zeal;

1. Martial, *Epigrams*, 9, xxii, 1-2. 'You think perhaps, pastor, that I ask for wealth for the same reason that the mob and the ignorant crowd ask for it.'
2. i.e. Delany himself.
3. Cardinal Richelieu (1585-1642), chief minister of France and virtual dictator from 1624 until his death; Lucius Ælius Sejanus (d. A.D. 31), Roman statesman.
4. Swift.

You hear, (whilst I sit by abash'd and mute)
With soft Concessions shortning the Dispute;
Then close with kind Enquiries of my State,
'How are your Tythes,[5] and have they rose of late?   20
Why *Christ-Church* is a pretty Situation,
There are not many better in the Nation!
This, with your other *Things*, must yield you clear
Some six — at least five hundred Pounds a Year.'

Suppose at such a Time, I took the Freedom
To speak these Truths, as plainly as you read 'em,
(You shall rejoin, my Lord, when I've replied,
And, if you please, my Lady[6] shall decide.)

'My Lord, I'm satisifed you meant me well,
And that I'm thankful, all the World can tell,   30
But you'l forgive me, if I own th'Event
Is short, is very short of your Intent;
At least I feel some Ills, unfelt before,
My Income less, and my Expences more.'

'How Doctor! double Vicar! double Rector!
A Dignitary! with a City Lecture —
What Glebes — what Dues — what Tythes — what Fines — what
                                                      Rent![7]
Why Doctor — will you never be content?'[8]

'Would my good Lord but cast up the Account,
And see to what my Revenues amount,   40
My Titles ample! but my Gains so small,
That one good Vicarage is worth 'em all —
And very wretched, sure, is he, that's double,
In nothing, but his Titles, and his Trouble.

5. An eighteenth-century clergyman received the bulk of his income from tithes, payments of 'a tenth' of their produce which parishioners were obliged to provide. Tithes were greatly resented and were often difficult to collect. At this time, Delany held not only the cure of Derryvullen, Co. Fermanagh, but also the chancellorship of Christ Church, Dublin.

6. i.e. Lady Carteret.

7. Delany imagines Carteret enumerating four further sources of income for a clergyman.

8. Delany held (or had held) other benefices and positions as well as his rectory and his chancellorship. These included the Archbishop King lecturership and the professorship of history, both at Trinity College, Dublin, the cure of St John's in Dublin and a prebendal stall in St Patrick's Cathedral.

Add to this crying Grievance if you please,
My Horses founder'd on FERMANAGH Ways;
Ways of well-polish'd and well-pointed Stone,
Where every Step endangers every Bone;
And more to raise your Pity, and your Wonder,
Two Churches — twelve HIBERNIAN Miles asunder![9]   50
With complicated *Cures*, I labour hard in,
Besides whole Summers absent from my Garden!
But[10] that the World would think I plaid the Fool,
I'd change with CHARLY GRATTAN for his School[11] —
What fine Cascades, what Vistos might I make,
Fixt in centre of th'IERNIAN Lake![12]
There might I sail, delighted, smooth, and safe,
Beneath the Conduct of my good Sir RALPH:[13]
There's not a better Steerer in the Realm;
I hope, my Lord, you'll call him to the *Helm* —'   60

'Doctor — a glorious Scheme to ease your Grief!
When *Cures* are cross, a School's a sure Relief.
You cannot fail of being happy there,
The Lake will be the *Lethe*[14] of your Care:
The Scheme is for your Honour and your Ease!
And Doctor, I'll promote it when you please.
Mean while, allowing Things — below your Merit,
Yet Doctor, you've a philosophick Spirit;[15]
Your Wants are few, and, like your Income, small,
And you've enough to gratify 'em all: 70
You've Trees, and Fruits, and Roots enough in store,
And what would a Philosopher have more?
You cannot wish for Coaches, Kitchens, Cooks —'

9. For the difference between 'English' and 'Irish' miles, see p. 160, n. 1.
10. except.
11. Charles Grattan was headmaster of Portora Royal School, Enniskillen, Co. Fermanagh.
12. A conflated adjective echoing 'Ierne', a poetic name for Ireland, and Lough 'Erne', the lake near Enniskillen.
13. Sir Ralph Gore (c. 1675-1732), Chancellor of the Exchequer in Ireland and speaker of the Irish House of Commons. Gore came from Manorhamilton, Co. Leitrim, not far from Enniskillen, and owned a villa on an island in Lough Erne.
14. In classical mythology, whoever drank the waters of Lethe (a river in hell) forgot everything.
15. calmness of spirit (as well as love of knowledge) cf. l. 72.

'My Lord, I've not enough to buy me Books —
Or pray, suppose my Wants were all supplied,
Are there no Wants I should regard beside?
Who's Breast is so unman'd as not to grieve,
Compass'd with Miseries he can't relieve?
Who can be happy — who would wish to live,
And want the Godlike Happiness to give?   80
(That I'm a Judge of this you must allow,
I had it once — and I'm debarr'd it now.)
Ask your own Heart, my Lord, if this be true —
Then how unblest am I! how blest are you!'

''Tis true — but, Doctor, let us wave[16] all that —
Say, if you had your Wish what you'd be at.'

'Excuse me, good my Lord — I won't be sounded,[17]
Nor shall your Favour by my Wants be bounded.
My Lord, I challenge nothing as my Due,
Nor is it fit I should prescribe to You.   90
Yet this might SYMMACHUS[18] himself avow,
(Whose rigid Rules are antiquated now):
My Lord, I'd wish — *to pay the Debts I owe*, —
I'd wish besides — to *build*, and to *bestow*.'

---

16. waive.
17. examined, questioned.
18. Quintus Aurelius Symmachus (c. 345-410), a famous Roman orator.

JONATHAN SWIFT

An Epistle upon an Epistle from a certain Doctor to a certain great Lord: being a *Christmas-Box* for D. *D[ela]ny*[1]

– Palatinæ Cultor facunde Minervæ,
Ingenio frueris qui propriore Dei.
Nam tibi nascentes DOMINI cognoscere Curas,
Et secreta DUCIS Pectota nôsse licet. Martial, Lib. 5, Ep. 5.[2]

As *Jove* will not attend on less
When Things of more Importance press:
You can't, grave Sir, believe it hard,
That you, a low *Hibernian* Bard,
Shou'd cool your Heels a while, and wait
Unanswer'd at your *Patron*'s Gate;
And wou'd my Lord vouchsafe to grant
This one, poor, humble Boon I want,
Free Leave to play his *Secretary*,
As *Falstaff* acted old King *Harry*:[3]   10
I'd tell of yours in Rhyme and Print:
Folks shrug, and cry, *There's nothing in't.*
And after several Readings over,
It shines most in the Marble Cover.

How cou'd so fine a Taste[4] dispense
With mean Degrees of Wit and Sense?
Nor will my Lord so far *Beguile*
The *Wise* and *Learned* of our *Isle*

1. This is Swift's response to the previous poem and his text often echoes it. For clarification of the place-names in this poem, see the notes to Delany's poem.
2. 'You, eloquent worshipper of Palatine Minerva, delight more nearly in the nature of the god; for you are allowed to know our lord's cares even as they are being born, and to be privy to the inmost feelings of our chief.'
3. This passage could be rendered as follows: 'If Carteret does grant your request, I want leave to impersonate his secretary (as Falstaff impersonated Prince Hal in Shakespeare's *Henry IV Part I*); I would say that your printed, poetic request had no substance. In fact, although your poem has been read several times, the best thing about it is the marbled paper on its cover.' (A specially bound copy of Delany's poem had, obviously, been presented to Carteret.)
4. i.e. How could as fine a Taste [as yours] dispense with even moderate degrees of wit and sense?

170

To make it pass upon the Nation,
By Dint of his sole Approbation.   20
The Task is Arduous, Patrons find,
To warp the Sense of all Mankind:
Who think your Muse must first aspire
E'er he advance the Doctor higher.

You've Cause to say he *meant you well*:
That you *are thankful* who *can tell*?
For still you're short (which grieves your Spirit)
Of his Intent, you mean, your Merit.
Ah! *Quanto rectiùs, Tu Adepte,*
Qui nil moliris tam ineptè?[5]   30
Smedley, thou *Jonathan* of *Clogher*,[6]
'When thou thy humble Lays do'st offer
To *G——f——n*'s Grace, with grateful Heart:
Thy Thanks and Verse, devoid of Art:
Content with what his Bounty gave,
No larger Income dost thou Crave.'

But you[7] must have Cascades, and all
Ierna's Lake, for your Canal,
Your Vistos, Barges, and (A Pox on
All Pride) our *Speaker* for your Coxon: 40
It's Pity that he can't bestow you
Twelve Commoners in Caps to Row you.
Thus *Edgar*[8] proud, in Days of Yore,
Held Monarchs labouring at the Oar;
And as he pass'd, so swell'd the *Dee*
Inrag'd, as *Ern* would do to thee.

---

5. An adaptation of two lines from Horace's *Ars Poetica*: 'How much more appropriate it would be if you, who want to be an expert in poetry, did not make such inept efforts.'
6. Here (and below ll. 49-58) Swift quotes from Smedley's *Epistle to Grafton* (see above pp. 147-50) and contrasts Smedley's modest request with Delany's.
7. i.e. Delany.
8. The reference is to Edgar, king of the English (944-75) who, according to the chroniclers, made six kings who had sworn loyalty to him row him up and down the river Dee at Chester while he held the tiller of the boat, like a coxwain. (See *Jonathan Swift: the complete poems* ed. Pat Rogers (Harmondsworth: Penguin, 1983), p. 806, n. 43.)

How different is this from *Smedley*?
(His Name is up,[9] he may in Bed lye)
'Who only asks some pretty Cure,
In wholesome Soil and Æther Pure;   50
The Garden stor'd with artless Flowers,
In either Angle shady Bowers:
No gay Parterre with costly Green,
Must in the Ambient Hedge be seen;
But Nature freely takes her Course,
Nor fears from him ungrateful Force:
No Sheers to check her sprouting Vigour,
Or shape the *Yews* to Antick Figure.'

But you forsooth, your *All* must squander,
On that poor Spot, call'd *Del-Ville*, yonder: 60
And when you've been at vast Expences
In Whims, Parterres, Canals and Fences:
Your Assets fail, and Cash is wanting
For farther Buildings, farther Planting.
No wonder when you raise and level,
Think this Wall low, and that Wall bevel.[10]
Here a convenient Box[11] you found,
Which you demolish'd to the Ground:
Then Built, then took up with[12] your Arbour,
And set the House to *R–p—t B—b–r.*[13]   70
You sprung[14] an Arch, which in a Scurvy
Humour, you tumbled Topsy Turvy.
You change a Circle to a Square,
Then to a Circle, as you were:
Who can imagine whence the Fund is,
That you *Quadrata* change *Rotundis*?[15]

9. This seems to mean that since Smedley's name has appeared, a rhyme must be found for it.
10. broken, not straight.
11. small shelter or shed. See *Memoirs of Laetitia Pilkington*, ed. A. C. Elias Jr. (Athens, Georgia, 1997), p. 392.
12. connected it with.
13. i.e. and then let (what was now big enough to be called) the house to Rupert Barber — husband of the poet Mary Barber.
14. An architectural term meaning to commence the curve of an arch.
15. The reference is to Horace *Epistles* I, i, 100; *mutat, quadrata rotundis*, 'changing square to round'.

To *Fame* a temple you Erect,
A *Flora*[16] does the Dome protect;
Mounts, Walks, on high; and in a Hollow
You place the *Muses* and *Apollo*;   80
There shining 'midst his Train, to Grace
Your Whimsical, Poetick Place.

These Stories were, of old, design'd
As Fables: But you have refin'd
The Poets Mythologick Dreams,
To real Muses, Gods, and Streams.
Who wou'd not swear, when you contrive thus,
That you're *Don Quixote Redivivus*?[17]

Beneath, a dry Canal there lies,
Which only *Winter*'s Rain supplies.   90
Oh! cou'd'st thou, by some Magick Spell,
Hither convey St. *Patrick*'s *Well*;[18]
Here may it re-assume its Stream,
And take a Greater *Patrick*'s Name.

If your Expences rise so high;
What Income can your Wants supply?
Yet still you fancy you inherit
A Fund of such Superior Merit,
That you can't fail of more Provision,
All by my *Lady*'s kind Decision.   100
For the more Livings you can fish up,
You think you'll sooner be a Bishop:
That cou'd not be *my Lord*'s *Intent,*
Nor can it *answer in the Event.*
Most think what has been heap'd on You,
To other sort of Folk was due:
Rewards too great for your Flim-Flams,[19]
Epistles, Riddles, Epigrams.

---

16. A statue of the goddess of flowers.
17. You are the reincarnation of Don Quixote (who could not tell fantasy from reality).
18. A well in the gardens of Trinity College, Dublin which suddenly dried up in 1729.
19. The name given to lightweight verses — used also by Swift of the poems of Ambrose Philips.

Tho' now your Depth must not be Sounded,
The Time was, when you'd have compounded[20]   110
For less than CHARLY GRATTAN's School:
Five hundred Pound a Year's no Fool.

Take this Advice then from your Friend,
To your Ambition put an End.
Be frugal, *Patt*: pay what you owe,
Before you *Build* and you *Bestow*,
Be Modest: nor Address your Betters
With Begging, Vain, Familiar Letters.

A Passage may be found, I've heard,
In some old *Greek* or *Latin* Bard,   120
Which says, wou'd Crows in Silence eat
Their Offals, or their better Meat,
Their generous Feeders not provoking
By loud and unharmonious Croaking:
They might, unhurt by Envy's Claws,
Live on, and Stuff, to Boot, their Maws.[21]

A LIBEL on D[octor] D[elany] and a Certain Great Lord[1]

Deluded Mortals, whom the *Great*
Chuse for Companions *tete à tete*,
Who at their Dinners, *en famille*,
Get Leave to sit whene'er you will;
Then, boasting tell us where you din'd,
And, how his *Lordship* was so kind;
How many pleasant Things he spoke,
And, how you *laugh'd* at every *Joke*:

---

20. been prepared to settle for.

21. The last line means: 'they might live on and be able to eat their fill, into the bargain'. The classical author referred to is Horace, *Epistles* I, xvii, 50-51, in a passage which Pat Rogers translates (p. 807, n. 120): 'But if the crow could feed in silence, he would have more of a meal, and far less brawling and unpleasantness'.

---

1. Swift's second response to Delany's poem to Lord Carteret. See notes to the two preceding poems.

Swear, he's a most facetious Man,
That you and he are *Cup* and *Cann*.[2]   10
You Travel with a heavy Load,
And quite mistake *Preferment*'s Road.

Suppose my *Lord* and you alone;
Hint the least Int'rest of your own;
His Visage drops, he knits his Brow,
He cannot talk of Bus'ness now;
Or, mention but a vacant *Post*,
He'll turn it off with; *Name your Toast*.
Nor could the nicest Artist Paint,
A Countenance with more Constraint.   20

For, as their Appetites to quench,
Lords keep a Pimp to bring a Wench;
So, Men of Wit are but a kind
Of Pandars[3] to a vicious Mind,
Who proper Objects must provide
To gratify their Lust of Pride,
When weary'd with Intrigues of State,
They find an idle Hour to Prate.
Then, shou'd you dare to ask a *Place*,
You forfeit all your *Patron*'s grace,   30
And disappoint the sole Design,
For which he summon'd you to *Dine*.

Thus, *Congreve*[4] spent, in writing Plays,
And one poor Office, half his Days;
While *Montague*,[5] who claim'd the Station
To be *Mæcenas* of the Nation,
For *Poets* open Table kept,
But ne'er consider'd where they Slept.
Himself, as rich as fifty *Jews*,
Was easy, though they wanted Shoes;   40

---

2. A proverbial expression meaning 'very friendly associates'. Swift is alluding, in the first ten lines of this poem, to Delany's boasting that he was on good terms with the lord lieutenant.

3. procurers (from the proper name Pandar in Chaucer's *Troilus and Criseyde*).

4. The playwright William Congreve (1670-1729), who had held a government sinecure.

5. Charles Montague, Earl of Halifax (1661-1715), poet, politician and patron. Mæcenas was a great patron of the arts in classical Rome; Horace dedicated his *Odes* to him.

175

And, crazy *Congreve* scarce cou'd spare
A Shilling to discharge his Chair,[6]
Till Prudence taught him to appeal
From *Pæn*'s Fire[7] to Party Zeal;
Not owing to his happy Vein
The Fortunes of his latter Scene,
Took proper *Principles* to thrive;
And so might ev'ry *Dunce* alive.

Thus, *Steel*[8] who own'd what others writ,
And flourish'd by imputed Wit,   50
From Lodging in a hundred Jayls,
Was left to starve, and dye in *Wales*.

Thus *Gay*,[9] the *Hare* with many Friends,
Twice sev'n long Years the *Court* attends,
Who, under Tales conveying truth,
To Virtue form'd a *Princely* Youth,
Who pay'd his Courtship with the Croud,
As far as *Modest Pride* allow'd,
Rejects a servile *Usher*'s Place,
And leaves *St. James*'s in Disgrace.   60

Thus *Addison*[10] by Lords Carest,
Was left in Foreign Lands distrest,
Forgot at Home, became for Hire,
A trav'lling Tutor to a *Squire*;
But, wisely left the *Muses* Hill,
To Bus'ness shaped the *Poet*'s Quill,

---

6. i.e. to pay for a sedan chair. Congreve suffered from gout.
7. A hymn to Apollo or (here) a poem.
8. Sir Richard Steele (1672-1729), playwright, journalist and politician, who died in Wales. He had been accused of publishing others' works as if they were his own.
9. John Gay (1685-1732), poet and dramatist. Gay had likened himself to a hare in one of his fables. In 1727, after several years apparently in royal favour, Gay had been offered only the post of tutor ('gentleman-usher') to the infant princess Louisa. Swift, like Gay's other friends, considered the offer insulting, and Gay declined it.
10. Joseph Addison (1672-1719), politician and writer. Swift is referring to incidents early in Addison's life; in 1702, he seems to have found himself stranded on the Continent without money because of a change in government, and later he was offered the post of tutor to the son of the Duke of Somerset. Addison was secretary to the lord lieutenant of Ireland 1708-10.

Let all his barren Lawrel's fade
Took up himself the *Courtier*'s Trade,
And grown a *Minister of State,*
Saw Poets at his Levee[11] wait.   70

Hail! happy *Pope,*[12] whose gen'rous Mind,
Detesting all the Statesmen kind,
Contemning *Courts*, at *Courts* unseen,
Refus'd the Visits of a Queen;
A Soul with ev'ry Virtue fraught
By *Sages*, *Priests*, or *Poets* taught;
Whose filial Piety[13] excels
Whatever *Grecian* Story tells:
A Genius for all Stations fit,
Whose *meanest Talent* is his *Wit*:   80
His Heart too Great, though Fortune little,
To lick a *Rascal Statesman*'s Spittle.
Appealing to the Nation's Taste,
Above the Reach of Want is plac't:
By *Homer* dead was taught to thrive,
Which *Homer* never cou'd alive.[14]
And, sits aloft on *Pindus* Head,[15]
Despising *Slaves* that *cringe* for Bread.

True *Politicians* only Pay
For solid Work, but not for Play;   90
Nor ever chuse to work with Tools
Forg'd up in *Colleges* and *Schools*.
Consider how much more is due
To all their *Journey-Men*[16] than you,
At Table you can *Horace* quote;
They at a Pinch can bribe a Vote:

---

11. An official or court reception. Addison was Secretary of State from 1717 to 1718, so would have held levees.
12. Alexander Pope (1688-1744), the most formidable poet of the age. It is probably not true that Pope went out when Queen Caroline came to visit him, though the rumour was widely believed. A dash replaces the word 'Queen' (l. 74) in early editions.
13. Pope was very attached to his mother.
14. Pope's translations of Homer made him a rich man.
15. A mountain, or rather a chain of mountains, in Greece, sacred to Apollo and the Muses.
16. Here the word means hack writers, paid for each day's work.

You show your Skill in *Grecian* Story,
But, they can manage *Whig* and *Tory*:
You, as a *Critick*, are so curious
To find a Verse in *Virgil* Spurious;   100
But, they can smoak[17] the deep Designs,
When *Bolingbroke* with *Pult'ney* Dines.[18]

Besides; your Patron may upbraid ye,
That you have got a Place already,
An Office for your Talents fit,
To Flatter, Carve, and shew your Wit;
To snuff the Lights, and stir the Fire,
And get a *Dinner* for your Hire,
What Claim have you to *Place* or *Pension*?
He overpays in Condescension.   110

But, Rev'rend *Doctor*, you, we know,
Could never Condescend so low;
The *Vice-Roy*,[19] whom you now attend,
Would, if he durst, be more your Friend;
Nor will in you those Gifts despise,
By which himself was taught to rise:
When he has Virtue to retire,
He'll Grieve he did not raise you higher,
And place you in a better Station,
Although it might have pleas'd the Nation.   120

This may be true — submitting still
To *Walpole*'s more than Royal Will.
And what Condition can be worse?
He comes to *drain* a *Beggar's Purse*:[20]
He comes to tye our Chains on faster,
And shew us, *England* is our Master:

17. uncover.
18. Henry St John, Viscount Bolingbroke (1678-1751), statesman and philosopher, had been
    one of Swift's political masters 1710-13. By the time of this poem, Bolingbroke was best
    known as an ex-Jacobite who was opposed to the powerful Prime Minister, Robert
    Walpole. William Pulteney (1684-1764) was another politician at this time opposed to
    Walpole.
19. Carteret.
20. Swift often repeated this view of the relationship between a lord lieutenant and the
    Ireland he was sent to govern. In early editions, *Walpole* (l. 122) appears as *W———le*,
    and England (l. 126) as *E———d*.

Caressing Knaves and Dunces wooing,
To make them work their own undoing.
What has he else to bait his Traps,
Or bring his *Vermin* in, but *Scraps*?   130
The Offals of a *Church* distress't,
A hungry *Vicarage* at best;
Or, some remote inferior *Post*,
With forty Pounds a Year at most.

But, here again you interpose;
Your favourite *Lord* is none of those,
Who owe their Virtues to their Stations,
And Characters to Dedications:[21]
For keep him in, or turn him out,
His *Learning* none will call in doubt;   140
His *Learning*, though a Poet said it,
Before a Play,[22] wou'd lose no Credit:
Nor POPE wou'd dare deny him Wit,
Although to Praise it PH——PS[23] writ.
I own he hates an Action base,
His *Virtues* battling with his *Place*;
Nor wants a nice discerning Spirit,
Betwixt a true and spurious Merit;
Can sometimes drop a *Voter*'s Claim,
And give up Party to his Fame.   150
I do the most that *Friendship* can;
I hate the *Vice-Roy,* love the Man.

But, You, who till your Fortune's made
Must be a Sweet'ner by your trade,
Shou'd swear he never meant us ill;
We suffer sore against his Will;
That, if we could but see his Heart,
He wou'd have chose a milder part;
We rather should lament his Case
Who must obey, or lose his *Place*.   160

21. i.e. Your favourite Lord (Carteret) is not one of those to whom qualities accrue only because of his position, or one of those whose character is made up of the attributes given to him in book dedications.
22. i.e. in a dedicatory prologue to a play.
23. Ambrose Philips (1674-1749). See p. 138.

Since this Reflection slipt[24] your Pen,
Insert it when you write agen:
And, to illustrate it, produce
This *Simile* for his Excuse.

'So, to destroy a guilty Land,
An *Angel* sent by *Heav'n*'s Command,
While he obeys *Almighty* Will,
Perhaps may feel *Compassion* still,
And wish the Task had been assign'd
To *Spirits* of less gentle kind.'   170

But I, in *Politicks* grown old,
Whose Thoughts are of a diff'rent Mold,
Who, from my Soul, sincerely hate
Both Kings[25] and *Ministers* of *State*,
Who look on *Courts* with stricter Eyes,
To see the Seeds of *Vice* arise,
Can lend you an Allusion fitter,
Though *flatt'ring Knaves* may call it *bitter*.
Which, if you durst but give it place,
Would shew you many a *Statesman*'s Face.   180
Fresh from the *Tripod* of Apollo,[26]
I had it in the Words that follow.
(Take Notice, to avoid Offence
I here except *His Excellence*.)

So, to effect his *Monarch*'s ends,
From *Hell* a *Viceroy* DEV'L ascends,
His *Budget*[27] with *Corruptions* cramm'd,
The Contributions of the *Damn'd*;
Which with unsparing Hand, he strows[28]
Through *Courts* and *Senates* as he goes;   190
And then at *Belzebub*'s *Black-Hall*,[29]
Complains his *Budget* was too small.

24. escaped.
25. Early editions print a dash instead of the word 'Kings'.
26. The seat of the oracle in the shrine dedicated to Apollo at Delphi.
27. Satchel or bag.
28. throws or casts (as if sowing corn).
29. The Devil's Black Hall, contrasted with Whitehall, the centre of English government.

Your *Simile* may better shine
In Verse; but there is *Truth* in mine.
For, no imaginable Things
Can differ more than GOD and *Kings*;[30]
And, *Statesmen* by ten Thousand odds
Are ANGELS, just as *Kings* are GODS.

30. Here, and in l. 198, early editions print a dash instead of the word '*Kings*'.

JONATHAN SWIFT, PATRICK DELANY, THOMAS SHERIDAN
AND OTHERS

Riddles, street cries and other short verses

When George Faulkner printed a selection of riddles in the second volume of his 1735 edition of Swift's *Works*, he prefixed it with a note which began: 'About Nine or Ten Years ago, some ingenious Gentlemen, Friends to the Author, used to entertain themselves with writing Riddles, and send them to him and their other Acquaintance, Copies of which ran about, and some of them were printed both here and in *England*. The Author, at his leisure Hours, fell into the same Amusement ...' The three riddles and other verses which follow are typical of many written and rewritten in Swift's circle. Although the first riddle is said to have been the work of Delany and the street cries the work of Swift, it is really impossible to assign any of them to a single author.

Three Riddles

In Youth exalted high in Air,
Or bathing in the Waters fair;
Nature to form me took Delight,
And clad my Body all in White:
My Person tall, and slender Waste,
On either Side with Fringes grac'd;
Till me that Tyrant Man espy'd,
And drag'd me from my Mother's Side:
No Wonder now I look so thin;
The Tyrant strip't me to the Skin: 10
My Skin he flay'd, my Hair he cropt;
At Head and Foot my Body lopt:
And then, with Heart more hard than Stone,
He pick't my Marrow from the Bone.
To vex me more, he took a Freak,[1]
To slit my Tongue, and made me speak:[2]
But, that which wonderful appears,
I speak to Eyes and not to Ears.
He oft employs me in Disguise,
And makes me tell a Thousand Lyes: 20

[1.] a capricious whim.

[2.] Some birds are natural mimics and can be taught to talk, but magpies and crows cannot talk unless their tongues are slit.

182

To me he chiefly gives in Trust
To please his Malice, or his Lust.
From me no Secret he can hide;
I see his Vanity and Pride:
And my Delight is to expose
His Follies to his greatest Foes.

All Languages I can command,
Yet not a Word I understand.
Without my Aid, the best Divine
In Learning would not know a Line: 30
The Lawyer must forget his Pleading,
The Scholar could not shew his Reading.
Nay; Man, my Master, is my Slave:
I give Command to kill or save.
Can grant ten Thousand Pounds a Year,
And make a Beggar's Brat a Peer.

But, while I thus my Life relate,
I only hasten on my Fate.
My Tongue is black, my Mouth is furr'd,
I hardly now can force a Word.   40
I dye unpity'd and forgot;
And on some Dunghill left to rot.[3]

[A second Riddle]

Begotten and born, and dying with Noise,
The Terror of Women, and Pleasure of Boys,
Like the Fiction of Poets concerning the Wind,
I'm chiefly unruly, when strongest confin'd.[1]
For Silver and Gold I don't trouble my Head,
But all I delight in is Pieces of Lead;
Except when I treat with a Ship or a Town,
Why then I make pieces of Iron go down.

---

3. The answer to the riddle is a quill pen.

1. In classical literature, Æolus, the god of the winds, confined them either in a bag (Homer) or in a cave (Virgil).

One Property more I would have you remark,
No Lady was ever more fond of a Spark;[2]   10
The Moment I get one, my Soul's all a-fire,
And I roar out my Joy, and in Transport expire.[3]

[Another Riddle]

We are little airy Creatures,
All of diff'rent Voice and Features,
One of us in Glass is set,
One of us you'll find in Jet,[1]
T'other you may see in Tin,
And the fourth a Box within,
If the fifth you shou'd pursue
It can never fly from you.[2]

[Two verses in Mock Latin]

As sonata in praes o Molli

Mollis abuti,
Has an accuti,
No lasso finis;
Molli divinis
Omi de armis tres,
Imi na Dis tres;
Cantu disco ver
Meas alo ver.

---

2. Playing on both meanings of this word, a spark of fire and a young gallant or lover.
3. The answer to the riddle is a cannon.

---

1. A hard, black stone.
2. The answer to the riddle is the vowels.

Jonathan Swift, Patrick Delany, Thomas Sheridan and others

A Love Song

Apud in is almi de si re,
Mimis tres I ne ver re qui re.
Alo veri findit a gestis,
His miseri ne ver at restis.

[Street Cries]

Herrings

Be not sparing,
Leave off swearing
Buy my Herring
Fresh from *Malahide*,[1]
Better ne'er was try'd.
Come eat 'em with pure fresh Butter and Mustard,
Their Bellies are soft, and as white as a Custard.
Come, Six-pence a Dozen to get me some Bread,
Or, like my own Herrings, I soon shall be dead.

Oranges

Come, buy my fine Oranges, Sauce for your Veal,
And charming when squeez'd in a Pot of brown Ale.
Well roasted, with Sugar and Wine in a Cup,
They'll make a sweet Bishop[1] when Gentlefolks sup.

Asparagus

Ripe 'Sparagrass,
Fit for Lad or Lass,
To make the Water pass;
O, 'tis pretty Picking
With a tender Chicken.

---

1. A small fishing port a few miles north of Dublin.

1. A sweet drink of mulled wine, oranges and sugar.

Oysters

Charming Oysters I cry,
My Masters come buy,
So plump and so fresh,
So sweet is their Flesh,
No *Colchester* Oyster,
Is sweeter and moister;
Your Stomach they settle,
And rouse up your Mettle,
They'll make you a Dad
Of a Lass or a Lad;   10
And, Madam your Wife
They'll please to the Life;
Be she barren, be she old,
Be she Slut, or be she Scold,
Eat my Oysters, and lye near her,
She'll be fruitful, never fear her.

THOMAS SHERIDAN

To the *Dean,* when in England, in 1726

You will excuse me, I suppose,
For sending rhyme instead of prose,
Because hot weather makes me lazy,
To write in metre is more easy.

While you are trudging London town,
I'm stroling Dublin, up and down;
While you converse with lords and dukes,
I have their betters here, my books:
Fix'd in an elbow chair at ease,
I chuse companions as I please.　　　　　　　　　　10
I'd rather have one single shelf,
Than all my friends, except your self;
For after all that can be said,
Our best acquaintance, are the dead.
While you're in raptures with Faustina,[1]
I'm charm'd at home, with our Sheelina;[2]
While you are starving there in state,
I'm cramming here with butcher's meat:
You say, when with those Lords you dine,
They treat you with the best of wine;　　　　　　　20
Burgundy, Cyprus, and Tockay,[3]
Why so can we, as well as they.
No reason, then, my dear Dean,
But you should travel home again.
What tho' you mayn't in Ireland hope,
To find such folk as Gay and Pope:
If you with rhymers here would share,
But half the wit, that you can spare;
I'd lay twelve eggs, that in twelve days,
You'd make a doz'n of Popes and Gays.　　　　　　30

---

1. Faustina Bordoni, a famous Italian singer who took London by storm in 1726.
2. The Irish name *Síle*, anglicised as Sheela or Sheila, was often taken as a generic name for an Irishwoman.
3. A sweet Hungarian wine.

Our weather's good, our sky is clear,
We've ev'ry joy, if you were here;
So lofty, and so bright a skie,
Was never seen by *Ireland's–Eye*![4]
I think it fit to let you know,
This week I shall to Quilca[5] go;
To see McFayden's horny brothers,[6]
First suck, and after bull their mothers.
To see alas, my wither'd trees!
To see what all the country sees!   40
My stunted quicks,[7] my famish'd beeves,[8]
My servants such a pack of thieves;
My shatter'd firs, my blasted oaks,
My house in common to all folks:
No cabbage for a single snail,
My turnips, carrots, parsnips, fail;
My no green pease, my few green sprouts,
My mother always in the pouts:
My horses rid, or gone astray,
My fish all stol'n, or run away: 50
My mutton lean, my pullets old,
My poultry starv'd, the corn all sold.

A man come now from Quilca says,
'*They've* stolen the locks from all your keys:'[9]
But what must fret and vex me more,
He says, 'They stole the keys before.
They've stol'n the knives from all the forks,
And half the cows from half the sturks;'[10]
Nay more, the fellow swears and vows,
'They've stol'n the sturks from half the cows'.   60

---

4. A joke. Ireland's Eye is the name of an island in the Irish Sea just north of Dublin.
5. Sheridan's small house in County Cavan.
6. Obviously the reference is to young bullocks; but MacFadden was the maiden name of Sheridan's wife.
7. quick = quicksets, young hawthorn trees planted to form a hedge.
8. bullocks.
9. George Faulkner added the following note in the first printed edition of this poem: '*They* is the grand thief of the county of Cavan; for whatever is stolen, if you enquire of a servant about it, the answer is, *They* have stolen it.'
10. young bullocks or heifers.

With many more accounts of woe,
Yet tho' the devil be there, I'll go:
'Twixt you and me, the reason's clear,
Because, I've more vexation here.[11]

A True and Faithful Inventory

of the Goods Belonging to Dr. Swift, Vicar of Laracor;
upon Lending His House to the Bishop of Meath, Until His Own Was Built[1]

An Oaken, broken Elbow-chair;
A Cawdle-Cup,[2] without an Ear;
A batter'd, shatter'd Ash Bedstead;
A Box of Deal, without a Lid;
A Pair of Tongs, but out of Joint;
A Back-Sword Poker,[3] without Point;
A Pot that's crack'd across, around,
With an old knotted Garter bound;
An Iron Lock, without a Key;
A Wig, with hanging, quite grown grey;   10
A Curtain worn to Half a Stripe;
A Pair of Bellows, without Pipe;
A Dish, which might good Meat afford once;
An *Ovid*, and an old *Concordance*;
A Bottle Bottom, Wooden Platter,
One is for Meal, and one for Water;
There likewise is a Copper Skillet,
Which runs as fast out as you fill it;
A Candlestick, Snuff dish, and Save-all,[4]
And thus his Household Goods you have all.   20
These, to your Lordship, as a Friend,
Till you have built, I freely lend:
They'll save your Lordship for a Shift;[5]
Why not, as well as Doctor Swift?

---

11. Perhaps because Sheridan's wife (with whom he had a stormy relationship) was in Dublin.

---

1. The Bishop of Meath was Henry Downes. Swift's house at Laracor was in County Meath near Trim, the bishop's seat. This poem was said to have been written by Sheridan as a counter to a similar unflattering list of the contents of Sheridan's house at Quilca which Swift wrote in 1724, but the case is not proven.

2. Caudle is a drink made with warm beer or wine, eggs, sugar and spices. It is drunk out of a two-handled cup with a narrow neck.

3. A poker made out of a back-sword, one which has only one cutting edge.

4. A device to hold a candle firmly so that it will burn to the very end.

5. i.e. this will do for your lordship as an expedient for the moment.

JONATHAN SWIFT

Mary the Cook-Maid's Letter to Dr Sheridan[1]

Well; if ever I saw such another Man since my Mother bound my
    Head,[2]
You a Gentleman! marry come up, I wonder where you were bred?
I am sure such Words does not become a Man of your Cloth,
I would not give such Language to a Dog, faith and troth.
Yes; you call'd my Master a Knave: Fie, Mr *Sheridan*, 'tis a Shame
For a Parson, who shou'd know better Things, to come out with
    such a Name.
Knave in your Teeth,[3] Mr. *Sheridan*, 'tis both a Shame and a Sin,
And the Dean, my Master, is an honester Man than you and all
    your Kin:
He has more Goodness in his little Finger, than you have in your
    whole Body,
My Master is a parsonable Man, and not a spindle-shank'd Hoddy
    doddy.[4]   10
And now whereby I find you would fain make an Excuse,
Because my Master one Day, in Anger, call'd you Goose.
Which, and I am sure I have been his Servant four Years since
    October,
And he never call'd me worse than *Sweet-heart*[5] drunk or sober:
Not that I know his Reverence was ever concern'd to my
    Knowledge,
Tho' you and your Come-rogues[6] keep him out so late in your
    wicked College.

---

1. In one of his many lighthearted poems sent to Swift, Sheridan had referred to him as a
goose. Swift here imagines the response of Mary, his cook (or 'cook-maid'), to her
master's being addressed in this way. Robert Hogan has examined the text in which
Sheridan called Swift a goose and noted that what was previously printed as one poem
is really three separate pieces. See *The Poems of Thomas Sheridan* ed. Robert Hogan
(Newark, 1994), pp. 77, 78, 84-5 and 279-80.
2. i.e. since I was born. The heads and bodies of new-born infants were often bound in long
bandages or swaddling clothes.
3. A defiant expression.
4. Physically, Sheridan was remarkably small, thin and bony.
5. Swift called his cook 'sweetheart'.
6. A Malapropism for 'comrades'.

You say you will eat Grass on his Grave:[7] a Christian eat Grass!
Whereby you now confess your self to be a Goose or an Ass:
But that's as much as to say, my Master should die before ye,
Well, well, that's as God pleases, and I don't believe that's a true
    Story,   20
And so say I told you so, and you may go tell my Master; what
    care I?
And I don't care who knows it, 'tis all one to *Mary*.
Every Body knows, that I love to tell Truth, and shame the Devil,
I am but a poor Servant, but I think gentle-Folks should be civil.
Besides, you found Fault with our Vittels[8] one Day that you was
    here,
I remember it was upon a *Tuesday*, of all Days in the Year.
And *Saunders* the Man[9] says, you are always jesting and mocking,
Mary, said he, (one Day, as I was mending my Master's Stocking,)
My Master is so fond of that Minister that keeps the School;[10]
I thought my Master a wise Man, but that Man makes him a Fool.   30
Saunders, said I, I would rather than a Quart of Ale,
He would come into our Kitchin, and I would pin a Dish-clout[11] to
    his Tail.
And now I must go, and get *Saunders* to direct this Letter,
For I write but a sad Scrawl, but my Sister *Marget* she writes
    better.
Well, but I must run and make the Bed before my Master comes
    from Pray'rs,
And see now, it strikes Ten, and I hear him coming up Stairs:
Whereof I cou'd say more to your Verses, if I could write written
    Hand,[12]
And so I remain in a civil Way, your Servant to command

                                              Mary

---

7. A quotation from the 'offending' poem: 'Though you call me a goose, you pitiful slave,// I'll feed on the grass that grows on your grave.'
8. victuals, food.
9. Swift's manservant.
10. i.e. Sheridan.
11. dishcloth.
12. i.e. with joined letters.

A Pastoral Dialogue

At Sir Arthur Acheson's house in the North of Ireland, Sept. 20, 1729[1]

A Nymph and Swain, *Sheelah* and *Dermot* hight,[2]
Who *wont* to weed the Court of *Gosford Knight*,[3]
While each with stubbed Knife remov'd the Roots
That rais'd between the Stones their daily Shoots;
As at their Work they sat in counterview,
With mutual Beauty smit, their Passion grew.
Sing heavenly Muse in sweetly flowing Strain,
The soft Endearments of the Nymph and Swain.

Dermot   My Love to *Sheelah* is more firmly fixt
            Than strongest Weeds that grow these Stones betwixt: 10
            My Spud[4] these Nettles from the Stones can part,
            No Knife so keen to weed thee from my Heart.

Sheelah   My Love for gentle Dermot faster grows
            Than yon tall Dock[5] that rises to thy Nose.
            Cut down the Dock, 'twill sprout again: but O!
            Love rooted out, again will never grow.

Dermot   No more that Bry'r thy tender Leg shall rake:
            (I spare the Thistle for Sir *Arthur*'s sake.)[6]
            Sharp are the Stones, take thou this rushy Mat;
            The hardest Bum will bruise with sitting squat.   20

Sheelah   Thy Breeches torn behind, stand gaping wide;
            This Petticoat shall save thy dear Back-side;
            Nor need I blush, although you feel it wet;
            Dermot, I vow, 'tis nothing else but Sweat.

---

1. Swift often visited Sir Arthur and Lady Acheson at Market Hill in County Armagh and many of his poems mention them or the way of life in the Irish countryside he observed around their estate. This poem is in the long line of mock-pastoral dialogues in English and Anglo-Irish verse.
2. i.e. called, a conscious and comic archaism, though Swift does not sustain the mock-medieval mood. wont = were accustomed to.
3. i.e. the courtyard of the Achesons, whose family name was Gosford.
4. weeding knife.
5. A large, coarse weed, common in Ireland.
6. A note in early editions points out that Sir Arthur was a great lover of Scotland — the national emblem of which is the thistle.

Dermot	At an old stubborn Root I chanc'd to tug,
	When the Dean threw me this Tobacco plug:[7]
	A longer Half-p'orth[8] never did I see;
	This, dearest *Sheelah*, thou shalt share with me.

Sheelah	In at the Pantry-door this Morn' I slipt,
	And from the Shelf a charming Crust I whipt: 30
	Dennis[9] was out, and I got hither safe;
	And thou, my Dear, shalt have the bigger Half.

Dermot	When you saw *Tady* at Long-bullets play,[10]
	You sat and lous'd him all the Sun-shine Day.
	How could you, *Sheelah,* listen to his Tales,
	Or crack such Lice as his betwixt your Nails?

Sheelah	When you with *Oonah* stood behind a Ditch,
	I peept, and saw you kiss the dirty Bitch,
	Dermot, how could you touch those nasty Sluts!
	I almost wisht this Spud were in your Guts, 40

Dermot	If Oonah once I kiss'd, forbear to chide:
	Her Aunt's my Gossip[11] by my Father's Side:
	But, if I ever touch her Lips again,
	May I be doom'd for Life to weed in Rain.

Sheelah	*Dermot*, I swear, tho' *Tady*'s Locks could hold
	Ten Thousand Lice, and ev'ry Louse was Gold,
	Him on my Lap you never more should see;
	Or may I lose my Weeding-knife — and Thee.

Dermot	O, could I earn for thee, my lovely Lass,
	A pair of Brogues[12] to bear thee dry to Mass! 50
	But see, where *Norah* with the Sowins[13] comes —
	Then let us rise, and rest our weary Bums.

---

7. A piece of cake or twist tobacco cut off for chewing.
8. i.e. what could be bought for a halfpenny.
9. Sir Arthur Acheson's butler.
10. Tady = Thady, an anglicisation of the Irish name *Tadhg*; long bullets = bowling (as still practised on the roads of counties Cork and Armagh).
11. A baptismal sponsor.
12. shoes. Ir. *bróg*. See Glossary.
13. A sort of flummery or gruel, often eaten on All Hallows Eve. cf. Ir. *samhain*.

MARY BARBER
(c.1685-**1728**-1755)

Mary Barber, who was born in Dublin, married an Englishman who had set up as a woollen draper in the city. Swift thought highly of her work, and her volume *Poems on Several Occasions* (1734) is prefaced by a commendatory letter from him. In fact, Swift advised and assisted Mary Barber over many years and arranged for his *Polite Conversation* to be printed in London for her benefit in 1737. As a poet, Mary Barber was not afraid to attack hypocrisy and injustice with a strong and individual voice, and she has been hailed by some modern critics as one of Ireland's earliest feminists.

An Unanswerable Apology for the Rich

'All bounteous Heav'n,' *Castalio*[1] cries,
With bended Knees, and lifted Eyes,
'When shall I have the Pow'r to bless,
And raise up Merit in Distress?'

How do our Hearts deceive us here!
He gets Ten Thousand Pounds a Year.
With this the pious Youth is able,
To build, and plant, and keep a Table.
But then, the Poor he must not treat;
Who asks the Wretch, that wants, to eat?   10
Alas! to ease their Woes he wishes,
But cannot live without *Ten* Dishes.
Tho' *Six* would serve as well, 'tis true;
But one must live, as others do.
He now feels Wants, unknown before,
Wants still encreasing with his Store.
The good *Castalio* must provide
Brocade, and Jewels, for his Bride.
Her Toilet shines with Plate[2] emboss'd,
What Sums her Lace, and Linen cost!   20
The Cloaths, that must his Person grace,
Shine with Embroidery and Lace.
The costly Pride of *Persian* Looms,
And *Guido*'s Paintings,[3] grace his Rooms.

---

1. A generalised name for a rich young man.
2. toilet = dressing-table; plate embossed = silver-plate engraved with a monogram.
3. i.e. paintings by Guido Reni of Bologna (1575-1642).

His wealth *Castalio* will not waste,
But must have every thing in *Taste*.
He's an Œconomist confest,
But what he buys must be the best.
For common Use, a Set of Plate;
Old China, when he dines in State.   30
A Coach and Six, to take the Air,
Besides a Chariot, and a Chair.[4]
All these important Calls supply'd,
Calls of Necessity, not Pride,
His Income's regularly spent;
He scarcely saves, to pay his Rent.
No Man alive wou'd do more Good,
Or give more freely, if he cou'd.
He grieves, whene'er the Wretched sue,
But what can poor *Castalio* do?   40

Wou'd Heav'n but send Ten Thousand more,
He'd give — just as he did before.

To Mrs Frances-Arabella Kelly[1]

Today, as at my Glass I stood,
To set my Head-cloths, and my Hood,
I saw my grizzled Locks with Dread,
And call'd to mind the *Gorgon*'s Head.[2]

Thought I, whate'er the Poets say,
Medusa's Hair was only gray:
Tho' *Ovid*, who the Story told,
Was too well-bred to call her old;
But, what amounted to the same,
He made her an immortal Dame.   10

---

4. chariot = a fast, four-wheeled horse-drawn vehicle; chair = a private sedan chair.

1. The beautiful and clever daughter of a rakish Jacobite, Frances Arabella Kelly got to know Swift, Patrick Delany, Mary Barber, Constantia Grierson and other members of their circle at about the beginning of 1733. Mrs Delany reported that 'Miss Kelly's beauty and good-humour have gained an entire conquest over him (i.e. Swift)'. (*The Autobiography and Correspondence of Mary Granville, Mrs Delany* ... ed. Lady Llanover, 6 vols. (London, 1861-62), I, 396).

2. The Gorgons were three hideous sisters of classical mythology. They were immortal and had serpents on their heads instead of hair. The sight of the severed head of one of the Gorgons, Medusa, was enough to turn anyone to stone. See Ovid, *Metamorphoses,* book iv.

Yet now, whene'er a Matron sage
Hath felt the rugged Hand of Age,
You hear our witty Coxcombs cry,
'Rot that old Witch — she'll never die!'
Tho', had they but a little Reading,
Ovid would teach them better Breeding.

I fancy now, I hear you say,
'Grant Heav'n, my Locks may ne'er be gray!
Why am I told this frightful Story?
To Beauty a *Memento Mori*?'[3]   20

And, as along the Room you pass,
Casting your Eye upon the Glass,
'Surely,' say you, 'this lovely Face
Will never suffer such Disgrace:
The Bloom that on my Cheek appears
Will never be impair'd by Years.
Her Envy, now, I plainly see
Makes her inscribe those Lines to me.
These Beldams,[4] who were born before me,
Are griev'd to see the Men adore me: 30
Their snaky Locks freeze up the Blood;
My tresses fire the purple Flood.

Unnumber'd Slaves around me wait,
And from my Eyes expect their Fate.
I own, of Conquest I am vain,
Tho' I despise the Slaves I gain.
Heav'n gave me Charms, and destin'd me
For universal Tyranny.'

The Recantation: to the same Lady

Forgive me, fair One, nor resent
The Lines to you I lately sent.
They seem, as if your Form you priz'd,
And ev'ry other Gift despis'd:
When a discerning Eye may find,
Your greatest Beauty's in your Mind.

3. A reminder of death.
4. ugly old women or hags.

MATTHEW PILKINGTON
(1701-**1731**-1774)

Matthew Pilkington was the son of a machine-maker from Ballyboy, Co. Offaly. He was educated at Trinity College, Dublin and ordained into the Church of Ireland. In 1725, he married Laetitia Van Lewen, daughter of a male midwife of Dutch origin who had settled in Dublin. Soon after their marriage, the Pilkingtons became favourites of Swift. Later, after they had separated, Swift disowned the couple, accusing them of dishonesty. Pilkington was a noted classical scholar and, in addition to two volumes of poetry, wrote the *Gentleman's and Connoisseur's Dictionary of Painters* (London, 1774). See *Memoirs of Laetitia Pilkington* ed. A. C. Elias Jr. (Athens, Georgia, 1997), pp. 832-34.

The Invitation:
To Doctor Delany at Delville, MDCCXXIX[1]

Excepto quod non simul esses, cætera lætus.[2]

While you, dear *Friend*, exempt from Care,
Delight to breathe the rural Air,
Where *Nature* pours her best Perfumes
From fragrant Flow'rs and op'ning Blooms,
While you, with Gardens, Groves and Plains,
And various Eye-bewitching Scenes,
Contrive politely how to please,
And charm the Soul a thousand Ways,
I wish, — nor let my Wish be vain, —
To tempt you back to Town again.   10

'Twere Condescension great in thee
To quit such Joys to pleasure me,
For here no stately Dome have I,
No Scenes to charm the roving Eye,
No Gardens fair, no Fields to roam,
Nor half the sweets you find at Home:
Yet if gay *Ovid* sings aright,
The Gods themselves wou'd oft delight,

---

1. Patrick Delany, a prominent member of Swift's circle who was famous for living beyond his means, had spent large sums of money on improving his house and garden at Delville, just north of Dublin. In this invitation full of exaggerated flattery, Pilkington compares his own house unfavourably with Delany's small estate. See also p. 164 above.

2. Horace, *Epistles* i, x, 50. 'Happy in other respects, except that you are not with me.'

Ev'n *Hermes* and *Apollo* too,[3]
(Both rival'd in their Arts by you,   20
Whether in Lays sublime you shine,
Or act the Orator Divine:)
These Gods, I say, wou'd now and then
Descend, to visit humble Men.

Oft it is pleasing in the *Great*
To live forgetful of their State,
To leave Abundance, and unbend
Their Minds to some inferior Friend,
Where blest with Health, and homely Fare,
They quaff Delight, and smile at Care,   30
And find that in an humble Cell
Mirth, Innocence, and Peace can dwell.

Oft in a *Toyshop* have you seen
A gawdy-painted, small Machine,
Where Man and Wife are plac'd together,
To tell by turns the Change of Weather;
No *Simile* could half so well
Describe the House in which I dwell.

O! would some *Zephyr*[4] waft, with Care,
My House and Garden thro' the Air,   40
To Lands encircled by the Main,
Where *Lilliputian* Monarchs[5] reign,
How wou'd it glad my Heart to see
Whole Nations — somewhat less than me?
My House wou'd then a Palace rise,
And *Kings* with Envy view my Size.

O thou, by every *Muse* inspir'd,
By ev'ry gen'rous Soul admir'd,
A while forsake the sylvan Scene,
And with the *Graces*[6] in thy Train,   50

---

3. Hermes was the Greek name for the god Mercury (the messenger of the gods) and Apollo was god of all the fine arts, including poetry. Various stories about both gods appear in Ovid's *Metamorphoses*.
4. The west wind.
5. i.e. very small monarchs (so called after the minute Lilliputians in Swift's *Gulliver's Travels*).
6. The *Gratiæ* or the three graces represented kindness and benevolence among friends.

Descend to make my Joys compleat,
And with thy Presence bless my Seat:
For thy enliv'ning Converse lends
Abundant Rapture to thy Friends,
Thy Words, express'd with graceful Art,
Improve the Head, and mend the Heart.

The more we know thee, still we find
Some new Perfection in thy Mind,
A rich, inestimable Store
Of Virtues, unperceiv'd before.   60

Thus o'er the Vault of Heav'n by Night,
We see a thousand *Orbs* of Light,
But when with nicer View we trace
That bright, interminable Space,
New Worlds of Glory there we spy,
That 'scap'd at first the wond'ring Eye.

Anacreon Paraphras'd, Ode viii[1]

'Twas when the mirth-exciting Bowl
Had sooth'd my Cares, and rais'd my Soul,
That I on purple Carpets spread
My Limbs at Ease, and lean'd my Head,
Till *Sleep*, that soft-wing'd Child of Night,
With Shades enveil'd my swimming Sight.

Then seem'd I swift in am'rous Play,
To run with Virgins, fair as Day,
While Youths, more delicately fram'd
Than that soft God *Lyæus*[2] named,   10
Reproach'd my too advent'rous Age,
That dare such Bloom and Youth engage,
For Love was a prepost'rous Crime
In one so silver'd o'er by *Time*.

---

1. The comparatively uninhibited odes of the Greek lyric poet Anacreon were frequently
   adapted or translated by Irish poets of the eighteenth century.
2. One of the names of Bacchus, the god who presided over wine.

But while, to perfect all my Bliss,
I wish'd to snatch a fragrant Kiss,
From these my Sleep-forsaken Eyes,
The *Fancy*'s fair Creation flies,
The sweet Illusions flit away,
And all the pleasing Forms decay.   20

Abandon'd, wretched, griev'd, alone,
I sigh'd, the lov'ly Phantoms flown,
I wish'd, I strove, but strove in vain,
To dream the Rapture o'er again.

LAETITIA PILKINGTON
(c.1708-**1732**-1750)

Laetitia Pilkington is best known to those interested in eighteenth-century Ireland for her highly entertaining three-volume *Memoirs of Laetitia Pilkington* ([London, 1748-54] and ed. A. C. Elias Jr. [Athens, Georgia, 1997]). In addition to its revelations about her own unconventional life, Mrs Pilkington's *Memoirs* contains what is, in effect, the first biography of Swift. Embedded in the text are many of her own poems and some by her friends; the one below was written before the acrimonious separation between Laetitia and her clergyman-poet husband, Matthew.

The Petition of the Birds
[to Mr Pilkington on his return from shooting]

Ah Shepherd, gentle Shepherd! spare
Us plum'd Inhabitants of Air
That hop, and inoffensive rove
From Tree to Tree, from Grove to Grove;
What Phrensy has possess'd your Mind,
To be destructive of your Kind?
Admire not if we Kindred Claim,
Our sep'rate Natures are the same;
To each of us thou ow'st a Part
To grace thy Person, Head, or Heart;   10
The Chaste, the fond, the tender *Dove*
Inspires thy Breast with purest Love;
The tow'ring *Eagle* claims a Part
In thy courageous, gen'rous Heart;
On thee the *Finch* bestow'd a Voice
To bid the raptur'd Soul rejoice;
The *Hawk* has giv'n thee Eyes so bright,
They kindle Love and soft Delight;
Thy snowy Hue and graceful Mien,
May in the stately *Swan* be seen;   20
The *Robin*'s Plumes afford the Red,
Which thy soft Lips and Cheeks bespread;
Thy filial Piety and Truth,
The *Stork* bestow'd to crown thy Youth.

Did we these sev'ral Gifts bestow
To give Perfection to a Foe?
Did we so many Virtues give,
To thee, too fierce to let us live?
Suspend your Rage, and every Grove,
Shall echo Songs of grateful Love.   30
Let Pity sooth and sway your Mind,
And be the Phœnix of Mankind.

CONSTANTIA GRIERSON
(c.1705-**1732**-1732)

Constantia Grierson is probably best known as a classical scholar and as editor, or perhaps more accurately as proof-corrector, of the many fine editions of classical texts published in Dublin by her husband, the printer George Grierson. Little is known of Constantia's life, and how she acquired her classical learning remains something of a mystery.[1] She was a valued member of Swift's circle and very friendly with Mary Barber. Some poems bearing her name appeared in Mary Barber's *Poems on Several Occasions* and in Laetitia Pilkington's *Memoirs*. Others remain unpublished.

To Miss *Laetitia Van Lewen*[2]

The fleeting Birds may soon in Ocean swim,
And *Northern* Whales thro' liquid Azure skim,
The *Dublin* Ladies their Intrigues forsake,
To Dress and Scandal an Aversion take;[3]
When you can in the lonely Forrest walk,
And with some serious Matron gravely talk
Of Possets, Poultices, and Waters still'd,[4]
And monstrous Casks with Mead and Cider fill'd;
How many Hives of Bees she has in Store,
And how much Fruit her Trees this *Summer* bore;　　　　　10
Or Home returning in the Yard can stand,
And feed the Chickens from your bounteous Hand:
Of each one's Top-knot tell, and hatching pry,
Like *Tully* waiting for an Augury.[5]

---

1. See A.C. Elias Jr., 'A Manuscript Book of Constantia Grierson's', *Swift Studies* II (1987), 33-56.
2. i.e. Laetitia Pilkington. In early editions, this poem was sometimes printed with the explanatory title 'To Miss *Laetitia Van Lewen* in a Country-Town at the time of the Assizes'.
3. i.e. birds will swim, whales will fly and Dublin ladies will forsake intrigues and take an aversion to clothes and scandal, if you continue in the country.
4. The vocabulary used in this passage — matron, possets, poultices — and the activities described — home distilling and brewing, farming and bee-keeping — are deliberately rural, contrasting vividly with life in metropolitan Dublin. A 'posset' is a hot milk drink.
5. i.e. treating the behaviour of each chicken as seriously as did Roman augurs, who sought to ascertain whether the gods were favourable to an undertaking by interpreting the behaviour of birds, especially chickens. Marcus Tullius Cicero ('Tully') wrote a famous treatise on divination and auguries.

When Night appoaches, down to Table sit
With a great Crowd, choice Meat, and little Wit;
What Horse won the last Race, how mighty *Tray*,[6]
At the last famous hunting, caught the Prey;
Surely, you can't but such Discourse despise,
Methinks, I see Displeasure in your Eyes: 20
O my *Lætitia*, stay no longer there,
You'll soon forget, that you yourself are fair;
Why will you keep from us, from all that's gay,
There in a lonely Solitude to stay?
Where not a Mortal thro' the Year you view,
But Bob-wigg'd Hunters,[7] who their Game pursue
With so much Ardor, they'd a Cock or Hare,
To thee, in all thy blooming Charms, prefer.

You write of Belles and Beau's that there appear,
And gilded Coaches, such as glitter here;   30
For gilded Coaches, each estated Clown
That gravely slumbers on the Bench[8] has one;
But Beaux! they're young Attorneys! sure you Mean!
Who thus appear to your romantick Brain.
Alas! no Mortal there can talk to you,
That Love or Wit, or Softness ever knew:
All they can speak of's *Capias*'s[9] and Law,
And Writs to keep the Country Fools in Awe.
And, if to Wit, or Courtship they pretend,
'Tis the same Way that they a Cause defend;   40
In which they give of Lungs a vast Expence,
But little Passion, Thought or Eloquence:
Bad as they are, they'll soon abandon you,
And Gain, and Clamour, in the Town pursue.
So haste to Town, if ev'n such Fools you prize;
O haste to Town! and bless the longing Eyes
         Of *your* Constantia.

---

6. The name of a hound.
7. i.e. huntsmen who wear old-fashioned wigs.
8. i.e. each stupid landlord who sleeps while acting as a magistrate.
9. Legal writs ordering an arrest (Latin: *capias*, take).

from: Lines to an unnamed Lady[1]

To you, Illustrious Fair, I tune my song;
To you alone, of right, my lays belong;
Attend and Patronise a work design'd
To free you from the Oppression of mankind.
And ye harmonious Nine, whose heavenly Fire
Does Mortal breasts with Godlike thoughts inspire,
To whom are Learning, Wit and Arts assign'd
To show th'extensive pow'rs of woman's Mind,
By your enliv'ning force assist my Lays;
Who praises Women does the Muses praise.   10

Could Sense refin'd and wit indeed bestow
Nought but precarious blessings here below,
If Mortals who attend the Muses seat
Were only by them render'd rich and great,
Men to themselves their learning might confine,
And Women with them need not wish to shine.
But Heav'n-sprung knowledge — say, celestial Guest,
Thou Grace, thou glory of the human breast![2]
Do brightest Minds consume their youthfull Days
In Homer's, Maro's, or in Flaccus' Lays?[3]   20
Do they in ancient Authors Strive to view
Whatever Romans did or Grecians knew,
Do they thro' nature cast their piercing Ey
And all her motions, laws and works descry
At the litigious bar at last to get
A Guilty Conscience and a vast Estate,
To tend the Sick man's mournfull couch, and gain
Prodigious Wealth by adding to his Pain? ...

---

1. The lady to whom this fragment is addressed is possibly Frances-Arabella Kelly (see
   above p. 195). The text is taken from Constantia Grierson's commonplace book. The poem
   is untitled in the manuscript, but the title above has been supplied for this, its first printing.
   For details of the manuscript, see Elias 'A Manuscript Book of Constantia Grierson's'.
2. The sentence is unfinished. The meaning is clearly that heaven-sprung knowledge is not
   confined to men. On the contrary, it is a celestial guest which is the glory of every human
   breast. Men, despite their education, end up being litigious oppressors with guilty
   consciences. Presumably if Mrs Grierson had finished the poem, she would have added
   lines praising the intellectual powers of the unknown lady, to whom she gave the name
   Astal, and contrasting her also with the vain, society women described in the last four
   lines of the fragment.
3. The authors listed are Homer, Virgil and Horace.

... Shall every fair who trifles time away,
Uselessly Good, impertinently Gay, 30
Whose life's to game, to sleep, to dress, to dine,
With Astal's Soul in equal Glory shine?

WILLIAM DUNKIN
(c.1709-**1734**-1765)

William Dunkin was born in Dublin in 1709. His parents died young and he was educated at Trinity College, Dublin, where he was a member of a group of lively young scholars who entertained each other, and those who frequented the Dublin coffee-houses, by publishing scurrilous verse satires. He joined the circle around Swift, and was described by the Dean as 'a Gentleman of much Wit, and the best English as well as Latin poet in this Kingdom' (*The Correspondence of Jonathan Swift*, ed. Harold Williams, 5 vols., second ed. (Oxford, 1965), V, 86). Dunkin's English verse is certainly ebullient, original and witty and he regularly exploited his classical learning by, for example, translating his own English poems into Latin and Greek and then back into English. He became headmaster of Portora Royal School, Enniskillen in 1746.

The first extract from Dunkin's work is from 'The Parson's Revels', a three-canto poem which describes, often in uninhibited Hiberno-English, an extended, riotous party given by an Irish country squire and attended by the local parson. In the tradition of the Martinus Scriblerus preface to Pope's *Dunciad,* the poem is preceded by a thirty-page 'Fragment of Perpetual Notes, Illustrations, and various Readings, taken from the best Critics, Commentators, and Grammarians, and collated with the most authentic Manuscripts'. Many (spurious) sources are quoted, in English, Greek, Latin and Irish, and there are parodies of Dryden, Milton, Pope and Virgil, and disparaging mentions of many 'modern' poets. Like most of Dunkin's work — and some of that of Swift and Sterne — the joke lies in the juxtaposition of musty learning and bawdry. The passage which follows comes from the second canto where Father Fegan or Fagan, the local catholic priest, joins the party.

from: The Parson's Revels

from: Canto II

... But enters now the Parish Priest,
Who was by Patrick[1] and by Chreest,
As great a wolf, as ever fleec'd
               The laity.

Although but little known to fame,
By birth and breeding he would claim
Profound respect; for why? his name
               Was Fegan:

---

1. St Patrick.

He swore, he travell'd many a league
To Paris, Antwerp, and the Hague,   10
And was descended from Sir Teague
         O Regan:[2]

His body-coat was fac'd with fat,
His head as grey, as any cat,
And belly big, to cupboard what
         He gathers.

His wit and humour much he smothers,
But numerates his learned brothers,
And quotes his venerable mothers,
         The fathers.[3]   20

Quoth he, 'I am vwell boarn and brid,[4]
Shur Teague O Regan vwash my hid,
Aldough, deer joay, I nivir rid
         Your Nhomars;

Yit Fegan can confabulaat
In Frinch and Laatin, dher mey faat,
And hild a Teshis at dhe graat
         Shaint Omars.

Yit, bey dhe bilt, fhwich Franshis vwoar,
Dhe crass ov Creest, fhwich Paatrick boar,   30
Dhe Baads ov Bridgit, and fwhat's moar
         Mey Vistimints,

2. A reference to this line in the prefatory material notes that Sir Teague O Regan was 'an Irish gentleman of remarkable courage and conduct, allowed to be one of the best officers in King James's army' and quotes his long Latin epitaph which is then translated into disrespectful English. The character is, however, an invented one. For 'Teague', see Glossary.

3. An Irish 'bull'. In the prefatory notes, these lines are said to have been 'plucked' from the verses of Moronides. The theft is described as 'a pleasurable felony'.

4. Father Fagan's speech is roughly equivalent to the following: 'I am well born and bred; Sir Teague O'Regan was my ancestor, although, dear joy [a typical Irish exclamation, meaning roughly 'my friend'; but see Glossary], I never read Homer; Yet Fagan can converse in French and Latin; they're my fate; and I defended a thesis at the great St Omers. [There was a famous Jesuit college at St Omer is northern France.] Yet by the belt which St Francis [of Assisi] wore, and by the cross of Christ which St Patrick bore, by the beads of St Brigid [abbess of Kildare in the fifth century] and, what's more, by my vestments, I really love your clergymen, who bow [at the name of] Jesus in the creed, although they let their laymen read the scriptures. God bless King George [i.e. George II] and his Lutherans, but curses on the presbyterians: those knaves are ugly Nolliverians [unexplained: perhaps linked with the name Oliver Cromwell], and like apes.'

I louv your clargymin indeed,
Fwho bovw to Jeshuz in dhe creed,
Aldough dhey lit dheir laamin reed
      Dhe Tistimints.

Gaad blish king Gaarge and hish Lutterians,
But cursh upon dhe Proshpiterians,
Dhe knaaves are oogly Nolliverians,
      And apish ——'   40

But Denison[5] began to chase here:
'A Turk, or Pagan must be safer
Than thee with all thy Gods of wafer,
      Vile Papish![6]

Thy brethren, void of faith, and hope,
And charity, deserve the rope;
Old Antichrist is but the Pope
      In scarlet:[7]

The rock,[8] which you would rest upon,
As I shall fairly prove anon,   50
Is but the spawn of Babylon,
      A harlot,[9]

Who curses with her blessings mixes,
Trick'd up with painted babies, pyxies,[10]
Indulgencies, and crucifixes,
      Her trapping.[11]

---

5. A presbyterian who is present at the feast.
6. papist. The reference in the previous line is to transubstantiation.
7. i.e. the Pope, dressed in his scarlet robes, is nothing but the devil.
8. i.e. the catholic church, the 'rock' of St Peter.
9. Protestants often described the catholic church as 'the whore of Babylon', using the name of the Mesopotamian city (which occurs in the Old Testament) to symbolise corruption.
10. A pyx is the box, cabinet or vessel in which the consecrated host is reserved in a catholic church.
11. This stanza lists some of the 'trappings' involved in catholic worship and ritual which offended presbyterians — angels in paintings and statues, containers in which the consecrated Host is kept, documents issued by the church which gave remission for sins, and images of the cross on which Christ was crucified.

A church, upheld by lying rumours,
Long bloated with unhealthy tumours,
And ripe (if you would purge her humours)
                    For tapping'[12]   60

He said, and in his fury collar'd
The Priest, who cry'd, 'I am a scollard,[13]
Na Manichæan, Arian, Lollard,[14]
                    Or Pagan.

Compeshe linquam, deshine[15]
Stultishiam, et probabo te
Shin — cate — gore — mati — she
                    A Dagon.

Shed, shee jam mavish dishputare
Pugnish, quam lagishe pugnare,   70
Tantundem dat, præsheptor chare,
                    Tanteedhem.

Etiam-shee veenee bibish undham,
Immundhum spiritum confundham,
Et shatanhem ex te contundham
                    Par feedhem.'

Thus Fegan, fraught with Latin, huffs,
And Presbyter as proudly puffs,
Preparing for conclusive cuffs
                    Their thumpers.[16]   80

---

12. i.e. bleeding or draining blood from patients in whom an excess of blood was thought to be causing illness.
13. scholar.
14. The names of three so-called heretical sects. Na = not.
15. Though both its vocabulary and its syntax are eccentric, Father Fagan's speech is roughly equivalent to the following: 'Check your tongue! Cease your folly, and I shall prove you consignificantly to be a dago! But if you prefer to dispute with fists rather than to fight with logic, he gives, dear instructor, tit for tat. Even if you drink an ocean of wine, I shall throw your filthy spirit into confusion, and I shall beat the devil out of you, on my oath!' **Notes:** The word *sincategorematice* is a genuine, if not a classical, word. In English, 'consignificantly' is a term used in theology meaning that two propositions are both significant. 'Dago' is a term which, though originally connected with the Spanish *Diego* = James, was used, in the eighteenth century, to refer to anyone of the Latin races.
16. fists.

But B—,[17] with pacific grace
Uprising, splits the doubtful case,
And reconciles them with a brace
        Of bumpers[18]....

... Leave wrangling to the bar and bench;[19]
With wine your melancholy drench:
Here's to the Spaniards, and the French
        A drubbing.[20]

At flowing bumpers who can carp,
Or in his jovial humour warp?[21]   90
Then fill your glasses: — tune your harp,
        O Murphy.

This Murphy, strolling up and down,
Had been a harper of renown,
And Bard as eloquent, as Crown,
        Or Durfy.[22]

About O Neal he kept a pother,[23]
For why? he was his foster-brother,[24]
Begotten on a base-born mother
        A spinster;   100

But, though reduc'd to live by strings,
Greater than great O Neal[25] he brings
His father's blood from antient kings
        Of Leinster.

---

17. The good-natured landlord.
18. large glasses of liquor or beer.
19. i.e. to lawyers.
20. i.e. here's to the defeat of the Spaniards and the French (traditional enemies of the English — though not of the native Irish).
21. go astray.
22. John Crowne (c. 1640-c. 1703) and Thomas D'Urfey (1653-1723), English playwrights and poets.
23. i.e. he kept making a fuss about one of the leaders of the O'Neill clan (of Ulster).
24. The medieval Gaelic custom of fosterage, by which strong bonds of loyalty were forged between fostered children and the fostering family, was mistrusted by the English colonisers of Ireland who recognised in it one of the main strengths of Gaelic society. Fosterage between Irish and Anglo-Irish families was forbidden. The custom continued into the seventeenth century, however.
25. Hugh O'Neill (1550-1616), Earl of Tyrone, famous for his opposition to various British incursions into Ireland in the late sixteenth century.

As ladies fair, of taste refin'd,
Their petted linnets often blind
To make them sing the sweeter, kind-
                            ly cruel:

To strike his mind with visions bright,
And give his hearers more delight,   110
Melpomene[26] depriv'd of sight
                            This jewel.

Quoth Oaf,[27] 'I hate him, and his kin,
To hear his music is a sin:
For bringing such a rebel in
                            Small thanks t'ye.

His harp is hollow; so is he;
Both make one popish jubilee:
What can he play, but Garran-buoy,[28]
                            Or Planksty?'[29]   120

At this O Murphy, like a nag
Spurr'd to his mettle, would not lag:
Quoth he, 'I am na ribil rag-
                            A-muffin,[30]

But ov dhe reight Hibarnian seed,
Aldough mey fadhir cud nat reed,
Nat lek yur black fanaatic breed,[31]
                            You puffin....'

His voice was brazen, deep, and such,
As well accorded with High-dutch,   130
Or Attic Irish,[32] and his touch
                            Was pliant:

26. Melpomene was the Greek muse associated with tragedy.
27. A presbyterian guest at the feast.
28. Ir. *Gearrán Buí*, 'yellow pony', a dance tune.
29. Ir. *Plancstaí*, a generic term for lively dance music performed on the harp.
30. malignant.
31. A rough equivalent of this speech is as follows: I'm no ribald ragamuffin, but of the true Irish race, although my father could not read — not like you 'black' fanatical lot [protestants] — you idiot!'
32. High Dutch: German; Attic Irish: common (spoken) Irish (as the commonest Greek was that of Attica).

Dubourgh[33] to him was but a fool;
He play'd melodious without rule,[34]
And sung the feats of Fin Macool,[35]
          The giant.

He sounds in more majestic strains,
How brave Milesians[36] with their skanes[37]
Had butcher'd all the bloody Danes
          Like weathers.[38]   140

While Bryan Borough[39] with a yell
Flat on the bed of honour fell,
When he might sleep at home as well
          On feathers:

He celebrates with lofty tone
Tyrconnel, Desmond, and Tyrone,[40]
Renown'd O Neal, who shook the throne
          Of Britain;

O Donnel, fam'd for whisky rare,
And then, O Rowrk,[41] thy noble fare   150
Of sheep and oxen, with no chair
          To sit on....

At last, though much against his heart,
His tongue and fingers act their part,
Displaying with Orphean art,[42]
          And cunning,

33. Matthew Dubourg (1703-67), 'Master of the State Musick' in Ireland in the 1730s.
34. i.e. he played his melodies without written music.
35. The legendary Irish hero, Fionn Mac Cumhail.
36. Native Irishmen. See Glossary.
37. Ir. *scian*, knife.
38. castrated rams.
39. Brian Boru, king of Ireland, who defeated the Vikings in the eleventh century.
40. Leaders of Gaelic Ireland in the sixteenth and early seventeenth centuries.
41. Brian O'Rourke, a chieftain of County Leitrim, gave a feast of legendary proportions in the late sixteenth century. This was celebrated in a poem by Hugh Mac Gauran, which Swift 'translated' as 'The Description of an *Irish-Feast*'. The Mac Gauran poem was popular in Irish and in other English translations as well.
42. i.e. skill like that of the mythological lyre-player, Orpheus.

How WILLIAM cross'd the Boyn to fight,
And how King James had beaten quite
His hot pursuers out of sight —

> By running. 160

He plays, and sings it o'er and o'er,
'Encore', quoth Denison, 'encore!
One Williamite would rout a score

> Of trimmers:[43]

Nassau, with bays immortal crown'd!'
'Nassau, Nassau' the guests resound;
The GLORIOUS MEMORY flows round

> In brimmers.[44]

A Receipt for Making a Doctor[1]

If you have nothing else to do,
Go travel for a year, or two,
At Paris spend a month at least,
In fashions to improve your taste;
Spunge upon Irish Priests and Friers,
And drink a health to all high-flyers;[2]
Stand firmly up for right divine,
Perpetual in the Royal Line,
Wishing (indeed as well they might)
The christian princes would unite, 10

---

43. Those who change allegiance so as to be always supporting the winning side.
44. Orange toasts included the words: 'To the glorious, pious and immortal memory of the great and good King William', and were drunk in glasses filled 'to the brim'.

---

1. Despite the existence of the Royal College of Physicians in Ireland (founded in 1654) and the presence in Dublin of several distinguished physicians in the late seventeenth and early eighteenth centuries — Dr Thomas Molyneux and Sir Patrick Dun for instance — the unqualified or under-qualified 'doctor' could still make a satisfactory living in eighteenth-century Dublin or London. Medical education remained haphazard and unregulated throughout most of Europe, and the licensing of medical practitioners was not effectively policed. When Goldsmith set himself up in practice in London in 1756, his only qualification seems to have been — like that of the young man to whom Dunkin addresses the poem which follows — that he had visited some of the European cities which had medical schools. Dunkin's poem is a satire on many such doctors. 'Receipt' means 'prescription'.
2. High-Churchmen or Tories: the next two lines refer to support for the doctrine of the divine right of kings, asserted by supporters of James II and his successors.

To carry on the gospel-work,
And join their arms, to rout the Turk.
From Coffee-Houses, without earning,
You may receive a world of learning:
But, lest in lies you should be found,
Visit the Hospitals once round,
And get some Connoisseur to tell,
Where all the best Physicians dwell:
Their names and families enquire,
Their tempers, persons, and attire,   20
And if they eat and drink by rule,
And at what times they go to st—l.[3]

From thence as straight, as you can steer,
Direct your course to Mont-Pelier;[4]
'Twill raise your spirits in a minute,
The very air has physic in it.
But there's a lesson worth a score,
I wonder, how I pass'd it o'er;
The hanging gardens at Versailles[5]
Would furnish out a thousand tales;   30
Nor will you give your hearers parley,[6]
When you have had a sight of Marlay;[7]
And then the Sorbonne,[8] so renown'd
For adepts in the art profound.
The God of wealth, who never sees
The worth of men, confers degrees,
And here a fidler, and the proctor
Unite in dubbing thee a doctor.[9]
The sage professors ne'er dispute
The title with a human brute,   40

3. i.e. to stool, to evacuate the bowels.
4. The French city of Montpellier was known as a place where would-be doctors could be trained.
5. The great palace built by Louis XIV near Paris, the gardens of which were particularly famous.
6. i.e. something to talk about (Fr. *parler*, to speak.)
7. Marlay-le-Roi, another superb palace built by Louis XIV not far from Paris.
8. The university in Paris.
9. A note at this point reads: 'Musical concerts are frequent at commencements [i.e. degree ceremonies] in the French academies', but the implication is that the degree of doctor could be bought — as it was reputedly for Rabelais' horse, Caballus (l. 44). proctor = a university official.

Nor would refuse it to a horse,
Provided he could send a purse,
And, if you will not take my word,
Caballus still is on record;[10]
(Tho' some physicians would explode him)
Full fam'd, as Rab'lais, who bestrode him.
Chiron[11] (whose pupil, fondly nurst,
Taught boys to ride their masters first)
In person, parts, profession, limb,
Was but the prototype of him.   50
To Spa[12] yet more successful fly hence,
To see, and to be seen is science.
The German counts, if ever able,
Are seldom from the gaming table,
Nor will the ladies fail to set
Their alimony at picquet.[13]
Should fortune second your endeavour,
Some hits may make you up for ever,
And if you fail, the public scoff,
Or decent drubbing gets you off.   60
Consider time is on the wing;
When you have taken there your fling,
To Leyden[14] hie; for know, Mynheer,
You must go through your courses here;
Here students learn the perfect art,
The mental, and the practic part;
The public lecture, licens'd brothel
Serve mainly to instruct you both well:
From thence, your time completely spent,
Come home as wise, as when you went,   70
Come home in haste, but first be sure have,
Or counterfeit some lines from Boerhaave.[15]
Buy books of physic, French, or German,
And swear you read them under Herman:

---

10. A note in early editions refers the reader to the life of Rabelais, prefixed to his *Works*.
11. A centaur who changed himself into a horse.
12. Spa, a town in Belgium well-known for its mineral waters, was one of the most fashionable medicinal resorts in eighteenth-century Europe.
13. A card game: the (separated) ladies are prepared to stake their alimony money as bets.
14. i.e. go to Leyden, a city in the Netherlands famous, in the eighteenth century, for its medical school. Mynheer: the Dutch equivalent of 'Sir' or 'Mr'.
15. Herman Boerhaave (1668-1738), famous Dutch physician and scientist.

216

Moreover, to enhance the lumber,[16]
Place Greek and Latin in the number:
The indexes, and title pages
Contain the wisdom of the sages.
And lastly, that it may be seen,
How nice, and curious you have been,   80
Procure (for it will well become ye)
A fragment of Ægyptian Mummy;[17]
A living tortoise, serpents' hide,
A human kidney petrify'd,
A leaf, that would perplex describers,
Anatomiz'd thro' all its fibres,
A butterfly, that far surpasses
The colours in prismatic glasses,
A flying fish with half a fin,
Th'embryo of a Sooterkin.[18]   90
An Elk's foot, and a Mare-maid's hand,[19]
With something from some new-found land,
So very strange in ev'ry part,
The deep professors of the art
Have not agreed, tho' often met,
What name it should be call'd as yet.

When furnish'd thus, desist to roam,
Triumphantly returning home.
But, in conjunction with these tools,
You must observe domestic rules.   100
Imprimis,[20] to attract the folk,
Bedeck thyself with scarlet-cloak:
A cloak, like Taylor's,[21] I would choose,
Down to the buckles in your shoes,
Broad-cap'd, wide-spreading o'er your shoulders,
And signifying to beholders,

16. rubbish.
17. Quack doctors or 'empirics' often collected useless but curious objects, such as are satirised in this list, to impress their clients.
18. 'An imaginary kind of afterbirth formerly attributed to Dutch women'. (*OED*)
19. i.e. the hand of a mermaid.
20. In the first place (*Latin*).
21. Probably a reference to John Taylor (1703-72), itinerant oculist and charlatan, who was the subject of many satires. See *DNB*.

Behind the long-projected shade,
The badge of your mysterious trade.
Transported with the pompous cheat,
The little vulgar, and the great   110
Around thee flock, nor dread mishap,
Like buzzing flies about a trap.
The heels of all the shoes you wear
Be high, the toes for ever square,
The thickest leather you can get,
Yet may it shine like polish'd jet:
Adorn your shoes with smallest buckles,
And let your ruffles hide your knuckles.
On either leg, to hide the flaw
Of calf, a pair of stockings draw,   120
Full long, and to avoid a blunder,
The upper silk, and worsted under:
So may you roll by just degrees
The duplicates above your knees.
Put on thy head a broad-brim'd hat,
About thy neck a fring'd cravat;
And, tho' an apple, fit to coddle,[22]
Be bigger than thy busy noddle,
Thy noddle, which (perhaps) contains
Proportionately much less brains,   130
Bedeck it with a wig as large,
As Wh—d's was,[23] nor grudge the charge....

Be often seen in hackney chair,
And, seen, assume a solemn air,
With hurry of important face,
Nor stay two minutes in one place,
Except it be to shew thy learning ——
With persons of the least discerning.
Where e'er you are, where e'er you pass,
Behold all objects through a glass,[24]   140

22. boil or bake.
23. This doctor has not been identified, though presumably Dunkin is referring to someone practising in Dublin; elsewhere in the poem he mentions Swift's Dublin friend, Dr Helsham.
24. A lens or magnifying-glass.

And add, that this defect of sight
Proceeds from rising in the night,
To visit men of high degrees,
Tho' then you only dreamt of fees....

A wise physician still consults
His patient's eyes, his tongue, and pulse,
And thinks it also not amiss
To view the colour of his piss,
Mark this, and what on that may border,
Nay condescend to taste the ord—e.[25]   150
Great Maro,[26] as you may be told,
From dung was wont to gather gold,
And mould it in his mint with pain,
But this was metaphoric gain;
The gold you rake from dung is sterling,
Such, as in time may buy a Berlin.[27]

Talk much of books, of men, and reading,
Despising narrow, inland breeding,
What great men are abroad, and —— (hem)
How very great you were with them: 160
Tho' Boerhaave and his sect (no doubt)
Are in some matters hugely out:
With doctor Halley[28] I agree,
And, —— sir, I thank you for my fee.

If ask'd to give your full opinion
Of any wretch in your dominion,
Stare east, and west, and north, and south,
And hold your cane up to your mouth;
Then pause awhile, and shake your head,
As if you give him up for dead;   170
At length your oracle deliver,
Discharging all your artful quiver

---

25. ordure.
26. The reference seems to be to the first book of *The Georgics* in which, when Virgil is writing about the tillage of the fields, he mentions the importance of manuring the ground.
27. A four-wheeled, covered carriage.
28. Dr Edmund Halley (1656-1742), one of the most distinguished English scientists of the day.

Of bolusses,[29] of pills, and clysters,
Decoctions, potions, julips, blisters,
With proper participles, pungents,
Abstersives, lenitives, emungents,
Cathartics, purgatives, emeticks,
With laxatives, and diuretics,
Descanting (while the man continues
Past hopes) on arteries and sinews;   180
At last demand a pen and ink,
And say —— you know not what to think,
The symptoms are so bad: —— his tongue's
So white, —— and then I fear his lungs ——
He seems to make a heavy moan,
And strain his breath, but I have known
Some people from a worse condition
Recover by a good physician....

Do this, and havock[30] as you will,
You shall be deem'd a man of skill;   190
Nothing can recommend you further,
You have full privilege to murther.

On the Omission of the Words *Dei Gratia* in the late Coinage of Half-Pence[1]

No Christian king, that I can find,
    However queer and odd,
Excepting our's, has ever coin'd
    Without the grace of God.

By this acknowledgement they shew
    The mighty King of Kings,
As him, from whom their riches flow,
    From whom their grandeur springs.

---

29. A list of the less common as well as the normal medical procedures of the day.
30. create havoc.

---

1. The Irish copper halfpence minted in 1736 were the first Irish coins not to carry the customary formal phrase 'Dei Gratia' (by the grace of God), after the name of the monarch. They were also the first coins to carry the head of George II, though he had been king since 1727.

Come then, Urania,[2] aid my pen,
    The latent cause assign;   10
All other kings are mortal men,
    But GEORGE, 'tis plain's, divine.

2. The muse of astronomy.

JONATHAN SWIFT

A Character, Panegyric, and Description of the LEGION CLUB

Written in the Year 1736[1]

As I strole the City, oft I
Spy a Building large and lofty,[2]
Not a Bow-shot from the College,
Half the Globe from Sense and Knowledge.
By the prudent Architect
Plac'd against the Church direct;
Making good my Grandame's Jest,
Near the Church — you know the rest.[3]

Tell us what this Pile contains?
Many a Head that holds no Brains.   10
These Demoniacs[4] let me dub
With the Name of *Legion Club*.
Such Assemblies, you might swear,
Meet when Butchers bait a Bear;[5]
Such a Noise, and such Haranguing,
When a Brother Thief is hanging.
Such a Rout and such a Rabble
Run to hear Jack-pudding[6] gabble;
Such a Croud their Ordure throws
On a far less Villain's Nose.[7]   20

---

1. The Church of Ireland and the Irish landlords were often at loggerheads over tithes — payments due from landowners and tenants to support the clergy. Without tithes, the church would have had little income and when, in 1736, the landlords who made up the Irish House of Commons set up a committee to see if they could remove pasturage tithes, Swift's fury at what he saw as secular attempts to ruin the established Church of Ireland burst forth in this famous attack on the Irish parliament for which he coined the name 'the legion club'. In Luke 8. 30, there is reference to a madman called Legion 'because many devils were entered into him'.

2. The new parliament house, designed by Sir Edward Lovet Pearce and now the headquarters of the Bank of Ireland, was begun in 1729 and completed in 1739. It is situated close to Trinity College and to St Andrew's Church.

3. The proverb is 'Near the Church, and far from God'.

4. madmen.

5. Butchers played a prominent part in bull- and bear-baiting.

6. A street clown or buffoon.

7. i.e. the condemned criminal (at whom people throw their rubbish) is far less guilty than these men.

Could I from the Building's Top
Hear the rattling Thunder drop,
While the Devil upon the Roof,
If the Devil be Thunder Proof,
Should, with Poker fiery-red
Crack the Stones, and melt the Lead;
Drive them down on every Skull,
While the Den of Thieves[8] is full,
Quite destroy that Harpies Nest,[9]
How might then our Isle be blest?   30
For Divines allow, that God
Sometimes makes the Devil his Rod:
And the Gospel will inform us,
He can punish Sins enormous.

Yet should *Swift* endow the Schools
For his Lunatics and Fools,
With a Rood or two of Land,
I allow the Pile may stand.[10]
You perhaps will ask me, why so?
But it is with this Proviso,   40
Since the House is like to last,
Let a royal Grant be pass'd,
That the Club have Right to dwell
Each within his proper Cell;[11]
With a Passage left to creep in,
And a Hole above for peeping.

Let them, when they once get in
Sell the Nation for a Pin;[12]

---

8. Jesus told the moneychangers in the temple: 'My house shall be called a house of prayer; but ye have made it a den of thieves'. (Matthew 21. 13).

9. In classical mythology, the Harpies were monsters, half-woman and half-bird, rapacious and filthy.

10. In fact, in his will, Swift endowed St Patrick's Hospital ('for Idiots and Lunaticks') with considerably more than a rood (a measure of about 80 square metres) or two of land. Pile = large building.

11. i.e. like madmen kept in solitary confinement.

12. Throughout this paragraph, Swift applies to the members of parliament the terms normally used to describe the behaviour of madmen in a 'bedlam', mischievously inserting into this mad world the parliamentary terms 'committee', 'Orders of the House' (i.e. standing orders) and 'Heads of Bills' (the summary of proposed legislation which the Irish parliament had to submit to the English Privy Council for approval).

While they sit a picking Straws
Let them rave of making Laws;   50
While they never hold their Tongue,
Let them dabble in their Dung;
Let them form a grand Committee,
How to plague and starve the City;
Let them stare and storm and frown,
When they see a Clergy-Gown.
Let them, 'ere they crack a Louse,
Call for th'Orders of the House;
Let them with their gosling Quills,
Scribble senseless Heads of Bills;   60
We may, while they strain their Throats,
Wipe our Arses with their Votes.[13]

Let Sir *Tom*,[14] that rampant Ass,
Stuff his Guts with Flax and Grass;
But before the Priest he fleeces
Tear the Bible all to Pieces.
At the Parsons, *Tom*, Halloo Boy,[15]
Worthy Offspring of a Shoeboy,
Footman, Traytor, vile Seducer,
Perjur'd Rebel, brib'd Accuser;[16]   70
Lay thy paltry Privilege aside,
Sprung from Papists and a Regicide;
Fall a working like a Mole,
Raise the Dirt about your Hole.

Come, assist me, Muse obedient,
Let us try some new Expedient;
Shift the Scene for half an Hour,
Time and Place are in thy Power.

---

13. In Swift's time, no written record of parliamentary proceedings was kept so that the printed 'votes' were one of the few tangible results of parliamentary activity. Both nouns are replaced by dashes in early printings.

14. Sir Thomas Prendergast (d. 1760), postmaster-general of Ireland, known to be strongly anti-clerical. Here, as throughout this printing of 'The Legion Club', proper names, which are protected by dashes in early printings, are supplied.

15. 'At the Parson's' and 'Halloo Boy' were typical cries of a huntsman in the field.

16. Prendergast's father, a Jacobite, was once described by Swift as a man 'who engaged in a Plot to murder King *William III* but, to avoid being hanged, turned Informer against his Associates, for which he was rewarded with a good Estate, and made a Baronet'. (Williams, *Poems*, p. 826). The plot took place in 1696.

Thither, gentle Muse, conduct me,
I shall ask, and you instruct me.   80
See, the Muse unbars the Gate;
Hark, the Monkeys, how they prate!

All ye Gods, who rule the Soul
Styx, through Hell whose Waters roll!
Let me be allow'd to tell
What I heard in yonder Hell.[17]

Near the Door an Entrance gapes,
Crouded round with antic Shapes;
Poverty, and *Grief*, and *Care*,
Causeless *Joy*, and true *Despair*;   90
Discord periwigg'd with Snakes,
See the dreadful Strides she takes.

By this odious Crew beset,
I began to rage and fret
And resolv'd to break their Pates,[18]
'Ere we enter'd at the Gates;
Had not *Clio*[19] in the Nick,
Whisper'd me, 'Let down your Stick;'
'What,' said I, 'is this the Mad-House?'
These, she answer'd, are but Shadows,   100
Phantoms, bodiless and vain,
Empty Visions of the Brain.

In the Porch *Briareus*[20] stands,
Shews a Bribe in all his Hands:
Briareus the Secretary,
But we Mortals call him *Cary*.[21]
When the Rogues their Country fleece,
They may hope for Pence a Piece.

---

17. In George Faulkner's printing of this poem, there is a note here drawing attention to parallels with Virgil's *Æneid* VI, 264ff.
18. heads.
19. The muse of history. In the Nick = in the nick of time.
20. A giant in classical mythology; he had fifty heads and one hundred hands.
21. Walter Carey (1685-1757), secretary to the lord lieutenant and a prominent Whig.

Clio, who had been so wise
To put on a Fool's Disguise,   110
To bespeak some Approbation,[22]
And be thought a near Relation,
When she saw three hundred Brutes,[23]
All involv'd in wild Disputes,
Roaring till their Lungs were spent,
'Privilege of Parliament',
Now a new Misfortune feels,
Dreading to be laid by th' Heels.[24]
Never durst a Muse before
Enter that Infernal Door;   120
Clio stifled with the Smell,
Into Spleen and Vapours fell;
By the *Stygian* Steams that flew,
From the dire infectious Crew.
Not the Stench of Lake *Avernus*,[25]
Could have more offended her Nose;
Had she flown but o'er the Top,
She would feel her Pinions drop,
And by Exhalations dire,
Though a Goddess, must expire.   130
In a Fright she crept away,
Bravely I resolv'd to stay.

When I saw the Keeper frown,
Tipping him with half a Crown,
'Now,' said I, 'we are alone,
Name your Heroes, one by one.'

'Who is that Hell-featur'd Brawler,
Is it Satan? No 'tis *Waller*.[26]
In what Figure can a Bard dress
Jack, the Grandson of Sir *Hardress*?[27]   140

---

22. i.e. to arrange that she might be approved of.
23. There were three hundred members of the Irish House of Commons.
24. arrested. The words 'Privilege' and 'Parliament' (l. 116) are protected by dashes in early printings.
25. A lake in Italy, said to be the entrance to the underworld.
26. John Waller, MP for Doneraile, Co. Cork.
27. Waller's grandfather, Sir Hardress Waller, had been a judge at the trial of Charles I.

Honest Keeper, drive him further,
In his Looks are Hell and Murther;
See the scowling Visage drop,
Just as when he murther'd Throp.[28]

'Keeper, shew me where to fix
On the Puppy Pair of *Dicks*;[29]
By their lanthorn Jaws and Leathern,
You might swear they both are Brethren:
Dick Fitz-Baker, *Dick* the Player,[30]
Old Acquaintance, are you there?   150
Dear Companions hug and kiss,
Toast *old Glorious*[31] in your Piss.
Tye them, Keeper, in a Tether,[32]
Let them stare and stink together;
Both are apt to be unruly,
Lash them daily, lash them duly,
Though 'tis hopeless to reclaim them,
Scorpion Rods[33] perhaps may tame them.

Keeper, yon old Dotard smoke,[34]
Sweetly snoring in his Cloak.   160
Who is he?' ''Tis hum-drum *Wynne*,
Half encompass'd by his Kin.'[35]
There observe the Tribe of *Bingham*,[36]
For he never fails to bring 'em;
While he sleeps the whole Debate,
They submissive round him wait;

---

28. Rev. Roger Throp, rector of Kilcorman, Co. Limerick, had stood up to Waller over tithes and, it was popularly believed, had been 'persecuted' to death by him.
29. Richard Tighe (c. 1678-1736), MP for Belturbet, Co. Cavan and Richard Bettesworth (1689-1741), MP for Midleton, Co. Cork. lanthorn (lantern) jaws are 'long, thin jaws giving a hollow appearance to the cheek' (*OED*).
30. The first of these nicknames refers to the fact that one of Tighe's ancestors had supplied bread to Cromwell's army, and the second to Bettesworth's theatrical manner when speaking in parliament.
31. Drink toasts to William III.
32. Swift addresses the keeper in the madhouse: the two Dicks should be tethered and whipped daily.
33. Medieval instruments of torture.
34. i.e. 'Keeper, find out who that old imbecile is.'
35. There were two members of parliament called Owen Wynne at this time, and one called John Wynne.
36. There were two members of parliament called Bingham, Sir John and Henry.

Yet would gladly see the Hunks[37]
In his Grave, and search his Trunks.
See they gently twitch his Coat,
Just to yawn, and give his Vote;   170
Always firm in his Vocation,
For the Court against the Nation.

Those are *Allens, Jack* and *Bob,*[38]
First in every wicked Jobb,
Son and Brother to a Queer
Brainsick Brute, they call a Peer.
We must give them better Quarter,
For their Ancestor trod Mortar;
And at *Hoath* to boast his Fame,
On a Chimney cut his Name.   180

There sit *Clements, Dilkes,* and *Harrison,*[39]
How they swagger from their Garrison.
Such a Triplet could you tell
Where to find on this Side Hell?
Harrison, and *Dilkes,* and *Clements,*
Souse them in their own Excrements.
Every Mischief's in their Hearts,
If they fail 'tis Want of Parts.[40]

Bless us, *Morgan!*[41] Art thou there, Man?
Bless mine Eyes! Art thou the Chairman?   190
Chairman to yon damn'd Committee?
Yet I look on thee with Pity.
Dreadful Sight! What, learned *Morgan*[42]
Metamorphos'd to a Gorgon!

---

37. An old miser.
38. John and Robert Allen, the son and brother of Lord Allen. An ancestor, another John Allen, had been the architect for part of Howth Castle (see ll. 179-80).
39. Henry or Nathaniel Clements, Michael O'Brien Dilkes and William Harrison, all MPs.
40. abilities, talents.
41. Dr Marcus Antony Morgan, MP for Athy, Co. Kildare, was made chairman of the committee set up by the House of Commons to look into the issue of the tithes.
42. Morgan was a graduate of Trinity College, Dublin (which was therefore his *Alma Mater*) where many of those who were later ordained into the Church of Ireland would have been his fellow students (see l. 200).

For thy horrid Looks, I own,
Half convert me to a Stone.
Hast thou been so long at School,
Now to turn a factious Tool!
Alma Mater was thy Mother,
Every young Divine thy Brother.   200
Thou a disobedient Varlet,
Treat thy Mother like a Harlot?
Thou, ungrateful to thy Teachers,
Who are all grown reverend Preachers!
Morgan! Would it not surprise one?
Turn thy Nourishment to Poison!
When you walk among your Books,
They reproach you with their Looks;
Bind them fast, or from the Shelves
They'll come down to right themselves: 210
Homer, Plutarch, Virgil, Flaccus,[43]
All in Arms prepare to back us:
Soon repent, or put to Slaughter
Every *Greek* and *Roman* Author.
While you in your Faction's Phrase
Send the Clergy all to graze;
And to make your Project pass,
Leave them not a Blade of Grass.[44]

How I want thee, humorous *Hogart*![45]
Thou I hear, a pleasant Rogue art;   220
Were but you and I acquainted,
Every Monster should be painted;
You should try your graving Tools,
On this odious Group of Fools;
Draw the Beasts as I describe 'em,
Form their Features, while I gibe 'em;
Draw them like, for I assure you,
You will need no *Car'catura*;[46]

---

43. The fourth of these classical authors is Quintus Horatius Flaccus, normally known as Horace.
44. The disputed tithes were those due to the clergy from graziers, i.e. those whose animals graze grass.
45. William Hogarth (1697-1764), painter and engraver.
46. The Italian version of the word 'caricature'.

Draw them so that we may trace
All the Soul in every Face.   230
Keeper, I must now retire,
You have done what I desire:
But I feel my Spirits spent,
With the Noise, the Sight, the Scent.'

'Pray be patient, you shall find
Half the best are still behind:
You have hardly seen a Score,
I can shew two hundred more.'
'Keeper, I have seen enough;'
Taking then a Pinch of Snuff;   240
I concluded looking round 'em,
May their God, the Devil, confound 'em.

JAMES ARBUCKLE
(c.1700-**1745**-c.1747)

James Arbuckle was the son of a Dublin Presbyterian minister in Dublin. He was educated at the university of Glasgow where he qualified as a doctor of medicine in 1724. Returning to Dublin, he became a well-known figure in the literary world as journalist and as poet. Arbuckle's commentary on Swift's will — in which he left money for the foundation of a hospital for 'Idiots and Lunaticks' — is the best of many such poems.

On Swift's leaving his Fortune to Build a Mad-House

> To Madmen Swift bequeaths his whole estate,
> Why should we wonder? Swift is right in that;
> For 'tis a rule as all our Law[y]ers know
> Men's Fortunes to their next of kin shou'd goe;
> And 'tis as Sure, unless old Bards have lyed,
> Great wit to madness is most near Allyed.[1]

---

1. cf. 'Great wits are sure to madness near allied', Dryden, *Absalom and Achitophel,* I, 163.

PART III
1735-60

HENRY BROOKE

(c.1703-**1735**-1783)

Henry Brooke was born in County Cavan, the son of a clergyman. He was educated at Trinity College, Dublin and soon became a prolific writer. In addition to his philosophical poem *Universal Beauty*, Brooke wrote plays (including the famous *Gustavus Vasa,* which was banned in London by Walpole because of its apparent criticism of him), novels (including *The Fool of Quality*) and many political pamphlets; as a pamphleteer, Brooke wrote in support of differing points of view at various times. His daughter Charlotte, famous for her *Reliques of Irish Poetry*, edited his works for publication and they appeared in four volumes shortly before he died in Dublin in 1783.

Universal Beauty is the most significant philosophical poem written by an Irish writer in the eighteenth century. Like Alexander Pope in *An Essay on Man*, Brooke uses the poem to survey God's creation in the universe, and to give an account of the forms of knowledge and of the nature of man. In the last of the six books of the poem, he contemplates the beauty of the design of the universe and, in the section printed below, expresses a typically Augustan wonder at the social order which exists in the world of bees; there are, the reader soon learns, lessons here for mankind.

from: Universal Beauty (book VI)

... Bear, bear my song, ye raptures of the mind!
Convey your bard thro' Nature unconfined,
Licentious[1] in the search of wisdom range,
Plunge in the depth, and wanton[2] in the change;
Waft me to Tempe,[3] and her flowery dale,
Born on the wings of every tuneful gale;[4]
Amid the wild profusions let me stray,
And share with Bees the virtues of the day.

Soon as the matin glory gilds the skies,
Behold the little Virtuosi[5] rise!   10
Blithe for the task, they preen their early wing,
And forth to each appointed labour spring.
Now nature boon[6] exhales the morning stream,
And glows and opens to the welcome beam;

1. unconfined.
2. play heedlessly or extravagantly.
3. The most delightful spot on earth, according to many poets in classical literature.
4. Used here in its poetic meaning, 'a soft or gentle breeze'.
5. learned persons, particularly those skilled in the sciences, in music or in collecting.
6. bounteous. Milton uses the same phrase, 'nature boon' in *Paradise Lost* IV, 242. The couplet means 'Now bounteous nature breathes forth the morning air ['stream'] and glows and opens [herself] to the welcome [sun] beams'.

The vivid tribes amid the fragrance fly,
And every art, and every business ply.
Each chymist[7] now his subtle trunk unsheathes,
Where, from the flower, the treasured odour breathes;
Here sip the liquid, here select the gum,
And o'er the bloom with quivering membrane hum.   20
Still with judicious scrutiny they pry,
Where lodg'd the prime essential juices lie;
Each luscious vegetation wide explore,
Plunder the spring of every vital store:
The dainty suckle, and the fragrant thyme,
By chymical reduction, they sublime;[8]
Their sweets with bland attempering[9] suction strain,
And, curious, thro' their neat alembicks[10] drain;
Imbibed recluse, the pure secretions glide,
And vital warmth concocts the ambrosial tide.[11]   30

Inimitable Art! do thou atone
The long lost labours of the Latent Stone;
Tho' the Five Principles so oft transpire,
Fined, and refined, amid the torturing fire.[12]
Like issue should the daring chymist see,
Vain imitator of the curious Bee,
Nor arts improved thro' ages once produce
A single drachm[13] of this delicious juice.
Your's then, industrious traders! is the toil,
And man's proud science is alone to spoil.   40
'Sweet's the repast where pains have spread the board,
'And deep the fund incessant labours hoard;
'A friendly arm makes every burden light;
'And weakness, knit by union, turns to might.'[14]

---

7. The bee is seen as a chemist or alchemist (i.e. one able to turn one thing into another).
8. i.e. they turn what they have gathered from the dainty honeysuckle and the fragrant thyme [i.e. nectar] into something higher, more excellent [i.e. honey].
9. modifying.
10. In these lines, Brooke is describing the transformation of nectar into honey in terms borrowed from alchemy. 'Alembicks' were instruments used in distillation.
11. i.e. Imbibed in secret, the pure secretions [from the nectar] glide [through the bees' bodies] and the living warmth digests them and turns them into liquid ambrosia. 'Ambrosia' was not only the food of the gods in classical mythology, but also, according to the *OED*, was another name for 'bee-bread', the mixture of honey and pollen consumed by the nurse-bees in a beehive.
12. The 'Latent Stone' and the 'Five Principles' are terms from alchemy.
13. drachm = dram, a small measure of liquid.
14. The source of this quotation is untraced.

Hail happy tribes! illustrious people hail!
Whose forms minute such sacred maxims veil;
In whose just conduct, framed by wondrous plan,
We read revers'd each polity of man.
Who first in council form'd your embryon state?
Who rose a patriot in the deep debate?   50
Greatly proposed to reconcile extremes,
And weave in unity opposing schemes?
From fears inferr'd just reason of defence,
And from self interest rais'd a publick sense;
Then pois'd his project with transposing scale,
And from the publick, shew'd the private weal?
Whence aptly summ'd, these politicians draw
The trust of power, and sanctitude of law;
Power in dispensing benefits employ'd,
And healing laws, not suffer'd, but enjoy'd.   60
The members, hence unanimous, combine
To prop that throne on which the laws recline;
The law's protected even for private ends,
Whereon each individual's right depends;
Each individual's right by union grows,
And one full tide for every member flows;
Each member as the whole communion great,
Back'd by the powers of a defending state;
The state by mutual benefits secure,
And in the might of every member sure!   70

The publick thus each private end pursues;
Each in the publick drowns all private views:
By social commerce and exchange they live,
Assist supported, and receiving give.

High on her throne, the bright Imperial Queen[15]
Gives the prime movement to the state machine;
She, in the subject, sees the duteous child;
She, the true parent, as the regent mild,
With princely grace invested sits elate,
Informs their conduct, and directs the state.   80

15. i.e. the queen bee.

Around, the drones who form her courtly train,
Bask in the rays of her auspicious reign;
Beneath, the sage consulting peers repair,
And breathe the virtues of their prince's care;
Debating, cultivate the publick cause,
And wide dispense the benefit of laws....

The clustering populace obsequious wait,
Or speed the different orders of the state;
Here greet the labourer on the toilsome way,
And to the load their friendly shoulder lay;   90
Or frequent at the busy gate arrive,
And fill with amber-sweets their fragrant hive;
Or seek repairs to close the fractured cell;
Or shut the waxen wombs where embryos dwell;
The caterers prompt, a frugal portion deal,
And give to diligence a hasty meal;
In each appointed province all proceed,
And neatest order weds the swiftest speed;
Dispatch flies various on ten thousand wings,
And joy throughout the gladsome region rings.   100

Distinctly canton'd is their spacious dome:[16]
Here infants throb within the quickening comb;
Here vacant seats invite to sweet repose,
And here the tide of balmy nectar flows;
While here the frugal reservoirs remain,
And not one act of this republick's vain....

When swarms tumultuous claim an ampler space,
And thro' the straitening citadel[17] increase,
An edict issued in this grand extreme,
Proclaims the mandate of the power supreme.   110
Then exiled crouds abjure their native home,
And sad, in search of foreign mansions roam;
A youthful empress guides their airy clan,
And wheels and shoots illustrious from the van.[18]

16. i.e. the spacious beehive. In the eighteenth century, beehives were made of thick straw-
    work in the shape of a dome.
17. i.e. the beehive.
18. The front position in the moving swarm of bees.

Fatigued at length, they wish some calm retreat,
The rural setlement and peaceful state;
When man presents his hospitable snare,
And wins their confidence with traitorous care.
Suspicion ever flies a generous breast ——
Betrayed, each enters an unwary guest;   120
Here every form of ancient maxim trace,
And emulate the glories of their race.

As when from Tyre imperial Dido fled,
And o'er the main her future nation led;
Then staid her host on Afric's meted land,
And in strait bounds a mighty empire plann'd;[19]
So works this rival of the Tyrian Queen;[20]
So founds and models with assiduous mien;
Instructs with little to be truly great,
And in small limits forms a mighty state.   130

Intent, she wills her artists to attend,
And from the zenith bids her towers descend:
Nor like to man's, the aerial structures rise;
But point to earth, their base amid the skies.[21]

Swift for the task the ready builders part,
Each band assigned to each peculiar art;
A troop of chymists scour the neighbouring field,
While servile tribes the cull'd materials wield,
With tempering feet the laboured cement tread,
And ductile[22] now its waxen foliage spread.   140
The geometricians judge the deep design,
Direct the compass, and extend the line;
They sum their numbers,[23] provident of space,
And suit each edifice with answering grace.

---

19. Virgil's *Æneid* tells the story of Dido, queen of Tyre, who was forced to flee to Africa with her followers, where she founded the city of Carthage. meted = measured, of limited extent.
20. i.e. the queen bee.
21. A bee colony builds its combs from the top downwards.
22. malleable, pliant.
23. i.e. do their calculations.

Now first appears the rough proportion'd frame,
Rough in the draft, but perfect in the scheme;
When lo! each little Archmedes[24] nigh,
Metes[25] every angle with judicious eye;
Adjusts the centering cones with skill profound,
And forms the curious hexagon around.   150

The cells indors'd[26] with double range adhere,
Knit on the sides, and guarded on the rear;
Nought of itself, with circling chambers bound,
Each cell is form'd, to form the cells around;
While each still gives what each alike demands,
And but supported by supporting stands;
Jointly transferring, and transferr'd exists;
And, as by magick union, all subsists.

Amazing elegance! transcendent art!
Contrived at once to borrow, and impart;   160
In action notable, as council great,
Their fabricks rise, just emblems of their state....

---

24. One of the greatest mathematicians of the classical world, Archimedes is often credited
    with being the inventor of both physics and mechanics.
25. measures.
26. indors'd = endorsed, i.e. back to back.

ANONYMOUS POEMS FROM THE 1730s AND 1740s

The Kerry Cavalcade: or, the High Sheriff's Feast[1]

Assist me, ye Muses, *F——ce*[2] to sing,
A Sheriff most glorious, as great as a King.
Tho' some of his Brethren were taller, and bigger,
Not one in all Ireland made half such a Figure.
As Folks may observe, when I've rightly display'd,
The wonderful Pomp of his grand Cavalcade;
O'er Mountains, and Quagmires, and Ditches he trudges,
To shew what a *Bow* he cou'd make to the Judges.
Now view his Attendance, and take them in Order,
As they march in Procession to *Kerry*'s wild Border;   10
Two Foot-men in White, ran puffing before,
Red Ribbons, red Sashes, deep Fringes all o'er.
To tell the Lords Judges (who little did mind 'em)
Their Master, the Sheriff, was coming behind 'em.
Four Grooms with four Horses, embroidered, advanc'd,
How stately they trotted, how proudly they pranc'd;
And, lest they shou'd fart in the Gentlemens' Noses,
Their Tails were adorn'd with Ribbands and Roses.
Next these came a Page in a Dress very odd,
And all that he bore was the Sheriff's white Rod;[3]   20
The Ladies of *Kerry* cou'd kiss the sweet Varlet,[4]
So pretty he look'd in his Silver and Scarlet.
Now see the High Sheriff most gloriously dress'd,
He's ev'ry Bit Scarlet, Coat, Britches and Vest;
His Sword was so dreadful, the Sight on't was felt,
As it clung to his Ribs in a broad Shoulder Belt;
In Velvet of Crimson it bloodily dangled,
As if a whole Army of Men it had mangled.

---

1. It was customary for a high sheriff to receive the judges of the assize court at the boundary of his county, though usually with less pomp than is described in this poem. See Charles Smith, *The Ancient and Present State of the County of Kerry* (Dublin,1756), p. 101, note q, and Constantia Maxwell, *Country and Town in Ireland under the Georges* (London, 1940), pp. 56-57.
2. Right Hon. John Fitzmaurice, High Sheriff of County Kerry, later Earl of Shelburne. At the time of this poem, Fitzmaurice was living at Lixnaw, the mansion near Listowel owned by his father, the Earl of Kerry.
3. The wand of office.
4. attendant, servant.

Now view his fine Stone Horse,[5] in *Turkish* fine Bridle,
A pawing the Ground, not a Limb of him idle;   30
And he who's upon him, as busy as he,
To keep in his Seat by the Clasp of his Knee.
The Reins were green Silk, with a Mixture of Gold,
As full of fine Figures as e'er they could hold;
The Caps and the Hoofings were Velvet in Green,
Yet cou'd scarce for the Gold and the Fringes be seen;
The Reason there's few but the Wise can discover,
Because it is thought they were cover'd all over.
Two Trumpeters, *Tantarrarara*, came after,
They sounded not Musick, but something like Laughter;   40
Profusely, in Silver, bedecked they were,
Which gave them a greater, and much better Air.
Twelve Men, in the Family Colours, true tawny,
On black Horses mounted, sleek, long tail'd, and brawny,
From Twenty to Forty Pound Price at the least,
And Roses of Ribbonds adorned each Beast.
The Crest of *F———e*, (O were it an Ass!)
On the Caps and the Hoofings was a *Centaur* in Brass;
With Hats lac'd with Gold, and with short Wiggs so bluff,[6]
Their Back-swords hung swaggering in broad Belts of Buff;[7]   50
Their Stocks, or black Cravats, genteely were put on,
And fasten'd behind with a Brace of Gold Button.
Each Man of the Twelve had of Pistols *a Brace*,
And a Carabine[8] fix'd in its own proper Place;
By the Learned in War ycleped[9] a Bucket,
A Socket of Leather where he carefully stuck it,
A Stopper of Red, mix't with White in each Muzzle,
So much like a Tulip, a Florist they'd puzzle.
Each Rider's fine Coat had a fine Scarlet Cape,
Roll'd up on the Rump of his Horse, in a Heap;[10]   60

5. stallion.
6. with broad, flattened fronts. Such wigs were obviously the latest fashion.
7. stout leather.
8. Carabine = carbine, a firearm used by mounted soldiers.
9. i.e. called — a conscious and humorous archaism.
10. Hiberno-English pronunciation would make this word rhyme with 'cape'.

The E—— of *K*——'s[11] own Gentleman single,
Came trotting up next with a *Jingle di Jingle*,
The Horse was a Stone-Horse he rid, and a Bay,
And a very fine Stone-Horse, as some People say —
The L—— *K*——'s Steward, and Gentlemen Waiters,
And other Domesticks, and other like Creatures;
O Lord, who wou'd think that his Lordship was able,
To mount Thirty-five of this Gang from one Stable!
The Gentlemen then of the County came cap'ring,
With twenty led Horses; and Field Cloths a vap'ring,[12]   70
When all of a sudden the Welking grew low'ring,[13]
And all of a sudden the Clouds fell a-pouring;
The Rain it was heavy, the Tempest blew so well,
It sous'd 'em, and dous'd 'em as far as *Listowel* ——
The Horses and Coaches thro' Puddles did paddle,
The Judges were forc'd to betake to their Saddle;
They gallop'd, and gallop'd, thro' Thick and thro' Thin,
All rough-cast with Mortar,[14] all wet to the Skin;
'Till they came to an Inn, where the Sheriff got ready
An Hundred and Twenty good Dishes, *Berlady*;[15]   80
All keen-set as Hawks, or as Pris'ners a-starving,
O Heav'ns what Clutter, what Cutting, what Carving!
But short the Repast, in the Midst of their Cheer,
As the Devil wou'd have it, there came a Courier,
Who told 'em a River was rising to drown 'em,
Which News did so terrify, fright, and confound 'em,
That they mounted their Horses, and flew off in haste,
Without saying Grace to the High Sheriff's Feast.

11. The Earl of Kerry.
12. i.e. showing off their pennants or flags.
13. i.e. black clouds were lowering overhead.
14. i.e. covered in mud so that they looked like statues rough cast in mortar.
15. 'By our Lady'.

from: The Upper Gallery[1]

... When Ev'ning Clouds condensing fall in Rain,
And draggled Crowds the cover'd Pent-house[2] gain:
Tradesmen take in their Goods, expos'd to sale,
And tuck'd-up Hoops the Maiden Leg reveal:
When Politicians into Shops repair,
And settle Nations, till the Sky grows clear.
Then no Walks please: All Nature seems to frown,
Black Kennels[3] swell, and Coaches shake the Town.
If *one fair Splendid* [4] in thy Pocket glows,
Fly to the Theatre's instructive Shows;   10
There some fam'd Heroe of a distant Age,
Revives in Verse, and pompous awes the Stage;
Or comic Scenes less solemn Joys dispense,
Please, to instruct, and laugh us into Sense.

While the spruce Beaus loll thoughtless in their Chairs,[5]
Wrapt in thick Rug, we whistle up the Stairs:[6]...
Now o'er the Seats in Ranks descending, creep,
Tread cautious, and beware the headlong Steep.
Oft some ill-fated Nymph, with careless Strides,
To the Wood's slipp'ry Verge her Foot misguides,   20
Supine she falls, her white Limbs lie display'd,
And shoot a sudden Lustre thro' the Shade:
Eager to see, the Youths assemble round,
And the throng'd Galleries with Laughter sound....
In the dim Shade we sit, a doubtful Race,
Disguis'd each Voice, and cover'd ev'ry Face,

---

1. This poem is unusual among poems about Dublin theatres in the eighteenth century (most of which are concerned with the wranglings of actors, actresses and managers) as it recounts the experience of attending the theatre. Although it seems, early in this extract, that the poet is going to describe young thugs breaking up a performance, in fact the poem goes on to give an account of an uninterrupted evening in the theatre and a glimpse of life in the streets of Dublin.
2. A covered walk, arcade or colonnade in front of a row of buildings.
3. gutters in the street, black with dirt.
4. A slang word for a small coin.
5. sedan chairs.
6. The young men are ascending to the highest part of the theatre, the 'gods'. Often, as in this case, patrons entered from the back and had to climb down past rows of steeply raked seats to reach their own. 'Wrapt in thick Rug' may mean that they had wrapped rugs around themselves or it may be connected with the gaming slang word 'rug' and mean 'all safe'.

Hid in the uncock'd Hats wide spreading Round,[7]
Or sunk in some old Tye's immense Profound;[8]
Beneath, thick Coats their friendly Capes expand,
And the Oak-Cudgel waves in ev'ry Hand....   30
Nor dare, rash Youth, by Love of Dress misled,
Cloth'd in thy best Array, our Realms to tread;
Whene'er some Fopling wou'd our Shade profane
By the white Ruffle, or the glancing Cane,
All fly his Touch, and with keen-stinging Jest
Torment the Wretch, who dares to be well-drest....

Now fills the Dome: They trim the languid Flames,
And the snuff'd Tapers call forth all their Beams;
Wedg'd eager in Front-seats, they throng, they squeeze,
And Fans, soft-waving, shed a gentle Breeze: 40
Pit, Boxes, Gall'ry shine with blended Rows,
Ladies, and Bawds, and Cits,[9] and Rakes, and Beaus;
'Tis smiling, curt'sying all. The Fiddles rise,
The wing'd Notes thicken, and the Musick flies.
When Orpheus[10] taught his tuneful Lyre to sound,
Thus Stones, Trees, *Bacchanals*[11] came dancing round.
Love, ever Dullness's most favour'd Theme,
Now burns the Fops with metaphorick Flame;
They woo the Fair with Fustian[12] and Grimace,
Attack with Nonsense, and subdue with Lace.   50
Women, like Magpies, full of Pride and Noise,
Stalk chatt'ring round, and follow glitt'ring Toys;[13]
Pleas'd with some shining Trifle, haste away,
Spread their gay Plumes, and hoard the Tinsel-Prey.[14]
Some thoughtless Hearts deceitful Nymphs ensnare
With Pomp of Dress, and Gayety of Air.
So, heedless of the Net, the Lark's betray'd,
Charm'd by the Glass, that sparkles in the Mead.

---

7. i.e. the brims of the hats were not cocked or turned up.
8. i.e. hidden deep behind some immense old cravat.
9. citizens, a word usually applied to shopkeepers.
10. The mythical lyre-player who could charm all nature with his playing.
11. Festivities in honour of Bacchus, the god of wine.
12. bombastic language.
13. i.e. as magpies steal and hoard glittering toys, so these women stalk and follow foolish young men who would be playthings for them.
14. i.e. hoard the gaudy, showy young men they have caught.

Secure from high we view th'amusing Scene,
Survey their Follies, and forsee their Pain.   60
Thus Mountain-Tops untroubled Quiet know,
While Tempests roar, and Lightnings flash below.
Pleas'd we elude the ling'ring Lapse of Day,
With jocund Catch, or am'rous Roundelay;[15]
Our tastes their throng'd *Hesperian*[16] Notes confound,
Lost in a trackless Labyrinth of Sound;
Gay native Tunes assert our worthier Choice,
And the *Black Joke*[17] resounds from ev'ry Voice....

The Play begins, now hush'd be ev'ry Sound,
Hush'd the Discourse of e'en that *Female Round*.   70
Now in fictitious Scenes our Minds engage;
Mourn with *Monimia*,[18] or with *Hamlet* rage!
Thee, *Brutus*, chief my ravish'd Soul admires,
Each Word transports me, and each Action fires;
Thy Death, great Patriot, still survives in Fame,
The noblest Drama, as the greatest Theme.
Now *Congreve*[19] charms us with less pompous Lines,
Art joyn'd with Nature, Wit with Humour shines;
Whether grave Sense, or mirthful Scenes he writes,
His Sense instructs us, and his Mirth delights....   80

High we preside, to give the Play-House Laws,
And call forth all the Tempest of Applause....
Oft' our Applause has found the Gall'ry fail,
And the torn Wainscot rattled with our Zeal:
We bid the Recompense of Wit go round,
And teach the doubtful Clappings where to sound:
From us deriv'd, like Warmth the rest employs,
And Hands colliding propagate the Noise....

15. A song with a refrain.
16. Of the Hesperides or western isles. The poet seems to be contrasting the music played by the orchestra in the pit with the songs sung by himself and his friends.
17. A slang phrase for indecent jokes.
18. Monimia is the title-character in Thomas Otway's *The Orphan or the Unhappy Marriage* (1680).
19. The plays of William Congreve (see above p. 67) were popular in eighteenth-century Dublin.

But now the Curtain falls, the Musick flies,
From their throng'd Seats the yawning Audience rise;   90
Whilst with slow Speed the rushing Crowds descend,
The Stairs sound hollow, and the Gall'ries bend....

The Beaus and Fair last quit the thinn'd Abode,
(The brawny Chairman pants beneath his Load)
Gay Creatures, proud of Dress and transient Bloom,
The light Things flutter round, and gold the Gloom.
So[20] where the Sew'rs thro' broken Channels glide,
And stagnant Filth coagulates the Tide,
Lur'd by the Stench unnumber'd Flies resort,
And wanton circling, mix in various Sport;   100
From Side to Side the humming Insects run,
Wave their gilt Wings, and glitter in the Sun.

But where shall hungry Bard for Refuge fly
From Paths nocturnal, and a wintry Sky?
Aghast I feel the Chairman's Pole behind,
And dread loud Coaches in each rustling Wind!
Thro' my rent Coat the chilling Tempests blow,
And gaping Shoes admit the Tide below![21]
Thus numb'd by Frosts, or drench'd in soaking Rain,
Oft' I explore my empty Purse in vain;   110
Alas! no Sixpence rises to my Hand,
Whose magick Force cou'd flying Cars command.[22]
At length, I come where 'mid th'admiring Round,
In Verse alternate, warbled Ballads sound,
Ballads my self had fram'd with wond'rous Art,
To gain a Supper, or a Milk-Maid's Heart!
I with the croud, the tuneful Sounds pursue,
What won't the Love of Fame and Musick do?
Now the arch Stripling from some neighb'ring Stand,
Hurles Flames malignant from his lifted Hand;[23]   120
Whizzing they fly; the Croud aghast retires
From the dread Squib, and future-spreading Fires.

---

20. i.e. thus. The next six lines constitute a parodic incursion into epic simile.
21. i.e. the water from the puddles.
22. i.e. I could afford to get a carriage home if I had sixpence.
23. i.e. a mischievous youth from nearby throws firecrackers into the crowd.

It bounces, bursts, and in a Flash is lost,
From Side to Side the reeling Crouds are tost;
Now heav'd on high, now trampl'd under Feet,
And *Poets* roll with *Coblers* in the Street....

An Elegy

on the much lamented Death of those excellent *Patriots* and Lovers of their Country
the Family of all the POTATOES in the Kingdom of Ireland,
who fell by a general Massacre, being confined and starved alive by Cold and Hunger
(cruellest of deaths!) between the 26th Day of *December*, and the 18th of *January*
in the Year 1739,[1] to the inexpressible Loss and Grief of the weeping, bleeding Country[2]

IF ever grief was great without Disguise,
If tears sincere e'er flow'd from Mourners Eyes,
Now is the Time ——! now Tyrant-Sorrow reign,
And from our Eyes the briny Ocean drain!

HIBERNIA ——! well dost Thou refuse to raise
Thy Head, to see the Sorrows of these Days,
Grave was thy *Harp* before, and half unstrung,
Slow mov'd the Finger, plaintive went the Tongue:
Now to deep Mourning tune thy future Lays,
With Frost-nipt *Shamrogs*[3] crown'd instead of *Bays*.   10

POTATOES ——! Kindly Root, most cordial Friend,
That ever Nature to this Isle did send!
Potatoes; oh hard Fate! all dead and gone?
And with them thousands of our selves anon!
'Twas you, deceas'd dear friends, kept us alive,
Vain, vain are all our Hopes long to survive!

1. i.e. between 26 December 1739 and 18 January 1740.

2. There were several serious famines in eighteenth-century Ireland, one of the worst of which occurred when the bad weather and poor harvest of 1739 was followed by an appallingly cold winter. This remarkable, heart-felt poem eloquently mourns the death of the entire Irish potato crop, frozen solid in the ground in the middle of that winter, and highlights the terrible plight of the hundreds of thousands at the lower end of the economic scale, for whom the potato had, by the 1730s, become not only the staple diet but also a vital part of everyday life. Louis Cullen estimates that there were probably more deaths in the Irish countryside in the famine of 1740-41 than in the great Famine of 1845-48 (*An Economic History of Ireland since 1660* (London, 1972), p. 69).

3. shamrocks — but here standing for potato plants.

Incense to living Benefactors paid
Uncertain is, till low their Heads are laid:
Low are the Heads of dear Potatoes laid,
Then Incense certain to them shall be paid.   20

Virgil, thy *Georgicks*, and thy *Muse* here bring,
While I the Praise of dead Potatoes sing.[4]
With grateful Sense (blest Root!) I must relate
Cheap was thy Culture, but thy Profit great,
Of Plough or Harrow, harness'd Ox or Steed,
Thy Cultivation did not stand in need:
Into poor Earth a Parcel of You flung
Thin-bedded with a Lock of half-made Dung,
Cover'd with one poor Shovel and a Spade
With small Expence of Time and Labour laid,   30
Nay, cut in Pieces (that, which kills most *Grain*,
Potatoes multiplies, and mends the Strain)
Did with the next approaching Summer's Sun
High with luxuriant Leaves, and Branches run,
Whereon thick Tufts of *Musky* Blossoms shoot,
Delicious in Smell, as strengthening is the Root.

The Blossoms wither'd, *Apples*[5] next succeed,
Whose viscous Balsam hectick Patients need:
Or, if regard to Luxury be paid,
Of them are beauteous rich Confections made.   40

The Apples ripe, the *Leaves*, as *Trefoil*[6] sweet,
The Cattle us'd with lowing Joys to meet.
Even in Corruption sweet the Stalks exhale
An aromatick Flavour thro' the Vale.
Useless no Part, the bleach'd *Haulm*[7] provides
White-Satin Litter for pet Heifers Sides.

4. Virgil's *Georgics* are poems in praise of agriculture and life on the land.
5. The small white apple-like 'fruit' of the potato which forms after the flower. They are no longer used in medicine or confectionery.
6. Clover, shamrock or any other wild, three-leafed plant.
7. The stalk of the potato plant.

The *Root*, the hidden Treasure, is behind,
Prop of the Poor, *Delight* of all Mankind!
A Tract of Ground, so planted, look'd with Scorn
On thrice the Quantity of *any* Corn.   50
Surprising Root ——! wherein Food has but Share,
Which does at once both *Food* and *Medicine* bear.
Prolifick Juices from it swell the Veins,
It *multiplies*, and Human Kind *maintains*.
Bruis'd, and to burn'd or scalded Parts apply'd,
To cool and heal them, is a Topick try'd.
In Leprous Ails[8] Potatoe-broth takes Place,
Abstersive,[9] healing, sovereign as *Lough Leichs*.[10]

Corn many Operations undergoes,
Before it can a single Loaf compose: 60
Potatoes no such Cost, Pains, Care demand,
Each being a Loaf born ready to the Hand:
One single Operation they require,
Bare Transplantation from their Beds to Fire,
Where soon they *Breaden*, cracking Skins disclose
Rich mealy Pulp, such as roast Chestnut shews.
No Salt, or Sugar, or a Grain of Spice
They need to cook them delicate and nice:
Tea ready done, Milk from the Cow is said,[11]
Potatoe justly roasted is *French Bread,*   70
And equally a *Pudding* of it made
Before the King (God bless him!) might be paid.[12]

The *Liquors* did our thriftless People know,
That from them in their native *India*[13] flow,
Where here by Art superior drawn might prove,
Such as the Poor, or higher Tastes might love.

8. ailments.
9. Having the quality of cleansing or purging.
10. This lake is unidentified. The water from many Irish lakes was reputed to have healing properties.
11. The couplet seems to mean that, though the people are actually consuming milk and potatoes, they say that their meal is of tea and French bread.
12. Before any taxes would be paid. Taxes could be levied only on a cash crop.
13. 'India' is here used as an emblem of a source of great wealth. The couplet means: 'If only our thriftless people knew the liquor which they could make from this native source of wealth ...' and the next ten lines refer to various practical uses to which all parts of the the potato plant might be put.

Thus, might they, from the same Potatoe heap
Variety of Life's best Comforts reap,
Bread, to enable them Labour to endure,
Drink, to forget that ever they were poor,   80
Starch[14] for their Linnen (such as *Linnen* wear!)
And for the spruce Ones, *Powder* for the Hair.
Let it suffice thus far with grief to tell
In what Potatoes *living* did excel!

Here stop and sigh ——! kind *Elegiac* Muse
A Mourners *last* Request do not refuse,
Now something like *last Speech* and *dying Words*[15]
(For little better now our State affords!)
Nay, for us now some *Elegy* contrive,
We are not *dead*, but who could say *alive*?   90
Our Hearts are with Potatoes dying dead,
Of half-dead creatures try what may be said.

Potatoes fed us, while the *Corn* we sow'd
Was to the Payment of the Rent bestow'd.[16]
What must we feed on now, when *both* are spent?
Oh cou'd our *Feasts* be now like old *black Lent*![17]
I must ——! I will to sad Remembrance bring
Our wonted *Irish* Olio[18] of the Spring,
Crown'd with a Herring; *Herring* King of Fish!
Potatoes Queen of Roots in wooden Dish!   100
Herrings, tho' gone this Year, we may regain,
Potatoes dead will never come again!
By angry Clergy will it now be said,
This comes a Judgement for the Tithe unpaid:[19]
Those who detain it timely shou'd repent;
Poor Tenants, don't they pay it in their Rent?

---

14. Potatoes also contain starch, and a white starchy powder can be made by drying them.
15. Broadsheets sold at executions often purported to be the 'last speech and dying words' of the malefactor.
16. The smaller Irish tenants commonly grew corn as a cash crop to pay the rent, and potatoes to feed themselves and their families.
17. i.e. a time of abstinence before a return to normal eating patterns.
18. A dish of various meats and vegetables stewed or boiled together (*OED*).
19. The payment of dues, known as tithes, to the clergy of the Church of Ireland was compulsory in eighteenth-century Ireland, and was much resented.

Oh bless'd Saint PATRICK, Guardian of this Isle,
Commiserate our Case, and on us smile!
Propitious *Nature*, may our Schemes succeed,
Inspire a Method to preserve some *Seed*!   110
With Care we must the thawing Clods explore,
Increase by small Plantations, as before:
If that shou'd fail ——! in Swarms we must repair
To *India*[20] strait, make up our Losses there,
There bidding to our Rent-rack'd[21] Lands adieu,
Potatoes eat, taste Flesh, Bread, Butter too.

EPITAPH

Beneath this *frozen* Sod, dead may be found,
Half of the real Wealth of *Irish* Ground!
Much might, but much, alas! need not be said
Here lie two Thirds of Ireland's *daily Bread.*   120

---

20. Presumably the poet means the West Indies,\ to which many Irish families and
individuals were emigrating at this time.
21. Excessively high or 'rack' rents were common throughout eighteenth-century Ireland.

JAMES STERLING
(1701-**1737**-1763)

James Sterling was born in 1701 in County Offaly, the son of a 'gentleman', according to the record in Trinity College, Dublin, from which he obtained his B.A. in 1720. His first play seems to have been performed in Dublin's Smock Alley Theatre as early as 1723; he contributed three poems to Matthew Concanen's *Miscellaneous Poems, original and translated* (London, 1724) and published several poems in Dublin in the 1720s. Later Sterling was ordained into the Church of Ireland and in 1733 he moved to London, where he wrote many political pamphlets and some more plays. He emigrated to Maryland in 1740 and spent the rest of his life as a minister there. The poem below, published anonymously, was probably written to order, for a fee; yet its proposal is framed in a refreshingly realistic view of Irish politics and economics, and the poem provides, as well, a memorable description of whaling off the coast of County Donegal. It is addressed to Arthur Dobbs (1689-1765), author of the most important economic tract written in eighteenth-century Ireland, *An Essay on the Trade and Improvement of Ireland*, 2 parts (Dublin, 1729, 1731) and, at this time, Surveyor General of Ireland.

A Friend in Need is a Friend in Deed:
or, a PROJECT, At this Critical Juncture, to gain the Nation a hundred thousand Pounds per Annum from the Dutch; by an IRISH WHALE FISHERY.

Nor Songs, nor Tales of Love delight the Muse,
Resolv'd a new, a useful Theme to Chuse;
She scorns those trite, those weatherbeaten Strains,
The Spurious Product of Fantastick Brains;
Who Fawn and Flatter, Creep and Cringe, and Lie
And place their Heaven in Fair *Chloe*'s Eye,
With base Submission, with Devotion paid,
They meanly seek t'immortalize the Maid;
But search the truth, the Reason's quickly Found,
'Tis said that *Chloe* has ten thousand Pound: 10
So Mean, so Mercenary are their Views,
It's scarce allow'd there is an honest Muse.
To prove the contrary, my Muse pretends,
Protests she's Byass'd by no servile Ends;
T'assert her Country's Good she pleads a Right,
To state her Case in clear, in honest Light.

Where Arts and Trade encrease, they always bring
Wealth to the Subject, Grandeur to the King;
Th'Improvement of a Fishery and trade,
In Holland, shews the vast Advantage made,   20
A Country whose intestine[1] Fruits and grain
Cou'd scarce its tenth inhabitant Maintain,
By care, tho' Lately indigent and poor,
All neighb'ring Lands outshines in wealthy Store;
Th'industrious *Dutch* have prov'd it very plain,
That Art with Diligence makes greatest Gain:
Full of this Maxim their yet Infant Rise,
Cautiously Prudent, providently Wise,
Proportion'd Premiums[2] to all Persons paid
Who or[3] invented, or improv'd a Trade;   30
Thus Daily grew the grandeur of the State;
Encouragement must be Perfection's Bait.

HIBERNIA too by Nature's liberal Hand,
Affording all that human wants demand,
Like *Holland* long oppress'd with hostile Rage
Appear'd no better than a publick Stage,
For Murder, Rapines, Massacres, Design'd
Rebellions, Schisms, Vice in every Kind,
Harrass'd with Ills by slow Degrees decay'd
She thus had perish'd. But with timely Aid   40
NASSAU[4] victoriously the Foe subdu'd
Restor'd her Peace, her former Trade Renew'd:
Kind Fortune too gave an auspicious Smile,
And growing Trade flow'd to enrich our Isle;
Our Parliament with due, with timely Care,
Did for a Future Growth in Arts prepare;
Their Laws and Edicts with due Premiums fraught,
Our Manufactures to Perfection brought,

---

1. internal. i.e. a country which can hardly feed one-tenth of its inhabitants from produce grown within its borders.
2. rewards or prizes. The Dublin Society (later the Royal Dublin Society), founded in 1731, was already beginning to provide prizes for improvements in agricultural and other useful arts in Ireland.
3. either.
4. i.e. William III (1672-1702) was fifth monarch in the house of Orange-Nassau, Stadholders of the Northern Provinces, as well as, from 1689, king of Britain and Ireland.

Their chiefest Aim to raise our *Woolen* trade
Which we with Freedom ev'ry where Convey'd;   50
In *Portugal* our Cloths great Prices bore,
And *Irish* Cloaks the Formal *Spaniard* wore.

Those Halcyon Days, alas! too good to hold!
Our *Irish* Cloths fetch no more Foreign Gold;
Our Wealth was envy'd; to exhaust our Store,
Our Trade was stopt by Laws unknown before.[5]
Altho' our Cloths might with the *English* Vie,
Our Colours with the fam'd *Venetian* Die,
Millions of Sheep upon our Mountains roam,
Their Fleeces now must be consumed at Home.   60

Our *Woolen* Trade thus lost, *Hibernia* mourn'd,
And to Improvement of our *Linen* turn'd.
Induc'd by Premiums first the Spinster[6] strove,
And for Encouragement the Artist wove;
Each glowing Breast hop'd to obtain the Prize,
And Emulation caus'd the Trade to rise;
That curious Art which long enrich'd the *Dutch*,
We have improv'd, and our Perfection's such
Their *Linen* priz'd so Justly many Years,
No longer now its wanted Value bears,   70
Ours gain'd the Preference in Ballance weigh'd,
Prov'd the chief Standard of our sinking Trade.

But this alone cannot our Wants supply,
We seem defective in a *Fishery*:
The Dutch have this Establish'd, whilst we may
Enjoy the like much easier than they.

Judicious DOBBS has this most fully prov'd,
By true Affection to his Country mov'd,
He gave his Thoughts, his Arguments more Strong
And more persuasive than the Muses Song;   80

---

5. The Woollen Act, passed by the Westminster parliament in 1699 to protect English mercantile interests, prohibited Ireland from exporting woollen goods. It destroyed the flourishing Irish woollen trade.
6. A woman (or man) who makes a living spinning wool.

How speedily might this our Isle be blest,
Were all her Sons with equal Love possess'd;
With what Affection are his Thoughts display'd!
In his ingenious Essays on our Trade.[7]
With Emulation thus, O DOBBS inflam'd,
My Muse has at her Country's Profit aim'd;
Nor sordid Int'rest, nor the love of Praise,
Cou'd e'er have forc'd her to attempt the Bays,
But filial Love alone, that bids her try
To Sing th'Advantage of a *Fishery*.   90
Thou hast indeed with great exactness shewn
Our vast Expenses paid for *Oil* and *Bone*,
And by a modest Computation found
The *Dutch* gain yearly Fifty Thousand Pound.
This might be sav'd did we but once agree
To Man a Fleet to attempt a *Fishery*.

Say now my Muse, what Numbers wilt thou bring,
Or in what Lines our Benefactor Sing,
Who thus has taught us of his own accord
What Plenty these our fertile Shores afford;   100
Who first discover'd *Whales* upon our Coast,
Such Quantities as *Britain* cannot Boast;
Ev'n *Donnegal* produces equal Store
To what is found on *Greenland*'s foreign Shore;
How great his Merits, who thus taught a Road
To Feed our wants at home, to send abroad
To save our Coin, and daily fetch home more,
Each tending to encrease the Publick store;
Yet farther, when a Stranger to the Coast,
He found the *Fish* which hitherto were Lost   110
Lost, or at least, they yet unheeded lay,
Tho' on the Shore they sported every Day,
And always undisturb'd enjoy'd the peaceful Sea.

If it be true what *Horace* sagely Notes,
His Heart was shielded in three Brazen Coats,
Who first adventur'd o'er the fickle Main,
And could intrepidly behold the Train

7. The two parts of Dobbs's *An Essay on the Trade and Improvement of Ireland* appeared
   in Dublin in 1729 and 1731.

Of Finny Monsters skim the glassy Plain,[8]
What had he said, to raise his Country's good,
Had he beheld our Fisher stem the Flood,   120
Of briny Waves, with what a Coat of Mail
Wou'd he have Arm'd him to attack a *Whale*.
On *Doren*'s Towering Mount[9] thus from afar
I view'd the Dangers of the wat'ry War,
No Ruffling Breeze disturb'd the Marble Sea,
Th' unwieldy Monster on the Surface lay,
The daring Fisher silently draws near,
Deep in his Back descends the bearded Spear;
Rouz'd with the Wound, incens'd with pungent Smart,
He plunges down, th'astonish'd Waters part;   130
Entomb'd in Floods he cuts his private Way,
The veer'd out Lines his private Paths betray,
The hurry'd Barge through yielding Water flies,
Deceives my Sight, deserts my wandring Eyes.
The Monster breathless now thrusts up his Nose,
The Barge emergent at a Distance Rows,
He Sneesing snorts, transparent Floods appear,
Which mounting up Illuminate the Air,
Repelled by Clouds they downward show'r again
In Sluicy heaps like spouts of Winter rain;   140
Th'enormous Monster thus expos'd to view
Th'audacious Fishers strait the War renew
Courageously against the Foe advance
Repeat their blow and leave the goring Lance;
Enrag'd with double Smart the Monster heaves,
A hoary Foam o'erspreads the curling Waves,
Downward he sinks, and instantly again
Upon the Surface Floats, the Whitening Main
Exagitated[10] with such vig'rous bounds
Assuming rage obstreperously Sounds;   150
Above, below, the Monster seeks in vain
To loose the Dart, or mollifie his Pain;
Nor ease, nor Rest, nor Mitigation found,
Inspir'd with Rage and Fiercer through the Wound,

8. Horace, *Odes* I, iii, 9.
9. A note at this point in the 1736 edition refers to 'Doren' as 'a Mountain in the County of Donnegal nigh Killibeggs, where the Whales are taken'. cf. Doorin Point, to the southeast of Killybegs.
10. stirred up.

All Efforts try'd, no more prepares to Fly,
Exerts his Strength and vainly beats the Sky;
His spatt'ring Tail whole Seas of Water throws,
The Waters sink and tremble at his blows;
Heated with frequent Strokes they raging boil,
Tumultuously like Pots of Spumy Oil.   160
With equal Courage but inferiour Force,
Th'undaunted *Fisher* steers his giddy Course,
Anxious again to wound the bulky Foe,
Rows boldly up and strikes another blow;
Again falls off his Forky Tail t'evade
Each dashing stroke is with a stroke repaid;
Till Sickening by degrees he Faintly heaves,
Whilst spouting Blood infects the Frothy Waves,
Gathering his wasting Strength he vaults the Skies,
Hangs in the Air, Expiring, falls and dies.   170
With Peals of shouts the hollow Heavens ring
When on the Prostrate Foe they joyful Spring,
Sweating to Land they tow the vanquish'd Prize,
Supine on Waves the Floating Monster lies;
But e'er they reach it, tumid[11] Billows Roar,
Hoarse, hideous Noises fill the sounding Shore;
Stern *Boras*[12] with despotick lawless Sway
Sweeps o'er the land, and Couches on the Sea;
Now spongy, gathering Clouds o'ercast the Light,
The Day serene sinks into gloomy Night,   180
While Waves on Waves ebullient[13] dreadful rise
And irresisted seem to dare the Skies,
The skilful Fisher tries his Art in vain
To save his Prey in the tumultuous Main;
The lines are cut, the Labours of the Day
Tost at the Pleasure of th'impetuous Sea.
Scarcely the Floods sustain the pond'rous Freight
But sink depress'd and groan beneath the weight,
Till by the assistance of the driving Blast,
The floating Mountain on the Shore is cast.   190
In vain the Seaman plies the bending Oar,
Tuggs hard and sweats to reach the wish'd for Shore,

11. swelling.
12. Boreas, the north wind in classical mythology.
13. agitated as if boiling.

Nor Helm, nor Oars, th'unstable Boat obeys,
But whirling drives before the boiling Seas,
Elate on Waves against the Sky she's tost,
Now low in Waters' darksome abyss lost.
Quite spent with Toile, oppress'd with anxious Care,
'Twixt glim'ring Hopes of Living and Despair,
The Seaman, now no more the Torrent braves
And but half dead escapes the gaping Waves.   200

Such are the Dangers of the faithless Sea
Through such as these the *Fisher* seeks his Prey.
Awake, HIBERNIA, ope thy Eyes and see
The vast Advantage of a *Fishery*;
With Speed prepare t'attack the Finny Foe,
From taking which such Benefits will flow;
Equip your Boats with sharp *Harpoon* and *Lance*,
Let's strive our publick Treasure to Advance;
So shall Returning Gold reward our Toil,
When *London Lamps* shall glow with *Irish Oil*[14]   210
To the *Undertaker*[15] let us shew Regard,
His Merits Value and his Pains Reward,
Who has a worthy *Publick Spirit* shewn
To raise the *Kingdom's Good* with Hazard of his *own*.

14. Whale-oil for use in oil lamps was an important commodity in the eighteenth century.
15. i.e. the person prepared to finance the undertaking.

WETENHALL WILKES
(fl.**1737**, d.1751)

Wetenhall Wilkes was an ambitious English miscellaneous writer, among whose works was *An Essay on the Existence of God* (1730) and *A letter of genteel and moral advice to a young lady* (1740). In 1737 he was in Dublin, confined in 'The Black Dog', a tavern which was used as a prison for debtors and for those accused of crimes before their cases came to court. From 'The Black Dog', Wilkes addressed the following poem to Swift requesting his assistance in obtaining his release. There is no record that Swift took any action; however, according to Wilkes's own testimony, the poem became something of a success and he sold 17,000 copies of it in two months. He published two further continuations to the poem, as well as other verses, including 'The prisoner's ballad: or welcome, welcome, brother debtor'. Wilkes later became a dissenting minister.

from: ## The Humours of the Black Dog
In a letter to the R.*J.S.*D.D.D.S.P.D.,[1] by a Gentleman in
Confinement: a new Poem

... Coup'd up with iron Barrs my drooping Muse
Dark Scenes of Wretchedness all round her views;
By which dispirited to touch the Lyre,
No more she warms my breast with sacred Fire;
No more inspires me with heroic Strain
But bids me write with a dejected Vein.
The tuneful Nine[2] require a Mind of ease;
But mine is wreck'd above a thousand ways.

Ye Gods! When first the *Grippers*[3] brought me here,
How were my sinking Spirits seiz'd with fear!   10
I felt an horror creeping through my Veins
And Phrenzy hurling through my shatter'd Brains.

---

1. The letters stand for 'Reverend *Jonathan Swift*, Doctor of Divinity, Dean of Saint Patrick's, Dublin'.
2. i.e. the Muses.
3. The Sheriff's men — a term used only in Ireland.

'Tis not amiss progressively to tell,
I hope, what some in my short time befell.
In came *John Moor*[4] to ask the Penny-Pot;
Which straight the *Lower House* in order got.
If this be once denied, up comes *Moll-Whip*:[5]
'Your Servant, Sir: the penny-pot or — strip.'
Plebeian shouts ring through the crowded Hall:
'So old, so good a Custom must not fall.'   20

Then comes in *Peter*,[6] with a leering Look:
'Sir, I presume you heard the words were spoke:
Long life t'you Sir; I want a little Chink:[7]
For upon Tick[8] I never draw my Drink.'
If out of Cash or in their answer short
E'er in the Morn they rise, they suffer for't.
Some miss their hats and wiggs and some their shoes;
Their stockings some, and others all their Cloaths:
Which, thus into the Huckster's[9] hands be'ng got,
Are pawn'd with *Peter* for the Penny-Pot.   30
Three loud Ho-yesses fill the dusty Hall
And ev'ry thirsty Throat obeys the Call.
He then, exerting all his homebred skill,
Takes constant care to draw — but not to fill.
After eight quarts are brought he stops[10] as due
For himself two-pence, and for *Betty*[11] two.
If he be checkd, with dreadful oaths and lies
The bother'd house his rusty throat supplies;
Not one among us all but daily talks
Of his bad measure and his double chalks:[12]   40

---

4. A newcomer was faced with a traditional demand from the other prisoners (in 'the Lower House') for the twenty pence necessary to purchase a 'penny-pot' (a measure of ale for all). An original note at this point describes John Moor as 'A long stick with a head and face cut on one end dress'd in a hat and wigg, which is brought in by the youngest Prisoner to make this demand.'
5. 'A fictitious name for a Broom which is brought in as a Symbol to signify it will sweep all before it and that there must be no Denial' (original note).
6. 'The Drawer and Deputy Turn-key' (original note). A 'turnkey' is a prison warder.
7. money.
8. credit.
9. A small shopkeeper — in this case one who buys old clothes for cash.
10. 'The usual penny-pot is twenty pence, out of which he makes those stoppages by a Rule of his own' (original note).
11. 'The Girl's name that makes the Beds' (original note).
12. A 'chalk' was a record of purchase 'chalked up' on a board at an alehouse.

In both which Articles he is by far
The greatest ——— that ever kept a Barr.
His surly Countenance and sawcy Tongue
Would make a stranger think all things go wrong:
With us that are confin'd indeed they do;
And that our Looks, our Words, our Actions shew.
Should I the progress of each Day rehearse,
'Twould prove at best a (melancholy) Farce.

Now, to proceed: (where other Dues were paid)[13]
The Turnkey (sneering) lighted me to bed.   50
A serious view be'ng taken of my —— Den,
At length I with reluctance tumbled in.
When to and fro I many hours had tost
I started up in stupid wonder lost;
And fretting did my various Cares bewail:
But fain would not believe I was in —— Jail.
When balmy slumbers are to me deny'd,
Oppress'd with grief I toss from side to side.
In dreams I oft am tortur'd on the Deep
And often wreck'd with visions in my sleep.   60
I oft on shaking Bogs and Quicksands tread
And am by violence to Vultures led.
On pointed Pyramids I often stand,
As if suspended 'twixt the Clouds and Land:
Thence through a Formless Void I tumble down
And am to Savages and Tygers thrown.
I from those slumbers start in wild surprize
While ghastly Horror stands before my Eyes.
But when the Dawn reveals the rosy East
(Since on my pillow I can find no rest,)   70
I rise and wander through my chearless Room;
Where Melancholly reigns in awful gloom.
Hungry Revenge, Spleen, Anguish, pale-fac'd Fear,
And self-consuming Envy govern here,
They all alternately my thoughts possess,
And rend my Soul with exquisite distress.

13. 'Three quarts of Ale and a large Candle' (original note).

Soon as I hear the sounding Doors unfold,
Increasing Tumults then invade my Soul.
My beating heart comes flutt'ring to my lips
And fear my Mind of all its vigour strips: 80
My Nerves unbrac'd forget their Office too,
And Madness lodges on my bristling Brow.

An Iron Chain still rattles at the Door
And ev'ry window massy Barrs secure.
All Rooms are lock'd and on each Case of Stairs
A Door our passage up and down debars:
But, though our Bodies closely are confin'd,
We still can freely exercise our Mind.

When ev'ry Morn the Turnkey comes up stairs
The Jingling keys in triumph still he bears.   90
Peter keeps Heaven's keys — Scriptureans[14] tell;
But here our *Peter* keeps the keys of ——.
As grim as *Cerberus*[15] he shakes those keys;
Growls at the Poor, but grins at him who pays.

The Doors unlock'd,[16] we Pris'ners all convene
At Change[17] and form a melancholly Scene.
Some slippers, nightcaps and some habits[18] wear;
And others in their usual dress appear:
But all look Pris'ner like. —— A wild amaze
Stares in the eyes and spreads o'er e'ry face; ...   100

... Up Stairs and down I stroll from Morn till Night;
But ev'ry where the barrs insult my sight.
I traverse all the Rooms in search of rest
While rude, convulsive doubts divide my breast.
Sometimes a cordial Friend (for none but such
The gloomy Chambers of a Jail approach)

14. Those who read the Scriptures, theologians.
15. In classical mythology, Cerberus was the dog stationed at the gates of hell.
16. 'The doors are never open'd till after eight in the morning' (original note).
17. 'A large common room where all meet to walk and converse ...' (original note). Eighteenth-century merchants met to conduct their business in the Exchange or Change.
18. The use of this word here is obscure. It may carry its usual meaning of the clothes of someone in a religious order, or, perhaps, refer to nightshirts or even to 'habits' wrapped around bodies for burial.

263

Industr'ously attempts my mind to ease ——
My sinking Spirits with new Mirth to raise.
If 'tis enquir'd — how we our Cares sustain,
We answer thus: — *'Tis folly to Complain.*[19]   110
In forced mirth sometimes an hour we pass
And sometimes take a recreating Glass.
Then from the pipe and flask I seek relief
And with Tobacco puff away my grief.
But when we part my agonies return;
My breast begins with double rage to burn:...
... Till healing slumbers bring to my relief
A sweet forgetfulness of all my Grief....

[19] 'A Phrase of Mr *Andrew Shannon*, a Fellow Prisoner' (original note).

ROBERT NUGENT, EARL NUGENT
(1702-**1740**-1788)

The son of a landowner in County Westmeath, Robert Nugent was involved with politics in both Ireland and England, where he accumulated various titles and eventually became one of the country's richest men. His witty speeches in the Westminster parliament were delivered in what was described as 'a rich Irish brogue'. Nugent was a prolific poet (though it was alleged by Thomas Gray that at least one of the poems published under his name was written by the poet David Mallet) and also befriended other writers including Goldsmith, who wrote 'The Haunch of Venison' in his honour. On its second appearance in print, in 1773, the poem which follows was dedicated not to an unnamed 'Pollio' but to Nugent's friend Philip Stanhope, fourth Earl of Chesterfield, author of the famous *Letters* to his natural son (1774). It was presumably written for Chesterfield in the first place, and the name 'Pollio' was used in the early printing to heighten the effect of classical idyll.

Epistle to Pollio, from the Hills of Howth in Ireland[1]

Pollio! would'st thou condescend
Here to see thy humble friend,
Far from doctors, potions, pills,
Drinking health on native hills;
Thou the precious draught may'st share,
Lucy shall the bowl prepare.
From the brousing goat it flows,
From each balmy shrub that grows;
Hence the kidling's wanton fire,
Hence the nerves that brace his fire.   10
Vigorous, buxom, young and gay,
Thou like him shalt love and play.

What, though far from silver Thames,
Stately piles, and courtly dames;
Here we boast a purer flood,
Joys that stream from sprightly blood;
Here is simple beauty seen,
Fair, and cloth'd like beauty's queen:
Nature's hands the garbs compose,
From the lily and the rose.   20

---

1. The title to the 1773 printing reads: 'Epistle to the Earl of Chesterfield from the Hills of Howth in Ireland, where the author was drinking Goat's whey. By Lord Viscount Clare (at that time Robert Nugent Esq.)'. Howth Hill is on the northern side of Dublin bay, about eight miles from the city.

265

Or, if charm'd with richer dies,
Fancy every robe supplies.
Should perchance some high-born fair,
Absent, claim thy tender care,
Here, enraptur'd shalt thou trace,
S———'s shape, and R———'s face;[2]
While the waking dream shall pay
Many a wishing, hopeless day.
Domes with gold and toil unbought,
Rise by magic pow'r of thought,   30
Where by artist's hand undrawn,
Slopes the vale, and spreads the lawn;
As if sportive nature meant,
Here to mock the works of Kent.[3]

Come, and with thee bring along
Jocund tale and witty song,
Sense to teach, and words to move,
Arts that please, adorn, improve;
And, to gild the glorious scene,
Conscience spotless and serene.   40

Poor with all a H———t's[4] store,
Lives the man who pines for more.
Wretched he who doom'd to roam,
Never can be blest at home;
Nor retire within his mind,
From th'ungrateful and unkind.
Happy they whom crowds befriend,
Curs'd who on the crowd depend;
On the great one's peevish fit,
On the coxcomb's spurious wit;   50
Ever sentenc'd to bemoan
Others failings in their own.

---

2. Obviously the coded names of London beauties; this line is among several omitted in the 1773 printing.
3. William Kent (1684-1748), a fashionable painter and landscape architect.
4. Perhaps a reference to Henry Herbert, ninth Earl of Pembroke (d. 1751). In the 1773 printing, the line is changed to 'Wretched with a W———'s store' where the missing word is probably 'Walpole's' i.e. Horace Walpole, Lord Orford (1717-97).

If, like them, rejecting ease,
Hills and health no longer please;
Quick descend! — Thou may'st resort
To the viceroy's splendid court.[5]
There, indignant, shalt thou see
Cringing slaves, who might be free,
Brib'd with titles, hope, or gain
Tye their country's shameful chain;   60
Or, inspir'd by heav'n's good cause,
Waste the land with holy laws:
While the gleanings of their power,
Lawyers, lordlings, priests devour.

Now, methinks, I hear thee say,
'Drink alone thy mountain-whey!
Wherefore tempt the Irish shoals?
Sights like these are nearer Paul's.'[6]

---

5. i.e. in Dublin. The next eight lines express a view of Irish political activity commonly
held at the time.
6. i.e. sights like these are more similar to those you see in London (near St Paul's
cathedral).

JOHN, EARL OF ORRERY
(1707-**1741**-1762)

The fifth earl of Cork and Orrery is probably best known as the author of an unflattering and, in places, malicious biography of Swift, whom he knew in the last decade and a half of Swift's life. Orrery's own literary ambitions were not inconsiderable and, in addition to verse translations from the classics such as that which follows, he translated the letters of the younger Pliny (1751). Among his interests was book collecting, and his wealth enabled him not only to acquire a fine library but to have the books magnificently bound. He knew most of the writers of the age and befriended, among others, Dr Johnson.

from: ## The First Ode of the First Book of Horace Imitated ...

O THOU![1] whose Virtues *Albion*'s[2] Sons can trace
Thro' an ennobled long descending Race,
Whose honour'd Friendship, and whose guardian Name
Open a Prospect to the Realms of Fame,
Observe the various Passions of the Mind,
That teize, delight, distract, and rule Mankind.

There are, 'tis strange to say it, but there are,
Who[3] place their Glories in the rowling Car,[4]
Who drive the flying Steeds with nicest Art,
And act the Charioteer's tyrannick Part.   10
Hark! Stranger, hark! the circling Scourges sound;
The bridles jingle, and the Horses bound:
In Clouds of Dust th'envelop'd Heroes fly,
Like Gods invisible to mortal Eye.
Now, now, they lash, and now with Pride elate,
Double the Corner, pass the streighten'd[5] Gate;
Now short or wide with rapid Quickness turn,
And for the Coachman's Lawrels drive and burn.
Oh! give them all the Honours They require!
Let other Heroes other Virtues fire;   20
Be These for matchless Skill in driving known
And bind their Temples with a Whipcord Crown.

1. The Earl of Chesterfield, to whom this poem (like that by Robert Nugent above) is inscribed.
2. A poetic name for Britain.
3. i.e. those who.
4. carriage.
5. narrowed.

Tempt with Ambition, if You can, the Soul
Whom neither Vanity, nor Wants controul,
Shew Him the azure Garter[6] dangling high,
Or shake the taper Staff[7] before his Eye,
Say, the Gold Key his Pocket-holes shall grace,
Promise the Gift of Gifts! Sir *Robert*'s Place;[8]
Calm and unmov'd the Baits He shall behold,
Despise the Ensigns,[9] and disdain the Gold,   30
Safe in a Corner humble Port He'll quaff,
And, whilst He pities Kings, at Statesmen laugh.

Or try another, try a Man, whose Rent
In spight of Taxes, yields him ten per Cent,
Bid him all lands, all Purchases forego,
And deal in South-Sea Bonds — He'll answer, No!

Suppose a Third, who plows his native Soil,
And shares the Landlord's Pride, and Tenant's Toil,
Is neither idly vain, nor humbly low,
Perhaps a Justice, or who might be so;   40
Shall such a Man be lur'd from Plenty's Ease,
Quit his own Hearth, and launch into the Seas!
No, not at VERNON's[10] Call, — let others roam;
He'll fight the *Spaniards*, if he must, at Home.

But see the Merchant trembling for his Store,
The Winds grow mighty, and the Tempests roar;
The freighted Vessel, where his Treasure lies,
Now sinks to Hell, now rises to the Skies;
Pale and aghast! his Thoughts averse to Gain
Seek but this once the Mercy of the Main,   50
Should bounteous *Neptune* waft the Bark to Land,
Safe from each threat'ning Storm, each latent Sand,

6. The ribband of the Order of the Garter is of dark blue velvet edged with gold.
7. A staff and a gold key were the symbols of office of certain officers of the English monarch.
8. i.e. the place of prime minister, at the time of this poem (1741) held by Sir Robert Walpole.
9. badges of office.
10. Admiral Edward Vernon (1684-1757) was still at the time of this poem regarded as England's greatest admiral; however, he was disgraced in 1746 after fleets under his command were defeated off Spain and the West Indies.

To Trade, to Avarice, He'll bid adieu,
Let Him but pay his Creditors their Due;
That done, He'll seek some rural, calm Retreat,
No painful Doubts molest a Country-Seat.
So vows the Trader, whilst immers'd in Fear,
The Bark once landed, other Scenes appear,
All rural Prospects vanish from his Mind,
Again he tempts the Seas, and trusts the Wind.   60
Why should he change his Schemes? his Vows recant?
No Storm so dreadful, as the Thoughts of Want....

JOHN WINSTANLEY
(1677-**1742**-1750)

John Winstanley is one of the most entertaining poets of eighteenth-century Ireland. He spent some years at Trinity College, Dublin but did not get any degree, though he later declared himself 'Apollo's and the Muses' Licensed Doctor', wrote the letters A.M.L.D. after his name, and used the title 'Doctor' when it suited him. He wrote many poems about events in Dublin, Cabra and Glasnevin, two villages just to the north of the city, where he lived for much of his life. His two published volumes contain poems by other hands as well as his own, but the poems included here seem to be his work. The first of them gives a rare insight into the daily life of (in this case obviously high-spirited) school-girls in eighteenth-century Dublin.

Miss Betty's Singing-Bird

A Pretty *Song*, this coming *Spring,*
A little chanting *Bird* will sing;
The *Bird* you've heard old Women say
Comes often down the Chimney-way,
Then flies or hops the house around,
Where Tricks or Pranks are to be found;
The same which does all Stories tell,
When little Girls do ill or well.

When they're obstrep'rous or loquacious,
Contrump'rous,[1] boist'rous or audacious;   10
With what is given 'em discontent,
Or say things of their own invent;
Fling off their Caps and Cloaks i' th' Street,
Beat little Children that they meet;
Call Aunt a Sow, or ugly Witch,
Cic'ly a Hussy, Slut or B——h,
Scratch, bite and pinch, or pull her Quoife,[2]
And lead her a most dreadful Life.
Saunter an Hour or two to School,
And when they come there, play the Fool,   20
The ramping Hoyden[3] or Miss Bumpkin,
The Girls they sit by, ever thumping;

---

1. An unrecorded word: possibly a nursery form of, or mistake for, contumelious, meaning insolent.
2. = coif, a close-fitting cap worn by women at this time.
3. A rude or ill-bred girl or woman, a romp (*OED*).

Call Masters 'Bastard' or such Name,
And ev'ry little Miss defame;
When Aunt can scarce on them prevail
To wear a Gown not rattle-tail,
Yet never want a daggled Tail;[4]
When they have got a knack of crying,
Their Stays a-lacing, or Hair tying,
Go oft to Bed with weeping Eyes,   30
Yet sigh and slobber when they rise;
When Raisins, Sugar-plums nor Figs
Will bribe them not to pull off Wiggs;
For which, their bawling and their yelping,
They surely get full many a Skelping,[5]
Are lock'd in Vault, or Hole o' th' Stairs,
To sigh, and fret, and melt in Tears,
To bawl and roar, and not let out
Till many a Tear is dropt about,
And after to their Mistress sent   40
For further Flogging Punishment;
Which Chastisements, if proving vain,
They never more must go again
To *Lecoudre* or *Delamain*,[6]
But carry'd be, from *City* far,
To *Jerrico* or *Mullingar*.[7]

These, and perhaps a bolder thing,
This little prating *Bird* will sing
Of naughty *Girls* this coming Spring.

But, if they're modest, mild and witty,   50
And do Things innocent and pretty,
Observing always what they're bid,
Never deserving to be chid,
Discreet and good, they will be then
By *Ladies* loved, admir'd by *Men*;
Indulg'd in ev'ry harmless Way,
And suffered now and then to play;

---

4. tail = the skirt of a woman's dress. Despite their aunt's admonitions, the girls dress untidily.
5. smacking.
6. Lecoudre is untraced but William Delamain performed as a dancer in the Smock Alley theatre in 1732 and gave dancing lessons to young ladies.
7. A 'Jericho' is 'a place of banishment some distance away' (Partridge). Mullingar is a town in the Irish midlands, fifty miles from Dublin.

Have all the finest, nicest Cloaths,
Rich Ribbons, Laces, Stockings, Shoes,
Gold Snuff-box, Watch and Diamond Pendant,   60
And Cross with Jewels at the end on't;[8]
Oft Coach abroad, to take the Air
At *Park* and *Strand*, when Weather's fair;
Go now and then, on Holidays,
To *Consorts*,[9] *Puppet-Shows* and *Plays*;
Be always fine, most nicely dress'd,
In what's most curious, rich and best.
    All these this pretty Bird will sing;
    All these and more will surely bring
    To Girls, if Good, this coming Spring.   70

Upon *Daisy*, being brought back from *New Park* to *Stoneybatter*[1]

... Most lovely *Daisy*! sprung of *lovely Race*!
(For many a Charm thy Mother, *Lovely*, grace)
A cherry red her shining Coat adorns,
Her Head, black Eyes, sleek Face, and stately Horns;
Her Body's comely, plump, both deep and round;
With Legs and Hoofs, strong, streight, and smooth, and sound:
Nor *Mountown Mully*,[2] fam'd for Beauty rare,
For Teats and Udders can with her compare:
Then, from her Breath, a spicy Odour flows,
Perfuming all around, where'er she goes.   10
Had *Jove* seen *Lovely*, when a *Bull* he turn'd,
Not for *Europa*, but for her, he'd burn'd;[3]
Neglected *Ĭo*, ne'er had made such Stir,
But jealous *Juno* run horn mad on her.

---

8. Miss Betty and her schoolfriends seem to be catholics, as Winstanley was himself.
9. i.e. concerts.

---

1. The cow has been brought back from pastures at New Park, some unidentified place outside Dublin, to Stoneybatter, near the city centre.
2. See above p. 61.
3. The god Jupiter turned himself into a bull to be able to seduce Europa and, in another story, he turned the priestess Ĭo (whom he loved) into a long-suffering heifer to protect her from the wrath of his wife, Juno.

Forgive me, *Daisy*! I a while digress,
Tho' *Lovely*'s Fame be great, thine is no less;
Thy Beauties too, anon shall grace my Song,
Tho' she, and *New Park*, yet my Verse prolong....

... *Daisy*! my worthy, my delightful Theme!
(For oft I've tasted, and shall taste thy *Cream*)   20
Long may thy swelling *Udders* spring with *Milk*;
Late, very late, the merry *Milk Maid* Bilk;[4]
But ready still, both Morn' and Ev'ning stand
With running Teats to meet *brisk Molly*'s Hand:
And *Molly*, in Return (as 'tis but meet)
Shall still take care to keep her *Vessels* sweet;
Her *Dairy* clean, her *Milk* from lavish Waste,
From all *Domestick Thieves* devouring Taste;
That arrant *Thief*, the bold voracious *Cat*,
That covets *Cream*, tho' cloyed with *Mouse* and *Rat*,   30
But *Puss* ('tis true) is dead, so there's no fear of that.

Ah! *Molly*! *Molly*! much, (let me advise)
Thy glorious *Fame* for *Cream* and *Butter* Prize:
For what avails the *China* rich and fine,
The burnish'd *Plate*, that on *Tea-tables* shine,
The various Sorts of costly, foreign *Tea*,
As *Green, Imperial, Hyson,* or *Bohea*,[5]
If thy *domestick Banquet* fail to feast,
With most substantial *Food*, the hungry *Guest*:
If thy delicious *Butter*, nicely spread   40
On many a thin-slic'd Piece of whitest Bread,
Thy sweetest *Cream*, do not the Table grace,
The rest, (to me) but fill an empty Space,
Is all but glitter, all a mere *Slop-bowl*;
Thy *Cream*, thy *Butter*, charm the *Poet*'s Soul,
Shall make thy *Fame*, thro' neighb'ring Houses ring,
And my glib Tongue thy lasting Praises sing.

4. i.e. only refuse to produce milk for the milkmaid very late in your life.
5. Four different kinds of tea available in Dublin at the time.

The Poet's Lamentation for the Loss of his Cat, which he us'd to call his Muse

Oppress'd with Grief, in heavy Strains I mourn,
The Partner of my Studies from me torn:
How shall I sing? what Numbers[1] shall I chuse?
For, in my fav'rite *Cat*, I've lost my Muse.
No more I feel my Mind with Raptures fir'd,
I want those Airs that *Puss* so oft inspir'd;
No crouding Thoughts my ready Fancy fill,
Nor Words run fluent from my easy Quill:
Yet shall my Verse deplore her cruel Fate,
And celebrate the Virtues of my *Cat*.   10

In Acts obscene she never took Delight,
No Catterwauls disturb'd our Sleep by Night;
Chaste as a Virgin, free from every Stain,
And neighb'ring *Cats* mew'd for her Love in vain.
She never thirsted for the *Chicken*'s Blood,
Her Teeth she only us'd to chew her Food;
Harmless as Satires which her Master writes,
A Foe to scratching, and unus'd to Bites.

She in the Study was my constant Mate,
There we together many Evenings sat.   20
Whene'er I felt my tow'ring Fancy fail,
I strok'd her Head, her Ears, her Back, her Tail;
And, as I strok'd, improv'd my dying Song,
From the sweet Notes of her melodious Tongue:
Her Purrs, and Mews, so evenly kept Time,
She purr'd in Metre, and she mew'd in Rhime.
But when my Dulness has too stubborn prov'd,
Nor cou'd by *Puss*'s Music be remov'd;
Oft to the well-known Volumes have I gone,
And stole a line from POPE, or ADDISON.   30

Oft-times, when lost amidst poetic Heat,
She, leaping on my Knee, has took her Seat;
There saw the Throes that rack'd my lab'ring Brain,
And lick'd and claw'd me to myself again.

1. Verse form, metre.

Then, Friends, indulge my Grief, and let me mourn;
My *Cat* is gone, ah! never to return.
Now in my Study, all the tedious Night,
Alone I sit, and, unassisted, write:
Look often round (oh greatest Cause of Pain!)
And view the num'rous Labours of my Brain;   40
Those Quires of Words[2] array'd in pompous Rhyme,
Which brav'd the Jaws of all-devouring Time;
Now undefended, and unwatch'd by *Cats*,
Are now doom'd Victims to the Teeth of *Rats*.

---

2. Unbound, loose sheets of paper, covered in words.

John Winstanley

To the Revd Mr ——— on his Drinking Sea-Water

Methinks, dear *Tom*, I see thee stand demure
Close by old Ocean's side, with arms erect,
Gulping the brine; and, with gigantic quaff,
Pledge the proud *Whale*, and from ten thousand Springs
Dilute the hyp,[1] concomitant unkind![2]

For thee th'*Euphrates*, from her spicy banks,
Conveys her healing stream: for thee the *Caspian*
Filters her Balsam; while the fragrant *Nile*
Tinges with balmy dew the greeting seas,
Conscious of thee; whose tow'ring Pyramids   10
Would pride to lodge thy consecrated Urn.

For thee the sage *Batavian*,[3] from his stern
With face distorted and convulsive grin,
Disgorges easterns Gums, in bowels pent,
And streaks the surge with salutary hue.[4]

For thee the *Thames*, impregnated with Steam
Mercurial, wafts her complicated Dose
From reeking Vaults, full copiously supply'd
By Bums venereal, ruefully discharg'd
By *Ward*'s mysterious Drop, or magic Pill.[5]   20

---

1. hypochondria.
2. i.e. at the same time (as you think drinking sea-water will make you healthy), you are being unkind to yourself.
3. Dutchman.
4. i.e. sewers stain the water which is, otherwise, health-promoting.
5. Joshua Ward (1685-1761), a famous English quack doctor, who claimed that his pills and drops (which were in fact a dangerous compound of antimony) could cure almost any ailment.

LAURENCE WHYTE
(c.1683-**1742**-c.1753)

Laurence Whyte, who was born in County Westmeath, became a teacher of mathematics in Dublin. He wrote a prodigious quantity of verse and described himself on the title pages of his two volumes as 'A Lover of the Muses and of Mathematics'. He was the author of two fascinating long poems, 'The Parting Cup' which gives a detailed description of the life of a substantial farming community in early eighteenth-century Ireland, and 'A Dissertation on *Italian* and *Irish* Musick, with some Panegyrick on *Carralan* our late *Irish Orpheus*'. Extracts from the first of these poems appear below, and the text of the second one, which links Irish and Italian culture in a way unique in Irish eighteenth-century verse, may be found in *The Field Day Anthology of Irish Writing* (1991), I, 412-15. 'There's scarce a *Forthman* or *Fingallian*, // But sings or whistles in *Italian*', Whyte wrote in 'A Dissertation on *Italian* and *Irish* Musick...' — which would be fascinating, if true.

The music hall to which the poem below refers was built in Dublin in 1741 by the members of the Charitable Musical Society for the Relief of Imprisoned Debtors, of which society Laurence Whyte was an enthusiastic member. Thomas Neal, the well-known Dublin music publisher, was treasurer of the society when the new hall was built, and the architect was Richard Cassels, who also designed the Rotunda, the Dining-Hall of Trinity College and Leinster House, all in Dublin. The new music hall in Fishamble Street became famous when Handel conducted the first performance of his oratorio *Messiah* there in 1742.

A POETICAL Description of Mr. NEAL's new Musick-Hall in Fishamble-street, Dublin,

being a Supplement to an Historical POEM, wrote in the Year 1740[1] on the
Rise and Progress of the Charitable and Musical Society, formerly kept at the
Bulls-head in said Street.

By an old MEMBER

As *Amphion*[2] built of old, the *Theban* Wall,
So *Neal* has built a sumptuous *Musick-Hall*;
The one by per'rful[3] Touches of his *Lute*,
The other by the *Fiddle* and the *Flute*,
Join'd with some others of harmonick Sound,
He rais'd this lofty Fabrick from the Ground;

---

1. This poem is in Whyte's *Poems on Various Subjects, Serious and Diverting, Never before Published* ... (Dublin, 1740).

2. In Greek mythology, Amphion was the son of Jupiter and Antiope. He is said to have been the inventor of music and to have built the walls of Thebes by the sound of his lyre. See ll. 3 and 6.

3. This spelling of 'powerful' may represent Hiberno-English pronunciation; see Bliss pp. 213-14.

Where heaps of Rubbish in confusion stood,
Old walls, old Timber, and some rotten Wood;
From their old *Chaos*, they new Forms assume,
Here stands the *Hall*, and there the *Drawing Room*,   10
Adorn'd with all that Workmanship can do,
By Ornaments, and Architecture too.

The Oblong Area runs from *East* to *West*,
Fair to behold, but hard to be exprest;
At th'*Eastern* end, the awful Throne is plac'd,[4]
With fluted Columns, and Pilasters grac'd,
Fit for the noblest *President* to rest,
Who likes the Arms of *Ireland* for his Crest.
In diff'rent Classes at the *Western* end
Musicians with their Instruments attend;   20
While they diffuse their Harmony around,
The concave *Arch* reverberates the Sound;
This charms the Soul, and tunes it to a Pitch,
Gives Emulation to the Poor and Rich,
Exalts their *Virtues* to a high Degree,
And fix their central point in Charity.[5]
Thus do the *Planets* in their *Orbits* move,
As Authors say, in Harmony and Love;
In certain *Periods*[6] they are sure to run,
Mov'd by the attractive Motion of the *Sun*.   30

Long had the *Goddess* wander'd here and there,
First from the *George* to anchor at the *Bear*,
Then from the *Bear*, she travel'd to the *Bull*,
And there her Train grew numerous and full,
Then hoist her Sails, to find a larger port,
Where she might rest and build a sumptuous Court.[7]
The Goddess here at length her Anchor fixt,
Both Sexes blended, and all Parties mixt,
She, without *Schism*, has brought them to agree,
To join and set the Captive *Debtor* free.   40

4. Presumably a high-backed chair for the president of the society to whom respect (awe)
  is due.
5. The society donated its proceeds to a fund for the relief of imprisoned debtors.
6. An astronomical term for the time in which a planet performs one revolution around the sun.
7. i.e. the musical society, personified in the 'Goddess' of music, had moved from tavern to
  tavern until membership had grown to such an extent that the society was able to occupy
  Neal's new music hall.

The Architect has here display'd his Art,
By Decorations proper for each Part,
The *Cornice*, *Dentills*, and the curious *Mould*,
The *Fret-work*, and the Vaulted Roof behold,
The hollow Arches, and the bold Design,
In ev'ry part with Symmetry divine.[8]

There stand fine Mirrors to reflect the Fair,
Lest they forget themselves, or where they are;
The precious *Curl* and *Lappets*[9] to adjust,
And to remind them that they are but Dust.   50
Here Men may know themselves, and what is more,
They may reflect what they have been before,
That as they've enter'd at the common Gate,
So sure are they to meet the common *Fate*,
How soon, how late, or where, or when, or how,
Are things too serious to dilate of now;
But Thoughts like these have made great *Xerxes*[10] weep,
To think that *Death* shou'd lay his *Host* asleep.
In all *Assemblies* where the brilliant *Fair*,
To hear and see, so eagerly repair,   60
Where *Beaux* in dress, do with each other vie,
I can't forbear to think, *that all must die.*
When *Man* of all his Wishes is possest,
Cloy'd with Enjoyments, lays him down to rest.

8. The various internal architectural features mentioned in this paragraph include plaster
   and woodwork decorations.
9. Streamers attached to women's head-gear — fashionable at this time.
10. Xerxes the Great (c. 519-165 B.C.), king of Persia.

from: **The Parting Cup or
The HUMOURS of Deoch an Doruis**[1]

alias Theodorus, alias Doctor *Dorus*, an old Irish Gentleman famous (about 30
Years ago) for his great Hospitality, but more particularly in Christmas Time.

Parum Vini acuit Ingenium, — Ergo Multum[2]

from: Canto I
Look back on Time; you see him bald,
He's never more to be recall'd.
Behold his Forelocks! how they play,
Which no Man's sure to grasp a Day;[3]
His Glass which never fails to run,
Measures the Motion of the Sun;
With Scyth so keen, he mows down all
The Inhabitants upon the Ball,[4]
And with his Wings flies on so fast,
That thirty Winters now are past,   10
Since Deoch an Doruis and his Spouse,
In Christmas time kept open house:
The Time when no Man shou'd be sad,
The Time when Younkers[5] all run mad,
By Light of Stars, or Silver Moon,
To serenade them with a Tune,
The Time for Merriment and Sport,
When Nights are long, and Days are short,

1. The first two cantos of this long and interesting poem depict life in County Westmeath
   in the early years of the eighteenth century. Whyte describes the world of a substantial
   Catholic farmer to whom he gives the unexpected name of 'Deoch an Doruis', which he
   translates as 'the parting cup'. The phrase 'The Tribe of Deoch an Doruis' occurs
   frequently throughout Whyte's verse and refers to those — particularly of earlier
   generations — for whom conviviality and generosity had been a way of life; the subject
   of this poem is the generalised leader of this clan. By the fourth canto of the poem,
   Deoch an Doruis and members of his tribe have been reduced to abject poverty by rack-
   renting landlords and unfavourable economic conditions. The contrasts in Whyte's poem
   between a life of plenty and a life of want, and the analysis of the economic and social
   causes of these devastating changes, were to be echoed eloquently in Goldsmith's *The
   Deserted Village* a generation later. Ir. *deoch an dorais* = a stirrup-cup or parting drink.
   The title means 'The entertaining qualities of life of someone who lived a hospitable life
   in County Westmeath thirty years ago'.
2. 'Too little wine sharpens the wits — therefore (drink) much.'
3. i.e. since 'Old Father Time' — whose traditional hour-glass and scythe are mentioned in
   the next lines — is bald, no one can catch him by the forelock to bring him back.
4. i.e. the earth.
5. young men.

When Northern Blasts are wont to blow
To ev'ry Hill a Cap of Snow,   20
To ev'ry Tree a frozen Wig,
And candy over ev'ry Sprig;
When Folks have little else to do,
But try what Ale their Neighbours brew,
To drink all Night, and sing in Chorus,
And when they part drink Deochadorus.

They were a thrifty loving Pair,
Who liv'd in plenty all the Year,
Stood at a mod'rate easy Rent,
Enjoying Life with vast Content.   30
They kept a Harp, and Pair of Tables,[6]
Good Oats, and Hay in Barns and Stables;
And all Extravagance to shun,
He wore the Cloth his Wife had spun;
By frugal Means kept out of Debt,
Nor was his Door with Duns[7] beset;
His Side Board was not Plate, but Wood,[8]
Which made his Payments very good,
Kept a good Cellar, Kitchen, Larder,
And those who will enquire farther,   40
His Birth, or Pedigree to trace,
Will find him of Milesian Race,
Descended from some Irish King,[9]
If all be true our Druids sing.
His Grandsier's Fate did oft bemoan,
Who forfeited in Forty one,[10]
Her Sire lost all in Eighty Eight,
Which we remember to be Fact;

---

6. Probably a backgammon board.
7. debt collectors.
8. i.e. the dishes on his sideboard were made of wood, not plated with silver.
9. i.e. descendants of the kings of ancient Ireland, or even of the fabulous King Milesius, founder of Ireland, and so of native Irish stock. See Glossary.
10. The references are to the land forfeitures which followed the Rebellion of 1641 and the war between King James and King William 1689-90 which was ended by the Treaty of Limerick in 1691.

Tho' he was in no Insurrection
But kept at home, and took Protection,   50
And was of the Strongbonian Race;
All cou'd not mitigate his Case.[11]

Then by Industry and by Farm,
They liv'd so comfortably warm,
The Landlord had his Rent well pay'd,
Nor had he any Cause to dread,
His Tenant to give up his Lease,
As now, too often, is the Case,
Run in Arrear, or fly away
To North or South America.   60
Whene'er the Squire was run a-ground,
He cou'd advance him fifty Pound,
And on a Pinch cou'd make a shift,
To give his Honour a good lift.

It was the humour of them both
To live upon their Country Growth,
And valu'd, not one pinch of Snuff,
Your Canisters of Indian Stuff,[12]
For they cou'd breakfast, sup or dine
Without a drop of Tea, or Wine,   70
And nothing foreign, she wou'd tell ye,
Shou'd cloath her Back, or fill her Belly.
Thus liv'd the happy loving Pair,
By their Frugality, and Care,
Their Undertenants at Command,
Or paid them Rent, or till'd the Land,
With many Servants in their Stations,
For all their servile Occupations,
That none in Idleness shou'd lurk,
They often made their Children work,   80
Lest they shou'd ever scorn to do it,
If by necessity put to it;...

---

11. The point being made is that, even though the family of the wife of Deoch an Doruis was of Norman, or 'Old English', rather than of native Irish stock — they were descendants of the Norman knights who came to Ireland with Strongbow (Richard FitzGilbert de Clare, earl of Pembroke) in 1169 — their lands were still taken from them in the forfeitures after the Treaty of Limerick.

12. i.e. crates of imported goods.

... He taught his Sons to hold the Plow,
To sow the Seed, to reap and mow,
To take the Area of a Field
Before it was manur'd or till'd;
They read the Irish, Latin spoke,
The Head of Priscian seldom broke;[13]
An Argument cou'd form and twist,
Like Sophister, or Casuist.[14]   90
They spoke it without Hesitation,
Tho' now a days 'tis not the Fashion,
Since Graduates tell us 'tis Pedantick,
And he who speaks it, must be Frantick,
A Jesuit, Conjuror, or Clown,
Who has no taste for Court, or Town.

His first born Pat — *diebus illis*,[15]
Wrote an Acrostic[16] upon Phillis,
And then presents her with some Lines,
In Epigrams, and Vallentines,   100
In such a soft pathetic stile,
As gain'd the Favour of a smile,
His Passions were so well display'd,
He gain'd th'Affections of the Maid,
Who did with curious Work emboss
For him a fine St. Patrick's Cross;[17]

Pat in Return sent, piping hot,
To *Phillis*, the True Lovers Knot,[18]
And at the wish'd-for time of Easter,
Slipt in her hand a Crooked Tester.[19]   110

---

13. Priscian was a Latin grammarian of the fifth century; the phrase 'to break Priscian's head' meant to violate the rules of Latin grammar.
14. Two classes of learned men who are said to use specious or quibbling learning and rhetoric. Senior students at Trinity College, Dublin are also known as Sophisters.
15. 'In those days.'
16. A short poem, common in eighteenth-century Ireland, in which the first letters of each line, read downwards, spell the name of the person to whom the poem is addressed.
17. A St Patrick's Cross, common in the eighteenth century, was a small cross made from red and green paper, pinned onto a white background and decorated with ribbons. It was commonly worn on the saint's day. (Dáithí Ó hÓgáin, *Myth, Legend and Romance: an Encyclopædia of the Irish Folk Tradition* (London and New York: Prentice Hall, 1991), p. 361.)
18. i.e. sent her immediately a true lover's knot — a double-looped bow — symbolising his true love for her.
19. A crooked six-penny piece — traditionally a lucky omen.

Gave her a Ribband, Gloves, and Ring,
As Earnest for some better thing.
Pat went to traffick[20] ev'ry Year,
To Fairs and Markets, far and near,
But never chas'd a Fox or Hare,
Nor kept a Racing Horse or Mare;
For he was very apprehensive,
Such Sports as these were too expensive,
Which ruin'd the Landlord's eldest Son,
By Bets and Racing quite undone,   120
Fulfilling all that wise Men say on
The common Fable of Actæon.[21]

They seldom did refuse a Summons,
To play at Foot Ball or at Commons,[22]
To pitch the Bar, or throw a Sledge,
To vault, or take a Ditch or Hedge,
At leisure Hours t'unfold a Riddle,
Or play the Bagpipes, Harp or Fiddle;
Pat played at Quoits, sometimes at Cat,
Cou'd catch it flying in his Hat.   130
Phillip the Cat cou'd pitch or roll,
At ten Yards distance, in the Hole,
Phœlix was dext'rous at a Trip,
With nimble foot, cou'd race or skip,
Pursue the Cat o'er Hedge or Plain,
And count the distance back again,
So sure and skilful in his Aim,
He never lost the Cat or Game.

20. to buy and sell.
21. In Greek mythology, Actæon was a keen hunter who, having been turned into a stag by the goddess Artemis, was chased and killed by his own hounds.
22. The game of hurling (Ir. *camán*: a hurley stick). The modern forms of the other sports mentioned in the next few lines are throwing the 'caber' or wooden pole, throwing the 'hammer', vaulting (the reference here is possibly to pole-vaulting over hedges), and discus-throwing ('quoits'). The game of 'cat' may be Gaelic Football (Ir. *caid*), or the English game of tip-cat (played with a 'cat' or tapered piece of wood), or perhaps a game similar to cricket played with a wooden 'cat' instead of a ball. However, in none of these games does a player score by pitching or rolling a 'cat' into a hole from a distance of ten yards, so the exact identity of the game described here is unclear. Perhaps it was a game similar to golf.

from: Canto II

Since Dechadorus play'd his Part,
To train his sons by Rules, and Art
By Precepts, and by good example,
Next comes his Wife to give her sample.
The female Issue were her Care,
With proper Documents to rear,
'Remember Child as you come in,
Hold up your Head, keep in your Chin;
Walk smooth and straight, keep out your Toes,
And see to manage well your Clothes!   10
To be good Housewives, you must learn,
To make and mend, to wash and darn,
No Child of mine, I do profess,
Shall eat the Bread of Idleness.
If you be handy, 'twill support you,
And draw industrious Lads to court you,
Pin up your Lappets,[1] dress you tighter,
And learn to walk a little slighter.
If you take Reason for your guide,
In Decency there is no Pride;   20
Let Virtue be your constant Rule,
Your guard from Vice, and Ridicule'.
A thousand other Things she said,
Wherein good Morals were convey'd,
And often brandishing her Rod,
To be observant — of a Nod.
She often made them labour hard,
To brew and bake, to spin and card,[2]
To dress a dish or two of meat,
Fit for the Squire himself to eat,   30
To use their Needle, read and write,
And dance the Irish Trot at night.
They made a Curtsy on a Pinch,[3]
Exceeding any country Wench,
Without a Hoop look'd prim and gay,
On Sunday or on Holy-day,

---

1. Streamers attached to ladies' head-dresses.
2. 'To card' is to prepare wool for spinning by combing and untangling it.
3. at a pinch.

At Patrons[4] danc'd a Jig or Horn-pipe,
Play'd on a Fiddle or [a] Cornpipe,[5]
Such Country dances as they play,
On Salt Box, or the Tongs and Key.[6]   40
Five Cards they play'd with Art and Skill,
As Ladies now do at Quadrill.[7]
They play'd for two-pence or a Groat,[8]
But never higher cou'd be brought;
Yet to their Praise it may be said,
They made good Butter, Cheese and Bread,
Good Iskebaha[9] cou'd distill,
Wherein they shew'd the utmost Skill.

   With Mien above the common Sort,
They mimick'd those who come from Court,   50
And walk'd a Minuet smooth and straight,
According to the Figure Eight,[10]
And that with better Grace and Airs,
Than some who dance at the Lord Mayor's.
Tho' never bred in Town or City,
With Repartee, or Pun cou'd fit ye,
And as their Heels denote them Dancers,
Their heads were turn'd for witty Answers.
And when at work cou'd sweetly chime
Their Irish songs in Tune and time   60
When e'er requested for a Song,
There was no need to teaze them long;
Such as they had, they gave it free,
Without a long Apology —,
For want of Skill, for Cough, or Cold,
With humours not too coy or bold,
The Song was always Short and Sweet,
Without Defect of Rhime or Feet;

---

4. i.e. patterns, the festivities surrounding the feast day of a patron saint.
5. A simple musical instrument, like the modern tin-whistle, but made out of a dried corn-stalk.
6. In traditional Irish music, domestic implements, such as a pair of spoons, are used to beat the rhythm. Tongs, keys and boxes (such as those in which salt was kept) could be similarly used.
7. Five Cards and Quadrille were, respectively, a simple and a complicated card game.
8. A coin worth four pence.
9. Ir. *Usquebaugh*: whiskey — in the eighteenth century, mostly home-distilled. See Glossary.
10. A reference to the pattern of steps in the dance, the minuet.

The Thoughts were good, and cou'd not cloy,
And when repeated gave new Joy, 70
Who ever wou'd cry out encore!
He had the same song o'er, and o'er,
And as they freely gave the song,
They were as free to hold their Tongue.
When Nature's kind, and does her Part,
She well supplies the Want of Art,
They had an Ear, good Voice, and Sense,
For Art, as ample recompense.

   Then Deochadorous ev'ry Year
Cou'd give his Landlord hearty Cheer, 80
A Cordial welcome to his Friend,
And gave himself at latter End;
You might as well hope to get free
From Newgate, or the Marshalsea,[11]
As strive to go by Force or Stealth,
'Till first you drink his Landlord's Health.
When that was down, then you were sure,
To meet his good Wife at the Door,
Who with full Brimmers[12] plies you fairly,
The Quintescence[13] of Irish Barley, 90
You must comply — *durante Lite*,[14]
To take a Cup of *Aquavitæ*,[15]
And tells you while it is a filling,
''Tis Water of my own distilling,
A perfect Cordial, and as such,
You need not fear to take too much.
Then take another Cup of it,
'Twill make you over-flow with Wit;
If any of the seeds remain,
Within the compass of your Brain, 100
These Waters quickly make them sprout,
And into Branches flourish out:
It gives them such a sudden Spring,
You cannot long forbear to sing,

11. Debtors' prisons in Dublin.
12. mugs or goblets filled to the brim.
13. Most refined essence.
14. 'While the argument lasts.'
15. Whiskey ('water of life').

It oils the Tongue, the Lungs, the Weason,[16]
And makes us exercise our Reason;
This makes the Learned and the Wise,
To argue and Philosophize.
Before we part — you'll find it true,
And now dear friend — I drink to you!'   110

   To drink her health you cannot fail,
Who brew'd such fine nectarean Ale,[17]
To toast her Daughters Ann and Joan,
And all the rest down one by one,
Each Nymph far brighter than Aurora,[18]
Especially her Eldest Nora,
Run high divisions on her Charms,
And wish her in her Lover's Arms....

... This brings of course another Mugg,
Which is succeeded by a Jugg,   120
And if you cannot take your flight,
You must sit down and stay all night,
To sing your Chorals, if you've any,
Or make a match for Jone, or Nanny,
Lest Folks shou'd think that you are dumb,
Then sing your Cronane[19] with a hum....

... When each drank more than twice enough
And Candles were burnt out to Snuff,
Our Heads grew heavy, Legs grew weak,
And no man cou'd his Exit make.   130
Our Eyes began to close and glew,
And what's more wonderful and true,
In this Recess from Cares and Trouble,
Each individual thing look'd double,
Appearing plainly to your View,
For ev'ry one you reckon'd two,
Such are the effect of Irish Ale,
To all you Topers I appeal! ...

16. throat.
17. i.e. a drink as delicious as that of the gods of Greek mythology.
18. Goddess of the dawn. Line 117 seems to mean that there were disagreements about Nora's beauty.
19. song. cf. Ir. *crónán*, a word denoting humming or crooning.

The Cask which horizontal lay,
And bore the Burden of the day,   140
Now lies Oblique, one end depress'd,
As if it were inclin'd to Rest:
The Liquor ran but very slow,
When Chaunticleer[20] began to crow,
To signifie our Cask of Stout,[21]
Was on the Stoop[22] and almost out.
The Harper lull'd some folks asleep,
Whose Ditty's make Old Women weep,
And then with touches brisk and nice,
Set them a dancing in a trice;   150
Altho' illiterate and blind,
He had the Gifts of Tongue and Mind,
Tho' poor, and humble his condition,
He was a Poet and Musician,
His Harp for Irish Hero's strung,
Their Fall he wept, and Zeal he sung:...
His Lamentations sung and play'd
Compos'd for valiant Hero's dead
Who fell in Aughrim's fatal plain,
Manur'd with blood of thousands slain,[23]   160
Recites the story to a truth,
The tragic End of Great St. Ruth;[24]...
E'en those who fled, he sung their Fate,
And made them Famous for Retreat,
Tyrconnell, Sarsfield,[25] and the Rest,
With loud Encomiums he blest,
With all his Hero's slain at Derry,
As if such Tales cou'd make us merry,
And those of Limrick and Athlone,
Concluded with *Oh Hone! Oh Hone!*[26]   170

20. The cock which crows to salute to dawn.
21. strong beer — not necessarily dark beer or porter.
22. propped up.
23. The battle of Aughrim (1691) at which 7,000 Irishmen perished.
24. Charles Chalmont, marquis de St Ruhe (known in Ireland as 'St Ruth'), the French commander at the battle of Aughrim, where he was decapitated by a cannonball.
25. Richard Talbot, Earl Tyrconnel (1639-91) and Patrick Sarsfield, Earl of Lucan (d. 1693), the two most important leaders of the Irish Jacobites in the period 1685-93.
26. Ir. *Ochón, Ochón*, Alas! alas!

The Harper, at each interval,
Had Dram or Madder[27] at his call,
Together with his Horn of Snuff,
Of each we saw he took enough,
And when he cou'd no longer play,
Speakshoyech[28] usher'd in the Day.

from: Canto IV

Thus Farmers liv'd like Gentlemen
E're Lands were raised from five to ten,
Again from ten to three times five,[1]
Then very few cou'd hope to thrive,
But tug[g]'d against the rapid Stream,
Which drove them back from whence they came;
At length, 'twas canted[2] to a Pound,
What Tenant then cou'd keep his Ground?
Not knowing which to stand or fly,
When Rent-Rolls[3] mounted Zenith high,   10
They had their choice to run away,
Or labour for a Groat a Day,
Now beggar'd and of all bereft,
Are doom'd to starve, or live by Theft,
Take to the Mountains or the Roads,
When banish'd from their old Abodes;
Their native Soil were forc'd to quit,
So Irish Landlords thought it fit,
Who without Cer'mony or Rout,
For their Improvements turn'd them out.[4]   20

---

27. i.e. 'dram' a portion (glass) of whiskey or 'meadar' a quadrangular wooden bowl of ale.
    Ir. *meadar*.
28. Ir. *Spéic Seoigheach*, an Irish tune the origin of which is obscure, but the title of which
    has been translated as 'The Humours of Joyce's Country'.

---

1. i.e. rents per acre were raised from five shillings to ten, to fifteen, and finally to twenty
   shillings (one pound) per annum.
2. sold at auction.
3. The rents payable on the rent-roll or landlord's list of rented land.
4. Whyte returned to this theme in a poem entitled 'Gaffer and Gammer, with the Humours
   of a bad Landlord: a Tale' in his 1742 *Original Poems on Various Subjects*, pp. 14-17. In
   that poem, he tells of an improving farmer who entertains his landlord well and, as a
   consequence, 'Next Year poor Gaffer was turn'd out // For brewing Ale so very stout, //
   For being generous and free, // As Farmers whilom us'd to be.'

Embracing still the highest Bidder,
Inviting all Ye Nations hither,
Encouraging all Strollers, Caitiffs,[5]
Or any other but the Natives.

Now Wooll is low, and Mutton cheap,
Poor Graziers can no Profit reap,
Alas! you hear them now complain,
Of heavy Rents, and little Gain,
Grown sick of bargains got by Cant,
Must be in time reduc'd to Want,   30
How many Villages they rais'd
How many Parishes laid Wast!
To fatten Bullocks, Sheep, and Cows,
When scarce one Parish has two Plows,
And were it not for foreign Wheat,
We now shou'd want the Bread we eat.
Their Flocks do range on ev'ry Plain,
That once produc'd all kind of Grain
Depopulating ev'ry Village,
Where we had Husbandry and Tillage,   40
Fat Bacon, Poultry and good Bread,
By which the Poor were daily fed.
The Landlords then at ev'ry Gale,[6]
Besides their Rent, got Nappy Ale,[7]
A hearty welcome and good Chear,
With Rent well paid them twice a Year.
But now the Case is quite revers'd,
The Tenants ev'ry Day distress'd,
Instead of living well and thriving,
There's nothing now but leading, driving.[8]   50
The Lands are all monopoliz'd,
The Tenants rack'd and sacrific'd,
Whole Colonies to shun the Fate,
Of being oppress'd at such a Rate

5. villains.
6. A periodical payment of rent.
7. A strong, home-brewed ale.
8. i.e. families evicted when they could not pay the higher rents are now forced to travel
   from place to place with their animals 'leading' and 'driving' them, seeking pasturage.

By Tyrants who still raise the Rent,
Sailed to the Western Continent,[9]
Rather than live at home like slaves,
They trust themselves to Wind and Waves....

... Our 'Squires of Late thro' Europe roam,
Are too well bred to live at home,   60
Are not content with Dublin College,[10]
But range abroad for greater Knowledge,
To strut in Velvets and Brocades,
At Balls, at Plays and Masquerades,
To have their Rents their chiefest Care is,
In Bills to London, or to Paris;
Their Education is so nice,
They know all Chances on the Dice,
Excepting when it is their Fate
To throw away a good Estate, ——   70
Then does the Squire with empty purse
Rail at ill Fortune with a Curse,
His Pride is fallen down a Peg,
And now must either starve or beg,
His greatest Cronies pass him by,
And ev'ry Friend he'd forc'd to try,
At length he turns out a Cadet,
To live upon a Groat a Day,
Rails at his Stars that he shou'd thus get
His Bread by lugging a brown Musquet.   80
He who turn'd out, a pretty Fellow,
Soon grows dejected, lean, and yellow,
If he survives but one Campaign,
Returns all tatter'd home again.
With all the Stock of Brains he had,
To get a Pension, or turn Pad;[11]
And shou'd he lose an Arm or Leg,
He is intitl'd then to beg.
If Random shot shou'd take his Head,
So full of Mercury, or Lead,   90

9. America or the West Indies.
10. Trinity College, Dublin.
11. Highway robber.

Windmills or Castles in the Air,
The World will say it was but fair,
Who liv'd at Random all his Life,
Shou'd die by Random in the Strife:
What can we further say of him,
There fell the Brave Sir Giddy Whim! ...
... These Absentees we here describe,
Are mostly of our Irish Tribe,
Who live in Luxury and Pleasure,
And throw away their Time and Treasure,   100
Cause Poverty and Devastation,
And sink the Credit of the Nation,
A Nation sunk for Want of Trade,
A Foot-stool to her Neighbours made;
And yet our Gentry all run wild,
And never can be reconcil'd,
To live at home upon their Rent,
With any Pleasure or Content....

... Their Mansions moulder quite away,
And run to Ruin and Decay,   110
Left like a Desert, wild and waste,
Without the Track of Man or Beast,
Where Wild Fowl may with Safety rest,
At ev'ry Gate may build a Nest,
Where Grass and Weeds on Pavements grow,
And ev'ry Year is fit to mow;
No Smoak from Chimneys do ascend,
Nor Entertainment for a Friend,
Nor Sign of Drink, or Smell of Meat,
For human Creatures there to eat;   120
There Rats and Mice no longer cou'd
Subsist, or live for want of Food,
Tho' undisturb'd by Cat or Dog,
Who perish'd there for want of Prog,[12]
The Garrison[13] at length they quit,
For there they cou'd not get a bit,
Unless they prey'd upon each other,
Like some who spare no Friend or Brother,

12. food. A term of unknown origin, widely used in the eighteenth century.
13. store-room.

Man-eaters who devour us all,
And thrive upon their Neighbours' Fall,   130
Live by Oppression, and by Guile.
Such is the Practice of our Isle,
Where scarce one Tribe of Deoghedorus,
But stands in Misery before us.

JAMES EYRE WEEKES
(c.1720-**1743**-c.1754)

There were probably, as Patrick Fagan has demonstrated (*Georgian Celebration*, pp. 120-
23), two eighteenth-century poets called James Eyre Weeks or Weekes, from Cork. The
livelier of the two, whose poems appear below, was a bawdy, irreverent poet of considerable
skill. If Fagan is correct, this poet was murdered in 1754.

from: The Intrigues of *Jove*: a Ballad

Ye humorous folks prepare,
I'll sing you the whoredoms of *Jove*;
To the many disguises give ear,
Which he put on to gratifie love.

First, there is his *shower* of *gold*
Which he *rain'd* into *Danae*'s lap,[1]
And was he not damnably fool'd,
I wish he had met with a c—p.[2]

With permission, this *Jove* was a cully,[3]
To give such a sum to a lass,   10
When nowadays every town bully
Can whore for six penn'worth of *brass*.

But some of my readers cry, 'Hold —
Consider the damsel was clean';
What then? For a *shower* of *gold*
I'd warrant to lye with a *Queen*.

And still, I insist, he's a ninny[4]
To cry up the bawdy-house *price*,
When the girl would have taken a *guinea*,
Ay marry, a whore's not so nice.[5]   20

---

1. According to Ovid (*Metamorphoses* 4, v, 611), Jove changed himself into a shower of
   golden rain in order to seduce Danae.
2. clap or venereal disease.
3. fool.
4. simpleton; the *OED* suggests the word comes from 'innocent'.
5. 'Ay marry' is an asseveration of surprise (originally referring to the Virgin Mary); nice =
   difficult to please.

Half-a-crown[6] to a whore once I offer'd,
I seldom give more to a whore;
With a sneer, she deny'd what I proffer'd
And bid me remember *Jove*'s *show'r*.

'The deuce', answer'd I, 'are you there?'[7]
Will only *Jove*'s *shower* content you?'
I ne'er knew the sex was so *dear*
Nor thought that the *gold* was so *plenty*.

Thus this oaf of a god is their sample,
And nothing but *gold* will go down,   30
While *Danae*'s a standing example
To ev'ry whore in the town[8]....

Two Poems

Left on a Lady's Toilette[1]

Oh that I was my *Silvia*'s stays!
To clasp her lovely waist,
To press those breasts, where rapture plays,
Where love and pleasure feast.

That I was but her smock so white,
To feel her velvet skin,
To bless my touch with soft delight,
And kiss it without sin.

Or that I was her stocking neat,
Garter'd above her knee,   10
That I, so near the happy seat,
The happy seat may see.

6. A coin worth one-eighth of a pound.
7. i.e. what's wrong with you?
8. The poem goes on to describe Jove's other amours and links them to night-life in Cork.

1. dressing-table.

Why am I not her lace, her ring,
Her dicky[2] or her fan,
Her dog, her monkey, any thing
But what I am — a *man*.

Answer'd by her WOMAN

Ah simple poet! ill-judg'd prayer!
How like an owl you sing ——
Better for thee the *ring* to wear
Than be thyself the *ring*.

Where is thy feeling, senseless stock?
Thou injudicious elf ——
Better for thee to *lift* the smock
Than be the smock thy self.

Wou'd you, fond simpleton, desire,
To be your mistress' fan,   10
If you wou'd rightly *cool* her *fire*,
Wish still to be a *man*.

---

2. A woman's under-petticoat (Partridge).

SIR ARTHUR DAWSON
(1698-**1749**-1775)

Arthur Dawson, son of Joshua Dawson, builder of Dublin's Dawson Street, was educated at Trinity College, Dublin. He was appointed a Baron of the Irish Exchequer in 1741 and was once described by Mrs Delany as 'a very clever, sensible man'. This fine Bacchanalian song, on which rests his fame, is said to have been composed when Baron Dawson and the Irish bard Turloch Carolan were both guests of Squire Jones at Moneyglass, Co. Antrim. Carolan, asked to produce a song in honour of his host, retired to bed with his harp and a bottle of whiskey. Here he composed the song, both words and music. Dawson, hearing the air, memorised it and composed a set of words for it in English, based loosely on the Irish words of Carolan. In the morning, Carolan sang his song, after which Dawson accused him of plagiarism and sang his own, to the amusement of the company and the fury of the bard. Sir Samuel Ferguson's account of the event (apparently backed by the authority of Dean Swift) completes the story: 'After Carolan's passion had been excited to the utmost pitch, an explanation took place which ended in a jovial night and pardon for the offence' (*Dublin University Magazine*, January 1841, pp. 15-16). Though written in the 1730s, the song did not appear in print until about 1749.

Bumpers,[1] 'Squire Jones

Ye good Fellows all
Who love to be told that there's Claret good Store,
Attend to the Call of one who's ne'er frighted,
But greatly delighted with six Bottles more:
Be sure you don't pass the good house *Money-glass*,
Which the jolly red God so peculiarly owns;
'Twill well suit your Humour, for pray what would you more
Than Mirth with good Claret, and Bumpers, 'Squire *Jones*.

Ye Lovers who pine
For Lasses who oft prove as cruel as fair,   10
Who whimper and whine for Lillies and Roses,
With Eyes, Lips and Noses, or Tip of an Ear;
Come hither, I'll shew you, how *Phillis* and *Chloe*,
No more shall occasion such Sighs and such Groans;
For what mortal so stupid as not to quit *Cupid*,
When call'd by good Claret, and Bumpers, 'Squire *Jones*.

---

1. Glasses filled to the brim for the drinking of toasts.

Ye Poets who write
And brag of your drinking fam'd *Hellicon*'s Brook,[2]
Though all you get by't is a Dinner oft times,
In Reward for your Rhimes, with *Humphrey* the Duke:[3]   20
Learn *Bacchus* to follow, and quit your *Apollo*,
   Forsake all the Muses, those senseless old Drones;
   Our jingling of Glasses your rhyming surpasses,
When crown'd with good Claret, and Bumpers, 'Squire *Jones*.

   Ye Soldiers so stout,
With Plenty of Oaths, though no Plenty of Coin,
Who make such a Rout of all your Commanders
Who serv'd us in *Flanders*, and eke at the *Boyne*,
Come leave off your rattling of sieging and battling,
   And know you'd much better to sleep with whole Bones,   30
   Were you sent to *Gibraltar*, your Note you'd soon alter,[4]
And wish for good Claret, and Bumpers, 'Squire *Jones*.

   Ye Clergy so wise,
Who Mysteries profound can demonstrate clear,
How worthy to rise, you preach once a Week,
But your Tythes never seek above once in a Year,
Come here without failing, and leave off your railing
   'Gainst Bishops providing for dull, stupid Drones,
   Says the Text so divine, what is Life without Wine,
Then away with the Claret, a Bumper, 'Squire *Jones*.   40

   Ye Lawyers so just,
Be the Cause what it will, who so learnedly plead,
How worthy of Trust, you know black from white,
Yet prefer Wrong to Right, as you're chanc'd to be feed,
Leave musty Reports, and forsake the King's Courts,
   Where Dulness and Discord have set up their Thrones,
   Both *Salkield* and *Ventris*,[5] with all your damn'd Entries,
And away with the Claret, a Bumper, 'Squire *Jones*.

---

2. Helicon was a spring on Mount Olympus, sacred to the muses.
3. No duke living in Ireland in the 1730s was called Humphrey, so this is probably a jocose name for one of Carolan's patrons.
4. Several regiments of Irish troops were sent to defend Gibraltar in the late 1720s.
5. William Salkeld (1671-1715) and Sir Peyton Ventris (1641-91) were legal writers.

Ye physical Tribe,
Whose Knowledge consists in hard Words and Grimace,   50
Whene'er you prescribe, have at your Devotion
Pills, Bolus[6] or Potion, be what will the Case:
Pray where is the Need to purge, blister and bleed,
When ailing yourselves, the whole Faculty owns
That the Forms of old *Galen*[7] are not so prevailing,
As Mirth with good Claret, and Bumpers, 'Squire *Jones*.

Ye Foxhunters eke,
That follow the Call of the Horn and the Hound,
Who your Ladies forsake before they're awake,
To beat up the Break where the Vermin is found,   60
Leave *Piper* and *Blueman*, shrill *Dutchess* and *Trueman*,[8]
No Music is found in such dissonant Tones,
Would you ravish your Ears with the Songs of the Spheres,[9]
Hark! away to the Claret, a Bumper, 'Squire *Jones*.

---

6. A large pill.
7. Some doctors were, at this time, still following the teachings of the Galen (c. 129-99 B.C.).
8. Typical names of foxhounds.
9. The music made by the spheres of the Ptolemaic universe as they move in unison with each other.

ANONYMOUS SONGS AND POEMS FROM THE 1750s

Drinking Song

Dear Ireland, now it is time to grow wise,
    Let us retrench
    Ev'ry thing French,
And all, and all their wines despise.
Let Noah's fortune be never thine,
Who left himself naked by drinking wine:
    Our soil and skill
    Our bumpers fill, our bumpers fill,
    With whiskey all divine.

Chorus: *Then toss off your bowls, then toss off your bowls,*   10
    To the good of the nation,
To all who promote it, to all, to all,
    All who promote it on ev'ry occasion.

Why should you be at hazard or cost
    Of bringing home
    Brandy or rum,
While we, while we our whiskey boast?
This is a spirit of a nobler kind,
For giving good spirits to heart and mind,
    Whate'er you crave,   20
    Or wish to have, or wish to have,
    In this alone you'll find.

Chorus: *Then toss off your bowls, then toss off your bowls, etc.*

With whiskey let your glasses run o'er:
    Then drink away
    Chearful and gay.
This is, this is your native store.
While wines give gouts and gravels[1] birth,
    This, thank the gods,
    Exceeds by odds, exceeds by odds,   30
    All liquors upon earth.

Chorus: *Then toss off your bowls, then toss off your bowls, etc.*

---

1. stones in the kidney or the gall-bladder.

On Deborah Perkins of the county of Wicklow

Some sing ye of Venus the goddess
Some chant ye of rills, and of fountains;
  But the theme of such praise,
  As my fancy can raise,
Is a wench of the Wicklow mountains.

Mount Ida they surely surpass,
With the Wood-nymphs recess, and their lurkings;[1]
  O! 'tis there that I play
  And wanton all day,
With little black[2] Deborah Perkins.   10

King Solomon, he had nine hundred, at least,
To humour his taste, with their smirkings;[3]
  But not one of 'em all,
  When she led up a ball,
Cou'd foot it like Deborah Perkins.

The fair Cleopatra, Anthony lov'd,
But, by heaven, I'd give him his jerkings;
  If that he was here,
  And shou'd think to compare
That trollop, with Deborah Perkins.   20

Bacchus he priz'd Ariadne the sweet,
But I wish we were now at the firkins;[4]
  I'd make him reel off,
  In contemptible scoff,
While I toasted plump Deborah Perkins.

---

1. Mount Ida was a wooded mountain near Troy, frequented by the gods.
2. This is probably a shortened form of the term 'black Moor' which, according to Partridge, was one of playful endearment.
3. 'King Solomon had seven hundred wives, princesses, and three hundred concubines', I Kings 11. 3.
4. Bacchus, god of wine, loved Ariadne, who had been forsaken by her husband; firkins = small ale-casks.

Might I have all the girls at command,
That boast of their Dresden,⁵ or markings;
    I'd rather feed goats,
    And play with the coats
Of cherry-cheek'd Deborah Perkins.   30

A fig for the eclogues of Maro,⁶
Or Ovid's fantastical workings;
    If I haven't their letters,
    I sing of their betters,
When I touch up young Deborah Perkins.

The Clerk's Song

King *David* was a psalmist rare,
    And many a psalm he made,
He both compos'd and sung with air;
    But singing's all our trade.

Yet as much greater our renown,
    As harder is our lot;
He got for's¹ pains a golden crown,
    We but a silver groat.²

That good king *David* lov'd his glass
    Is very plain, for why ah!   10
He drank one night to such a pass,
    That he fuddled poor *Uriah*.³

King David longed for a drink,
    And really so do I:
'Tis all good singers fate, I think;
    For singing makes us dry.

---

5. Dresden china is white and delicate so, allusively, the reference here is to delicate, white skin.
6. Publius Virgilius Maro (70-19 B.C.), normally known as Virgil.

---

1. i.e. for his.
2. A small coin worth four pence.
3. II Samuel 11. 15. David ate and drank with Uriah and 'made him drunk'.

Then if you'll give me t'other tift[4]
I'll give you t'other strain:
I sing to drink, for that's my gift,
    And drink to sing again.   20

TIT for TAT; or the Rater rated:

A new Song, in Way of Dialogue, between a Laggen Farmer and his Wife[1]

HE   'Ye're welcome hame, my *Marg'y*,
        Frae the grim craving clergy;
        How deeply did they charge ye,
            Wi' sair oppressive tythe?
        While some are chous'd,[2] and cheated;
        Some rattled are, and rated;
        Ye hae been better treated,
            I trow, ye luick sae blythe'.[3]

SHE   'I hae been wi' the rector;
        His wife did scould and hector;   10
        Instead o' a guid lecture ——
            Quo' she, "Ye go too fine,[4]
        With scarlet cloaks and bedgowns,
        With velvet puggs[5] and plaid-gowns,
        With ruffled sleeves and headrounds,[6]
            More rich and gay than mine".

---

4. tift = tiff, a small draught of liquor (James Orchard Halliwell, *A Dictionary of Archaic and Provincial Words*, two vols. (Brixton Hill, 1852), p. 873).

1. Like everyone involved in farming in eighteenth-century Ireland, the speakers in this poem, who come from the Lagan valley in County Donegal, found the payment of tithes to support the local Church of Ireland rector irksome. The title of the poem could be translated: 'Tit for tat, or the berating of those who demand the rates or tithes ...'. This poem is in the energetic and vigorous language of the northern fringe of Ireland, Ulster Scots; words and phrases not explained in the notes will be found in the Glossary.

2. defrauded.

3. i.e. Some are defrauded and cheated, some are scolded and berated: [but] you have been treated better, I think, because you look so happy.

4. i.e. are going around dressed too finely. (The rector's wife speaks in English rather than Ulster Scots.)

5. An article of women's clothing, the exact meaning of which is uncertain.

6. headrounds = headbands — ornamental bands worn around the head.

"Forbear, proud madam Persian,[7]
Take back ye'r ain aspersion,
Wi' tea, ye'r chief diversion,
    Ye waste ye'r time awa: 20
While dressing ye're and pinning,
I'll spin, and bleach my linnen,
And wear my ain hands winning,
    Ye rector's lazy daw.[8]

I rise e'er the cocks craw day;
My hands I spare not a' day,
And wi' my farmer laddie
    At night I take my ease:
My husband plows and harrows,
He sows and reaps and farrows,   30
Shame fa' them wad change marrows,[9]
    For rector's gown and chaise.[10]

Sure some kind deel has brought us
Yon yellow chiel,[11] that taught us
To cleek the tythe potatoes
    Frae ilk a greedy gown!
Nae bishop, dean, or rector,
Nae vicar, curate, proctor,[12]
Dare ettle[13] now to doctor[14]
    Our skeedyines[15] under ground.'   40

HE   'Dear *Madgie*, e'en fairfaw ye!
            I'm blest that e'er I saw ye!

---

7. i.e. you who are as proud as a Persian.
8. i.e. '... and I wear my own hands [to the bone] gathering crops — you're the rector's lazy
   slut.'
9. companions, equals.
10. i.e. 'shame fall on those who would exchange their equals for the comforts of life with a
    rector.' The implication is that the rector's wife was herself, from a farming family.
11. A footnote at this point in the 1752 printing of the poem refers to a lawyer 'who went by
    the name of Yellow Rowan'. The lines mean: 'Sure some kind devil has brought us
    "Yellow Rowan" who has taught us to take for ourselves the potatoes which should have
    been paid as a tythe to every greedy clergyman.'
12. an agent for the collection of tythes.
13. have it in mind to.
14. tamper with.
15. potatoes, Ir. *sceidíní*, small potatoes.

A braid-cloth coat I aw ye,
    Fac'd wi' a velvet cape:[16]
May milk and meal ne'er fail ye,
May loss of yews[17] ne'er ail ye,
But geer[18] grow on ye daily,
    For birking madam *Crape*.[19]

On the *Spaw*[1] at *Castle-connel*, in the County of *Limerick*

Ye beaux and belles, of Mallow-well,[2]
    Who daily ill heap on-ill;[3]
If you've a mind, true health to find,
    Come quick to Castle-Connell.

Such beauties here, around appear,
    That you can scarce go one-ell,[4]
But you must swear, for water, air,
    There's nought like Castle-Connell.

Here numbers come, on saddle some,
    And some without one pannel;[5]   10
But all are found, soon heal[6] and sound,
    By wond'rous Castle-Connell.

---

16. A cape is, here, a long narrow strip of cloth around the shoulder of a coat. The lines mean: 'I owe you a coat of broadcloth (a fine, woven black cloth) trimmed ('faced') with velvet.'

17. ewes.

18. = gear, possessions and property.

19. birking = (strictly) birching, punishing by beating with a rod; Madam Crape = the rector's wife. In the eighteenth century, clergymen's clothes were sometimes made of a woven fabric called crape, and a clergyman might be referred to as 'Mr Crape' (*OED*).

1. An eighteenth-century spelling of the word 'spa'.

2. The poet hopes to attract patrons from the spa at Mallow, Co. Cork to that at Castleconnell.

3. As in other poems on spas (by Swift and Sheridan for instance), the name of the spa completes each stanza, and the poet is often forced to commandeer strange words to rhyme with it. This line seems to mean 'Who daily add to your ills (by staying at Mallow)'.

4. A measure of about 45 inches.

5. A kind of saddle.

6. A Scots and Ulster form of the word 'hale' = cured.

If pox or stone,[7] with many a groan,
    Obstruct your aching channel;
By drinking free, you'll quickly see,
    The effects of Castle-Connell.

Oft have I seen, the sickness green,
    And beau, wrapp'd up in flannel,[8]
Without a drug, look fair and smug,
    And all by Castle-Connell.   20

Our waters can soon make a man,
    Brisk as the fam'd MacDonnell,[9]
And ladies may, I boldly say,
    Get heirs at Castle-Connell.

Let empty blades,[10] with addled heads,
    Swill liquors like a funnell,
We at this spring, quaff health and sing,
    Success to Castle-Connell.

Our bark we steer, with mirth, good cheer,
    Whilst love sits on the gunnel;[11]   30
Thus spend the day, in sportive play,
    And health, at Castle-Connell.

---

7. i.e. venereal disease or kidney stones, both of which cause pain in the urinary tract ('the channel').
8. i.e. in bandages made of flannel.
9. A note in the original edition reads: 'Alluding to a Song on the Earl of Antrim, whose Family name is MAC DONNELL'. There are several eighteenth-century songs about the family.
10. 'Gallant, free and easy fellows' (*OED*).
11. The gunwale (pronounced 'gunnel') is the topmost piece of timber around the side of a small boat (or 'bark').

A New Ballad on the Hot-Wells at Mallow[1]

Ye nymphs deprest
With want of rest,
And with complexion sallow,
Don't waste your prime
With chalk or lime;[2]
But drink the springs at *Mallow*.

They cure all hues,
Blacks, greens, and blues,
The dun,[3] the pale, the yellow:
Nay, in their room,   10
Will raise a bloom,
And make you shine at *Mallow*.

All you, that are
Both lean and bare,
With scarce an ounce of tallow;[4]
To make your flesh
Both plump and fresh,
Come drink the springs at *Mallow*.

For all that you
Are bound to do,   20
Is just to gape and swallow,
You'll find by that,
You'll rowl in fat,
Most gloriously at *Mallow*.

Or if love's pain
Disturbs your brain,
And makes your reason shallow:
To shake it off,
Gulp down enough
Of our hot springs at *Mallow*.   30

---

1. A town in County Cork.
2. Both chalk and lime, dissolved in water, were used to alleviate indigestion.
3. A dingy brown colour, 'like the hair of a mouse' (*OED*).
4. fat.

309

Ye ladies fair,
Who want an heir,
Whose fruitful fields lie fallow,
Leave spouse at home,
And hither come,
To drink the wells at *Mallow*.

These springs you'll find
So good in kind,
They make you soon cry, ballow![5]
To lull and keep   40
Your babe asleep,
Which you may get at *Mallow*.

A doctor true
You may go to;
One that will lay you all low;
Then take his juice
Of sov'reign use,
To give new life at *Mallow*.

The Rakes of Mallow

Beauing, belling, dancing, drinking,
    Breaking windows, damning, sinking,[1]
Ever raking, never thinking,
    Live the Rakes of *Mallow*.

Spending faster than it comes,
    Beating Bawds, and Whores, and Duns,[2]
Bacchus' true begotten Sons,
    Live the Rakes of *Mallow*.

One time nought but Claret drinking,
    Then like Politicians thinking   10
To raise the Sinking-fund,[3] when sinking,
    Live the Rakes of *Mallow*.

---

5. A bellowing, bull-like roar. The word is coined as a rhyme for Mallow.

---

1. Degenerating into an 'inferior or unsatisfactory state or condition' (*OED*).
2. debt-collectors.
3. A fund of revenue saved and set aside for the purpose of reducing the national debt.

One Time flush with Money Store,
  Then as any poet poor,
Kissing Queens,[4] and then the Whore,
  Live the Rakes of *Mallow*.

When at home with Dadda dying,
  Still for *Mallow* water crying,
But when there, good Claret plying,
  Live the Rakes of *Mallow*.   20

Living short but merry Lives,
  Going where the Devil drives,
Keeping Misses, but no Wives,
  Live the Rakes of *Mallow*.

Racking tenants,[5] Stewards teizing,[6]
  Swiftly spending, slowly raising,
Wishing to spend all our Days in
  Raking thus at *Mallow*.

Thus to end a raking Life,
  We grow sober, take a Wife,   30
Ever after live in strife,
  Wish again for *Mallow*.

4. Young women, probably of good reputation — in contrast to the whore.
5. i.e. extracting extortionate rents from tenants.
6. teasing, pestering.

Scew Ball[1]

Come gentlemen sportsmen, I pray listen all,
I will sing you a song in praise of Scew Ball,[2]
And how he came over[3] you shall understand,
It was by Squire Merwin[4] the pearl of our land.

And of all his late actions that I've heard before,
He was lately challenged by one Sir Ralph Gore,[5]
For five hundred guineas on the plains of Kildare,
To run with Miss Sportly, that charming grey mare.

Scew ball he then hearing the wager was laid,
Unto his kind master said, 'Don't be afraid,   10
For if on my side you thousands lay would,
I will rig[6] in your castle a fine mass of gold.'

The day being come, and the cattle[7] walk'd forth,
The people came flocking from East, South and North,
For to view all the sporters, as I do declare,
And venture their money all on the grey mare.

Squire Merwin then smiling unto them did say,
'Come gentlemen all that's got money to lay,
And you that have hundreds, come I'll lay you all,
For I will venture thousands on famous Scew Ball.'   20

---

1. Throughout the eighteenth century (as still today), the Curragh, a plain in County Kildare about thirty miles west of Dublin, was a popular venue for horse racing. Despite the fact that Arthur Mervin and Sir Ralph Gore were prominent members of the Irish racing fraternity in the mid eighteenth century, this ballad celebrates a race which seems to have been rigged.
2. A scewbald horse is a white horse with irregular markings of red or brown.
3. i.e. got the better of his opponent.
4. *Pue's Occurrences* (4 April 1752) reported that Arthur Mervin's horse 'Scuball' had beated Ralph Gore's mare the previous Monday. Arthur Mervin or Marvyn was president of the Irish branch of the Jockey Club in the late 1750s.
5. Sir Ralph Gore of Belleisle, Co. Fermanagh, was Ranger of the Curragh from 1756 to 1760 and succeeded Arthur Mervin as president of the Irish Jockey Club in 1759.
6. To manipulate something or someone illegally or illicitly (Partridge). The implication is that the race was rigged.
7. animals — in this case, horses.

Squire Merwin then smil'd, and thus he did say,
'Come gentlemen sportsmen, to-morrow's the day,
Your horses and saddles and bridles prepare,
For we must away to the plains of Kildare.'

The day being come, and the cattle walk'd out,
Squire Merwin he order'd his rider to mount,
And all the spectators for to clear the way,
The time being come, not one moment delay.

These cattle were mounted, and away they did fly,
Scew Ball like an arrow past Miss Sportly by,   30
The people went up for to see them go round,
They said in their hearts that they ne'er touched the ground.

But as they were running, in the midst of the sport,
Squire Mirwin to his rider began this discourse,
'O loving kind rider come tell unto me,
How far is Miss Sportly this moment from thee?'

'O loving kind master you bear a great stile,[8]
The grey marc's behind me a long English mile,[9]
If the saddle maintains, I'll warrant you there,
You ne'er will be beat on the plains of Kildare.'   40

But as they were running by the distance chair,[10]
The gentlemen cry'd out, 'Scew Ball never fear,
Altho' in this country thou wast ne'er seen before,
Thou has beaten Miss Sportly, and broke[11] Sir Ralph Gore.'

---

8. 'The manner of action of a racehorse' (*OED*).
9. An English mile was 1200 paces, an Irish mile 1500 paces.
10. Presumably a marker around which the horses raced; cf. the obsolete word 'chare' = a turn.
11. ruined. cf. the phrase 'to break the bank'.

THOMAS MOZEEN
(fl.**1750**, d.1768)

Thomas Mozeen was an English actor who lived in Dublin for two years in the 1740s. He seems to have spent his time drinking and riding, and was well known to several residents of counties Wicklow and Dublin, including the sixth earl of Meath and Owen Bray, the hospitable landlord of a public house at Loughlinstown. Mozeen's most famous poem, a song normally known as 'The Kilruddery Hunt', celebrates a fox hunt which took place in 1744. The persons named were all well-known in hunting circles at the time and the places named can be traced today.

A Description of a Fox-Chase
that happened in the County of *Dublin*, 1744, with the Earl of *Meath*'s Hounds

Hark, hark, jolly Sportsmen, a while to my Tale,
Which, to claim your Attention, I hope, will not fail:
'Tis of Lads, and of Horses, and Dogs, that ne'er tire
O'er Stone Walls, and Hedges, thro' Dale, Bog and Briar:
A Pack of such Hounds, and a Set of such Men,
'Tis a shrewd Chance if ever you meet with again.
Had *Nimrod*,[1] the mightiest of Hunters, been there,
'Fore gad he had shook like an Aspen for Fear.
La, la, la, &c.

In Seventeen Hundred and Forty and Four,   10
The Fifth of *December* —— I think 'twas no more,
At Five in the Morning, by most of the Clocks,
We rode from *Kilruddery*,[2] to try for a Fox; ——
The *Laughlin's* Town Landlord, the bold *Owen Bray*,
With 'Squire *Adair*, sure, was with us that Day;
Jo Debill, *Hall Preston*, that Huntsman so stout,
Dick Holmes, (a few others); and so we set out.
La, la, la, &c.

We cast off the Hounds for an Hour or more,
When *Wanton* set up a most tuneable Roar: 20
Hark to *Wanton*! cry'd *Jo* —— and the rest were not slack,
For *Wanton*'s no Trifler esteem'd by the Pack:

---

1. A descendent of Noah and a 'mighty hunter' (Genesis 10. 9).
2. The seat of the earls of Meath, in north County Wicklow.

Old *Bonny* and *Collier* came readily in,
And every Dog join'd in the musical Din.
Had *Diana*[3] been there, she'd been pleas'd to the Life,
And some of the Lads got a goddess to Wife——
       La, la, la, &c.

Ten Minutes past Nine was the Time o' the Day,
When *Reynard* unkennell'd, and this was his Play;
As strong from *Killeagar*, as tho' he could fear none; 30
Away he brush'd round, by the House at *Kilternan*;
To *Carrick Mines* thence, and to *Cherrywood* then;
Steep *Shank Hill* he climb'd, and to *Ballyman Glenn.*
Bray Common he past; leap'd Lord *Anglesea*'s Wall;
And seem'd to say, 'Little I value you all.'
       La, la, la, &c.

He ran Bushes, Groves, up to *Carbury Bourns*;[4]
Jo Debill, and *Preston*, kept leading by Turns;
The Earth it was open,[5] —— but *Reynard* was stout,
Tho' he cou'd have got in, yet he chose to keep out: 40
To *Malpass*'s Summits[6] away then he flew;
At *Dalkey*'s Stone Common, we had him in View.
He shot on thro' *Bullock* to *Shrub Glenagary*,
And so on to *Mount Town*, where *Larry* grew weary.
       La, la, la, &c.

Thro' *Roche*'s Town Wood, like an Arrow he past,
And came to the steep Hills of *Dalkey* at last;
There gallantly plung'd himself into the Sea,
And said in his Heart, 'Sure none dare follow me'.
But soon, to his Cost, he perceiv'd that no Bounds 50
Cou'd stop the Pursuit of the staunch mettl'd Hounds.
His Policy here didn't serve him a Rush:
Five Couple of Tartars[7] were hard at his Brush.
       La, la, la, &c.

3. The mythological goddess of the hunt, normally depicted naked and carrying a bow and arrows.
4. A note in early editions of the poem indentifies Carbury Byrne as a carpenter who lived in the area.
5. i.e. the fox's earth or hole had not been stopped up to prevent his returning. stout = brave.
6. What is now Killiney Hill was owned, at this time, by a Colonel Malpass.
7. tartars = savage animals.

To recover the Shore, then again was his Drift,
But e'er he could reach to the Top of the Clift,[8]
He found both of Speed, and of Cunning a Lack;
Being way-laid, and kill'd by the rest of the Pack.
At his Death there were present the Lads that I've sung,
Save *Larry*, who, riding a Garron,[9] was flung.   60
Thus ended, at length, a most delicate Chace,
That held us five Hours and ten Minutes Space.

La, la, la, &c.

We return'd to *Killruddery*'s plentiful Board,
Where dwells Hospitality, Truth, and my Lord[10] ——
We talk'd o'er the Chace, and we toasted the Health
Of the Man who ne'er vary'd for Places or Wealth.
Owen Bray baulk'd a Leap; said *Hal Preston,* — 'twas odd;
'Twas shameful, cry'd *Jack* —— by the great living God!
Said *Preston,* I halloo'd, Get on, tho' you fall;   70
Or I'll leap over you, your blind Gelding, and all.

La, la, la, &c.

Each Glass was adapted to Freedom and Sport;
But party Affairs we consign'd to the Court.[11]
Thus we finish'd the rest of the Day and the Night,
In gay flowing Bumpers, and social Delight.
Then till the next Meeting, bid Farewell each Brother;
So some they went one Way, and some went another.
And as *Phœbus* befriended our earlier Roam,
So *Luna* took Care in conducting us Home.[12]   80

La, la, la, &c.

8. cliff.
9. small horse; cf. Ir. *gearrán*, gelding or small horse.
10. Chaworth Brabazon (1686-1758), sixth Earl of Meath and owner of the Kilruddery hunt.
11. i.e. we did not discuss politics, which would be discussed at court.
12. Phoebus = the sun; Luna = the moon.

Thomas Mozeen

An Invitation to OWEN BRAY's at Laughlin's town

Are ye landed from England, and sick of the seas,
Where ye rowl'd, and ye tumbl'd all manner of ways?
To Laughlin's-town then, without any delays,
For you'll never be right, till you see Owen Bray's,
     With his *Ballen a mona*,[1] &c.,
     A glass of his claret for me.

Were ye full of complaints from the crown to the toe?
A visit to Owen's will cure ye of woe;
A buck of such spirits ye never did know,
For let what will happen they're always in flow,   10
     When he touches up *Ballen* &c.,
     The joy of that fellow for me.

You may talk of Italians, whatever you will,
I'd not give a fig to be crown'd with their skill;
Nay, sooner than hear 'em I'd gulp down a pill;
For who wou'd compare a damn'd unmeaning thrill,
     To *Ballen a mona,* &c.,
     The grounds of a ballad for me.

Fling leg over garron, ye lovers of sport,
True joy is at Bray's, tho' there's little at Court;   20
'Tis thither the lads of brisk mettle resort,
For there they are sure that they'll never fall short,
     Of claret, and *Ballen* &c.,
     The eighty-fourth bumper for me.

The days in December are dirty and raw,
But when we're at Owen's we care not a straw;
We bury the trades of religion, and law,
And the ice in our hearts, sure, we presently thaw
     With good claret and *Ballen* &c.,
     The quick moving bottle for me.   30

---

1. The tune 'Ballinamona' is in Burk Thumoth's *Twelve English and Twelve Irish Airs* (London, c. 1745). A character called Father Luke sings a song called 'Ballinamona, or, You Know I'm your Priest, and your Conscience is mine' in the second act of *The Poor Soldier* by John O'Keeffe (London, 1783).

Mean-spirited reptiles deservedly sink,
But Owen shall sing, and shall hunt, and shall drink,
The boy that from bumpers yet never did shrink,
Nor till threescore and ten, shall he venture to think
  Of leaving off *Ballen* &c.,
  Long life to gay fellows for me.

THOMAS NEWBURGH
(c.1695-**1758**-1779)

Thomas Newburgh was born in Dublin, the son of the chairman of the Linen Board. He was educated at Oxford but returned to Ireland when he inherited an estate in County Cavan. The poem which follows is one of very few describing Irish eighteenth-century buildings or monuments. It comes from a volume of Newburgh's miscellaneous work entitled *Essays Poetical, Moral and Critical* (Dublin, 1769) which is sometimes catalogued as the work of his father, Brockhill Newburgh.

In the eighteenth century, the Dublin park of St Stephen's Green was surrounded on each side by a tree-lined walk, Beaux Walk on the north (the most fashionable of the walks), Monk's Walk on the east, Leeson's Walk on the south, and French Walk on the west. Between the walks and the central meadow was a ditch, or 'ha-ha', and in the centre of the green was an equestrian statue of George II. Erected in 1758, this statue was blown up in 1937.

The BEAU WALK, in STEPHEN'S GREEN

'Mid Trees of stunted Growth, unequal Roes,
On the coarse Gravel, trip the Belles and Beaus.
Here, on one Side, extends a length of Street,
Where Dirt-bespattering Cars and Coaches meet.
On t'other, in the Ditches lazy Flood,
Dead Cats and Dogs lie bloated; drench'd in Mud.
But lo! a Statue from afar salutes your Eyes,
To which th'Inclosure all Access denies.
So distant, whose, or whom, no Eye can ken,
Plac'd in the Centre of a marshy fen.   10
But know, 'tis Royal George[1] on whom you stare,
Tho' oft mistaken for some good Lord Mayor:
And tho' his Charger foams in ductile Brass,
The Charger for an ambling Pad[2] may pass;
The whole equestrian Statue for a Toy,
A Horse of Hobby, mounted by a Boy.
For shame, ye Cits,[3] where meet th'assembl'd Fair,
Fill up your Dikes and purge th'unwholsome Air.
Let George's royal Form be fairly shewn,
And like his Virtues, be reveal'd and known.[4]   20

[1.] George II (1683-1760), king of Great Britain and Ireland 1727-60.
[2.] A charger is a horse ridden by an army officer in battle, whereas a pad is a slow, steady, reliable one.
[3.] A (derogatory) term for a citizen of a town.
[4.] The poet is urging the citizens to fill in the ha-ha and make the green (and the statue) accessible.

SAMUEL WHYTE
(1733-**1758**-1811)

Samuel Whyte was born in a ship crossing the Irish Sea and first 'touched land' in Liverpool. He was brought up by the Sheridan family in Dublin and became one of the most influential schoolmasters in eighteenth-century Dublin. His pupils included Richard Brinsley Sheridan, Thomas Moore and many of the sons and daughters of the Anglo-Irish gentry. Whyte was an accomplished poet and also wrote on education and rhetoric. He published the poetry of many of his pupils in *The Shamrock or Hibernian Cresses* in 1772.

from: A Familiar Epistle to J.H. Esq; near Killarney
[A Description of Dublin in 1758]

... From this dull Town's unvarying Scene,
Where Smoke, and Noise, and Folly reign;
Where Virtue's hallow'd Flames expire;
And Health, and Joy, with Sighs, retire;
Where Cards infernal Vigils keep;
And Politics have '*murder'd Sleep*';[1]
Where Fogs and Mists, in black Array,
With horrid Gloom obscure the Day;
And Clouds of Dust, or Floods of Rain,
Gay Fancy's magic Power restrain;   10
From such a Place, O say, my Friend,
What Present can the Poet send?
No Fragrance here the Morn supplies,
No Lustre gilds the Evening Skies;
Nor verdant Field, nor Summer Flower,
Nor Music, floating through the Bower,
One pleasing Image can suggest,
Or waken Rapture in the Breast:
Instead of these, from Sleep I start,
Rouz'd by the Rattling of a Cart;   20
The Hoarseness of the Dirt-man's[2] Throat,
The Chimney-Sweeper's piercing Note,
With 'Shoes to mend', and 'Cloaths to sell',
In Union harsh the Concert swell;

1. An echo of *Macbeth* II, i, 36: 'Macbeth does murder sleep'.
2. The collector of night-refuse.

Sounds void of Harmony and Grace,
That fright the Muses from the Place....

Sick of the Joys, and tasteless grown
To all the Follies of the Town;
Vex'd with the Scene of endless Strife,
You'll ask me — How I spend my Life?   30
Know then, my Friend — In Garret high,
Three Stories mounted to the Sky;
A *Prior* here; a *Plowden* there;[3]
And Cloaths and Books on every Chair;
As Fancy leads, in various Way,
I pass the Morning of the Day....

When *Sol* his broader Face displays,
And Westward slopes his Evening rays,
I sometimes ramble, 'till 'tis dark,
In the *New-Garden*, or the *Park*;   40
Chat with the Girls of Dress or Place;
Direct a Patch; admire a Lace;
And, with a well-feign'd Rapture, view
A Flounce, a Ribbon, or a Shoe;
As Whim directs, I blame, or praise;
And say — whate'er the Circle says —
'The prettiest Hat — the finest Fan'
And — '*Barry* is a charming Man!'[4]
And, while their Humours thus I hit,
Lord! How they wonder at my Wit!   50

Or, sometimes to the Globe[5] I stray,
To hear the Trifle of the Day;
There learned Politicians spy,
With thread-bare Cloaks, and Wigs awry,
Assembled round, in deep Debate
On *Prussia*'s Arms, and *Britain*'s Fate[6]

---

3. i.e. the works of the poet Matthew Prior (1664-1721) and the legal writer Edmund
   Plowden (1518-85).
4. Spranger Barry (1719-77), a well-known Dublin actor.
5. A footnote identifies this as 'The Globe Coffee-House, in *Essex-street, Dublin*'.
6. At the time of this poem, England and Prussia were at war with France, Austria, Russia,
   Sweden and Saxony in what became known as the Seven Years War (1756-63).

Whilst one, whose Penetration goes,
At best, no farther than his Nose,
In pompous, military Strain,
Fights every Battle o'er again;   60
Thence marks *Intrenchments*, *Posts*, and *Lines* —
Here mounts the *Breach* — *there* springs the *Mines* —
And bustling, arrogant, and loud,
Thus dictates to the gaping Crowd —
'The *Austrian* Foot[7] was posted *there* —
The *King* attacked them in the *Rear*'....
Such Folks there are, my Friend; and you
Have seen the like in *London* too;...

Tir'd of the Noise, the Smoke, the Men,
I leave the Coffee-House at Ten;   70
Retire to rest about Eleven;
And seldom wake 'till Six or Seven....

---

7. i.e. regiment of foot-soldiers.

ART MAC CUMHAIDH
(c.1715-**1760**-1773)

The unusual macaronic poem which follows is said to have been composed by Art Mac
Cumhaidh, who lived in the Fews area of south County Armagh. The religious and political
issues of the times are presented in the form of a dialogue between two buildings, the new
protestant church in Forkhill, Co. Armagh, which was built in 1767 and which speaks in
English throughout the poem, and the nearby catholic chapel at Fraughart, which was falling
into desrepair at the time, and which speaks in Irish. The metre in both Irish and English is
a regular form of the Irish stress metre known as *Ochtfhoclach*.

Tagra an Dá Theampall
(The Disputation of the Two Churches)

An Róimhchill:[1]   Eadar Foirceal na cléire is Fochairt na nGael
             'Sé chodail mé aréir ar lóistín,
      Is le fáinne an lae 'sé chuala mé an ghéag
             Cur ceisteanna i gcéin ón Róimhchill,
      Dá fiafraí den téa'pall galánta gléasta
             Chonaic sí réidh de chomhgar:
      'Cé acu sliocht Gael a dheasaigh do thaobh,
             Clann Liútair nó fréamh Strongbownians?'[2]

An Teampall Gallda:[3] You silly old dame, I would have you forsake
             Your ignorant papish notions,   10
      For all your sliocht Gael[4] are declining away
             From Popery's vain devotion.
      My Protestant states are thriving each day,
             Since Rome and they divorcèd;
      Your church is decayed and ever shall fade
             Under our Lutheran forces.

---

1. The catholic chapel.
2. *Stanza 1*: I slept last night in a house between Forkhill of the clerics and Faughart of the
   Irish, and at day break I heard someone asking questions from afar from the Roman
   church, enquiring of the fine well-built church that she saw ready nearby: 'Was it the
   Irish who fixed your walls, or the followers of Luther or the descendants of the
   Strongbownians?'
3. The protestant church.
4. offspring of Gael (for whom see next note).

An Róimhchill: D'fhreagair mé a scéala sa teanga fuair Gael
Mac Eathair ar Mhaigh Séanair óirearc:
'Tabhair aire dhuit féin nach scaipfidh do shréad
Mar Nimrod is a shaoraibh róghlic.   20
Ach is cosúil gur éag siad maithe Síl Néill
Is clann Anluain fuil tréanrí Óirthear,
Mac 'Naosa na stéad, na n-ollamh 's na dtead,
Tráth deasadh do leithéid sa chló sin.'[5]

An Teampall Gallda: In spite of your beads, my English shall reign,
Whilst Irish grows daily odious:
England and Wales have riches in heaps,
To flourish away most glorious.
My flock has estates, with land and demesnes,
All riding in state in their coaches,   30
While taxes, arrears, and cesses severe
Upon your Gaelian broaches.[6]

An Róimhchill: An gcuala tú scéala sa Scrioptúir dá léamh
Ar phobal na hÉiphte i mbeobhruid,
Gurb iomaí sin gléas ler coscradh an réacs,
Sul fár scaradh go léir uaidh an cóige,
Is le cumas na n–éacht gur chruinnigh siad laochra
I gcarbaid go gléasta in ordú,
'S in ainneoin a dtréas go dtáinig siad saor
Tríd thonnaibh geal tréan na bóchna.[7]   40

---

5. *Stanza 3*: I answered his tale in the language Gael Mac Eathair received on the illustrious
plain of Prophecy (in Athens): 'Look after yourself that your flock is not scattered as
happened to Nimrod and his nobles.' But it seems that the O'Neills had died as well as
the O'Hanlons, powerful kings of the east part of the province, and MacGuinness, who
had horses, poets and harps around him, when the likes of you was adorned like that.
Notes to stanza 3: The implication of this stanza is that, if these local chieftains had
been alive, a protestant church would not have been built at all; Gael Mac Eathair: This
is a reference to Fenius Farsa, the king of Scythia who, according to the traditional
history of Ireland, founded a school for languages in Athens. He instructed Gael Mac
Eathair, the eponymous ancestor of the Gaelic Irish, to preserve the language of his
people; Nimrod: Nimrod, the mighty hunter, is credited with building the tower of Babel
(Genesis 10. 8-9).
6. i.e. while taxes, unpaid debts and the obligation to provide provisions to soldiers (an
obligation known as a cess) pierce your Irish people.
7. *Stanza 5*: Did you hear the story being read from Scripture about the people in bondage
in Egypt, how the Pharaoh was assailed by many means before the province was
completely sundered from him, and how by the power of their deeds they gathered
warriors lined out in order in chariots, and how despite their betrayal they came safely
across the powerful bright waves of the sea?

An Teampall Gallda: Your clergy maintains the Scripture contains
But mystical dreams and stories;
False doctrine that leads your senses away
From heavenly grace and glory.
Inventing such schemes for money to gain,
Of Limbo they treat laborious,
Until Luther the great, and Calvin of late,
Renounced their shameful chorus.

An Róimhchill: 'Sé mo thuirse gur tréaghdadh maithe na nGael
In Eachroim 's ar thaobh na Bóinne,   50
'S nach maireann i gcéim Eoghan an Chogaidh
Ó Néill
Chuirfeadh Cromail i bpéin 's a shlóite.
Cha lasfadh King Harry, Beelsebub éitheach,
Nó Liútar a bhuaradh Fódla,
New Lights nó Seceders, Old Presbyterians,
Swaddlers nó Quakers leofa.[8]

An Teampall Gallda: Luther was great in virtue and fame,
And high potentates adored him.
From Germany great to England he came,
Until he would plainly show them   60
How they might ease King Henry's reign
Concerning Queen Kate's divorcement,
By marrying the fair Anne Boleyn of fame,
In spite of proud Spain's reinforcement.

An Róimhchill: Bhí an iomad den chléir in eagna 's i léann
Ag teagasc i dtéa'pall Rómha,
Ag Nice is ag Éphesus thart timpeall fán réim
Go Constanti — Ghréagach — nople,

---

8. *Stanza 7*: It's my sorrow that the Gaelic nobles were wounded at Aughrim and by Boyneside, and that Owen Roe of the Battles O'Neill does not live in power, for he would hurt Cromwell and his hosts. King Harry would not have ignited deceitful Beelzebub or Luther to trouble Ireland with New Lights or Seceders, Old Presbyterians, Swaddlers or Quakers. **Note to stanza 7**: <u>O'Neill</u>: Owen Roe O'Neill, (c. 1590-1649) commander of the Irish Confederate army, who never lost a battle in Ireland; <u>Harry</u>: King Henry VIII (1491-1547), king of England 1509-47; <u>New Lights or Seceders, Old Presbyterians, Swaddlers or Quakers</u>: the names of various non-conformist sects active in seventeenth-century Ireland and England.

Sul fá dtainig an fear claon sin, Liútar na mbréag,
A mhilleadh an mhaighdean ró-ghlan.   70
Is má d'imigh le baos na Huguenots gan chéill,
Char cailleadh mo shréadsa i gcónaí.[9]

An Teampall Gallda: Your whimsical brain, with wrath or disdain,
                     It never will change my notion:
                     For you have no more share with us to compare
                     Than the purling stream to the ocean,
                     In Hibernia fair, in Scotland we reign,
                     In England great, and Hanover;
                     So what need we care for France or for Spain,
                     Or for Charley, your rakish rover?   80

An Róimhchill: Níl gar dom bheith 'dréim le creideamh gan chéill
                Nach nglacann uaim scéal nó comhairle,
                Nó go dtiocfaidh na méara chonaic an tréanfhear,
                Baltassar ar thaobh a lóistín,
                Dá noctadh dhuit féin, 'réir chothrom an scéil,
                Gurb atuirseach mé faoi Sheoirse,
                Is ar fheartaibh Mhic Dé, nár mhairidh tú i gcéim,
                Nó go gcuirfidh Rí Séarlas brón ort.[10]

---

9. *Stanza 9*: Many clerics, wise and learned, were teaching in the Roman church at Nicea (325 A.D.), Ephesus (481 A.D.) and Grecian Constantinople (381 A.D.), before that evil man, Luther of the lies, came to desecrate the pure virgin (church). And even if the senseless Huguenots went after folly, my flock were not lost for ever.

10. *Stanza 11*: It's no use for me to vie with a senseless creed that will take from me neither knowledge nor advice, until the fingers that the strongman Belshazzer saw on the side of his house come and show it to yourself, according to the truth of the story, that I being dejected about George, wish by the miraculous powers of the Son of God, that you not remain in high station until King Charles brings you to grief. **Notes to Stanza 11**: <u>Belshazzar</u>: In the book of Daniel, Belshazzar the king sees 'the fingers of a man's hand' writing on the plaster of the wall (Daniel 5. 5.); <u>George</u>: i.e King George III (1738-1820), king of Great Britain and Ireland 1760-1820; <u>King Charles</u>: Charles Edward, the Young Pretender (1720-88), ('Bonnie Prince Charlie') titular king of Great Britain and Ireland after the death of his father, the Old Pretender, in 1766.

LIAM INGLIS
(1709-**1760**-1778)

Liam Inglis was born in County Limerick and became a schoolmaster in Castletownroche, Co. Cork. He was ordained a priest in Rome in 1749, and entered the Augustinian Order. He returned to Ireland and became assistant prior of the Augustinian house in Cork. He wrote poetry in his youth and after 1760, but seems to have spent his middle years working at church affairs.

Do Tharlaigh Inné Orm
[I met yesterday]

Do tharlaigh inné orm is mé im' aonar sa ród,
Fánach beag béithe agus éistigh lem' ghlór,
Ba bhreá deas a béal is ba craorac mar rós,
Is ba lách deas a claonrosc ag géilleadh don spórt.[1]

Do bheannaigh go tapa is chuir maig ar a beol,
'Sir, I am your servant, how far do you go?'
'Béarla níl agam is ní chanaim a shórt,
Ach Gaeilge liom labhair is freagra gheobhair.'[2]

'As I hope to be married, a word I can't speak
Of that silly language, which makes my heart ache.   10
Therefore I entrust you some pity to show,
For I have the colic and I cannot well go.'

'Ná trácht liomsa ar chailligh ní maith liom féin iad,
Oirbheart is easpa is galar is pian;
Do b'fhearr liomsa ainnir a mbeadh lasadh ina ciabh
Is dhá mhama gheala mar shneachta ar shliabh.'[3]

---

1. *Stanza 1*: I met yesterday, while I was travelling, a wandering little maid and, listen to my voice, her mouth was nice and fine and red like a rose, and her eye was nice and pleasant, agreeable to fun.
2. *Stanza 2*: She promptly greeted me with a smile on her lips. '*Sir, I am your servant, how far do you go?*' 'I have no English, and I don't speak like that, but speak Irish to me and you'll get an answer.'
3. *Stanza 4*: Don't mention 'hags' [Ir. *chailligh*; cf. the word 'colic' in l. 12] to me, I don't like them; [they involve] deviousness and want and disease and pain. I'd prefer a maiden with shining curls and two bright breasts like snow on the mountainside. **Note to Stanza 4:** *Double-entendres* are common in macaronic poems of this type.

'Don't talk of my mama,[4] but prithee draw near,
For I am a poor creature that's raving with fear,
Therefore I beg, sir, some token you'll make,
Whereas of English[5] a word I can't speak.'   20

'Is English mo shloinne is ní shéanfad go brách,
A bhruinneall na finne is a chéadshearc thar mhnáibh.'
Do rugas go cluthair is go séimh ar mo ghrá
Is do thit sise is mise in éineacht ar lár.[6]

'O Lord, be quiet sir, what is all that?'
'Ní gá dhuit, a radharc ghil, tógfad gan stad
Do hoop is do ghúna is do chóta go pras',
Is go súgach do mhúineas dom stórach a ceacht.[7]

'If that be your Irish, 'ógánaigh a chroí,
I vow and declare I'll learn it of thee.'   30
Is é deir mo réilteann bheag bhéaltana bhinn,
'Ceacht eile den Ghaeilge, más féidir é, arís.'[8]

Do chromas dá mhúineadh go lúfar gan stad,
Is cúrsa na n-údar do thuig sí go glan,
Do thaitnigh gach véarsa dár léas di go mór,
Is do b'aite léi Gaeilge ná Béarla céad uair.[9]

---

4. cf. Ir. *mhama*, breasts in l. 16.
5. Though the sense seems to demand the word 'Irish' here, the fact that the poet jokes in the next line about his name Inglis (pronounced 'English') suggests the reading is correct. The humour of the line may be connected with the fact that the Irish word for 'English', *Béarla*, also means 'language'.
6. *Stanza 6*: '*English* is my surname, and that I'll never deny, O fair maiden and most loved among women.' I cosily and gently took hold of my love and she and I together fell down on the ground.
7. *Stanza 7*: '*O Lord, be quiet sir, what is all that?*' 'Don't worry, my bright-eyed one, without delay I'll swiftly lift your hoop and gown and petticoat.' And merrily I taught my treasure her lesson.
8. *Stanza 8*: '*If that be your Irish*, O youth of my heart, *I vow and declare I'll learn it of thee.*' This is what my little sweet-lipped fair one says: 'Another Irish lesson, if possible, again.'
9. *Stanza 9*: I set to teach her promptly and lively, and she understood clearly the works of the writers. She enjoyed greatly every verse I read to her, and Irish was a hundred times more pleasant to her than English.

PART IV
1760-90

DOROTHEA DUBOIS
(1728-**1764**-1774)

Dorothea was the eldest daughter of Richard Annesley, later sixth earl of Anglesea (1694-1761), and Ann Simpson, daughter of a wealthy Dublin merchant. When she was about twelve years old, Dorothea's father repudiated his marriage to Ann Simpson, declaring that it was bigamous. He subsequently lived with Juliana Donovan whom he married in 1752. Together they had further children, the eldest of whom succeeded to his father's Irish titles and estates, despite the claims of Dorothea and her mother and despite also a series of famous court cases involving a James Annesley, who appeared in 1740 claiming to be the true heir, and asserting that he had been kidnapped by Dorothea's father (his uncle) and sold into slavery in America.

Once Annesley had abandoned his 'Simpson' family, Dorothea, her mother and her two sisters found themselves penniless. Dorothea started writing in the 1760s, probably to support her family — though she was also determined to expose her father as a scoundrel. In addition to *Poems on Several Occasions* (1764), which contains a vivid account of her life story (see below 'A True Tale'), Dorothea published an autobiographical novel *Theodora* (1770), two plays and *The Lady's Polite Secretary, Or, New Female Letter-Writer* (1771), an interesting guide to self-expression and letter-writing for women. She had married a musician named Dubois in 1752, but her finances remained desperate and she died in poverty in Dublin.

The Amazonian Gift[1]

Is Courage in a Woman's Breast,
    Less pleasing than in Man?
And is a smiling Maid allow'd
    No Weapon but a Fan?

'Tis true, her Tongue, I've heard 'em say,
    Is Woman's chief Defence;
And if you'll b'lieve me, gentle Youths,
    I have no Aid from thence.

And some will say that sparkling Eyes,
    More dang'rous are than Swords;   10
But I ne'er point my Eyes to kill,
    Nor put I trust in Words.

---

1. The Amazons were legendary female warriors.

331

Then, since the Arms that Women use,
    Successless are in me,
I'll take the Pistol, Sword or Gun,
    And thus equip'd, live free.

The Pattern of the *Spartan* Dame[2]
    I'll copy as I can;
To Man, degen'rate Man, I'll give
    That simple Thing, a *Fan*.   20

Song

A Scholar first my Love implor'd,
And then an empty titled Lord;
The Pedant talk'd in lofty Strains;
Alas! his Lordship wanted Brains:
I list'ned not to one or t'other,
But strait referr'd them to my Mother.

A Poet next my Love assail'd,
A Lawyer hop'd to have prevail'd;
The Bard too much approv'd himself,
The Lawyer thirsted after Pelf:[1]   10
I list'ned not to one or t'other,
But still referr'd them to my Mother.

An Officer my Heart wou'd storm,
A Miser sought me too, in Form;
But *Mars* was over-free and bold,
The Miser's Heart was in his Gold:
I list'ned not to one or t'other,
Referring still unto my Mother.

2. The inhabitants of Sparta, in ancient Greece, were renowned for their simplicity and courage.

1. riches.

And after them some twenty more
Successless were, as those before;   20
When *Damon*, lovely *Damon*, came,
Our Hearts strait felt a mutual Flame;
I vow'd I'd have him, and no other,
Without referring to my Mother.

from: A True Tale
An autobiographical poem

Nature had form'd *Anglesus*[1] full of Grace,
Both as to Understanding, Form and Face,
Pleasing Wit, quick Penetration, and
Such jocund Humour, as wou'd Mirth command;
He wedded with a Fair and spotless Maid,
In blooming Youth and Innocence array'd;
Obtain'd a Fortune to his Wish — nay more
Than he cou'd then expect, for he was poor
In point of Fortune, altho' nobly born;
But lovely Anna[2] might a Crown adorn,   10
So was the Fair-one call'd; and many a Swain
Strove for her Love, whom *Anglesus* did gain.
Some Years they liv'd in Happiness and Peace,
And Heaven bless'd their Marriage with Encrease;
Three Daughters (out of Seven) gave them Joy,
But both were anxious to obtain a Boy.
Tho' these sweet Pledges, he wou'd often swear,
To his fond Heart, were equally as dear.

Soon to a Title and a great Estate
Angles' succeeded,[3] by the will of Fate.   20
His lovely Wife and infant Daughters shone
In all the Pomp that Grandeur cou'd put on;
At Court, at ev'ry public Place, appear'd,
Admir'd by all, by ev'ry one rever'd.
But who'd on human Happiness depend?
This short-liv'd, glitt'ring Scene was soon to end.

---

1. i.e. Dorothea's father, Richard Annesley, sixth earl of Anglesea.
2. i.e. Ann Simpson, Dorothea's mother.
3. Richard Annesley became earl of Anglesea in April 1737.

Transient Felicity! *Anglesus* grew
Unkind to *Anna*, sigh'd for something New;
Beheld a Tenant's Daughter[4] with Desire,
Nor scrupled to indulge the guilty Fire.   30
Tho' mean the *Nymph*, and common to Mankind
She gain'd an Empire o'er his fickle Mind;
Contriv'd such Schemes, and us'd such subtile Art,
She soon, alas! occasion'd them to part.

The faithful Wife, the tender Mother, view
Now exil'd from her Lord, and Children too;
To his Inconstancy a Victim made,
Forsaken, comfortless, to Want betray'd.
Her hapless Daughters now, like tender Plants,
The Sun-shine of a Parent's Kindness wants;   40
From Place to Place, the wretched Suff'rers tost,
By Heav'n unless preserv'd, had sure been lost.
Dorinda[5] now (the eldest of the Three)
Began to feel the Force of Misery;
Mourn'd her sad Fate, to be expos'd to Woe
Ere her weak Years, the Task cou'd undergo.
Scheme after Scheme was for her Ruin laid,
But Virtue guarded still the tim'rous Maid;
Attempts proved fruitless; cautiously she trod,
Entrusting still her Innocence to GOD.   50
The pow'rful Guardian, watchful on her side,
Preserv'd the Maid, who sought Him for her Guide.

The King[6] to *Anna*, bless'd his Mem'ry be,
A Pension gave; and, when at Liberty,
The anxious Mother to her Children came,
Shelter'd their Youth, and rescu'd them from Shame.
But *Anglesus* the younger Two retakes,
(Some three Years after) and the First forsakes....

4. In fact, Juliana Donovan was descended from Donel Oge Na Cartan O'Donovan, chief
   of the Clan Lochlin.
5. i.e. Dorothea herself.
6. George II.

Dorinda, who continues to live with her mother, soon marries a young foreigner (in real life, Dorothea's husband, Dubois). Some time later, her father, 'enfeebled by Disease', suffers a stroke and the doctors proclaim him to be in 'instant danger'. Dorinda, overcome with sympathy for her father and imagining he might want to make his peace with her, persuades her mother and her husband to let her go and see him before he dies.

> ... Soft'ned at length, the kind Permission giv'n
> They recommend her to the Care of Heav'n!   60
> And each, by Turn, fast hold her in their Arms,
> Beseeching God to shield her from all Harms.
> Dissolv'd in Tears, they parted — swift she flew
> T'experience Villainy of deepest Hue.
> Sh' obtained the sight, so earnestly she sought,
> But at the Hazard of her Life 'twas bought.
> The cruel Father imprecating lay,
> Disowning Nature, order'd her away;
> Tho', to Appearance, ready just to go
> And pay that debt which all to Nature owe.   70
> A num'rous Throng of Ruffians now surround
> The sad *Dorinda*, prostrate on the Ground.
> His base-born Son,[7] a Pistol e'en presents,
> Behind her Head; but watchful Heav'n prevents
> The Fiend from executing his Intents.
> They pull and drag her, tear her Hands and Cloak,
> Nay dare uplift their own to give a Stroke:
> Force her from Room to Room, then down the Stairs,
> Nor heed her piteous Cries, nor flowing Tears.
> Some, more humane, now shook indeed their Head   80
> As they pass'd by, but nothing still they said.
> (Scarce two Months past a dang'rous Lying-in,
> Such cruel Usage surely was a Sin.)
> Now driv'n from the House, Dorinda sate
> And humbly warmed her at the Kitchen Grate.
> While ev'ry Word was followed by a Sigh,
> Behold her Woes draw Tears from ev'ry Eye.
> Her Servants now are ty'd, her Horse's Ear
> Inhumanely cut off: 'tis much they spare
> *Dorinda*'s Life, whom thus they seem to hate   90
> With Spleen, uncommonly inveterate....

7. i.e. Arthur, son of the sixth earl of Anglesea and Juliana Donovan.

Dorinda is kept prisoner for two days and nights and undergoes various hardships. At last, exhausted and 'madly raving', she is released, though her servants are still detained. She manages to reach Ferns, Co. Wexford, a 'well-affected Town' where she is, at last, offered some protection.

... Th'enrag'd Inhabitants together rose,
And their *Dorinda*'s Enemies oppose.
Fierce Anger blaz'd in each resenting Eye,
And Stones, in Show'rs, at her Oppressors fly.
Is this, cry'd they, for Duty a Reward,
This a Return for such a Child's Regard?
A Child, which once he doated on so much,
Can we believe our Eyes, his Nature's such,
That to so dutiful a Daughter, he   100
Can so unnatural a Father be?...

... But now, to sum up all Dorinda's Woe,
Anglesus really dies,[8] 'twas order'd so;
Offended Heav'n wou'd no longer see
A Man absorb'd in Vice and Infamy:
His Talents buried, his Genius cramp'd,
And by base Influence, each Virtue damp'd....

... But ere he dy'd, some nine Years, as they say,
She[9] o'er his Mind, obtain'd so great a Sway
That, tho' already marry'd (to her Shame   110
Be't spoken) she obtain'd the shadowy Name
Of Wife, altho' he had no Right to give
That name to any one, and *Anna* live.
But, so infatuated was he grown,
He fear'd her Pow'r, and quite forgot his own.
His Will, or rather her's, she next has done,
And leaves th'Estate to her ill-gotten Son,
Whom in it she stiles L[or]d; her daughters too
She titles Ladies; what won't Cunning do?
The artful Wretch obtains whate'er she craves;   120
Then as a Tyrant, to her Dupe behaves.
Thus she, who once wou'd to his Foot-men yield,
Becomes his Queen, and doth his Sceptre wield;
Exerts a Power, by few Wives assum'd,
Or rather none, it is to be presum'd.

8. 4 February 1761.
9. Juliana Donovan, described in the poem as 'the vicious *Devilyn*'.

336

To Law, voracious Law, fair *Anna* now
Must have Recourse; it cannot disallow
Her Right, which on its own Foundation lies,
And can't be deaf to Truth's distressful Cries.
Dorinda and her Sisters too appeal   130
To Truth and Justice, these must strait prevail
O'er Vice and Perjury, for sure in vain, ⎫
Distressed Virtue never can complain, ⎬
Where soft Compassion, well is known to reign. ⎭

ANONYMOUS POEMS FROM THE 1760s

Description of Dublin[1]

Mass-houses, churches, mixt together;
Streets unpleasant in all weather.
The church, the four courts, and hell[2] contiguous;
Castle, College green, and custom-house gibbous.[3]

Few things here are to tempt ye:
Tawdry outsides, pockets empty:
Five theatres, little trade, and jobbing arts,
Brandy, and snuff-shops, post-chaises, and carts.

Warrants, bailiffs, bills unpaid;
Masters of their servants afraid;   10
Rogues that daily rob and cut men;
Patriots, gamesters, and footmen.

Lawyers, Revenue-officers, priests, physicians;
Beggars of all ranks, age, and conditions,
Worth scarce shews itself upon the ground;
Villainy both with applause and profit crown'd.

Women lazy, dirty, drunken, loose;
Men in labour slow, of wine profuse:
Many a scheme that the public must rue it:
This is Dublin, if ye knew it.   20

---

1. This unflattering poetic portrait of eighteenth-century Dublin is a re-writing of a description of London by John Bancks or Banks (1709-51). See *The New Oxford Book of Eighteenth-Century Verse*, ed. Roger Lonsdale (Oxford, 1984), p. 275.

2. The name of a passage-way leading from Fishamble Street to the old Four Courts (the main law-courts). See John T. Gilbert, *A History of the City of Dublin,* 3 vols, revised edition (Dublin, 1978) I, 67.

3. Shaped like a hump.

The Rakes of Stony Batter[1]

Come all you roving blades, that ramble thro' the City,
Kissing pretty Maids, listen to my Ditty,
Our time is coming on, when we will be merry,
Kitty, Poll, and Nan, will give us Sack and Sherry.
   Hey for Bobbin Joan, Hey for Stony Batter,
   Keep your Wife at home or else I will be at her.

There's Bridget, Peg, and Nell, with Nancy, Doll, & Susan,
To please their sweethearts well, sometimes will go a boozing,
But when their cash is gone, they'll hunt for a Cully,[2]
And bring the splinters[3] home, to their beloved Bully.[4]   10
   Hey for Bobbin Joan, Hey for Stony Batter,
   Keep your Wife at home or else I will be at her.

In Summer Lasses go, to the Fields a Maying,
Thro' the Meadows gay, with their Sweethearts playing,
Their smiling winning ways, shew for game they're willing,
Tho' Jenny cries 'Nay, I won't F—k for a shilling',
   Hey for Bobbin Joan, Hey for Stony Batter,
   Keep your Wife at home or else I will be at her.

'Go you cunning Knave, no more of coax nor wheedle,
By those Buttons in my Sleeve, I'll prick you with my needle,   20
What will you still be bold, Mammy call to[5] this Man,
For shame my hands don't hold, I vow my breath is just gone.'
   Hey for Bobbin Joan, Hey for Stony Batter,
   Keep your Wife at home or else I will be at her.

There's Joan a buxom Lass, met with lusty Johnny,
They went to take a glass, he call'd her dear and honey,
She said 'You silly Clown, take me round the middle,
Play me Bobbin Joan, or else I'll break your fiddle.'
   Hey for Bobbin Joan, Hey for Stony Batter,
   Keep your Wife at home or else I will be at her.   30

1. This well-known bawdy song dates from the mid-century when Stonybatter, a district of Dublin on the north side of the Liffey, was famous as a centre of a certain kind of night life.
2. A fool — particularly, in the eighteenth century, a man who is duped by a woman (Partridge).
3. money.
4. A protector and exploiter of prostitutes, a pimp (Partridge).
5. Reprimand this man or, perhaps, give him his account (*OED*).

He gently laid her down, and he pull'd out his scraper,
He play'd her such a tune, which made her fart and caper;
She said 'My dearest John, you're such a Jolly rover,
My cloak and gown I'll pawn, that you would ne'er give over.'
    Hey for Bobbin Joan, Hey for Stony Batter,
    Keep your Wife at home or else I will be at her.

Come let us take a roam, up to Stony Batter,
Keep your Wife at home, for humpers will be at her,
Hey for cakes and ale, Hey for pretty misses,
That will never fail, for to crown our wishes.   40
    Hey for Bobbin Joan, Hey for Stony Batter,
    Keep your Wife at home or else I'll stop her water,
    Is your apples ripe, are they fit for plucking,
    Is your maid within, ready for the F——g?

The May Bush[1]

The Night before de first of May
    Riggy dee di di dum tum de,
To cut a brave Bush we all did agree,
    Riggy dee di dum de;
We being all in a fighting mood,
We straight set out for Santry wood,[2]
To fetch home a Bush, or spill de last drop of our blood,
    Ri diggy doe di dum de.

---

1. This song gives a vivid account of one of the regular feuds between factions in eighteenth-century Dublin, this time over the setting up of a May-bush by the butchers' boys of Smithfield (on the north side of the Liffey) and the attempt to cut it down by the tailors and weavers of the Coombe (known as 'the Liberty boys', and from an area south of the river). The song was very popular and an even more vigorous, though unfortunately only fragmentary, version beginning 'De nite afore de fust of Magay' appears in John Edward Walsh's *Sketches of Ireland Sixty Years Ago* (Dublin, 1847), pp. 99-101.
2. Santry House and wood were a few miles north of the centre of Dublin.

Bill Durham he being de stoutest[3] about, *etc.*,[4]
He search'd, till he found a clever[5] Bush out, *etc.*,   10
Wid our saws and our hatchets we all did prepare,
And we cut de brave[6] Bush wedout[7] dread or fear,
And wid Pipers and Fidlers we home did it bear, *etc.*[8]

But when we came to old Lough-boy,[9] *etc.*,
De Girls and Boys all jump'd for joy, *etc.*,
But when to Smithfield we drew near,
De Boys of the Market all met us there,
Dey pull'd off their mitres[10] and gave us three cheers, *etc.*

As soon as we got this clever Bush up, *etc.*,
We splic'd all our makes 'till we ris a sup,[11] *etc.*,   20
De Girls of Stoney[12] all came down,
Wid daisies and butter-cups to deck the Bush round,
Den dous'd all their sieves 'till dey ris a crown,[13] *etc.*

De next day being Monday, we all did agree, *etc.*,
For to go to Stoney de May-maids to see, *etc.*,
But bad chance to de Liberty, when dey did hear,
Dat we went to Stoney widout dread or fear,
Wid swords, sticks, and folchions to Smithfield did steer, *etc.*[14]

---

3. bravest. Walsh describes Bill Durham as 'a distinguished man at that time in the Liberty riots' (p. 99).

4. The three lines of repeated refrain (as in the first stanza) are marked by '*etc.*' in subsequent stanzas.

5. suitable.

6. fine.

7. without.

8. At this point, Walsh quotes another verse which describes how Bill Durham rode the May-bush in triumph as it was born back to Smithfield: 'Bill Durham, he sat astride on his bush // Ri rigidi ri ri dum dee, // And dere he kept singin', as sweet as a trush, // His faulchin in one hand, his pipe in his mush // Ri rigi di dum dee!' [trush = thrush; faulchin or falchion (see l. 34) = sword; mush = mouth, from Fr. *mouche*.]

9. Lough Buoy was a street near the Smithfield market.

10. hats.

11. i.e. we joined together (spliced) all our halfpennies (makes) until we had raised (ris) enough to buy a drink (sup).

12. Stonybatter, a district near Smithfield. See p. 339.

13. i.e. then pawned (dous'd) all their Sieves (used here to mean 'measures for various kinds of produce' (*OED*)) until they had raised a crown (five shillings).

14. At this point, this version lacks a stanza describing how the Liberty boys stole the May-bush while the Smithfield boys were visiting the 'May-maids' of Stonybatter.

Bill Durham, who was up the whole night before, *etc.*,
Was now in his Quarry lying taking a snore, *etc.*,   30
And hearing the noise go by his door, *etc.*,
Den out of his Flea-bag[15] he straight flew,
And over his shoulder his Skin-bag[16] he threw,
And from out of the Chimney his falchion he drew, *etc.*[17]

Wid his hat in his hand by way of a shield, *etc.*,
He never cried stop 'till he came to Smithfield, *etc.*,
But finding none of the Boys at home,
Oh! Gog's blood,[18] says Bill Durham, am I left alone?
Oh! be de hoky,[19] the glory of Smithfield is gone, *etc.*

For the love of our Bush revenge we must get, *etc.*,   40
In slaughtering season we'll tip dem a fret,[20]
We'll wallop a Musey round Meath-street in tune,[21]
And we won't leave a weaver alive on the Coombe, *etc.*,
But we'll rip up their paunches, and burn their looms, *etc.*

---

15. bed.
16. 'Skin-bag' is unrecorded, but Walsh's text gives 'flesh-bag' which = a shirt or chemise (Partridge).
17. The text is corrupt here and this stanza includes an extra line. falchion = sword.
18. God's Blood!
19. An expletive fairly common in Ireland, said to be a contraction of "Holy poker!" See Bernard Share, *Slanguage: a Dictionary of Slang and Colloquial English in Ireland* (Dublin, 1977), p. 19.
20. i.e. when the time comes for cattle to be slaughtered, we'll give them something to worry about.
21. i.e. we'll beat (wollop) a bull (a Musey or mosey) round Meath Street (in the Coombe) properly (in tune).

OLIVIA ELDER
(fl. **1769**-80)

Olivia Elder, who is only known from the manuscript volume of her poems in the National Library of Ireland, lived in County Derry. Her poems, some of which are written in Ulster Scots, are mostly addressed to neighbours in the area and are in the form of verse epistles. They are full of vivid detail and provide a rare glimpse of life in rural Ireland in the 1770s.

from: To Mrs D.C.H., an account of the Author's manner of spending her time.
Written October 20th 1769

When far from you, dear Anna, plac'd,
Think not my life I idly waste;
But when I tell you how it's pass'd,
You'll say it is an odd contrast,
And that I strangely spend my time
Between the mean and the sublime.

I oft forsake both Pope and Swift
The House to sweep, and Pots to lift;
With Princely Queensbury leave his Gay,[1]
To call the folks from making hay;   10
Or Young[2] upon the morning star
To help the boy down with the Car;[3]
Quit tragic Queens in all their clutter,
And help to churn, or dress, the butter.

Oft from my hand the Pen I whisk out,
And in its place take up the Dishclout;[4]
For spite of all sublimer wishes,
I needs must sometimes wash the dishes.
No wonder if my work but trash is
When I'm obliged to lift the ashes: 20

---

1. The Duke and Duchess of Queensbury were patrons of the poet and dramatist John Gay (1685-1732).
2. Edward Young (1683-1765), one of the most popular poets of the late eighteenth century.
3. cart.
4. dishcloth.

Or that I sing in homely lays,
I'll site the Besom[5] with the Bays.
Unfinish'd I must leave a fable,
To go and scour the kitchen table,
Or from the writing of a Poem,
Descend my Neighbour's turf to throw 'em,
For trust me, I'm not quite unskilled in
A good turf stack the art of building.
And yesterday, a sight uncommon,
I help'd with one a poor old Woman.   30
Nay, at this very present Writing,
As this Epistle I'm inditing,[6]
When all are busy bearing hay to us,
I'm forced to go and boil Potatoes.

In politics I never dabble,
Nor e'er in party matters squabble,
But sometimes curious, read the news,
Then take a Brush and clean my Shoes.

Tho' never at a school or College,
Of ancient fables I've some knowledge;   40
Yet Beauties Queen, and wisdom's Goddess[7]
I quit, to mend my whale-bone bodice;
Or like the Shepherd God Apollo,
Leave wit and verse a Cow to follow[8]....

... I sometimes sew, and sometimes knit,
And oft in social circle sit;
Leave mending of the kitchen fires
And pay a visit to the Squire's;
Drink tea and coffy, laugh and chat,
And hear his talk of this and that;   50
How he himself must prime the Pudding[9]
Or else he never gets a good one;

5. A sweeping broom made of a bunch of twigs tied to a handle. The bay tree was sacred to
   Apollo, the god of the muses and of poetry. Thus the poet puts her sweeping brush beside
   her poetic talent.
6. composing.
7. Venus and Minerva.
8. Apollo was the god of shepherds as well as of poetry.
9. A note at this point reads: 'His Phrase for putting Brandy in it'.

Of method new his meat to cure up,
Then swears it is the best in Europe;
How cheap he purchases things new,
Doubt if all he says is true;
Or hear dull Storys where no wit is
From stupid Rector,[10] who more fit is
For feasting Aldermen than Preacher,
Else of good eating make his teacher.   60

But to return from these digressions,
Were I to tell of my professions,
Of Cook, Slut,[11] Butter, Laundry Maid,
Of ricks and huswifery my trade
You'd hear, I was the perfect ape
Of Proteus, god of changing shape.[12]
What need I speak of candles dripping,
Of brewing, baking, and tea sipping
With Ladies, then entreat excuse
'Till I shew Nan to kill a Goose;   70
Or how I went from spinning tow[13]
To entertain a Paris Beau;
For once, when thus employ'd, I hopt on[14]
A visit from the sprightly Captain[15]
Who comes with fishing tackle here,
And likes to taste my Bottled Beer;
Or how from whitewashing a wall
I'm dress'd and dancing at a Ball;
Sometimes engaged in Mirth and folly,
And oft immersed in melancholy.   80

10. A note explains that the reference is to the Revd Mr Barnard, son of Bishop William
    Barnard (1697-1768); this cleric was the brother of Dr Samuel Johnson's friend, Thomas
    Barnard (1728-1806), at the time of this poem the dean of Derry.
11. i.e. kitchen-maid or drudge (*OED* sv. slut.2), a more playful word in the eighteenth
    century than now.
12. ape = imitator; Proteus was a mythological sea deity who assumed different shapes (a
    tiger, a fiery flame, a whirlwind or a stream).
13. The fibre of flax.
14. hopt on = happed on, came upon by chance.
15. This is, according to a note in the manuscript, a Major W—d, nephew of Robert Wood
    (c.1717-71), traveller and politician.

You with my skill would never quarrel
In tighting hoops upon a Barrel,
Nor would believe with what art
I play the Manteau maker's part,[16]
What pictures of old fans have made,
And grottos in the rural shade;[17]
How catgut envied work have wrought on[18]
For working muslin, how thin cotton,
Now spring[19] a gown, and now an apron,
And now a steed I sometimes leap on,   90
Or learn to do some Dresden stitches,[20]
Then go and mend an old man's Britches.
And then begin the very trade
In t'other world of ancient Maid[21]....

16. dressmaker. A manteau was a loose upper garment worn by women.
17. 'A method of making pictures out of old broken china.' [original note]
18. i.e. how I have wrought work which has been admired on catgut (a coarse cloth of thick cord [*OED*]) as if it had been worked on muslin or thin cotton.
19. to increase or extend in height or length (*OED*).
20. embroidery.
21. i.e. spinning; cf. spinsterhood.

OLIVER GOLDSMITH
(1728-**1770**-1774)

Goldsmith, the son of a clergyman, spent his childhood in counties Longford and Westmeath. He attended Trinity College, Dublin after which he went to Edinburgh to study medicine. He travelled widely on the Continent, finally settling in London where he earned a precarious living as a writer. He became a trusted member of the circle of writers around Samuel Johnson. *The Deserted Village*, probably Goldsmith's best-known work, draws heavily on his memories of childhood in the Irish midlands though, as Katharine Balderston points out, there is probably a considerable difference between 'the coarse Irish reality of the 1730s' and the 'refined and idealized memories' of the poem (*The Collected Letters of Oliver Goldsmith* (Cambridge, 1928), p. x).

from: The Deserted Village

Sweet AUBURN,[1] loveliest village of the plain,
Where health and plenty cheared the labouring swain,
Where smiling spring its earliest visit paid,
And parting summer's lingering blooms delayed,
Dear lovely bowers of innocence and ease,
Seats of my youth, when every sport could please,
How often have I loitered o'er thy green,
Where humble happiness endeared each scene!
How often have I paused on every charm,
The sheltered cot,[2] the cultivated farm,   10
The never failing brook, the busy mill,
The decent[3] church that topt the neighbouring hill,
The hawthorn bush, with seats beneath the shade,
For talking age and whispering lovers made!
How often have I blest the coming day,
When toil remitting lent its turn to play,
And all the village train from labour free
Led up their sports beneath the spreading tree,
While many a pastime circled in the shade,
The young contending as the old surveyed;   20
And many a gambol frolicked o'er the ground,
And slights[4] of art and feats of strength went round.

1. Traditionally closely associated with Lissoy, Co. Westmeath, where Goldsmith spent his childhood.
2. cottage.
3. not ostentatious, appropriate.
4. Examples of skill or skilfulness.

347

And still as each repeated pleasure tired,
Succeeding sports the mirthful band inspired;
The dancing pair that simply sought renown
By holding out to tire each other down;
The swain mistrustless of his smutted face,
While secret laughter tittered round the place;[5]
The bashful virgin's side-long looks of love,
The matron's glance that would those looks reprove!   30
These were thy charms, sweet village; sports like these,
With sweet succession taught even toil to please;
These round thy bowers their chearful influence shed,
These were thy charms — But all these charms are fled.

Sweet smiling village, loveliest of the lawn,
Thy sports are fled, and all thy charms withdrawn;
Amidst thy bowers the tyrant's hand is seen,
And desolation saddens all thy green:
One only master grasps the whole domain,[6]
And half a tillage stints thy smiling plain;[7]   40
No more thy glassy brook reflects the day,
But choaked with sedges, works its weedy way;
Along thy glades, a solitary guest,
The hollow sounding bittern[8] guards its nest;
Amidst thy desert walks the lapwing[9] flies,
And tires their ecchoes with unvaried cries.
Sunk are thy bowers,[10] in shapeless ruin all,
And the long grass o'ertops the mouldering wall;
And trembling, shrinking from the spoiler's hand,
Far, far away thy children leave the land.   50

5. The group is laughing at someone whose face has been smeared with smuts without his knowing it.
6. A single landowner has replaced several.
7. i.e. The single landowner's action in ploughing only half the land ('half a tillage') brings to an end ('stints') the cheerful appearance of the plain.
8. A large wading bird. Goldsmith elsewhere described the bittern's booming call as 'dismally hollow' (*A History of Earth and Animated Nature* 6 vols. (London, 1774), VI, 1-2).
9. A bird of the plover family which breeds on islands 'where men seldom resort' (*A History of Earth and Animated Nature*, VI, 32).
10. humble cottages — here probably referring to the temporary structures of landless migrant workers.

Ill fares the land, to hastening ills a prey,
Where wealth accumulates, and men decay;
Princes and lords may flourish, or may fade;
A breath can make them, as a breath has made;
But a bold peasantry, their country's pride,
When once destroyed, can never be supplied....

Sweet was the sound when oft at evening's close,
Up yonder hill the village murmur rose;
There as I past with careless steps and slow,
The mingling notes came softened from below;   60
The swain responsive as the milk-maid sung,
The sober herd that lowed to meet their young;
The noisy geese that gabbled o'er the pool,
The playful children just let loose from school;
The watch-dog's voice that bayed the whispering wind,
And the loud laugh that spoke the vacant mind,[11]
These all in sweet confusion sought the shade,
And filled each pause the nightingale had made.
But now the sounds of population fail,
No chearful murmurs fluctuate in the gale,[12]   70
No busy steps the grass-grown foot-way tread,
For all the bloomy flush of life is fled.
All but yon widowed, solitary thing
That feebly bends beside the plashy spring;
She, wretched matron, forced, in age, for bread,
To strip the brook with mantling cresses spread,[13]
To pick her wintry faggot from the thorn,
To seek her nightly shed, and weep till morn;
She only left of all the harmless train,
The sad historian of the pensive plain.   80

Near yonder copse, where once the garden smil'd,
And still where many a garden flower grows wild,
There, where a few torn shrubs the place disclose,
The village preacher's[14] modest mansion rose.

---

11. i.e. the loud laugh of the village simpleton.
12. In eighteenth-century poetic usage, a gale was a gentle breeze, rather than a violent wind.
13. The old woman picks the watercress which now grows all over the surface of the stream.
14. Goldsmith's sister, Catherine, stated that this was a portrait of his father (Balderston, p. 162).

A man he was, to all the country dear,
And passing rich with forty pounds a year;
Remote from towns he ran his godly race,
Nor e'er had changed, nor wish'd to change his place;
Unpractised he to fawn, or seek for power,
By doctrines fashioned to the varying hour;   90
Far other aims his heart had learned to prize,
More skilled to raise the wretched than to rise.
His house was known to all the vagrant train,
He chid their wanderings, but relieved their pain;
The long remembered beggar was his guest,
Whose beard descending swept his aged breast;
The ruined spendthrift, now no longer proud,
Claimed kindred there, and had his claims allowed;
The broken soldier,[15] kindly bade to stay,
Sate by his fire, and talked the night away,   100
Wept o'er his wounds, or tales of sorrow done,
Shouldered his crutch, and shewed how fields were won.
Pleased with his guests, the good man learned to glow,
And quite forgot their vices in their woe;
Careless their merits, or their faults to scan,
His pity gave ere charity began....

Beside yon straggling fence that skirts the way,
With blossomed furze[16] unprofitably gay,
There, in his noisy mansion, skill'd to rule,
The village master taught his little school;[17]   110
A man severe he was, and stern to view;
I knew him well, and every truant knew;
Well had the boding tremblers learned to trace
The day's disasters in his morning face;
Full well they laughed with counterfeited glee,
At all his jokes, for many a joke had he;
Full well the busy whisper circling round,
Conveyed the dismal tidings when he frowned;
Yet he was kind, or if severe in aught,
The love he bore to learning was in fault;   120

15. Discharged, presumably after being wounded.
16. gorse.
17. Goldsmith's sister stated that this was a portrait of the schoolmaster at Lissoy,
Co. Westmeath (Balderston, p. 164).

The village all declared how much he knew;
'Twas certain he could write, and cypher[18] too;
Lands he could measure, terms and tides presage,[19]
And even the story ran that he could gauge.[20]
In arguing too, the parson owned his skill,
For even tho' vanquished, he could argue still;
While words of learned length, and thundering sound
Amazed the gazing rustics ranged around;
And still they gazed, and still the wonder grew,
That one small head could carry all he knew.   130

But past is all his fame. The very spot
Where many a time he triumphed, is forgot.
Near yonder thorn, that lifts its head on high,
Where once the sign-post caught the passing eye,
Low lies that house where nut-brown draughts[21] inspired,
Where grey-beard mirth and smiling toil retired
Where village statesmen talked with looks profound,
And news much older than their ale went round.
Imagination fondly stoops to trace
The parlour splendours of that festive place;   140
The white-washed wall, the nicely sanded floor,[22]
The varnished clock that clicked behind the door;
The chest contrived a double debt to pay,
A bed by night, a chest of drawers by day;
The pictures placed for ornament and use,
The twelve good rules, the royal game of goose;[23]
The hearth, except when winter chill'd the day,
With aspen boughs, and flowers, and fennel gay,[24]
While broken tea-cups, wisely kept for shew,
Ranged o'er the chimney, glistened in a row.   150

18. undertake arithmetical calculations.
19. i.e. foretell how long astronomical phenomena would last, and the time of high and low tides.
20. calculate of the area of land.
21. ale and beer.
22. Goldsmith sent a more vivid and energetic version of the lines describing the alehouse (lines 140-50) to his brother Henry in a letter written in January 1759 (Baldeston, pp. 64-65). The third and fourth lines of the earlier version read: 'The sanded floor, that grits beneath the tread, // The humid wall with paltry pictures spread.' Goldsmith used the lines again in *The Citizen of the World*, Letter 30.
23. 'The twelve good rules' were rules for good conduct said to have been written by Charles I; 'the royal game of goose' was a board game played with dice.
24. i.e. branches from the poplar tree, wild flowers and stems of fennel, a herb with spectacular yellow flowers which grows wild in parts of Ireland

Vain transitory splendours! Could not all
Reprieve the tottering mansion from its fall!
Obscure it sinks, nor shall it more impart
An hour's importance to the poor man's heart;
Thither no more the peasant shall repair
To sweet oblivion of his daily care;
No more the farmer's news, the barber's tale,
No more the wood-man's ballad shall prevail;
No more the smith his dusky brow shall clear,
Relax his ponderous strength, and lean to hear;   160
The host himself no longer shall be found
Careful to see the mantling[25] bliss go round;
Nor the coy maid, half willing to be prest,
Shall kiss the cup to pass it to the rest....

As some fair female unadorned and plain,
Secure to please while youth confirms her reign,
Slights every borrowed charm that dress supplies,
Nor shares with art the triumph of her eyes,
But when those charms are past, for charms are frail,
When time advances, and when lovers fail,   170
She then shines forth sollicitous to bless,
In all the glaring impotence of dress.
Thus fares the land, by luxury betrayed;
In nature's simplest charms at first arrayed,
But verging to decline, its splendours rise,
Its vistas strike, its palaces surprize;
While scourged by famine from the smiling land,
The mournful peasant leads his humble band;
And while he sinks without one arm to save,
The country blooms — a garden, and a grave.   180

Where then, ah, where, shall poverty reside,
To scape the pressure of contiguous pride?
If to some common's fenceless limits strayed,
He drives his flock to pick the scanty blade,
Those fenceless fields the sons of wealth divide,
And even the bare-worn common is denied.

---

25. foaming, from the word 'mantle', the foam which covers the surface of liquor (*OED*).

If to the city sped — What waits him there?
To see profusion that he must not share;
To see ten thousand baneful arts combined
To pamper luxury, and thin mankind;   190
To see those joys the sons of pleasure know,
Extorted from his fellow-creature's woe.
Here, while the courtier glitters in brocade,
There the pale artist[26] plies the sickly trade;
Here, while the proud their long drawn pomps display,
There the black gibbet[27] glooms beside the way.
The dome where Pleasure holds her midnight reign,
Here, richly deckt, admits the gorgeous train;
Tumultuous grandeur crowds the blazing square,
The rattling chariots clash, the torches glare.   200
Sure scenes like these no troubles e'er annoy!
Sure these denote one universal joy!
Are these thy serious thoughts? — Ah, turn thine eyes
Where the poor houseless shivering female lies.
She once, perhaps, in village plenty blest,
Has wept at tales of innocence distrest;
Her modest looks the cottage might adorn,
Sweet as the primrose peeps beneath the thorn;
Now lost to all; her friends, her virtue fled,
Near her betrayer's door she lays her head,   210
And pinch'd with cold, and shrinking from the shower,
With heavy heart deplores that luckless hour
When idly first, ambitious of the town,
She left her wheel[28] and robes of country brown....

Even now the devastation is begun,
And half the business of destruction done;
Even now, methinks, as pondering here I stand,
I see the rural virtues leave the land:
Down where yon anchoring vessel spreads the sail,
That idly waiting flaps with every gale,   220
Downward they move, a melancholy band,
Pass from the shore, and darken all the strand.[29]

26. artisan.
27. gallows.
28. spinning-wheel.
29. beach or shoreline.

Contented toil, and hospitable care,
And kind connubial tenderness, are there;
And piety, with wishes placed above,
And steady loyalty, and faithful love:
And thou, sweet Poetry, thou loveliest maid,
Still first to fly where sensual joys invade,
Unfit in these degenerate times of shame,
To catch the heart, or strike for honest fame;   230
Dear charming nymph,[30] neglected and decried,
My shame in crowds, my solitary pride;
Thou source of all my bliss, and all my woe,
That found'st me poor at first, and keep'st me so;
Thou guide by which the nobler arts excell,
Thou nurse of every virtue, fare thee well.
Farewell, and O where'er thy voice be tried,
On Torno's cliffs, or Pambamarca's side,[31]
Whether where equinoctial fervours glow,
Or winter wraps the polar world in snow,   240
Still let thy voice prevailing over time,
Redress the rigours of the inclement clime;
Aid slighted truth, with thy persuasive strain,
Teach erring man to spurn the rage of gain;
Teach him, that states of native strength possest,
Tho' very poor, may still be very blest;
That trade's proud empire hastes to swift decay,
As ocean sweeps the labour'd mole[32] away;
While self dependent power can time defy,
As rocks resist the billows and the sky.   250

30. i.e. the muse of poetry.
31. The references are to the river Torneälv in Sweden (where 'the polar world' is wrapped in snow) and to Mount Pambamarca in Ecuador (where 'equinoctial [i.e. tropical] fervours glow').
32. A man-made breakwater.

Song

from *She Stoops to Conquer*[1]

Let school-masters puzzle their brain
With grammar, and nonsense, and learning;
Good liquor, I stoutly maintain,
Gives genius[2] a better discerning.
Let them brag of their Heathenish Gods,
Their Lethes, their Styxes, and Stygians;[3]
Their Quis, and their Quaes, and the Quods,
They're all but a parcel of Pigeons.
  Toroddle, toroddle, toroll.

When Methodist preachers come down,   10
A preaching that drinking is sinful,
I'll wager the rascals a crown,
They always preach best with a skinful.[4]
But when you come down with your pence,
For a slice of their scurvy religion,
I'll leave it to all men of sense,
But you, my good friend, are the pigeon.
  Toroddle, toroddle, toroll.

Then come, put the jorum[5] about,
And let us be merry and clever,   20
Our hearts and our liquors are stout,
Here's the Three Jolly Pigeons[6] for ever.
Let some cry up[7] woodcock or hare,
Your bustards, your ducks, and your widgeons;[8]
But of all the birds in the air,
Here's a health to the Three Jolly Pigeons.
  Toroddle, toroddle, toroll.

---

1. Goldsmith's most famous comedy, *She Stoops to Conquer*, was first produced in London on 15 March 1773.
2. Some early editions mistakenly read 'genus'.
3. A lighthearted list of classical persons and places (and in the next line of Latin words) constantly referred to or used by schoolmasters.
4. i.e. when they are drunk.
5. A large drinking vessel.
6. A public house which still exists near Ballymahon, Co. Longford.
7. extol the praises of.
8. Woodcock, bustard, duck and widgeon are all game birds.

RICHARD BRINSLEY SHERIDAN
(1751-**1771**-1816)

Sheridan was born into the most literary family in eighteenth-century Ireland; his grandfather
was Thomas Sheridan the elder (1687-1738), poet, translator of Persius and friend of Swift, his
father was Thomas Sheridan the younger (1719-88), playwright, actor, manager of the Smock
Alley theatre, biographer of Swift, lexicographer and writer on elocution, and his mother was
the novelist and dramatist Frances Sheridan née Chamberlaine (1724-66). The family moved
to Bath when Sheridan was about twenty and he lived the rest of his life in England where,
after a successful career as a dramatist, he entered political life in 1780 and rose to the position
of secretary of the treasury. Though he is best remembered for sparkling comedies, such as *The
School for Scandal* (1777), Sheridan also wrote some entertaining occasional verse.

Lines by a Lady of Fashion

Then behind, all my hair is done up in a plat,
And so, like a cornet's,[1] tuck'd under my hat.
Then I mount on my palfrey[2] as gay as a lark,
And, follow'd by John, take the dust in High Park.[3]
In the way I am met by some smart macaroni,[4]
Who rides by my side on a little bay pony —
No sturdy Hibernian, with shoulders so wide,
But as taper and slim as the ponies they ride;
Their legs are as slim, and their shoulders no wider,
Dear sweet little creatures, both pony and rider!   10

But sometimes, when hotter, I order my chaise,[5]
And manage, myself, my two little greys.
Sure never were seen two such sweet little ponies,
Other horses are clowns, and these macaronies,
And to give them this title, I'm sure isn't wrong,
Their legs are so slim, and their tails are so long.
In Kensington Gardens[6] to stroll up and down,
You know was the fashion before you left town, —

---

1. The reference seems to be to the way a 'cornet', a junior officer in a cavalry troop whose
   job was to carry the colours, tucked his pigtail into his hat.
2. A small saddle-horse for ladies.
3. i.e. Hyde Park, the fashionable place for riding in eighteenth-century London.
4. A fop or dandy who had travelled to the Continent, and affected continental fashions.
5. A light, open carriage.
6. Like Vauxhall and Ranelagh Gardens, mentioned later in the poem, Kensington Gardens
   were a place where the 'beau monde' of London went 'to be seen'.

The thing's well enough, when allowance is made
For the size of the trees and the depth of the shade,   20
But the spread of their leaves such a shelter affords
To those noisy, impertinent creatures called birds,
Whose ridiculous chirruping ruins the scene,
Brings the country before me, and gives me the spleen.

Yet, tho' 'tis too rural — to come near the mark,
We all herd in *one* walk, and that, nearest the Park,
There with ease we may see, as we pass by the wicket,
The chimneys of Knightsbridge and — footmen at cricket.
I must tho', in justice, declare that the grass,
Which, worn by our feet, is diminished apace,   30
In a little time more will be brown and as flat
As the sand at Vauxhall or as Ranelagh mat.[7]
Improving thus fast, perhaps, by degrees,
We may see rolls and butter spread under the trees,
With a small pretty band in each seat of the walk,
To play little tunes and enliven our talk.

Song

from *The School for Scandal*

Here's to the maiden of bashful fifteen,
Here's to the widow of fifty;
Here's to the flaunting extravagant quean,[1]
And here's to the housewife that's thrifty.
Chorus: Let the toast pass, —
Drink to the lass,
I'll warrant she'll prove an excuse for a glass.

Here's to the charmer whose dimples we prize,
Now to the maid who has none, sir;
Here's to the girl with a pair of blue eyes,   10
And here's to the nymph with but *one*, sir.
Chorus: Let the toast pass, &c.

---

7. Vauxhall Gardens had sandy walks and Ranelagh Gardens contained a building called the Rotunda where concerts and dances took place. Other writers also mention the mats on the floor.

---

1. This word can mean both a healthy young woman and a prostitute — here with the second meaning.

Here's to the maid with a bosom of snow;
    Now to her that's as brown as a berry:
Here's to the wife with her face full of woe,
    And now to the damsel that's merry.

Chorus: Let the toast pass, &c.

For let 'em be clumsy, or let 'em be slim,
    Young or ancient, I care not a feather;
So fill a pint bumper[2] quite up to the brim,   20
    And let us e'en toast them together.

Chorus: Let the toast pass, &c.

---

2. A large glass filled to the brim and used for a toast.

GERALD FITZGERALD
(1740-**1773**-1819)

Gerald Fitzgerald entered Trinity College, Dublin as a sizar (a student who undertook menial tasks and received a free education) in 1759. He became a fellow of the college in 1765, professor of Law in 1783 and of Hebrew in 1790. He retired at the age of sixty-six and spent the last thirteen years of his life as a country clergyman. The poem which follows recounts the events of a day's expedition from Dublin; the poet and his friend leave Trinity College early in the morning and, after shooting snipe and woodcock in the Dodder valley, climb the Dublin mountains where 'many a shot repays the pleasing toil'. In the late afternoon, the two friends are still in the Dublin mountains; they have a fine view over the countryside and can see the city in the distance, but they are tired and in need of some refreshment.

from: The Academick Sportsman

... The Day advanc'd, and waning to the West,
Demands a thought for respite, and for rest,
Back to the city calls a sudden eye,[1]
Where vary'd beauties all in prospect lie;
The pointed Steeples menacing the Skies,
The splendid Domes, that emulously rise,
The lowly Hamlets scatter'd here and there,
That scarcely swell to breathe refreshing air;
The hedge-row'd Hills, and intermingled Vales,
The distant Villas fann'd by floating Gales;   10
And Eastward still, along the Bay serene,
Attendant Commerce crowns the solemn scene.[2]

These to behold may please the vacant mind,
More pleasing far the Cottage of the Hind,[3]
That yonder smokes,[4] by russet Hawthorn hedg'd,
By hay-yard back'd, and side long cow-shed edg'd:
Oft have I there my thirst and toil allay'd,
Approach'd as now, and dar'd[5] the dog that bay'd;
The smiling Matron joys to see her Guests,
Sweeps the broad hearth, and hears our free requests,   20

---

1. i.e. the poet suddenly turns his eyes to look at the city.
2. They can see commercial shipping in Dublin Bay.
3. 'A married farm-servant for whom a cottage is provided' s.v. 'hind' 2 (*OED*).
4. i.e. smoke from the hearth fire rises either through the chimney or, more probably, through the thatch.
5. challenged.

Repels her little Brood, that throng too nigh,
The homely board prepares — the napkin dry,
The new-made butter — rasher's[6] ready fare,
The new-laid egg, that's dress'd with nicest care;
The milky Store, for cream collected first,
Crowns the clean noggin[7] and allays our thirst;
While crackling Faggots, bright'ning as they burn,
Shew the neat cup-board, and the cleanly churn —
The modest Maiden rises from her wheel,
Who, unperceiv'd, a silent look would steal;   30
Call'd she attends, assists with artless grace,
The Bloom of Nature flushing in her face,
That scorns the die,[8] which pallid pride can lend,
And all the Arts which Luxury attend.

With fuel laden from the brambly rock,
Lo! forward comes the Father of his flock,
Of honest front:[9] salutes with rustic gait,
Remarks our fare, and boasts his former state,
When many a cow, nor long the time remov'd,
And many a calf his spacious pasture rov'd,   40
'Till rising Rents reduc'd him now to three,
Abridg'd his Farm, and fix'd him as we see;
Yet thanks his GOD, what fails him in his wealth
He seeks from labour, and he gains from health:
Then talks of sport; how many Wild-ducks seen!
What flocks of Widgeon,[10] too, had fledg'd the green!
'Till ev'ry 'Prentice dar'd the city shun,
Range the wide field, and lift the level gun.

While thus amus'd, and gladden'd with our lot,
The hasty Ev'ning calls us from the Cot;   50
A small gratuity dilates their heart,
And many a blessing follows as we part.
Nor you, ye Proud! their humble state disdain,
Their state is Nature's, hospitable, plain,

---

6. Thin slices of bacon or ham.
7. A small drinking vessel.
8. i.e. cosmetics.
9. expression, appearance.
10. A particular kind of wild duck.

Transmitted pure from Patriarchal times,
Unfram'd, unfashion'd to Corruption's Climes —
To you unknown their sweets from Toil's release —
To you unknown their Innocence and Peace —
Secure from Danger, as remov'd from Fame,
Their Lives calm Current flows without a name.   60

With limbs refresh'd, with lively tales and gay,
We homeward haste, and guile the tedious way;
Each object view, in wintry dress around,
And eye the Dogs, that wanton o'er the ground;
The pensive Red-breast on the leafless bough,
And, just beneath, the fragrance-breathing cow,
While still more grateful, with her cleanly pail,
The ruddy Milkmaid hears a tender tale
From the lov'd Swain, who swells th'alternate sigh,
Leans on his staff, and lures her side-long eye,   70
With artless guile, his passion to impart,
With looks that speak the passion of his Heart....

... Lo! yonder come — yet distant to the eye,
The vagrant PLOVER wafted thro' the sky;
Swift to the hedge, on diff'rent sides we run,
That skirt the copse, and hide the deadly gun;
Onward they move regardless of their state,
A single Guide conducts them to their fate —
The sudden Thunder bursts upon their head —
The foremost fall and all the rest are fled....   80

At length arriv'd, where DUBLIN's boasted Square
Rears its high domes, yet, spreads a healthful air,
O'er the wide view my willing eyes I cast,
And fill remembrance with its pleasures past,
Its shady walks, that lure the Noontide gale,
And sweeter breath of Love's enraptur'd tale;
Its sparkling Belles, that, arm'd in beauty's pride,
Wound as they pass, and triumph on each side;
But now no more these glories gild the Green —
Chill night descends, and desolates the scene.   90

361

The rising moon, with delegated sway,
Supplies the radiance of the distant Day,
Smiles on our path, directs our weary feet
Thro' all the busy tumults of the street —
With head-long pace, *here*, vagrant *Hawkers* scour,
And *bloody News* from lungs horrific pour,
There, dull, discordant Ballad-Notes annoy,
That mock the crowd, with love's fantastick joy;
The cumb'rous coach, the blazon'd chariot shows
Where lazy pride, or lordly state repose;   100
While, close behind, and heedless of her way,
We see the friendless, shiv'ring female stray:
She, once, the darling of her mother's arms,
Her father's pride, and blest with blooming charms,
Thro' all the village known for spotless fame,
Fair was her beauty, fairer still her name;
'Till the Tempter urg'd insidious suit,
And lur'd her weakness to forbidden fruit,
There perish'd grace, her guardian honour fled,
And sad remembrance mourns each blessing — dead!   110
Expell'd from Paradise of native sway,
She wanders now to ev'ry vice a prey —
A prey to yonder terror of the Night,
(Avert, ye Gods! such monsters from my sight,)
The Bully[11] dire! whose front the furies swell,
And scars dishonest mark the son of Hell —
In vain! she shrinks to shun his luckless pace,
Aw'd by the terrors of his vengeful face;
To scenes TARTAREAN,[12] see! the wretches hie,
Where, drench'd in vice, they rave — or rot — or die.   120

Heav'n! how unlike the pure, the tranquil plain,
Where rural mirth, and rural manners reign;
Where simple cheer disclaims the cares of wealth,
And fresh'ning gales diffuse the glow of health;
Where, undisturb'd, unenvy'd, unconfin'd,
Calm reason rules each movement of the mind;
Where mock'd ambition seeks her last retreat,
And proves the world, a bubble or a cheat.

---

11. One who protects and lives on the earnings of prostitutes. front (here) = forehead.
12. hellish. In classical mythology, Tartarus was one of the regions of hell.

As op'ning streets with brighter aspect smile,
Lo! ALMA MATER[13] rears her rev'rend Pile,   130
Unfolds the portals of her awful Square,
Where Arts and Science own her fost'ring care;
Struck with the scene that boasts ELIZA's name,
We pause, and praise the consecrated name,
The hallow'd ground, with softer footsteps, tread
Where BERKELEY reason'd, and where USHER read,
Where, born to combat an untoward age,
Indignant SWIFT explor'd the classic page —
Hail! happy Shade! — with griefs that once were thine,
IERNE[14] bends beneath thy patriot shrine;   140
In times like these, when gath'ring woes impend,
She mourns her Dean, her Draper, and her Friend,
Her exil'd commerce, half-deserted land,
Her harp unstrung, and manacled her hand,
While her pale Artists,[15] ev'ry comfort fled,
Droop in her streets, and die — for want of bread.

Thus past the day, and paid the pious tear
To worth deceas'd — to virtues ever dear,
Each fond Reflection, rising in our breast,
At length subdues, and yields to soothing rest;   150
Pleas'd we behold the bright'ning fuel blaze,
And hot repast, that challenges our praise,
While keenest appetites a zest bestow,
Which listless luxury can never know:
The cloth remov'd, with blessing for our fare,
We, next, the Bowl's convivial juice prepare,
Or, the rich Grape's nectareous bev'rage pour,
To raise the heart, and cheer the social hour,
When toil declining claims refreshment's smiles,
And mirthful innocence the time beguiles....   160

13. i.e. Trinity College, Dublin, founded in the reign of Queen Elizabeth I ('Eliza') and boasting among its teachers or graduates the philosopher Bishop Berkeley, Archbishop James Ussher and Swift.
14. A poetic name for Ireland.
15. artisans, tradesmen.

MARY SHACKLETON
(1758-**1774**-1826)

Mary Shackleton was the daughter of the master of the Quaker school at Ballitore, Co. Kildare where Edmund Burke, among others, received his early education. Mary herself attended the school and, from an early age, wrote about her life and feelings in her journal, in poems and in letters. The first of the poems which follows, written when she was sixteen, concerns her emotions on discovering that one of her schoolfellows, 'Lysander', had been untrue to her, and the second and third poems show her reactions to other domestic events. As a whole, Mary Shackleton's early poems give an unusual and vivid insight into the mind of a young woman in rural eighteenth-century Ireland. Mary Shackleton married William Leadbetter in 1791 and her *Poems* appeared in 1808.

The Welcome to Liberty

With smiles I greet thy glad approach,
And gladden at thy gentle touch,
    Delightful Liberty;
More welcome than returning light
To those who painful pass the night
    Is Freedom unto me.

While sighing lovers round me pine,
I join not in their plaintive whine,
    But laugh at all their pain;
No cares of love my peace molest,   10
But sweet Contentment in my breast,
    Now holds her gentle reign.

Lysander[1] has a heavenly face,
In every feature shines a grace,
    He has a noble mien.
And more than all, he said he lov'd;
My heart his fancy'd flame approv'd,
    And pleas'd, I wore his chain.

---

1. The identity of 'Lysander' has not been established.

Lysander, being false to me
I do not so much blame in thee,   20
     As saying that thou lov'd;
Before thou did my face behold,
A Maiden's in a finer mould
     Thy tender heart approv'd.

When my resolves I first did take
The chains which thou imposed, to break,
     It tore my heart, I own.
To ease the Tooth-ache's raging pain
We that of drawing[2] glad sustain,
     Which soon to tire[3] is known.   30

'Twas wondrous kind to set me free,
To school I'll go, nor think of thee,
     Though thou before me stands;
My sums, my books, my globes I'll ply,[4]
Nor let my pen (to view thy eye)
     Lie useless in my hands.

Of Mars and Jupiter I'll tell,
Venus and Saturn, knowing well
     More radiant than thy eyes
Which once I said (but 'twas a lie)   40
Outshone these lamps which hang on high
     To light the sable skies.

'Tis true the lilly and the rose
In thy sweet face their charms disclose,
     And graceful is thy air,
Though the black sloe rolls in thy eye,
But yet I truly think that I
     May meet with some as fair.

---

2. i.e. extracting a tooth.
3. diminish.
4. Terrestrial and celestial globes were widely used to teach geography and astronomy in eighteenth-century schools.

Free as the Tenants of the grove
Who sing of Liberty and love,   50
     The latter I disclaim.
Delightful, charming Liberty,
The gentle joys which flow from thee
These, these shall be my theme.

On the Murder of a Cat[1]

To doleful strains, ah, strains of woe
    I tune my trembling string;
The hapless end and cruel fate
    Of murdered Puss I sing.

Her Form was elegant, and green
    As emerald was her eye;
And well I ween her coat so gay
    Might with the Tortoise vie.

Ah, what avails thy coat so gay,
    Or eke[2] thy emerald eye?   10
Thy beauty could not save thy life,
    But thou alas must die.

Fate guides her steps one fatal morn;
    She bends her harmless way
To the French-room, where in their beds
    Her cruel murderers lay.

Ah, had she in the Kitchen staid
    She'd met a milder fate;
What needeth this reflection now,
    For 'tis, alas, too late.   20

Soon from their beds her murderers start,
    Resolv'd poor Puss to slay,
Alas! 'tis for so small a fault
    Her dearest blood must pay.

---

1. References to the killing, and sometimes the eating, of domestic cats, occur elsewhere in eighteenth-century Irish verse. See also Robert Darnton, *The Great Cat Massacre and other Episodes from French Cultural History* (New York, 1984), p. 90.
2. even.

Large Phibbs and Toby, Thacker, more
    Whose names I now forget,
With bloody minds on mischief bent
    The hapless beast beset.

Mary who, lighting up the fire
    Was busy in the Hall,   30
Above her heard a thundering noise
    As though the loft would fall.

Pat Rogers[3] went the cause t'explore;
    When he appear'd in view,
They fell to dress, when he retir'd
    Their cruel sport renew.

Williams was there, tho' in her Death
    I own he had no part,
Yet will not scenes of cruelty
    Awake a feeling heart?   40

He, though he might, ne'er op'd the door
    To set the Captive free,
But let her be the helpless sport
    Of wanton cruelty.

And now the bloody deed is done,
    The wretched victim slain,
The bloody floor and curtains torn
    Her monuments remain.

Oh what a mighty Conquest's won!
    A Conquest won so cheap,   50
O'er a weak, harmless animal
    That had no way to scape.

When not for use, but brutal sport
    A living thing you slay,
Not you that cannot give a life
    Should take a life away.

3. A senior servant in the house.

To Sarah Shackleton[1]
on her beating me with the bed-stick as she lies in Bed at her ease

Ah, why thy cruel rage to bend
Against a sister and a friend
Who never did in thought offend?
That when into my bed I creep,
And think to lay me down to sleep,
Thou from thy bed which joins me nigh
Stretches thy arm, and waving high
The dreaded Bed-stick, to my woe,
Doth give me many a heavy blow;
Ah, prithee, say, what is the cause   10
Of all this wondrous waste of blows?
Is it because thy bed is found
With dreadful Bed-sticks guarded round
That thou dost chuse to let me see
Thy great superiority?
At the Retreat,[2] too, much I fear,
My bed will join thine very near.
Ah, let me rest within my bed,
Nor with thy Bed-stick break my head,
And, prithee, very soon have done   20
With whacking Mary Shackleton.

---

1. Mary's elder sister. A bed-stick or bed-stave was a stick kept beside the bed, handy, according to the *OED,* 'as a weapon'.
2. A house to which the Shackleton family went in the summer-time.

WILLIAM PRESTON
(1753-**1776**-1807)

William Preston was born in Dublin and educated at Trinity College. He became a lawyer and was the first secretary to the Royal Irish Academy (1786). Some of his serious poems appeared in the Academy's *Transactions*, but he was more successful as a satirist, and his satirical verses appeared regularly in Dublin in the last two decades of the century. Preston also wrote a widely acclaimed tragedy based on the French Revolution; he died, according to the *DNB*, of overwork.

The poem below is a satiric attack on the miscellaneous English writer, Richard Twiss, whose *Travels through Portugal and Spain* (London, 1775) was followed in 1776 by his *Tour in Ireland in 1775*. Twiss's account of Ireland was less than flattering to the land or its inhabitants, and the book was vigorously attacked by several Irish writers, including William Preston in this poem. In Twiss's earlier account of his travels in the province of Murcia in Spain, he had noted that he had spent 'every evening at the house of Donna Teresa Pinna y Ruiz'. The poet imagines Donna Teresa's dismay at Twiss's departure from Spain: 'Half naked, shiv'ring at the midnight air, // With mangled bosom and dishevell'd hair, // One stocking off — I sit — and weep — and write, // The streaming tears have drown'd my taper's light'. However, '*Hibernia* calls him', and Donna Teresa wonders what charms Twiss will find in Ireland to compete with those he has left in Spain.

from: An heroic Epistle from Donna Teresa Pinna ÿ Ruiz

To gain the notice of an F.R.S.,[1]
Th' *Iernian* plains do teeming wonders bless,
Such potent drugs as ancient *Colchis*[2] bore,
The venom'd herbage of *Thessalian*[3] lore?
With alligators swarms the river's side,
Do winged basilisks[4] the breezes ride?
In vain, in vain you tread the barren plains;
Nor asp, nor tumbledung[5] rewards your pains.
The wretched vales nor snake nor scorpion boast,
Saint *Patrick* chas'd them from the guilty coast,   10

---

1. i.e. to gain the notice of a Fellow of the Royal Society (Twiss had been elected to the Royal Society in London in 1774), do the plains of Ireland boast prolific wonders such as the potent drugs ...
2. A country in Asia famous in classical lore for its poisonous herbs.
3. Thessaly, now part of Greece. The inhabitants were renowned as magicians and herbalists.
4. fabulous reptiles.
5. Twiss's excited description of the American tumbledung beetle (*Travels in Portugal and Spain* (hereafter *TPS*), II, 14) is given in a footnote at this point.

Mere *common* flies the noontide shambles[6] breed,
Mere *vulgar* lice on *Irish* beggars feed:
In vain your teeth, your microscope you try,
They seem but *English* to the taste and eye.

While Pinna[7] weeps to Murcian[8] vales and bow'rs,
What cares, what studies fill the wanderer's hours!
Dost thou, with learn'd and deep precision, mark
The length of turkey, and the breadth of lark?[9]
Thy sumptuous board do rotten viands load,
And writhing maggots feed thy darling toad?[10]   20
Dost thou thy muster-roll of beauties frame,
And call to judgement each aspiring dame?[11]
A second *Paris*[12] — on thy dread commands,
In naked glory wait the shining bands.
A thousand nymphs, *Ierne*'s proudest boast,
A thousand nymphs — and every nymph a toast[13] —
While nice discernment, in impartial scale,
The tooth of *Phillis* weighs with *Mira*'s nail,
Adjusts the credit and the debt of charms,
The legs of *Portia* with *Calista*'s arms,   30
Blondina's lily with *Belinda*'s rose,
And *Laura*'s pretty foot with *Flavia*'s nose.
But can'st thou, fond and feeling as thou art,
Survey the charmer, and preserve thy heart?
Some secret spell the homeliest maidens find
To fire the tinder of thy yielding mind,
Each stature, colour, feature, age and shape;
Brown as they were, not gypsies could escape:

---

6. abattoirs.
7. i.e. Donna Teresa.
8. The province in south-eastern Spain where Twiss had encounted Donna Teresa.
9. Twiss had measured the wing-span of larks he had shot in Spain (*TPS*, I, 66).
10. Twiss's description of feeding toads with maggots (*TPS*, II, 96) is given at this point.
11. The original note at this point reads: 'Mr Twiss had seriously conceived a design of making a catalogue of beauties, ranked according to their respective merits, for the imbellishment of his intended book of travels through Ireland.'
12. In classical literature, Paris, son of Priam king of Troy, had to decide which was the most beautiful of three goddesses, Juno, Venus and Minerva, who appeared naked before him.
13. The lady whose health is proposed and drunk to.

Their smutty charms your wandering eyes betray'd,
And oft and oft you wronged the *Murcian* maid.[14]   40
With soothing speech you woo'd the tawny train,
And sometimes too — you mourn'd their proud disdain.
In some cook's shop, thus roves th' inconstant fly,
From cate[15] to cate he darts an eager eye,
Now soars to ven'son, with a humming flight,
Now feasts on bull-beef with a cheap delight;
Well-pleas'd he sucks, and buzzes as he blows,
And maggots mark him, whereso'er he goes.
Distracting thought! Some *Irish* damsel's thrall,
Perhaps this moment at her feet you fall;   50
Or on the footstool of her chariot stand,[16]
Sigh, chatter, flirt her fan, and squeeze her hand,
When city belles in Sunday pomp are seen,
And gilded chariots troll round Stephen's-green.
Ye gods above! Ye blackguard boys below!
Oh, splash his stockings, and avenge my woe.
Perhaps some Siren[17] wafts thee all alone,
In magic vehicle, to cates unknown;
High low machine, that bears plebeian wight[18]
To distant tea-house, or funereal rite: 60
Still as it moves, the proud pavilion nods,
A chaise by mortals, NODDY term'd by gods.[19]
Where *Donnybrook* surveys her winding rills,
And *Chapel-izod*[20] rears her sunny hills;

---

14. The footnote at this point refers to Twiss's having constantly stayed with gypsies in Spain, and to his remark that he has *'more than once* known *unsuccessful attempts* made for a *private interview* with some of their young females, who virtuously rejected both the courtship and the money'.

15. A choice delicacy.

16. The original footnote refers to Twiss's account (*TPS*, I, 257) of his participating in the Spanish custom by which, while the ladies were taking the air in their carriages, gentlemen sometimes got onto the footsteps of the carriages, *'cortejando las sennoras'* or *'cicisbeing the ladies'*. (A 'cicisbo' was, in Italy, 'the recognised gallant of a married woman' (*OED*).)

17. In classical literature, the Sirens — beautiful maidens who were partly woman and partly bird, lured sailors to destruction by their singing.

18. person.

19. A 'Noddy' was a light two-wheeled vehicle used in Ireland. Twiss described 'Noddies' in his *Tour in Ireland*.

20. Donnybrook and Chapelizod were two villages near Dublin, popular for day-trips in the summer.

Thy sumptuous board the little loves prepare,
And *Sally Lunn*,[21] and *saffron cake* are there.
Blest saffron cakes! from you may *Dublin* claim
Peculiar pleasure, and peculiar fame.
Blest cates! plump, yellow, tempting as the breast
Of gypsey, heaving thro' the tatter'd vest!   70
Once smocks alone neglected saffron dy'd,[22]
(Unwash'd to wear them was the maiden's pride)
The generous drug,[23] more honour'd than of yore,
Now fills the bellies it adorn'd before.

Yet shall our lemons to potatoes bend?
With Spanish dames shall Irish maids contend?
Or *Dublin* beggars boast an equal part
With *Murcian* gypsies in my *Richard's* heart?
Are fairer throngs at play than bull-fight see?
Or yield our Alamedes[24] to Stephen's-green?   80
The rocket's blaze shall dim the comet's tail,
When Liffey's banks contend with Murcia's vale;
And lemons crown the bleak Hibernian coast,
E're Irish miss[25] the charms of Pinna boast.
Let birth, let grandeur strike thy lifted eye,
And say, what maiden shall with Pinna vie?
The best, the proudest of your Irish dames,
Reflected pride from Spanish lineage claims.[26]
What are the glories of Milesian blood?
A scant infusion of our generous flood —   90
But so debas'd, so lost, you vainly trace
The genial currents in the mongrel race....

Come, *Richard*,[27] come, no more perplex thy head
With writing books that never shall be read.
What joys, what sports can *Irish* plains afford,
What tender lady, or what treating lord?

21. A kind of light, sweet teacake containing sultanas, which is eaten with butter.
22. A note reads: 'Alluding to the custom which anciently prevailed among the Irish of dying their linen with saffron.'
23. i.e. saffron, which is used for colouring food and is made of the dried stigmas of the autumn crocus flower.
24. An alameda is the Spanish name for a public walk shaded with trees.
25. maiden.
26. Milesius, legendary founder of the Irish race, is said to have come to Ireland from Spain. See Glossary.
27. i.e. Richard Twiss.

At twilight hour what painted Floras rove;
Oh, where shall traveller taste the joys of love?
In what kind tavern shall he wear the night;
Where find a bagnio[28] fit for Christian wight?   100
What beggar maid shall fire him with her charms;
Or what soft gypsie fill his longing arms?
The gypsie damsel tyrant Houghton[29] claims,
And, envious caitiff! mars thy rising flames.
The sable cart — detested object — rolls,
And rumbles dire dismay to vagrant souls;
The mutes around it stalk — a griesly band —
The bloody halberd[30] arms each iron hand.
All, all the ragged to their empire bend,
Old, young, blind, lame, the fatal cart ascend.   110
Not shrieking infant for his youth he spares,
Not bearded grandsire for his silver hairs,
Not maiden coy, with rage and terror pale,
He dooms, he bears her to his proud serail.[31]
E'en when the ballad-singer's note is loud,
And fears and wishes sooth the melting croud,
When artless love, and love's disport, she sings,
Or heroes pendent in unworthy strings;
Sudden the cart — the fatal cart appears, —
The captive minstrel steeps her song in tears.   120
But ah! my fears, my boding fears arise,
(Within the vagrant act my Richard lies)
Lest thou the cart's unenvied height shouldst gain,
And ride triumphant through the hooting train.
Once only skilled to feed the toad and asp,
Say, canst thou oakum pick, or logwood rasp?[32]....

---

28. A brothel.

29. A 'sable cart', manned by armed men, collected vagrants from the streets of Dublin every evening and brought them to the House of Industry, which was managed by a Mr Houghton. According to a droll footnote later in the poem, 'the late Alderman Faulkner' had written that the House of Industry was 'for taking up cripples that lie in the streets, folks without legs that stand at the corners, and such like vagrants. We have pleasure to hear that all the ballad-singers, blind harpers, Hackball, and many other nefarious old women, are in there already....'

30. A fearsome military weapon which combines a battleaxe with a spear.

31. = seraglio or a place where women are confined — as in the harem of an eastern potentate.

32. The original notes explains that the paupers in the House of Industry were often employed to pick old ropes to pieces to obtain the fibres (oakum) and also to scrape logs of the American logwood tree (*Hæmatoxylon Campechianum*) to obtain a dye or drug found inside them.

Come, *Richard*, come, forget *Hibernian* charms,
And close thy wanderings in *Teresa*'s arms.
No critics here in coffee-houses rage,
No classic females learned warfare wage;   130
But ball and bull-fight charm the courtly throng,
The midnight chorus, and the matin song.
Here tune thy fiddle, here refit thy bow,
And pitch thy printer to the fiends below[33]....

33. In fact, Twiss responded to this poem with one entitled 'An Heroic Epistle from R. Twiss Esq., to Donna Teresa' (Dublin, 1776).

LADY CLARE
(c.1755-**1776**-1844)

Such was the Irish reaction to Richard Twiss's *Tour in Ireland in 1775* that a Dublin earthenware manufacturer had the idea of painting the offender's portrait on the bottom of chamber-pots. Beside the portrait appeared the following verse, said to be the work of Anne Whaley, who was later the wife of John Fitzgibbon Lord Clare, lord chancellor of Ireland 1789-1802 and architect of the Act of Union. Constantia Maxwell prints the verse because, as she puts it wryly, 'it illustrates the aristocratic humour of the time' (*Dublin under the Georges* (Dublin, 1936) p. 276).

Motto inscribed on the bottom of chamber-pots beside a portrait of Richard Twiss

> Here you may behold a liar,
> Well deserving of hell-fire:
> Every one who likes may p——
> Upon the learned Doctor T——.

TURLOGH CAROLAN
(1670-1738: translated by Joseph Cooper Walker in **1776**)

When writing for his patrons, the famous Irish harper Turlogh Carolan normally composed the words of his songs as well as the melodies to which they were sung. The first appearance in print of English versions of Carolan's Irish words was in Joseph Cooper Walker's remarkable *Historical Memoirs of the Irish Bards* (Dublin, 1776). Charlotte Brooke later translated many of the same Carolan verses in her *Reliques of Irish Poetry* (Dublin, 1789).

Carolan's Receipt

When by sickness or sorrow assail'd,
    To the mansion of Stafford[1] I hied;
His advice or his cordial n'er fail'd
    To relieve me — nor e'er was denied.

At midnight our glasses went round —
    In the morning a cup he would send —
By the force of his wit he had found,
    That my life did on drinking depend.

With the spirit of Whiskey inspir'd
    By my Harp e'en the pow'r is confess'd —   10
'Tis then that my genius is fir'd: —
    'Tis then I sing sweetest and best.

Ye friends and ye neighbours draw near;
    Attend to the close of my song: —
Remember, if life you hold dear,
    That drinking your life will prolong.

---

1. Dr John Stafford of Elphin, Co. Roscommon was, according to Donal O'Sullivan (*Carolan: the Life, Times and Music of an Irish Harper*, 2 vols. (London, 1958) I, 103), a life-long friend of Carolan. He attended him in his last illness and was a coffin-bearer at his funeral.

ELIZABETH RYVES
(c.1750-**1777**-1797)

Elizabeth Ryves was born in Ireland, 'of a good family', according to biographical accounts of her (see D. J. O'Donoghue, *The Poets of Ireland* (Dublin, 1912) and *DNB*). She was apparently swindled out of her Irish property and moved to London where she earned a precarious living as a writer and translator. Apart from several translations from French, she also wrote political articles, plays, a novel and seven volumes of poetry. Elizabeth Ryves is said to have been a generous and kind-hearted person of considerable ability, but she died in poverty.

Ode to Sensibility

The sordid wretch who ne'er has known
To feel for miseries not his own,
Whose lazy pulse serenely beats
While injured worth her wrongs repeats;
Dead to each sense of joy or pain,
A useless link in nature's chain,
May boast the calm which I disdain.

Give me a generous soul, that glows
With others' transports, others' woes,
Whose noble nature scorns to bend,   10
Tho' Fate her iron scourge extend,
But bravely bears the galling yoke,
And smiles superior to the stroke
With spirits free and mind unbroke.

Yet by compassion touched, not fear,
Sheds the soft sympathizing tear
In tribute to affliction's claim,
Or envied merit's wounded fame.
Let Stoics scoff! I'd rather be
Thus curst with sensibility   20
Than share their boasted apathy.

JAMES DELACOURT OR DE-LA-COUR
(1709-**1778**-1781)

The Rev. James Delacourt (the name is spelt in several different ways) was a native of Cork and was educated at Trinity College, Dublin. He wrote poetry from his student days and was a great admirer of the English poet James Thomson, to whom he addressed several poems. According to John O'Keeffe's *Recollections* (London, 1826), Delacourt was 'a dapper little man'; other commentators refer to his eccentricities. His poems were collected in a volume published in Cork in 1778.

In praise of a Negress

What shape I have, that form is all my own
To art a stranger, and to modes unknown;
To paint or patches,[1] perfum'd fraud, no friend,
Nor know what stays and honey-water mend;
No spotted moons deform my jetty face,
I would be blacker than that speckled race!
My simple lotion is the purer rain,
And e'en that wash is labour took in vain.
But my pearl teeth, without tobacco's aid,
O'er snow or Indian iv'ry cast a shade!   10
My eyes eclipse the stars in all their flame,
Such as may not e'en Albion's daughters[2] shame!
My softer skin with the mole's velvet vies,
Ah! who will on these altars sacrifice?
But if I please less in the sultry day,
My colour with the candles dies away;
Since to our hue the light is deem'd a foe,
Night will a THAIS[3] in my charms bestow.

---

1. Eighteenth-century beauties would often affix artificial patches to their faces (sometimes large enough to be called 'spotted moons', as in line 5) to make themselves look more interesting. The references in the next few lines are to beauty aids and cosmetics of various kinds.
2. i.e. the daughters of Britain.
3. Thais was a famous Athenian courtesan who accompanied Alexander the Great in his expedition to Asia.

GEORGE SACKVILLE COTTER

(1755-**1778**-1831)

Rev. George Sackville Cotter was the son of Sir George Cotter of Cork and was educated at
Cambridge. His two-volume *Poems consisting of Odes, Songs, Pastorals, Satyrs. &c...*
(Cork, 1788) is full of interest; the first volume contains, for instance, a long and detailed
poetic account of an Irish country house of the 1770s ('The Squire's Habitation: a Satyr', I,
133-73) as well as poems about night-life in eighteenth-century Cork, with accounts of its
alcoholics, its coffee houses and its gambling.

The bulk of the volume is taken up with a long poetic epistle to an unnamed friend, in
which Cotter recounts the adventures and upsets experienced by visitors to the spa of
Swanlinbar in County Cavan. After a general introduction to life at the spa in Epistle I,
Cotter uses Epistle II to tell his friend what happened in the 'place of amusement for ladies'.
Epistle III gives a vivid account of breakfast in the spa hotel and Epistle IV describes a day-
trip on nearby Lough Erne.

from: Epistles from Swanlinbar

address'd to Richard ———— Esq.

from: Epistle II

Lo! a place of amusement for ladies hard by,
Where they mount on a swing and are toss'd up on high;
All give their assistance, and many a thump
The Miss, as she's flying, receives on the rump;
Miss Kitty Virago[1] ascended one day,
With her heels in the air she was rattled away;
Before she was seated, the barbarous pack
Set her off with a violent jerk at her back;
She screech'd and she squall'd, said her head turn'd round,
But still they would not let her get to the ground;   10
A rapid Phænomenon borne to the moon!
While every one gaz'd at the mighty Balloon
Her feathers so high, and her Cork spread behind
Were so light as to fly on the wings of the wind.
The joke was too near being serious it's true,
As forth from the rope she unluckily flew;
And dreadful to think on, so great was the clatter,
That nobody tried, or[2] to save, or come at her;

---

1. Miss Kitty Virago is, like all the characters in this poem, a thinly disguised portrait of
   someone known to both Cotter and his correspondent.
2. either.

Half naked she flew in a terrible plight,
While ev'ry one stood all astonish'd with fright;   20
And worse would have been the disaster, but Lo!
In the front runs a deep little river below;
In the middle she fell on a sudden slapdash,
And we who stood by, were all wet by the splash....

from: Epistle III

Now a bustle ensued at the table where meet
All the parties, and strive who shall get the best seat;
All running and striding o'er benches and table,
They crowd for a breakfast, as well as they're able.
Lord Snuffle sat down at the top of the row,
And Mrs Bumshuffle a little below; ...
Now the fiddle and dulcimer enter'd, and soon
Serenaded the eaters with many a tune:
With talking and Music there rose such a clatter,
Outside you'd have wonder'd what could be the matter.   10
In a simile, let me compare it to hell,
In a hubbub when headlong the Devils all fell;
'Twas impossible even to hear conversation,
But a scrap now and then of some silly narration;
Or calling out, 'Tea, Ma'am, or Chocolate, say!'
'I never take Sugar — some Coco, Ma'am, pray!'
'Fill the teapot, I'll thank ye — don't stir Sir, I beg' —
'O Dear Sir, I fear I have scalded your leg' —
'Here waiter, where are you?' 'Cream, Ma'am, do you wish?'
'Is the tea to your liking? pray take t'other dish;'   20
'Bring Chocolate here to the top of the table' —
'More toast — and of muffins as much as you're able;'
'Lady Brilliant, you've eaten no breakfast; I feel
'For your headache;' — 'Dear Madam, I've eaten a deal;'
Then loud play'd the fiddlers, tho' bad at the best,
As if they would make all the victuals digest;
The clamour continued, till all were supplied
With tea, toast and butter, and muffins beside;
Some had bowls full of milk, nicely fill'd to the brim,
Others whetted their stomacks, with cake they call Slim,   30

But as cakes for a breakfast are quite a delusion,
Eggs were added to these in the utmost profusion.
At length all was hush'd, as tempestuous gales
Sudden sink to a calm, and a silence prevails....
E'en the music left off, and how happy was I
When they laid both their bows and their violins by....

from: Epistle IV

... At length we arrived on the banks of the lake,
All eager the fresh water voyage to take,
Some gay-headed sparks took the ladies in charge,
And safely conducted them down to the barge
Supplied by his Lordship[1] who dwells by the lake,
For the company thither their parties to make;...

O could I set down ev'ry word that was spoke,
I'd tell you of many an excellent joke;
Some modest, but some beyond decency's laws
To which all the men gave the loudest applause,   10
And the women by tittering seem'd to declare,
Such gaieties scarce disagreeable were....

After a while, the barge is caught in a squall and overturns — luckily close to the shore
where the water is only a few feet deep.

The Gentlemen tried the poor Ladies to haul in,
Who sat in the water all screeching and squalling;
Captain Spindle the tallest in company bore
An old lady aloft on his back to the shore;
While my Lord most politely conducted the daughter
With scraping and bows thro' the midst of the water.
The remainder succeeded all shaking their clothes,
Drag'd forth in a crowd by the wet dripping beaus,   20
The Ensign[2] was highly successful that day,
Or else a life might have been lost in the fray;

1. William-Willoughby Cole, second Viscount Enniskillen and Baron Mountflorence, of
   Florence Court, Co. Fermanagh.
2. A junior army officer.

Mrs Drippin was sunk in deep water, it's true,
But she drag'd herself forth by the hair of his queue![3]
Loud crying 'O what shall I do? What a dipping?
'Twere better to stay with my dear Mr Drippin,
Alas he knows nothing of this sad mishap,
For now he is taking his afternoon's nap.'
Then grasping her cloak in the fear of being lost,
Tuck'd up, shewing legs nearly thick as a post.　　　　30
She sigh'd and she sobb'd, took the offer'd relief,
And waddled out slowly, an emblem of grief.
Mr Bruin cried, 'Haste, Madam, out of the way go!'
Then clim'd o'er the back of Miss Kitty Virago;
And where alongside, by a ponderous charge
Of water upturn'd, lay the sorrowful barge,
He stept on its bottom, secure from the shock,
And stood like a cormorant perch'd on a rock.
Meantime in the water lay feminine squallers;
Oh! how did I pity the dear caterwaulers!　　　　40
'Twould have melted your heart, to have seen the sad thumps
That the rude fancy billows bestow'd on their rumps;
Then each as she rose 'mid the boisterous din,
How closely the drapery stuck to her skin!
Nor plainer was once by artificer's whim
Mark'd out the proportion of figure and limb.
Nor finer did Græcian Statue disclose,
The vest or the shape from the head to the toes....

3. pigtail.

GORGES EDMOND HOWARD
(1715-**1782**-1786)

Gorges Edmond Howard, the son of an army officer, was born in Coleraine. He was educated at Thomas Sheridan's school in Dublin and became a successful lawyer. He wrote a number of legal works but, according to the *DNB*, was 'ridiculed for worthless tragedies and occasional verse'. In fact, the satires written on him and George Faulkner by the dramatist Robert Jephson still make entertaining reading.

The Modern Lass in High Dress in MDCCLVI

Haste all ye bucks and lads of fire
And view a modern nymph's attire;
Here's every charm to win the sight,
And give to sense and heart delight.

Behold my jet-black locks that flow,
In sportive curls on neck of snow!
My polish'd shoulders plump and bare,
And swelling hills beneath, so fair!

Adown my back, ev'n to my waist,
With boundless joys your fancy feast!   10
Through plackets[1] then, those juts descry,
Would lure the pious hermit's eye.

The beauties too of limbs below,
Which friendly, curtail'd garments show;
And if th'indulgent gale blows high,
Others, that there adjacent lie.

So little art our grandames knew,
That ev'n a foot, man must not view,
And straight, would make a wond'rous rout,
If bubby peep'd from tucker out.[2]   20

---

1. A placket is normally a slit at the top of an apron or petticoat to make it easier to put it on or take it off; but here the slits seem to be in the girls' blouses and it is their 'jutting' breasts which can be seen through them.
2. i.e. if a nipple appeared above the top of the bodice of a dress.

But we their offspring far more sage,
Than that prepost'rous prudish age,
From old or young, the gay and grave,
Veil not the charms kind Nature gave.[3]

3. The reference is to the revealing women's fashions of the 1750s.

EOGHAN RUA Ó SÚILLEABHÁIN
(c.1748-**1782**-1784)

Eoghan Rua Ó Súilleabháin (O'Sullivan), one of the best Irish-language poets of the
eighteenth century, came from County Kerry. He was a scribe and a poet, as well as a
schoolmaster and, like other Irish poets of his day, had a command of English superior to
most Irish-speakers. He also had a reputation as a rake, and seems to have spent much of his
life wandering. He served in the British navy for a while, and wrote a famous poem, in
English, praising Admiral Rodney. In the poem which follows, it is interesting to see
Ó Súilleabháin emphasising the practical side of the training offered in his hedge-school.

Letter to Father Fitzgerald

Reverend Sir —
    Please to publish from the altar of your holy Mass
    That I will open school at Knocknagree Cross,
    Where the tender babes will be well off,
    For it's there I'll teach them their Criss Cross;[1]
    Reverend Sir, you will by experience find
    All my endeavours to please mankind,
    For it's there I will teach them how to read and write;
    The Catechism I will explain
    To each young nymph and noble swain,   10
    With all young ladies I'll engage
    To forward them with speed and care,
    With book-keeping and mensuration,
    Euclid's Elements[2] and Navigation,
    With Trigonometry and sound gauging,[3]
    And English Grammar with rhyme and reason.
    With the grown-up youths I'll first agree
    To instruct them as well in the Rule of Three;[4]
    Such of them as are well able,
    The cube root of me will learn,   20
    Such as are of tractable genius,

1. A children's game played on a slate.
2. The *Elements* of the classical Greek mathematician Euclid (fl. c.300 B.C.) was the standard geometry book in the eighteenth century.
3. Calculating the area of land or the capacity of a container.
4. 'A method of finding a fourth number from three given numbers, of which the first is in the same proportion to the second as the third is to the unknown fourth' (*OED*).

With compas and rule I will teach them,
Bills, bonds and informations,[5]
Summons, warrants, supersedes,
Judgement tickets, good
Leases, receipts in full,
And releases, short accounts,
With rhyme and reason,
And sweet love letters for the ladies.

5. The poet lists all the minor legal documents which anyone working as a land agent or middleman in eighteenth-century Ireland might be expected to encounter. A 'supersedeas', for instance, was a writ commanding the stay of legal proceedings which ought otherwise to have proceeded, and the other terms have similarly precise meanings.

CHAPBOOK VERSE OF THE 1780s[1]

The anonymous verse which follows is taken from chapbooks printed in the 1780s in Irish provincial centres such as Monaghan, Newry and Limerick. The verse concerns local events, people and products, and was clearly composed in the towns where it was printed. The frail, crudely printed chapbooks were sold to travelling chapmen who, in turn, sold them on to ballad-singers active in the countryside so that the songs would have been heard at fairs and in country ale-houses all around Ireland. The poems exude a fierce vigour unique in eighteenth-century Irish verse in English, and are valuable not only because they bring us poetic voices of originality and freshness, but also as a source of information on a side of Irish cultural life about which little has been written.

The mother-tongue of the poets whose work appears in these chapbooks was Irish rather than English, as is clear from their use of the language. In addition, many of the verses are in the *amhrán* or song metres of Irish verse rather than those of English verse. In several poems, for instance, the rhythmic units are linked by assonance and alliteration rather than by end-rhyme, which is typical of Irish rather than English verse.

Connelly's Ale: a new song

One fair summer's morn, bright Phœbus adorn
When mass it is over to Lurgan we go,
To see all the lasses as thro the street passes
I'm sure they will treat us to brandy I know;
Their mothers pursuing for fear of their ruin
A stick in her hand and a drab on her tail[2]
She hops on her crutches: 'Get home you dam'd bitches,
You'll surely be ruin'd by Connelly's Ale.'

There's a man in this town and his name I'll mention
And all his delight is in bunging of Ale;[3]   10
He has a daughter both comely and handsome,
You'd know by her eyes she had gig in her tail.
Kiss her and press her and do what you will,
Brush her up tight I'll be bound she wont fail;
Of a Saturday night she's as willing as I am
To take a fresh jorum[4] of Connellys Ale

---

1. For a discussion of these chapbooks, the terms used to describe them, and the poems they contain, see introduction, pp. 19-20.
2. meaning uncertain. The 'tail' is the back part of the mother's skirt and 'drab' probably means dirt.
3. i.e. filling himself with ale.
4. A large drinking vessel.

387

First when they drink it makes their heads dissy,
Then after that it will go to their tail;
And many a one it does swell in the belly,
I will leave the blame to Connelly's Ale.   20
It's our country lasses their silks and dresses
That wears a high crown to set out their tail,
When they meet a young Weaver he views their behaviour,
Then he does treat them to Connelly Ale,

You Farmers that's wealthy and has daughters plenty,
They dress up their heads with a flying topsail
Whilst bread and tea they must have in the morning
Yet nothing will do them but Connellys Ale;
Theyre mammy's is kindly and dresses them finely
To light wakes and dances they never will fail,   30
The boys find them willing that has but one shilling,
They will give them their fill of Conne[ll]ys Ale

The Connaughtman's Visit to DUBLIN

This is one of many eighteenth-century poems about countrymen visiting Dublin or Belfast.
The characteristics of the orthography are those of Hiberno-English, though the lack of
normal English spellings is obviously designed to add to the comic effect of the verse. The
poem is easier to read if the following substitutions of consonants are made: b = p; d = th;
f = wh; t = th or d; sh = s, j or ch; wh = f or v; v = f or w. For further clarification and for
word-lists, see the Glossary.

You people of Dublin who whollies[1] the rules,
Of canting[2] poor strangers and humbugging fools;
If ever you cath me vonst more on your stones,[3]
I'll give whree leave whor to broke all my bones.

Vidh a good house and garden I lived at my ease,
But those wordly pleasures my mind could not please;
To frends and to neghbors I did bid adieu,
And set off to Dublin to see the review.[4]

1. follows.
2. deceiving, double-crossing.
3. i.e. if ever you catch me once more on your (paving-)stones.
4. i.e. a review of the Volunteers in Dublin's Phoenix Park.

I whodered[5] my brogues and I pushed to the road,
And parted sweet Leitrim my place of abode,   10
My time being short I kept still in a trot,
'Till at last I arrived at the wery same spot.[6]

Vidh a trembling aspect into town did advonce,
And arrived at a soop-maker's celler by chance,
There vas cows heads, lambs puddings and what tripes,
Dis dillusious[7] sight gave my belly the gripes.

Vith mazement and vonder I viewed all over, 'till
A woman [I] spy'd at the door, who said, Vill
You vak[8] down here sir, there is everything nice,
You may eat a good dinner at a small price.   20

I turn'd down stairs and I'll pull of[f] my hat,
And immediately down by the whire I sat;
I lesh than five mienets she did brought me a plate,
Overflown vid black pratie, fite cabitch and meat.[9]

She'l tolt me in Leitrim she vas born'd and bread,
And that she would comodate me with a good bed,
I thank'd her and then straight to bed I did fly,
And there lay as snug as a pig in a stie.

My shides they had not long lay down on the bed,
Fen a regiment of varriors my body over-spread;   30
They kept such retreating and fighting all night,
T'as ten times more greater nor Aughrim's fight.[10]

---

5. This is probably a coinage based on the Ir. *fuadar*, haste or hurry. The word 'fuadar' and the verb 'footering' are both recorded in Hiberno-English. See Diarmaid Ó Muirithe, *A Dictionary of Anglo-Irish: words and phrases from Gaelic in the English of Ireland* (Dublin, 1996) and Bernard Share, *Slanguage* (Dublin, 1997).

6. i.e. the place the poet has been talking about, Dublin.

7. An unrecorded word, perhaps an antonym for 'delicious' or a mistake resulting from the poet's unfamiliarity with the English language.

8. walk.

9. i.e. overflowing with black potatoes, white cabbage and meat.

10. The reference is to the great battle of Aughrim in 1691.

Fen whirst I lay down oh! but she[11] vas hard,
For every fedder vood measure von yard;[12]
Ten thousand black troops my body overspread,
And had lik vor to tumble me out of the bed.

But de morning being come I jump'd up in a whrite,[13]
I dressed me and call'd for my bill upon sight;
My hostage[14] made answer as we vere from one town,
'And as your an acontance[15] I'll charge you but a crown.'   40

'Oh! that's beyond reason and conshence to boot!'
Then I and my hostage began to dispute;
She tolt me my wrangling vid soon have an end,
So streightway for shistance her dater did send.[16]

In lesh than three minuets how I was conwounded,
To whind myself then by a gard close surrounded;
I took them whor nearls nor peers ov the land,[17]
They vore drab coats vith fite cabes[18] and guns in their hands.

Says one 'My good fellow, come make no delay,
But pay your reckoning and march away;   50
For if you refuse for to pay her the whole,
By George you must shirtinly march to the gaol.'

'Pleash your honour, I'm a poor Conought-man
Before in my life I was never trepan;'[19]
But she svore by her jakers[20] she vood have her due,
So I paid her and then vent off to the review.

---

11. i.e. the bed. The Irish word for 'bed', *leaba*, is a feminine noun.
12. i.e. the feathers in the mattress were a yard long — not the small, soft downy feathers from the breast of the bird, but the large feathers from its back.
13. fright.
14. hostess. Another example of uncertain command of English.
15. i.e. as you are an acquaintance.
16. i.e. so straight away she sent her daughter to get assistance.
17. i.e. I took them for earls or peers of the land.
18. i.e. they wore yellowish-brown coats with white capes.
19. I was never tricked in my life before.
20. A softening of the oath 'By Jesus'; see Bernard Share, *Slanguage* (Dublin, 1977), p. 150.

I dived in to town like an eel in the mud,
Kept moving my limbs wholl as fast as I could;
To drive away sorrow I fishled a-pace,
Filst the nails in my brogu's and the flags join'd in base.[21]　　60

I whinding myself vas out of her reach
Whor the plash[22] of reviewing I went in search,
I still kept runing pursuing my whate,
'Till at lasht I derived[23] at the Whenix Park gate.

Fon[24] I entered the Park I whirst cast round my eyes,
And view'd all about me with strange surprize,
Such standing of Whiskey and Sheeben[25] vas there,
I thought on my shoul it vas sweet Leitrim whair.

I wholow'd the croud across ditch and hedge
Sometimes being up to my knees in the sledgs[26]　　70
Altho' being whatagu'd[27] I kept still on my heels,
'Till at last I deriv'd at the grand review wheelds.

But fen I came therc I vas whilled vide such vonder,
Their damnable guns did rattle like thunder,
And made such a nois by their rattling of drums,
I thougt that the end of the Vorld vas come.

Sich plenty of fiders[28] the most ov them did vore,
I'm sure they had turkeys and hens to galore[29]
And Reynard had dare at their roosts been to steal,
Whor great many more on their heads vore his tail.　　80

---

21. i.e. I whistled immediately, while the sound of the nails in my brogues (boots) on the flagstones made harmony.
22. place.
23. arrived. Another example of uncertain command of English.
24. when.
25. stands selling whiskey, and shebeens (Ir. *síbín*), tents or stalls for the sale of ale or liquor.
26. meaning unclear. Perhaps a mistake for 'sloughs'.
27. fatigued.
28. feathers. The Volunteers had splendid uniforms, often with large plumes or (if this writer is to be believed) fox's brushes fastened to their hats or helmets.
29. See Glossary.

They fir'd vith sich spirits and marshed up so tight,
I'm sure they're boys that Ireland ve'd white;[30]
I gave dem my blessing whor wearing the fleece,
Obtaining whree trade and proticting dere geese.[31]

The General gave orders whor closing the ranks,
At hearing of silch[32] I jumped in the flanks;
Fair von at my but made a ram of his gun,[33]
And bid me run home for my praties was dun.

'Dog you', says I, 'if you vear fear I know,[34]
But I would make you pay very well whor that blow';   90
At hearing of silch, in a passion he flew,
And a long carving knife[35] on my own self he drew.

I took to my heels full as fast as I coud,
And I never cry'd stop 'till I'll get in a vood,
Where being whatagued on my sides down I lay,
And fell fast asleep and slept there till next day.

My heart being represt[36] and my pockets being low,
I gader'd my sences to know fat I wood do;
My whine pair of brogues that cost me half-a-crown,
I solt whor tin-pence[37] and so quit the town.   100

Now I thank my good fortune that I got home,
And lives at more ease nor the King on his Throne,
To all whoolish whancies I now bid adieu,
And silsh ever I live[38] I will think of the raveiw.

---

30. i.e. that would fight for Ireland.
31. The rallying cry of the Volunteers was 'Free trade'; the countryman's own concerns show in his idea that a man fights to protect his own geese.
32. such; but here, and in l. 91, the word means 'that'.
33. i.e. for one rammed his gun against my backside.
34. The text reads 'he' and 'is', which seem to be errors and have been amended to 'I' and 'if'. The line could mean: 'If you were where I know' i.e. in my home area.
35. presumably a bayonet.
36. depressed — another example of incorrect English.
37. The poet sold his fine pair of brogues for tenpence.
38. i.e. as long as ever I live.

The Maiden's Resolution or an Answer to the Farmer's Son

Draw near each constant female, while I my ruine revealing,[1]
My grief's beyond concealing, for ever I'm undone;
As on my bed I leaned, of my darling's pain I dreamed,
My mind was then enflamed to love my Farmer's Son.

Venus now convey me to my love and don't deceive me,
Since Cupid has enslav'd me I'm in chains for evermore;
Grant me but my desire, it's all that I require,
For gold I don't admire, but a man I do adore.

My life runs so uneasy, nothing in life can please me,
Cupid strongly does tease me, his arrow pierc'd my breast;   10
By the gray light of the morning, I went to see my darling,
His person seem'd quite charming, tho' in a homely dress.

Blessed was the hour, I entered his sweet bower,
Bedeckt with fragrant flowers where silver streams do run;
And Sol's beams were shining with beauty most surprising,
All things were still delighting my country Farmer's Son.

Tho' my ambitious parents doth like for to make varience,[2]
Who said he was inferior to their great dignity;
Cupid has inspir'd me and Hyme[3] has desir'd me,
To hail[4] the wound I gave him with sweet chestity.   20

The Sailor Dear

Ye maidens pretty in town and City,
Pray hear with pity my mournful strain,
A Maid confounded in sorrow drowned,
And deeply wounded with grief and pain.

---

1. The metre, rhythm and assonantal rhyming patterns of this poem (and of the two which
   follow it) are those of the Irish *Ochtfhoclach*. See introduction.
2. trouble.
3. i.e. Hymen, the classical god of marriage.
4. i.e. 'heal', an Hiberno-English pronunciation.

'Tis for the sake of a lovely sailor,
I'm still bewailing, melting in tears,
Whilst other maidens are fondly playing,
I'm grieving for my Sailor Dear.

In dales and allies thro' shades and vallies
And all around each pleasant grove,   10
Roll'd in sweet flowers and rural bowers,
We've spent soft hours in mutual love;
But now my dear has crost the ocean,
And left his jewel residing here,
Cursed war's alarms deprived my arms,
Of my sweet charming Sailor dear.

Tho' he did leave me I don't blame him
Because my darling was forced away,
'Twas to save my fortune my greedy parents,
Contriv'd to have him sent to sea;   20
Five thousand Pounds left by my uncle,
Besides four Hundred Pounds a year,
'Tis for that reason they do disdain him,
As he's beneath them my Sailor dear.

May every vengeance be his[1] attendants,
That sent my jewel to plough the main,
For worldly treasure and my displeasure,
They'd forfeit all for the sake of gain.
Could I command the wealth of India,
And once my darling to appear,   30
I would resign the golden mines,
And in marriage join my Sailor dear.

---

1. i.e. their. This usage may reflect the fact that, in Irish, there is only one word, 'a', to represent the English possessive adjectives 'his', 'her' and 'their'.

The Coughing Old Man

Each female so pretty in country and city,
I pray you will pity a languishing maid,
That is daily vexed and nightly perplexed,
All by my old husband — I wish he were dead.
He's cross grain'd and crooked and doating[1] stupid,
And has no more sense than a young sucking calf,
Altho' he lies by me he ne'er can enjoy me,
For still when he is noodling[2] he is killed with the cough.

The very first night that he came to bed to me,
I longed for a trial at Venus's game,   10
But to my sad vexation and consternation,
His hautboy[3] was feeble & weak in the main.
For instead of pleasing he only kept teazing;
To him then I turned my back in a huff,
But still he did cry, 'twill do by-and-by,
A chusla se sthere![4] I am killed with the cough.

This doating old creature a remnant of nature,
His shins are so sharp as the edge of a knife,
His knees they are colder than snow on a mountain,
He stands more in need of a nurse than a wife;   20
I by him sit weeping whilst he lies a sleeping,
Like a hog in a sty he does grunt and puff,
A wheezing and harking both sneezing and farting,
And worse than all that he's killed with the cough.

His breath it does stink like asafœtadu,[5]
His blobbring and slobbring I can't bear,
For each night when I lie beside him,
He must have a spitting cup placed on his chair;
His nose and his chin are joined together,
His tawny old skin is yellow and tough,   30
Both trembling and shaking like one in the ague,
Still smothering and spitting and killed with the cough.

---

1. i.e. a man in his dotage.
2. = canoodling, 'indulging in caresses and fondling endearments' (*OED*).
3. oboe.
4. Ir. *A chuisle is a stór*, my pulse and my treasure. A common endearment in Irish.
5. A strongly garlic-flavoured gum used in medicine and in cooking.

For sake of cursed money my father has undone me,
By making me wed this doating old man,
Altho' some might shame me, what Maid can blame me,
To crown him with horns[6] as soon as I can;
What signifies treasure without any pleasure,
I'm young and would have enjoyed enough,
And not to be tied to a gouty old fellow,
That's withered and worn and killed with the cough.   40

Since fortune to me has proved so cruel,
In brief my intention to you I'll relate.
If he does not alter and fare the better,
No longer on him I mean to wait.
I'll have a look out for some rousing young fellow,
That's able to give me some reason to laugh;
If such I can find than I'll swap my old cuckold,
And pitch to the vengeance himself and his cough.

A Drop of Dram[1]

Says Moll Drew to Widney, my husband's a sad man,
He ne'er allows me to take a drop of dram,
And when that I do get it, 'tis little that I take,
And then it's all for the company's sake,
With your tittle tattle, prittle prattle, o'er a cup of tea,
I cannot abide such nonsense I say;
Come o'er across to Crowe's, he is a civil man,
And has got a very private place to take a drop of dram.

Says Widney to Moll Drew, my husband's a sad lout,
For it's once in the month that we have a merry bout,   10
I'd die of the hips[2] if I didn't get a sup,
For Moll you know, a drop is good, to keep the spirits up,

---

6. i.e. to be unfaithful to him, to make him a cuckold.

1. A small measure of liquor — but the word is used here to mean the liquor (whiskey) itself.

2. = hyp or hyps, a common eighteenth-century term for low spirits, from the word 'hypocondria'.

Your Cyder and your Toddy,[3] and your smoking slops of ale,
I cannot quit, nor will I quit, until I drink my fill,
For whilst I have got a bowl to pledge, a poringer[4] or pan,
I'll comfort my sick stomach with a little drop of dram.

When Moll and I have drunk enough, we then call in poor Luke,
Then Moll and he and I do drink, untill we all puke,
All that we have for it, is to stretch upon a sod,
But not until upon my word we finish e'ery drop,   20
Craw sick[5] Luke he wakens, and he call for mugs of ale,
Moll or I dont relish it, it looks so weak and pale,
I wou'd not give a needle for't, a devil or a dam,
The devil a thing cares Moll or I, but for a drop of dram.

It was about last hollintide,[6] that poor Moll Drew fell sick,
She sent for Doctor R——, who swore her pulse was quick,
He order'd her a two-milk whey, and plenty of tezan,[7]
And yet I heard Peg Whalen say that Noll's a skilful man:
Poor Moll grew worse and worse, till the Doctor gave her up,
But I who knew my neighbours way brought in the old sup,   30
Your pills and your bolus's,[8] or doctor's but a sham,
The devil a thing cares Moll, Luke or me but for a good dram.

The parson of the parish says that drinking is a sin,
But Joe his clerk the night before swore he had a full bowl in;
Our husbands and our neighbours scold, and says our names are up,
God knows the parish old and young, begrudges us a sup,
But let them scold and rave away and bluster as they will,
We will not quit nor cannot quit untill we drink our fill,
For Moll and Luke are flatly of opinion as one,
That it's neither sin nor shame for to take a drop of dram.   40

3. A drink of whiskey mixed with hot water and sugar.
4. A small basin (often belonging to a child) from which porridge, soup or soft food is eaten.
5. i.e. sick in his stomach.
6. = Hollantide, the time of All-Hallows, 31 October, now generally celebrated as Hallowe'en.
7. Fr. *tisane*, an infusion of herbs.
8. large tablets or pills.

Corporal Casey

When I was at home, I was merry and frisky,
My dad kept a pig, and my mother sold whiskey,
My uncle was rich, but would never be easy,
'Till I was inlisted by Corporal Casey:
    Oh! Rub a dub, row de dow, Corporal Casey,
    Rub a dub, row de dow, Corporal Casey,
My dear little Sheelah I thought would run crazy,
Oh! when I trudg'd away with tough Corporal Casey.

I march'd from Kilkenny, and as I was thinking,
On Sheelah, my heart in my bosom was sinking;   10
But soon I was forc'd to look fresh as a daisy,
For fear of a drubbing[1] from Corporal Casey.
    Oh! rub a dub, row de dow, Corporal Casey
    Rub a dub, row de dow, Corporal Casey!
The devil go with him, I ne'er could be easy,
He stuck in my skirts so, ould Corporal Casey.

We went into battle, I took the blows fairly
That fell on my pate,[2] but he bother'd me rarely:
And who should the first be that dropt? — Why an't please ye,[3]
It was my good friend, honest Corporal Casey.   20
    Oh! rub a dub, row de dow, Corporal Casey,
    Rub a dub, row de dow, Corporal Casey!
Thinks I, you are quiet, and I shall be easy;
So eight years I fought without Corporal Casey.

1. beating.
2. head.
3. = why, and may it please you! a colloquial expression equivalent to 'And would you believe it?'

Darby O'Gallagher, or the Answer to Morgan Rattler

There are many eighteenth-century responses to 'Morgan Rattler', a well-known bawdy song about a virile weaver. This one, like the songs 'Manus M'Allister' and 'Paddy O'Slattery' has, until now, successfully evaded all anthologists except John Wardroper. (See his *Lovers, Rakes and Rogues: Amatory, Merry and Bawdy Verse from 1580 to 1830* (London, 1995), p. 171 and p. 342.) This version of the text is taken from a chapbook printed by W. Goggin in Limerick in about 1785.

> Great boasting of late we have heard of the fates,[1]
> Of the comical rake called Morgan Rattler,
> But now we have found one will cut him down
> Well known by the name of young Darby O'Gallagher.
>
> He is a brisk blade and a black-smith by trade,
> Well known by the ladies to be a gay frolicker;
> As he passes by the ladies replies,
> There goes the bold hammerman Darby O'Gallagher.
>
> His music excels all carillon bells,[2]
> His stroke's more sweet than the warbling chorister.   10
> No flute or guitar can ever compare
> To the musical hammer of Darby O'Gallagher.
>
> At Mullingar fair young Dermot was there,
> With Nancy Adair that well noted smaliker;[3]
> Her gown she did pledge for the triangle wedge,
> That was drove by the sledge of Darby O'Gallagher.
>
> If you would see him dandle that yellow sledge handle,
> As stiff as the leg of a stool in a wallet,[4] sir,
> Each maid with surprize does twinkle their eyes,
> At the wonderful size of his D. O'Gallagher.   20

1. i.e. feats.
2. This stanza comes from the version of the text printed by Wardroper (p. 171).
3. frolicker. Cf. Ir. *smalcaire*, a beater, a boxer, a stout, strong man.
4. A bag for carrying clothes.

His excellent musick is good for the tisick,[5]
It works the fair maids like a dose of jallip,[6]
No Doctor of skill can cure it so well,
As the two smacking hammers of Darby O'Gallagher.

A maid most rare with a languishing air,
Whose skin was fair and locks were black sir,
She being distrest did beg the request
Of a blast of the bellows from D. O'Gallagher.

So now to conclude girls don't think it rude
For singing the praise of this sporting frolicker;   30
Now Morgan may sleep, he's the boy that can sweep
Twelve shillings away with his Darby O'Gallagher.[7]

The New Dhooraling[1]

You maidens pretty attend this ditty
And 'twill make you smile,
'Tis of a rattling roving blade
That's well beloved by each fair maid,
The sporting girls take great delight
In his sweet company day and night.
On his bagpipes he plays them a tuneful spring,
While he muffles the tune on his Dhooraling.

Too long the Doodeen[2] was the toast
Altho' no more than an empty boast,   10
Sweet Dhoora now is the pleasing toy
Diverts the girls tho' ever so coy,
The Piper's fees they never dispute
When he plays them a lilt on his German flute,
Then away with M'Teague and his Doodeen Pin
And left[3] room for M'Lean and his Dhooraling.

---

5. phthisic: consumption or a wasting disease of the lungs.
6. jalap: a purgative drug.
7. As Wardroper notes (p. 172), twelve shilling coins measured twelve inches when laid beside each other.

---

1. An unrecorded word; probably a diminutive based on the Ir. *dúr*, hard or stiff, so meaning 'a little, stiff thing'.
2. cf. Ir. *dúidín*, a short-stemmed clay pipe. The word is the diminutive of *dúid*, a stumpy object or protuberant part. See also Share, *Slanguage* (Dublin, 1977), p. 81.
3. i.e. make room for.

In Patron,[4] Market, Town or Fair,
The girls do treat him every where,
His chanter[5] is of the largest size,
And for it they'd freely part their eyes, 20
When to M'Lean they do repair,
For money or liquor they never spare,
The price of the yarn they to him bring
For a musical lilt on his Dhooraling.

Of all other music that ever was known,
They give the degree to the Piper's drone,[6]
With a blast of his bellows he fills the bag,
Then his triangle Chanter begins to wag,
Each bar on the Gamot[7] he plays so true,
        [line missing],
No harpsichord, fiddle or tuneful spring 30
Can equal M'Lean and his Dhooraling.

A buxom widow below Coleraine[8]
Heard several talk of young Dan M'Lean
Resolved she was no time to waste
But sent for the Piper to come in haste.
He squeezed up his pipes without delay,
With his bags and his drones he leathered away,
Five guineas in gold and a diamond ring
She gave for a trust[9] of his Dhooraling.

He met an old woman in Portadown,[10] 40
Who had not a tooth in her jaw but one,
Tho' she mumbled her meat with a horn spoon,
Yet this merry going heiffer she liked the tune,
Altho decripid, blind and lame
She longed for a touch of the sporting game,
Her pipe and tobacco away she did fling,
And beat time with her crutch to his Dhooraling.

---

4. On Patron or Pattern Day, large numbers of people would attend masses in honour of the patron saint of a church, after which there would be revelry.
5. The chanter is the finger-pipe of a bagpipe, on which the tune is played.
6. The bass pipe of a bagpipe.
7. gamut: i.e. each bar on the musical scale.
8. A town in County Derry.
9. i.e. thrust.
10. A town in County Armagh.

One night dancing at a ball,
A youthful Lady chanced to fall,
Young Dan to her assistance went   50
Which filled this fair one with content,
She slipped him into a private room,
Where he blew up his bags like an air balloon,
In raptures round him she did cling,
Whilst he played her the humours of Dhooraling.

But least[11] I should detain you long
I'll here conclude my merry song.
In hopes I have offended none
By praising of the Piper's drone,
The prudent maids that seem so shy   60
Are willing the game to try,
And when alone they'll merrily sing
Concerning the fate of Dhooraling.

Hush Cat from under the Table

You jolly young rake who loves for to freak
To sport and play with the girls so pretty,
Attend to my tale, while I shall reveal,
A humourous sonnet both pleasant and witty;
I happen'd of late a ramble did take,
And met with a maid, upon the highway sir,
I address'd her so sly, she soon did comply,
To lye in my arms until break of day sir.
    'Hush', she did cry 'My Mammy's hard by,
    Come with me to night, you shall have good quarters;   10
    Lye down very snug, like a bug in a rug,
    And I will lye by you to tie up my garters.'

To Newry[1] I came along with my dame,
She went to a lane and I follow'd after,
The old woman sure she run to the door
While I on the floor was kissing her daughter:

---

11. lest.

---

1. A town in County Down.

The cat run about, and made such a rout
While she in a pout, with a stick then did storm her,
Cups and Saucers were broke, I laugh'd at the joak,
While the old woman groap'd for puss in the corner.   20
    Hush cat come out in a crack,
    Hush cat from under the table;
    Hush cat I smiled at that,
    If you had been there you'd laugh while you're able.

At dawning of day I slipped away,
Without any delay I set to the road sir;
To Lurgan[2] I came, and met with a dame,
I asked her name, and place of abode sir,
I had excellent room to wave[3] in her loom,
A girl in full bloom, her name it was Nancy.   30
I pleas'[d] her so well that e'er long she did swell,
For I was the lad that cou'd tickle her fancy.
    When three quarters[4] were gone, she had a young son
    Her mother cry'd 'Hush a ba', rocking the cradle!
    Hush cheep cat, at every whack,
    That eat the child's pap in under the table.

Away to Belfast I came at the last,
And there I did court my old landlady's daughter,
A comely young Girl and fit for an Earl,
So trim and so plump made my teeth to water,   40
She soon did comply and never seem'd shy,
'Saying f[or]ty good pounds there is left me to marry;
Now you are the lad that has my maiden head,
I'll sure be a mother if I don't miscarry.'
    Hush puss come out of the bush,
    Her mother did scold, [ ]od[5] brawl'd while able,
    And ever since that she never cry'd stop,
    But whacking the cat from under the table.

2. A town in County Armagh.
3. i.e. weave.
4. i.e. nine months.
5. illegible.

While she was in this pout, we then slipped out,
To a beer house hard by where a room we did call for,   50
We there took our sport and had no resort;
Shortly the old woman she miss'd her daughter,
Then out she did run, in her smock to us come,
In such a fret that I laughed while able,
To see the rare fun, while the girl did run,
And cunningly slipped in under the table.

   Hush cat get into the sack,
   Hush my poor pussy, lye still while you're able,
   I thought it no crime to wait for my time,
   To slip her poor kitten from under the table.   60

Her portion[6] I got and it was my lot,
Next day to be married to fair lovely Nancy,
A house and good room she furnished soon,
And three excellent looms which pleased my fancy,
Her time being come she had a brave son,
And still at the fun we laugh while we're able,
But it was my lot a good fortune I got,
By hushing the cat from under the table.

   Hush cat be merry and fat,
   You shall have milk while to take it you'er able,   70
   We laugh at the frolick without spleen or cholick
   At hushing the cat from under the table.

---

6. marriage portion, dowry.

ANONYMOUS VERSE FROM NEWSPAPERS AND BOOKS OF THE 1780s

Description of a Country Assizes

Ye heav'nly nymphs, Æonian maids,[1] descend,
Inspire my lays, your kind assistance lend,
Whilst I, your humble bard, in flowing strains,
Of *Courts* of *Justice* sing, and lawyer's gains;
How long-rob'd judges thro' the country ride,
Whilst country lobbies grace the coach's side:
What preparation's made in ev'ry town;
How all's got ready 'gainst *My Lord* comes down.[2]
Their houses whitewash'd and well scour'd their floors,
Their windows brighten'd, and well swept their doors;   10
Each dunghill, too, is far remov'd with care;
No noisome smells now taint the ambient[3] air.

The sheriff next collects his motly crew,
Some glare in scarlet, some in brown or blue:
With wand in hand, and all his friends around,
He meets the judges at the county's bound.[4]
Fierce, neighing coursers scamper o'er the plain,
And, like a snow-ball, swells the' unpolish'd train.
Some days before, as heralds to a court,
The stragg'ling pedlars to the town resort: 20
Hackney attornies,[5] by degrees, walk in,
And thus give notice of th'approaching din.

At length arrives the cavalcade: and slow,
In marshall'd order rang'd, to court they go.
Four halberd-men,[6] like knaves in packs of cards,
March on before, and some each passage guards.
The thrilling trumpet thro' the streets resounds,
And ev'ry female heart with joy rebounds.

1. Either 'Ionian', i.e. from a part of Greece celebrated for the genius of its inhabitants, or 'Æonian', meaning the daughters of Æon, the first woman, according to Greek mythology; or, perhaps, just a loose reference to the Muses who inspire poetry.
2. i.e. how all is got ready for my Lord's arrival (from Dublin).
3. surrounding.
4. See above p. 241 for a description of a sheriff's meeting with assize judges.
5. i.e. lawyers who hang around outside the court waiting to be hired by defendants.
6. Men carrying halberds, long spear-like weapons which also incorporate a battle-axe.

Crouds throng on crouds, and round the judges press,
'Squires in shoals advance, — can country 'squires do less?   30
All pay their homage; then salute their friends,
And news to learn, each eagerly attends.
Some by the hand their old acquaintance shake,
Whilst others kiss and slobber, e'er they speak:
For shame, *Hibernians*! give this custom o'er;
Men kissing men, I've seldom seen before:
Kisses for girls should be reserved alone,
Who often twenty will return for one.

A troop of lawyers now the circle grace,
With plodding[7] heads, and consequential face: 40
Well powder'd perukes[8] hide their shallow crowns,
The rest's conceal'd beneath their threadbare gowns;
Hands ever open to receive their fees,
A cause to varnish, or a purse to squeeze.
A heap of pettifoggers[9] next appears;
To set good folk together by the ears
Their sole delight: a wretched, shameless crew,
As ever deed, or bills or answers drew....

The clod-pate[10] squire, who scarcely knows to read,
With joy elate, now mounts his ill-broke steed;   50
Flies to the town to shew his wond'rous parts,
Swears, drinks, and games, with puppies, prigs, and smarts.[11]
A fierce-cock'd hat, with gold and silver lace,
And well-dress'd bob,[12] sets off each pimping face.

At night, to crouded card-rooms they repair,
Some to be seen, whilst others round them stare;
Brag, whist, or quadrille,[13] now their hands employ,
And the sly coquet cheats the country boy,
Laughs in his face, and wins his little hoard,
His brain and pocket equally well stor'd.   60

7. stolid, monotonous — an epithet transferred from the lawyers to their heads.
8. wigs.
9. Legal practitioners of inferior status, those who deal with petty cases in minor courts.
10. thick-headed, stupid.
11. Those who affect smartness in dress or behaviour.
12. A knot of hair.
13. Three fashionable card games.

Next night the assembly attracts them all,
And each fond swain doth on his partner call,
Oft on the fair-one casts his sheepish eye,
Talks much of love, and swears for her he'd die:
She, silly fool, his homage glad receives,
His nonsense swallows, and each word believes.
Both sexes now with equal joy advance,
And fly thro' th'ringlets of the mazy dance,
Whilst wretched fidlers, wretched music brings
From shocking instruments, and ill-tun'd strings.   70
In giddy whirls some hop and skip about,
And call it dancing, tho' they're always out; ...

Mean while the bus'ness of the court goes on;
Some gain their suit, some lose, and are undone.
Each *nisi-prius*[14] try'd with care and cost;
Gain, lose, who will, —— the lawyers get the most.
With noise and clamour they expound the laws,
And well-pack'd juries finish ev'ry cause.
Poor rogues are punish'd, rich ones seldom try'd,
Beneath the golden bribe each fault they hide.   80
The smooth-tongu'd barrister each point explains,
That black is white, that right is wrong maintains:
Quirks, turns, and quibbles, with many loopholes made,
O'erthrow all systems, and support the trade.

Feasts, now, and treats are ev'ry where prepar'd,
At which no cost in meat or wine is spar'd.
Three days in drink and wrangling thus they spend,
The fourth's bright sun sees all contentions end.
Judges, councils, attorneys, now depart;
Peace, ease, and rest's restor'd to ev'ry heart.   90
Silence and dirt their former seats attain,
Men turn to slovens, women grow sluts again;
Dunghills, once more, in heaps around us rise,
And joyful pigs! are loosen'd from their styes.

14. Legal actions tried by the judges in the assize court.

The Agent's Downfall: a new ballad[1]

Let us sing of a sporting, brave swaggering blade,
With pistols, bright cuteau,[2] and fine shewy parade:
His address and his voice were as milky and mild,
As were the old Serpent's, when poor Eve he beguil'd.

Derry down,[3] *&c.*

Though proud, he is humble enough to superiors,
And to carry a point, he'd kiss their p———rs:
Once angry his spirit's too high to forgive,
So pray always beware of the stone in his sleeve.

His delight lies in cards, horses, hounds and in dice,   10
And our hero would knock a man down in a trice,
To Bacchus and Venus, no subject more loyal;
Nor you or I, Sir, to the Family Royal.

But his temper in truth was not always alike,
A great man he'd flatter, when a poor man he'd strike.
None dare to provoke him, for if in a fury,
He'd flog, then indict them before the grand jury.

A great agent he was, and a justice of peace,
The tenant's all trembl'd when they saw his police,[4]
With drivers and bailiffs, and warrants all ready,   20
In hunting down game, he was 'Steady, boys, steady'.

For many a year this Tartar[5] had flourish'd,
Both tenants, and all who offended him punish'd.
At balls and at races, he was fine as a jay;
Though his feathers were borrow'd, he figur'd away.[6]

---

1. Land agents were almost universally hated in eighteenth-century Ireland, and it is unusual to come across a poem which shows any sympathy for the plight of an agent whose luck has run out.
2. Fr. *couteau*, knife; here meaning a sword.
3. The song is sung to a well-known tune, 'Derry Down', and it is the chorus from that song which is to be inserted here.
4. The last word in this line is illegible in the original, and the word 'police' is conjectural.
5. The Tartars of central Asia were renowned as particularly fierce warriors.
6. i.e. cut a fine figure.

So old Æsop[7] assures us, the carrion crow,
Once in feathers he plunder'd, dress'd nice as a beau,
Till vex'd at the greedy, conceited, bold vermin,
The birds who were owners, to strip him determine.

Alas! 'tis too true, that our great brigadier,   30
Will just in the trim of the scald[8] crow appear.
His best feather is pluck'd, he's steward no longer,
In spite of his claws, he's o'ermatched with a stronger.

And what's worst of all, a sad reck'ning remains,
For to shame our poor scald crow, and puzzle his brains,
The two eagles deputed to pluck him, have found
All his tricks and his pranks, his small wits to confound.

Another misfortune, although he can write,
No steward alive can worse reck'ning indite.[9]
To move pity then, what can this poor fellow say,   40
But forgive me, my Lord, or I must run away.

No estate have I bought, nor no friends have I made,
Nor of Mammon[10] unrighteous, sav'd cash in my trade.
Drivers[11] fees and discounts, I have squeez'd to be sure,
But they went as they came; for what's past there's no cure.

My play-purse now is weak, which before never fail'd;
For while Tom brought the rents in, my grandeur prevail'd.
Now adieu to the Curragh, to Daly's,[12] and all
Jocky clubs and bye-matches, and masquerade ball.

So which way I turn me; how shall I decide?   50
For I cannot escape a deep wound to my pride.
I know this is truth, by thousands attested,
The great hold me cheap, by the poor I'm detested.

---

7. Originally a slave, the Greek writer Æsop became famous for his fables.
8. i.e. in the same condition as a scalded crow.
9. i.e. the agent is not good at keeping accounts.
10. The god of money.
11. 'Drivers' here may be overseers of gangs of workmen.
12. The most famous racetrack in Ireland and the most notorious gaming-club in Dublin.

How the tenants and rogues of K———ss will frout[13] me,
Like a cur with a bone to's tail, they will scout me;[14]
They will spurn at my warrants, they will sneer at my frown,
Since they beat me before, they'll now trample me down.

But to try one push more, I'll put on a bold face,
And pretend that I feel neither loss nor disgrace.
To th'assizes once more I will stoutly repair,   60
And if things there don't please me, I'll bully and swear.

If I find matters come to the worst, I can't fail,
To die like a man, and to keep out of a gaol,
I'll apply to my pistol, or else buy a rope,
So end all my fears in this forlorn hope.

Take a Cobler's advice,[15] all ye agents so bold,
While such stations of pow'r from great men ye hold,
Be honest, have pity, be quiet and humble,
You'll meet with compassion if ever you stumble.

Description of an Unfortunate Woman of the Town

'Twas at that Time when Letchers seek the Park,
Dreading the Light, because their Deeds are dark
I went to Mortimer, poor Girl! — so high,
I found her parlour nearest to the Sky!
Oh! what a wretched Falling-off is here,
From her the Brilliant, her the Debonair!
She, whom a Monarch might have wished to court,
Though living dead; alive without Support;
On whom a Levée[1] once of Lovers hung,
Sipping, like Bees, the Honey of her Tongue;   10

---

13. annoy. It is impossible to identify K——ss with certainty.
14. i.e. they will make sport of me as if I were a dog with a bone tied to its tail.
15. The meaning of this phrase is unclear, but it probably refers to the seventeenth-century
    'cobbler's law', which was that 'he that takes money must pay the shot' or to the well-
    known proverb that 'the cobbler should stick to his last', i.e. one should mind one's own
    business. The latter saying is first found in Pliny's *Natural History*, xxxv, 85.

1. i.e. a whole room full of fashionable young men.

Alas! here pinch'd with all the Pains of Need;
Cast from the Garden like a noxious Weed;
The Crimson Cov'ring, and the downy Bed,
Where oft thy lovely Limbs were lewdly spread,
Are chang'd to wretched Straw upon the Floor;
The Casement[2] broke, the Room without a Door;
Dead Flies, dead Spiders, fill the wretched Haunt,
Sad, sorry Emblems of the House of Want.
No brilliant Equipage,[3] no Tea-cups charm;
A Tin-pot full, without a Fire to warm;   20
A broken Jordan,[4] and a three-legg'd Chair,
A Bottle shew'd a Candle had burnt there;
The broken Bellows, like their Mistress kind,
By Time and Use had almost lost their Wind.
Thus sat the fallen Fair, with comely Mien,
Amidst her Penury — her Raiment clean:
Shock'd at a Visit from a Friend, she tries
To hide the melting Rhet'ric of her Eyes,
Which stole adown her Cheeks, still smooth, still fair,
And wiped them with the Tresses of her Hair;   30
(The first repenting Sign in Eve of Grace)
Which, though disorder'd, deck'd her pretty Face.
She gaily bred,[5] completed[6] to the Joy
Of am'rous Appe[ar]ence,[7] to play, to toy,
To sing, to lisp, to troll the Tongue, to dress,
And roll the Eye of Love with sure Success —
O lovely Mortimer! ignobly lost!
Once, 'midst the fairest Fair, the fairest Toast.[8]

---

2. window.
3. A carriage with servants or, perhaps, simply clothing and surroundings.
4. chamber-pot.
5. i.e. smartly bred, bred in good society.
6. educated, brought up.
7. Conjectural reading because of damage to the text.
8. A noted beauty whose health is drunk in toasts.

The Lord Mayor's Ball[1]

All you who would wish to be merry,
    Take a trip to the Lord Mayor's ball;
Then jigg it until you are weary,
    Being fellows at foot-ball all.
        Sing natherum doodle, nagetty tragedy mum,
        my ditherum doodle, fidgetty nigetty mum.

Here ev'ry one jostles his neighbour,
    And strives to preserve his own toes;
He hops it without any labour,
    Ask with whom, then nobody knows.   10
        Sing natherum doodle, &c.

Such circles, such squares, and such bounces,[2]
    Would even laid Euclid astray;[3]
Such jostles, such shoves, and such pounces,
    Each striving to make out his way.
        Sing natherum doodle, &c.

Miss jiggs it from corner to corner,
    She's press'd on from shoulder to flank;
Mamma must take[4] to adorn her,
    To enter her in this grand rank.   20
        Sing natherum doodle, &c.

The mamma now views her fair daughter,
    And sees her retreat and advance;
The more she can hobble and totter,
    More graces she adds to the dance.
        Sing natherum doodle, &c.

---

1. Many visitors to eighteenth-century Dublin commented on its varied and vigorous social life. Balls, levées and other fashionable events took place regularly at Dublin Castle. However, the balls which took place under the patronage of the Lord Mayor of Dublin seem to have been less exclusive.
2. leapings.
3. i.e. even the famous geometrician Euclid would not be able to recognise as squares or circles the patterns in which people are dancing.
4. devote herself.

Dear Ona[5] will trip it together,
   Tho' Swift may condemn our splish splash;
We'll keep from our skins the cold weather,
   From couple to couple we'll dash.   30
     Sing natherum doodle, &c.

The Weaver aside lays his shuttle,
   Who wishes to shake a loose leg;
And why not, he's gay and he's subtle,
   'Tis better jog her than go beg.
     Sing natherum doodle, &c.

The Council Men flock here like bum-bees,
   The Freemen like suds in a cinque;
The Beadles like mites in cream cheese,
   The Warkawks with these you may think.[6]   40
     Sing natherum doodle, &c.

Should you come off free from contusion,[7]
   Kind fortune must be at your call;
All you who admire confusion,
   Be sure trip to the Lord Mayor's ball.
     Sing natherum doodle, &c.

5. The Irish proper name Úna. The reference in the next line is to a well-known quatrain in Swift's version of 'O'Rourke's Feast': 'The Floor is all wet // With Leaps and with Jumps, // While the Water and Sweat // Splish splash in their Pumps' (pumps = light dancing shoes).

6. i.e. 'The members of the common council (the governing body of the Dublin Corporation) flock here like humble-bees, and the freemen of the city (i.e. those who had voting rights) are like the foam or soap-suds in a sink; the beadles (town-criers and minor parish officials) are as numerous as cheese-mites in cream cheese and, as you would expect, there are also young dandies.' The word 'Warkawk' is probably a composite one incorporating the names 'Mohawk' and 'Hawkabite' — two of the Indian tribes after which the more dissolute young aristocrats of the day called their clubs and associations.

7. bruising.

A New Song[1]

A set of young bloods sallied out t'other night,
 Galloping dreary dun,
A set of young bloods sallied out t'other night,
All Colonels and Captains, and men of great might.
 With their haily, gaily, gamborely
 Gigling, nigling, galloping, galloway,
 Draggle tail dreary dun.

From the Barracks of Dublin they stagger'd away,
Ripe ranting and roaring adown Ormond-quay.
 With their mad haily gamborely, etc.   10

Like Heroes pot valiant they all had agreed,
To act in the city some praise-worthy deed.
 With their stout haily, gamborely, etc.

Just now in a Shop a fair Dame they espied,
'Here's game', they all swore and into it hied.
 With their hot haily, gamborely, etc.

Stout, clever and clean, they assaulted the Fair,
They frowzled and towzl'd, and rumpled her hair.
 With their damn'd haily, gamborely, etc.

Her husband in haste he came now to her aid,   20
For though they were seven he was not afraid.
 Of their haily, gamborely, etc.

But when on his neck a black stock they espied,
The rascal's a Volunteer, surely, they cried.[2]
 With a damn'd haily, gamborely, etc.

---

1. Almost all accounts of late eighteenth-century Dublin comment on the lawlessness of the city and blame gangs of young aristocrats, often English army officers stationed in Dublin barracks, for at least some of the trouble.

2. From the mid-1770s, British troops were withrawn from Ireland to fight in the American War of Independence. This laid Ireland open to the threat of invasion by France and Spain, and Irish protestants soon formed themselves into armed volunteer corps to protect their property. The Volunteers were soon strong enough to demand free trade and other concessions from the Westminster parliament. Volunteers wore distinctive uniforms when on parade, and black stocks around their necks when not in uniform. There was, from time to time, local tension between these Irish volunteers and officers of the British army in Ireland, whose behaviour could be loutish.

It is so, cries the boldest, and up to him goes,
I'll see how he looks when I've hold of his nose.
  With his haily, gaily, gamborely, etc.

But so it fell out, as 'twill quickly appear,
Our hero had got the wrong sow by the ear,   30
  With his haily, gaily, gamborely, etc.

'Are you there', says the VOL. as he gave him a bang,
Which together knock'd two of their heads with a twang,
  Of his strong haily, gamborely, etc.

Then out flew their swords, and they curst and they swore,
They'd have full revenge on this son of a whore.
  For his damn'd haily, gamborely, etc.

But now to his aid a brave youth did appear,
Soon they were join'd by a stout Volunteer.
  With his haily, gaily, gamborely, etc.   40

And quickly the shop it was cleared of the rout,
For Colonels and Captains were all tumbled out.
  With their poor haily, gamborely, etc.

'O Gentlemen dear, our lives do but spare,
I'm a Lord of Great Britain, old Harrington's heir,'[3]
  With my haily, gaily etc.

Our heroes were now turn'd o'er to the mob,
Where with stones they got wherrits and raps on the nob,[4]
  With their sad haily, gamborely, etc.

---

3. The young man pleading for his life is Charles, Viscount Petersham (1753-1829), eldest son of William, second earl of Harrington, and grandson of William Stanhope, first earl of Harrington, who had been lord lieutenant of Ireland 1746-51. Viscount Petersham succeeded to the earldom in 1779 and had a distinguished career in the British army.
4. i.e. gave them sharp blows and raps on the head.

Advertisement Extraordinary[1]

Come, ye lads of elegance and spirit,
Seek you nymphs of beauty, wit, and merit;
I'm the mart that such in taste can furnish,
With worth innate, and well as outside burnish:
Tho' various charms your different fancies ask,
To please you all I'll find an easy task;
My store's so rich, of which observe these samples,
That well may serve as patterns, not examples:
Let him who swells with self-important pride,
Deriv'd from birth, or wealth, or star on side,   10
From W–ng——d learn such folly to correct,
Who's rightly taught that nought can claim respect,
But mental virtues, or polite address,
How large a share of each doth she possess?
If spleen annoys, or langour 'press your mind,
With sprightly E–ll–s quick relief you'll find;
Or, does your taste on striking objects dwell,
'Tis I can shew a brilliant proper B–lle.
Is there a youth of heart inform'd to feel,
At Cr–mpt–n's strains? tho' obdurate as steel,   20
He'd quickly melt, and new sensations know,
Her song wou'd make his frozen passions glow:
But who, amidst his gay pursuits, wou'd seek,
A maid that's modest, curteous, fair and meek?
If e're he bends his ear to reason's voice,
On Sk–rr–tt sure, he'll rest his happy choice;

1. This poem is more complex than it seems. Eighteenth-century Dublin was famous for its prostitutes (see *The Memoirs of Mrs Leeson, Madam, 1727-97* ed. Mary Lyons, Dublin, 1995) and, at first sight, this poem seems to be a witty advertisement for the ladies who worked in William Street (now South William Street). However, none of the girls named in this poem — Wingfield, Ellis, Bell, Crampton or Skerritt — is named in Mrs Leeson's *Memoirs* and a search of the Dublin street directories of the period reveals citizens called Wingfield, Bell, Crampton and Skerritt carying on legitimate business, or residing, in William Street. Wingfield was the family name of Lord Powerscourt who built a magnificent mansion in William Street in 1771, a dentist called John Crampton was practising at 16 William Street in the 1780s, and Sir Thomas Bell, physician and practitioner in midwifery lived at No. 13. Joseph Skerritt (a very uncommon name in Dublin), an attorney, also lived in the street. Other residents included a bishop and at least two members of the Irish parliament, so it seems an unlikely location for the activities advertised. A close reading of the poem shows links between the proper names and the activities of the respectable citizens — the connection of Wingfield with birth, wealth, and 'star on side', for instance. It seems fair to conclude that, behind this address to young men of elegance and spirit, is a complex joke the point of which is now lost.

Whose well-form'd mind a sure resource wou'd prove,
To soften care, and anxious thought remove:
What native elegance her form displays!
What varying graces all her movements sways! —   30
None better knows domestic cares to mind,
Nor none to move in circles more refin'd;
'Tis few like her, with blooming youth can blend ⎫
Those virtues that maturer years attend,   ⎬
And sure must charm, as parent, wife, or friend: ⎭
But now, methinks the Lads impatient say,
Who's he that thus to bless can guide our way;
I grant that you shou'd know your chap, 'tis meet,
Then at your service, Sirs, I'm
                        WILLIAM-STREET.   40

Garry Own Naugh Glora
or The Limerick Rakes[1]

You jolly jovial sporting blades,
    Bacus' son[2] be ne'er dismay'd,
Drink and sing and lend your aid,
    Help me with your Chorus.
Whilst seated round a flowing bowl,
    Toast a health without controul,
I mean to every jovial soul,
    In Garry own naugh Glora.

To mirth and sport they all attain,
    The Country round do sound their fame;   10
For actions that are so glorious,[3]
No honest heart we do offend,
    We'd venture life to save a friend,
Our money freely we do spend,
    In Garry own a Glora.

---

1. Garryowen, now a district of Limerick city, was common land in the eighteenth century.
   Garry Own Naugh Glora = Ir. *Garraí Eoghain na Glóire*, glorious Garryowen. This song
   is widely known, but in the later, more polished version, collected by Crofton Croker
   (*Popular Songs of Ireland*, pp. 236-37). This text dates from 1785.
2. son(s) of Bacchus, god of wine.
3. There is a line missing in this stanza, and in stanzas 3 and 7.

417

If by our King we'er call'd to sea,
   We'er ne'er dismay'd but post away,
And always prove victorious;
We're sprightly boys, stout hearts of fame,
   We're known all over France and Spain   20
Where e'ere we go, they dread the name,
   Of Garry own naugh Glora.[4]

Crusing, Boozing, raking, paying,
   Music for us sweetly playing,
Thro' the streets at night serenading,
   Seeing who dare oppose us,
The Mayors and Sheriffs we make run,
   We beat the Constables and Bums,[5]
We are the boys to shew them fun,
   In Garry own na Glora.   30

We break windows and kip[6] doors,
   We beat the bullies, bawds and whores,
We pay the Doctors for the cures,
   And teized[7] by pills and bolus.
Instead of Spa,[8] we drink Ale,
   And pay the reckoning on the nail,
For debt we're never sent to Jail,
   From Garry own naugh Glora.

Singing, drinking, bucking, fighting,
   Thro' the streets with cudgels rioting,   40
Breaking Limerick lamps if lighting,[9]
   And tearing all before us;
Thus we pass our time away,
   Seldom sleeping night or day,
From Mallow rakes we bear the sway,
   In Garry own naugh Glora.

4. It is not clear if the king in this stanza is James III — in which case the rakes are catholics
   and they have a fearsome reputation among their *allies* in France and Spain — or George III,
   in which case they are protestant and are feared by their *enemies* in France and Spain.
5. bumbailiffs — those employed to arrest malefactors.
6. put a stick through; cf. Ir. *cipín*, a little stick.
7. teased, annoyed.
8. i.e. spa water — probably from Castleconnel, Co. Limerick.
9. According to Crofton Croker (quoting John Ferrar's 1766 *History of Limerick*), lamps
   were first erected in Limerick in 1696.

As topers brave we spend our life,
 Free from worldly care and strife,
Whilst bumpers flow before us.
 So let the sparkling glass go round,   50
Glass to glass we like the sound,
So may this day with peace be crowned,
In Garry own naugh Glora.

ANONYMOUS IRISH/ENGLISH POEMS FROM THE 1780s

These poems come from the chapbooks and manuscripts of the late eighteenth century and are, like the earlier examples, the work of bilingual poets writing for a bilingual audience. The metrical elements are, again, borrowed from Irish *amhrán* or song metres.

The second, fourth and sixth stanzas of this first song are in Irish, but the text is not written in Gaelic script. Instead, the sounds of the Irish are represented on the page according to the conventions of English spelling so that, if read or sung aloud, the text should be recognisable as Irish. However, the system used is erratic and inconsistent which makes the reconstruction of the Irish text very difficult and, in parts of stanzas 4 and 6, impossible. In the notes to the poem, stanza 2 is reconstructed as well as possible and is also translated into English, but the Irish text to stanzas 4 and 6 is so garbled that these stanzas are merely loosely paraphrased in English.

The Rake's Frolick or *Stauka an Varaga*[1]

Through nations ranging, raking elements,
Spending my days in peace and fellowship,
    Oro,[2] and plenty good store.
In each company fill your bumpers high,
With pleasing jollity toast the lasses free,
    Oro, and drink your store.
Through Munster I roved with jovial company,
Rowling in sport, resorting pleasantly,
In each barony through the country,
Boozing heartily, cruising gallantly,   10
    Oro, and pleasure galore.

Es Buohileen fast ha saar arr chanosagh,
Da hanigh oan Monister faulhe ee yhallo room,
    Oro, gus thouir dhum pog.
Neer vadah lume eihe Ueenthe er liooba lath
Cush thieva varileh en eenthing maroga,
    Oro, es da y laning da score,
Prabig noor see agus leenther knogarea,
Gallim oam chree ga niolodb a tharigid,
Thiogh a saggarth es bemesth cagilthe,   20

---

1. 'The market post or stake'.
2. An exclamation like 'Oho!'.

Me vouhill cabshagh sheen er liobha lume.
　　Oro, es na scar lume gidhio.[3]

When first I set sail to range the barony,
From sweet Farihy to Kildoray,[4]
　　Oro, and from that to red chair.
It's there the fair maids do treat me heartily,
With full glasses free and impartiality,
　　Oro, the truth I'll declare.
On the high road to Castle Oliver[5]
I met a coaxing, roving froliker,　　　　　　　　　　　30
Her mode denoted she was a Palentine,[6]
She wore deep ribbons her clothes in fashion sir,—
　　Oro, her love she received.

Boadha ma raee, three claar na Banaba,
Oan ra Chariges dhan thraid shin Chasnal,
　　Oro, es ga dreliceh ra slardh.
Na danea yhan rith shin no knaulioh challiogs er,
Da har vaccasa an erraen's an arrigadh,
　　Oro, es da nearing neas moe,

3.　　Is buachaillín fásta é is sárfhear ceannsa,
　　　　Do tháinig ón Mainistir, fáilte Uí Cheallaigh romham,
　　　　　　Oró, agus tabhair dom póg.
　　　　Níorbh fhada liom oíche Aoine ar leaba leat
　　　　Cois taobh an bharraille an aontóinn margadh
　　　　　　Oró is dá nglanfainn do scór,
　　　　Preabaigh in bhur suí agus líontar cnagaire
　　　　Geallaim óm chroí go ndíolfad an t-airgead
　　　　Tiocfaidh an sagart is bímis ceangailte
　　　　Mo bhuachaill caimseach sín ar leaba liom
　　　　　　Oró is na scar liom go deo.

He is a grown boy and a fine, mild man who came from Mainistir [perhaps
Monastanenagh Co. Limerick, or any site of a monastery] *and greeted me well; 'Oho!
and give me a kiss! Friday night in bed with you was not boring for me. Beside the
barrel,* [i.e. here in the tavern] *I would make a deal, Oho! and would I pay your price?
Sit up there, and let a naggin* [a container of whiskey] *be filled. I promise from my heart
that I'll pay the money. The priest will come and we will be joined.' 'My curly-headed
boy, lie down on the bed with me, Oho! and never leave me!'*

4.　A Farahy and Kildorrery are communities in north county Cork, near the Limerick border.
5.　Near Kilfinane, Co. Limerick.
6.　A Palatine. Several hundred German protestant families from the Palatine, refugees after
　　their province was overrun by the French, settled in County Limerick in the early
　　eighteenth century. They retained German customs, including modes of dress,
　　throughout the eighteenth century.

Been affran leh foule gagh law o haggirth aun   40
An Maraga's faar you laulau sathaugh thin aun,
Straidh van calkes es ee er liabha,
Mydhen d eass es mea a veh na hanea shea,
        Oro da baith ea mr [*sic*] skiole.[7]

There I perceived her state and stature,
Her stately carriage and face most flattering,
        Oro, she wounded me sore.
There I engaged her close in garrison,
In the tavern where she followed me,
        Oro, we had whiskey galior,[8]   50
Who'd refuse such boozing lasses free,
With wnom I'd chuse to cruise most gallantly
Win or lose I'd scourge them heartily,
Their curiosity drowns all poverty,
        Oro, tis time I adore.

Voulas me laave le stauka an varaga,
Hagass marthan ga braugh na carring lea,
        Oro, es nie yeaning gadhio,
Baar lume agum ee no estate na banada,
No croan na sasaugh, es moer ydldh Allabin.   60
        Oro es dah nearing nees moe.
Ma challias an eelan da vie an a muallen gum
Pheelimea a reesth a caun three shaughthinea
Beengh a tharigadn creeng a dhaskea guth,
        [*line missing*]
        Oro, es buckum a roadh.[9]

---

7. It is impossible to reconstruct the full Irish text of this stanza. A rough paraphrase would
   be: *My road shall be through the plain of Ireland from the foot of Carrig* [possibly a local
   name for a peak in the Galtee or Knockmealdown Mountains] *to that street of Cashel*
   [a town in Co. Tipperary]. *Oho! ... The people of that journey ... She was better than I
   saw all over Ireland and across the sea; Oho! and if I were to say more! There's a mass
   to be got there every day from a priest; It's the best market ever ... A stately woman* [or
   '*a street woman*'], *her skin chalk-white, and she on the bed having good desire, and me
   to be beside her; Oho! that was the story!*

8. See Glossary.

9. It is impossible to reconstruct the full Irish text of this stanza. A rough paraphrase would
   be: *I touched my hand on the market post. I gave my* [*word*?] *that I wouldn't ever leave
   her. I'd prefer to have her than the land of Ireland, or the crown of England or the
   majesty of Scotland; Oho! if I said any more! If I lose the fair one that was on the hill
   with me.... 'I will return again in three weeks' time; you'll have the correct money in
   store for you. Oho! let's get going!'*

422

It was on a day where play was publickly
With great pleasantry, mirth and jollity,
  Oro, and dancing also.
While we were skipping and kissing heartily
Staka an varaga aside she carried me,   70
  Oro, ma chree Saun Roe.[10]
It's into a chamber neat she follow'd me,
Told me her peas[11] was fit for trashing[12] free,
To tell you in plain I tasted them certainly,
My flail she fractur'd, I'm teaz'd with doctors fee, —
  Oro, which makes me condole.[13]

The Answer to *Stauka an Vauraga*

I am a fair maid that loves good Company,
Such as would chuse a girl of quality,
  Oro, and the Boys I adore.

I travel'd this Nation submissive and complesant,
From Country to City I roll'd in great merriment,
  Oro, and am killing galore.

All those who navigates in the Seas of tranquility,
Furls their Sails in the midst of extremity,
Steers by their Compass unto the lower country.
When the Tempess's[1] over we'll drink in great jollity: 10
  Oro, and had pleasure galore.

One day as I rov'd by an ancient brave Castle sir,
I met a young lad and he drest in the Fashion sir,
  Oro, and his eyes they did roul.

He handles me jently, carouses me hartily,
Praises my Beauty, and Hugs me quite lovingly;
  Oro, he is the joy of my soul.

---

10. Ir. *mo chroí Suibhán Rua*, my love, red-haired Joan.
11. cf. Ir. *pit, pis*, pudenda.
12. thrashing.
13. The poet complains that he has been infected with venereal disease.

1. tempest's.

He says my fair maid, if you join me in company,
To Munster we'll go for to see that fair country;
It's the province we'll roul in great jolity,   20
And back we return to sweet [?]ildo[?]ery,[2]
       Oro, and the lip of a Bowl.

He is as handsome a lad as any in this Country,
He singles, he doubles, he tribles it handsomely;
       Oro, he is valiant and bold.

He lies in my arms without dread or danger
I lend him some coals to keep fire in his Chamber;
       Oro, there was snow on the ground.

While we were a kissing and hugging quite heartily,
Rouling and sporting under Venus's liberty;   30
I kindled his Coals with a bunch of Curiosity,
Sits at his own Fire, and keeps me in memory:
       Oro, I am afraid he'll get cold,

Tis now I will leave off my raking and rambling,
To Munster I'll go for to set up a Standing;
       Oro, and I'll pass for a maid.

'Tis there the boys out of pleasure will leasure me,
With joy out of measure they'll dingle and gingle[3] me,
With Bottles and Glasses we'll pass the night merrily;
Saying here's a good health to the boy in obscurity,   40
       Oro, my Harvest is made.

---

2. Text damaged. The reference may be to Kildorrery, Co. Cork (see l. 24 of previous poem).
3. dangle and jingle me (shake me around).

Pléaráca an Bhráthar:[1]

A New Song called the Friar's Jigg or Plearaca an Vrathar

There are some who sing of Moreen and others of Grainne too[2]
And third of Andrew Cary;[3] but I will give you what is new:
It is of that base negro[4] who lately from the Church has ran —
That you may know him plainly, he's Patrick O'Finegan.

Ná luaitear feasta Móirín, nó seancheol ar bith mar sin
Ach bímid anois ag tráchtadh ar ní nach raibh i bhfad ó shin:
Níl i mbéal mná nó páiste, ó Dhroichead Áth' go Muineachán,
Ach mire agus pléaracha Phádraig Uí Fhionagáin.[5]

A curse upon you Patrick! how shamefully you went to work!
A job of such performance you would not hear of Jew or Turk;   10
But take this as a warning, when you shall be no longer man,
You'll damn the day you were born, poor Patrick O'Finegan.

Níl baile mór nó clúideán sa taobh sin nár chaith sé tráth
Ag radaireacht go lúbach is go cluainteach ag mealladh mná;
I léim sé as an ord, 'sé dóigh liom go gcríonfaidh an crann;
Ach rug an t-ainmhian buaidh ort, a Phádraig Uí Fhionagáin.[6]

One time you were a gauger[7] and teasing each landlady;
Again a yarn-seizer, ranging through each barony;
A smuggler bold next day, no gauger can you trepan;[8]
And on Sunday you are a preacher, brave Patrick O'Finegan.   20

---

1. 'The Friar's Revelry'. This bilingual attack is aimed at Patrick O'Finegan, a friar who left the catholic church and conformed to the Church of Ireland.
2. i.e. some sing of traditional Irish heroes and heroines.
3. Andrew Cary was another renegade priest.
4. Not used literally, but as a general term of disapproval.
5. *Stanza 2:* Henceforth don't talk of Moreen, or any other old tune, but let us tell of something that happened not long ago. There's no story in the mouth of woman or child from Drogheda to Monaghan but the madness and the revelry of Patrick O'Finegan.
6. *Stanza 4:* There's not a large town or a corner in that land that he didn't spend some time revelling deceitfully and seducing women. Since he jumped from the order, I thought the tree would wilt; but lust got the better of you, Patrick O'Finegan.
7. One who measures land or quantities; also an exciseman, the sense in which it appears here.
8. swindle.

Is maith an t-ábhar spóirt tú, a dhreoláin, 's do leabhar leat,
Ag rá nach bhfuil spré beo sa Róimh mhóir nach bhfuil caite amach!
Má bhuain dóibh ganntan guail 's gan iad stuama ar a lasadh ann,
Dhéanfaidh tú féin 's do ghúna toiteach ann, a Phádraig Uí
Fhionagáin.[9]

Now since you are grown blind and inclined to increase your guilt,
And the curses of old Egypt down on your perjured head are spilt,[10]
Go corded off to Rome[11] and make what penance there you can;
Your end is to be roasted, poor Patrick O'Finegan.

A Phádraig, is gan chéill duit, 's nach léir dhuit ach ag déanamh cleas;
Bhéara duit comhairle agus seoladh dhuit go dté do leas: 30
Gluais leat 'un na Rómha is crios S.P. fá do lár go teann
Nó tachtfaidh corda cnáibe thú, a Phádraig Uí Fhionagáin.[12]

So now, my Reverend Father, as you are past all sound advice,
I lave[13] you to the swarm, to be consumed by nits and lice.
As for your filthy writings, all know they are not worth a damn;
So ply them to your scabby rump, poor Patrick O'Finegan.

Is aontas insan áit do phléaráca agus gúna leat,
Ag rith ar fud na sráide ar pháistí agus garsúin bhochta;
Scuir dod chosanairde is tabhair aire do do sheáps beag fánach,
Nó brisfear do dhrandal gránna, a Phádraig Uí Fhionagáin.[14]   40

---

9. *Stanza 6:* You're a figure of fun, you silly person, with your book saying that there is no
    live spark in Rome that has not been thrown out! If they have a shortage of coal and they
    are not able to light up, you and your dress will make smoke for them, Patrick
    O'Finegan.
10. A reference to the plagues endured by the people of Egypt until Pharaoh agreed to
    release the children of Israel (Exodus chapters 8-12).
11. O'Finegan had been a friar, and so had worn a knotted cord around his waist. He is urged
    to go to Rome (where he could find the pope) with his friar's habit on, to do penance for
    his apostasy.
12. *Stanza 8:* O Patrick, it is foolish for you that trickery is all you can see. I'll give you
    advice and direction that will be for your good. Go to Rome with St Francis's belt about
    your middle, or else a hempen rope will choke you, Patrick O'Finegan.
13. leave.
14. *Stanza 10:* Your revelry and wearing a dress are one and the same, as you run up the
    street into children and young people. Give up your arrogance and take care of your poor
    little shop, or your ugly mug will be broken, Patrick O'Finegan.

'Twas better, I am sure, from your youth you had herded swine
Than now to pervert the truth and abuse all laws divine.
Sure if a roving journeyman, you made the awls and last your plan,[15]
You would not be scoffed by all, poor Patrick O'Finegan.

Nárbh fhearr dhuit le do ré leis an éill is do mheana beag,
Nó ag dreas ar phobal Dé in aghaidh na cléire is bean agat?
Seacht scalladh ar do cháir! a phlaigh, is déas an Diabhail thú féin is
do chlann,

Is tú féin an giolla gránna, a Phádraig Uí Fhionagáin.[16]

---

15. i.e. Sure, if you were a travelling journeyman using (a carpenter's) awls or (a shoemaker's) last...
16. *Stanza 12:* Would it not be best for you to spend your time with your strap and little awl than to incite God's people against the clergy, and you with a wife? Seven scaldings on your mouth, you plague; you and your children are weapons of the Devil, and you yourself his ugly servant, Patrick O'Finegan.

JOHN TAYLOR
(fl. **1787**)

John Taylor was a stay-maker who lived in Limerick and who seems to have had a deserved reputation as an eccentric. In the poem below, he directs an elaborate curse at the man who stole, apparently from the house of his benefactor Stephen Creaghe, a leg of beef which had been promised to him.

On a Beef's being stole which was promis'd to the AUTHOR

Curse on the harden'd, unrelenting thief,
That stole poor honest Taylor's promised beef,
Whose happy loins, I did so often boast,
Shou'd grace my board with sumpt'ous boil'd and roast;
On which (vain hope) from eve 'till dawn of day,
My inmost thoughts were fix'd, O! sad idea!
Now snatch'd by thee, no prospect of another
Have I in view, from friend, or ev'n brother;
Cou'd you[1] not search the lawns of Colonel Green?[2]
Mount-pleasant, Shannon-grove, or Ballisteen?   10
If these cou'd not supply your darling sport,
The member's well supplied at Ballinort:
At Colonel Waller's, or at fam'd Adare,
In each you'd find the best of butcher's fare,
At gen'rous D———'s too, you can't but know,
Beef's but a drug, his ton's[3] a sporting doe;
Cou'd none of these thy thirst for theft supply,
And pass the once gay, sporting Taylor by?
'But turn thy foot-steps from yon flow'ry mead,[4]
Of princely Stephen's hospitable shade,   20
Where dwells the friendly, gen'rous, just and good,
And all that's by true greatness understood,

---

1. Taylor is addressing the thief.
2. Green and Waller were landlords with properties near Limerick, and the houses named in the next few lines were local demesnes.
3. 'Ton' is a French word meaning 'fashion' or 'vogue' and is used incorrectly here. The line seems to mean that D——— does not want beef since his (fashionable) taste inclines to venison.
4. In the lines in inverted commas, the poet seems to imagine what he would say to the thief if he could address him before the deed were done. A note at l. 20 identifies 'Stephen' as *Stephen Creaghe, Esquire*.

There smiling charity her vigils keep,
To guard her true born offspring whilst asleep.'
Ten thousand curses light upon thee down,
A stroling vagrant be from town to town;
And all thy kin (tho' thousands now were living)
Be struck to death, nor see the gates of Heav'n;
Thy heart and mind with ranc'rous malice torn,
Of ev'ry class and sect, the scoff and scorn;   30
And may old time ne'er stop thy pois'nous breath,
'Till tired of life, you'll vainly call for death;
In pain and torture all your days to spend,
Then at the gallows, close thy shameful end:
Thus may the Gods, thou damn'd infernal thief,
Afflict thee sore for stealing of my beef.

FOUR DUBLIN UNDERWORLD POEMS FROM THE 1780S

The first of the poems which follows is one of the most anthologised of eighteenth-century Irish poems in English, though little is known about the circumstances of its composition. Conjectures about its authorship have been widespread, but it is probable that this poem, like the three which follow it, was a genuine street poem, 'collected' in Dublin by someone whose identity is unknown, and written down in a way which reflects the pronunciation and vocabulary of the speech of the late eighteenth-century Dublin underworld. By 1788, the poem is described as being 'all the *ton*' (i.e. all the rage) in Dublin. The texts reproduced here are the earliest available and are taken from manuscripts or early chapbooks. They are left unedited so that their vigor is not diminished in any way, but paraphrases are provided in the notes. The last line (or prose passage) in each stanza of all four poems, was meant to be said 'Newgate style' — that is, spoken rather than sung, and inserted as comic relief.

Like other similar poems of the period, those in this section exhibit a shockingly casual attitude to the brutal realities of public executions and of street violence; but life for the poor in Dublin in the late eighteenth century was nasty, brutish and short. Many accepted that they were likely to meet a violent end and retained, even in the presence of death, a sense of humour and a delight in the ridiculous.

In the first poem, Larry's friends visit him in gaol the night before his execution and, as was common at the time, bring drink, cards and candles to 'wake' him. His coffin, sent by the authorities to remind him of impending death, is turned upside-down and used as a card-table. Larry was said by John Edward Walsh (*Sketches of Dublin sixty years ago* (Dublin, 1847), p. 84) to have been a cripple named Lambert, 'paralytic on one side, but of irreclaimable habits'.

De Nite afore Larry was stretch'd

De night afore Larry was stretch'd
de Boys de all ped him a visit
bait too in dir Sacs de all fetch'd
de sweated dir duds till de ris it
for Larry was ever de Lad.
when a Boy was condemd to de squeezers
he'd swet all de duds dat he had
to help his poor friend to a sneezer
and warm his Gob fore he died.[1]

---

1. *Stanza 1*: The night before Larry was hanged, the boys all paid him a visit. They all brought provisions in their bags and had pawned their clothes to raise enough money — for Larry was always 'the lad'. When a boy was condemned to be hanged, his friends would pawn all their clothes to help get drink for him to warm him up before he died. **Notes on stanza 1**: The pronouns in lines 7 and 8 (third person singular) should obviously be in the third person plural; bait: provisions; to sweat your duds: to pawn your clothes.

De Boys de came crowding in fast   10
de drew all dir Stools round about him
nine Glims round his trapcase were plac'd
he could not be wakd well widout em.
whin one of us axd could he die
widout having truely repinted
O say's Larry dats all in my Eye
and first by de Clargy invinted
to get a fat bit for dirselves.[2]

Im sorry dear Larry says I
to see you in dis Situation   20
and blister my Limbs if I lie
If I live it will be my own Station
Uchone its all over says he
de neckcloth Ill be forced to put on
By dis dime to morrow youll see
poor Larry as ded as de mutton
bekase why his courage was good.[3]

Den Ill be cut up like a pye
and my nob from my Body be parted
your in the rong box den says I   30
for de never will be so hard hearted
a Chalk on de back of your neck
Is all dat Jack Ketch dare to give you
den mind not such trifles a feck
for why should de likes a dem greif you
and now boys come tip us de deck[4]

---

2. *Stanza 2*: The boys came crowding in fast and they drew their stools round about him. Nine candles were placed on his coffin — for he couldn't be properly 'waked' without them. When one of them asked whether or not he could die without having truly repented, Larry said: 'O, that's all rubbish; it was invented by the clergy to get money for themselves.'

3. *Stanza 3*: 'I'm sorry, dear Larry,' says I, 'to see you in this situation — and blister my limbs if I am not telling the truth! If I live, that is what will happen to me.' 'Alas, it's all over,' says he; 'I'll be forced to put on the noose. By this time tomorrow, you'll see poor Larry as dead as mutton. Why? Because he was brave!'

4. *Stanza 4*: 'Then I'll be cut up like a pie, and my head will be parted from my body!' 'That would be all wrong,' says I, 'for they will never be as hard-hearted as that! All that Jack Ketch dares to give you is a mark on the back of your neck. So don't give a damn about such little things — why should they worry you? Now, boys, tip out the deck of cards!' **Notes on stanza 4:** Larry is assured that he will only be hanged and that he will not, like those guilty of treason or poisoning, be hanged, drawn, quartered and beheaded; Jack Ketch was a famous executioner and his name was used to apply to any hangman. (Hangmen marked the neck of a condemned man to show where they should place the knot of the noose.)

De Cards being call'd for we pled
till Larry vount one a dem cheated
a dart ad is napper he made
de boy being easily heated   40
and ses be do hoky you teef
Ill splinter your skull wid my daddle
you cheat me bekase Im in Greif
but soon Ill demolish your noddle
and tip you Your Claret to drink[5]

De gownsman step'd in wid his book
and spoke him so neat & so civil
Larry tipt him a Kilmainham look
and pitchd his big wig to de devil
den raising a little his head   50
he took a sup out a de bottle
and sighing most bitterly said
Oh de hemp will be soon round my throttle
and squeeze my poor windpipe to det.[6]

But sure dis de best way to die
oh de devil a better a livin
for when on de Gallows so high
de way is de shorter to heaven
but what harrashes Larry de most
& makes his poor soul malankolly   60
wen he dinks on de dime dat his Gost
shall come in a Sheet to his Molly
O sure it will kill her alive[7]

5. *Stanza 5*: The cards being called for, we played until Larry found that one of them was cheating. He hit out at the swindler — Larry always had a short temper — and said: 'By the devil, you thief! I'll splinter your skull with my hands! You're cheating me because I'm depressed. But I'll crush your skull and give you your own blood to drink!'

6. *Stanza 6*: The clergyman stepped up to Larry with his prayer book, and spoke to him politely. But Larry gave him a Kilmainham look and tipped his big wig off his head with an oath. Then, raising his head a little, he took a swig out of the bottle he had and, sighing most bitterly, said: 'O, the rope will soon be round my throat and will squeeze my poor windpipe to death.' **Notes on stanza 6:** <u>A Kilmainham look</u> is a contemptuous look such as felons about to be executed might give to the clergy attending them. Kilmainham Gaol, west of Dublin, was the place of execution of felons from County Dublin. Until 1783, Dublin city criminals (like Larry) were executed either at a site between present-day Upper Fitzwilliam Street and Lad Lane or at St Stephen's Green.

7. *Stanza 7*: 'But sure, this is the best way to die, and it's a devil's sight better than living! For when you are high up on the gallows, it's a shorter distance to heaven! But what worries Larry most, and makes his poor soul melancholy, is thinking about the time when his ghost will come in a sheet to visit his Molly — O sure, that will frighten her to death!'

Deeze words were so meltingly spoke
our Grif it found vent in a Shower
for my part I dot my hart broke
to see him cut down like a flower
On his travels I watchd him next day
de trottler I tot to have kilt him
But Larry not one word did say   70
nor changed till he kem to king William
and den why his kuller grew white[8]

When he kem to the nubbing chit
he was tuckd up so neat & so pritty
de rumbler shuot off from his feet
& he died wid his feet to the sitty
he kick'd too but dat was all pride
for soon you may say twas all over
and whin the noose was untyd
at home why we wak'd him in clover   80
and sent him to take a Ground sweat.[9]

---

8. *Stanza 8*: These words were spoken with so much feeling that we all started to weep. For my part, I thought my heart would break to see him cut down like a flower! Next day, I watched him on his travels: I thought I would have killed the hangman! But Larry didn't say a word or change his appearance until he came to King William — and then, why, his colour turned white. **Notes on stanza 8:** Larry's change in colour occurs as the procession taking him to the gallows passes the statue of King William III, which stood in College Green, outside Trinity College. Since the last such procession took place in 1783, the poem must have its origins before that date.

9. *Stanza 9*: When he came to the gallows, he was hanged neatly enough; the cart shot away from beneath him, and he died with his feet pointing towards the city. He kicked too — but that was his pride, for you may say that it was all over soon, and when the noose was untied, we took him home and 'waked' him in comfort and safety. Then we buried him in a grave. **Notes on stanza 9:** the nubbing-cheat: the gallows; to tuck up: to hang; before the invention of 'the drop', condemned malefactors would be standing on a cart which was driven out from under them; to take a ground sweat: to be in a grave.

Luke Caffrey's Kilmainham Minit[1]

When to see Lukes Last Gig we agreed
we tipd all our Gripes in a tangle
and mounted our trotters wid speed
to squint at de Snub as hed dangle
for he was de Smart on de Gap
he boozled de Bull & pinners
and when dat he milld a fat Slap
he merrily melted de winners
to snack wid de boys of de pad[2]

In a Giffee we blinkd at de Speed   10
where de Quod its glum Phiz did exhibit
wid a facer we coddled our blood
for de wind it blowd cold from de Jibbet
de boy he had traveld afore
like Rattlers we after him ped'd it
for it to miss us would greev him full sore
kase why as a fevur he begd it
Wed tip him de fives 'fore his det[3]

1. This poem concerns Luke Caffrey's hope that, like at least one other Dublin eighteenth-century felon for whom the operation had been successful, he might be revived after being hanged if one of his veins were to be opened. In the event, though his friends 'lent him a Snig' in 'de Juglar' after the execution, they found him 'quite ded'. The 'Minit' of the title is a macabre reference to the 'minuet' or apparently dance-like movements of the felon's body as he is actually being hanged. Again, this early manuscript text is presented unedited.

2. *Stanza 1*: When we agreed to see Luke's last dance, we all shook hands on it, and set off on foot to look at the lad as he dangled. For Luke was always the one for a joke, good at outwitting bailiffs and gaolers, and whenever he had a good haul, he would happily spend his 'winnings' and share them with the rest of the gang. **Notes on stanza 1:** to tip the gripes: to shake hands; mounted our trotters: mounted our horses, a jocular phrase meaning that they went on foot; Smart on de Gap seems to mean 'clever with his mouth', but may be obscure; Bull: police officer or bailiff; pinner: gaoler; to mill a fat Slap: to get a good haul of stolen goods; to melt de winners: to spend the winnings (by metonomy); pad: a gang of footpads or highwaymen.

3. *Stanza 2*: Immediately, we went as quickly as we could past the Spud to the grim-looking prison; we had a drink to warm up our blood, for the wind blows cold from the gallows. But Luke had set out from the gaol already; so we raced after him as fast as carriages would go, for it would have grieved him if we had missed his hanging. Why? because he had begged us to be there as a favour, so we could shake hands with him before his death. **Notes on stanza 2:** The meaning of the first line is obscure. Other versions of the text (and the rhyme) make it clear that the last word should be 'Spud' rather than 'Speed', but its meaning is still not clear. Could it be a name for the New Hall Market which was next to Newgate prison? Quod: prison, in this case Dublin's Newgate prison; to ped: (probably) to go on foot; Rattlers: carriages; to tip the fives: to shake hands (the fives being the five fingers).

When we came to de mantrap & saw
poor Luke look so blue in de Gabbard   20
to save him I tot I cud draw
me toaster fm out a de Sgappart
Oh Luky sis I do you see
be de Iron & Steel in my daddles
If I tot I cud once set you free
de Scarlets should smoke in dir Saddels
your Gullet to save fm de noose[4]

Your Soul Id fight blood to de Eyes
you know it I would to content you
but foul Play I always despise   30
dats for One for to fall upon twenty
Sis he tis me fate for to die
I knowd it when I was committed
but yet if de Slang you run sly
de Scragboy may still be outwitted
and I scout again on de lay[5]

When I dance chuxt de Ert an de Skies
de Clargy may bleat for de Strugler
but when on de ground your frend lies
Oh! tip me a snig in de Jugler   40
you know dat it is me last hope
as de Surjins of Natomy tell us
dat whin Im cut down fm de Rope

---

4. *Stanza 3*: When we came to the gallows and saw poor Luke looking so blue in the mouth, I thought I might be able to save him if I drew my sword out of its scabbard. 'O Luke,' says I, 'do you see — by the iron and steel in my hands — that, if I thought I could set you free and save your gullet from the noose, the soldiers would suffer in their coats.' **Notes on stanza 3:** <u>mantrap</u>: gallows; <u>Gabbard</u> probably means 'mouth'; <u>toaster</u>: toasting-fork, a jocular word for a sword; <u>daddles</u>: hands; <u>Scarlets</u>: soldiers in scarlet coats; <u>to smoke</u>: to smart or suffer; <u>Saddels</u> could mean coats or saddles.

5. *Stanza 4*: 'By your soul, I'd fight till there was blood in my eyes — you know I would, to please you. But I always despise foul play — and it would be foul play for one to attack twenty!' Says Luke 'It's my fate to die; I knew it once I was in gaol. But yet if you can (i.e. if I can) escape the handcuffs, the hangman might still be outwitted, and I might go searching for booty again.' **Notes on stanza 4:** <u>to run sly</u>: to escape; <u>Slang</u> = slangs: handcuffs; <u>Scragboy</u>: hangman; <u>lay</u>: a criminal occupation.

you'll bring back de puff to my Bellows
and set me once more on my pins[6]

He finishd dis speech wid a sigh
we saw de poor fellow was funking
a drizzel stole down from his Eye
do we tot he had got better spunk in
wid a tip a de slang we reply'd   50
an a Blinker dat nobody noted
de Clargy step'd down from his Side
and de Gabbard fm under him floated
Oh! twas den me port Royal run cold[7]

Pads foremost he div'd & den Round
he caper'd de Kilmainham Minit
but when dat he lay on de Ground
our business we tot to begin it
wid de Stiff to a Sheebeen we hied
But det had shut fast evry Grinder   60
his Brainbox hung all a one Side
an no Distillers pig could be Blinder
but dat we must all come to[8]

His pushing block pissey came in
after tipping de Scragboy a dusting

6. *Stanza 5*: When I dance between the earth and the sky, the clergy may bleat about the one who is dying; but when your friend lies on the ground, O, make a small cut in my jugular vein. You know, that's my last hope, as the surgeons of anatomy tell us, that when I'm cut down from the rope, you could bring back the wind to my lungs and set me once more on my legs. **Notes on stanza 5:** Strugler is obscure, but the context seems to suggest the one who is struggling for life as he is being hanged.

7. *Stanza 6*: He finished this speech with a sigh, and we saw the poor fellow was afraid. He began to cry — though we had thought he was braver than that! We replied by shaking his hand, and giving him a wink that nobody noticed; then the clergyman stepped down from his side and the cart pulled away from under him: O! then my blood ran cold. **Notes on stanza 6:** a tip a de slang is obscure here; it seems to be a conflation of parts of two phrases, 'to slang one's mauleys' and 'to tip the mauley', both of which mean 'to shake hands with'; gabbard means, from the context, the cart on which Luke was standing; port Royal refers not to the place in France but, jocosely, to the poet's 'royal' blood, as red as port wine.

8. *Stanza 7*: He dived down feet first, and then his body swung round, dancing the 'Kilmainham Minuet'. But when he lay on the ground, we thought we would begin our business and took the body off to an alehouse. But death had closed his jaws, and his head hung all to one side; no distiller's pig could be blinder — but that's what we must all come to! **Notes on stanza 7:** grinder = tooth, but in this context = jaws; distiller's pig is obscure but may refer to a pig roasted whole at a fair (cf. a 'Bartholomew's pig' which was a pig roasted whole and sold piping hot at Bartholomew Fair in London).

Her Stuff Shop was up to her Chin
like a Cramd foul wid tinderniss brusting
we lent him a Snig as he sed
in de Jugler tis here dat de mark is
but whin dat we found him quite ded   70
in de dustcase we bundled his Carcase
and sent him to Sleep in de Clay[9]

A New Song call'd Luke Caffrey's Gost

Oh! de time piece had cum to the twelve
De fardins burn'd blue in their sockets,
When Reraw and I be ourselves,
De bottle took out of our Pockets
De Stiff was betwuxt where we sat,
As blind as the box of a pedler;
We drank to his helt for all dat,
While we cust de neck-hamp'ring medler,

Dat stood upon the green clot, bodgered poor Luke's stags out of count,
and took away his precious life, for de valiation of a few hump back'd
Williamites, and a bloody queen Anne's tester, your soul.[1]

---

9. *Stanza 8*: After she had thrown abuse at the hangman, his partner came in. Her belly's up to her chin and she looks like a stuffed chicken, bursting with tenderness (i.e. she is expecting a baby soon). We made a cut in his jugular vein where the hangman's mark was, as he had told us to do. But when we found that he was quite dead, we put his body into the coffin and buried him. **Notes on stanza 8:** pushing block is a phrase connected with sexual activity (cf. pushing-school = brothel); pissey: companion; to tip de Scragboy a dusting: to pelt the hangman with abuse and filth, a common activity at hangings; Stuff Shop: belly; Cramd foul wid tinderniss brusting: a stuffed (roasted) chicken, bursting with tenderness; Snig: cut; mark is either the mark made by the hangman on the condemned man's neck, or a mark made by someone else to show the position of the jugular vein.

1. *Stanza 1*: O, it was twelve o'clock and the candles burned blue in their sockets, when Reraw and I, by ourselves, took the bottle out of our pockets. The corpse was between us where we sat, as blind as a pedlar's box. We drank to his health, nonetheless, while we cursed the meddlesome, neck-destroying hangman who stood on the green cloth, bothered Luke's friends more than one can measure, and took away his precious life, for the price of a few hump-backed Williamite coins and a bloody sixpence from Queen Anne's reign, by your soul! **Notes on stanza 1:** A sequel to the previous poem. The prose passage at the end of each stanza is spoken. Reraw, Cf. Ir. *rí-rá*, commotion; As blind as the box of a pedler: this phrase almost certainly had a specific meaning, now lost; the green clot: the scaffold was sometimes covered in a green cloth; bodgered poor Luke's stags out of count is obscure, and the paraphrase given above is merely conjectural; hump back'd may carry echoes of the fact that a hangman wore a mask and a false hump on his back to protect him from missiles.

We look'd at him once, den sat down,
And sqib'd it 'till greef made us mellow;
No bull-dog that barks in the town,
Could ever secure de poor fellow;
For when be de scruff of de neck,
You know, in Ram-alley, dey pin'd him;
Do dey had de mob at dir beck,
Who would in a giffee, have skin'd him,

He squar'd up to the two Bailes, tip'd one of dem a loving sqeeze; den gave him a cut of bread and butter over de elbow, and a back sprang in de mazzard, dat made his day lights dance to de tune of de old cow and de hay-stack, set him spinning like a whirligig, and laid him down, your soul, amongst de mud larks: where he slept like a daisy. He den tip'd de oder a long-arm leg, wid a dig in de smellers, dat laid him on his face in a foundling manufacturing postur, when he gave dem leg bail for his appearance at de next crak-neck assembly be de hoky![2]

On a sudden de wind shook de house,
De devil was taught in a hurry,
Dat struck us as mute as a mouse,   30
I'd blew in a damnable flurry:
But making a pitiful moan,
We soon saw de poor Operation:
De dust case he view'd wid a groan,
To see himself in that condishain.

His eyes were swell'd in his brain-box, like two scalded goose-berries in a mutton tart; his face look'd for all de world like de rotten rump of a Thomas-street blue-arse, and his grinder rattled in his jaw wags, like a pair of white headed fortune tellers in an elbow-shaker's bone box.[3]

2. *Stanza 2*: We looked at him once, then sat down and drank until grief made us mellow. No bailiff that works in this town could ever secure the poor fellow; for when, you know, they pinned him by the scruff of the neck in Ram-alley, though they could call on the support of the mob who would have skinned him in a trice, he squared up to the two bailiffs, got one of them around the neck, then gave him a hard blow over the elbow and hit him in the face with the back of his hand so hard that his eyes danced to the tune of the old cow and the haystack, setting him spinning around like a whirligig and threw him down, by my soul, into the gutter, where he slept like a daisy. Then he kicked the other bailiff violently, and hit him on the nose, which sent him sprawling on his face in an indecent posture, so that he couldn't appear at the next hanging, by God! **Notes on stanza 2:** squib[b]'d: (from the context) drank it back; <u>Ram-'Alley</u>: Ram Lane in Dublin (later known as Schoolhouse Alley) ran between Cook Street and Merchant's Quay; <u>a cut of bread and butter</u>: though the general meaning of the phrase itself is clear enough, its detailed meaning is obscure; <u>mazzard</u>: face; <u>mud-larks</u>: men who scavenge in gutters or in the mud; <u>to give leg-bail</u>: to escape from something; <u>crack-neck assembly</u>: public hanging.

3. *Stanza 3*: Suddenly, the wind shook the house — we thought the devil must have been in a hurry! That struck us mute as a mouse, and I was pretty frightened immediately. But

'Oh! boys, don't be fiekend'd,' sis he,   40
''Tis Luke, your poor friend, dats cum to you;
Like me you bot shortly will be,
For de neck-crack will shortly undo you;
So 'fore all your coppers are spint,
Take warning in time as I charge you;
On your marrow bones down and repint,
And take the advice of the Clargy.'

But that you know, is what he did not do himself; for he was steel in de
hart, blood to de back bone, flint in de nuckle-dabbers, Manley's mettle in
his lims, your soul! every inch of him, and he died hard, like a pancake
cock on a game Tuesday.[4]

Sis he, — 'I've got one ting to say, —
You know One-ey'd Bid of the alley:
De heffer was mine on de lay,
Kase why, we was bot made to tally;
De dog-days aint over wid her;
I fear dat you bot will be at her;

But don't, your souls! don't!   [*spoken*]

---

we soon saw the poor apparition, moaning pitifully; he looked into the coffin with a
groan to see himself in that condition. His eyes were all swollen in his head, like two
scalded gooseberries in a mutton tart; his face looked, for all the world, like the rotten
backside of a blue-bottle fly from Thomas Street, and his teeth rattled in his jaws like a
pair of little white dice when shaken by a gambler in a dice-box. **Notes on stanza 3:**
Thomas Street was famous for butchers' stalls; white headed fortune tellers in an elbow-
shaker's bone box is obscure and the interpretation above is conjectural.

4. *Stanza 4*: 'O, boys, don't be frightened,' says he. ''Tis Luke, your poor friend, that's
come to you. You will both soon be like me, for you too will be hanged. So, before all
your pennies are spent, take warning in time, as I tell you; get down on your knees and
repent; take the advice of the clergy.' But that, you know, is what he did not do himself;
for he had steel in his heart, blood to his backbone, flint in his fists, and was as spirited
as Manley in his limbs, your soul! every inch of him. And he died hard, like a brave cock
in a festival cockfight. **Notes on stanza 4:** nuckle-dabbers: (from the context) fists;
Manley's mettle: the significance of Manley is not clear: was he perhaps a local hero —
a boxer, a brave street fighter? In Wycherly's play *The Plain Dealer*, there is a strong
character called Manly, but this allusion seems too literary; like a pancake cock on a
game Tuesday is another obscure phrase, though its general meaning is clear enough,
and the phrase comes from cock-fighting. However, 'to die game' meant 'to suffer at the
gallows without shewing any signs of fear or repentance' (*A Dictionary of Buckish
Slang*, London, 1811), so the phrase may carry echoes of this meaning.

For if by an inch dat you stir;
De devil your wig-blocks shall batter,   60
And white-wash de wall wid your brains.[5]

Oh! she was my own herts delight,
For her on the padroul I scamper'd;
And do dat she seem'd in a fright,
On de day my poor gullet was hamper'd
Yet now dat my herts dead and gone
(Do, your souls! ther was never a bolder,)
I see dat she looks out for one
To cumfort her 'fore she grows older,
And make her forget all her greefe.[6]   70

O! tell her, den, not to forget
Poor Luke, if she sullies her Carcase:
I'll haunt her, bekase of my det,
De minit I see dat de dark is.'
In a flash as he vanish'd away,
Wid a sigh to our ail-pumps he beckoned:
We bot to[o]k de culler of clay,
Kase why, we were bloodily freckin'd.

No wonder! — Oh! Murder! Murder! to tink of de barbarous finis dat he
treatend'd us wid. But der needed no operation to cum to tell us dat, for
let us when we will upon the padding course, Neck-lace is de Word! and
we must all be in at de Hemp post in de end.[7]

5. *Stanza 5*: Says he, 'I've got one thing to say. You know one-eyed Bid of the alley; she
was living with me. Do you know why? We were both made to be together. Her heyday
is not over yet and I fear you will both try and get at her. But don't, on your souls, don't!
For if you stir an inch towards her, the devil will crush your skulls and whitewash the
wall with your brains!'
6. *Stanza 6*: 'O, she was my heart's delight! For her I went out on patrol [to rob], and though
she seemed frightened on the day my poor neck was throttled, yet now that my heart's
dead and gone (though, your souls! there was never a bolder one), I see that she is looking
out for someone to comfort her before she grows older, and make her forget all her grief.'
7. *Stanza 7*: 'O, tell her then not to forget poor Luke. If she defiles her body, I'll haunt her
the minute I see it's dark, because I'm dead.' In a flash, as he vanished, he pointed, with
a sigh, at our necks; we both turned white. Why? Because we were bloody frightened!
No wonder! O murder, murder! To think of the barbarous end that he threatened us with!
But we didn't need an apparition to come to tell us that, for although we will go out
robbing whenever we want, we know the word 'noose', and that we must all be there at
the gallows in the end. **Notes on stanza 7:** to our ail-pumps he beckoned is obscure and
can be interpreted only conjecturally in the context of the whole stanza.

440

Den hearing a noise at the door,
Our tipple was quickly prevented:
Our barkers, do rusty were sure,
We taut dat M'Kinly had scented;
We prim'd, and as sure as a gun,
Thro' de key-hole we peep'd ad de pinners;
Den out of de window we run,
And left them to laugh at dir winners. 90

But den, boys, 'twas no shame to take to our scrapers — neck or nothing
was de word! — and you know we disvalid dem in de regard of fair play,
dats man to man — stiff and stout — tree down anoder cum — No pegs,
your soul! below de nable![8]

O says Luke which have you seen poll,
The whore when I catch her I will kill her,
She is this half hour and full,
Away for the Weed and the Steamer,
Without she has pick'd up a Cull,
And dye for his gold or his tatler, 100
Her eyes with bruis'd blood I will fill;
And with my two maulers I'll ratler her,[9]

And make her remember this night.

His trunk was half mounted you know,
We had all the molls of the City;
Thro' the Streets there was never such a show
With whores pimps padmen and bullies;

8. *Stanza 8*: Then, hearing a noise at the door, we quickly stopped drinking. Our pistols, though rusty, were sure enough. We thought that McKinley had sniffed us out. We primed our pistols and, as sure as a gun, when we peeped through the keyhole, we saw the police. Then we hopped out of the window and left them to laugh at their winnings (i.e. the dead body). But then, boys, it was not shameful to take to our heels — neck or nothing's the word! And, you know, the contest would have been invalid by the rules of fair play, that is man to man, stiff and stout, three down and another to come.... No blows, your soul, below the navel!

9. *Stanza 9*: 'O', says Luke, 'Which of you has seen my woman? When I catch the whore, I'll kill her. She's been in 'The Weed and the Steamer' for an hour and a half. Unless she has picked up a client, and will let him sleep with her for money or his watch, I'll give her two black eyes and shake her with my two hands, and make her remember this night.' **Notes on stanza 9:** This stanza seems out of place in the chapbook version of the poem printed here, and may be an interpolation from another version of the text. poll: a generalised name for an immoral woman; 'The Weed and the Steamer' seems to be the name of a Dublin public house — an even more colourful name than most; dye = die = have sexual intercourse; without means 'unless' here, which makes Luke a pimp or, in eighteenth-century Dublin slang, a 'bully'.

Poll ask'd me into drink but
I swore by the holy saint people,
One drop should not enter my gote   110
Until I would leave him in sweet bullies acre[10]

And tip him to bed wid de shovel.

From de burying ground as we came home,
I look'd wid my eyes all round me;
Every Cull with his Whore on his back,
Taking his pleasure in comfort,
I slipt my heel under molls gown,
Down on the ground she tumbled;
Her petticoats up to her Chin,
I soon found the way to her toll de roll.[11]   120

Lord Altham's Bull[1]

'Twas on the fust of sweet Magay,
It being a high holiday,
Six and twenty boys of de straw
Went to take Lord Altham's bull away.

I being de fust in de field, who should I see bud de mosey wid his horns
sticking in de ground. Well becomes me, I pinked up to him, ketched him
by de tail, and rode him dree times round de field, as well as ever de
master of de tailor's corporation rode de fringes; but de mosey being

---

10. *Stanza 10*: [After his execution] Luke's body was exhibited for a while, you know. We
had all the girls of the city. There was never such a show of whores, pimps, robbers and
procurers through the streets. The girl asked me in for a drink, but I swore by the holy
saints that a drop wouldn't enter my guts until I had left him in the graveyard and tipped
him into bed with a shovel. **Notes on stanza 10:** <u>sweet bullies acre</u> seems to have been
a jocular name for a Dublin graveyard.

11. *Stanza 11*: As we came home from the graveyard, I looked with my eyes all around me
and saw every fellow lying down with his whore, enjoying himself. I slipped my heels
under Moll's gown and down she tumbled onto the ground, with her petticoats up to her
chin. I soon found the way to her 'toll de roll'.

1. Bullbaiting was fairly common in eighteenth-century Dublin. Bulls were often stolen,
during the night, from herds being driven into the city for slaughter, and were baited
either in special bull-rings or in the streets. This poem dates from after 1771 when the
Brownes became earls of Altamont (i.e. Altham) and before 1773 when the old Newgate
prison, mentioned towards the end of the poem, was demolished. It was probably first
printed in the 1780s. For the links between this poem and 'Trickster' poems in several
cultures, see Alan Harrison, *The Irish Trickster* (Sheffield, 1989), chapter 6.

game to de back bone, de first rise he gev me in de elements, he made a
smash of me collar-bone. So dere being no blunt in de cly, Madame
Stevens was de word, where I lay for seven weeks in lavendar, on de
broad of me back, like Paddy Ward's pig, be de hokey.[2]

> We drove de bull tro many a gap,
> And kep him going many a mile,
> But when we came to Kilmainham lands,
> We let de mosey rest awhile.

Oh! boys, if de mosey was keeper of de ancle-spring warehouse, you cud
not help pit[y]ing him; his hide smoked like Ned Costigan's brewery, and
dere was no more hair on his hoofs dan dere's wool on a goose's gams, be
de hokey.[3]   20

> We drove de bull down sweet Truck-street,
> Widout eider dread or figear,
> When out ran Mosey Creathorn's bitch,
> Hand cotched de bull be de year.

Hye, Jock — dat dog's my bitch — spit on her nose to keep her in wind —
fight fair, boys, and no stones — low, Nettle, low — shift, shift, my beauty,

2. *Stanza 1*: It was on the first day of the sweet month of May, a high holiday, that twenty-six straw-boys went to take Lord Altham's bull away. I was first into the field, and who should I see but the bull with its horns sticking in the ground. As befits me, I crept up to him, caught him by the tail and rode him three times round the field, as well as ever the master of the tailor's corporation rode the franchises. But the bull was full of life, and the first time he tossed me up in the air, I smashed my collar-bone. Since I had no money in my pockets, I had to go to Mrs Stevens's hospital where I lay for seven weeks in luxury, flat on my back like Paddy Ward's pig, by heaven! **Notes on stanza 1:** Magay: May; boys of de straw: It is tempting to see this as a reference to the 'straw-boys', groups of young bachelors dressed in garb made of straw, who were permitted to behave in a riotous manner at certain times of year under the general direction of someone called the 'Mayor of the Bull-ring'. See J. E. Walsh, *Ireland Sixty Years Ago* (Dublin, 1847), p. 94 and Harrison, chapter 6; however, since those involved in the stealing of the bull are transported to Virginia at the end of this poem, the reference may be to boys employed in the Dublin straw-market at Smithfield; Lord Altham: Lord Altamont; mosey: a common name for a bull; de master of de tailor's corporation rode de fringes: every three years, members of the Dublin guilds rode arounds the bounds of the city in a ceremony known as beating the bounds, franchises or 'fringes', (see above p. 103); blunt in de cly: money in the pocket; Madame Stevens was de word refers to Dr Steevens' Hospital; endowed by Dr Richard Steevens (1653-1710) and built by his sister, Grizell (the 'Madam Stevens' of the text), the hospital opened in 1733; Paddy Ward's pig: the meaning of this is obscure.

3. *Stanza 2*: We drove the bull through many a gap, and kept him going many a mile. But when we came to the fields at Kilmainham, we let him rest. O, boys, if the bull was the keeper of the stocks, you could not help pitying him. His hide smoked like Ned Costigan's brewery and there was no more hair on his hoofs than there is wool on the legs of a goose, by heaven! **Notes on stanza 2:** de ancle-spring warehouse: the stocks; Ned Costigan's brewery was famous for the smoke it discharged over Dublin according to Walsh (p. 96).

and keep your hoult. Oh! boys, your souls, I tought de life ud leave Mosey Creathorn's glimms, when he saw his bitch in de air; 'Oh! Larry Casey, happy det to you, and glory may you get, stand wide and ketch her in your arms — if her head smacks de pavement, she's not worth lifting up — dat's right, yer sowls, now tip her a sup a de blood while it's warm'.[4]

> We drove de bull down Corn-market,
> As all de world might segee,
> When brave Tedy Foy trust his nose tro' de bars,
> Crying 'High for de sweet liberty.

Oh! cruel Coffey, glory to you, just knock off my darbies — let me out on padroul of honour — I'll expel de mob — kill five, skin six, and be fader of de scity, I'll return like an innocent lamb to de sheep-walk. Oh! boys, who lost an arm, who lost five fingers and a tumb?' 'Oh!' says Larry Casey, 'it belongs to Luke Ochy, I know it by de slime on de slieve'.[5]

> De mosey took down Plunket-street,
> Where de clothes on de pegs were hanging,
> Oh! den he laid about wid his nob,
> De shifts around him banging.

Oh! Mrs Mulligan, jewel, take in de bits o' duds from de wall, out o' de way o' de mosey's horns — be de hokey, he'll fly kites wid dem, and den poor Miss Judy will go de Lady Mayress's ball, like a spatchcock.[6]

---

4. *Stanza 3*: We were driving the bull down sweet Tuck Street without either dread or fear, when out ran Mosey Creathorn's bitch, and caught the bull by the ear. 'Hi, Jock, that dog's my bitch! Spit on her nose to help her to breathe! Fight fair, boys, and no stones! Low, Nettle, low! Shift, shift my beauty, and keep your hold!' O boys, your souls, I thought the life would leave Mosey Creathorn's eyes when he saw his bitch in the air! 'O, Larry Casey, may you have a happy death, and may you get glory! Stand with your legs wide and catch her in your arms! If her head smacks the pavement, it's not worth lifting her up! That's right, now give her a little of the blood while it's warm!' **Notes on stanza 3:** spit on her nose could mean 'blow in her nostrils'.

5. *Stanza 4*: We drove the bull down Cornmarket, as all the world might see, when brave Teddy Foy thrust his nose through the bars, crying 'Hey for sweet liberty! O cruel Coffey, glory to you, just knock off my handcuffs, let me out on parole! I'll get rid of the mob in the street, will kill five of them and skin six! I'll be the father of the city and will return like an innocent lamb to the sheep-walk. O, boys, who lost an arm, who lost five fingers and a thumb?' 'O', says Larry Casey, 'it belongs to Luke Ochy; I know it by the slime on the sleeve'. **Notes on stanza 4:** Teddy Foy is a prisoner in the Newgate prison and Coffey is presumably the gaoler there.

6. *Stanza 5*: The bull took off down Plunket Street where the clothes were hanging on the pegs. O, then he laid about him with his head, with petticoats flapping around him. 'O, Mrs Mulligan, dear, take in the bits of clothes from the wall, out of the way of the bull's horns! By heaven, he'll make kites out of them, and then poor Miss Judy will go to the Lady Mayoress's Ball like a spatch-cock.' **Notes on stanza 5:** Plunket Street was a centre for second-hand clothes stalls; a spatch-cock: a fowl killed, dressed and grilled at short notice, so here the phrase means 'naked as a spatch-cock', i.e. with no clothes on.

Lord Altham is a very bad man,
As all de neighbours know,
For driving white Roger from Kilmainham lands,   50
We all to Virginy must go!

Well! boys! — suppose we go for seven years, an't dere six of us! Dat's just fourteen monts a-piece. I can sail in a turf-kish, and if ever I come back from his Majesty's tobacco-manufactory, I'll butter my knife in his tripes, and give him his guts for garters. All de world knows I've de blood of de Dempseys in me.[7]

---

7. *Stanza 6*: Lord Altham is a very bad man, as all the neighbours know. For driving white Roger from Kilmainham lands, we are all to be transported to Virginia! Well, boys! Suppose we go for seven years – aren't there six of us? That's just fourteen months each! I can sail in a turf-basket, and if ever I come back from his Majesty's tobacco-manufactory, I'll butter my knife with Lord Altham's intestines and give him his guts for garters. All the world knows that I've the blood of the Dempseys in me. **Notes on stanza 6:** white Roger is the name of the bull.

445

BRIAN MERRIMAN
(c.1749-**1789**-1805)

from: The Midnight Court
[translated in 1789 by Denis Woulfe]

Cúirt an Mheán Oíche or *The Midnight Court* is the masterpiece of eighteenth-century poetry in the Irish language. Its author, Brian Merriman, was a schoolteacher and farmer who lived at Feakle, Co. Clare. The poem was written about 1780 and translated in 1789, according to a note on the manuscript from which this text is taken, by Denis Woulfe who was the schoolmaster in the neighbouring parish of Sixmilebridge.

In a dream, the poet is forced to attend the 'court', an assembly of women, at which Aoibheall, queen of the fates or fairies of Thomond (a lordship which comprised most of what is now County Clare) acts as judge. The assembly is protesting at the fact that men marry old women for their money and leave young women starved of love and sexual pleasure. A young woman is about to give her evidence.

from: Canto I

A crowded court anon appeared,
All impatient to be heard;
And on the bench, in royal state,
Benignly sat the Queen of Fate;
A female guard with arms advanced
And swords full drawn, her cause enhanced.
A brilliant, blooming, youthful maid,
With silks illumined and arrayed,
With strength of frame, had gained the lists,[1]
Disposed to swear the evangelists.   10
Her hair in tresses loosely flowing,
Her face with ire and anger glowing,
Her looks disdainful, unrelenting,
Her scolding nature representing.
No utterance or words had she,
From violent hate and enmity;
But death would be a consolation
From racking grief and sad vexation,
As on the table firmly mounted,
Her hands she clapped and facts recounted,   20

---

1. The place of combat or contest — in this case, the court.

446

'Til tears bedewed her rueful face,
And sighs renewed her speech apace;
Her visage cleared, her sobs abated,
Her woeful wants she thus related:
'A thousand welcomes to thee I count,
O Joval! of the airy mount;[2]
Thou morning star of brilliant hue;
Our health, our wealth, and refuge true.
Thou mighty Queen! bound advocate!
Your kind relief we now entreat.   30
The cause which makes my tears to flow
And human nature wrapped in woe;
Which did my faculties impair,
And filled my heart with deep despair,
Is the number of the female train
Rank[3] old maids that now remain.
Grey gloomy hags all antiquated
That married life in no wise hated;
As in my travels I have learned
That thousands have for mankind yearned;   40
And I, for one, do surely cry;
No husband's care or heir have I.
Alas! how dismal to narrate
The doleful ills and hardships great
Each dreary night that I endure;
Yet no ease find, nor speedy cure,
But tossing, turning all alone,
All social pleasure from me flown.
Observe with care, O, gracious queen!
The Irish fair inflamed most keen;   50
But if the men thus persevere,
We must prevent,[4] and them ensnare;
They are urged by heat and strange desire,
When no soft maid would them admire,
When no fond pleasure would proceed
From dry old bones as weak as reed!
If perchance in youthful years,
When beard protruding first appears,

2. i.e. Aoibheall, who is acting as judge.
3. mature.
4. i.e. go before them.

447

That one is seven, with open arms,
Would join a maid of graceful charms,   60
A model fair one interesting,
Her manners rare all manifesting,
No tawny brownish budget[5] despised
Who pinched got pounds, had realised.
My brain is racked, my heart is torn,
My mind relaxed and long forlorn;
My wit decayed, my fame declining,
In sad extremes I'm daily pining
When prolific youth I view betrothed
To impotent fools, profusely loathed;   70
Frolicsome, social, jovial blades,
All married to slothful, moping jades;[6]
A dashing, sightly, scion allured,[7]
Of handsome size, and mind matured,
Is often yoked in chains, 'tis true,
To a wrinkled hag, or cankered shrew.
Or yet a greasy, lazy load
Of fleshy frame, or hateful toad;
An overbearing, beastly drone,[8]
To rash extremes from nature prone.   80
O! galling news, a stupid bride,
Of legs awry, and coarse-grain hide,[9]
Tonight in state will married be;
O! hapless fate, not fancy me!
Why not admire my size and gait,
My skin so white, my smile so neat,
My teeth so fair, of ivory hue,
My smirking face, compared by few;
My hazel eye, that brightly rolled,
My neck designed in beauty's mould;   90
My symmetry in grand array;
My dimpled cheeks the rose display;

---

5. wallet or leather pouch. These lines mean that only one young man in seven marries a
   maid of graceful charms and does not get for himself ('realise') a tawny, despised,
   brown-skinned old bag who has gathered ill-deserved riches to herself.
6. older women.
7. i.e. an heir who has been allured or enticed.
8. an idler.
9. skin.

My fingers long, and hands imposing,
My rising breast, to ruth disposing;[10]
My slender waist, and graceful parts,
No bent, no base, no stain imparts.[11]
My members[12] all the laurel claim,
With beauties still I will not name;
No stupid, sluggish, slovenly maiden,
But a charming creature, mild and pleasing.   100
Count me not a cranky stake,[13]
A drowsy gad,[14] or rank old rake;[15]
A haughty hulk, or humdrum hateful,[16]
Brawling Butt,[17] or Slut deceitful;
Or slothful Ape, devoid of glee,
But the loveliest maid that eye could see.
Had I been loose, or coarse, or painless,
Young men to woo, or truly brainless,
Void of wit or cunning ways,
In frantic fits I'd end my days.   110
None as yet did me behold
At watch[18] or wake of young or old,
At pattern,[19] goal,[20] long-dance or race,
Where hearty folk do crown a pace,
But decked most gay in grand attire
In hopes that they would me admire.
My powdered hair I daily dusted;
My high-cauled cap[21] with starch encrusted.

---

10. i.e. disposed to be compassionate or kind.
11. i.e. show that there's nothing crooked or ignoble or stained about me.
12. limbs, but the word can also mean 'the private parts'; 'to claim the laurel' is to win a contest. Frank O'Connor translated these lines: 'There's bottom and belly that claim attention, // And the best concealed that I needn't mention.'
13. old stick.
14. A sleepy, tough old rope. cf. Ir. *gad*, a withe or tough cord made of woven twigs or branches.
15. A lusty and dissipated old woman.
16. A big, haughty, unwieldy person or a hateful old bore.
17. A person who fights and is the object of jokes.
18. All-night devotional ceremony or 'wake'; also, perhaps, the all-night revels associated with midsummer.
19. The revelry following the celebration of the festival of a patron saint.
20. The start of a race.
21. i.e. a woman's cap with a high caul or back to it.

My hood all round with ribbons streaming,
My cotton gown with flounces beaming;   120
My Cardinal,[22] the best in kind,
With scarlet-red, superbly lined.
My apron round of cambric lawn,[23]
With herbs, and flowers, and poultry drawn;
My high-heeled shoes, with screws embraced,
With shining hue, securely laced;
With rings and ruffles, gloves and laces,
Fringes, buckles, bobs and braces.
Fancy me not a heedless creature,
Barren of speech or feeling nature,   130
A fearful, fanciful, fantastic fair,
Unskilled in planning or planting a snare.
I would not hide from Adam's race
My forehead high, or smiling face.
To hurling feats throughout the year
I do repair[24] both far and near,
At goaling, racing, feasting, dancing,
And bonfires blaze, my claims advancing.
At market fair, and sabbath meeting,
Counting, gazing, glancing, greeting;   140
But all in vain, no game in view;
My artful schemes have failed anew.
After all the love unfeigned
That I for men have entertained,
And after all my various losses
By dummies, cards, and tea-cup tosses,[25]
No ancient trick or heathen rite
At coming moon, or purely bright,
On All-Saints' Day, or change of weather,
But were vexatious[26] altogether.   150
Underneath my pillow clothes,
With herbage gay I stuffed my hose;

22. A short cloak worn by ladies, originally of scarlet cloth, with a hood.
23. A type of very fine linen.
24. go.
25. Methods of fortune-telling.
26. A source of trouble or distress. i.e. she tried every possible love-charm at the right
    moments — when the moon was new, and when it was full, and on All Saints' Day, and
    when the weather was changing — though it was a nuisance to do so.

At feasting meals, a fair divide
For conjuration laid aside.[27]
My chemise steeped against the streams,
My love to see in pleasant dreams;
With broom I cleared around the mow;
My hair and nails in ashpit low;
The flail I placed upraised from earth,
The spade concealed beneath the hearth;   160
My distaff stowed beneath the hill;
My bottom thrown in limestone kiln;
In open street I flax-seed shed,
And covered close the cabbage head;
In every stage my rage provoked;
Infernal aid I oft invoked.
O! painful strife! O! dire reflection!
No marriage rite, nor kind protection;
My sad relation analysed,
My years increased unharmonised.   170
To silver locks I'm fast approaching,
And no fond spark my passion broaching.
O! lustrous gem of radient light,
My soul forfend from fell afright;[28]
Dispel with speed my deep decay;
Reflection keen to me pourtray.[29]
The scowling brow, if doomed to roam,
No soothing spouse or friendly home;
By blood of Kings! fire! thunder! air!
I'm fairly duped, I solemnly swear.   180
The meanest dregs of human kind
I see caressed by husbands kind;
Sally hath her bumpkins braced,[30]
Merlin and Dorah to husbands faced;

---

27. In lines 151-66, the girl lists the love-charms and magical actions she used to attract a
lover. She stuffed fresh plants and herbs into her stockings and put them under her pillow;
she kept part of the food served at feasts to use in magic spells; she soaked her underwear
in stream water; she cleared a space around the stack of hay or grain in the barn with a
broom; when she cut her hair or nails, she put the clippings into the ashpit; she stuck the
flail upright in the ground; she concealed a spade under the hearth; she hid her distaff
beneath the hill; she threw a ball or skein of thread ('a bottom') into the limestone kiln;
she cast down flax-seed in the street and she covered a cabbage-head closely. She was
very angry whenever she did these things — and she also called on the devil.
28. i.e. protect my soul from terrible fear.
29. i.e. let me see what I will look like (if I never get married).
30. i.e. her children well cared for.

Matilda and Margery much more elated,
Who at me sport[31] — being so ill-fated.
Slaney and Julia have wealth unbounded,
Cecilia and Hannah with guests surrounded,
With many more in social glee,
And I controlled impatiently;   190
Tho' keen my rueful, ruthless rage,
A speedy cure I do presage.
With herbs, and spells, and magic charms,
That will compel into my arms
A handsome youth, a rural swain,
Whose love profound will drown my pain;
For many tried the like expedient,
And I could find each fine ingredient;
A powerful means that mainly grapples,[32]
Are powdered leaves concealed in apples;   200
The merry mandrake by cow-dung fed,
The great fig-wort with flower not shed;
Sweet woodbine berries, and ozier[33] flowers,
With yellow cumin, and other powers;
Herbs and flowers well pulverised
With strange receipts not advertised.[34]
'Tis wonderful yet all Thomond[35] round,
How Brimstone-Bet a husband found;
But she to me in secret told,
That Planksty[36] fair, her mate so bold,   210
Was hook'd at once, tho' strong and hale,
By boggy roots infused in ale.
I'm labouring long in sad suspense,
Delay me not, but right dispense,
Remove in time my rising pain,
Or in despite, a prize I'll gain....'

---

31. i.e. who make fun of me.
32. that catches them perfectly.
33. osier, willow.
34. The aphrodisiacs in these lines include powdered leaves concealed in apples, the mandrake root (*Mandragora*), the greater fig-wort (*Scrophularia*), the berries of the common honeysuckle (*Lonicera Periclymenum*), the flowers of the willow (*Salix viminalis*), and the yellow cummin (*Cummin Cycinum*).
35. The lordship of Thomond which comprised most of County Clare.
36. Planxty is normally the name given to a lively tune played on the harp, but here it is a proper name.

CHARLOTTE BROOKE
(c.1740-**1789**-1793)

Charlotte Brooke was the youngest of the twenty-two children of Henry Brooke, the novelist, poet, playwright and pamphleteer (whose works she edited). She published a translation of a poem by Carolan (anonymously) in Joseph Cooper Walker's *Historical Memoirs of the Irish Bards* (1786) and, in 1789, brought out her famous *Reliques of Irish Poetry*. Her translations in that volume may seem rather conventional beside the originals, but she also wrote an introduction in which she wrote passionately of the 'various and comprehensive powers' of which 'this neglected language is possessed'. She provided enthusiastic and knowledgeable notes to the translations, as well as some texts in Irish. Her praise of Irish poetry helped change attitudes towards the Irish culture of the period.

Song for Gracey Nugent [1]
(translated from the Irish of Carolan)

Of Gracey's charms enraptur'd will I sing!
Fragrant and fair, as blossoms of the spring;
To her sweet manners, and accomplish'd mind,
Each rival Fair the palm of Love resign'd.

How blest her sweet society to share!
To mark the ringlets of her flowing hair;[2]
Her gentle accents, — her complacent mien! —
Supreme in charms, she looks — she reigns a Queen!

That alabaster form — that graceful neck,
How do the Cygnet's down and whiteness deck! —   10
How does that aspect shame the cheer of day,
When summer suns their brightest beams display.

Blest is the youth whom fav'ring fates ordain
The treasure of her love, and charms to gain!
The fragrant branch, with curling tendrils bound,
With breathing odours — blooming beauty crown'd.

---

1. The subject of the song was the sister of John Nugent of Castle-Nugent, Coolamber, Co. Westmeath.
2. Brooke's note reads: 'Hair is a favourite object with all the Irish Poets, and endless is the variety of their description: — "Soft misty curls" — "Thick branching tresses of bright redundance" — "Locks of fair waving beauty" — "Tresses flowing with the wind like the bright waving flame of an inverted torch". They even affect to inspire it with *expression*: as "Locks of *gentle* lustre" — "Tresses of *tender* beauty" — "The Maid with the *mildly* flowing hair" &c. &c.'

Sweet is the cheer her sprightly wit supplies!
Bright is the sparking azure of her eyes!
Soft o'er her neck her lovely tresses flow!
Warm in her praise the tongues of rapture glow!   20

Her's is the voice — tun'd by harmonious Love,
Soft as the Songs that warble through the grove!
Oh! sweeter joys her converse can impart!
Sweet to the *sense*, and grateful to the *heart*!

Gay pleasures dance where'er her foot-steps bend;
And smiles and rapture round the fair attend:
Wit forms her speech, and Wisdom fills her mind,
And *sight* and *soul* in her their object find.

Her pearly teeth, in beauteous order plac'd;
Her neck with bright, and curling tresses grac'd: —   30
But ah, so fair! — in wit and charms supreme,
Unequal Song must quit its darling theme.

Here I break off; — let sparking goblets flow,
And my full heart its cordial wishes show:
To her dear health this friendly draught I pour,
Long be her life, and blest its every hour!

THOMAS DAWSON LAWRENCE
(c.1730-**1789**-c.1810)

According to D. J. O'Donoghue, Thomas Lawrence was at school with Goldsmith in Ballymahon, Co. Longford. He later joined the British army and rose to the rank of colonel. Lawrence lived in Banbridge, Co. Down, and his *Miscellaneous Works* (Dublin, 1789) were published for the benefit of the Sunday School there.

Epitaph on an orphan beggar child

To find an earthly home in vain I tried,
But heav'n has granted what the world denied;
No sorrowing friends surround my gloomy bier,
No parent wrings the hand, or drops the tear;
An orphan, friendless here, shall now no more
His absent parents, or his fate deplore.
Hear! pamper'd slaves of luxury and pride,
Ye who in gorgeous palaces reside!
The same Creator bounteously has giv'n
A wand'rer here, a passport safe to Heav'n.   10

PART V
1790-1805

L. O'REILLY
(fl. **1790**)

The verse which follows is one of the few poems written in English by itinerant Irish-speaking ballad-makers to have survived unaltered and unedited. In form, style and subject matter, this poem is an English-language version of an Irish elegy. The poet would probably have learned what English he knew from books, rather than from native speakers, which would explain his misunderstanding of the meanings of certain English words and of the syntax of standard English; the rules he is applying thoughout the poem are those of Irish rather than English prosody.

A headnote in the first printing of this poem explains how it came to be preserved. A company of ladies, who were taking an evening's walk in the Irish countryside, happened to meet 'a poor mad itinerant Ballad-maker' and purchased all his compositions from him. The elegy on the death of Miss Burne happened to be the first poem read aloud, and the company amused themselves by laughing at it. A poet called William Ball,[1] who was present, defended the poem, 'extolled its excellences' and 'dared to hint something about the taste of ladies for fashionable dress and frippery'. As a penance for his remarks, or perhaps to support his argument, Ball was required by the company to 'translate' the elegy into the conventional poetic language and metre of the day. Joshua Edkins, when he included Ball's poem in the second volume of his *A Collection of Poems, mostly original, by several hands* (two vols, Dublin, 1790, I, 141-49) printed the original poem and the 'translation' on facing pages, and gave the name of the ballad-maker as L. O'Reilly.

Elegy
on the death of the late good and truly pious Miss Bridget Burne[2]

Unhappy Hibernia mourn, O mourn and do not cease!
Thus and only thus can you equitably appease
The throbs and griefs of all that lov'd the good,
The seraphick spirit that from you alas! is fled.
Mourn ye widows, your comfortress is gone;
Ye orphans mourn, thrice orphantized again;
Lament ye poor; ye lost her tender-looking charity,
Who pity'd your wants, distress and misery:
In all your griefs, along with you she would grieve,
Oppress'd with distress until yours she would relieve: 10

---

1. William Ball was the third son of Rev. Thomas Ball of Dublin. He was educated at Trinity College, Dublin and was called to the Irish Bar in 1775.
2. The poet's unfamiliarity with standard English is seen in the vocabulary and syntax of the poem. However, unless the meaning is obscure, individual words and phrases are not explained in the notes, though the rather eccentric punctuation of the original has been amended in places.

Ye pious christians, great and small, lament.
She is gone whose Heavenly spirit gave you all content.
Unhappy Hibernia! Ominous Ominous is your fate,
Since you have lost that celestical Heavenly spirit,
Unless she works your patronage with God above
Who again may take you into his love.
On earth her virtuous parallel she scarce did leave.
Her acquaintance (no wonder) do not — can not, cease to grieve.
Good natured, tender, pious, affectionate, sincere,
In charitable deeds incessant, and in prayer,   20
She lov'd God and truth to that high degree
Could her seraphick soul heat, she hated but hypocricy.
Her desires, thoughts, words, and actions only sought
God's honour and glory to promote.
She was sincere, good hearted, hospitable, kind,
Her serafick soul with every grace and virtue shined.
She spoke the French and learned the Irish to perfection,
Weekly taught crouds of children there christian docterene.
She studied physick on purpose to relieve the poor;
She kept always medicens their Languers for to cure;   30
The loathsomests ulsers that would the poor oppress,
With her own blessed hands she would dress.
The sovereign Lord, whose immence wisdom did ordain
Different herbs various virtues to retain,
The indefaticable labours of Miss Burne so did bless,
To cure her patients she always had success.
In the happy youth of her domestick abode,
The seeds of every christian virtue she has sowed;
Her domesticks before bed-time every night,
In mutual, reciprocal prayer she would unite,   40
With holy conversation and pure integrity.
She done all her works to God's honour and glory.
To speak God's praises was her greatest joy,
This was her chief employment and felicity.
Pure joy, tenatious of a certain certitude,
To be enraped coheir[3] in Christ's celestial abode,
During immemorable ages, Angels shall celebrate her immortal fame,
Her victores and virtues memorable ever shall remain.

---

3. i.e. to be included as a joint heir.

O ye her friends, if ye can cease to grieve,
Raise now your mournful thoughts from the grave!   50
Her glorious soul in spetious mantions of Heaven's immencity,
In angelick consort shall reign for all eternity.
There grief shall find no place, nor joy shall have an End,
Never-ending delights the blessed there ever find;
In frequence of eternal day, in great transending joys,
Unremitting echoes there rowls never failing Allelujahs.
Thro' the sublimest pleasures of celestial felicity,
Every moment to augment as immence as eternity;
No space can bound Heaven's sublimest atmosphere,
Nor tongue can speak what God does prepair   60
For those who do him love and does his Law preserve;
With Christ coheir they Eternally shall live.
Could good nature recoil that joy, grief should preponderate,
Her presant glory that we should congratulate;[4]
Good nature must have its way, reason still shall joy,
And thus we all congratulate her felicity.

---

4. As they stand, these lines are unintelligible. However, Ball's rather free 'translation'
   removes the obscurity: 'Cease then thy tears, good nature! And instead, // With joy let
   ev'ry friendly bosom glow'.

MARY O'BRIEN
(fl. **1790**)

Little is known about Mary O'Brien except that she lived in Ireland for some years. She is said to have been the wife of a Patrick O'Brien and to have written novels and plays in addition to *The Political Monitor*, her volume of poems inspired by the regency crisis of 1788 and published in Dublin. The poem which follows is as vivid a caricature of the blustering 'John Bull' (a personification of England) as that achieved by many of the cartoonists of the day in their satirical drawings and prints.

The Freedom of John Bull

As poets write, and painters tell,
In form some heads are like a well;
Round as scoop'd Pumpkins in the hull,
Fat brains, thick sinews form a skull,
With every wit so near a kin,
You'd swear, if swearing was no sin,
Genius was in a *fog* within.
A face! for so the stories run,
Resembling much a midday sun;
Broad chin, plump cheeks ascending rise,   10
Sinking the twinkling of two eyes:
Such Jacky Bull, so soft and mellow
He's a mere woolsack[1] of a fellow.
With belly not unlike a butt,[2]
Behold him oft in elbow strut,
Discoursing on Britannia's laws,
A counsellor in freedom's cause;
As Bacchus on a barrel rides
So he on liberty bestrides,
Trotting with hobby horse's motion   20
To mount the cliffs of mother ocean.
Firm on a rock, a Briton born,
A foreign coast he views with scorn;

---

1. The English lord chancellor traditionally sits on a woolsack when in the House of Lords; but a woolsack is all bulk and no substance.
2. barrel — but also an object of ridicule.

There 'tween roast beef and porter[3] hung,
Each sense suspended, but the tongue,
Free 'midst a load of ills he reigns,
Tax'd at all points except his brains.
Were Billy Pitt[4] but to propose,
A tax on breathing thro' the nose,
Compliant to the youth's[5] intent,   30
He'd snuffle freedom in his scent;
So proud of his politic fate,
He'd boast tho' sinking with the weight.
Thus Billy, happily befriended,
Patches that fame but last year mended;[6]
As prudes in thread-bare estimation,
Clout up[7] their worn out reputation.

---

3. dark ale.
4. William Pitt (1759-1806), prime minister of England 1783-1801 and 1804-06.
5. Pitt had been only twenty-four when he became prime minister in 1783.
6. Pitt had been in political danger while King George III was temporarily insane in 1788/89, but returned to favour on the king's recovery in April 1789.
7. patch up.

HENRIETTA BATTIER
(1751-**1791**-1813)

Henrietta Battier was born in County Meath and married the son of a Huguenot banker in Dublin. Though she once described herself as 'a better housewife than poet', Mrs Battier is remembered today as the author of the best Irish satirical verse of the late eighteenth century. She was an ardent Irish nationalist and entered the political and social debates of the day with gusto; 'The Lemon', her spirited answer to John Giffard's ultra-loyalist poem 'The Orange', is highly entertaining, though its many specific political allusions limit its appeal for a modern reader. Despite the fact that she was paid for much that she wrote, Mrs Battier's fortunes gradually declined after the death of her husband in 1794, and when she died in Sandymount, near Dublin, she was apparently destitute.

In the two parts of *The Kirwanade* (Dublin, 1791), Mrs Battier attacked Rev. W.B. Kirwan, a famous preacher who had left the catholic priesthood and conformed to the Church of Ireland. The poem first appeared under the pseudonym of 'Patt Pindar', a name which thoroughly baffled the critics, who thought the author was certainly male and probably a clergyman. However, in the following passage from the second part of the poem, Mrs Battier puts the record straight.

from: The Kirwanade

Have at you, *K——N*!: — I'm myself again,
Nor has a cobweb dar'd to touch my pen:
Let envy burn her bowels to a cinder,
I still am *PATT*; — and while it pleases, *PINDAR*.
The public like me, and I'm grown in favour
As much as you are, so I must endeavour
To keep the gen'rous Bookseller's good-will,
Who well rewards the labours of my quill.
I do not want a plain expression twisted,
And tho' nor Priest nor Levite[1] has assisted   10
My flights of fancy or proscrib'd my game,
I wrote for *profit*, and Fate added *fame*.
'Living', I own's a very good reward,
Be it in the gift of Mr. or My Lord,[2]
For all the journey-work this pen of mine
Has ever done for the Olympian nine.[3]

1. Levites assisted the priests in Jewish religious ceremonies in the Old Testament.
2. Kirwan had accepted a 'living' from his new church and was, by 1791, both incumbent of the Dublin parish of St Nicholas Without and holder of the prebendal stall of Howth in the chapter of St Patrick's Cathedral.
3. i.e. she too, deserves to make a 'living' out of her work for the poetic muses.

And tho' no *gownsman*,[4] as your champions call me,
Yet, if a Sinecure[5] should over-haul me,
I think I know my own wild heart so well
That all the powers combin'd of earth and hell   20
Should never make its grateful pulses bend
To breathe a calumny against that friend
To whose benevolence of heart I ow'd
The streams of plenty that around me flow'd.

But whither has egotism borne my pen?
Forgive my rudeness, — most admir'd of men!
And give me leave to introduce myself —
Amongst some other maggots on your shelf.

The woman lately carried such a farce on
That, 'spite of common sense, they dubb'd me 'parson';   30
'Tis false tho', κ——ν; and I here make known,
I wear no petticoats except my own;
I am no mannish, het'rogeneous creature,
But truly feminine in limb and feature;
Thin as yourself, as waspish too at times,
And just as flippant in my tongue and rhymes.
My fortune's humble, but my spirit's high,
Nor can I brook the least indignity;
More of the mastiff than the spaniel breed,[6]
A whip shan't drive me, tho' a straw may lead.   40
Grateful myself, when I behold another
Maltreat his patron — were that man my brother,
For ever after I'd despise and hate him,
And like a Bear for ever seek to bait him;
With my last breath I'd justify my friend,
And mourn the faults I could no more defend.

I'm not ambitious — and a tiny thing
Makes me as pleased and happy as a king.
These are my principles — now, could there be
The smallest union between *you* and *me*?...   50

---

4. clergyman.
5. The implication is that Kirwan's prebendal stall of Howth was a sinecure. At a meeting of the chapter of St Patrick's in 1791, Kirwan had insulted the archbishop of Dublin who had given him the appointment.
6. Mastiffs are large, fierce dogs whereas spaniels are smaller and are said to fawn.

Lines addressed to the late Lord Clifden,

in behalf on the Three Young Men, *who ran away with the* Miss Kennedy's,
were written at the request of Miss Byrn, who was Sister *to one of them, and a
most amiable woman.*[1]

Oh! Thou in whom united virtues shine,
To Mercy's pleadings let thy heart incline,
Thy goodness oft prevented[2] my request,
This is the last and grant it — 'tis the best;
A word from you, my honour'd friend, may save
Three wretched youths from an untimely grave,
What tho' offended Justice turns away,
From all their kindred or the world can say,
Yet thou wert made in Mercy's happier hour,
Nor vainly just, nor arrogant of power;   10
The clay was purcelain,[3] of which you were form'd,
And gentler passions have they bosom warm'd,
And Mercy mark'd her character in vain
In Clifden's[4] face, if blood those marks should stain.
Think not, my friend, I dare point out to you,
Where mercy most, or retribution's due;
But yet, in equity, you'll own, my Lord,
That greater crimes oft scape a just reward;
Had brutal force, preventing an escape,
Compell'd their persons to a marriage rape,   20
Then every honest, generous breast must own,
No death but CHRIST's could for the crime atone;

---

1. On 12 April 1779, in one of the most famous abductions of eighteenth-century Ireland, Catherine and Anne Kennedy, aged fifteen and fourteen respectively and heirs to a fortune of £2,000, were abducted while visiting family friends at Graiguenamanagh, County Kilkenny. The two girls were taken away on horseback, forcibly married to their abductors by a 'couple-begging' priest, and violated. They were rescued five weeks later and their abductors, James Strange and Garret Byrne (with James Strange's brother Patrick), were tried for the crime and sentenced to death. Garret Byrne's sister persuaded (or, more probably, paid) Henrietta Battier to send the following poetic request for clemency to the local MP, James Agar, who had been elevated to the peerage as Baron Clifden in 1776. But all appeals failed, and the three young men were executed in Clonmel on 2 December 1780. See James Kelly, 'The Abduction of Women of Fortune in Eighteenth-Century Ireland', *Eighteenth-Century Ireland / Iris an dá chultúr*, ix, 1994, 7-43 (pp. 31-32). This poem did not appear in book form until after Lord Clifden's death.
2. i.e. forestalled.
3. porcelain — i.e. of the finest quality.
4. James Agar of Gowran Castle, Co. Kilkenny, MP for Kilkenny in the Irish parliament, was created Baron Clifden in 1776 and Viscount Clifden in 1781. He died 1 January 1789.

But think, my Lord, they were their willing wives,[5]
And spare, oh! spare, their wretched husbands' lives;
Justice has past her sentence, now, my Lord,
Let Mercy sheath the all avenging sword.
From the dark horrors of those dreadful cells,
Where dire Remorse, and black Conviction dwells
The sad triumvirate for mercy sue;
Their mothers, kinsmen, and a sister too;   30
Unhappy girl, oh! Clifden, had you seen
The wild distress, which mark'd her graceful mien,
The storms of sorrow that convulsed that breast,
Where all the friend and sister stood confest,
A mind, less amiably kind than yours
Would soothe the anguish that her soul endures.
Think then, my friend, when that all pleasing form,
Which Clifden owns, and many virtues warm,
Has past the pleasures of his youth and prime,
And waits the sure, tho' slow award of time,   40
When silver age has dim'd those speaking eyes,
And every joy must from reflection rise;
Think then, I say, how exquisitely great,
Beyond the glories of terrestrial state,
Will be the memory of an act like this,
That brings a foretaste of eternal bliss.
Oh! then anticipate the dear delight
Of conscience telling you, you acted right!
For power's best charter, rightly understood,
Is the prerogative of doing good;   50
Think not presumption has inspir'd my pen,
Thou most benignant of the sons of men,
Nor let my noble generous friend refuse,
The meek intreaties of the suppliant Muse.

---

5. Anne Kennedy, whose determination to prosecute her abductors gave the authorities the courage to proceed with the trial and, when a conviction was secured, with the execution, would not have agreed with this interpretation of events.

PAT O'KELLY
(1754-**1791**-c.1812)

Pat O'Kelly was one of the more colourful characters of late eighteenth-century Ireland. He lived as a wandering bard, in the tradition of the Gaelic poets, and travelled around Ireland on a piebald pony seeking patrons for his poems. His volumes of poetry are full of fascinating glimpses of ordinary life in Ireland. In 'The Itinerary', O'Kelly recounts his travels from Roscommon to Dublin via Galway, Limerick, County Kerry, Cork, Clonmel and Kilkenny; it is clear that, on the way, he stopped for generous refreshment at almost every town and country house of any significance. He also solicited subscriptions for the volume of verse which would follow the ramble, and the subscribers' list of his 1791 *Poetical Miscellanies*, which contains nearly two thousand names, including remarkable numbers from provincial towns, shows how successful he was.

from: The Itinerary

With thee fond *Roscommon*, thou seat of the *muses*,
Where claret to no man its genius refuses,
My song shall commence — and commencing shall tell
What beauties and heroes thy catalogue swell.
Thy *Frenches* and *Croftons*,[1] so dear to fair fame,
Shall ever the wreath of intelligence claim;
Hence parting, and parting with genuine sorrow,
Tho' fraught with a head that ne'er thinks of to-morrow,
All musing and thinking, unheard and alone,
The *muse* made her speediest way to *Athlone*;   10
Where fancy and wit, and the gen'rous board,
The elegant flights of rich genius afford;
Here the Nine[2] with O'KELLY a fortnight resided,
While wit, and good humour, and fortune presided.
His friends reckon'd many, and each friend subscribing,[3]
Whose hearts, and whose hands, shall be still worth describing.
With these I now part — tho' my heart shall remain,
And hold up their goodness in splendor's bright train.
DUNLOE,[4] to thy seats, next our journey we take,
Where freedom and friendship an holyday make;   20

1. The main landowning families in County Roscommon.
2. i.e. the nine muses.
3. i.e. buying a subscription to the volume of poems.
4. William-Power-Keating Trench (of the Le Poer-Trench family), Viscount Dunlo and Earl of Clancarty, who lived at Garbally, Co. Galway.

Where SKERRIT[5] of elegant mind — as of form
Still blossoms to forward delight and to charm....

Sweet KERRY — thou fav'rite spot of the Nine!
Where wit is still sparkling and glows like its wine,
Where HOGAN[6] of classical genius and skill,
Turns learning's best periods[7] and thoughts at his will!
From genial enchantments so frequent in KERRY,
And all the endearments of claret and sherry
We part — and we visit the banks of the LEE,[8]
Where CORK holds her commerce and liberties free....   30
What friendship, what virtues, here ope on the mind!
Where elegant figures are noble as kind.
The men fraught with spirit, the women with wit,
And beauty that stoics can annually hit!
Dear DALY[9] thy coffee and news are so good,
That every VISITANT praises thy food: —
That a *bard* be it ever and candidly known,
Thinks you prize ev'ry merit — forgetting your own! ...

Fair CARLOW we next thy lov'd buildings behold!
Where *Staunton*[10] despises each pomp, pride and gold!   40
Where learning displays ev'ry skill of a college,
And friendship and genius unite with true knowledge.
To SALLINS[11] where barges and dearness unite,
And bells only tinkle the dreary long night
Our passage we take, and to *Castletown*[12] come,
That seat of the *muses* and charity's home:
Where lovely LOUISA deals many a blessing,
And patriot THOMAS[13] shines each worth possessing.

---

5. Hyacinth Skerrett of Finavara, Co. Clare.
6. Edmond Hogan of Killarney.
7. sentences.
8. The river Lee flows through Cork city.
9. The owner of a coffee-house in Cork city.
10. Rev. Henry Staunton of Carlow.
11. A town in County Kildare, on the Grand Canal.
12. Castletown House, Celbridge, Co. Kildare, the home of the Conolly family.
13. Lady Louisa Conolly (1743-1821) and her husband, the Right Hon. Thomas Conolly (1737-1803).

To DUBLIN — the favourite rise of the *Graces*![14]
Where guineas are free[15] as are beauteous the faces!   50
KILLARNEY came *greeting* to elegant HOEY[16]
Whose *standard impression* secur'd us much joy.

The Litany for Doneraile[1]

Alas! how dismal is my tale,
I lost my watch in Doneraile.
My Dublin watch, my chain and seal,
Pilfer'd at once in Doneraile.
May Fire and Brimstone never fail,
To fall in show'rs on Doneraile.
May all the leading fiends assail,
The thieving Town of Doneraile.
As light'nings flash across the vale,
So down to Hell with Doneraile.   10
The fate of Pompey at Pharsale,[2]
Be that the curse of Doneraile.
May Beef, or Mutton, Lamb, or Veal,
Be never found in Doneraile,
But Garlic Soup and scurvy Cale,[3]
Be still the food for Doneraile.
And forward as the creeping snail,
Th'industry be, of Doneraile.   ·
May Heav'n a chosen curse entail,
On rigid, rotten Doneraile.   20
May Sun and Moon for ever fail,
To beam their lights on Doneraile.

---

14. The classical goddesses of beauty and inspiration of poets.
15. i.e. are bestowed freely.
16. This poem appears in the 'standard edition' of O'Kelly's *Killarney, a descriptive poem*, printed for him by the Dublin printer Peter Hoey, of Ormond Quay.

---

1. This famous curse was written in 1808 after O'Kelly had visited the town of Doneraile in County Cork. When she read the poem, Lady Doneraile sent O'Kelly a watch and seal as replacements for those stolen and he, in response, wrote a companion poem pouring blessings on the town. As in many other similar poems, the poet's ingenuity is taxed in finding rhymes for the place-name at the centre of the poem.
2. The army of Julius Caesar inflicted a crushing defeat on that of Pompey at Pharsalus in 48 B.C.
3. i.e. kale, an edible, cabbage-like plant.

May ev'ry pestilential gale,
Blast that curs'd spot called Doneraile.
May not a Cuckoo, Thrush or Quail,
Be ever heard in Doneraile.
May Patriots, Kings and commonweal,
Despise and harass Doneraile.
May ev'ry post, Gazette and Mail,
Sad tidings bring of Doneraile. 30
May loudest thunders ring a peal,
To blind and deafen Doneraile.
May vengeance fall at head and tail,
From North and South at Doneraile.
May profit light and tardy sale,
Still damp the trade of Doneraile.
May Fame resound a dismal tale,
Whene'er she lights on Doneraile.
May Egypt's plagues at once prevail,
To thin the knaves of Doneraile. 40
May frost and snow, and sleet and hail,
Benumb each joint in Doneraile.
May wolves and bloodhounds trace and trail,
The cursed crew of Doneraile.
May Oscar with his fiery flail,
To Atoms thresh all Doneraile.[4]
May every mischief fresh and stale,
Abide henceforth in Doneraile.
May all from Belfast to Kinsale,[5]
Scoff, curse, and damn you Doneraile. 50
May neither Flow'r nor Oatenmeal,
Be found or known in Doneraile.
May want and woe each joy curtail,
That e'er was known in Doneraile.
May no one coffin want a nail,
That wraps a rogue in Doneraile.
May all the thieves that rob and steal,
The Gallows meet in Doneraile.
May all the sons of Granuwale,[6]
Blush at the thieves of Doneraile. 60

4. This reference seems to be to a comet.
5. i.e. from the north of Ireland to the south.
6. Grainne O'Malley (Gráinne Mhaol), famous for a life of piracy and plunder along the
west coast of Ireland during the 1580s and 1590s.

May mischief big as Norway whale,[7]
O'erwhelm the knaves of Doneraile.
May curses wholesale and retail,
Pour with full force on Doneraile.
May ev'ry transport wont to sail,
A convict bring from Doneraile.
May ev'ry churn and milking pail,
Fall dry to staves in Doneraile.[8]
May cold and hunger still congeal,
The stagnant blood of Doneraile.   70
May ev'ry hour new woes reveal,
That Hell reserves for Doneraile.
May ev'ry chosen ill prevail,
O'er all the Imps of Doneraile.
May no one wish or pray'r avail,
To soothe the woes of Doneraile.
May th'Inquisition strait impale,
The rapparees[9] of Doneraile.
May curse of Sodom now prevail,[10]
And sink to ashes Doneraile.   80
May Charon's[11] Boat triumphant sail,
Completely mann'd from Doneraile.
Oh! may my couplets never fail,
To find new curse for Doneraile.
And may grim Pluto's inner gaol,[12]
For ever groan with Doneraile.

---

7. The rorqual or fin-whale, formerly common in waters off Norway.
8. In eighteenth- and early nineteenth-century Ireland, pails, churns and buckets were all made of wooden staves held together by metal bands; if the wood dried out, the utensil fell to pieces.
9. outlaws or bandits. By 'Inquisition', O'Kelly means, of course, the authorities in Ireland.
10. The city of Sodom was destroyed by fire and brimstone from heaven because of the wickedness of its inhabitants (Genesis, 19).
11. In classical mythology, Charon was the ferryman who conducted the souls of the dead in a boat over the river Styx to the infernal regions.
12. Pluto, the god of the infernal regions, lived in the centre of hell, where he sat on a throne of sulphur.

ELLEN TAYLOR
(fl. **1792**)

Written by the Barrow side, where she was sent to wash Linen[1]

Thy banks, O Barrow, sure must be
    The Muses' choicest haunt,
Else why so pleasing thus to me,
    Else why my soul enchant?

To view thy dimpled surface here,
    Fond fancy bids me stay;
But Servitude, with brow austere,
    Commands me straight away.

Were Lethe's virtues[2] in thy stream,
    How freely would I drink,   10
That not so much as on the name
    Of books I e'er might think.

I can but from them learn to know
    What misery's complete,
And feel more sensibly each blow
    Dealt by relentless fate.

In them I oft have pleasure found,
    But now it's all quite fled.
With fluttering heart, I lay me down,
    And rise with aching head.   20

For such a turn ill suits the sphere
    Of life in which I move,
And rather does a load of care
    Than any comfort prove.

---

1. Though she later seems to have kept a school, Ellen Taylor was employed as a maid in a house near Graiguenamanagh, Co. Kilkenny when she wrote this poem. She explains, in the introduction to *Poems by Ellen Taylor, the Irish Cottager* (1792), that it was a guest in the house who encouraged her to write poetry. The same unknown benefactor may have been behind the attempt to raise money for her through the publication of her work. Only forty copies of her *Poems* were printed and it is remarkable that such a slight, cheaply printed pamphlet has survived. The river Barrow flows through Graiguenamanagh.
2. The rever Lethe was one of the rivers of hell in classical mythology. Those who drank its waters forgot all that they had done, seen or heard.

Thrice happy she, condemned to move
        Beneath the servile weight,
Whose thoughts ne'er soar one inch above
        The standard of her fate.

But far more happy is the soul,
        Who feels the pleasing sense;   30
And can indulge without control
        Each thought that flows from thence.

Since naught of these my portion is,
        But the reverse of each,
That I shall taste but little bliss,
        Experience doth me teach.

Could cold insensibility
        Through my whole frame take place,
Sure then from grief I might be free:
        Yes, then I'd hope for peace.   40

HENRIETTA O'NEILL
(1758-**1792**-1793)

Henrietta Boyle was the grand-daughter of the fifth earl of Cork and Orrery, Swift's biographer. In 1777, she married John O'Neill of Shane's Castle, Co. Antrim, who became Baron O'Neill in 1793 and Viscount O'Neill in 1795. He later died of wounds received during the rising of 1798. Henrietta, who was an excellent amateur actress and who patronised, among others, the young Thomas Dermody, is remembered now for two remarkable poems, the 'Ode to the Poppy' and lines 'Written on Seeing her Two Sons at Play' (*Eighteenth-Century Women Poets*, ed. Roger Lonsdale (Oxford, 1989), p. 459). The 'poppy' celebrated in this poem is the opium poppy.

Ode to the Poppy

Not for the promise of the labour'd field,
Not for the good the yellow harvests yield,
    I bend at Ceres[1] shrine;
    For dull, to humid eyes, appear
    The golden glories of the year;
Alas! a melancholy worship's mine;
I hail the goddess for her scarlet flower;
    Thou brilliant weed!
    That dost so far exceed
The richest gifts gay Flora[2] can bestow;   10
Heedless I pass'd thee in life's morning hour,
    Thou comforter of woe!
Till sorrow taught me to confess thy power.

    In early days, when Fancy cheats,
      A various wreath I wove
    Of laughing spring's luxuriant sweets,
      To deck ungrateful love:
    The rose or thorn my numbers[3] crown'd,
    As Venus smil'd, or Venus frown'd;
But Love, and Joy, and all their train are flown.   20
    E'en languid Hope no more is mine,
    And I will sing of thee alone;

---

1. The classical goddess of corn and cornfields. Poppies commonly grow in cornfields.
2. The goddess of flowers.
3. verses.

Unless, perchance, the attributes of grief,
    The cypress bud, and willow leaf,
Their pale funereal foliage blend with thine.
      Hail, lovely blossom! thou canst ease
      The wretched victims of disease,
Canst close those weary eyes in gentle sleep
      Which never open but to weep;
          For, oh! thy potent charm   30
      Can agonizing pain disarm;
Expel imperious memory from her seat,
And bid the throbbing heart forget to beat.

Soul-soothing plant! that can such blessings give;
      By thee the mourner bears to live;
         By thee the hopeless die;
      Oh! ever friendly to despair,
      Might Sorrow's pallid votary dare,
Without a crime, that remedy implore,
Which bids the spirit from its bondage fly;   40
I'd court thy palliative aid no more;[4]
      No more I'd sue that thou should'st spread
      Thy spell around my aching head,
      But would conjure thee to impart
      Thy balsam[5] for a broken heart;
      And by thy soft Lethean power,[6]
         Inestimable flower!
Burst these terrestrial bonds, and other regions try.

---

4. i.e. might the pale-faced, devout worshiper of sorrow dare call — without its being a crime — for that remedy which bids the spirit fly from its captivity, I would not seek the palliative aid of opium any more. (O'Neill means that, if suicide were not a crime, she would seek that instead of opium.)

5. soothing ointment.

6. Those who drank the waters of Lethe (a river in hell) forgot everything they had ever experienced.

THOMAS DERMODY

(1775-**1792**-1802)

Dermody was born in Ennis, Co. Clare, the son of a hedge-schoolmaster. A child prodigy, he learned Latin and Greek early in life and taught in his father's school before he was ten. He then ran away to Dublin where he lived as a poor wandering scholar and poet. He attracted the notice of various patrons, but his erratic behaviour and heavy drinking alienated them all. He died in England at the age of twenty-seven. Dermody's brief, passionate, self-destructive life was probably less romantic than later commentators would like to believe.

An Ode to Myself

Thrice hail, thou prince of jovial fellows,
Tuning so blithe thy lyric bellows,
Of no one's brighter genius jealous;
        Whose little span
Is spent 'twixt poetry and alehouse,
        'Twixt quill and can.

Reckless howe'er the world may fadge,[1]
Variety thy only badge:
Now courting Susan, Kate, or Madge,
        Or black-eyed Molly;   10
For living in one sullen lodge
        Is downright folly.

Thy classics sleeping on the shelf,
Thou'rt muse and patron to thyself:
Aye frolic when profuse of pelf;[2]
        Grim as the gallows
When dunned by that obstreperous elf,
        False-scoring Alice.[3]

---

1. agree.
2. money.
3. The keeper of the alehouse is chasing him for debts which he asserts were falsely added to his account.

Long may'st thou punch ambrosial swill,
Drinking no water from that hill   20
By temperate bards recorded still
        In tasteless rhyme;[4]
For noble punch shall sweetly fill
        The thought sublime.

By many wrong'd, gay bloom of song,
Thou yet art innocent of wrong,
Virtue and truth to thee belong,
        Virtue and truth;
Though Pleasure led thy step along,
        And trapp'd thy youth.   30

With Baynham,[5] social spring of wit,
Thou hadst full many a merry fit,
And whether haply thou shalt sit
        With clown or peer,
Never shall lingering honour quit
        Thy heart sincere.

Ode to the Collegians[1]

SQUARECAPS, and round,[2] all honest boys,
May Tutors ne'er cry down your joys,
Or study, which bright Jest destroys,
        Teaze ye, when mellow!
Nor SATAN come, with sawcer eyes,
        In shape of Fellow!

---

4. Dermody contrasts the pleasures of drinking punch (fit for the gods) with the lack of delight in drinking water, even if the water is that of poetic inspiration and comes from the fountain of Hippocrene near Mount Helicon, the mountain sacred to the Greek muses.

5. John Baynam, a drinking companion of Dermody, was parish clerk of Killeigh, Co. Offaly.

1. This, probably because it is the work of an outsider, is the least serious of many eighteenth-century poems concerning the students of Trinity College, Dublin.

2. Undergraduate and graduate students wore caps of different shapes.

No Porter,[3] with obstrep'rous summons,
Startle your nap, with early drummings;
Be yours, short lectures, and long Commons,[4]
        To gar[5] you cheary!   10
For, in this life, whatever comes on's,
        Let's e'en be merry;

Let all your chamber-girls be pretty,
Your chums facete,[6] and free, and witty;
Your Masters not inclin'd to fret ye,
        Wi' too much knowledge;
And then, mon dieu! old Dublin City,
        May boast her College!

3. The keeper of the main gate, who also carried out various duties around the college.
4. Commons was (and is) the main formal, daily meal in the dining hall of Trinity College.
5. make.
6. facetious.

EDWARD RUSHTON
(1756-**1793**-1814)

The song which follows has often been stated to be the work of George Nugent Reynolds (1771-1802), a well-known poet and song-writer from County Leitrim. However, in *The Poets of Ireland* (Dublin, 1912), D. J. O'Donoghue states categorically (though without citing his evidence) that it was not by Reynolds but was the work of Edward Rushton. Rushton was an Englishman from Liverpool, who lost his sight on a slaving expedition to Guinea in 1774 (Roger Lonsdale, *The New Oxford Book of Eighteenth-Century Verse* (Oxford, 1983) p. 855). He later became a bookseller and journalist in his native city and, apparently, recovered his sight in 1807 after being blind for thirty-three years. Rushton's father is said to have been from Ireland, which would help explain why he wrote a song such as this.

Mary le More

As I stray'd o'er the common on Cork's rugged border,[1]
    While the dew-drops of morn the sweet primrose array'd,
I saw a poor maiden whose mental disorder,
    Her quick-glancing eye and wild aspect betray'd.
On the sward she reclined, by the green fern surrounded,
At her side speckled daisies and wild flow'rs abounded:
To its utmost recesses her heart had been wounded;
    Her sighs were unceasing — 'twas Mary le More.

Her charms by the keen blasts of sorrow were faded,
    Yet the soft tinge of beauty still play'd on her cheek;   10
Her tresses a wreath of pale primroses braided,
    And strings of fresh daisies hung loose on her neck.
While with pity I gazed, she exclaim'd, 'O my mother!
See the blood on that lash, 'tis the blood of my brother;
They have torn his poor flesh, and they now strip another —
    'Tis Connor, the friend of poor Mary le More.

'Though his locks were as white as the foam of the ocean,
    Those wretches shall find that my father is brave;
My father!' she cried, with the wildest emotion,
    'Ah! no, my poor father now sleeps in the grave!   20

---

1. i.e. the border between counties Cork and Kerry.

They have toll'd his death-bell, they've laid the turf o'er him,
His white locks were bloody! no aid could restore him;
He is gone! he is gone! and the good will deplore him,
    When the blue waves of Erin hide Mary le More.'

A lark, from the gold blossom'd furze that grew near her
    Now rose, and with energy caroll'd its lay;
'Hush! hush!' she continued, 'the trumpet sounds clearer;
    The horsemen approach! Erin's daughters away!
Ah! soldiers, 'twas foul, while the cabin was burning,
And o'er a pale father a wretch had been mourning —   30
Go, hide with the sea-mew,[2] ye maids, and take warning,
    Those ruffians have ruin'd poor Mary le More.

Away, bring the ointment — O God! see those gashes!
    Alas! my poor brother, come dry the big tear;
Anon we'll have vengeance for these dreadful lashes;
    Already the screech-owl and raven appear.
By day the green grave that lies under the willow
With wild flow'rs I'll strew, and by night make my pillow,
Till the ooze and dark sea-weed beneath the curl'd billow,
    Shall furnish a death-bed for Mary le More.'   40

Thus raved the poor maniac, in tones more heart-rending
    Than sanity's voice ever pour'd on my ear,
When, lo! on the waste, and their march tow'rd her bending,
    A troop of fierce cavalry chanced to appear;
'O ye fiends!' she exclaim'd, and with wild horror started,
Then through the tall fern, loudly screaming, she darted!
With an overcharged bosom I slowly departed,
    And sigh'd for the wrongs of poor Mary le More.

2. sea-gull.

481

SAMUEL THOMSON
(1766-**1793**-1816)

Samuel Thomson lived all his life in a small thatched cottage at Carngranny near
Templepatrick, Co. Antrim. Unlike most other self-taught 'weaver-poets' of his time,
Thomson was an educated man and he ran a small school in his house. Though he also wrote
in English, Thomson's best work is in Ulster-Scots. He greatly admired Robert Burns whom
he visited in Scotland in 1794. Thomson's own verse has a sprightly force and a delight in
language like that of Burns.

To a Hedge-hog

Unguarded beauty is disgrace   Broome[1]

While youthful poets, thro' the grove,
Chaunt saft their canny lays o' love,[2]
And a' their skill exert to move
           The darling object;
I chuse, as ye may shortly prove,
           A rougher subject.

What sairs to bother us in sonnet,
'Bout chin an' cheek, an' brow an' bonnet?
Just chirlin like a widow'd linnet,
           Thro' bushes lurchin;   10
Love's stangs are ill to thole, I own it,
           But to my hurchin.

Thou grimest far o' grusome tykes,
Grubbing thy food by thorny dykes,
Gudefaith *thou* disna want for *pikes*,
           Baith sharp an' rauckle;
Thou looks (L—d save's) array'd in spikes,
           A crecpin' heckle!

1. 'The Coquette', line 15, *The Works of the Poets of Great Britain and Ireland*, 8 vols.
(Dublin, 1793-1804), V, 470. William Broome (1689-1745), an 'excellent versifyer'
according to Dr Johnson, was one of the two poets employed by Alexander Pope to
translate Homer's *Odyssey* for the edition that Pope published as his own work
(1715-20). Broome also wrote all the notes for the work.
2. The Ulster-Scots words and expressions are explained in the Glossary

Some say thou'rt sib kin to the sow,
But sibber to the de'il, I trow;   20
An' what thy use can be, there's few
                    That can explain;
But naithing, as the learn'd allow,
                    Was made in vain.

Sure Nick[3] begat thee, at the first,
On some auld *whin* or thorn accurst;
An' some horn-finger'd harpie nurst
                    The ugly urchin;
The Belzie,[4] laughin, like to burst,
                    First ca'd thee *Hurchin*!   30

Fok tell how thou, sae far frae daft,
Whar wind fa'n fruit lie scatter'd saft,
Will row thysel', wi' cunning craft,
                    An' bear awa
Upon thy back, what sairs thee aft
                    A day or twa.

But whether this account be true,
Is mair than I will here avow;
If that thou stribs the outler cow
                    As some assert,   40
A pretty milkmaid, I allow,
                    Forsooth thou art!

I've heard the superstitious say,
To meet thee on our morning way,
Portends some dire misluck that day —
                    Some black mischance;
Sic fools, howe'er, are far astray
                    Frae common sense.

3. 'Old Nick', the devil.
4. Beelzebub, the devil.

Right monie a hurchin I hae seen,
At early morn, and eke at e'en,   50
Baith setting off, an' whan I've been
                    Returning hame;
But Fate, indifferent, I ween,
Was much the same.

How lang will mortals nonsense blether,
And sauls to superstition tether!
For witch-craft, omens, altogether,
                    Are damn'd hotch-potch mock,
That now obtain sma' credit ether
                    Frae us or Scotch fok.[5]   60

Now creep awa the way ye came,
And tend your squeakin pups at hame;
Gin Colley[6] should o'erhear the same,
                    It might be fatal.
For you, wi' a' the pikes ye claim,
                    Wi' him to battle.

The Hawk and Weazle[1]

To town ae morn, as Lizie hie'd,
          To sell a pickle yarn,
A wanton *Whiteret* she espy'd,
          A sportin at a cairn.
Alang the heath beskirted green,
          It play'd wi' monie a wheel:
She stood and dighted baith her een,
          An' thought it was the Diel
          She saw at freaks!

---

5. Thomson felt close ties with Scotland, with its people and its language. He once said of
   himself: 'Yet tho' I'm *Irish* all without, I'm every item *Scotch* within.'
6. The name of the poet's dog.
1. The Ulster-Scots words and expressions in this poem are explained in the Glossary.

Her doubts, howe'er were soon dismiss'd;　　　　10
　　　A gled cam whist'ling by,
And seiz'd the weazle: — ere it wist,
　　　'Twas halfway at the sky.
But soon the goss grew feeble like,
　　　And syne began to fa',
Till down he daded on a dyke,
　　　His thrapple ate in twa;
　　　　Let him snuff that.[2]

The weazle aff in triumph walks,
　　　An' left the bloodless glutton,　　　　　20
A warning sad to future hawks
　　　That grien for weazle's mutton.
Thus reprobates, that spitefu' cross,
　　　Decree their nibour's ruin,
Are aften forc'd, like foolish goss,
　　　To drink o' their ain brewin',
　　　　And just it is.

The Country Dance

O! ye douce fok, that live by rule,
Grave, tideless-blooded, calm an' cool,
Compar'd wi' you — O! fool! fool! fool!
　　　　　　　How much unlike!
Your hearts are just a standing pool,
　　　　　Your lives, a dyke!
　　　　　　　　　　BURNS[1]

Come muse, wha aft in merry tift,[2]
　　　Has ventur'd on the lyre;
Wha aft frae laverocks in the lift,
　　　Has snatch'd *poetic fire*:

---

2. An expression meaning, roughly, 'Let him put that in his pipe and smoke it!'

1. 'To J.S.****', lines 150-56, *The Complete Poems and Songs of Robert Burns* ed. James Kinsley (Oxford University Press, 1969), p. 147.

2. The Ulster-Scots words and expressions in the poem are explained in the Glossary.

Come ye wha snug in hawthorn shade,
    Sworn foe to spleen an' care,
Enraptur'd e'ed the corny glade,
    An' sung 'The Simmer Fair'[3]
        Ance on a day.

But Simmer fairs an' wabster louns   10
    Maun a' be laid aside:
Or basted ribs an' broken crowns
    Will aiblins us betide —
We'll drap the silly theme at ance,
    The merry maids an' swains,
For singing quaint o' Habbie's dance,
    Will thank us for our pains,
        An' stroak our head.

Aurora[4] fair had quat the plain,
    And harrowers lous'd their naigs,   20
And seeds-men set, their supper taen,
    To smoak an' rest their legs:
Whan lads an' lasses blythe an' kin',
    To Habbies[5] wad repair,
A few short hours to ease their min'
    O warl'y moil a' care,
        An' dance that night.

To see them scourin' doun the dykes,
    In *shauls* an' *aprons* glancin,
An' here an' there the cottage tykes   30
    Ay yelping at a chance ane:
An' ithers rantin' o'er the braes,
    Their hearts as light as cork-wood,
An' whistling some o'er bogs an' leas,
    Ye'd true the fok were stark-wood
        On sic a' night.

3. The reference is to Thomson's long poem 'The Simmer Fair' which describes the summer fair in Templepatrick, Co. Antrim. A passage in that poem about a fight between a weaver and a shoemaker had angered the weavers of Templepatrick who, as Thomson explains in a note relating to the second stanza of this poem in the first edition, had threatened him to 'within an inch of his life' for introducing them into the earlier poem.

4. Though Aurora was the classical goddess of the dawn, Thomson just means that the sun had set.

5. Habbie (the name given to an inhabitant of Kilbarchan, Scotland and to a stanza form much used by Burns) is here merely the name of the owner of the barn where the dance takes place.

There at Hab's yard the *rural group,*
    In merry mood convene,
Whar some are at hap-step-an'-loup
    While ithers put the stane:[6]   40
But soon the fiddle's dainty dint,
    Recalls the *halewar* in,
What pauky R——- wi' double squint,
    Invites them to begin
            The sport this night.

Come muse, we'll o'er to Habbie's hie,
    The e'ening's calm an' fair,
At hame what need we snoaring lie —
    An sican *pastime* there:
We'll aiblins meet wi' L—— an' J——   50
    That dainty, *social pair,*
And get wi' them a dance an' crack,
    Weel worth our gangin' there
            This bonie night.

Here some are come to crack an' joke,
    An' toy amang the lasses;
An' some to blether, spit an' smoak,
    An' bray like highland asses.
An' some to tauk o' ky an' corn,
    Potatoes, sheep an' horses,   60
An' some as thrawn wi' spleen an' scorn
    As they'd been fed on curses
            Since their first day.

Now o'er the floor in wanton pairs,
    They foot it to the fiddle;
The maidens muster a' their airs
    The young men skip an' striddle;
Ah! simple young things, ay beware
    O' lurking INCLINATION!
The clergy say, whan hobblin' there,   70
    Ye're wabblin' temptation
            To ane anither.—

---

6. i.e. some play at hop-step-and-jump while others put the shot or stone.

At *countra' dances*, jigs an' reels,
    Alternately they ranted;
Lads nimbly ply'd their rustic heels,
    An' maidens pegh'd an' panted —
Here *Rabin* lap wi' buxom *Jean*,
    An' *Liza* wi' her *Johney*,
While *Willy* in the neuk unseen,
    Kiss'd *Meg* as sweet as honey   80
        To her that night.

Kings may roll in state, an' Lords
    Enjoy their ill-got treasures;
Compar'd to this, their wealth affords
    But superficial pleasures.
Such happiness with pomp an' pride,
    Is seldom ever seen,
As here with rural swains abide,
    In countra' barns at e'en,
        On sic an night.   90

O Burns![7] had I but half thy skill —
    Thy bonie, silken stile,
Description here shou'd flow at will,
    In numbers smooth as oil: —
But here I'll ask my reader's leave,
    To make a small digression,
It aiblins may in future prieve
    To some a warnin' lesson
        Anither night.

Behind a noest[8] o' drawn strae,   100
    I' the end o' Habbie's stack-yard,
Poor simple Maggy a' night lay
    Wi' Dick, that squintin' black-guard;
Fair maidens oft may *sport* an' *dance*,
    Their min's but little harm in,
But ah! the dolefu' consequence,
    Three quarters[9] did determine
        To Maggy strang.

7. Thomson was a great admirer of Burns, whom he visited in Scotland in 1794.
8. nest, though here it means a pile or heap.
9. nine months.

Poor Meg! the scoff o' ilka chiel,
    Forgrutten, pale an' shabby,   110
Now ca's[10] about her lonely wheel
    An' rocks asleep her babby!
Frae her, ye maids, a lesson glean
    An' trust yoursels wi' no man,
'Bout *strae* or *bourtray neuks alane*
    At dancings i' the gloamin',
            For fear o' skaith.

It's weel, wat I, the lee-lang night,
    They neither fash'd nor tired;
A gayer groupe, 'tis true, ye might   120
    But neededna desired. —
Here, far remov'd from city's strife,
    Gay health an' young content,
With pleasure gilds the shepherds's life,
    While worldlings hearts are rent
            Wi' care an' fear.

Now rosy morn frae th'eastern steeps,
    The shades o' night gan tirl,
An' larks began wi' tunefu' cheeps,
    Their morning springs to skirl: 130
The lasses a' grown brave an' tame,
    Alang the dewy fields,
With kilted coaties[11] hie them hame,
    Escorted by the chiels
            In monie a pair.

Thus ilka ane for hame o'erhies,
    Some near, an' some a mile-hence:
Whilst meagre R———b, wi' heavy eyes,
    Gies o'er the Barn to silence.
Ill satisfy'd — in's *craving purse*,   140
    The Cappers up he clinks!
The haf' o't's *raps*[12] — he gies a curse!
    Then girnin', grumbling! slinks
            O'er next the Miltoun.[13]

10. calls, though here it means she sets her spinning wheel in motion.
11. i.e. with their petticoats tucked up.
12. i.e. half of them are 'raps' — counterfeit halfpennies.
13. Presumably the setting for the next barn-dance.

EDWARD WALSH
(1756-**1793**-1832)

Edward Walsh was born in Waterford. He was educated in England and qualified as a doctor
in Edinburgh, after which he spent his life as a physician in the army. He travelled widely
with his regiment — to Holland, Denmark, Russia, Canada (where he spent six years and
learned much from the Indians), Spain (during the Peninsular War), Belgium (where he was
at the Battle of Waterloo) and Holland. He was an accomplished artist and a discerning
collector of paintings. He retired to Dublin.

Rapture!

The evening spent in Chloe's arms
   Unheeded pass'd away;
No pause we knew from love's alarms,
   'Till rose the dawning day;

Then to the lovely Girl I cry'd,
   'For blissful Joys like these,
No splendid gift shall be deny'd,
   That may the Fancy please;

What brilliant *Gem*, what lust'rous *Pearl*
   Shall deck thy white Ear's tip?   10
Or grace thy waving auburn Curl?'
   I said, and press'd her lip;

'Nor *Gin* nor *Purl* will I receive,'
   (She answer'd, with a frown)
'You'll surely give what others give?
   Come — give me *Half-a-Crown*.'

Edward Walsh

The Epigram

An Epigram should be — if right,
Short, simple, pointed, keen and bright,
    A lively little thing!
Like wasp with taper body — bound
By lines — not many, neat and round,
    All ending in a sting.

JOHN ANKETELL
(c.1750-**1793**-1824)

John Anketell was born in County Monaghan and educated at Trinity College, Dublin. He was ordained into the Church of Ireland and held curacies and a benefice in the north of Ireland. His most interesting poems are the description of a traditional 'pattern' in Co. Monaghan which he probably experienced as a child in the 1760s and his description of a Sunday evening in Dublin, presumably from the early 1770s when he was at university.

from: ## Stramore Patron[1]

In bless'd *Hibernia's* thrice-renowned isle,
Where hospitality and plenty smile;
Thro' whose rich plains clear, fertile rivers flow,
Whose happy lands no pois'nous creatures know;
Whose hardy soldiers roaring cannons dare,
And face, undaunted, all the rage of war;
Where *Ulster* stretches its fair pastures forth,
To the cool climate of the wholesome north;
The county *Monaghan* is known to fame,
For yarn, flax, linen cloth, and store of game;   10
Here lies the barony of *Trugh*,[2] of old
Replete with sportsmen, resolute and bold;
Who fearless follow'd their sure-scented dogs,
O'er hills and dales, thro' valleys, glens, and bogs....
Their sons still own the ardour of their fires,
Their gen'rous breasts glow with *Nimrodian* fires;[3]
And in like sports some vacant hours employ,
To banish trouble and afford them joy.

Large shoals of fishes gambol in each flood,
Here crooked eels quick wallow thro' the mud;   20
In crystal brooks there darts the speckled trout,
The wide-mouth'd pike here rears his rav'nous snout;
The finny brood, the roach, the tench, and breme,[4]
Plunge thro' each lake, and play in ev'ry stream;

---

1. i.e. pattern, the religious and secular festivities associated with the feast day of the 'patron' saint of a church.
2. Trough or Truaghs is the most northerly of the five baronies of County Monaghan.
3. Nimrod was 'a mighty hunter' (Genesis 9. 7).
4. bream. The list is of freshwater fish.

And all conspire to please the angler's eye,
To seize the bait, or catch the cheating fly.
Here basks the partridge in the stubble field,
Great store of grouse the heath-clad mountains yield;
The woodcock flushed from the close-set brake;
See from the marsh the snipe to flight betake!   30
Ducks, teal, and widgeon wing their airy round,
And rails and plover cop'ously abound.

In lower *Trugh*, near the *Black-water*⁵ side,
A verdant plain extendeth far and wide,
Known by the appellation of *Stramore*,
A place ne'er spoken of in verse before.
On *Easter Monday* hither thousands run,
To be spectators of, or join the fun.
Here limping fidlers haste as well as able,
To glean some coppers from the giddy rabble;   40
And here the blind pipers merrily repair,
To charm the rustic's truly rustic ear.
The sports begin; the music plays; and lo!
The lively lads and lasses in a row
Form the light dance, and trip it on the ground,
To the sad bagpipes' or harsh fiddle's sound;
And for their dance the stated tribute pay,
The sum an half-penny — then march away;
For here no formal complaisance is shewn,
Nor female partner paid for by the clown.   50
What tho' no master ever taught them how
To drop a court'sy, walk genteel, or bow;
In sprightly measures on the green they move,
And cheerful hop, as they themselves approve.

Here *Oonagh* stands; her pumps,⁶ you see, are new,
Her gown stripp'd linen, and her stockings blue;
Last week in *Glasslough*⁷ were her buckles bought,
How bright they shine, tho' purchased for a groat!⁸

---

5. The river Blackwater marks the boundary between the counties of Monaghan and Tyrone.
6. Light leather shoes.
7. A small town in County Monaghan. The buckles were probably bought in a market held there.
8. A coin worth fourpence.

With three-cock'd hat, and smooth-comb'd, flowing hair,
Her partner *Paddy* hands along the fair;   60
His brogues are half-soal'd,[9] and at ev'ry bound
Their firm-nail'd heels imprint the beaten ground.
Dolly with care her scarlet cloak displays,
Lac'd tightly in her mistress' cast-off stays;
While *Laughlin* struts, and seemingly looks big,
With coarse black stockings, and his one-row wig.
Here *Peggy* skips, dress'd in a yellow gown,
Which cost in *Skernageerah*[10] just a crown;
New cap and ribands set her off with grace,
And add fresh honors to her rosy face;   70
While *Denis* smartly trips along to shew
His sheep-skin breeches, bought some weeks ago.
With nimble steps see *Bridget* next advance,
And gladly enter on the pleasing dance;
A new green petticoat proclaims her fine,
And gloves and ruffles render her divine!
Lawrence beholds her with a lover's eye,
And 'cuts his capers' as his sweetheart's nigh;
Displays his bath-rug[11] coat with artful care,
And laughs with joy to see her fondly stare.   80
There *Sheelah* moves with awkward, sheepish mien,
Her handkerchief and apron, though, are clean;
And then who can unmov'd, uncharm'd withstand
The penny ring that decks her yellow hand!
Terrence the lightening of her eyes receives,
And swears for her alone he dies or lives;
While his red waistcoat shoots a pointed dart,
Which pierces her, kind fair one! thro' the heart.

Following the dancing, there are games of hurling and football, after which the participants
'sit them down, and gladly rest awhile'.

Here crowds divert themselves at pitch-and-toss,
All wish to win, tho' to their neighbours' loss.   90
Here *Philip* squanders all his cash away,
The price of his good yarn, at idle play.

9. Shoes soled with leather and nails would have been a luxury at the time.
10. Another small community in County Monaghan.
11. 'Bath-coating' was a material formerly fashionable for male attire (*OED*).

Behold how *Miles* his rent and tythe forgets,
And ventures all his money here on betts!
See *Murtoagh* risk the purchase of his shoes,
And very justly ev'ry farthing lose;
While *Dermot's* fleec'd of what should buy some meal,
And is compell'd to beg, work hard, or — steal;
And *Teague* rejoices at his lucky fate,
Five shillings won, make him with bliss elate.   100

Together there a group of little boys
In their train'd hands the well-shap'd cocksticks poise.[12]
A circle's swept upon the beaten land,
And in its centre, lo! a prop does stand:
On this a piece of lead, or button's laid,
The stated length is measur'd on the mead,
O'er which they throw; three casts for ev'ry pin;
Happy's the lad who can the trifle win!
Well pleas'd is he, compleated is his joy,
Who from the circle drives the worthless toy!   110

Lo! here are troops of brawny rustics seen,
Who with agility spring on the green.
Some with hop-step and-leap themselves divert,
Others at running-leaps are most expert:
Here sev'ral hold a staff in either hand,
With which they bound far o'er the level land:
Some throw the drawing, some the shoulder stone,[13]
And inactivity is felt by none.

Here fortune's wheel is quickly turn'd about,
Round which the gulls[14] raise at themselves a shout;   120
While its proprietor, with merry heart,
Acts, as prime gainer in the farce, chief part.
How prone are we to aid the wily foe,
Who for *Eve's* offspring plots unceasing woe!...

---

12. The game described is a form of cockshy – the game of flinging a stick or stone originally at a live cock (once popular at fairs held on Shrove Tuesday), or at any object set up for the purpose.

13. Throwing the shoulder-stone is a form of putting the shot: but throwing the drawing stone is obscure; perhaps the 'drawing-stone' was thrown like a discus.

14. i.e. those foolish enough to be 'gulled' into parting with their money at the wheel of fortune.

The sun now streaks the skies with ruddy light,
And yields its empire to the pow'r of night;
In splendid pomp the silver moon is crown'd,
And twinkling stars emit their beams around;
When to the tents the men and women drive,
Like bees in summer clust'ring at the hive.   130
Around they ply with whiskey, rum, and beer,
While cyder, wine, and brandy join the cheer;
With jokes and tales the meeting they prolong,
And crown their revels with an *Irish* song;
Make love by turns, and sometimes hop and prance,
And blithsome grown, again renew the dance;
Bagpipes and fiddles, with their grating notes,
Join in full concert with the rustics' throats;
They curse, tell lies, dispute, talk loud, and laugh,
Till urg'd to madness by the drink they quaff,   140
To blows and furious combat they proceed;
Friends fall by friends, and sons by fathers bleed;
Their angry strokes to all alike they deal,
The liquors o'er their senses so prevail.
The knotty sloe-tree cudgel bruises sore,
And from their heads draws floods of crimson gore;
Tough ash and hazle give a desp'rate wound,
And stout shilelahs[15] on their skulls resound:
With jars and tumults thus they end the play,
And fights and bloodshed close the parting day....   150

from: Description of Sunday Evening, spent in a Coffee-House in the City of Dublin

'Tis Sunday ev'ning, and when pray'rs are done,
Straight to the coffee-house crowds thronging run,
Where from their minds they utterly discard
Texts which in church they heard without regard.
Call for the news, and 'Is the packet come?'
With waiters' 'Here, Sir!' echo thro' the room.

---

15. shillelagh: a blackthorn club named after the village of Shillelagh, Co. Wicklow.

The tawdry fops, with sneering, vain grimace,
Adorn'd with ignorance — and flimsy lace,
Strut in mock majesty, and view with scorn
The *lower* creatures who this scene adorn.   10

Here the old dotards sip their capilaire,[1]
And talk of politics with lofty air;
On state affairs importantly proceed,
And pore on papers which they cannot read.

The spruce apprentice, from his master free,
In his best cloths hastes here with merry glee;
With powder'd hair resolv'd to cut a dash,
And treat of money — tho' he has no cash:
But as the coxcomb will not want his tea,
He must be trusted — as he cannot pay.   20

Thus when some hours in idleness they spend,
Their steps in sullen mood all homewards bend;
Or to some tavern, or curs'd stew[2] repair,
To banish langour — by increasing care....

1. Syrup flavoured with orange-flower water.
2. brothel.

FOUR ANONYMOUS 'RAMBLING' SONGS

The Peregrinations of Fiachra McBrady,
literally translated from the Original Irish[1]

If ye heard each disaster, of your poetaster,
And Irish scholmaster, since leaving Stradone;[2]
Thro' thick and thin splashing, the rain on him dashing,
My friends in compassion, you'ld Brady bemoan.
The bri'rs my cloaths tatt'ring, my new nail'd brogues clatt'ring,
The mud my legs spatt'ring, I strove to grope home;
Whilst tir'd, wet and weary, I'd rather, I swear ye,
Be 'n the cabin with Mary, than bishop of Rome.
I got over mountains, thro' bogs, and by fountains,
Pierc'd woods without counting, to Croghan, alone;   10
Whence to Arran I scamper'd, with baggage not hamper'd,
To Sligo's sea rampart, Kinnard and Tyrone.
Continuing my hurry, I dash' on to Newry,
Thence to Down like a fury, where they robb'd me *oghone!*[3]
O'er Sliav Gullin[4] I darted, from Drogheda parted,
Where against a ship carted,[5] I broke my jaw bone.
I shouted out murder, to the ship's crew if further,
I got near the border,[6] I'd fall in and drown;
Whilst the rascals kept funning, never fear, you're too cunning,
And the people came running, from all parts of the town.   20
For fear of no quarters,[7] from this crew of sea tartars,

---

1. The 'rambling' song, in which the poet recounts his adventures as he visits various parts of Ireland, was popular throughout the eighteenth century. Though the Irish text of this poem had been current in manuscript since the early eighteenth century, it only appeared in print in the October 1793 issue of the *Anthologia Hibernica* where the editor requested a translation. The English text he received — a remarkable *tour de force* — follows closely the complex *amhrán* or song metre as well as the assonantal rhyming patterns of the Irish original.
2. A market town in County Cavan. The poet's 'peregrinations' follow a relaxed route around Ireland starting in County Cavan and travelling through Ulster and then via Dublin, Waterford, Cork and Killarney to Galway and, eventually, back to Stradone.
3. See Glossary.
4. Slieve Gullion, the name of mountains in both County Derry and County Armagh — probably the latter here.
5. This line seems to mean that the poet's jaw was broken when he got caught between a cart and the side of a ship at Drogheda docks.
6. Meaning uncertain, through from the context it seems to mean the quayside.
7. i.e. for fear this fierce crew would show me no mercy.

I swam o'er the waters, in stockings and shoes;
Thence to Garristown common, where I met an old woman,
Who told me my coming was announc'd in the news.[8]
'Tis not to be wondered, that I found myself founder'd,[9]
Like a horse that on ground hard, had plough'd by the tail;
But St. Patrick's bells ringing, my heart set a springing,
And I reach'd Dublin singing *'Brave Grainne Weal'*.[10]
The first thing I'll mention, that gain'd my attention,
And my eyes kept in tension an hour I swear;   30
'Twas king William of Britain, on an iron horse sitting,
As fierce as a kitten, the post-office near.[11]
Desirous of knowledge, I went to the college,
Where I am forc'd to acknowledge, but little I found;
So sooner than argue, I steer'd for Portlarga,[12]
With of whiskey a cargo, my sorrows to drown.
I drank till quite mellow, then like a brave fellow,
Began for to bellow, and shouted for more;
But my host held his stick up,[13] which soon cur'd my hiccup,
As no cash could I pick up, to pay off the score.   40
To prison he sent me, here I 'gan to repent me,
I knew I must lent keep,[14] until my release;
But the next day they stript me, and out of doors kick'd me,
So my choler to quit, see, I damn'd the police.
With wet and cold, shiv'ring, my broken jaw quiv'ring,
I thought oft the river in, my body to throw;
And it still is a mist'ry, when I con o'er[15] my hist'ry,
By what means I mist free, the waters below.[16]
I visited Blarney, Birr, Cork, and Killarney,

---

8. The meaning of this is uncertain. Garristown is near Dublin and the bells of St Patrick's cathedral might just be audible there, so the line might mean that the poet interpreted the ringing of bells as an announcement of his arrival.

9. A horse forced to plough rough ground with the plough fastened to its tail might well 'founder', i.e. break down or go lame.

10. A song recounting the distresses of Gráinne Mhaol, Grace O'Malley (c.1530-c.1600).

11. i.e. the equestrian statue of William of Orange in College Green outside Trinity College, Dublin.

12. *Port Láirge*, the Irish name for Waterford.

13. The innkeeper held up the tally stick on which was recorded the amount owed.

14. i.e. abstain from drink as if it were Lent.

15. examine.

16. i.e. It is a mystery to me how I missed the waters of the river Styx (the river which, according to classical mythology, flows round hell seven times). The poet also wonders what prevented him from drowning himself.

Mc Mahon of Farney, and Galway's rich shore;   50
From Croagh Patrick with hot head, to Dromole I trotted,
With an oak stick well knotted, and so to Balore.
Here a lodging I'd taken, but lothe to awaken,
For fear of my bacon, or man, wife, or babe;
Brush'd on in a passion, and thro' the ford dashing,
I reach'd the mud mansion of Brian McCabe.
The potatoes were boiling, but his brats kept such squalling,
With the itch[17] their hands mawling,[18] the road I set to;
And at home found Moll Brady, with Owen and Thady,
As they'd heard I was drowned, all crying *Whillaloo*.[19]   60

I remember McBrady[20] — no lady, or village queen
But wish'd on a May-day, or play-day, his choice to've been;
To a barrel of liquor, none quicker, to run was seen,
Nor at fairs had a stick or club thicker, or brogues more clean;
Like a halfpenny candle, he'd handle his sapling green
Now alas! in Dunsandle,[21] a bramble his grave doth screen.

The Irish man's Ramble: a new song[1]

When forth in my Ramble intending to gamble,
To an ale house I rambled most freely,
I set with the Toppers[2] and Drunk of full bumpers,[3]
Till I became fudled most realey.

The Drawer[4] did say 'The Reckoning come Pay,
For that is the best Play most truely,
Or else I will strip you, and heartily whip you,
And out of Doors kick you most sure Sir.'

---

17. Many common skin disorders were called 'the itch' in the eighteenth century.
18. mauling, scratching.
19. Alas! (The poet has returned to his wife and children.)
20. As was common in Irish verse of the period, the finishing stanza (or *ceangal*, binding) — here spoken by someone who has outlived McBrady — is in a different metre.
21. A townland near Loughrea, Co. Galway.

---

1. Although the text of this poem is obviously corrupt, its charm would be greatly diminished by heavy editing; thus neither spelling nor syntax have been amended.
2. topers, drinkers.
3. Large glasses filled to the brim and used for the drinking of toasts.
4. ale-house assistant.

The landlady with a frown said 'The money lay down
Or your Clothes I will have for the Score Sir,   10
Your Coat, Briches and Hatt, your Shirt and Cravat,
I will have from your back most sure Sir.'

'Zouns' says the Clown,[5] 'the Stairs kick him Down,
Till wiser he growd:' this alarmed —
Like a Stag from a gun through the Streets I did run,
My Carkas and bum was well warmed.

The brats of the Town with pudel[6] and stone
Belabourd my bones severely,
The Dogs and the Hounds my body surrounds,
Thus I pay'd for my Jaunt most dear Sir.   20

There was Teag[7] with a Shovel and Bryun with a ladle,
And Dermot with a wattle[8] persued me,
And old Mother Trimble, and Joan with the spindle,
And Nora the bich sore abused me.

Old Couckold Roger as gray as a badger,
Close followed after to Shoot me,
And Nora my miss, that I youst[9] for to kiss,
She would galop and trot to come to me.

This is a rambler and also a gambler,
A knave or a blockhead so fitted,   30
To see London facion[10] the best in the nation,
My Policy there they out-witted.

But at last, by my Soul, my dear Joy, to condole
My misfortunes I met with a Ladey
That got me a login[11] that Night with-out Dogin
The Prince of all stalions most greasy.

5. uncouth fellow.
6. paddle, a small, spade-like instrument with a long handle, for clearing a ploughshare,
   etc. (*OED*).
7. See Glossary.
8. a rod or stick.
9. used.
10. fashion, i.e. ways and customs.
11. lodging.

McClure's Ramble

Of late a strong notion of rambling entangled my mind,
To seek out Dame Fortune my strong resolution inclin'd,
I set to the road like a rover with staff in my hand,
And I never delay'd till I came to the town of Strabane.[1]

Good yarn there plenty I thought I would do pretty well,
With a widow so dainty to journey-work instantly fell,
The best entertainment and whiskey provided for me,
Which help'd our engagement, indeed she was handsome and free.

Six months did I tarry, a second piece put in the loom,
I of weaving grew weary when spring made the trees for to bloom,   10
I'd been prone to hard labour and this to my mistress did say,
'Come pay me my wages, I'm instantly going away.'

She says, 'My dear Johnny, oh! why are you going so soon,
I'd have you to tarry and work out the piece in the loom,
But here is your cash and a present to buy you a spade,
Come lay me your shuttle to keep me in mind of the trade.'

I gather'd the mettal and found that the cash was five pound,
No old coin to rattle, nor in it light shillings were found;[2]
I pack'd up my wallet just like a brave journey-man,
In the sweet month of April it's then I set off from Strabane.   20

Unto Ballygally[3] I thought I would next take my way.
I met with a farmer and bargain'd with him by the day;
Great wages he gave me and ample reward for my toil,
And a stout agriculture I freely bestow'd on his soil.

He had a young daughter as sweet as the roses in June;
I strove for to gain her — at length she gave ear to my tune;
I wrought her plantation with good cultivation around,
But I could not well tarry to see her wheat harvest cut down.

---

1. In County Tyrone. This ramble takes place in Ulster.
2. i.e. the coins were good and valid.
3. A townland near Downpatrick, Co. Down.

The first of June coming I thought to myself I wou'd go
Down to Dungannon,[4] and there the green meadows to mow;   30
My master with honour my wages he instantly paid,
His daughter she purchas'd a scythe to blossom my trade.

My scythe in good order, my striekle[5] and stone at command,
I cut round the border before that I enter'd the land,
Six weeks and some better it's there with a maid I remain'd,
Demanding my wages, and home to Rathfryland[6] again.

Adieu Ballygally, Strabane and the county Tyrone,
Likewise Dungannon, where kindness unto me was shown,
And if I return my wages to augment, be sure,
The widows do mourn the loss of their Johnny McClure.   40

Now winter's approaching and home to Rathfryland must go,
No more be a weaver, nor yet the green meadows to mow,
I'll be a flax-dresser until that my trade it does fail,
Then for the pea-thrashing, good business in sweet Islakeale.[7]

All you Strabane weavers give over your bouncing and pride,
For I'm the bold shaver that near to Rathfryland reside,
For weaving and mowing I always do merit the praise,
In Ballynagappog,[8] McClure can sit at his ease.

Shales's Rambles, or the Lurgan Weaver

You ladies free of each degree, now hear my invitation,
I am a lad tho' trade is bad, that's known by reputation,
If you comply and wont deny, and wants your work done neatly,
Your looms I'll square to half a hair, and wave[1] your webs completely.

---

4. In County Tyrone.
5. 'Strickle', a dialect word from the North of England, is a whetstone for a scythe.
6. Rathfriland, Co. Down.
7. The text is defective at this point, so that this place-name is conjectural.
8. A townland near Newry, Co. Down.

---

1. weave.

So now you maids that love the trade, and now has took the notion,
Apply to me we'll soon agree, I'll put your loom in motion,[2]
If your geers be struck to fit the work, I'll do my best endeavour
To raise a twill with art and skill, for I'm the Lurgan weaver.[3]

I your beams will streatch in the broad reach, I'll pick and dress your yarn,
Your sliders raise will cloath with ease, in cellers shops or barns,   10
One I have to graze and stave, [I] use no comb or sheers,
My pullies hings your yarn springs, when e'er I touch your geers.

My slays will play without a stay, my headless falls a working,
Both right and left throws in the weft, without the temples bursting,
My bore staff's long, both stiff and strong, my shuttle still in order,
With open shades I'll fall to trade, and selvage neat your border.

You diaper[4] boys that make such noise, with lambs coupers and peacans,
With ratling slates your works compleat, to dress fine parlour tables
If one cord you streach, you make a breach, and hover round your burches,
But your toiling crafts and puzling drafts will never please the wenches.   20

For I served my time to coarse and fine, not like you stroling rakers,
That Shillaley clown[5] I'll pull him down, likewise the dirty baker,
My plan is new both nice and true, I am the boy that's ready,
M'Cuskers plough is over now, and likewise threshing neddy.[6]

If Neal appear or Downey here, to seize up cloth or yarn,
I'm on my oath to break them both, their trade they have to learn,
Apply to me I ask no fee, your time is only wasting,
The work I seal, you shall have bail,[7] will stand the winter bleaching.

---

2. Throughout this text, and particularly in lines 5-20, the poet uses (and finds double-meanings for) many of the technical terms associated with weaving and with looms. These are so specific that they are not glossed here.

3. Though this poet starts in Ulster, he moves throughout Ireland apparently earning a living as a weaver in every part of the country. The spelling of the names of several of the places he visits is such that they are impossible to identify.

4. Diaper is a kind of linen cloth so 'diapers' must mean those who weave this cloth. It is not clear why the looms for this work should be noisy; the term 'lambs coupers' is obscure but seems to mean something which made a noise (like a tin pea-can would if rattled) when used for beating ('lambing' or 'couping') someone or something.

5. i.e. that fellow from Shillelagh, Co. Wicklow (?)

6. 'threshing neddy' is obscure, though donkeys were sometimes used in the threshing of corn. However, the whole line is more likely to refer to some process connected with weaving.

7. i.e. you may be sure. Finished linen was left out-of-doors to bleach.

When Flora[8] queen with mantle green, bedecks the fields and meadows,
And Aurora fades in lonesome shades, I toy with buxom widows,   30
In house or tent I pay no rent, no dues or tythe to Rectors,
From hearth money I'm always free, I value no inspectors.[9]

Last year mispent I ne'er relent, I think not on to-morrow,
Each blooming day brings in new pay, I'm free from care and sorrow,
But here and there among the fair, to rid myself of trouble,
If they do scold or be too bold, I give my usual double.

But seen[10] my fame began to reign, all through this Irish nation,
Through villages and seaport towns, and all the corporations,
From Bellibough I then set off, to seek for new adventures,
Be not dismayed I'll show you trade, I carry my indentures.[11]   40

To Hilsborough I then did go, and manly I behaved,
And in Dromore both hard and sore, the yarn there I slaved,[12]
Then to Newry along the quay, the sailors seemes to grumble,
But with surprize the maids did rise, their pride I soon did humble.

As for my walk unto Dundalk, I was a noted ranger,
And from all round the mountains down, I dressed[13] their danger,
To Drogheda I took my way from that to Dublin city,
I was envy'd but still could hide among the maidens pretty.

In the town of Naas as I did pass, I raised the lasses wages,
In Mayborough[14] and through Carlow, I done my work courageous,   50
In Kilkenny I staid a day, to Gorden's town I hoofed,
And Waterford I will record, the maids was all apprized.[15]

---

8. Flora, queen of flowers, and Aurora, the dawn, often appear together in popular verse in the late eighteenth century, linked by their assonance and rhyme.
9. Hearth-tax was levied on those whose houses had a fireplace.
10. i.e. seeing — another example of English written down by someone who has learned it aurally.
11. Documents showing that the weaver had served his apprenticeship.
12. obscure, though it may mean that he 'sleeved' the flax, i.e. worked at the machine which turned it into the long thread known as a 'sliver'.
13. to 'dress' cloth is to finish it, but the word here seems to carry the additional meaning of 'addressed'.
14. Probably Maryborough, now Port Laois, Co. Laois.
15. The lack of end-rhyme in this couplet shows the text to be corrupt here.

Then to Clonmell and through Cashel, I wetted up their sheeting
On Youghall shore I drank galore, I use no thumbs or bating,
To Cork and Cove I there did rove, Bandon, Tralee and Dingle,
In Limerick I staid a week, and made their looms to jingle.

To Iniss[16] and Clare I did repair, I decently was used,
In Banagher I was Journeyman, my shuttle ne'er refused;
In Athlone when I was known, the men they strove to slay me,
Unto Loughreagh without delay, the females did convey me.   60

In Athenrea and Golaway,[17] I friendly there was treated,
Then through Headford and Balinrobe, my work I there completed,
Then to Westport I did resort and Bellinatiredy,[?]
All through Sligo my work did shew, the clowns I did not value.

All jobs did get in Belturbet, at threshing up their bedding,
And through Cavan I taught a plan, that took the best of trading,
I was three days in Ballibays, a month in Clownish[18] working,
In Smithsborough I was not slow, in dressing up their shirting.

In Monaghan the ladies ran, I kindly was received,
And from Glastlough unto Armagh, both night and day I weaved,   70
And round Richhill I showed my skill, I thought no crime to flatter,
I crossed the Bann to Ligoland, and spent the winter quarter.

I am roving Sheales that never fails, though Misers do envy me,
They need not fret their gold I'll get, their daughters still employ me;
In Lurgan town I will set down, in back lane I'll tarry,
And with young maids I'll always trade, but hang me if I marry.

16. Ennis, Co. Clare.
17. Galway.
18. Clones, Co. Monaghan.

ANONYMOUS POEMS FROM THE 1790s

The Colleen Rue[1]

As I roved out on a summer's morning,
    A specalating most curiously,
To my surprize I soon espied,
    A charming fair one approaching me,
I stood awhile in deep meditation,
    Contemplating what I should do,
Till at length recruiting all my sensations,
    I thus accosted the Colleen Rue.
'Are you Aurora or goddess Flora,[2]
    Eutarnatia or fair Venus bright,[3]   10
Or Helen fair beyond compare,
    That Paris stole from the Grecians sight?[4]
Thou fairest creature you've enslaved me;
    I am intoxicated by Cupid's clue,
Whose golden notes and infatuations,
    Deranged my ideas for you, colleen rue.'
'Kind sir, be easy and do not tease me,
    With your false praises most jestingly;
Your dissimulation or invocation,
    Are vaunting praises seducing me.   20
I'm not Aurora or beautious Flora,
    But a rural female to all men's view,
That's here condoling my situation,
    My appelation is the Colleen Rue.'
'Was I Hector that noble victor,
    That died a victim by a Grecian's skill,[5]

---

1. Ir. *cailín rua*, the red-haired girl. This is an early and 'unimproved' version of a famous song. The influence of the Irish verse tradition of the eighteenth century can be seen in the playful use of assonance and internal rhyme throughout the poem and in the innocent (or perhaps intentional) misuse of many English words and phrases. The artlessness of language and the use of completely unexpected allusions 'heterogeneously linked together', give this version of the text a memorable freshness and directness.

2. See above p. 505, n. 8.

3. 'Eutarnatia' is probably a mistake for Euterpe, the muse who presided over music; Venus was the goddess of love.

4. Helen, the most beautiful woman of her age, was carried off by Paris, son of Priam, king of Troy.

5. Hector, the bravest of the Trojan chiefs, was killed by Achilles, who spotted a weak point in his armour.

O was I Paris whose deeds were various,
    As an arbitrator on Ida's hill,[6]
I'd range through Asia likewise Arabia
    Or Pensylvania seeking for you,   30
The burning regions like famed Orpheus[7]
    For one embrace of you, Colleen Rue.'
'Sir, I'am surprized and dissatisfied,
    At your tantalizing eloquence.
I'm not so stupid or inslaved by Cupid,
    As to be a dupe to your insolence.
Therefore desist your solicitations,
    For I am pre-engaged — I declare it is true —
To a lad I love above all earthly treasure,
    And he'll soon enjoy his Colleen Rue.'   40
Now ye deities whose power is prevailing
    I pray give heed to my feeble frame,
Likewise ye muses who never refuses,
    The wounds of Cupid I pray ye hail.[8]
A peregrination to foreign nations,
    Determining and may prove true,
In hopes to find a maid more kind
    Than the blooming fair one, the colleen rue.

The Irish Phœnix[1]

Once more kind Muses it is your duty, for to infuse me with verse sublime,
My subject surely is now amusing, as you have chose me for to repine;
Ye mangling poets don't dare oppose me, for now my notions are raised
    on high,
Kind Gods support me through these my posies,[2] in you I glory and still
    rely.

---

6. In his youth, when he was living on Mount Ida, Paris had been called upon to decide
which of the three naked goddesses, Juno, Minerva or Venus, was the most beautiful.
7. Orpheus travelled through the underworld seeking his wife, Eurydice.
8. i.e. heal (pronounced 'hale' in Ireland in the eighteenth century).

---

1. This song is even closer to the Irish-language verse tradition of the eighteenth century
than the 'Colleen Rue'. The metre, the assonance and the vocabulary all show it to be the
work of a poet used to writing within the native tradition, one for whom English was a
foreign language.
2. This word, presumably, means 'verses'. As in several instances in this poem, it is probably
the sound of the word rather than its meaning which lies behind the poet's choice.

One pleasant evening for recreation, as I was ranging down by the shore,
I spied a maiden a lovely fair one, I thought her Venus sprung from the
    foam,
In admiration on her I gazed, in deep amazement I stood to view,
This second Phœnix exceeding nature and for to praise her it is my due.

To you fair Sabra in all her charms or chaste Diana cant equalize,[3]
Nor she whom Paris as is recorded was pleased to order the
    Golden Prize;[4]   10
The bright Aurora in all her glory or Goddess Flora[5] you far outvie,
My brain is roving in sad emotions I must adore you untill I die.

You are an angel, your good and pleasing, your fine behaviour
    enchanted me,
Your chains are really, I'm doomed to wear them, I wish sincerely
    for liberty.
These wounds you gave me, say will you heal them, you have
    enslaved me, now set me free,
It's you can ease me, from bonds release me, and let me gain my tranquility.

My jewel and darling, more fair than morning, or orient radient
    you far outshine,
Your eyes transparent has me alarmed, I wish, my charmer, that
    you were mine;
Your swan-like bosom, your neck including, your cheeks are
    blooming vermillion red,
Sure every feature new beauty graces, and auburn tresses flow
    from your head.   20

My breast is loaded with discomposure, in love sick motion I now
    complain,
Sly Cupid sporting at my corrodings,[6] that brat he glory's in giving pain;
Will you relieve me, from death reprive me, your captive bleeder I now
    remain,
I'm always weeping and still am grieving, but it's when sleeping of you
    I dream.

---

3. The references are to Diana, goddess of the chase and probably to Sabina Julia, a Roman matron celebrated for her virtues.
4. i.e. Venus, whom Paris adjudged to be the most beautiful of the goddesses and who therefore received the prize of a golden apple.
5. See above p. 505, n. 8.
6. A coinage meaning that Cupid is enjoying the sight of the poet's heart being corroded or destroyed by his love.

All recreations I'll now reneague[7] them, in silent places I mean to rove,
My prayers compleatly I'll offer daily, in adoration near Willow grove,[8]
Ye Supreme Deities say will I gain her, will I obtain her, can I intrude,
On you my fairest what shall I say love, but that I'm almost crazy for
    Mary Booth.

The Siege of Troy[1]

I sing of a war set on foot for a toy,[2]
And of Paris and Helen and Hector and Troy,
Where on women, kings, gen'rals, and coblers you stumble,
And of mortals and gods meet a very strange jumble.
    Sing didderoo, bubberoo, Oh, my joy,
    How sweetly they did one another destroy,
    Come fill up your bumpers,[3] the whiskey enjoy,
    May we ne'er see the like of the siege of Troy.

Menelaus was happy wid Helen his wife,
Except dat she led him a devil of a life;   10
Wid dat handsome taef[4] Paris she'd toy and she'd play,
Till they pack'd up their awls[5] and they both ran away,
    Sing didderoo, &c.

Agamemnon, and all the great chiefs of his house,
Soon took up the cause of this hornified spouse;
While Juno said this thing and Venus said that,
And the Gods fell a wrangling they knew not for what.
    Sing didderoo, &c.

---

7. renege, renounce.
8. A place in County Wicklow.

---

1. This is one of the liveliest of several late eighteenth-century songs which make playful
use of the material of Homer's *Iliad*. The poet delights in the contrast between the heroic
deeds and emotions normally associated with the Greeks of the original story and the
very unheroic 'stage' Hiberno-English used to describe them here. For a list of common
Hiberno-English spellings, see the Glossary.
2. A piece of amorous dallying, a whim (*OED*).
3. large glasses.
4. thief.
5. 'To pack up one's awls and be gone' is a seventeenth-century colloquial expression
meaning 'to depart for good'. Partridge suggests that 'awls' is a corruption of 'alls'.

Oh den such a slaughter and cutting of trotes,⁶
And slaying of bullocks and off'ring up goats,   20
Till the cunning Ulysses the Trojans to cross,
Clapt forty fine fellows in one wooden horse.
    Sing didderoo, &c.

Oh den for to see the maids, widows and wives,
Crying some for their virtue, and some for their lives;
Thus after ten years they'd defended the town,
Poor dear Troy in ten minutes was all burnt down.
    Sing didderoo, &c.

But to see how it ended's the best joke of all;
Scarce had wronged Menelaus ascended the wall,   30
But he blubb'ring saw Helen, and, oh strange to tell,
The man took his mare, and so all was well,
    Sing didderoo, bubberoo, Oh my joy,
    How sweetly they did one another destroy,
    Come fill up your bumpers, the whiskey enjoy,
    May we ne'er see the like of the siege of Troy.

Paddy MacShane's Seven Ages¹

If my own botheration don't alter my plan,
I'll sing seven lines of a tight Irishman,
    Wrote by old Billy Shakespeare of Ballyporeen.²
He said while a babe I lov'd whiskey and pap,
That I mewled and puk'd in my grandmother's lap;
She joulted me hard just to hush my sweet roar,
When I slipp'd through her fingers down whack on the floor,
    What a squalling I made sure at Ballyporeen.

---

6. throats.

---

1. Though the 'stage Irishman' song is usually associated with the nineteenth rather than
the eighteenth century, many such songs have their roots firmly in the rural Ireland of the
1780s and 1790s when they were already current. The one which follows is typical of the
type in its irreverent absurdities, in its use of word-play, and in the fact that it uses
apparently authentic details of life in late eighteenth-century rural Ireland to give colour
to the story.
2. A village in County Tipperary.

When I grew up a boy, with a nice shining face,
With my bag at my back, and a snail-crawling pace,   10
    Went to school at old Thwackum's[3] at Ballyporeen.
His wig was so fusty, his birch was my dread,
He learning beat *out* 'stead of *into* my head.
'Master Macshane', says he, 'you're a great dirty dolt,
You've got no more brains than a Monaghan colt;[4]
    You're not fit for our college at Ballyporeen.'

When eighteen years of age, was teas'd and perplext
To know what I should be, so a lover turn'd next,
    And courted sweet Sheelah of Ballyporeen.
I thought I'd just take her to comfort my life,   20
Not knowing that she was already a wife:
She ask'd me just once that to see her I'd come,
When I found her ten children and husband at home,
    A great big whacking chairman of Ballyporeen.

I next turn'd a soldier, I did not like that,
So turn'd servant, and liv'd with the great Justice Pat,
    A big dealer in p'ratoes at Ballyporeen.
With turtle and venison he lin'd his inside,
Ate so many fat capons, that one day he died.
So great was my grief, that to keep spirits up,   30
Of some nice whiskey cordial I took a big sup,
    To my master's safe journey from Ballyporeen.

Kick'd and toss'd so about, like a weathercock vane,
I pack'd up my awls,[5] and I went back again
    To my grandfather's cottage at Ballyporeen.
I found him, poor soul! with no legs for his hose,
Could not see through the spectacles put on his nose;
With no teeth in his head, so death cork'd up his chin;
He slipp'd out of his slippers, and faith I slipp'd in,
    And succeeded poor Dennis of Ballyporeen.   40

---

3. cf. Mr Thwackum, the heavy-handed schoolmaster in Henry Fielding's *Tom Jones* (1749).
4. Swift used the phrase 'a perfect Monaghan' to mean 'a fool'. *A Dialogue in Hybernian Stile Between A & B and Irish Eloquence by Jonathan Swift*, ed. Alan Bliss (Dublin, 1977), p. 69.
5. i.e. I packed up everything.

Sally Mac Gee

You sporting young girls, give ear to my ditty,
Pray listen a while you may smile at the same;
I'm a buxom young girl just come from the city,
I love for to play at young Venus's game;
I sport and carouse in jovial merriment,
With buxom young rakes of every degree,
In drinking and carousing is all my element,
I am the girl called Sally Mac Gee.

When forced from the town I came to the country,
I met a young Draper, who did me salute,   10
He lovingly embraced me, and shew'd his gallantry,
With plenty of liquors and money to boot;
The night being come, to sport we went merrily,
And while we were playing, I sure did make free,
His pockets did plunder of guineas in number,
Which makes him to think of Sally M'Gee.

The next was a lawyer, and with law attornies,
Came bowing and scraping, and making quite free,
With fifty bright shiners in good ready rhinos,[1]
He down on the table did tender to me;   20
I gave him diversion, and pleased him quite heartily,
Right willingly he paid me a double fee,
I scorch'd his quil with the coal of curiosity,
Which makes him to think on young Sally M'Gee.

The next was a miser, who thought himself wiser,
Than all the whole world, so griping was he;
His bags he did open, and as a love token,
A two hundred pound note he gave unto me;
I gave diversion, and pleas'd him quite heartily,
I surely did please him, and that to a tee,   30
I gave him the slip, and a smoking hot pip,
Now run to the doctor, says Sally M'Gee.

---

1. 'shiners' = coins, especially gold and silver ones; 'ready rhinos' = ready money
(Partridge). (The origin of 'rhinos' with this meaning is obscure.)

The next was an aleseller with a wife and fortune,
Who had set up that business two years or three,
With fifty bright shiners he came on to court me;
And his fortune he left it, [he left it] with me;
But I thought it pity to wrong wife and children,
Within my breast I did quickly agree,
I sent her the booty, word how I came by it,
Which makes her right thankful to Sally M'Gee.   40

The next was a farmer, and he was a charmer,
And then with his person I did quickly agree,
I liked well his courage, and joined him in marriage,
And ever right constant to him I will be;
Fifty bright pounds I got in my rounds,
I gave him for portion, so pleasing was he,
I live in the county Tyrone, 'tis very well known,
More luck and good fortune to Sally McGee.

Paddy the Piper

When I was a boy in my father's mud edifice,
    Tender and bare as a pig in a stye,
Out at the door as I look'd with a steady phiz,[1]
    Who but Pat Murphy the piper came by?
Says Paddy, 'But few play this music; can you play?'
    Says I, 'I can't tell, for I never did try.'
        He told me that he had a charm,
            To make the pipes prettily speak,
        Then squeez'd a bag under his arm,
            And sweetly they set up a squeak.   10
            With a faralla, laralla loo,
                Och hone, how he handled the drone!
            And then such sweet music he blew,
                'Twould have melted the heart of a stone.

1. face.

'Your pipe,' says I, 'Paddy, so neatly comes over me,
    Naked I'll wander wherever it blows,
And if my father should try to recover me,
    Sure it won't be by describing my clothes:
The music I hear now, takes hold of my ear now,
    And leads me all over the world by the nose.'   20
        So I followed his bagpipe so sweet,
           And sung, as I leapt like a frog,
        Adieu to my family seat,
           So pleasantly plac'd in a bog.
            With my faralla, laralla loo,
               Och hone, how he handled the drone!
            And then such sweet music he blew,
               'Twould have melted the heart of a stone.

Full five years I follow'd him, nothing could sunder us,
    Till he one morning had taken a sup,   30
And slipp'd from a bridge in a river just under us,
    Souse to the bottom, just like a blind pup.
I roar'd out, and bawl'd out, and hastily call'd out,
    'O Paddy, my friend, don't you mean to come up?'
        He was dead as a nail in a door;
           Poor Paddy was laid on the shelf;
        So I took up his pipes on the shore,
           And now I've set up for myself —
            With my faralla, laralla loo,
               To be sure, I have not got the knack,   40
            To play faralla, laralla loo, aye,
               And bubberoo, dideroo whack.

The Ladies Dress, or the Downfall of the Stay-Makers[1]

The Ladies of Dublin they are all growing wild,
Both maids wives and widows seem to be with child,
They'r thick in the waist as a Cow I declare,
For want of their stays how the people do stare.

---

1. This strange poem is included because it is an example of what was being sung on the streets of Dublin in the 1790s. The text was, in effect, 'collected' in 1795 and has not been interfered with in the course of transmission since. Its very artlessness and incoherence lend it an authenticity often lacking in more polished texts. It is presented here in unedited form.

The bunches of ribbands that hangs to their backs,
They look like Jack Daws when dress'd up in rags,
And as for the veils that the Ladies do wear,
It makes them look cleaver I vow and declare.

The trades men of Dublin they are very low,
For want of employment they were forced to go,   10
To serve King and Country they always proved true,
Long life and success to the orange and blue.[2]

If the Ladies of Ireland would please to wear stuff,[3]
The trades men of Dublin would shortly be up,
But those foreign dresses the Ladies does wear,
Which leaves our poor Tradesmen in grief and despair.

When the Farmer goes home poor Sheela replies
'A what way[4] to Dublin Markets', she cries,
The markets run high and provisions so dear,
For want of trade stirring I vow and declare.   20

When the Countryman came to Dublin to fair,
He looked all around him, and how he did stare,
A loaf in a window by chance he espys,
'A what you want for it dear Madam', — he cries.

'A Sixpence my dear, and it is GOOD Bread',
'O Lord!' says the Countryman, 'I'm almost dead!'
He took to his heels and he never cried stop
Till he came to a place that they now call Kilcock.[5]

---

2. Orange in support of the succession from William of Orange, blue linked to presbyterianism.
3. i.e. cloth spun in Ireland, instead of imported from abroad.
4. cf. Ir. *Cén tslí*, which way?
5. A town in County Kildare.

A New Song call'd
The Lord Lieutenant's Farewell to the Kingdom of Ireland[1]

You Natives of Ireland unto me now attend,
You have lost the worthy noble great wou'd be a loyal Friend;
I planely say Fitzwilliam bold, who'd stand his Country's Friend,
Our Lord Lieutenant really thought the penal laws to mend.

When I did land in Dublin, most candid just and free,
Our gracious King did send me hear [*sic*] to reign Exellency;
I found my Country was deceived such things there may not be,
Bad fortune may attend the foes of Irish liberty.

The Irish Roman Catholics, address'd me which is known,
To serve both King and Country, Fitzwilliam he was prone: 10
The Catholics of Ireland, deserves a just applause,
They'd boldly stand their Country's right, in defence of King George.

The Irish Roman Catholics truly would defend,
Because in heardship [*sic*] always they, stood King Georges[2] Friend,
Affrontcd in my Native land, the cause I'll not explain,
Farewell adieu sweet Irish Souls, I'll short return again.

I came as Lord Lieutenant, the King order'd it so,
I thought to save my Country, and not to be a foe;
The Irish Bill[3] I thought to pass, just and deservedly,
Examine how they boldly Fought, for King and Country.   20

1. Before his arrival in January 1795 as lord lieutenant of Ireland, rumours that the fourth
   Earl Fitzwilliam (1748-1833) would bring about the repeal of the Penal Laws against
   catholics had spread wildly. Though Fitzwilliam was certainly in favour of reform, the
   Westminster cabinet showed that it would not support him, and in March of the same
   year Fitzwilliam resigned in disgust and left Ireland. This loyal song in praise of the
   departing lord lieutenant is the work of a barely educated street singer and, though the
   lack of distinction between various speaking voices makes the text confusing at first
   reading, the poem in included because it casts valuable light on a side of Irish cultural
   life about which very little is known. The hurt and bewildered voice of the creator of this
   song emerges clearly from this text, unaffected by later events and unaltered by the
   additions of later singers. The text is presented here unedited.
2. King George III.
3. A bill to remove the penal legislation against catholics.

517

Adieu sweet Irish Grattan,[4] Fitzwilliam he did say,
And to each worthy member,[5] that his Country wont betray,
Stick true like loyal Irish Souls, fear God and serve your king,
Your Bill will pass undoubtedly, then let the Nation ring.

My Lady[6] thought for to be gay, unto the Irish Poor,
She said to me that Charity, was still laid up in store;
I knew it well and did rejoice, to hear her Charity,
You Irish Souls be always true, to King and Country.

Farewell bold Irish Heroes, God prosper long the Isle,
You'll find in course of time, that fortune yet will smile: 30
The loyalty you shew'd to me, I always shall retain,
In peace and joy I hope I'll come, to see you all again.

A New Song on the Half-pence being cry'd down or, a Peep into a Whiskey-Shop[1]

Your welcome to Dublin dear harry what news have you for me I pray,
In troth cousin Davy your city is worse than the country I say;
I met with a friend as I landed a walking through old thomas-street,
Pray where is the best sup of whiskey, its long before since we did meet.

We stept into Maddins for certain, sir fill half a pint of sweet Pea.[2]
We drank it together contented, just five-pence I charge he did say,
The half-pence to him then I handed, he said friend now this will not do,
I just then had good looking ten pence, he swore the[y] were damnable
    blue.[3]

---

4. Henry Grattan (1746-1820), parliamentarian and leader of those seeking Ireland's legislative independence.

5. i.e. member of the Irish parliament.

6. Charlotte, Lady Fitzwilliam (d.1822).

1. It is hard to date this interesting song. Copper coinage was revalued in 1737 and it is possible that this song was written then, though the only known printed copy of it dates from 1795. There were several hundred whiskey shops in eighteenth-century Dublin, but this is one of very few contemporary accounts of them. The text is presented unedited.

2. whiskey. Partridge notes this as an Anglo-Irish word, quoting *Life in Ireland* (1822), and explains that the name comes from 'the colour of the resultant urine'.

3. Though the coins being tendered to him look good, the landlord says they are not acceptable.

I told him that I had no better, he said the[y] were lately cry'd
    [d]own,[4]
Cammacks[5] or good silver he said you must surely find for
    this town;   10
My hat and my wig both he seized, and kick'd me away from his
    door,
To the market house bare headed rambled, first call'd him a blood
    of a whore.

A tinker and cobler together were there in a damnable stew,
Their coppers the landlord refused which made them cry what shall
    we do,
The cobler cry'd sir I just took them, for mending a pair of old
    shoes,
The tinker cry'd hell sweat your leather how dare you such
    half-pence refuse.

His budget[6] was kept for a token he cryed cobler what shall I do,
A man without tools cannot work you know it is certainly true,
Stand by at the bulk[7] said the cobler untill this old pair I do mend,
I'll act as a true hearted fellow while I have got wax, awl or end.[8]   20

Old Cathy the chaunter[9] was drinking with tommy the noted
    news-boy,
Three naggins[10] they punish'd in pleasure but mark now my dear
    little joy,
Two shillings they both had in copper the devil a twopence would
    pay,[11]
Bad luck to the first that condemn'd them, the one to the other did
    say.

4. i.e. a public proclamation had been made changing the value of the coins.
5. cammack = a sixpenny piece.
6. A leather bag in which a tradesman carried his tools.
7. A framework projecting from the front of a shop, a stall.
8. Three things used in shoe-making; an awl is a sharp tool to make holes in leather and a wax-end is a thread coated with cobbler's wax.
9. piper or, possibly, singer.
10. naggin = noggin, a small horn drinking vessel, especially for whiskey, or the measure of as much whiskey as would fit in a naggin.
11. i.e. though they had two shillings' worth of copper, it was now worth less than two pence.

Poor larry the sweep had a penny he call'd for a jolly half throw,[12]
He guzel'd it up in a hurry the landlord cry'd larry hullow,
Some better come hand out, be handy, the devil a better have I,[13]
His brush then he snapt[14] in a fury, but larry soon blackened his eye.

The news boys are all in confusion by crying the new copper down,[15]
The ballad singers all are bedevil'd, scarce able to walk from
    swifts-town,[16]   30
The shoe boys is now going in mourning, their trade is remarkable blue,[17]
It's better be idle than work, since the half pence we get will not do.

So now to conclude my dear neighbours it causes stagnation in town,
And old Peggy Dod the tripe woman, it makes her to look with a frown,
This song it is pleasing and hearty its also remarkable true,
Come hand out the good looking coppers as bad ones for whiskey wont do.

Sweet Castle-Hyde[1]

As I roved out of a summer's morning,
    Down by the banks of Black-water side,
To view the groves and the meadows charming,
    And pleasure gardens of Castle-hyde.
There I heard the thrushes warbling,
    The dove and partridge I now describe;
The lambkins sporting every morning
    All to adorn sweet Castle-hyde.

12. half a glass of whiskey.
13. i.e. The landlord cried 'Hey, Larry! Come along, hand out some better coins! Hurry up!' Larry replies that he does not have any.
14. i.e. the landlord snapped the handle of the sweep's brush.
15. i.e. because the new copper has been devalued.
16. The reference is probably to the Liberty of St Patrick's, where Swift had been dean 1713-45.
17. i.e. very bad.

1. This is another interesting survival from the world of the travelling poet of late eighteenth-century Ireland. An itinerant balladeer composed the song in praise of Castle Hyde, the seat of the Hyde family on the river Blackwater in County Cork. Instead of being paid for his work, as he expected, the poet was driven from the gate by order of the owner, who thought the poem so absurd that he suspected it was meant as a joke. The author, highly offended, composed an additional verse against the owner and sang the song at every opportunity. (That verse is not in the version printed here.) The song as a whole became well enough known to be preserved and later parodied by Richard Milliken.

There are fine walks in these pleasant gardens,
    And seats most charming in shady bowers,   10
The gladiator,[2] who is bold and daring,
    Each night and morning to watch the flowers.
There's a church for service in this fine arbour,
    Where nobles often in coaches ride,
To view the groves and pleasure gardens,
    That front the palace of Castle-hyde.

If noble princes from foreign places,
    Should chance to sail to our Irish shore,
'Tis in this valley they would be feasted,
    As often heroes have been before.   20
The wholesome air of this habitation
    Would recreate your heart with pride;
There is no valley throughout this nation,
    In beauty equal to Castle-hyde.

There are fine horses and stall-fed oxes
    A den for foxes to play and hide,
Fine mares for breeding, and foreign sheep,
    With snowly fleeces, in Castle-hyde.
The grand improvements there would amaze you,
    The trees are drooping with fruit of all kind,   30
The bees harmonizing the fields with music,
    Which yields more beauty to Castle-hyde.

The richest groves throughout this nation,
    In fine plantation you will see there,
The rose, the tulip, and sweet carnation,
    All vying with the lily fair;
The buck and doe, the fox and eagle,
    They sleep and play by the river side,
The trout and salmon are always sporting,
    In the clear streams of Castle-hyde.   40

2. i.e. a statue of a gladiator.

I rode from Blarney to Castle-barnet,[3]
    To Thomastown and sweet Doneraile,
To Kilshannick that joins Rathcormack,
    Besides Killarney and Abbeyfeale.
The flowing Nore and the rapid Boyne,
    The river Shannon and the pleasant Clyde,
But in all my ranging and serenading,
    I saw none equal to Castle-hyde.

---

3. The places and rivers listed in this stanza are in the southern and central parts of Ireland.

RICHARD ALFRED MILLIKEN
(1767-**1800**-1815)

Richard Milliken was born in County Cork and trained as a lawyer, but was more interested in painting, music and literature than the law. He lived in Cork city most of his life where, in 1797/98, he ran a literary magazine called *The Casket or Hesperian Magazine* with his sister. He wrote several plays and five volumes of poetry, but is best remembered for 'The Groves of Blarney', his parody of 'Sweet Castle-Hyde'. According to Crofton Croker (*Popular Songs of Ireland* (London, 1886) p. 137), Milliken was present at a 'convivial meeting' of gentleman at which 'Sweet Castle-Hyde' was sung and laughed to scorn. Milliken undertook to produce another song 'at least equal in absurdity', and took Blarney Castle and its grounds as his subject.

Croker asserts that 'Milliken's intention was to ridicule the songs which ignorant Irish village bards — with a vast fondness for rhyme, an imperfect knowledge of the English language, and a pedantic ambition to display the full extent of their classical knowledge — were, and still are, in the habit of composing.' The song is far more interesting than Croker implies, however, and its praise of the radical Arabella Jeffreys, of Blarney Castle, suggests an anti-establishment message hidden in a seemingly nonsensical poem. See the interesting note by W. J. Mc Cormack in the *Field Day Anthology of Irish Writing* 3 vols (Derry, 1991), I, 1102.

The Groves of Blarney

The groves of Blarney they are so charming
    All by the purling of sweet silent streams;
Being banked with posies that spontaneous grow there,
    Planted in order by the sweet rock close.
'Tis there the daisy, and the sweet carnation,
    The blooming pink, and the rose so fair;
The daffodowndilly, besides the lily, —
    Flowers that scent the sweet fragrant air.
             Oh, ullagoane,[1] *&c.*

'Tis Lady Jeffreys[2] that owns this station,   10
    Like Alexander, or Queen Helen fair;
There's no commander throughout the nation
    For emulation can with her compare.

---

1. cf. Ir. *ulagón*, alas!
2. Mrs Arabella Jeffreys was the eldest sister of John Fitzgibbon, first Earl of Clare, and was known as a supporter of those, like the Whiteboys, who opposed the payment of tithes and clerical dues in the 1780s.

She has castles round her, that no nine-pounder
　　Could dare to plunder her place of strength;
But Oliver Cromwell he did her pummell,
　　And made a breach in her battlement.[3]
　　　　　　　　Oh, ullagoane, &c.

There's gravel walks there for speculation,
　　And conversation in sweet solitude;　　　　　　　　20
'Tis there the lover may hear the dove, or
　　The gentle plover, in the afternoon.
And if a young lady should be so engaging
　　As to walk alone in those shady bowers,
'Tis there her courtier he may transport her
　　In some dark fort, or underground.
　　　　　　　　Oh, ullagoane, &c.

For 'tis there's the cave where no daylight enters,
　　But bats and badgers are forever bred;
Being mossed by natur', that makes it sweeter　　　　30
　　Than a coach and six, or a feather bed.
'Tis there the lake that is stored with perches,
　　And comely eels in the verdant mud;
Besides the leeches, and the groves of beeches,
　　All standing in order for to guard the flood.
　　　　　　　　Oh, ullagoane, &c.

'Tis there's the kitchen hangs many a flitch in,[4]
　　With the maids a stitching upon the stair;
The bread and biske',[5] the beer and whisky,
　　Would make you frisky if you were there.　　　　40

---

3. Though there is no truth in the story, it was generally believed that Oliver Cromwell (1599-1658) 'pummelled' Blarney Castle during his Irish expedition in 1649.

4. This stanza is said to have been added later as an intended insult to the first Lord Donoughmore (1756-1825), alluding to what was termed his 'mean descent'. flitch = a side of bacon hanging above the kitchen fire to be cured.

5. biscuit.

'Tis there you'd see Peg Murphy's daughter
    A washing *praties* forenent the door,[6]
With Roger Cleary, and Father Healy,[7]
    All blood relations to my lord Donoughmore.
                Oh, ullagoane, &c.

There's statues gracing this noble place in,
    All heathen goddesses so fair, —
Bold Neptune, Plutarch, and Nicodemus,[8]
    All standing naked in the open air.
So now to finish this brave narration,   50
    Which my poor geni' could not entwine;
But were I Homer, or Nebuchadnezzar,
    'Tis in every feature I would make it shine.
                Oh ullagoane, &c

---

6. i.e. washing potatoes in front of the door.
7. Murphys, Clearys and Healy are all names of catholic families, whereas the family name of the (protestant) Earls of Donoughmore was Hely-Hutchinson.
8. The juxtaposition of Neptune (the Roman god of the sea), Plutarch (the ancient historian), Nicodemus (a pharisee mentioned in St John's gospel), Homer (the classical Greek poet) and Nebuchadnezzar (conqueror of the Jews in the Old Testament) is, and is meant to be, ridiculous.

SAMUEL BURDY

(c.1754-**1796**-1820)

Samuel Burdy was born in County Down, of Huguenot descent. He was educated at Trinity College, Dublin and ordained into the Church of Ireland. He wrote a life of the eminent theologian and hymn-writer, Philip Skelton (1707-87) and several volumes of poetry. When, in 1796, the old gaol in County Down was no longer needed for prisoners, it was turned into 'an elegant Hotel'. This transformation struck Samuel Burdy as 'a fit subject for poetry', and he wrote a long and entertaining poem about the change. The passage which follows describes a dinner served to the members of the Down Hunt in the newly converted hotel.

from: The Transformation

... Sport concluded, daub'd with mire,
Horses smoking like a fire,
After different hares run down,
They return to country-town;
Take off dirty boots and spurs,
Lay by whips that lash the curs,
Buck-skin breeches, tight and neat,
Hunting-caps to save the pate.
Clergy also, fam'd for leaps,
Take off jackets, and black-caps,   10
Fam'd too for *reforming* sinner,
Now prepare themselves for dinner,
As do noble lords and squires,
Youthful sons and aged sires.

Hunting dress now laid aside,
In the mansion, splendid, wide,
All assemble, deck'd as gay,
As great courtiers on birth day.
After waiting past their power,
While each minute seems as hour,   20
Lacquey sleek, or negro sable,
Tells them, dinner's on the table.
Up they start at joyful news,
Haste like people from their pews,

When they seek for better fare
Than dry preaching and dull prayer.
To dinner now they all sit down,
As hungry each as country clown,
Appetites as keen as razor,
Caus'd by running close to Cæsar[1].....   30

Brown and white soup handed round,
First took in the distant ground;
These remov'd from head and foot,
Turbot at the head was put,
Dainty fish of costly price,
Lobster sauce to make it nice.
At the foot was smoking sirloin,
That would glutton tempt to purloin,
As I've seen at borough feast,
When each voter prov'd a beast.   40
Sides were deck'd with ham and chickens,
Where you'd find some pleasant pickings;
Corners too with tongue and turkey,
Fit to please them, e'en if murky,
Turkey boil'd, with sauce of celery,
That would dine a judge at Hilary;[2]
T'other corners chickens roasted,
Potatoes bak'd, and also toasted.
Turbot taken from the head,
Turkey roast was placed instead.   50
From head to foot in order stood,
Of their kind both rare and good,
Jelly, minc'd pies, and plumb-pudding,
Each to stuff like gun with wadding.
In the middle too was sallad,
Health to serve, and please the palate.
On side-table round of beef
Was of dishes there the chief;
Also there was leg of mutton,
Both prepar'd for solid cutting.   60
First with cabbage well was garnish'd,
T'other too with turnips furnish'd.

1. A typical name of a hound.
2. i.e. at the dinner celebrating the Hilary (spring) law term.

Sugar, pepper, salt and mustard,
Butter melted, capers, custard,
And such articles at table,
Strings of rhymes would take like cable....

Now they hob-nob with champaign,
Red and white, brought o'er the main,
With good port, madeira, sherry,
That, if dull, would make you merry,   70
Wines salubrious, rich and neat,
To digest delicious meat.
Drink at dinner, ale and beer,
Cider, porter, perry³ dear.

When the first course was completed,
And keen appetites were sated;
It remov'd, now comes the second,
Dishes nice, but eas'ly reckon'd.
At the head was good roast hare,
Foot was deck'd with lobsters rare,   80
Ta'en in *creels*⁴ at Strangford tide,
Where my kindly friends reside,
Social, hospitable, gay; —
Gently stole my hours away.
Corners too were deck'd with shrimps,
Caught in nets, as wily crimps⁵
Catch recruits within their meshes,
By fine promises and sashes.
At sides, and near to head and foot,
Tarts of different sorts were put.   90
Th' almonds, sweetmeats too and celery,
Merit praise, and without raillery,
Stretch'd far out, just like a cable,
All along th' extended table.

3. Cider made of pears rather than apples.
4. Wicker-work lobster pots. Strangford Lough is a large sea-water inlet in County Down.
5. Recruiting officers or members of a press-gang who trap men for the army or navy.

It remov'd, were I expert,
Soon I would describe dessert.
Apples, cakes, at head and foot,
Walnuts at the sides were put.
Raisins, cheese, and charming chestnuts,
By nice judges deem'd the best nuts,   100
In the middle had their station,
And of dinner made completion....

Now the guests, that drink good claret,
Boast and talk as glib as parrot,
Not of crimes,[6] but feats and leaps,
How they scorn'd to take the gaps,
Leapt o'er ditches, hedges, drains,
Scamper'd o'er the open plains,
In pursuit of puss or reynard,[7]
Darting horse with spurs like poniard,[8]   110
Pleas'd with harmony of Hounds,
And diversity of sounds....

Thus in gambling, handy-capping,
Drinking, boasting of their leaping,
Join'd with bawdy toast and song,
Roll'd their jovial hours along,
Till the dawn, in crimson clad,
Sent them reeling to their bed....

6. Crimes had been the main subject of conversation in the gaol before its conversion.
7. hare or fox. 'Puss' was a common name for a hare in the eighteenth century.
8. a dagger.

JANE ELIZABETH MOORE
(1738-**1796**-?)

Jane Elizabeth Moore was of English extraction. She gives a vivid account, in her *Genuine Memoirs of Jane Elizabeth Moore* (1785) of her work as a clerk in her father's business. She also makes it clear, in comments on her relationship with her husband, that she was determined not to be 'obligated' to any man. She moved to Dublin where she apparently bored Thomas Moore by insisting on reading her poems to him. Her *Miscellaneous Poems* (Dublin, 1796) contain poetic celebrations of the discovery of gold in County Wicklow and of the opening of Maynooth College, Co. Kildare. She also engaged in the following unusual exchange of verse letters with an unknown Dublin freemason. The date of Mrs Moore's death is not known.

A Question to the Society of Freemasons
by Jane Elizabeth Moore

Ye Brethren Masonic of ancient degree,
Who for ages have boasted of being 'quite free';
But whence, my good Sirs, does this freedom arise?
When so many thousands, who wish to be wise,
Are suing[1] instructions you boldly deny;
The answer is tacit, pray tell me for why?
The knowledge you prize were it once but made known,
Might soften the manners and model the clown;[2]
The secret so valu'd, once known to the fair,[3]
Might improve on ideas by feminine air;   10
Then why were your tenets so cruelly prest,
As not to admit of a plume in your crest?
Then an emblem of union would boldly proclaim,
By admitting, 'quite freely', each well-inform'd dame,
Who such secret would keep on the terms of admission,
And her sacred word pledge on obtaining permission:
Your answer is claim'd, why you thus should refuse,
The requests of the fair, who were born to amuse.

1. i.e. asking for.
2. An ignorant or ill-bred person, often a countryman.
3. i.e. to women. The Freemasons do not admit women to their ranks.

Answer
By T.W.M——a Esq.[1]

You've asked why our secrets are kept from the clown,
And why to the fair we do not make them known;
That a clown should partake of our mystery divine,
As well might you bid us cast pearl before swine:[2]
And as to the fair, why since truth I must tell,
Their foibles and frailties we all know too well;
But as Masons should ever from babbling forbear,
I'll pass by in silence the faults of the fair;
Their merits acknowledge, nor can I do less,
They were born to amuse us, but never to bless.   10

To T.W.M——a, Esq.
By Jane Elizabeth Moore

Your answer I've read, and lament with surprize,
That the fair should appear so frail in your eyes;
Reflect, that the errors you so keenly scan,
Are such as are taught them by still frailer man;
If the clown you could polish from nature's rude mass,
It would greatly embellish your much renown'd class.
Your secret, how futile soe'er it may be,
Savors not of *pro bono*[1] we all daily see;
And since Heaven's gifts you so badly define,
I fear 'tis our sex are as 'pearls before swine'.   10

---

1. The exact identity of this freemason remains unknown: however three prominent citizens of Dublin in 1796 had the right initials and the right letters in their surname to be candidates, Thomas Murtha, ironmonger, Thady MacNamara, attorney, and Theobald McKenna, physician. The third of these is the most likely candidate.
2. cf. Matthew vii. 6.

---

1. *pro bono publico*, for the public good.

531

A Rejoinder to Mrs Jane Eliz Moore's Repledum[1]

By T.W.M——a, Esq.,

I've read your reply, fraught with humour and taste,
And now to join issue permit me to haste;
When first mother Earth was call'd up by a nod
From chaos, and shap'd by Jehovah, our God!
Who made man his own image, with reason endow'd,
And surveying the whole, proclaim'd all his works good:
Who form'd our rules and imparted the same
To a chosen few, from the rest did retain
Our secrets mysterious, who his word issu'd forth,
They should not be revealed but to men of true worth;   10
That a man without principle, reason or thought,
To guide him to speak, or to act as he ought,
Should not be admitted our Lodge to disgrace,
It's harmony blast, or it's beauties deface;
That the faults of the fair sex are taught them by man,
I deny, for their crimes with creation began.
Mother Eve, who was made to encrease human kind,
To soften and solace man's trouble of mind;
Who tho' form'd his equal in reason and soul,
No mandate divine could her conduct controul;   20
Till banish'd from Eden, on herself and her race,
Brought the first curse on man, with th'Almighty's disgrace:
Tho' as Masons we're ever attach'd to the fair,
Their sorrows still soothe, still assuage every care;
Their weakness protect from the vulgar and rude,
Their joys still increase, nay their every good;
Yet our secrets and rites we can never impart
To the sex, for whose sin all mankind feel smart;
Altho' we lament we the fair can't admit,
Convinc'd that *a few* possess merit and wit;   30
That our secrets partaking, the brighter wou'd shine,
But we're barr'd by our rules, form'd by precepts Divine.

---

1. second pleading or rejoinder.

Answer to the above Replication[1]
by Jane Elizabeth Moore

Due thanks I acknowledge for your compliment paid,
But my sex still demanding the best of my aid,
A champion, I see, I must again forward stand,
For the crude observations receiv'd at your hand,
That Eve was a sinner to the world is known,
A fault Adam shou'd have reprov'd with a frown;
But like her he'd a *goût*[2] for what was forbid,
For which they both paid when in banishment hid;
Yet for one sin Eve committed, arithmetic rules
Will prove, men are adepts in criminal schools.   10
When the work was found good and the whole was survey'd,
You say that for *Masons* selection was made;
A chosen few might at the first be confin'd,
Yet enlarging the list there was evil combin'd;
The perspective, I fear, will exhibit a scene,
That will prove them familiar with sin in their mien;
If their merit they prize that a secret they keep,
And in mystery of science are known to dip deep;
Believe me in wine as in science, their skill
Proves too oft that o'er women they'd have their own will.   20
You say mother Eve to encrease human kind,
Was sent by her Maker in contract to bind,
To sooth and to soften the ills of mankind;
Yet as precept is weak, 'tis example should shew,
What lessons of virtue our sex should pursue;
The reason is plain, give but women their way,
And there's few who will not with pleasure obey;
Hostility does but the fuel encrease,
Moderation it is that promotes lasting peace.
The scene is now clos'd as the work is compleat,   30
And I trust that in friendship we ever shall meet;
No evil is meant in this jocular flight,
The protection we claim which you hold to our sight,
For the present, my friend, I will wish you good night.

1. reply.
2. taste.

As theory alone a good Mason will make,
And the scale and the compass like the prong and the rake,
May by strangers be handl'd, why not women pursue,
T'have a Lodge [3] of their own, with the tinsel and shew;
The fringe and the flounces, the jewels and toys,
The ladies may please, and add much to their joys.   40
Still of this be assured, by themselves they will shine,
As you say union's bar'd by a 'precept divine'.

3. The place where meetings of Freemasons are held; also the members composing a
branch of the Freemasons.

WILLIAM DRENNAN
(1754-**1797**-1820)

William Drennan was born in Belfast, the son of a dissenting minister. He was educated at the universities of Glasgow and Edinburgh and settled in Dublin, where he practised as a doctor. He was one of the founders of the United Irishmen and was tried for sedition in 1794, though acquitted. He later moved to Belfast and founded *The Belfast Magazine*. 'The Wake of William Orr', his most famous poem, commemorates the execution in 1797 of a United Irishman who had been convicted of nothing more serious than administering an illegal oath.

The Wake of William Orr

Here our murdered brother lies —
Wake him not with women's cries;
Mourn the way that manhood ought;
Sit in silent trance of thought.

Write his merits on your mind —
Morals pure and manners kind;
In his head, as on a hill,
Virtue placed her citadel.

Why cut off in palmy youth?
Truth he spoke, and acted truth —   10
Countrymen, 'Unite!' he cried,
And died — for what his Saviour died.

God of Peace, and God of Love,
Let it not thy vengeance move!
Let it not thy lightenings draw —
A Nation guillotin'd by law!

Hapless nation! rent and torn,
Thou wert early taught to mourn,
Warfare of six hundred years —[1]
Epochs marked with blood and tears!   20

1. i.e. since the 'conquest' of Ireland in 1189.

Hunted thro' thy native grounds,
Or flung reward to human hounds;
Each one pull'd and tore his share,
Heedless of thy deep despair.

Hapless Nation — hapless Land,
Heap of uncementing sand!
Crumbled by a foreign weight,
And, by worse, domestic hate.

God of Mercy! God of Peace!
Make the mad confusion cease;   30
O'er the mental chaos move,
Through it speak the light of love.

Monstrous and unhappy sight,
Brothers' blood will not unite;
Holy oil and holy water,
Mix, and fill the world with slaughter.

Who is she with aspect wild?
The widow'd mother with her child —
Child new stirring in the womb!
Husband waiting for the tomb!   40

Angel of this sacred place,
Calm her soul and whisper peace,
Cord, or axe, or guillotin'
Make the sentence — not the sin.[2]

Here we watch our brother's sleep;
Watch with us, but do not weep;
Watch with us thro' dead of night,
But expect the morning light.

Conquer fortune — persevere! —
Lo! it breaks, the morning clear!   50
The cheerful cock awakes the skies,
The day is come — arise! — arise!

---

2. i.e. the sentence of death is made, not by the sin (which does not exist) but by the
methods of execution.

MARY ALCOCK
(c.1742-**1798**-1798)

Mary Alcock was the daughter of Dr Denison Cumberland, an Englishman who became bishop of Clonfert and of Kilmore. Though her brother, Richard Cumberland (1732-1811), was a prolific dramatist, Mary published only two slight volumes of poetry. However, they show her to have been sensitive to the plight of the oppressed, and offended by the bigotry she found in Ireland. Her niece affixed a biographical memoir of her to the posthumous (1799) edition of her poetry which has, incidentally, an enormous subscription list, including four members of the British royal family.

The Chimney-Sweeper's Complaint

A chimney-sweeper's boy am I;
    Pity my wretched fate!
Ah, turn your eyes; 'twould draw a tear,
    Knew you my helpless state.

Far from my home, no parents I
    Am ever doom'd to see;
My master, should I sue to him,
    He'd flog the skin from me.

Ah, dearest Madam, dearest Sir,
    Have pity on my youth;   10
Tho' black, and cover'd o'er with rags,
    I tell you nought but truth.

My feeble limbs, benumb'd with cold,
    Totter beneath the sack,
Which ere the morning dawn appears
    Is loaded on my back.

My legs you see are burnt and bruis'd,
    My feet are gall'd by stones,
My flesh for lack of food is gone,
    I'm little else but bones.   20

Yet still my master makes me work,
     Nor spares me day or night;
His 'prentice boy he says I am,
     And he will have his right.

'Up to the highest top,' he cries,
     'There call out "chimney-sweep!"'
With panting heart and weeping eyes
     Trembling I upwards creep.

But stop! no more — I see him come;
     Kind Sir, remember me!   30
Oh, could I hide me under ground,
     How thankful should I be!

JOSEPH ATKINSON
(1743-**1798**-1818)

Joseph Atkinson was born in Dublin. He entered the army as a young man and rose to the rank of captain. He wrote a number of comic operas and several long poems, including an extended description of County Wicklow, *A Poetic Excursion* (Dublin, 1818). Atkinson was a friend of Thomas Moore and of Moore's patron, the Earl of Moira. He first wrote about Killarney when stationed there as a young officer in the late 1770s, but he returned to the theme in the 1790s. Unlike many of his contemporaries, who, when writing on Killarney concentrated on the sublime effect produced on sensitive minds by the wild scenery of the area, Atkinson was interested in the field sports available. He died in England.

from: **Killarney: a poem**

... *Then* spring the grouse, the heaths impurpl'd hold
And their bright plumage to the sun unfold;
Go flush the partridge, mark the pheasant's flight,
And from their terror catch a wild delight:
Then quick discharge the whizzing fatal lead,
And gain new life from the mute victims dead.

  Or, if a nobler game thy wish pursues,
(Nature has amply given thee here to chuse)
Rouz'd by the concert of the hounds and horn,
When the lark soaring hails the green-ey'd morn;   10
The stag awaits thee on the mountains' side,
The lofty groves his spreading antlers hide:
A gay flotilla on the lake appears,
Crowds to the sport, and each spectator cheers....

  The stag in view, behold the glorious game,
Let the pursuit thy kindling soul inflame:
How Echo sighs to hear his plaintive groans,
And, as in sympathy, his fate bemoans.
The well-staunch'd hounds, now join'd in tuneful cry,
With eager speed and fierce impatience fly: 20
How the stag trembles for his threaten'd fate,
Where can he rest, how combat or retreat?

In vain below the ardent chace to shun,
Up the steep precipice in vain to run;[1]
For there the rustic multitude combines
To guard the passes, and defend the lines;
By terror hurried, and o'erspent with toil,
Sudden he plunges in the cooler soil.

Fly swift, ye barges, o'er the billows skim,
See where your hunted martyr strives to swim: 30
The vig'rous rowers ev'ry nerve distend,
Now with full voice your cheering plaudits lend.

Behold him near, encrease your joyful cries,
Almost with fear your timid victim dies:
No more he swims, but panting now for breath,
Laments in tears a base, a barbarous death.

But spare, ah! spare this monarch of the chace,
The noblest, strongest, swiftest of his race;
And while triumphant and secure you float,
Ah! spare the dumb complainer's downy throat;   40
Be truly brave, not prodigal of blood,
Dismiss the ranger to his native wood.
Bound by a wreath the hand of beauty gave[2]
He'll own your bounty, and be mark'd your slave;
Amongst his wild companions long to live,
He to your sons a future chace may give.
Exulting clamours from the shores rebound,
And from the barges to the hills resound;

Tir'd with the noise of this tumultuous sport,
Some to the lake for calmer joys resort;   50
Whilst contemplation and amusement join'd,
New string the nerves and tranquilize the mind.

---

1. A note in the 1798 edition reads: 'When a stag chace is ordered for any visitor on the lake, it is crowded with boats from the neighbouring shores; and there are men ranged on the tops of the mountains to keep the stag from crossing them, and to drive him down to the lake.' Accounts by other eighteenth-century visitors confirm these details.
2. A note at this point explains that there was a custom which allowed ladies to bind the head of the stag with a ribbon.

Now bend the angle,[3] cast your mimic flies
And midst the rippling wave the fish will rise:
Th'aquatic brood perceive the tempting bait,
(But ah! what frauds on proffer'd bounty wait)
Now fondly eager to devour their prey,
They leap the pleasing but the fatal way;
Too late they find the treach'rous hook is there,
In vain they plunge to snap the twisted snare.   60

   Give line enough, let loose the twirling wheel,
Nor let them sudden all thy prowess feel;
In vain they struggle to preserve their life,
If cool experience rule the playful strife;
First to indulge, and next their course restrain,
'Till they flag gasping with fatigue and pain:
The speckled trout your landing net may wield,
Like the snar'd covey on the stubbl'd field.
If the large salmon thy temptation court,
A nobler game! a more delightful sport!   70
He through the liquid maze for hours will play,
Your keen impatience and your toil repay;
Whilst you, to make your noble captive sure,
With the barb'd gaff your struggling prey secure;
And whilst admiring friends your triumph hail,
The friendly theme becomes the friends' regale....

3. fishing-rod.

JAMES ORR
(1770-**1798**-1816)

James Orr, a poor weaver who never went to school and who lived almost all his life in a small community in County Antrim, is generally considered the best of the Ulster weaver poets of the late eighteenth and early nineteenth centuries. Like many of his brother poets, Orr was a radical, and he joined the United Irishmen. He fought at the battle of Antrim in June 1798, after which he went to America for a short while. He recorded his experiences on the emigrant ship from Larne in two poems, one in English and the other in Ulster-Scots; both poems are printed below. Orr's poetry is full of interesting details about life in Ulster and shows him to have had a strong social conscience.

Song composed on the Banks of Newfoundland[1]

In Ireland 'tis evening. From toil my friends hie[2] all,
    And weary walk home o'er the dew-sprinkled lea;
The shepherd in love tunes his grief-soothing viol,
    Or visits the maid that his partner will be:
The blythe milk-maids trip to the herd that stands lowing,
    The West finely smiles,[3] and the landscape is glowing,
The sad-sounding curfew, and torrent fast-flowing,
    Are heard by my fancy, tho' far, far at sea.

What has my eye seen since I left the green vallies
    But ships as remote as the prospect could be?   10
Unwieldy huge monsters,[4] as ugly as *malice*,
    And planks of some wreck, which with sorrow I see?
What's seen but the fowl that his lonely flight urges,
    The light'ning that darts thro' the sky-meeting surges?
And the sad scouling sky, that with bitter rain scourges
    This cheek Care sits drooping on, far, far at sea?

1. Shallow 'banks' off the coast of Newfoundland, famous fishing grounds.
2. hasten.
3. Evening light over the west of Ireland.
4. Whales seen from the deck of the ship.

How hideous the hold is! — Here, children are screaming,
    There dames faint thro' thirst, with their babes on their knee;
Here, down ev'ry hatch the big breakers are streaming,
    And, there, with a crash, half the fixtures break free: 20
Some court — some contend — some sit dull stories telling —
    The mate's mad and drunk, and the tar's task'd and yelling:[5]
What sickness and sorrow, pervade my rude dwelling! —
    A huge floating lazar-house,[6] far, far at sea.

How chang'd all may be when I seek the sweet village![7]
    A hedge-row may bloom where its street us'd to be;
The floors of my friends may be tortur'd by tillage,
    And the upstart be serv'd by the fallen grandee:[8]
The axe may have humbled the grove that I haunted,
    And shades be my shield that as yet are unplanted;   30
Nor one comrade live, who repin'd when he wanted
    The sociable suff'rer, that's far, far at sea.[9]

In Ireland 'tis night. On the flow'rs of my setting[10]
    A parent may kneel, fondly praying for me:
The village is smokeless, the red moon is getting
    The hill for a throne, which I yet hope to see:
If innocence thrive many more have to grieve for,
    Success, slow but sure, I'll contentedly live for —
Yes, Sylvia![11] we'll meet, and your sigh cease to heave for
    The swain, your fine image haunts, far, far at sea.   40

---

5. i.e. sailors are yelling as they rush about their tasks.
6. A hospital or place for poor and diseased persons.
7. The poet imagines himself returning to his home village.
8. In his imagination, the poet sees the land he knows taken over by some new landowner, who plants fields and hedgerows where there are now houses.
9. Lines 31-32 mean: 'Nor one comrade who was unhappy when he missed the company of the sociable man who was suffering far out at sea (i.e. the poet) be still left alive.'
10. The place where the poet was born.
11. Despite this call to 'Sylvia', Orr never married.

The Passengers

Down where yon anch'ring vessel spreads the sail,
That, idly waiting, flaps with ev'ry gale,
Downward they move, a melancholy band,
Pass from the shore, and darken all the strand.

GOLDSMITH[1]

How calm an' cozie is the wight[2]
    Frae cares an' conflicts clear ay,[3]
Whase settled headpiece never made
    His heels or han's be weary!
Perplex'd is he whase anxious schemes
    Pursue applause, or siller,
Success nor sates, nor failure tames;[4]
    Bandied frae post to pillar
        Is he, ilk day.

As we were, Comrades, at the time   10
    We mov't frae Ballycarry,[5]
To wan'er thro' the woody clime
    Burgoyne gied oure to harrie.[6]
Wi' frien's consent we prie't a gill,
    An' monie a house did call at,
Shook han's an' smil't; tho' ilk fareweel
    Strak, like a weighty mallet,
        Our hearts, that day.

On shore, while ship-mates halt, tho' thrang't,
    Wi' lasses hearts to barter;   20
Nybers, an' frien's, in boatfu's pang't,
    Approach our larboard quarter;[7]

---

1. *The Deserted Village*, ll. 219-22.
2. person.
3. Ulster-Scots words and expressions are explained in the Glossary.
4. i.e. success does not sate him, nor does failure tame him.
5. The community in County Antrim where Orr was born.
6. i.e. to wander through the wooded countryside (in America) it was beyond Burgoyne's power to plunder. Orr uses the name of General John Burgoyne (1722-92), the surrender of whose British troops to the forces of the American colonists at Saratoga in October 1777 marked a turning point in the War of American Independence, to symbolise the British forces defeated in America.
7. The left-hand side of the ship.

Syne speel the side, an' down the hatch
　　To rest, an' crack, an' gaze on
The boles o' births, that monie a wratch
　　Maun squeeze in, for a season,
　　　　　By night, an' day.

'This is my locker, yon'ers Jock's,
　　In that auld creel, sea-store is;
Thir births beside us are the *Lockes*,[8]
　　My uncle's there before us;
Here, hang my tins an' vitriol[9] jug,
　　Nae thief's at han' to meddle 'em.'
'L—d, man, I'm glad ye're a' sae snug;
　　But och! 'tis owre like Bedlam[10]
　　　　　Wi' a' this day.'

'All boats ashore!' the mate cries stern,
　　Wi' oaths wad fear a saunt ay:
'Now Gude be wi' ye, Brice,[11] my bairn' —
　　'An' Gude be wi' ye, Auntie.'
What *keepsakes*,[12] an' what news are sent!
　　What smacks, an' what embraces!
The hurryin' sailors sleely sklent
　　Droll leuks at lang wry faces,
　　　　　Fu' pale that day.

While 'Yo heave O!' wi' monie a yell
　　The birkies weigh the anchor;
Ilk mammies pet conceits itsel'
　　The makin' o' a Banker;[13]

30

40

8. A note in the original edition explains that this family had sailed for America in 1798.
9. This must be a mistake for a 'vitreous' jug, i.e. one made of, or looking as if it is made of, glass.
10. A mad house.
11. Bruce.
12. gifts.
13. i.e. one who fished on the Newfoundland 'Banks'.

They'll soon, tho', wiss to lieve at hame,   50
    An' dee no worth a totam,[14]
When brustin' breast, an' whamlin' wame,
    Mak' some wise men o' Gotham[15]
        Cry halt! this day.

Some frae the stern, wi' thoughts o' grief
    Leuk back, their hearts to Airlan';[16]
Some mettle't bucks, to work ay brief,
    At en's o' rapes are harlin';
Some haud aback frae dangers brow
    Their toddlin' o'er, no cautious;   60
An' some, wi' monie a twine an' throe,
    Do something wad be nauceous
        To name, this day.

Meanwhile, below, some count their beads,
    While prudes, auld-light[17] sit cantin';
Some mak' their beds; some haud their heads,
    An' cry wi' spite, a' pantin'!
'Ye brought us here, ye luckless cauf!
    (Aye did he; whisht my darlin'!)
L—d sen' me hame! wi' poke an' staff,   70
    I'd beg my bread thro' Airlan',
        My lane, that day.'

In twathree days, the maist cam' to,
    Few heads were sair or dizzy;
An' chiel's wha scarce a turn cud do,
    Begoud to be less lazy;
At night (to tell amang oursel's)
    They crap, wi' fandness fidgin',
To court — or maybe something else,
    Gif folk becam' obligin',   80
        Atween an' day.

---

14. i.e. and be no more use than a small child.
15. 'The wise men of Gotham' is a traditional phrase meaning 'fools'; the inhabitants of the village of Gotham successfully prevented an English king from building a hunting lodge in their village by pretending to be half-witted.
16. Ireland.
17. i.e. members of the 'Old Light' (strict) sects of the nonconformist churches.

Roun' the camhouse[18] what motley ban's
 At breakfast-time cam' swarmin'!
Tin, tankards, kettles, pots, an' pans,
 The braid flat fire was warmin':
The guid auld rule, 'First come first ser't,'
 Was urg't by men o' mettle;
An' ay whan callens grew mislear't,
 The arm o' flesh boost settle
   Th' affray, that day.   90

A bonie sight I vow it was,
 To see on some lown e'nin',
Th' immense, smooth, smilin' sea o' glass,
 Whare porpoises were stenin':
To see at night the surface fine
 That Cynthia[19] made her path on;
An' snove, an' snore thro' waves o' brine,
 That sparkle't like a heath on
   A bleaze some day.

But now a gale besets our bark,   100
 Frae gulph to gulph we're tumblc't;
Kists, kits, an' fam'lies, i' the dark,
 Wi' ae side-jerk are jumble't:
Some stauchrin' thro' a pitch[20] lays laigh —
 Some, drouket, ban the breaker;
While surge, on surge, sae skelps her — Hegh!
 Twa three like that will wreck her
   A while ere day.

Win's, wives, an' weans, rampage an' rave,
 Three score at ance are speakin';   110
While blacks wha a' before them drave,
 Lye cheepin' like a chicken.
'What gart us play? or bouse like beasts?
 Or box in fairs wi' venom?'[21]

---

18. caboose, the cooking area on the open deck of the ship.
19. i.e. the moon.
20. The downward plunge of the ship into a wave.
21. These lines seem to mean: 'What made us boil up inside or swing around like animals or be so venomously sick in our journey?'

Hear how the captain laughs an' jests,
 An' bit a bord between him
  An' death, this day.

'Tis calm again. While rightin' things,
 The heads o' births are bizziet,
The seaman chews his quid, an' sings,   120
 An' peys his fren's a visit.
'Eh! dem my eyes! how is't, goodman?
 Got clear of *Davy*'s locker?[22]
Lend me a facer till we lan',
 'Till blind as Newgate's knocker
  We'll swig,[23] that day.'

Here, gash guidmen, wi' nightcaps on,
 At ance baith pray an' watch;
An', there, for light, sits monie a loun
 At Cartes beneath the hatch: 130
Here, some sing sangs, or stories tell,
 To ithers bizzy knittin';
An', there some readin' to themsels,
 Nod owre asleep, while sittin'
  Twa fold that day.

Now Newfoun'lan's becalmin' banks
 Our ship supinely lies on;
An' monie a ane his lang line fanks,
 Whase heuk some captive dies on:
An' now, disguis't, a fore-mast-man   140
 Shaves dry, the churls unwillin'
To pay the poll-tax on deman'—
 A pint, or else a shillin'
  A piece, that day.[24]

---

22. i.e. Did you escape drowning? Davy Jones is a term for the evil spirit of the sea and 'Davy Jones's Locker' refers to the sea as a grave for drowned sailors.

23. A 'Newgate Knocker' was normally a description of a lock of hair, curled in a particular way. Here, however, the lines mean: 'Lend me a drink until we land and I can get as drunk as a blind knocker on a prison door.'

24. A note at this point reads: 'It has been a long established custom for the seamen, on reaching the banks of Newfoundland, to exact a shilling, or a shilling's worth of liquor, from every passenger; and to shave, without soap, those who refuse to contribute their quota'. fore-mast-man = a sailor below the rank of petty officer.

Aince mair luck lea's us (plain 'tis now
    A murd'rer in some mess is)[25]
An English frigate heaves in view,
    I'll bail her board,[26] an' press us:
Taupies beneath their wives wha stole,
    Or 'mang auld sails lay flat ay,   150
Like whitrats peepi' frae their hole,
    Cried, 'Is she British, wat ye,
            Or French, this day?'

'Twas but a brig frae Baltimore,
    To Larne wi' lintseed steerin';
Twa days ago she left the shore,
    Let's watch for lan' appearin':
Spies frae the shrouds, like laigh dark clouds,
    Descried domes, mountains, bushes;
The Exiles griev't — the sharpers thiev't —   160
    While cronies bous't like fishes,
            Conven't that day.

Whan glidin' up the *Delaware*,[27]
    We cam' forenent [28] *Newcastle*,
Gypes co'ert the wharf to gove, an' stare,
    While out, in boats, we bustle:
Creatures wha ne'er had seen a black,
    Fu' scar't took to their shankies;
Sae, wi' our best rags on our back,
    We mixt amang the Yankies,   170
            An' skail't, that day.

---

25. i.e. it is plain now that a murderer is taking his meals in a mess (a group eating together) on board the ship.
26. i.e. I'm certain ('would go bail') that she will board our ship and press us into military service.
27. The Delaware river.
28. opposite, over against.

The Execution

Awake my lire, and sing his fall
      Who on yon tree must yield his breath:
Nor censure me, you hearts of gall;
      I blame his deeds, but mourn his death.

The bosoms that fine feelings bless,
      Must grieve to see an erring swain
Ascend the climax of distress,
      Disgrace, remorse, affliction, pain.

The warlike guard, the sable priest,[1]
      The false-fac'd fiend, and warping mob,[2]   10
That scare the safe, must shock the breast
      Which long e'er night shall cease to throb.

The deep, damp cell in twilight furl'd,
      The filth that rots, the bolt that galls,
He's grieved to leave; and with a world
      Would buy a week within these walls.

Ah! see him led to life's last scene
      Thro' Carrickfergus' far-fam'd wall;
Whose mart is copious, fair her fane,[3]
      Her fortress firm, and just her hall.   20

Amid the circle see him bend
      His neck, now bare, the noose to meet:
And now the steps he'll ne'er descend,
      He climbs with loth and lingering feet.

Where should he turn? His actions here
      A woeful retrospect supply;
Confronting what is dark and dread
      Hereafter, shocks his mental eye!

1. i.e. the priest in his black robes.
2. i.e. the crowd whose mind is distorted.
3. church. (The church of St Nicholas in Carrickfergus, Co. Antrim is famous for its architecture and its monuments.)

Heaven's azure arch he dreads to scan,
      Heaven's easy laws he held in strife,   30
With shame he views the cruel clan
      Intent to see him lose his life.

Where e'er he looks his heart must bleed;
      He sees the ruffian who betrayed;
He sees th' accomplice of the deed;
      He sees his friends and favourite maid.

He sees his father. Torments move
      His inmost soul, as near he draws:
To see them grieve whom much we love
      Is death. 'Tis worse when we're the cause.   40

His last address had power to reach
      Ev'n scornful hearts, tho' void of art:
Affecting still must be the speech
      That simply leaves a feeling heart.

The choral psalm with sad delight
      Consol'd the breasts his speech had riv'n,
To hear him sing an angel might
      Lean from the battlements of heaven.

In plaintive and pathetic strains,
      To Being's source he wills his soul;   50
A long last gaze o'er hills and plains
      His sad eyes take, and cease to roll.

He hestitates, and looks again,
      Then veils the cheek where blooms the rose,
His pendant form with pungent pain
      Convulsive writhes, and wildly throes.

Heav'ns! see him struggle, spring, and stretch,
      Now swell, now sink, now scarcely shake;
So, on the hook, the finny wretch
      Hangs trembling o'er its parent lake.   60

HUGH PORTER
(1780-**1799**-1812)

Hugh Porter lived all his life as a weaver in Moneyslane, a small community in County Down. Though he probably had little education, Porter began writing poems in his teens and in 1799 presented this poem to the local rector, the Rev Thomas Tighe. Tighe, whose sister-in-law was the poet Mary Tighe, was an active supporter of several writers in the area, as well as being part of a circle which included Thomas Percy, poet and bishop of Dromore, whose *Reliques of Ancient Poetry* (1765) had changed the view of the age towards poetry in English. Porter's best verse is in Ulster Scots and, supported by Tighe and other patrons, he published poems in various newspapers, as well as a volume entitled *Poetical Attempts* (1813).

To the Reverend T[homas] T[ighe], Parson's Hill

REVEREND SIR, I would be laith[1]
Your honour in the least to skaith[2]
Tho' I repining bend beneath
 The want of rare things;
But ye hae wealth and honour baith[3]
 An' mony mair things.

Few persons can wi' you compare
In what the great and worthy share,
Yet och! if I had but the lear[4]
 That ye hae gotten,   10
I would not value a' your gear[5]
 An eyeless button.

For then I could baith write and spell,
An' speak, and leuk,[6] grammatical,
An' would sic rhyming blethers tell[7]
 'Tween truth and lies,
As Maister Dick, or e'en yoursel',
 Might may-be please.

1. loath. See Glossary for Ulster-Scots words and phrases.
2. damage.
3. both.
4. learning.
5. riches.
6. look.
7. i.e. and would tell such idle, rhyming tales.

But let us first our tale declare:
Ae[8] Sunday night to banish care,   20
I to your dwelling-house repair,
    Wi' right guid will,
An' if it was for sake o' prayer
    That's better still.

I entered in your parlour door,
And as I stalked owre the floor,
I saw — but sic a sight before
    I ne'er had seen;
A thousand beuks[9] I'm sure, and more,
    Surpriz'd my een.[10]   30

Thought I: 'If e'er it be my lot
To be a prisoner, here's the spot
Of a' the world I would have got
    To be my jail.
Here heart-corroding care should not
    My soul assail:

I could spen' mony a cheerfu' summer
To crack[11] wi' Virgil, Pope, an' Homer,
It raises in my brain a rumour
    To hear them talk'd o'.   40
But waes my heart[12] — what fits my humour
    I'm often baulk'd o'.'

While I survey'd this pompous pile
O' beuks in order, rank and file,
This sweet reflection made me smile:
    'He's condescendin',
An' will, perhaps, for a short while
    Vouchsafe to lend ane.

8. one.
9. books.
10. eyes.
11. converse.
12. i.e. my heart is sorrowful.

553

Amang the rest that me attracts
There's ane, of which I hear great cracks,   50
An' that's the *Elegant Extracts*,[13]
    So, if ye hae[14] it,
Your humble Rhymer, Sir, expects
    Or hopes ye'll gie[15] it.

I'll read as much o't as I can,
An' what I canna read — maun stan',[16]
I'll keep it clean wi' carefu' han',
    Nor tear nor burn it,
An' ony time that you deman',
    I will return it.   60

Now gin[17] your Reverence would please
To grant me this but twa-three days,
I'll teach the lanely burns and braes[18]
    The heights an' hollows,
To join wi' me in Scottish lays,
    An' sing as follows:

"Oh! may your reverence be blest
Wi' health, an' strength, an' peace, an' rest;
An' may contention ne'er infest
    Your social meetings,   70
But mutual love be aye exprest
    In kindly greetings.

---

13. *Elegant Extracts: or useful and entertaining pieces of poetry, selected for the improvement of youth*. The first edition of this widely popular selection, edited by V. Knox, appeared in London in about 1770, and the first Dublin edition is dated 1789.
14. have.
15. give.
16. must stand. i.e. 'What I can't understand must be left alone.'
17. if.
18. i.e. the lonely streams and hillsides.

An' may ye lang enjoy wi' credit
The douse[19] black gown, for weel ye set it,[20]
May nane ye wish weel e'er be fretit,[21]
    I pray most fervent,
For want of lear, or means to get it
    As is your servant,

                HUGH PORTER."'

19. sober. The reference is to the black cassock of the preacher.
20. i.e. for it suits you well.
21. i.e. may none of those whom you wish well be vexed by lack of learning (lear) or the means to acquire it.

JOHN PHILPOT CURRAN
(1750-**1799**-1817)

John Philpot Curran was born near Cork and educated at Trinity College, Dublin and the Middle Temple. He became a member of the Irish parliament in 1783, but resigned in 1797 because he realised he could never bring about reform of that corrupt institution. As a lawyer, he defended many of the United Irishmen, including William Drennan. Though best known for his speeches, Curran is also remembered for the poem below which is written in a form of the stressed Irish metre, the *ochtfhoclach*.

The Deserter's Meditation

If sadly thinking, with spirits sinking,
      Could, more than drinking, my cares compose,
A cure for sorrow from sighs I'd borrow,
      And hope tomorrow would end my woes.
But as in wailing there's nought availing,
      And Death unfailing will strike the blow,
Then for that reason, and for a season,
      Let us be merry before we go.

To joy a stranger, a wayworn ranger,
      In ev'ry danger my course I've run;   10
Now hope all ending, and death befriending,
      His last aid lending, my cares are done.
No more a rover, or hapless lover,
      My griefs are over — my glass runs low;[1]
Then for that reason, and for a season,
      Let us be merry before we go.

---

1. The image is of one half of an hourglass from which the sand has almost drained.

NATIONALIST VERSE OF THE 1790s

The success of the revolutions in America and in France in the 1770s and 1780s had a profound effect on Irish politics, and many Irish nationalist songs of the early 1790s reflect the aspiration that the liberty which had been won by the sword in America and in France might be won also by the sword in Ireland. Equally, the 'tree of liberty', planted in America in the 1770s and again in France in 1789, was often used as a powerful symbol for the freedom which replaces oppression. As the decade progressed and brutal skirmishes became common in Ireland, the songs become less idealistic and give instead sorrowful or defiant accounts of various tragedies and betrayals.

Liberty and Equality or Dermot's Delight

As *Teague*[1] and his comrade were digging potatoes,
  One fine morning lately, unclouded and gay,
Says *Dermot*, 'Come *Teague*, let us not over-rate us,
  And I'll tell you fine news that I heard yesterday!
Sure a wonderful hubbub has happen'd in *France*, boy:
  Neither King, Lord nor Priest there they value a straw —
But all ranks to the tune of EQUALITY dance, boy!
O! it does my heart good just to hear how they prance, boy!
  Round Liberty's Tree night and morning!

Bold Bobadil *Brunswick* and *Fred'ric* of *Prussia*,[2]   10
  With emigrant Princes — a runagate[3] crew,
Egg'd on by the *Pope* and the *Empress* of *Russia*,[4]
  Had swore that they'd make them their merriment rue.
So (*glunta me, Teague*)[5] without any formality,
  They march'd into *France* their design to fulfil —
But they met a reception from these Commonality,[6]
Not at all to the liking of such high-bred quality,
  For all their bravadoes and scorning!

---

1. See Glossary.
2. Karl Wilhelm Ferdinand, duke of Brunswick (1735-1806), one of the best generals and most widely respected rulers of eighteenth-century Europe, and Frederick William II, king of Prussia (1744-97) who invaded revolutionary France. The use of the appellation 'Bobadil' for the duke of Brunswick is obscure.
3. = renegade.
4. Pius VI (1717-99) and Catherine the Great (1729-96), empress of Russia.
5. Ir. *An gcluin tú mé*, Do you hear me?
6. i.e. from the 'common' (non-aristocratic) people of revolutionary France.

Thus cool'd, now the hot-headed heroes repented
    Their hatred of Liberty led them so far;   20
To get out of the scrape they were all well contented,
    For they found it was vain against Freedom to war.
Then they strove to retreat — when a dismal disaster
    Those ill-fated dupes of ambition befel —
By fatigue and disease, want of food and of pasture,
In their camp men and horses die faster and faster —
    To tyrants a terrible warning!

Mean time at their heels like a tempest came thund'ring,
    Old *Kellerman, Jourdain* and brave[7] *Dugomier;*[8]
Whilst each puny despot fled trembling — and wond'ring   30
    That nothing could stop their triumphant career:
Strong fortresses yield to their arms in a crack, boy,
    That cost many a long and a[9] bloody campaign! —
For the Governors fear'd to withstand their attack, boy,
As they found their own people still ready to back, boy,
    The *Friends of Mankind* night and morning.

More and more may the Tree of French Liberty flourish,
    And shield with its branches the nations around,
Soon may all the poor slaves that to tyranny *turrish,*[10]
    Restor'd to their Rights, with its blessings be crown'd!   40
May poor IRELAND, (I hope, *Teague,* the wish is no treason),
    Whose *shamrocks* her foes have so long trodden down,
Spring up to the rank of POLITICAL REASON,
Before the Potatoe be blossom'd next season —
    Her sinew, support, and adorning!

7. Word added in later editions.
8. Three great French generals, François Christophe Kellermann, Duke of Valmy (1735-1820), Count Jean Baptiste Jourdain (1762-1833), and Jean François Coquille Dugommier (1736-94).
9. Word added in later editions.
10. Obscure. Perhaps linked to the Ir. *turnamh,* falling.

The Star of Liberty

O'er the vine-cover'd hills and gay regions of FRANCE,
    See the day Star of LIBERTY rise;
Thro' the clouds of detraction, unwearied, advance,
    And hold its new course thro' the skies.
An effulgence so mild, with a lustre so bright,
    All Europe, with wonder, surveys;
And from desarts of darkness, and dungeons of night,
    Contends for a share of the blaze.

Let BURKE,[1] like a Bat, from its splendour retire,
    A splendour too strong for his eyes,   10
Let pedants and fools his effusions admire,
    Intrapt in his cobwebs, like flies:
Shall frenzy and sophistry hope to prevail
    Where reason opposes her weight —
When the welfare of millions is hung in the scale,
    And the balance yet trembles with fate?

Ah! who 'midst the horrors of night wou'd abide,
    That can taste the pure breezes of morn;
Or who, that has drunk of the chrystalline tide,
    To the feculent[2] flood would return?   20
When the bosom of beauty the throbbing heart meets,
    Ah! who can the transport decline?
Or who that has tasted of Liberty's sweets,
    The prize, but with life, wou'd resign?

But 'tis over; — high Heav'n the decision approves —
    Oppression has struggled in vain:
To the hell she has form'd, superstition removes;
    And tyranny bites its own chain.
In the records of time a new æra unfolds, —
    All nature exults in its birth —   30
His creation, benign, the CREATOR beholds,
    And gives a new charter to earth.

---

1. Edmund Burke (1729-97) is here attacked for his dislike of the French Revolution.
2. foul, full of impurities.

O catch its high import, ye winds, as ye blow!
    O hear it, ye waves, as ye roll!
From regions that feel the sun's vertical glow,
    To the farthest extremes of the pole.
Equal rights — equal laws — to the nations around,
    Peace and *friendship*, its precepts impart —
And wherever the footsteps of *man* shall be found,
    May he bind the DECREE ON HIS HEART.   40

Paddy's Advice to John Bull [1]

Now, arrah,[2] John Bull, I would have you be easy,
    Brave Paddy no longer will suffer your yoke,
With taxes and tithes, and bastiles[3] so cruel,
    You long plunder'd Paddy, and laughed at the joke.
        Sing ditheru, Johnny Bull, can't you be easy,
        When will you let honest Paddy alone?
        With a drop of old whiskey, if e'er he gets tipsy,
        By the holy Saint Patrick, he'll alter your tone.

Long time have ye fought with the French without reason,
    Because they presume to make laws of their own;   10
They want all men equal — Oh! that would be treason,
    For then each great monarch must jump from his throne;
        Sing ditheru, &c.

John, what do you think of the national convention?[4]
    They plundered the bishop for starving the poor,
Deprived every knave of his title and pension,
    And turned all the nuns and the monks out of door;
        Sing ditheru, &c.

1. i.e. Ireland's advice to England.
2. Ir. *ara*, a mild expletive, often put into the mouths of stage-Irishmen by English writers.
3. prisons.
4. The French National Convention was elected under universal suffrage. It sat from 21 September 1792 to 26 October 1796 and, despite the bloodshed and upheaval of the times, succeeded in preserving the main principles of the French Revolution — civil liberty and the sovereignty of the people. As such, it was a potent symbol for Irish nationalists.

Of treason, 'tis thought, John, a king can be guilty,
    By robbing the people of what is their right: 20
Then see you be heedful, and mind the thing needful,
    For in your own country the times may be tight.
                Sing ditheru &c.

from: The United Irishmen: A Tale, founded on Facts

This long and vivid poetic account of the realities of the skirmish between British troops and
local people at Hacketstown, Co. Carlow in 1798 begins with a description of a prosperous,
well-stocked farm 'near Wicklow', belonging to Patt B———n. Some friends and relatives
from Wexford, including one called Terence and a Hugh O'Flaherty, call to the house, and
are treated to a hearty welcome. The talk turns to politics and there is fierce criticism of the
government, the established church and the land settlements currently in force. A map of
Ireland which shows land ownership as it was before the confiscations of the seventeenth
century is produced, and the story of the French Revolution is told. Patt's patriotism is
aroused and he agrees to join the forces of insurrection. Terence is speaking:

        ... 'There you may see, — tho' we're derided,
        How Ireland's lands are all divided;
        Mark'd with the names of Old Proprietors,
        Which, on pretence that they were rioters,
        Were forfeited, were seiz'd, were given,
        To any scoundrel under heaven.
        If these a'n't grievances, I wonder
        What worse, could any labour under:
        But from all these, I hope our nation,
        Will soon obtain *Emancipation*.'   10

        To TERENCE ended, — PATT reply'd:
        'What you have said, can't be deny'd.
        We labour, to support a Crown,
        That with oppressions bear us down.
        Too true it is, — but I'm unletter'd,
        And cannot tell, how 'twill be better'd.
        For Government is still the winner,
        So let us now sit down to dinner.'

Then, down they sat about the table,
Each help'd himself, as he was able,   20
And freely, to their trenchers¹ take on,
Plenty of turkey, greens, and bacon:
With quick dispatch, they eat their meal,
And mix'd it well with good stout ale:
Then off went cloth, and plates and mug,
And in their room, a smoaking jug
Of whiskey punch, appear'd to crown,
Th'entertainment, and to drown,
For a short time, in dissipation,
The sorrows of the Irish nation.   30
Now, glasses round the table coasted,
GRATTAN² and FOX³ were loudly toasted,
And heartily they drank, and carol'd,
HARVEY,⁴ ROACH,⁵ and Lord FITZGERALD.⁶

When HUGH O'FL——Y said: 'PATT,
I took some notice, you said, that
You could not tell, as you're unletter'd,
How poor old Ireland might be better'd.
Now I will tell you, — don't you see
How France has gain'd her liberty?   40
'Twas not by humble mean submission,
That they obtain'd a quick transition
From slavery to liberty, that now
The trembling nations round them bow
To their controul, and vanquish'd, yield,
To them the honours of the field.

1. wooden platters on which food was served.
2. Henry Grattan (1746-1820), patriot and orator, who asserted Ireland's right to legislative independence in 1782 and was the most powerful voice in the Irish parliament known as 'Grattan's parliament' 1782-99.
3. Charles James Fox (1749-1806), English politician and statesman, who steered the measures for Irish legislative independence through the Westminster parliament.
4. Beauchamp Bagenall Harvey (1762-98), a landowner and lawyer who allowed himself to be made commmander-in-chief of the United Irishmen in the Wexford area, although he was quite unsuited to the task. He was executed after the failure of the rising.
5. The reference is either to Fr Philip Roche, who replaced Bagenal Harvey as field commmander of the rebel forces on 18 June 1798, or to Edward Roche of Garrylough, Wexford, a leading United Irishman, who took a prominent part in the defeat of the North Cork Militia at Oulart Hill near Enniscorthy, Co. Wexford in May 1798.
6. A note at this point in the first edition explained that the group had not heard of the death of Lord Edward Fitzgerald — which had taken place on 4 June 1798.

No. — It was by force they broke,
From off their necks, the galling yoke
Of tyranny. — That, only can
Recover the lost *Rights of Man*;   50
And shew the world, what now they see,
The *people*'s high *sov'reignity.*
By this, friend PATT, we shall be better'd,
And all our limbs from chains unfetter'd;
This, only this, can set us free,
And save from English tyranny.
And now, — for this we are preparing,
Ready our standard is for rearing;
We've made a noble large subscription,
Arms are prepar'd, of each description,   60
In vast abundance, firelock, pike,
They wait for us, — then let us strike,
The blow decisive, that shall be,
The Æra of our liberty;
The English then shall know and rue,
What our *united* force can do.

I wonder, you have not observ'd
What TERENCE said; it might have serv'd
To ope your eyes. — *It was to quiet us,*
Lest we should happen to grow riotous,   70
That they were lib'ral. Let our powers,
Increase their fears, and all is ours.
Now, PADDY, we've no time to lose;
Call for your boots, take off your shoes,
And come to *Hacket's-town,*[7] and see,
What mighty power, and force have we.'

He said, — and drinking the last sup,
With one accord, they all got up, —
Took horse in haste, and off they went,
Big, with the prospect of th'event.   80
There, when they came, — PADDY soon found,
A Num'rous force spread all around;
Such force as he had never seen,
Four thousand men upon the green,

---

7. A town in County Carlow.

With *pikes* and *guns* completely arm'd,
He saw, — and with the sight was charm'd;
His friends receiv'd his warmest thanks,
And with glad heart, he join'd the ranks.

My Readers now, no doubt, will think,
That night afforded much good drink,   90
And so it did; — for ev'ry store,
Was drain'd and search'd to find out more.

The morning came, — a day of doom,
A day of darkness and of gloom;
For ever be that day forgot!
From under Heaven, its record blot!
Day of defeat, distress and fear,
Be it not number'd in the year!

The morning came. — Th'united force
March'd forward with a steady course;   100
On their approach, — the Army[8] fell
Back to their Barrack: — who can tell
The joys, — the shouts, — that then resounded,
Of victory, and foes confounded?
But O! — delusive expectation,
Their joy was but of short duration;
HUME,[9] with his troop, fell on their rear,
The broad sword knew not how to spare;
HARDY, and GARDINER, quick return'd,
Each breast with martial fury burn'd, —   110
The infantry came forward firing,
The ground was strew'd with men expiring;
The rest, defenceless, unprotected,
Fled ev'ry way, as fear directed.
PATT ran as fast as heels could carry,
Nor did his friends behind him tarry;
They fled together in a group,
'Till overtaken by a troop

8. i.e. the government troops.
9. Hume, Hardy and Gardner were officers on the government side. In this skirmish, as throughout the campaign, victorious troops on either side slaughtered the enemy rather than taking prisoners.

Of horse — a pistol bullet
Found passage thro' poor PADDY's gullet.   120
Lifeless he fell upon the ground,
And his last breath pass'd thro' the wound.

O'F——Y turning quick about,
His pointed pike held fiercely out,
Thrust at an horse-man; — miss'd his aim,
Then down the weighty sabre came,
Full on his shoulder, — quite unstrung
His arm, — on bleeding sinews hung;
Then falling, in the mortal strife,
The horses trampled out his life.   130

TERENCE alone, of all that went
With PADDY, liv'd to tell th'event,
For him it was reserv'd to tell,
How his dear friends and cousins fell.
How shall I tell it? oft he cried,
To her who, late an happy bride,
Enjoy'd his love, and tender care,
Who never had a thought to spare
Ought, that his wife, or children needed,
But still, in acts of love exceeded.   140
Yet she must hear it, soon or late,
'O BIDDY! BIDDY! what sad state
Has our mad folly brought you to?
That day, that fatal day, I rue,
When we — received with friendship kind,
In your full house, so freely din'd;
Where all was plenty, all was peace.
O now! how alter'd is the case?
Your husband dead, your prospects ended,
No hope, that they will e'er be mended: 150
Your children, now, no more will see
Their father, — on whose cheerful knee
They've often sat; — or if they should,
'Twill be his corse,[10] besmear'd with blood; ...

10. corpse.

565

Are these the *rights* we vainly sought for,
The liberty we madly fought for?
Say, — have the dead at length enjoy'd it,
Or, rather, have we not destroy'd it?
With a mild Government not content,
And fiercely on rebellion bent;   160
Forth to the war we went, and we,
Have met our fatal destiny.
We've sacrific'd our lives, and all,
That ever man could precious call;
For what? — for meer delusive dreams,
Of greater liberty — for schemes
Republican, or *Catholic* — they're fled,
Like empty visions of the head,
And we're now number'd with the dead.'...

Come all you Warriors[1]

Come all you warriors, and renowned nobles,
    Who once commanded brave warlike bands;
Lay down your plumes, and your golden trophies,
    Give up your arms with a trembling hand,[2]
Since Father Murphy, of the County Wexford,
    Lately roused from his sleepy dream,
To cut down cruel Saxon persecution
    And wash it away in a crimson stream.

Sure Julius Caesar, nor Alexander,
    Nor renowned King Arthur e'er could equal him;   10
For armies formidable he has conquered,
    Though with two gunmen he did begin.
Camolin cavalry he did unhorse them,[3]
    Their first lieutenant he cut him down;
With shattered ranks and with broken columns
    They retreated home to Camolin town.

1. This poem was probably written soon after the decisive engagement of the 1798 Rising, the battle of Vinegar Hill near Enniscorthy (21 June 1798), at which the rebels were comprehensively defeated. But their spirit was not broken, as the final line of the poem makes clear.
2. These lines, addressed to all military heroes, show the poet's unrealistic assessment of the effect of the Rising.
3. The inhabitants of Boulavogue, led by their parish priest, Father John Murphy, defeated a corps of cavalry from nearby Camolin on 26 May 1798.

On the Hill of Oulart[4] he displayed his valour,
 Where one hundred Corkmen lay on the plain,
And at Enniscorthy,[5] his sword he wielded,
 And I hope he'll do it once more again.   20
The loyal townsmen gave their assistance,
 We'll die or conquer, they all did say,
The yeomen's cavalry made no resistance,
 While on the pavement their corpses lay.

When Enniscorthy became subject to him,
 'Twas then to Wexford we marched our men,
And on the Three Rocks[6] took up our quarters,
 Waiting for daylight the town to win.
With drums a-beating the town did echo,
 And acclamations from door to door;   30
On the Windmill Hill[7] we pitched our tents,
 And we drank like heroes, tho' paid no score.

On Carrig-ruadh[8] for some time we waited,
 Then next for Gorey we did repair,
In Tubberneering we thought no harm,
 The bloody army was waiting there.
The issue of it was a close engagement,
 While on the soldiers we played warlike pranks,
Thro' sheepwalks, hedgerows, and shady thickets,
 There were mangled bodies and broken ranks. 40

The shudd'ring cavalry, I can't forget them,
 We raised the brushes on their helmets straight,
They turned about, and they scud[9] for Dublin
 As if they ran for a ten-pound plate;[10]

---

4. Father Murphy's followers defeated three detachments of militia, including some of the North Cork Militia, at Oulart Hill, near Camolin, on 27 May.
5. Father Murphy's men took the town of Enniscorthy, with considerable loss of life, the next day.
6. The Mountain of Forth, or Three Rocks Mountain, is two miles from Wexford town.
7. Also known as Vinegar Hill.
8. Carrigrew Hill near the town of Gorey where the rebel forces gathered before inflicting a resounding defeat on government forces at Tubberneering on 4 June.
9. move rapidly.
10. i.e. as if they were running in a horse race.

Some got to Donnybrook, and some to Blackrock,
    And some up Shankhill[11] without wound or flaw;
And if Barry Lawless be not a liar,
    There's more went grousing up Luggelaw.[12]

With flying colours we marched on Limerick,[13]
    And to Kilcavan we did repair;   50
'Twas on Mount-Pleasant[14] we called the county,
    And pointed cannons at the army there.
When we thought fit, we marched on Gorey;
    The next was Arklow we did surround.
The night being coming, we regretted sorely,
    Tho' one hundred soldiers lay on the ground.[15]

The towns of England were left quite naked
    Of all its army, both foot and horse;[16]
The highlands of Scotland were left unguarded,
    Likewise the Hessians,[17] the sea they crossed.   60
To the Windmill Hill of Enniscorthy
    Their British fencibles[18] they fled like deers;
And our ranks were tattered, and sorely scattered
    For the loss of Kyan and the Shelmaliers.[19]

11. Three villages on the southern outskirts of Dublin, fifty miles north of Gorey; it is totally unrealistic for the poet to assert that the fleeing soldiers would have travelled so far.

12. A peak in the Wicklow Mountains.

13. Not the city in the west of Ireland but a small river in north County Wexford. Kilcavan is in the same area.

14. A place close to Tinahely, Co. Wicklow.

15. The insurgents failed to take the town of Arklow from government forces.

16. These few lines emphasise the effect which the need to send troops to Ireland had on the British army.

17. In the 1760s, England had hired 22,000 mercenaries from the the German prince Frederick II of Hesse-Cassel to assist in the war against the North American colonies. These were now deployed in Ireland.

18. Soldiers liable only for service at home.

19. Esmond Kyan of Mount Howard, Co. Wexford, a catholic landowner and United Irishman, leader of a band of soldiers from the village of Shelmalier. Kyan's failure to get his men into position at Vinegar Hill contributed to the defeat of the insurgents there on 21 June.

But if the Frenchmen they had reinforced us —
    Landed their transports in Ballybunn,[20]
Father John Murphy he would be their seconder,
    And sixty thousand along with him come;
Success attend the sweet county Wexford,
    Throw off its yoke and to battle run.   70
Let them not think we gave up our arms,
    For every man has a pike or gun.

Dunlavin Green[1]

In the year of one thousand seven hundred and ninety eight,
A sorrowful tale the truth unto you I'll relate,
Of thirty-six heroes to the world were left to be seen,
By a false information were shot on Dunlavin Green.

Bad luck to you, Saunders, for you did their lives betray;
You said a parade would be held on that very day,
Our drums they did rattle — our fifes they did sweetly play;
Surrounded we were and privately marched away.

Quite easily they led us as prisoners through the town,
To be slaughtered on the plain, we then were forced to kneel down,   10
Such grief and such sorrow as never before there seen,
When the blood ran in streams down the dykes of Dunlavin Green.

There is young Matty Farrell, has plenty of cause to complain,
Also the the young Duffys, who were shot down on the plain,
And young Andy Ryan, his mother distracted will run
For her own brave boy, her beloved eldest son.

Bad luck to you, Saunders, bad luck may you never shun!
That the widow's curse may melt you like snow in the sun,
The cried of the orphans whose murmurs you cannot screen,
For the murder of their dear fathers, on Dunlavin Green.   20

---

20. Baginbun, a headland in south County Wexford where the insurgents expected French revolutionary troops to land and bring reinforcements. No such landing occurred.

1. In May 1798, thirty-six members of the Narraghmore and Saunderstown Corps of the normally loyal yeomanry were made prisoners, as suspected United Irishmen, by their captain, a man named Saunders. They were taken to the fair green of the County Wicklow town of Dunlavin and shot dead by their yeoman colleagues without a trial.

Some of our boys, to the hills they are going away,
Some of them are shot, and some of them going to sea,
Micky Dwyer[2] in the mountains to Saunders he owes a spleen,
For his loyal brothers, who were shot on Dunlavin green.

The Croppy Boy[1]

'Good men and true! in this house who dwell,
To a stranger *bouchal*,[2] I pray you tell
Is the priest at home? or may he be seen?
I would speak a word with Father Green.'

'The Priest's at home, boy, and may be seen;
'Tis easy speaking with Father Green;
But you must wait till I go and see
If the holy father alone may be.'

The youth has entered an empty hall —
What a lonely sound has his light foot-fall!   10
And the gloomy chamber's chill and bare,
With a vested Priest in a lonely chair.

The youth has knelt to tell his sins;
'*Nomine Dei*',[3] the youth begins:
At '*mea culpa*' he beats his breast,
And in broken murmurs he speaks the rest.

'At the siege of Ross did my father fall,
And at Gorey my loving brothers all,
I alone am left of my name and place,
I will go to Wexford and take their place.[4]   20

2. Michael Dwyer (1771-1826) took part in the rising of 1798, and for five years evaded capture by hiding in the Wicklow Mountains. He was later transported to Australia.

1. There are many versions of this famous account of treachery. The rebels of 1798, who often kept their hair cropped short to show sympathy with the French revolution, were called the 'croppy' boys.

2. Ir. *buachaill*, boy, young man.

3. 'In the Name of God ...' and 'It is my fault ...', two phrases from the Latin rite of confession.

4. Wexford was one of the towns where the rebels planned to regroup after various defeats.

I cursed three times since last Easter day —
At mass-time once I went to play;
I passed the churchyard one day in haste,
And forgot to pray for my mother's rest.

I bear no hate against living thing;
But I love my country above my King.
Now, Father! bless me, and let me go
To die, if God has ordained it so.'

The priest said nought, but a rustling noise
Made the youth look above in wild surprise;   30
The robes were off, and in scarlet there
Sat a yeoman captain with fiery glare.

With fiery glare and with fury hoarse,
Instead of a blessing, he breathed a curse: —
''Twas a good thought, boy, to come here and shrive,
For one short hour is your time to live.

Upon yon river three tenders[5] float,
The Priest's in one, if he isn't shot —
We hold his house for our Lord the King,
And, amen, say I, may all traitors swing!'   40

At Geneva Barrack that young man died,
And at Passage they have his body laid.[6]
Good people who live in peace and joy,
Breathe a prayer and a tear for the Croppy boy.

The Patriot Mother

'Come, tell us the name of the rebelly crew,
Who lifted the pike on the Curragh[1] with you;
Come, tell the treason, and then you'll be free,
Or right quickly you'll swing from the high gallows tree.'

---

5. Small military vessels.
6. Geneva Barracks were near the village of Passage East, Co. Waterford, on the shore of
   Waterford Harbour.

---

1. A large plain in County Kildare.

'*Alanna*! *alanna*![2] the shadow of shame
Has never yet fallen upon one of your name,
And O! may the food from my bosom you drew,
In your veins turn to poison, if *you* turn untrue.

The foul words — O! let them not blacken your tongue,
That would prove to your friends and your country a wrong,   10
Or the curse of a mother, so bitter and dread,
With the wrath of the Lord — may they fall on your head!

I have no one but you in the whole world wide,
Yet false to your pledge, you'd ne'er stand at my side:
If a traitor you lived, you'd be farther away
From my heart than, if true, you were wrapped in the clay.

Oh! deeper and darker the mourning would be
For your falsehood so base, than your death proud and free,
Dearer, far dearer than ever to me,
My darling, you'll be on the brave gallows tree!   20

'Tis holy, *agra*,[3] from the bravest and best —
Go! go! from my heart, and be joined with the rest,
Alanna machree![4] O *alanna machree!*
Sure a 'stag'[5] and a traitor you never will be.'

There's no look of a traitor upon the young brow
That's raised to the tempters so haughtily now;
No traitor e'er held up the firm head so high —
No traitor e'er show'd such a proud flashing eye.

On the high gallows tree! on the high gallows tree!
Where smiled leaves and blossoms, his sad doom met he!   30
But it never bore blossom so pure or so fair
As the heart of the martyr that hangs from it there.

2. Ir. *a leanbh*, my child.
3. Ir. *a ghrá*, my love.
4. Ir. *a leanbh mo chroí*, child of my heart.
5. An informer.

Green upon the Cape

I'm a lad that's forced an exile from my own native land,
For an oath that's passed against me in this country I can't stand:
But while I'm at my liberty I will make my escape;
I'm a poor distressèd Croppy, for the Green on my cape.
     For the Green on my cape, for the Green on my cape,
I'm distressed, but not disheartened, for the Green on my cape!

But I'll go down to Belfast, to see that seaport gay,
And tell my aged parents in this country I can't stay:
Oh! 'tis dark will be their sorrow, but no truer hearts I've seen,
And they'd rather see me dying than a traitor to the Green.   10
     Oh! the wearing of the Green, Oh! the wearing of the Green!
May the curse of Cromwell darken each traitor to the Green!

When I went down to Belfast, and saw that seaport grand,
My aged parents blessed me, and blessed poor Ireland.
Then I went unto a captain, and bargained with him cheap:
He told me that his whole ship's crew wore Green on the cape!
     Oh! the Green on the cape, Oh! the Green on the cape!
God's blessing guard the noble boys with Green on the cape!

'Twas early the next morning our gallant ship set sail;
Kind Heaven did protect her, with a pleasant Irish gale.   20
We landed safe in Paris, where victualling was cheap —
They knew we were United — we wore Green on the cape!
     We wore Green on the cape, we wore Green on the cape!
They treated us like brothers for the Green on the cape!

Then forward stepped young Boney,[1] and took me by the hand,
Saying, 'How is old Ireland, and how does she stand?'
'It's as poor distressed a nation as you have ever seen,
They are hanging men and women for the wearing of the Green!
     For the wearing of the Green, for the wearing of the Green!
They are hanging men and women for the wearing of the Green!'   30

---

1. Napoleon Bonaparte (1769-1821), emperor of France. In other versions of this song, the narrator meets Napper Tandy (1740-1803), a prominent United Irishman who was condemned to death after leading a small, abortive invasion of Ireland; Tandy was not executed but was extradited to France.

573

'Take courage now, my brave boys, for here you have good frien's
And we'll send a convoy with you, down by their Orange dens;
And if they should oppose us, with our weapons sharp and keen,
We'll make them rue and curse the day that e'er they saw the Green!
    That e'er they saw the Green, that e'er they saw the Green!
We'll show them our authority for wearing of the Green!'

Oh! may the wind of Freedom soon send young Boney o'er,
And we'll plant the tree of Liberty upon our Shamrock shore;
Oh! we'll plant it with our weapons, while the English tyrants gape,
To see their bloody flag torn down, to Green on the cape!   40
    Oh! the wearing of the Green, Oh! the wearing of the Green!
God grant us soon to see that day, and freely wear the Green!

The Exiled Irishman's Lamentation

Green were the fields where my forefathers dwelt, O;
    Erin ma vourneen! slan leat go brach![1]
Tho' our farm it was small, yet comfort we felt, O,
    Erin ma vourneen! slan leat go brach!
At length came the day when our lease did expire,
And fain would I live where before lived my sire;
But ah! well-a-day, I was forced to retire,
    Erin ma vourneen! slan leat go brach!

Though all taxes I paid, yet no vote could I pass, O;
    Erin ma vourneen! slan leat go brach!   10
I aggrandized no great man[2] — and I felt it, alas! O;
    Erin ma vourneen! slan leat go brach!
Forced from my home, yea, from where I was born,
To range the wide world, poor, helpless, forlorn,
I look back with regret, and my heart-strings are torn,
    Erin ma vourneen! slan leat go brach!

With principles pure, patriotic and firm,
    Erin ma vourneen! slan leat go brach!
Attached to my country, a friend to reform,
    Erin ma vourneen! slan leat go brach!   20

1. i.e. Ireland, my darling, for ever adieu!
2. i.e. I did not increase the power or wealth of any great man.

574

I supported old Ireland, was ready to die for't;
If her foes e'er prevail'd, I was well known to sigh for't;
But my faith I preserved, and I'm now forced to fly for't,
  Erin ma vourneen! slan leat go brach!

In the North I see friends — too long was I blind, O;
  Boie yudh ma Vourneen! Erin go bragh![3]
The cobweb is broken, and free is my mind, O;
  Boie yudh ma Vourneen! Erin go bragh!
North and South, here's my hand, East and West, here's
        my heart, O;
Let's ne'er be divided by any base art, O;   30
But love one another, and never more part, O;
  Boie yudh ma Vourneen! Erin go bragh!

But heark! I hear sounds, and my heart strong is beating,
  Boie yudh ma vourneen! Erin go brach!
Friendship advancing, delusion retreating,
  Boie yudh ma vourneen! Erin go brach!
We have numbers, and numbers do constitute power;
Let's will to be free, and we're free from that hour.
Of Hibernia's sons, yes, we'll then be the flower,
  Boie yudh ma vourneen! Erin go brach!   40

Too long we have suffered, and too long lamented;
  Boie yudh ma vourneen! Erin go brach!
By courage undaunted it may be prevented,
  Boie yudh ma vourneen! Erin go brach!
No more by oppressors let us be affrighted,
But with heart and with hand let's be firmly united;
For by *Erin go bragh*, it is thus we'll be righted!
  Boie yudh ma vourneen! Erin go brach!

3. i.e. Victory to you my darling! Ireland for ever!

575

THREE ORANGE SONGS

Lisnagade

On 12 July 1791, a group of Defenders (members of one of the predominantly catholic secret societies dedicated to improving agrarian conditions by violent means) took over the old fort at Aghaderg, Co. Down, and tried to prevent the local Orangemen from celebrating the anniversary of the battle of the Boyne. The Orangemen, as this song makes clear, won the day.

Ye Protestants of Ulster, I pray you join with me,
Your voices raise in lofty praise and show your loyalty;
Extol the day we march'd away with Orange flags so fine,
In order to commemorate the conquest of the Boyne.

The first who fought upon that day the prince of Orange was,
He headed our forefathers in his most glorious cause,
Protestant rights for to maintain and pop'ry to degrade,
And in memory of the same we fought at Lisnagade.

'Twas early in the morning, before the rise of sun,
An information we receiv'd, our foes each with his gun   10
In ambush lay, near the highway, entrenched in a fort
For to disgrace our Orange flag, but it chanc'd they broke their oath.

We had not march'd a mile or so when the white flag[1] we espied,
With a branch of podereens[2] on which they much relied,
And this inscription underneath 'Hail Mary! unto thee,
Deliver us from these Orange dogs, and then we will be free'.

At half an hour past two o'clock the firing did commence,
With clouds of smoke and showers of ball, the heaven was condens'd;
They call'd unto their wooden gods, to whom they us'd to pray,
But my Lady Mary fell asleep, and so they ran away.   20

1. White, the colour of the Jacobites, was also used by the Defenders.
2. Ir. *paidrín*, rosary beads.

Protestant Boys

Tell me, my friends, why are we met here?
    Why thus assembled, ye Protestant Boys?
Do mirth and good liquor, good humour, good cheer,
    Call us to share of festivity's joys?
        Oh no! 'tis the cause,
        Of king, freedom, and laws,
That calls loyal Protestants now to unite;
        And Orange and Blue[1]
        Ever faithful and true,
Our king shall support, and sedition affright.   10

Great spirit of William! from heaven look down,
    And breathe in our hearts our forefathers' fire —
Teach us to rival their glorious renown,
    From Papist or Frenchman ne'er to retire.
        Jacobin — Jacobite —
        Against all to unite,[2]
Who dare to assail our sovereign's throne?
        For Orange and Blue
        Will be faithful and true,
And Protestant loyalty ever be shown.   20

In that loyalty proud let us ever remain
    Bound together in truth and religion's pure band;
Nor honour's fair cause with foul bigotry stain,
    Since in courage and justice supported we stand.
        So heaven shall smile
        On our emerald isle,
And lead us to conquest again and again;
        While Papists shall prove
        Our brotherly love; —
We hate them as masters — we love them as men.   30

1. Blue was the colour favoured by staunch presbyterians in the eighteenth century, since the Scottish Covenanters of the seventeenth century had adopted blue as their colour as opposed to red, the royal colour.
2. The link is between the revolutionary tendencies of the Jacobins, the most famous of the political clubs of the French revolution, and of the Jacobites, followers of the exiled James II and his heirs.

By the deeds of their Fathers to glory inspired,
    Our Protestant heroes shall combat the foe;
Hearts with true honour and loyalty fired,
    Intrepid, undaunted, to conquest will go.
        The shades of the Boyne
        In the chorus will join,
And the welkin[3] re-echo with God save the king.

The Tree of Liberty[1]

Sons of Hibernia, attend to my song,
Of a tree call'd th'Orange, it's beauteous and strong;
'Twas planted by William, immortal is he!
May all Orange brothers live loyal and free.
    Derry down, down, traitors bow down.[2]

Around this fair trunk we like ivy will cling,
And fight for our honour, our country, and king;
In the shade of this Orange none e'er shall recline
Who with murd'rous Frenchmen have dar'd to combine.
    Derry down, down, Frenchmen bow down.   10

Hordes of barbarians, Lord Ned in the van,[3]
This tree to destroy laid an infamous plan;
Their schemes prov'd abortive, tho' written in blood,
Nor their pikes, nor their scythes could pierce Orange wood.
    Derry down, down, rebels bow down.

---

3. the heavens.

1. The Tree of Liberty (a potent symbol of opposition to 'English tyranny' when it appeared in America between 1765 and 1775, and of opposition to tyranny in general when used in France after the Revolution) was more frequently employed by the United Irishmen than by Orangemen (see Georges-Denis Zimmermann, *Songs of Irish Rebellion: Political Street Ballads and Rebel Songs 1780-1900* (Dublin, 1967), pp. 41-43, 303-04 and 310-11).

2. The refrain shows that the song was to be sung to the air 'Derry down'.

3. Lord Edward Fitzgerald (1763-98), who, inspired by the ideals of the French Revolution, became a leader of the United Irishmen. He was captured and died in custody. 'in the van' = in the front line of the battle.

While our brave Irish tars[4] protect us by sea,
From false perjur'd traitors this island we'll free;
Priest Murphy's[5] war-vestment they'll find of no use,
Whenever we meet them they're sure to get goose,[6]
    Derry down, down, priestcraft bow down.   20

Hundreds they've burned of each sex, young and old,
From Heaven the order — by priests they were told;
No longer we'll trust them, no more to betray,
But chase from our bosoms those vipers away.
    Derry down, down, serpents bow down.

Rouse them my brothers, and heed not their swearing,
Absolv'd they have been for deeds past all bearing;
Mercy's misplac'd, when to murderers granted,
For our lands and our lives those wretches long panted.
    Derry down, down, reptiles bow down.   30

Then charge[7] high your glasses, and drink our Great Cause,
Our blest Constitution, our King, and our Laws;
May all lurking traitors, wherever they be
Make the exit of Sheares,[8] and Erin be free.
    Derry down, down, traitors bow down.

---

4. sailors.
5. Father John Murphy (c.1753-98), parish priest of Boulavogue, Co. Wexford who, at the head of his parishioners, defeated a corps of the Camolin cavalry on 26 May 1798.
6. i.e. run away like geese.
7. fill.
8. Henry Shears (1753-98) and his brother John (1766-98), two protestant United Irishmen, were executed in Dublin in 1798.

ROBERT EMMET
(1778-**1799**-1803)

Robert Emmet was born and educated in Dublin, where he became a leader of the United
Irishmen at Trinity College. He organised an unsuccessful rising against the English forces
in Dublin in July 1803, was captured and executed. Emmet's passionate conviction that
Ireland should be freed from English domination suffuses his poetry, as it does his more
famous 'Speech from the Dock'.

Lines written on the Burying-Ground of Arbour Hill in Dublin,
where the Bodies of Insurgents shot in 1798 were interred[1]

No rising column marks this spot,
   Where many a victim lies;
But oh! the blood which here has streamed,
   To Heaven for justice cries.

It claims it on the oppressor's head,
   Who joys in human woe,
Who drinks the tears by misery shed,
   And mocks them as they flow.

It claims it on the callous judge,
   Whose hands in blood are dyed,   10
Who arms injustice with the sword,
   The balance throws aside.

It claims it for his ruined isle,
   Her wretched children's grave,
Where withered Freedom droops her head,
   And man exists — a slave.

O sacred Justice! free this land
   From tyranny abhorred;
Resume thy balance and thy seat —
   Resume — but sheathe thy sword.   20

---

1. The small cemetery at Arbour Hill (behind the Royal — now Collins — Barracks in
Dublin) contains the remains of the United Irishmen executed by the authorities after the
1798 Rising.

No retribution should we seek,
    Too long has horror reigned;
By mercy marked may freedom rise,
    By cruelty unstained.

Nor shall the tyrant's ashes mix
    With those our martyr'd dead;
This is the place where Erin's sons
    In Erin's cause have bled.

And those who here are laid at rest,
    Oh! hallowed be each name;   30
Their memories are for ever blest —
    Consigned to endless Fame.

Unconsecrated is this ground,
    Unblest by holy hands;
No bell here tolls its solemn sound,
    No monument here stands.

But here the patriot's tears are shed,
    The poor man's blessing given;
These consecrate the virtuous dead,
    These waft their fame to heaven.   40

EDWARD LYSAGHT
(1763-**1800**-1810)

Edward Lysaght was the son of a landowner in County Clare. He was educated at Trinity College, Dublin and at Oxford, and became a successful lawyer. From about 1797, Lysaght lived in Dublin where he became well-known as a writer of society verses and of songs. He was a strong opponent of the Union and the song below paints, in caricature, a picture of the desolation which the ordinary citizens of Dublin imagined might follow the removal to London of the Irish parliament and its many hangers-on.

Song

How justly alarm'd is each Dublin cit,[1]
    That he'll soon be transform'd to a clown,[2] Sir!
By a magical move of that conjurer, Pitt,[3]
    The country is coming to town, Sir!
        Give Pitt, and Dundas,[4] and Jenkin[5] a glass,
        They'll ride on John Bull, and make Paddy an ass.

Through Capel-street[6] then you may *rurally* range,
    You'll scarce recognize the same street;
Choice turnips shall grow in the Royal Exchange,
    Fine cabbages down along Dame-street.   10
        Give Pitt, &c.

Wild oats in your College[7] won't want to be till'd;
    And *hemp* in your Four Courts[8] may thrive, Sir;
As of old shall your markets with muttons[9] be fill'd,
    By St. Patrick, they'll graze there alive, Sir!
        Give Pitt, &c.

1. citizen.
2. rustic.
3. William Pitt the younger (1759-1806), prime minister of England 1783-1801 and 1804-06, who brought about the Union between Great Britain and Ireland.
4. Henry Dundas, first Viscount Melville (1742-1811), secretary for war in the British cabinet 1794-1801.
5. This must refer to Robert Jenkinson, second Earl of Liverpool (1770-1828), British foreign secretary 1801-03, 1804-06 and 1807-09.
6. A street in Dublin, like all the other streets and places mentioned in the poem.
7. Trinity College.
8. The law courts. The hemp is that of the hangman's rope.
9. A note at this point in the 1811 edition of this poem reads: 'The word by which the Irish understand *sheep*, probably taken from the French *moutons*'.

In the Parliament-house, quite alive, shall there be
    All the vermin your island e'er gathers;
Full of rooks, as before, Daly's club-house[10] shall be,
    But the *pigeons* won't have any *feathers*.   20
        Give Pitt, &c.

Your Custom-house quay, full of weeds, oh! rare sport!
    While the minister's minions, kind elves! Sir,
Will give you free leave all your goods to export,
    When they've left none at home for yourselves, Sir!
        Give Pitt, &c.

The alderman cries, 'Corn will grow in your shops;
    This Union must work our enslavement;'
'That's true', says the sheriff, 'for *plenty of crops*[11]
    Already I've seen on your pavement.'   30
        Give Pitt, &c.

Ye brave loyal yeomen, dress'd gaily in red,
    This Minister's plan must elate us;
And well may John Bull, when he's robb'd us of bread,
    Call poor Ireland '*The land of Potatoes*'.
        Give Pitt, &c.

Love *versus* the bottle

Sweet Chloe advised me, in accents divine,
    The joys of the bowl to surrender;
Nor lose in the turbid excesses of wine,
    Delights more ecstatic and tender;
She bade me no longer in vineyards to bask,
Or stagger at orgies, the dupe of the flask,
For the sigh of a sot's but the scent of the cask,
    And a bubble the bliss of the bottle.

---

10. The most celebrated gaming-house in late eighteenth-century Dublin.
11. i.e. 'croppies', a term for those who took part in the 1798 Rising (who wore their hair close cut).

To a soul that's exhausted, or sterile, or dry,
    The juice of the grape may be wanted;   10
But mine is revived by a love-beaming eye,
    And with Fancy's gay flow'rets enchanted.
O, who but an owl would a garland entwine
Of Bacchis's ivy — and myrtle resign?
Yield the odours of love for the vapours of wine,
    And Chloe's kind kiss for a bottle!

MARY TIGHE
(1772-**1800**-1810)

Mary Tighe was the daughter of the Rev. William Blatchford, librarian of Marsh's Library Dublin, and of Theodosia Tighe, a descendent of the first Earl of Clarendon. She received a better education than most women of her time and knew not only the literatures of classical Greece and Rome but also those of modern Europe and that of England. She married her cousin Henry Tighe, but the marriage was unhappy and, in addition, Mary Tighe developed consumption. Her most considerable poetic achievement is the long poem *Psyche: or the Legend of Love* which was admired by many poets of the age, including Thomas Moore and John Keats. In addition, Mary Tighe wrote several shorter poems, many of them sonnets inspired by the Irish countryside.

Written at Rossana,[1] November 18, 1799

Oh my rash hand! what hast thou idly done?
   Torn from its humble bank the last poor flower
   That patient lingered to this wintry hour:
Expanding cheerly to the languid sun
It flourished yet, and yet it might have blown,[2]
   Had not thy sudden desolating power
   Destroyed what many a storm and angry shower
Had pitying spared. The pride of summer gone,
   Cherish what yet in faded life can bloom;
And if domestic love still sweetly smiles,   10
If sheltered by thy cot he yet beguiles
   Thy winter's prospect of its dreary gloom,
Oh, from the spoiler's touch thy treasure screen,
To bask beneath Contentment's beam serene!

1. The Tighe family home was at Rossana, near Ashford, Co. Wicklow.
2. flowered.

Written at Killarney, July 29, 1800

How soft the pause! the notes melodious cease,[1]
   Which from each feeling could an echo call;
   Rest on your oars; that not a sound may fall
To interrupt the stillness of our peace:
The fanning west-wind breathes upon our cheeks
   Yet glowing with the sun's departed beams.
   Through the blue heavens the cloudless moon pours streams
Of pure resplendent light, in silver streaks
Reflected on the still, unruffled lake.
   The Alpine hills in solemn silence frown,   10
   While the dark woods night's deepest shades embrown.
And now once more that soothing strain awake!
Oh, ever to my heart, with magic power,
Shall those sweet sounds recall this rapturous hour!

---

1. Mary Tighe seems to be recounting hearing real music while being rowed on the Lake of Killarney in the moonlight. In fact, William Ockenden reports (*Letters describing the Lakes of Killarney and Mucross Gardens* (Cork, c.1760), p. 13) that Lord Kenmare, the largest landowner in the Killarney area, would sometimes arrange for a French horn player to play beside the waters of the Lakes of Killarney while his guests were being rowed around the lake, presumably to heighten the romantic effect of the experience. Though Ockenden was writing about forty years before Mary Tighe, it seems clear that the custom continued. I am grateful to Luke Gibbons for this reference. See also the account of Edward Willis in *The Letters of Lord Chief Baron Edward Willis to the Earl of Warwick, 1757-62*, edited by James Kelly (Aberystwyth, 1980), pp. 63-64.

DANIEL RODERICK O'CONOR
(fl.**1800**)

Nothing definite is known of this poet, though he explains in a footnote to the poem which follows that his 'Fore-Fathers being stripped of their Property through the effect of the Penal laws, left me, an humble Literary Adventurer, as a Dependant only on Dame Fortune.' He bewails the lack of patronage for poetry in Dublin, and gives this as the reason for his decision to quit the capital.

from: The Author's Farewell to Dublin: a poem

... On Liffey's Banks good Heav'ns! what was my Lot,
Where ev'ry Muse is slighted and forgot;
Where with such state New Lordlings seem to frown,
And scarcely will on Swinish Worlds look down?
Thro' pride first to the Capital I came,
To learn more Wisdom and exalt my Fame;
To view Clontarff, and Aughrim's fatal plain,[1]
The haughty Liffey and the princely Slane.[2]
Some fav'rite passion urg'd me to behold
These Hills, renown'd in tuneful song of old,   10
Ben-Hedar's[3] pomp, and Bray's majestick side,
And Dalky's head, which overhangs the tide.

On ev'ry side gay Circles strike my eyes,
And Wits, in crowds, before me seem to rise:
Here stands a Patriot, Orator, and Sage:
But, here what Patriot feeds the Poet's rage?
Since but too few admire the tuneful song,
Say, where's the Bard, who figures in the throng;
Who sings great names, that in our Senate frown'd
On guilty Laws, and justly grew renown'd?   20

1. Sites of two famous battles (in 1014 and 1691 respectively)
2. Slane, Co. Meath, the site of Slane Castle, the seat of the Conyngham family. The first Marquess of Conyngham (1766-1832) – owner of the castle at the time O'Connor was writing – has been described as a 'European princeling' (Mark Bence-Jones, *A Guide to Irish Country Houses* (London, 1978), p. 260).
3. *Beann Éadair*, the Irish name for Howth Head, a promontory on the north side of Dublin Bay. Bray Head is a promontory south of Dublin, and Dalkey Hill overlooks Dublin Bay.

'Tis Britain's glory to advance her fame,
To rouse her Heroes, and the Poet's flame;
To lift the Olive, or disdain alarms,
And purchase Wreaths by noblest deeds of Arms.

On Scotland's warlike, hospitable ground,
For Heroes, Sages and great Chiefs renown'd,
The Arts are cherish'd — Science is admir'd —
The Muse applauded — and the Bard inspir'd.

Ill-fated Sister, Ireland, dumb alone,
Alas! to Fame or Fortune long unknown: 30
What drowns thy Genius? — Why to Science dead?
Lo! from thy coast th'insulted Muse hath fled;
Then will those Chiefs, whom publick weal inspir'd,
Whom Erin's wrongs with sense of glory fir'd,
With all their fame to dark oblivion creep,
In some dull page, or drowzy Annals sleep.

The Muse oft' thought her Labours would be crown'd,
Whilst in this Isle a VOLUNTEER was found;
Alas! too soon their glory died away;
Their eyes were clos'd 'gainst Fame's eternal day!   40
Those warlike Patriots rose to guard the State,
Stood fierce in arms, and labour'd to be great:
Astrea⁴ smil'd — GREAT GEORGE Ierne free'd;
In Heav'n an Angel then records the deed....

... but no one does so properly on earth, since poets are not paid to record such events.
Undaunted, O'Conor calls on all his poetic skills for the remainder of the poem to recount
the glories of Ireland's recent past, but ends still bewailing the state's unwillingness to
recognise the importance of poetry or to support its poets.

4. Astræa was the classical goddess of justice, but the name was also applied, symbolically,
   to Queen Elizabeth I as symbol of England. O'Connor uses it to mean England. 'Great
   George' is George III, who had signed the legislation granting Ireland limited legislative
   independence.

THOMAS MOORE
(1779-**1800**-1852)

Tom Moore was the son of a grocer and was born in Aungier Street, Dublin. When at Trinity College, Dublin, though a close friend of Robert Emmet, he shunned the activities of the United Irishmen. In 1799, Moore went to London to study law and in 1800 published his translations of Anacreon. These were followed in 1801 by the *Poetical Works of Thomas Little*. By 1807, Moore was writing the Irish melodies for which he became famous, and he went on to live the life of a man of letters in London. Below are two examples of his early work, both written before 1801.

Translation of Ode IX by Anacreon

I pray thee, by the gods above,
Give me the mighty bowl I love,
And let me sing, in wild delight,
'I will — I will be mad tonight!'
Alcmæon[1] once, as legends tell,
Was frenzied by the fiends of hell;
Orestes too, with naked tread,
Frantic pac'd the mountain-head;
And why? a murder'd mother's shade
Before their conscious fancy play'd.   10
But I can ne'er a murderer be,
The grape alone shall bleed by me;
Yet can I rave, in wild delight,
'I will — I will be mad tonight.'
The son of Jove, in days of yore,
Imbru'd his hands in youthful gore,
And brandish'd, with maniac joy,
The quiver of th'expiring boy.[2]
And Ajax, with tremendous shield,
Infuriate scour'd the guiltless field.[3]   20
But I, whose hands no quiver hold,
No weapon but this flask of gold;

1. According to classical mythology, Alcmæon and Orestes, both of whom murdered their mothers, were pursued by the furies.
2. Dardanus, son of Jupiter (Jove) and Electra, killed his brother Iasius to obtain the kingdom of Etruria.
3. Ajax who was, next to Achilles, the bravest of the Greeks at the Trojan war, was famous for his large shield.

The trophy of whose frantic hours
Is but a scatter'd wreath of flowers;
Yet, yet can sing with wild delight,
'I will — I will be mad tonight!'

Song

Away with this pouting and sadness,
    Sweet girl! will you never give o'er?
I love you, by Heaven! to madness,
    And what can I swear to you more?
Believe not the old women's fable,
    That oaths are as short as a kiss;
I'll love you as long as I'm able,
    And swear for no longer than this.

Then waste not the time with professions,
    For *not* to be blest when we can   10
Is one of the darkest transgressions
    That happen 'twixt woman and man.
Pretty moralist! why thus beginning
    My innocent warmth to reprove?
Heav'n knows that I never loved *sinning* —
    Except little sinnings in love!

If swearing, however, will do it,
    Come, bring me the calendar,[1] pray —
I vow, by that lip, I'll go through it,
    And not miss a saint on my way.   20
The angels shall help me to wheedle,
    I'll swear upon every one
That e'er danc'd on the point of a needle,[2]
    Or rode on a beam of the sun!

1. i.e. a calendar which lists the feast day of every saint.
2. The first edition notes that the allusion is to 'a famous question among the early schoolmen' about how many thousand angels could dance on the point of a very fine needle without jostling one another.

Oh! why should Platonic control, love,
    Enchain an emotion so free?
Your soul, though a very sweet soul, love,
    Will ne'er be sufficient for me.
If you think, by this coldness and scorning,
    To seem more angelic and bright,   30
Be an angel, my love, in the morning,
    But, oh! *be a woman tonight!*

W. KERTLAND
(fl. **1807**)

This extraordinary poetic advertisement gives a vivid picture of what was available in Dublin shops just after the Act of Union, which came into effect on 1 January 1801. The readers would, presumably, have recognised the misquotation from the first paragraph of Milton's *Paradise Lost* as a joke.

The DUBLIN Fancy WARE-HOUSE, No. ONE, *Lower* ORMOND-QUAY

'Things unattempted yet in Prose or Rhyme
'Of WATER and of FIRE — of Odours sweet —
'Of FASHION — FANCY — TRADE, and GRATITUDE,
'Sing heavenly Muse!!'   MILTON

> DEAR me! what mighty curious ways
> Men take for money now-a-days![1]
>
> The Muse, on Liffey's side, (they say)
> Is heard upon a *Minor Key*,
> A *Trading Muse*! (but truce with pun)
> She sings the Wares at NUMBER ONE;
> Such as in common times were told
> In cards and catalogues *of old*,
> But now as *manners change* with *times*,
> She *soars* from humble *Prose* to *Rhymes*.   10
> Here choicest articles you'll find
> To please the eye, amuse the mind;
> Goods both for ornament and use,
> Such as few other Shops produce: —
> As BOTTLED FIRE, a precious treasure!
> To light a candle at your pleasure;
> And Ink for Lovers when they choose
> To write their SWEETHEARTS *Billets doux*;

1. A footnote reads: 'Horace or Virgil, or some one of those *Geniuses* with whom *Trades People cannot possibly* be acquainted has, I am told, the following similar idea, "Quid non mortalia pectora cogis AURI sacra fames!!" — *very cogent reasons* embolden me to assure the *Classic Reader* that this passage is not purloined.' (The quotation is from Virgil, *Aeneid* iii, 56-57. 'To what do you not drive mortal hearts, accursed hunger for gold.')

('Tis used in various secret tricks,
But most in *Love* and *Politics*.)   20
Pencils of Fire to write i' th' dark;
Permanent Ink, your clothes to mark;
(*Mark* what you would with safety use,
Leave *unmarked* what you *wish to lose*.)
Canes, *empty* Purses, Gloves and Garters,
Fine Lavender and Honey Waters,
Silk Handkerchiefs, Snuff Boxes, Scissors,
Fruit Knives, Pencils, Tooth-Picks, Tweezers,
Rich *oily* Polish for your Shoes,
Boot-top *Restorer*, all should use;   30
With Pocket Books, each sort and size,
And Skipping Cords for exercise;
But *Hempen Rope* I never sell,
I love my Customers too well;
And tho' I've Gallowses (*for Breeches*),
I hate your doleful dying Speeches.[2]

LADIES! to you our high respects
We pay, as *gallantry* directs;
Wanton *Zephyr*'s[3] balmy wing,
For you Arabia's stores shall bring,   40
Wafting, in luxurious breeze,
Fragrance of ambrosial trees.
Lillies, and a thousand Flowers,
Cull'd in Rose and Jasmine Bow'rs
These to KERTLAND's Chymic Art[4]
All their od'rous powers impart,
Hence the choicest Perfumes flow,
Hence Soaps, Pomades, and Lip Salves glow
(To guard Hibernia's Daughters fair
From tanning sun-beams — frosty air,)   50
With Rouge, Carmine[5] and Milk of Roses,
Pungent Salts to *sting* your noses.

---

2. 'Hempen' rope was used by hangmen, and broadsheets containing the 'dying speeches' of malefactors were sold to the crowd at executions. 'Gallowses' were suspenders or braces to hold up trousers, but there is also a pun on the word 'gallows'.
3. The west wind.
4. i.e. Kertland's skill as a chemist (in making perfumes and toilet water).
5. Face colouring made of a crimson pigment obtained from cochineal. 'Milk of Roses' is another face cream or ointment.

With Grecian Water fresh and fair,
To turn to *black* the *greyest* hair;
And Water, which to hearts delight,
Will bleach the darkest linen white;
And Salt of Lemons, in a *twink*
To banish Iron Mould or Ink;
With *Lozenges* to cure a cold,
And *Horehound*,[6] good for young and old.   60

Patience! my kind and gentle reader,
For, Fashion is a *special Breeder*,
Of other GOODS I wish to tell
Oh! 'tis an EVIL not to sell.
'Twould pose e'en P———s *pericrany*,[7]
To sing of ev'ry *Miscellany*.

Here's Parapluie's[8] and Parasols,
Nice Fancy Papers, Prints and Drolls,
With Combs of Silver, Gilt or Shell,
To suit the Taste of *Beau* or *Belle*;   70
Dress Ornaments and *Wedding Rings*!
Beads, Bracelets, and a thousand things, —
Laid in as Fashion gives the hint,
Too *tedious* to appear in Print.

And then, to gratify *all* palates,
We've Vinegars, and Oils for Sallads,
Green Girkins, Capers, Macaroni
And rich Anchovies from Gorgona,[9]
Anchovy Essence, Cappillaire,[10]
True Usquebaugh and French *Liquere*.[11]   80

---

6. A cough remedy made from the horehound plant.
7. P——— is an unknown figure: *pericrany* is a joking word for the pericranium or skull — here 'the brain'.
8. umbrellas.
9. A city in Italy.
10. A syrup flavoured with orange-flower water.
11. Irish whiskey and French liqueurs.

If then for these you have occasion,
Accept this humble invitation,
Drawn out in jingling *spitter-spatter*
Like acid flash of — *Soda Water*,
And tho' but little you select,
E'en trifles have their due effect;
My heart with gratitude shall flow,
For every favour you bestow,
And, in all instances expedient,
I'll ever prove — your most obedient,   90

W. KERTLAND

Glossary

A) Hiberno-English

Commonly found Hiberno-English words and expressions

bonny-clabber	(Ir. *bainne clabair*) thick, naturally soured milk (Bliss, pp. 271-72).
brogue	(Ir. *bróg*) shoe (Bliss pp. 268-69).
Dear-Joy	A name for an Irishman, apparently used only before 1700 (Bliss, pp. 264-65); so widespread was the use of this Irish endearment in the late seventeenth century that Laurence Eachard states in his *Exact Description of Ireland* (London, 1691) that the Irish 'are vulgarly called by the names *Teague* and *Dear-Joy*' (Bliss, p. 265).
Galiore	(Ir. *go leor*) plenty, lots of (Bliss, p. 276).
Milesian	Milesius was the mythological ancestor of the Gaelic Irish race, so the adjective is used to distinguish those descended from the founders of that race from all later invaders.
Ohone! O hone! ochone! etc.	(Ir. *ochón*) alas! (Bliss, p. 256).
rapparee	(Ir. *rapairí*) outlaw (Bliss, p. 267).
Tadhg	Irish proper name. This anglicised form was a common pejorative term for any Irishman. See 'Dear-Joy' above.
Trews	(Ir. *triús*) close-fitting Irish trousers (Bliss, pp. 268-69).
Usquebaugh, uisce beatha, iskebah etc.	(Ir. *uisce beathadh*) 'water of life' i.e. whiskey (Bliss, p. 274). Irish whiskey was flavoured with raisins and herbs in the seventeenth and eighteenth centuries.

Word-list of common Hiberno-English spellings

1. Consonants. The most common substitutions of one consonant for another in the written Hiberno-English in this anthology are as follows:

    (i) 'd' for 'th' as in the following examples:

broder	brother	dis	this
dare	their	dish	this
dat	that	dose	those
de	the	dus	thus
dem	them	Fader	Father
den	then	fedder	feather
der	their	fiders	feathers
dere	their	gader'd	gathered
dey	they		

597

(ii) 'sh' for 's' as in the following examples:

curshed	cursed	shay	say
forsht	forced	shaying	saying
hash	has/have	sheal'd	sealed
her'sh	here's	shick	sick
Kingshail	Kinsale	shides	sides
lasht	last	shirtinly	certainly
lesh	less	shistance	assistance
losh	loss	shorrow	sorrow
nailesh	nails	shoul	soul
peash	peace	ush	us
plash	place	Wailesh	Wales
shaint	saint		

and of 'sh' for 'j' or 'ch' as in the following examples:

marshed	marched	shentry	gentry
Sheat	cheat	Shesuit	Jesuit
sheif	chief		

(iii) 'f' is substituted for 'wh' as in the following examples:

fat	what	fishled	whistled
fear	where	fite	white
fen	when	fon	when
filst	whilst		

and, in reverse, 'wh' can be substituted for 'f':

conwounded	confounded	whire	fore
whair	fair	whirst	first
whancies	fancies	white	fight
whatagued	fatigued	wholl	full
whate	fate	whollies	follows
wheelds	fields	wholow'd	followed
Whenix	Phoenix	whoolish	foolish
whind	find	whor	for
whinding	finding	whree	free
whine	fine	whrite	fright

(iv) 'v' is also substituted for 'w' as in the following examples:

svore	swore	ve'd	would
vak	walk	vell	well
varriors	warriors	ven	when
vas	was	vere	were
vat	what	vhile	while
ve	we	vid	would
vear	were	vide	with

vidh	with	vood	wood
vill	will	vood	would
vith	with	vore	wore
von	one	vorld	world
vonder	wonder	vud	would

(v) Another substitution is of 't' for 'th' or 'd':

bot	both	Tivel	Devil
solt	sold	tolt	told
tink	think	tunder	thunder

(vi) Other substitutions include 'b' for 'p'; 'v' for 'f'; 'w' for 'v':

cabes	capes	deveat	defeat
debittie	deputy	wery	very

2.   Vowels. Many vowels carried different values in eighteenth-century Hiberno-English from both modern Hiberno-English values and those of present-day Standard English. A sample of such differences follows:

acontance	acquaintance	tin-pence	ten-pence
advonce	advance	dees	does
fiders	feathers	dater	daughter
mate	meat	fair	for
prat	prate	firsht	forced
proticting	protecting	Chreist	Christ
raview	review	sich	such

The epenthetic or additional vowel, a feature of 'interference' from Irish, also occurs:

Galloway	Galway	nailesh	nails
Ingalish	English	Wailesh	Wales

3.   The texts also contain a number of phonetic spellings:

cabitch	cabbage	neghbors	neighbours
Ierish	Irish	ov	of
mienets	minutes		

4.   Mistakes occur quite frequently in written eighteenth-century Hiberno-English, caused by genuine (or feigned) lack of familiarity with uncommon or polysyllabic English words. Some speakers and writers were also prepared to coin words from Latin or Irish, or contract or expand words, as it suited them. A few examples are:

derived	arrived	Limbrick	Limerick
dispense	dispensation	represt	depressed
hostage	hostess		

5. Some users had — again either real or feigned — problems with correct use of verbs, either misunderstanding tenses or agreements or using Irish verb forms. 'To broke' exists for 'to break' for instance, and 'The Connaughtman's Visit to Dublin' contains the following lines: 'She'l tolt me in Leitrim she was born'd and bread' and 'Reynard had dare at their roosts been to steal'. Readers interested in a full discussion of the verb forms of spoken English in eighteenth-century Ireland are referred to Bliss, pp. 290-309.

6. Finally, and not surprisingly, the texts contain many Hiberno-English words, expressions and usages of which the following is a sample:

appace	at once	silsh ever I live	as long as I live
greater nor	greater than	to take a swear	to swear
parted	parted from	Yeamus	Seamus
pratie	potatoes		

B) Ulster-Scots words and expressions

a'	all	birkies	energetic ones
ae	one	birth	berth
aff	off, often	bizziet	busied
aften	often	black	blackguards; negro
aiblins	perhaps	bleaze	blaze, fire
ain	own	blether	to talk foolishly
aince	once	blythe	cheerful
Airlan'	Ireland	boatfu's	boats full
alang	along	bole	small recess
amang	among	bon(n)ie	fair, pretty
an'	and, one	boost	must
ance	once	bord	to board
ance on a day	once upon a time	bourtray	elder bush
ane	one	bouse, bowse	to bounce, to drink
anither	another		heavily
atween	between	box, bock	to vomit
auld	old	brae	hill, hillside
aw	to owe	braid	broad
awa	away	breaker	wave
ay	always	brief	for a short time
'aye	indeed	brustin'	bursting
		buck	dashing young fellow
bairn	child		
baith	both	ca'	to call
ban	band, group	cairn	a heap of stones
ban	to curse	callen	youths
bast	to beat soundly,	cam	came
	to cudgel	cam' to	came to (their right
beads	rosary beads		minds)
begoud	began	canny	(i) shrewd (ii) lucky
birk	to birch, to beat with a		(iii) pleasant
	cane	cant	to chant, to sing

cappers	copper coins	fair	fair (but in 'The
cartes	cards		Passengers', = fare,
cauf, calf	dolt		a journey)
chaunt	to sing	fairfaw, fair fa'	may good happen to
chiel	young fellow		you!
chirl	to chirp or warble	fa'n	fallen
churl	man, fellow	fandness	fondness
cleek	to seize, to take for	fank	to twist, entangle
	oneself	fash	to bother, trouble, get
co'ert	covered		angry
conceits itsel'	has a good opinion of	fear	to frighten
	itself	fidgin'	itching
conven't	convened	fok	folk
cozie	sheltered	forgrutten	forgotten
crack	talk, entertainment	frae	from
crap	to creep	freaks	capers
crave	to press for payment of	frien	friend
	a debt	fu'	full, very
craw	crow		
creel	basket	gan	began
cud	could	gangin	going
		gar	to make, compel
		gash	respectable
daded	thudded	gies	goes
daft	stupid	gif	if
dainty	pleasant	gill	half-a-pint
daw	lazy person, slut	gin	if
dee	to do	girnin'	grimacing
deel, de'il, diel	devil	glancin'	flashing by
dight	to rub (the eyes)	gled	kite, hawk
dint	occasion	goss	goshawk
disna	did not	gove	to stare
douce	sober	graft	cunning
doun	down	grien	to crave
drap	to drop	grimest	grimmest
droll	amusing, amused	grusome	rough-looking
drouket	drenched	Gude	God
dyke	dry stone wall, wall	gudefaith	Good heavens!
	with a hedge on top of	guid	good
	it	gypes	foolish people
e'ed	eyed	hae	to have
e'en, een	(i) eyes (ii) even	halewar	the whole company
en	end	hame	home
ether	either	han's	hands
ettle	to intend, plan to do	harlin'	trolling for fish
		harpie	harpy, monstrous old
fa'	to fall, to happen to		woman
facer	a dram or a glass of	harrie	to ruin, make poor,
	whiskey punch		plunder

harrowers	men who harrow the fields	mock	rubbish, abuse
haud	to hold	moil	clod of earth
headpiece	head	monie	many
heckle	hackle or flax-comb	mutton	flesh
hie	to go	my lane	by myself
hobblin'	bobbing up and down		
hold	hold (in a ship)	nae	no
hurchin	hedgehog	naig	horse
		nauceous	nauseous, disgusting
ilk	each, every	neuk	nook, corner
ilka	every	nibour	neighbour
ill	difficult	no	now
ithers	others	noest	nest
		no worth	no more use than
kin'	kind	nybers	neighbours
kist	chest		
ky(e)	cows	o'	of
		o'erhie	to go
laigh	low	oursel's	ourselves
lan	land	outler	a farm animal which remains outside during the winter
lang	long		
lap	leaped		
laverocks	skylarks	owre	too much
lay	song		
lea	untilled ground left fallow, pasture	pang't	packed tight
		pauky	cunning, crafty, sly
lea's	leaves	pegh	to puff
lee-lang	live-long, whole	peys	pays
leuk	to look, a look	pickle	a small amount of
lieve	to live	pikes	spines
lift	sky	plaid	woollen cloth
lintseed	flax seed	play	to boil
loun	fellow	poke	a beggar's bag
lous, lowse	to unyoke a horse from a plough or harrow	poll-tax	tax levied on each person
lown	calm, peaceful	press	to impress (someone) for the armed forces
luckless	unfortunate		
luick	to look	prie	to taste
		prieve	to prove
mair	more	prove	to sample
maist	most		
marrow	companion, equal	quaint	skilfully
maun	must	quat	to quit
meagre	miserable	quid	a piece of tobacco chewed in the mouth
meal	oatmeal		
mettle't	mettled, spirited	quo'	quoth, said
min'	mind		
mislear't	unmannerly, mischievous	rant	to play and sing the tune for a dance
		rantin'	romping

602

rape	rope	strib	to squeeze the last drop
rate	to berate		of milk out of
rattle	to strike or beat	striddle	to step out
	repeatedly	syne	soon, directly
rauckle	strong		afterwards
row	to roll, to trundle		
		taen	taken
sae	so, such	taupie	awkward fellow
saft	soft, softly	thir	these
sair	sore, severe; to serve	thole	to put up with
sauls!	upon my word!	thrang't	busy with work
scar't	scared	thrapple	throat
scourin'	rushing, roistering	thrawn	distorted
sea-store	stores for the voyage	throe	a twisting of the body,
sen'	to send		a spasm
set	sat	tift	fit
shankies	legs	tirl	to strip off
sib	related by blood to	toddlin	toddling, walking
sic	such	totam	a small child
sican	such-like	toy	to flirt
siller	silver, money	trew, true, trow	to believe
simmer	summer	twa	two
skail't	scattered	twa fold	bent double
skaith	harm, damage	twathree	two or three, a few
skeedyin	scideen, a small potato	twine	a wriggling of the body
	(Ir. *sceidíní*, small	tyke	(i) dog (ii) animal
	potatoes)		
skelp	to strike	wabblin	dangling
skirl	to sing, to shriek	wabster	weaver
sklent	to look sideways, to	wad	would
	squint	wame	belly, stomach
sleely	slyly	want for	to lack or be short of
sma'	small	wanton	frisky
smacks	kisses	warl'y	worldly
smil't	smiled	wat	know
snoove, snove	to glide	wean	young child
snore	to move at speed with	weel	well
	a rushing sound	ween	to think
speel	to clamber up	wha	who
spite	disappointment	whamlin	wammling, turning
sport	to play		over and over (of a
spring	lively tune		stomach)
stang	pain	whan	when
stark-wood	stark mad	whar	where
stauchrin'	staggering	whase	whose
sten	to leap	wheel	to pirouette
stern	sternly	whin	gorse bush
strae	straw	whisht	to be quiet
strak	struck	whiteret, whitrat	weasel
strang	strong(ly)	wi'	with

win	people one is fond of; wind; to earn by labouring, to gather in crops	wrang	wrong
		wratch	wretch
		ye'r	your
wiss	to wish, want	ye're	you are
wist	knew	yon	that one (over there)
wi' venom	violently	yon'ers	yonder is

Sources of the texts

Part I

Six poems from the Williamite wars
(i) 'Lilliburlero', *The Historical Songs of Ireland* ... ed. T. Crofton Croker (London, 1841), pp. 6-9; (ii) 'A Cruel and Bloody DECLARATION', Broadside (Dublin, 1725), Huntington Library, San Marino, California; (iii) from: *The Irish Hudibras* (London, 1689), pp. 100-05 and 144-51; (iv) 'The Irishmen's Prayers', *The Pepys Ballads* edited by W.G. Day (Cambridge, 1987) [facsimile edition], V, 69; (v) 'Epitaph on the Duke of Grafton', *State Poems: continued* (London, 1702), pp. 259-60; (vi) 'An *Irish* Song', *Wit and Mirth: or Pills to Purge Melancholy* (London, 1720), VI, 281.

Nahum Tate
(i) from: *Panacea: A Poem upon Tea* (London, 1702); (ii) 'Song of the Angels', *A Supplement to the New Version of Psalms by Dr Brady and Mr Tate*, 3rd edition (London, 1702).

John Toland
from: 'Clito', *Poems on Affairs of State* (London, 1703), II, 179-86.

William King
from: 'Mully of Mountown', *Miscellanies in Prose and Verse by William King* (London, 1707), pp. 359-66.

George Farquhar
'To a Gentleman' and 'An Epigram', *The Works of George Farquhar* ed. Shirley Strum Kenny (Oxford, 1988), II, 448 and 314.

William Congreve
'Doris', *The Works of Mr William Congreve*, 3 vols. (London, 1710), III, 992-95.

Thomas Parnell
(i) 'To ————', *Collected Poems of Thomas Parnell* eds. Claude Rawson and F.P. Lock (Newark, 1989), pp. 354-55 with punctuation added. (ii) 'On the Castle of Dublin', Rawson and Lock, p. 327. (iii) 'Bacchus', *The Posthumous Works of ... Parnell* (Dublin, 1758), pp. 277-82, with some corrections from *Works* (1755).

Mary Monck
'An Elegie on a Favourite Dog' and 'A Tale', *Marinda: Poems and Translations on Several Occasions* (London, 1716), pp. 67-71 and 110.

James Ward
from: '*Phoenix* Park', *Miscellaneous Poems* ed. Matthew Concanen (London, 1724), pp. 379-91; 'The Smock Race at Finglas', ibid., pp. 321-27.

Morrough O'Connor
'An Eclogue in Imitation of the first Eclogue of Virgil', *The Petition of Morrough O'Connor to the Provost and Senior Fellows of Trinity College* (Dublin, 1740), pp. 7-16 (first published 1719), Foxon O9.

Matthew Concanen
from: *A Match at Football* (Dublin, 1720).

Anonymous poems current 1710-25

(i) from: 'The Signior in Fashion', T.J. Walsh, *Opera in Dublin 1705-97* (Dublin, 1973), pp. 313-16. (ii) 'A Petition to the Ladies', Broadsheet (Dublin, c.1720) TCD Press A.7.4. #145. Foxon P193. (iii) from: 'The Cavalcade', Broadsheet (Dublin: c.1717) [UCD W1.C.3.24], compared with later text in J.J. Webb, *The Guilds of Dublin* (Dublin, 1929). (iv) 'An Irish Wedding', *The Whimsical Medley* TCD Manuscript 879, I, 123-28 also printed in *Anthologia Hibernica* for December 1794. (v) 'The Irish Absentee's new Litany', *The Pall-Mall Miscellany* (London and Dublin, 1732), pp. 10-13. (vi) 'The Humble Petition', Broadside (Dublin, 1725), TCD Press A.7.6. #18. (vii) from: *Hesperi-Neso-Graphia, or, A Description of the Western Isle* (London, 1716), pp. 3-15 (compared with Dublin 1735 and Cork 1795 printings). (viii) 'The Royal Black Bird', broadsheet, N.L.I. (L.O.) (compared with Georges-Denis Zimmermann, *Songs of Irish Rebellion: Political Street Ballads and Rebel Songs 1780-1900* (Dublin, 1967), pp. 119-20).

Nicholas Browne

from: 'The North Country Wedding', *The North Country Wedding and the Fire* ... (Dublin, 1722), Gilbert Collection 7a(1), #27, compared with the 'corrected' text in Concanen, *Miscellaneous Poems* (London, 1724).

Mary Davys

from: 'The Modern Poet', *The Works of Mrs Davys* (London, 1725), I, 277-80.

Ambrose Philips and Henry Carey

(i) 'To Miss Georgiana', *Pastorals, Epistles, Odes and other original Poems by Mr Philips* (Dublin, 1768), pp. 108-110, compared with text in *The Poems of Ambrose Philips*, ed. M. Segar (Oxford, 1937). (ii) 'Namby Pamby', Broadside (Dublin, c.1725), Foxon C49, Huntington Library, California, #143234.

Part II

Jonathan Smedley

(i) 'Verses fix'd on the Cathedral Door', *Gulliveriana* (London, 1728), pp. 77-79; (ii) 'An Epistle to his Grace', Broadside (Dublin, 1724), Foxon S499.

Jonathan Swift

(i) 'His Grace's Answer to Jonathan', Broadside (Dublin, 1724), Foxon S858; (ii) 'To Charles Ford Esq.', *Works of ... Swift ...* (Dublin: Faulkner, 1762), XIV, 186; (iii) 'Stella at Wood-Park', *Works of ... Swift ...* (Dublin: Faulkner, 1735), II, 212; (iv) 'An Epistle upon an Epistle', Broadsheet (Dublin, 1730); (v) 'A LIBEL on D[octor] D[elany]', *Works of ... Swift ...* (Dublin: Faulkner, 1735), II, 255; (vi) [Swift, Delany, Sheridan and others] Riddles, street cries, etc., 'In Youth exalted high in Air', *Works of ... Swift ...* (Dublin: Faulkner, 1735), II, 380-82; remaining riddles, street cries etc. from *Works of ... Swift ...* (Dublin: Faulkner, 1772), VIII, 249; VIII, 253; XVI, appendix, p. 13; VIII, 272; VIII, 215; VIII, 216; VIII, 214; and VIII, 214-15; (vii) 'Mary the Cook-Maid's Letter', *Works of ... Swift ...* (Dublin: Faulkner, 1735), II, 163; (viii) 'A Pastoral Dialogue', *Works of ... Swift ...* (Dublin: Faulkner, 1735), II, 220; (ix) 'A Character, Panegyric, and Description of the LEGION CLUB', *Works of ... Swift ...* (Dublin: Faulkner, 1772), XI, 346-55.

Esther Johnson

'To Dr Swift', Deane Swift, *Essay upon ... Dr Jonathan Swift* (London, 1755), pp. 81-83.

Thomas Sheridan
(i) 'A Description of Doctor Delany's Villa', *Miscellaneous Poems ... Published by Mr. Concanen* (London, 1724), pp. 239-42; (ii) 'To the Dean', *Works of ... Swift ...* (Dublin: Faulkner, 1767), XVI, appendix, p. 17; (iii) 'A True and Faithful Inventory', Broadside (Dublin, 1726).

Patrick Delany
'An Epistle to His Excellency ... *Lord* Carteret', Broadside (Dublin, 1729).

Mary Barber
(i) 'An Unanswerable Apology for the Rich', [Mary Barber] *Poems on Several Occasions* (London, 1734) pp. 17-19; (ii) 'To Mrs. Frances-Arabella Kelly' and 'The Recantation', ibid., pp. 151-54.

Matthew Pilkington
(i) 'The Invitation', *Poems on Several Occasions* (London, 1731), pp. 41-42; (ii) 'Anacreon Paraphras'd', ibid., pp. 125-26.

Laetitia Pilkington
'The Petition of the Birds', *Memoirs of Mrs Laetitia Pilkington* 2 vols. (Dublin, 1749), I, 38-40.

Constantia Grierson
(i) 'To Miss *Laetitia Van Lewen*', *The Memoirs of Mrs Laetitia Pilkington* (Dublin, 1776), pp. 25-26; (ii) from: 'Lines to an unnamed Lady', Constantia Grierson's Manuscript Book [private collection].

William Dunkin
(i) from: 'The Parson's Revels', *Select Poetical Works of William Dunkin*, 2 vols. (Dublin, 1770), II, 25-49. (ii) from: 'A Receipt for Making a Doctor', ibid., II, 275-86; (iii) 'On the Omission of ... *Dei Gratia*', ibid., II, 274.

James Arbuckle
'On Swift's leaving his Fortune', National Library of Wales, Aberystwyth: holograph in PR 4116.A47.

Part III

Henry Brooke
from: 'Universal Beauty' in *A Collection of the Pieces formerly published by Henry Brooke Esq.*, 4 vols. (London, 1778), I, 116-23.

Anonymous poems from the 1730s and 1740s
(i) 'The Kerry Cavalcade', Foxon K30, Broadside (Dublin, 1734); (ii) from: *The Upper Gallery* (Dublin, 1733); (iii) 'An Elegy on the much lamented Death of ... all the *Potatoes*', Broadside (Dublin, 1740).

James Sterling
from: *A Friend in Need is a Friend in Deed ...* (Dublin, 1737).

Wetenhall Wilkes
from: *The Humours of the Black Dog* (Dublin, 1737), Foxon W464.

Robert Nugent, Earl Nugent
'Epistle to Pollio, from the Hills of Howth', *A Collection of Poems* ed. Robert Dodsley and others, 6 vols. (London, 1770), II, 207-10.

John, Earl of Orrery
from: *The First Ode of the First Book of Horace Imitated* ... (Dublin, 1741), pp. 2-8.

John Winstanley
(i) 'Miss Betty's Singing-Bird' *Poems written occasionally by John Winstanley ... interspers'd with many others ... by several Ingenious Hands* (Dublin, 1742), pp. 177-79; (ii) 'Upon *Daisy*, being brought back from *New Park* to *Stoneybatter*', ibid., pp. 170-74; (iii) 'The Poet's Lamentation for the loss of his Cat', *Poems written occasionally by the late John Winstanley ... interspers'd with many others, ... by several Ingenious Hands,* Vol II (Dublin, 1751), pp. 293-96; (iv) 'To the Revd Mr ——— on his Drinking Sea-Water', ibid., pp. 82-83.

Laurence Whyte
(i) 'A POETICAL Description of Mr. NEAL's new Musick-Hall', *Original poems on Various Subjects ... Part the Second* ... (Dublin, 1742), pp. 21-23. (ii) from: 'The Parting Cup or The HUMOURS of Deoch an Doruis', *Poems on Various Subjects, Serious and Diverting, Never before Published* ... (Dublin, 1740), pp. 68-99.

James Eyre Weekes
from: 'The Intrigues of *Jove*: a Ballad', *Poems on Several Occasions* (Cork, 1743), pp. 127-29; 'Left on a Lady's Toilette' and 'Answer'd by her WOMAN', ibid., pp. 53-54.

Sir Arthur Dawson
'Bumpers, 'Squire Jones', *The Muses Holiday or the Polite Songster* (Dublin, c.1750), pp. 28-29.

Anonymous songs and poems from the 1750s
(i) 'Drinking Song', *The Ulster Miscellany* (Dublin?, 1752), pp. 276-77; (ii) 'On Deborah Perkins', *The Merry Fellow or the Jovial Companion* [by Luke Lively] 2 vols. (Dublin, 1756), I, 293-94; (iii) 'The Clerk's Song', *The Ulster Miscellany* (Dublin?, 1752), p. 339; (iv) 'TIT for TAT; or the Rater rated', *The Ulster Miscellany* (Dublin?, 1752), pp. 380-81; (v) 'On the *Spaw* at *Castle-connel*, in the County of *Limerick*', *The Muses Holiday or the Polite Songster* (Dublin, c.1750), pp. 52-53; (vi) 'A New Ballad on the Hot-Wells at Mallow', *The Ulster Miscellany* (Dublin?, 1752), pp. 342-44; (vii) 'The Rakes of Mallow', *A New Academy of Compliments or the Lover's Secretary* ... 19th ed. (Dublin, 1768), pp. 129-30; (viii) 'Scew Ball', *Later English Broadside Ballads* (2 vols), vol. 2, eds. John Holloway and Joan Black (London: 1975).

Thomas Mozeen
(i) 'A Description of a Fox-Chase', *A Collection of Miscellaneous Essays* by T[homas] Mozeen (London, 1762), pp. 33-36; (ii) 'An Invitation to OWEN BRAY's at Laughlin's town', *The Merry Fellow or the Jovial Companion* [by Luke Lively], 2 vols. (Dublin, 1765), I, 250-51.

Thomas Newburgh
'The BEAU WALK, in STEPHEN'S GREEN', *Essays Poetical, Moral and Critical* (by Thomas Newburgh) (Dublin, 1769), p. 215.

Samuel Whyte
from: 'A Familiar Epistle to J.H. Esq.', *The Shamrock or Hibernian Cresses* [ed. and partly written by] Samuel Whyte (Dublin, 1772), pp. 57-61.

Art Mac Cumhaidh
'Tagra an Dá Theampall', *Dánta Tiadha Uladh*, ed. Énrí Ó Muirgheara (Baile Átha Cliath, 1936), pp. 375-79.

Liam Inglis
'Do Tharlaigh Inné Orm', Diarmaid Ó Muirithe, *An tAmhrán Macarónach* (Baile Átha Cliath, 1980), pp. 65-66.

Part IV

Dorothea Dubois
(i) 'The Amazonian Gift', *Poems on Several Occasions by a Lady of Quality* [Lady Dorothea Dubois] (Dublin, 1764), pp. 85-86; (ii) 'Song', ibid., pp. 102-04; (iii) from: 'A True Tale', ibid., pp. 1-27.

Anonymous poems from the 1760s
(i) 'Description of Dublin', *The New Foundling Hospital for Wit, part the second* (London, 1768), pp. 49-50; (ii) 'The Rakes of Stony Batter', *Later English Broadside Ballads* (2 vols), vol. 2, eds. John Holloway and Joan Black (London, 1975); (iii) 'The May Bush', from a volume of Irish-printed chapbooks (c.1810), Trinity College Dublin 66.u.165.

Olivia Elder
from: 'To Mrs D.C.H., an account of the Author's manner of spending her time', NLI MS 23254, pp. 7-11.

Oliver Goldsmith
(i) from: *The Deserted Village* (London, 1770); (ii) 'Let school-masters puzzle their brain', *She Stoops to Conquer* (Dublin, 1773).

Richard Brinsley Sheridan
(i) 'Lines by a Lady of Fashion', *The Plays and Poems of Richard Brinsley Sheridan*, ed. R. Crompton Rhodes, 3 vols. (New York, 1962), III, 241-42; (ii) 'Here's to the maiden of bashful fifteen', *The School for Scandal* (Dublin, 1777).

Gerald Fitzgerald
from: *The Academick Sportsman*, second edition (Dublin, 1797), pp. 11-23.

Mary Shackleton
(i) 'The Welcome to Liberty', NLI MS 23574, pp. 63-65; (ii) 'On the Murder of a Cat', ibid., pp. 74-77; (iii) 'To Sarah Shackleton on her beating me with the bed-stick', ibid., p. 192.

William Preston
from: 'An heroic Epistle from Donna Teresa Pinna ÿ Ruiz', *Poems on Several Occasions* (Dublin, 1781), pp. 15-25.

Lady Clare
'Motto inscribed on the bottom of chamber-pots', Constantia Maxwell, *Dublin under the Georges* (Dublin, 1936), p. 276.

Turlogh Carolan
'Carolan's Receipt', Joseph Cooper Walker, *Historical Memoirs of the Irish Bards* (Dublin, 1776), appendix p. 87.

Elizabeth Ryves
'Ode to Sensibility', *Poems on Several Occasions* (London, 1777) — but this text is taken from *The Cabinet of Irish Literature*, second edition, ed. Katharine Tynan Hinkson, 4 vols. (London, 1903), I, 235.

James Delacourt or De-La-Cour
'In praise of a Negress', *Poems by the Revd. James De-La-Cour A.M.* (Cork, 1778) p. 98.

George Sackville Cotter
from: 'Epistles from Swanlinbar', *Poems, consisting of Odes, Songs, Pastorals, Satyrs &c ... by the Reverend George Sackville Cotter A.M. ...* 2 vols. (Cork, 1788), I, 181-224.

Gorges Edmond Howard
'The Modern Lass in High Dress in MDCCLVI', *The Miscellaneous Works in Verse and Prose of Gorges Edmond Howard Esq.*, 3 vols. (Dublin, 1782), I, 28-29.

Eoghan Rua Ó Súilleabháin
'Letter to Father Fitzgerald', Daniel Corkery, *The Hidden Ireland* (Dublin, 1924), pp. 200-01.

Chapbook verse of the 1780s
(i) 'Connelly's Ale: a new song', Chapbook (Dublin, c.1785) Gilbert Library Dublin, 7a1/8; (ii) 'The Connaughtman's Visit to DUBLIN', Chapbook (Limerick, c.1785) BL 11622.df.34/3; (iii) 'The Maiden's Resolution or an Answer to the Farmer's Son', Chapbook (Dublin, 1784) Gilbert Library Dublin 7a1/10; (iv) 'The Sailor Dear' Chapbook (Limerick, c.1785) BL 11622.df.34/23; (v) 'The Coughing Old Man' Chapbook (Limerick, c.1785) BL 11622.df.34/8 with some amendments from another version of the text at BL 11622.df.34/20 (Monaghan, 1788); (vi) 'A Drop of Dram', Chapbook (Limerick, c.1785) BL 11622.df.34/15; (vii) 'Corporal Casey', *Crosby's Irish Repertory* (London, 1808), pp. 135-37; (viii) 'Darby O'Gallagher, or the Answer to Morgan Rattler', Chapbook (Limerick, c.1785) BL 11622.df.34/7; (ix) 'The New Dhooraling', Chapbook (Limerick, c.1785) BL 11622.df.34/21; (x) 'Hush Cat from under the Table', Chapbook (Monaghan, 1787) BL 11622.df.34/29.

Anonymous verse from newspapers and books of the 1780s
(i) 'Description of a Country Assizes', *Flora's Banquet: A Collection of Poems,* 2 vols. (Belfast, 1782), I, 130-35; (ii) 'The Agent's Downfall: a new ballad', Gilbert Library Dublin, 'Gleanings from Newspapers' (four volumes of Dublin newspaper cuttings from 1780-96), IV, 58-59; (iii) 'Description of an Unfortunate Woman of the Town', ibid., IV, 139-40; (iv) 'The Lord Mayor's Ball', ibid., IV, 115-16; (v) 'A New Song', ibid., IV, 54-56; (vi) 'Advertisement Extraordinary', ibid., IV, 97-98; (vii) 'Garry Own Naugh Glora, or The Limerick Rakes', Chapbook (Limerick, c.1785) BL 11622.df.34/23.

Three anonymous Irish/English poems from the 1780s
(i) 'The Rake's Frolick or *Stauka an Varaga*' Chapbook (Limerick, c.1785) BL 11622.df.34/14; (ii) 'The Answer to *Stauka an Vauraga*' Chapbook (Monaghan, c.1787) BL 11622.df.34/34; (iii) '*Pléarácá an Bhráthar*: A New Song called the Friar's Jigg', C. Mhág Craith, *Dán na mBráthar Mionúr I* (Baile Átha Cliath, 1967).

John Taylor
'On a Beef's being stole which was promis'd to the AUTHOR', *The Miscellaneous Works of John Taylor* (Limerick, 1787), pp. 54-56.

Four Dublin underworld poems from the 1780s
(i) 'De Nite afore Larry was stretch'd', NLI MS G482, pp. 81-86; (ii) 'Luke Caffrey's Kilmainham Minit', ibid., pp. 90-94; (iii) 'A New Song call'd Luke Caffrey's Gost', Chapbook (Dublin, 1795), Trinity College Dublin, EPB Librarian's office; (iv) 'Lord Altham's Bull', John Edward Walsh, *Sketches of Ireland 60 Years Ago* (Dublin, 1847), pp. 94-98.

Brian Merriman
from: *The Midnight Court* (tr. Denis Woulfe in 1789), UCD Add Irish MS 11.

Charlotte Brooke
'Song for Gracey Nugent' (tr. from the Irish of Carolan), *Reliques of Irish Poetry* (Dublin, 1789), pp. 246-49.

Thomas Dawson Lawrence
'Epitaph on an orphan beggar child', *The Miscellaneous Works of Thomas Dawson Lawrence Esq. ...* (Dublin, 1789), p. 59.

Part V

L. O'Reilly
'Elegy on the death of ... Miss Bridget Burne', *A Collection of Poems, mostly Original,* [ed. Joshua Edkins], two vols. (Dublin, 1790), II, 140-48.

Mary O'Brien
'The Freedom of John Bull', *The Political Monitor or Regent's Friend ...* (Dublin, 1790), pp. 27-28.

Henrietta Battier
(i) from: *The Kirwanade*, Number II (Dublin, 1791), pp. 1-4; (ii) 'Lines addressed to the late Lord Clifden', *The Protected Fugitives: A Collection of Miscellaneous Poems, the Genuine Productions of a Lady* (Dublin, 1791), pp. 139-42.

Pat O'Kelly
(i) from: 'The Itinerary', *O'Kelly's Poetical Miscellanies* [the second part of] *Killarney: A Descriptive Poem* by Pat O'Kelly (Dublin, 1791), pp. 111-16; (ii) 'The Litany for Doneraile', *The Hippocrene: a collection of Poems* by Patrick O'Kelly Esq. (Dublin, 1831), p. 116.

Ellen Taylor
'Written by the Barrow side', *Poems by Ellen Taylor, the Irish Cottager* (Dublin, 1792), p. 8.

Henrietta O'Neill
'Ode to the Poppy', *Anthologia Hibernica*, November 1793, pp. 384-85.

Thomas Dermody
(i) 'An Ode to Myself', *1000 Years of Irish Poetry* ed. Kathleen Hoagland, second edition (New York, 1962), pp. 372-73; (ii) 'Ode to the Collegians', Thomas Dermody, *Poems ...* (Dublin, 1792), p. 55.

Edward Rushton
'Mary le More', *1000 Years of Irish Poetry* ed. Kathleen Hoagland, second edition (New York, 1962), pp. 366-67.

Samuel Thomson
(i) 'To a Hedge-hog', *New Poems on a Variety of Different Subjects* ... (Belfast, 1799), pp. 126-28; (ii) 'The Hawk and Weazle', ibid., pp. 212-13; (iii) 'The Country Dance', *Poems on Different Subjects* ... (Belfast, 1793), pp. 63-69.

Edward Walsh
'Rapture!', *Bagatelles or Poetical Sketches by E. Walsh M.D.* (Dublin, 1793), p. 60; 'The Epigram', ibid., p. 50.

John Anketell
(i) from: 'Stramore Patron', *Poems on Several Subjects* (Dublin, 1793) pp. 209-17; (ii) from: 'Description of Sunday Evening, in ... Dublin', ibid., pp. 132-33.

Four anonymous 'rambling' poems
(i) 'The Peregrinations of Fiachra McBrady', *Anthologia Hibernica,* December 1793, p. 458; (ii) 'The Irish man's Ramble: a new song', from: *Later English Broadside Ballads* eds. John Holloway and Joan Black, vol. II (London, 1979); (iii) 'McClure's Ramble', Songsheet (Downpatrick, c.1804), collection Irish Folk Music Archive, Dublin; (iv) 'Shales's Rambles, or the Lurgan Weaver', Chapbook (n.p., 1795), TCD uncatalogued.

Anonymous poems from the 1790s
(i) 'The Colleen Rue', Chapbook (Dublin, c.1810), TCD 66.u.165; (ii) 'The Irish Phœnix', Chapbook (Dublin, c.1795), TCD uncatalogued; (iii) 'The Siege of Troy', *The Edinburgh Miscellany* ... (Edinburgh, 1792), pp. 253-54; (iv) 'Paddy MacShane's Seven Ages', *Crosby's Musical Repertory* (London, 1808), pp. 13-15; (v) 'Sally Mac Gee', *Later English Broadside Ballads* eds. John Holloway and Joan Black, vol. I (London, 1975); (vi) 'Paddy the Piper', *Crosby's Irish Repertory* (London, 1808), pp. 275-77; (vii) 'The Ladies Dress, or the Downfall of the Stay-Makers', Chapbook (n.p., 1795), TCD uncatalogued; (viii) 'A New Song call'd The Lord Lieutenant's Farewell to the Kingdom of Ireland', Chapbook (n.p., 1795), TCD uncatalogued; (ix) 'A New Song on the Half-pence being cry'd down or, a Peep into a Whiskey-Shop', Chapbook (n.p., 1795), TCD uncatalogued; (x) 'Sweet Castle-Hyde', Chapbook (n.p., c.1810), TCD CC.m.77.

Richard Alfred Milliken
'The Groves of Blarney', *Popular Songs of Ireland* ed. Thomas Crofton Croker, second edition (London, 1886), pp. 142-44.

Samuel Burdy
from: 'The Transformation', *Ardglass, or The Ruined Castles; also The Transformation* by the Revd. Samuel Burdy (Dublin, 1802), pp. 79-85.

Jane Elizabeth Moore
'A Question to the Society of Freemasons', with its answers, *Miscellaneous Poems on Various Occasions* by Jane Elizabeth Moore, second edition (Dublin, 1797), pp. 26, 28, 82-83 and 84-85.

612

William Drennan
'The Wake of William Orr', *The Dublin Book of Irish Verse 1728-1909*, ed. John Cooke (Dublin, 1909), pp. 12-14.

Mary Alcock
'The Chimney-Sweeper's Complaint', *Poems by Mary Alcock* (London, 1799), pp. 22-24.

Joseph Atkinson
from: *Killarney: a poem* by Joseph Atkinson Esq. (Dublin, 1798), pp. 11-15.

James Orr
(i) 'Song composed on the Banks of Newfoundland', *Poems on Various Subjects* by James Orr, new ed. (Belfast, 1936) (reprint of Orr's *Poems on Various Subjects* [Belfast, 1804]), pp. 167-68; (ii) from 'The Passengers', *The Country Rhymes of James Orr, the Bard of Ballycarry*, ed. Philip Robinson (Bangor, Co. Down, 1992), pp. 18-24; (iii) 'The Execution', ibid., pp. 108-10.

Hugh Porter
'To the Reverend T[homas] T[ighe], Parson's Hill', *The Country Rhymes of Hugh Porter, the Bard of Moneyslane*, eds. Amber Adams and J.R.R.Adams (Bangor, Co. Down, 1992), pp. 1-3.

John Philpot Curran
'The Deserter's Meditation', *The Dublin Book of Irish Verse 1728-1909,* ed. John Cooke (Dublin, 1909), pp. 5-6.

Nationalist verse of the 1790s
(i) 'Liberty and Equality or Dermot's Delight', *Paddy's Resource* (Belfast, 1795), pp. 1-3; (ii) 'The Star of Liberty', ibid., pp. 20-22; (iii) 'Paddy's Advice to John Bull', *Paddy's Resource* (Belfast, 1812), p. 105; (iv) from: *The United Irishmen: A Tale, founded on Facts* (Dublin, 1798), pp. 5-14; (v) 'Come all you Warriors', *Field Day Anthology of Irish Writing*, 3 vols. (Derry, 1991), I, 1099-1100; (vi) 'Dunlavin Green', *The Faber Book of Ballads*, ed. M. Hodgart (London, 1965), p. 202; (vii) 'The Croppy Boy', *Irish Minstrelsy ...* ed. H. Halliday Sparling, second ed., revised (London and New York, n.d.), pp. 34-36; (viii) 'The Patriot Mother', ibid., pp. 286-87; (ix) 'Green upon the Cape', ibid., pp. 11-14; (x) 'The Exiled Irishman's Lamentation', *Paddy's Resource* (Belfast, 1812), pp. 111-13.

Three Orange Songs
(i) 'Lisnagade', *The Patriotic Songster* (Strabane, 1816), p. 91; (ii) 'Protestant Boys', *Irish Minstrelsy*, pp. 327-28; (iii) 'The Tree of Liberty', *A Collection of Loyal Songs* (Dublin, 1798), pp. 44-45.

Robert Emmet
'Lines written on the Burying-Ground of Arbour Hill', *The Cabinet of Irish Literature*, revised edition, ed. Katharine Tynan Hinkson, 4 vols. (London, 1903), I, 273-74.

Edward Lysaght
(i) 'Song', *Poems by the late Edward Lysaght Esq.* (Dublin, 1811), pp. 95-97 compared with, and in places amended from the text in Carr's *The Stranger in Ireland* (London, 1808), pp. 229-30; (ii) 'Love *versus* the Bottle', *Irish Minstrelsy*, pp. 199-200.

Mary Tighe
(i) 'Written at Rossana, November 18, 1799', *Psyche with Other Poems*, third edition (London, 1811), p. 230; (ii) 'Written at Killarney, July 29, 1800', ibid., p. 233.

Daniel Roderick O'Conor
from: 'The Author's Farewell to Dublin: a poem', *The Works of Mr Daniel Roderick O'Conor ...* two volumes (Cork, n.d.), I, 208-10.

Thomas Moore
(i) 'Translation of Ode IX by Anacreon', *Odes of Anacreon translated into English verse ...* by Thomas Moore Esq. (Dublin, 1804), pp. 48-49; (ii) 'Song', *The Poetical Works of the late Thomas Little* (i.e.Thomas Moore) (Dublin, 1804), pp. 26-27.

W. Kertland
'The DUBLIN Fancy WARE-HOUSE', from: *The Monthly Pantheon* no. 9, February 1809 (Dublin, 1809), p. 155.

INDEX OF TITLES AND FIRST LINES[1]

A Band of Cupids th'other Day 76
A Chappel of the Riding-House is made 66
A chimney-sweeper's boy am I 537
A crowded court anon appeared 446
A Nymph and Swain, Sheelah and Dermot hight 192
A Pretty Song, this coming Spring 271
A Scholar first my Love implor'd 332
A set of young bloods sallied out t'other night 414
Academick Sportsman, The 359
Advertisement Extraordinary 416
Agent's Downfall, The: a new ballad 408
Ah, why thy cruel rage to bend 368
Ah Shepherd, gentle Shepherd! spare 201
Ah simple poet! ill-judg'd pray'r! 297
Alas! how dismal is my tale 470
'All bounteous Heav'n,' Castalio cries 194
All Hail ye soft Mysterious Pow'rs, which charm 99
All ye Poets of the Age 140
All you who would wish to be merry 412
Amazonian Gift, The 331
An Epigram should be — if right 491
An Oaken, broken Elbow-Chair 189
Anacreon Paraphras'd, Ode viii 199
Answer 531
Answer to 'Stauka an Vauraga', The 423
Answer to the above Replication 533
Answer'd by her Woman 297
Apud in is almi des ire 185
Are ye landed from England, and sick of the seas 317
As Amphion built of old, the Theban Wall 278

As Bacchus ranging at his leisure 72
As I roved out of a summer's morning 520
As I roved out on a summer's morning 507
As I stray'd o'er the common on Cork's rugged border 480
As I strole the City, oft I 222
As Jove will not attend on less 170
As poets write, and painters tell 462
As sonata in praes o Molli 184
As Teague and his comrade were digging potatoes 557
Assist me, ye Muses, F——— to sing 241
Author's Farewell to Dublin, The 587
Awake my lire, and sing his fall 550
Away with this pouting and sadness 590
Bacchus or the Drunken Metamorphosis 72
Be not sparing 185
Bear, bear my song, ye raptures of the mind! 235
Beau Walk in Stephen's Green, The 319
Beauing, belling, dancing, drinking 310
Begotten, and Born, and dying with Noise 183
Behind moth-eaten Curtain, 'stead of Press 135
Beneath this place 51
Bumpers, 'Squire Jones 299
But enters now the Parish Priest 207
Carolan's Receipt 376
Cavalcade, The: A Poem On the Riding the Franchises 103
Character, Panegyric, and Description of the Legion Club, A 222
Charming Oysters I cry 186
Chimney-Sweeper's Complaint, The 537
Clerk's Song, The 304

1. Titles are in italics, first lines in roman type.

Clito: a Poem on the Force of Eloquence 58

Colleen Rue, The 507

Come, be content, since out it must 153

Come, buy my fine Oranges, Sauce for your Veal 185

Come, ye lads of elegance and spirit 416

Come, tell us the name of the rebelly crew 571

Come all you roving blades, that ramble thro' the City 339

Come all you warriors, and renowned nobles 566

Come all you Warriors 566

Come gentlemen sportsmen, I pray listen all 312

Come muse, wha aft in merry tift 485

Connaughtman's Visit to Dublin, The 388

Connelly's Ale: a new song 387

Corporal Casey 398

Coughing Old Man, The 395

Country Dance, The 485

Coup'd up with iron Barrs my drooping Muse 260

Croppy Boy, The 570

Cruel and Bloody Declaration, A 39

Curse on the harden'd, unrelenting thief 428

Darby O'Gallagher, or the Answer to Morgan Rattler 399

De night afore Larry was stretch'd 430

Dear Doctor, here comes a young Virgin untainted 115

Dear Ireland, now it is time to grow wise 302

Dear me! what mighty curious ways 592

Dear Smed I read thy Brilliant Lines 151

Deluded Mortals, whom the Great 174

Description of a Country Assizes 405

Description of a Fox-Chase, A 314

Description of an Unfortunate Woman of the Town 410

Description of Doctor Delany's Villa, A 164

Description of Dublin 338

Description of Sunday Evening,... in the City of Dublin 496

Deserted Village, The 347

Deserter's Meditation, The 556

Disputation of the Two Churches, The 323

Do Tharlaigh Inné Orm 327

Do tharlaigh inné orm is mé im' aonar sa ród 327

Don Carlos in a merry Spight 160

Doris, a Nymph of riper Age 67

Doris 67

Draw near each constant female, while I my ruine revealing 393

Drinking Song 302

Drop of Dram, A 396

Dublin Fancy Ware-House, The 592

Due thanks I acknowledge for your compliment paid 533

Dunlavin Green 569

Each female so pretty in country and city 395

Eadar Foirceal na cléire is Fochairt na nGael 323

Eclogue in Imitation of the first Eclogue of Virgil, An 83

Elegie on a Favourite Dog, An 75

Elegy on the death of ... Miss Bridget Burne 459

Elegy on the much lamented Death of ... all the Potatoes, An 248

Epigram, The 491

Epigram on the Riding-House in Dublin, An 66

Epistle to His Excellency John Lord Carteret, An 166

Epistle to his Grace the Duke of Grafton, An 147

Epistle to Pollio, from the Hills of Howth in Ireland 265

Epistle upon an Epistle from a certain Doctor, An 170

Epistles from Swanlinbar 379

Epitaph on an orphan beggar child 455

Epitaph on the Duke of Grafton 51

Execution, The 550

Exiled Irishman's Lamentation, The
574

*Familiar Epistle to J. H. Esq; near
Killarney, A* 320

*First Ode of the First Book of
Horace Imitated, The* 268

For here the Old Scullogues were all
42

Forgive me, fair One, nor resent 196

Freedom of John Bull, The 462

Friend in Need is a Friend in Deed, A
253

From a Country full of Rebellion and
Treason 112

From this dull Town's unvarying
Scene 320

*Garry Own Naugh Glora, or The
Limerick Rakes* 417

Good men and true! in this house
who dwell 570

Great boasting of late we have heard
of the fates 399

Green upon the Cape 573

Green were the fields where my
forefathers dwelt, O 574

Groves of Blarney, The 523

Hark, hark, jolly Sportsmen, a while
to my Tale 314

Haste all ye bucks and lads of fire
383

Have at you, K——N!: — I'm
myself again 464

Hawk and Weazle, The 484

Here our murdered brother lies 535

Here you may behold a liar 375

Here's to the maiden of bashful
fifteen 357

*Heroic Epistle from Donna Teresa
Pinna ÿ Ruiz, An* 369

*Hesperi-Neso-Graphia: or A
Description of the Western Isle*
116

Heu dolor anxietas! Suspira rumpite
pectus 39

His Grace's Answer to Jonathan 151

Ho! brother Teague, dost hear de
decree 37

How calm an' cozie is the wight 544

How justly alarm'd is each Dublin
cit 582

How soft the pause! the notes
melodious cease 586

Hub ub, ub, boo 53

*Humble Petition of a Beautiful
Young Lady, A* 115

Humours of the Black Dog, The 260

Hush Cat from under the Table 402

I am a fair maid that loves good
Company 423

I met yesterday 327

I pray thee, by the gods above 589

I sing of a war set on foot for a toy
510

I sing the Pleasures of the Rural
throng 90

I'm a lad that's forced an exile from
my own native land 573

I've read your reply, fraught with
humour and taste 532

If ever grief was great without
Disguise 248

If my own botheration don't alter my
plan 511

If sadly thinking, with spirits sinking
556

If ye heard each disaster, of your
poetaster 498

If you have nothing else to do 214

In bless'd Hibernia's thrice-
renowned isle 492

In common Words I vulgar things
will tell 58

In Ireland 'tis evening. From toil my
friends hie all 542

In praise of a Negress 378

In the year of one thousand seven
hundred and ninety eight 569

In Western Isle renown'd for Boggs
116

In Youth exalted high in Air 182

Intrigues of Jove, The: a Ballad 296

*Invitation, The: To Doctor Delany at
Delville, MDCCXXIX* 197

*Invitation to Owen Bray's at
Laughlin's town, An* 317

Irish Absentee's new Litany, The 112

Irish Hudibras, The 42

Irish man's Ramble, The: a new song
500

Irish Phoenix, The 508

Irish Song, An 53
Irish Wedding between Dick and Moll, An 107
Irishmen's Prayers to St. Patrick, The 49
Is Courage in a Woman's Breast 331
It was my Lord, the dextrous Shift 147
Itinerary, The 468
Kerry Cavalcade, The: or the High Sheriff's Feast 241
Killarney: a poem 539
King David was a psalmist rare 304
Kirwanade, The 464
Ladies Dress, The, or the Downfall of the Stay-Makers 515
Left on a Lady's Toilette 297
Let school-masters puzzle their brain 355
Let that Heroick Muse that sings 107
Let us sing of a sporting, brave swaggering blade 408
Letter to Father Fitzgerald 385
Libel on D[octor] D[elany] and a Certain Great Lord, A 174
Liberty and Equality or Dermot's Delight 557
Lilliburlero 37
Lines addressed to the late Lord Clifden 466
Lines by a Lady of Fashion 356
Lines to an unnamed Lady 205
Lines written on the Burying-Ground of Arbour Hill in Dublin 580
Lisnagade 576
Litany for Doneraile, The 470
Little charm of placid mien 138
Lo! a place of amusement for ladies hard by 379
Look back on Time; you see him bald 281
Lord Altham's Bull 442
Lord Mayor's Ball, The 412
Love Song, A 185
Love versus the Bottle 583
Luke Caffrey's Kilmainham Minit 434
Maiden's Resolution or an Answer to the Farmer's Son, The 393
Mary le More 480

Mary the Cook-Maid's Letter to Dr Sheridan 190
Mass-houses, churches, mixt together 338
Match at Football, A 90
May Bush, The 340
McClure's Ramble 502
Methinks, dear Tom, I see thee stand demure 277
'Mid Trees of stunted Growth, unequal Roes 319
Midnight Court, The 446
Miss Betty's Singing-Bird 271
Modern Lass in High Dress in MDCCLVI, The 383
Modern Poet, The 135
Mollis abuti 184
Most lovely Daisy! sprung of lovely race! 273
Motto inscribed on the bottom of chamber-pots 375
Mountown! Thou sweet Retreat from Dublin Cares 61
Mully of Mountown 61
My old acquaintance and my dearest friend 83
Namby Pamby: or a Panegyric on the new Versification 140
Nature had form'd Anglesus full of Grace 333
New Ballad on the Hot-Wells at Mallow, A 309
New Dhooraling, The 400
New Song, A 414
New Song, call'd The Lord Lieutenant's Farewell, A 517
New Song call'd Luke Caffrey's Gost, A 437
New Song on the Half-pence being cry'd down, A 518
Nite afore Larry was stretch'd, De 430
No Christian king, that I can find 220
No rising column marks this spot 580
Nor Songs, nor Tales of Love delight the Muse 253
North Country Wedding, The 128
Not for the promise of the labour'd field 475

Now, arrah, John Bull, I would have you be easy 560
Now did the bag-pipe in hoarse notes begin 79
Now through the Welkin wide the rosy Morn 128
O broder Teague, and Teague my Roon 49
O Thou! whose Virtues Albion's Sons can trace 268
O'er the vine-cover'd hills and gay regions of France 559
Ode to Myself, An 477
Ode to Sensibility 377
Ode to the Collegians 478
Ode to the Poppy 475
Of Gracey's charms enraptur'd will I sing! 453
Of late a strong notion of rambling entangled my mind 502
Oh, my rash hand! what hast thou idly done? 585
Oh that I was my Silvia's stays! 297
Oh! de time piece had cum to the twelve 437
Oh! Thou in whom united virtues shine 466
On a Beef's being stole which was promis'd to the Author 428
On Deborah Perkins of the county of Wicklow 303
On Liffey's Banks good Heav'ns! what was my Lot 587
On Swift's leaving his Fortune to Build a Mad-House 231
On the Castle of Dublin, Anno 1715 71
On the Murder of a Cat 366
On the Omission of the Words Dei Gratia in the late Coinage 220
On the Spaw at Castle-connel, in the County of Limerick 307
Once more kind Muses it is your duty 508
One fair summer's morn, bright Phoebus adorn 387
Oppress'd with Grief, in heavy Strains I mourn 275
Paddy MacShane's Seven Ages 511
Paddy the Piper 514

Paddy's Advice to John Bull 560
Panacea: A Poem upon Tea 54
Parson's Revels, The 207
Parting Cup or The Humours of Deoch an Doruis, The 281
Passengers, The 544
Pastoral Dialogue, A 192
Patriot Mother, The 571
Peregrinations of Fiachra McBrady, The 498
Petition of the Birds, The 201
Petition to the Ladies of Dublin, A 101
Phoenix Park 77
'Pléaráca an Bhráthar': A New Song called the Friar's Jigg 425
Poet's Lamentation for the Loss of his Cat, The 275
Poetical Desciption of Mr Neal's new Musick-Hall, A 278
Pollio! woulds't thou condescend 265
Protestant Boys 577
Question to the Society of Freemasons, A 530
Rakes Frolick or 'Stauka an Varaga', The 420
Rakes of Mallow, The 310
Rakes of Stony Butter, The 339
Rapture! 490
Recantation, The 196
Receipt for Making a Doctor, A 214
Rejoinder to Mrs Jane Eliz Moore's Repledum 532
Reverend Sir, I would be laith 552
Reverend Sir — Please to publish from the altar of your holy Mass 385
Rich in Improvements of his well-spent Time 54
Ripe 'Sparagrass 185
Royal Black Bird, The 126
Sailor Dear, The 393
Sally Mac Gee 513
Says Moll Drew to Widney, my husband's a sad man 396
Scew Ball 312
Shales's Rambles, or the Lurgan Weaver 503
Shall Cooper's-hill majestick rise in Rhyme 77

Siege of Troy, The 510
Signior in Fashion, The 99
Smock Race at Finglas, The 79
Some sing ye of Venus the goddess 303
Song (from *She Stoops to Conquer*) 355
Song (from *The School for Scandal*) 357
Song 332
Song 582
Song 590
Song composed on the Banks of Newfoundland 542
Song for Gracey Nugent 453
Song of the Angels at the Nativity of Our Blessed Saviour 56
Sons of Hibernia, attend to my song 578
Sport concluded, daub'd with mire 526
Squarecaps, and round, all honest boys 478
St. Patrick's dean, your country's pride 158
Star of Liberty, The 559
Stella at Wood-Park 160
Stramore Patron 492
Street Cries 185
Sweet Auburn, loveliest village of the plain 347
Sweet Castle-Hyde 520
Sweet Chloe advised me, in accents divine 583
Tagra an Dá Theampall 323
Tale, A 76
Tell me, my friends, why are we met here? 577
Thanks to the Friend whose happy Lines cou'd cheer 70
The Day advanc'd, and waning to the West 359
The evening spent in Chloe's arms 490
The fleeting Birds may soon in Ocean swim 203
The groves of Blarney they are so charming 523
The Ladies of Dublin they are all growing wild 515

The Night before de first of May 340
The sordid wretch who ne'er has known 377
Then behind, all my hair is done up in a plat 356
Then spring the grouse, the heaths impurpl'd hold 539
There are some who sing of Moreen and others of Grainne too 425
There you may see, — tho' we're derided 561
This House and Inhabitants both well agree 71
Thou wise , and learned Ruler of our Isle 166
Three Riddles 182
Thrice hail, thou prince of jovial fellows 477
Through nations ranging, raking elements 420
Thy banks, O Barrow, sure must be 473
'Tis Sunday ev'ning, and when pray'rs are done 496
Tit for Tat: or the Rater rated 305
To ————— 70
To a Gentleman who had his Pocket Pick'd 65
To a Hedge-hog 482
To Charles Ford Esqr. on his Birth-day 153
To doleful strains, ah, strains of woe 366
To Dr Swift on his Birth-day 158
To find an earthly home in vain I tried 455
To gain the notice of an F.R.S. 369
To Madmen Swift bequeaths his whole estate 231
To Miss Georgiana 138
To Miss Laetitia Van Lewen 203
To Mrs D.C.H., an account of the Author's manner of spending her time 343
To Mrs Frances-Arabella Kelly 195
To Sarah Shackleton on her beating me with the bed-stick 368
To T. W. M———a, Esq. 531
To the Dean, when in England, in 1726 187

To the Revd Mr ——— on his Drinking Sea-Water 277

To the Reverend T[homas] T[ighe], Parson's Hill 552

To town ae morn, as Lizie hie'd 484

To you, Illustrious Fair, I tune my song 205

Today, this Temple gets a Dean 145

Today, as at my Glass I stood 195

Transformation, The 526

Translation of Ode IX by Anacreon 589

Tree of Liberty, The 578

True and Faithful Inventory, A 189

True Tale, A 333

'Twas at that Time when Letchers seek the Park 410

'Twas on the fust of sweet Magay 442

'Twas when the mirth-exciting Bowl 199

Unanswerable Apology for the Rich, An 194

Unhappy Hibernia mourn, O mourn and do not cease! 459

United Irishmen, The 561

Universal Beauty 235

Upon a fair morning for soft recreation 126

Upon Daisy, being brought back from New Park to Stoneybatter 273

Upper Gallery, The 244

Verses fix'd on the Cathedral Door 145

Wake of William Orr, The 535

We are little airy Creatures 184

Welcome to Liberty, The 364

Well; if ever I saw such another Man 190

What shape I have, that form is all my own 378

When by sickness or sorrow assail'd 376

When Ev'ning Clouds condensing fall in Rain 244

When far from you, dear Anna, plac'd 343

When forth in my Ramble intending to gamble 500

When I was a boy in my father's mud edifice 514

When I was at home, I was merry and frisky 398

When to see Lukes Last Gig we agreed 434

While Shepherds watch'd their Flocks by Night 56

While you, dear Friend, exempt from Care 197

While youthful poets, thro' the grove 482

Who can forbid the Muses Tears to Flow? 75

With smiles I greet thy glad approach 364

With thee fond Roscommon, thou seat of the muses 468

Would you that Delville I describe? 164

Written at Killarney, July 29, 1800 586

Written at Rossana, November 18, 1799 585

Written by the Barrow side, where she was sent to wash Linen 473

Ye beaux and belles, of Mallow-well 307

Ye Brethren Masonic of ancient degree 530

Ye Females of Dublin make Haste and repair 101

Ye good Fellows all 299

Ye heav'nly nymphs, Æonian maids, descend 405

Ye maidens pretty in town and City 393

Ye nymphs deprest 309

Ye Protestants of Ulster, I pray you join with me 576

Ye Tuneful Nine, your Poet's Mind inspire 103

Ye're welcome hame, my Marg'y 305

You humorous folks prepare 296

You jolly jovial sporting blades 417

You jolly young rake who loves for to freak 402

You know the Ancient Writings say 65

You ladies free of each degree, now
hear my invitation 503
You maidens pretty attend this ditty
400
You Natives of Ireland unto me now
attend 517
You people of Dublin who whollies
the rules 388
You sporting young girls, give ear to
my ditty 513
You will excuse me, I suppose 187
You've asked why our secrets are
kept from the clown 531
Your answer I've read, and lament
with surprise 531
Your welcome to Dublin dear harry
518

INDEX OF AUTHORS

Alcock, Mary 537-38
Anketell, John 492-97
Anonymous 37-53, 99-127, 241-52,
302-13, 338-42, 387-427, 430-45,
498-522, 557-579
Arbuckle, James 231
Atkinson, Joseph 539-41
Barber, Mary 194-96
Battier, Henrietta 464-67
Brooke, Henry 235-40
Brooke, Charlotte 453-54
Browne, Nicholas 128-34
Burdy, Samuel 526-29
Carey, Henry140-42
Carolan, Turlogh 376
Clare, Lady 375
Concanen, Matthew 90-98
Congreve, William 67-9
Cotter, George Sackville 379-82
Curran, John Philpot 556
Davys, Mary 135-37
Dawson, Sir Arthur 299-301
Delacourt, James 378
Delany, Patrick 166-69, 182-86
Dermody, Thomas 477-79
Drennan, William 535-36
Dubois, Dorothea 331-37
Dunkin, William 207-21
Elder, Olivia 343-46
Emmet, Robert 580-81
Farquhar, George 65-6
Fitzgerald, Gerald 359-63
Goldsmith, Oliver 347-55
Grierson, Constantia 203-06
Howard, Gorges Edmond 383-84
Inglis, Liam 327-28

Johnson, Esther 158-59
Kertland, W. 592-95
King, William 61-4
Lawrence, Thomas Dawson 455
Lysaght, Edward 582-84
Mac Cumhaidh, Art 323-26
Merriman, Brian 446-52
Milliken, Richard 523-25
Monck, Mary 75-6
Moore, Jane Elizabeth 530-34
Moore, Thomas 589-91
Mozeen, Thomas 314-18
Newburgh, Thomas 319
Nugent, Robert, Earl 265-67
Ó Súilleabháin, Eoghan Rua 385-86
O'Brien, Mary 462-63
O'Connor, Morrough 83-89
O'Conor, Daniel Roderick 587-88
O'Kelly, Pat 468-72
O'Neill, Henrietta 475-76
O'Reilly, L. 459-61
Orr, James 542-51
Orrery, John, Earl of 268-70
Parnell, Thomas 70-4
Philips, Ambrose 138-40
Pilkington, Matthew 197-200
Pilkington, Laetitia 201-02
Porter, Hugh 552-55
Preston, William 369-74
Rushton, Edward 480-81
Ryves, Elizabeth 377
Shackleton, Mary 364-68
Sheridan, Thomas 164-65, 182-89
Sheridan, Richard Brinsley 356-58
Smedley, Jonathan 145-50
Sterling, James 253-59

Swift, Jonathan 151-57, 160-63,
   170-86, 190-93, 222-30
Tate, Nahum 54-7
Taylor, John 428-29
Taylor, Ellen 473-74
Thomson, Samuel 482-89
Tighe, Mary 585-86
Toland, John 58-60

Walsh, Edward 490-91
Ward, James 77-82
Weekes, James Eyre 296-98
Whyte, Laurence 278-95
Whyte, Samuel 320-22
Wilkes, Wetenhall 260-64
Winstanley, John 271-77